The Handbook of
SECONDARY
GIFTED
EDUCATION

The Handbook of
SECONDARY
GIFTED
EDUCATION

edited by

Felicia A. Dixon, Ph.D.
& Sidney M. Moon, Ph.D.

PRUFROCK PRESS INC.
WACO, TEXAS

Library of Congress Cataloging-in-Publication Data

The handbook of secondary gifted education / edited by Felicia A. Dixon & Sidney M. Moon.
    p. cm.
  Includes bibliographical references and index.
  ISBN 1-59363-178-2 (pbk. : alk. paper)
  1. Gifted children—Education (Secondary)—United States—Handbooks, manuals, etc.
I. Dixon, Felicia A., 1945– II. Moon, Sidney M.
  LC3993.23.H36 2006
  371.95'73—dc22

2005027212

ISBN 1-59363-178-2

At the time of this book's publication, all facts and figures cited are the most current available. All telephone numbers, addresses, and Web site URLs are accurate and active. All publications, organizations, Web sites, and other resources exist as described in the book, and all have been verified. The authors and Prufrock Press, Inc., make no warranty or guarantee concerning the information and materials given out by organizations or content found at Web sites, and we are not responsible for any changes that occur after this book's publication. If you find an error, please contact Prufrock Press, Inc. We strongly recommend to parents, teachers, and other adults that you monitor children's use of the Internet.

PRUFROCK PRESS INC.
P.O. Box 8813
Waco, TX 76714-8813
(800) 998-2208
http://www.prufrock.com

DEDICATION

For John Feldhusen, our mentor, whose research in and advocacy for secondary
gifted education provided inspiration for our work in this volume.

and

For our families: David, Diane, and Deirdre (Felicia) and Doug, Alex, Jeff, Mark,
and Rob (Sidney) who encouraged us in this endeavor and continue to remind us
of why gifted education is important throughout life.

Contents

PART 2: TALENT DEVELOPMENT IN ADOLESCENCE

INTRODUCTION

by Felicia A. Dixon
& Sidney M. Moon

*T*he title of this book, *The Handbook of Secondary Gifted Education,* is indicative of the collaborative efforts of many researchers who have contributed time and expertise to informing others of the issues related to adolescent gifted students in secondary schools. It is the right time for this book. President George W. Bush's No Child Left Behind: High Quality, High School Initiatives act (January, 2005) has shifted the focus to accountability for secondary schools; the publication of the Templeton National Report on Acceleration (Colangelo, Assouline, & Gross, 2004) has asserted that schools hold back their brightest students, allowing their educational progress to be determined by the pace of their less able peers; and Davidson, Davidson, and Vanderkam (2004) have written that American students lag behind students in other industrial nations, and the brightest learn to coast through school, seldom stretching their brains. Indeed, the picture presented of gifted education at the secondary level is dismal.

The President's plan for high schools includes encouraging the growth of Advanced Placement (AP) and International Baccalaureate (IB) programs, and training teachers in low-income schools to teach these courses. Another stated goal is to enhance math and science achievement for high school graduates, along with bolstering the level of teaching of these subjects in the middle and high schools. These goals address deficiencies in schools and propose much needed reforms. However, they are not specifically targeted at the gifted adolescent. While many gifted adolescents take AP and IB classes, these classes are not specifically differentiated for gifted adolescents (Callahan, Hertberg, & Kyburg, 2005). This book focuses on gifted adolescents, a group that Colangelo et al. (2004) described as "currently invisible on the national agenda" (p. 2), and on those who teach and guide them.

The Handbook of Secondary Gifted Education is divided into four parts. Part I, "On Being Gifted and Adolescent," provides the foundation for the rest of the book. It covers conceptions of giftedness in adolescence, general developmental themes, and individual differences. The chapters in Part I provide insight into the great potential that these students exhibit and highlight individual and cultural factors that influence their development. Part II, "Talent Development in Adolescence," presents several different domains, including academic, visual arts, personal, social, and sports, and how talent develops in each of these. These chapters are written to give educators a sense of the complete talent development process in different talent domains. Since adolescence is a catalytic period in talent development, understanding the big picture is important. Part III, "What Schools Can Do: Curriculum and Instruction," is the longest portion of the book, and presents the content domains, cross-disciplinary skills (i.e., critical and creative thinking), out-of school activities, affective curriculum interventions, models, and special schools for gifted adolescents. All chapters center on the gifted adolescent and specific needs that must be met in school and understood by all who teach or mentor these students. The final part, Part IV, "What Teacher Education Can Do: Professional Development," targets teachers and administrators (i.e., superintendents, principals, and counselors), discussing how these professionals can become more aware of gifted adolescent student issues. Part IV also addresses the need for advanced training to enable teachers, counselors, and administrators to be more effective in guiding gifted adolescents in secondary schools.

Each separate part of the book overviews the chapters contained in it, citing relevant literature to introduce the topic of the section. Our goal in this book is to focus on the secondary student. Because much of the research literature in the field of gifted education focuses on young children, our challenge is to fill a much-needed gap. By creating one volume with a central focus on the gifted adolescent, our hope is that all those interested in gifted adolescents will be able to have ready access to a variety of essential topics. A second goal is to give direction to teachers of the gifted secondary student, suggesting what they can do to meet these students' needs both within the classroom and in the school culture in general.

We define secondary as including both middle school (grades 6–8) and high school (grades 9–12). In our work with secondary teachers, we have heard the expressed need for far greater specificity with respect to both domain and developmental level than elementary school teachers express. This book accommodates the need for specificity by addressing both talent development and curriculum and instruction in domain-specific, rather than domain-general terms. In addition, our chapters on curriculum and instruction include activities devoted to each of the two secondary levels, because there are differences in student needs and recommended instructional strategies by developmental level.

We have asked chapter authors to include a review of relevant empirical literature on their topic. In this way, we seek to establish this book as a text grounded in empirical research and sound theory relevant to teachers, counselors, and administrators interested in gifted adolescents. In addition, students in graduate training programs in gifted education and researchers who focus on gifted and talented adolescents may find great insight from the variety of topics focusing on gifted adolescents at the secondary level.

We have worked extensively with secondary gifted students and know the pure joy working with them can bring. We have also seen the stress and anxiety they manifest when they have to cope with their exceptionalities in environments that do not understand them or their unique talents. Often gifted education is treated as if it ends in middle school. In high school, many administrators are content with depositing these students into AP or honors classes that focus on rigorous content with little or no focus on gifted qualities and how adolescence affects giftedness. While we respect all schools that try to offer something different educationally for these students, we know schools could do better. The purpose of this book is to suggest ways schools can improve services for and understanding of gifted adolescents and the talent development process.

Two years ago, we decided to collaborate on this edited book. We knew the book was needed in the field of gifted education then, and we are certain it is needed now. The time is right for this book, and we are proud to present it to you.

References

Callahan, C., Hertberg, H., & Kyburg, R. (2005). AP and IB courses: A fit for gifted learners? Paper presented at the annual meeting of the American Educational Research Association, Montreal, Canada.

Colangelo, N., Assouline, S. G., & Gross, M. U. M. (2004). *A nation deceived: How schools hold back America's brightest students.* Iowa City, IA: The Connie Belin & Jacqueline N. Blank International Center for Gifted Education and Talent Development.

Davidson, J., Davidson, B., & Vanderkam, L. (2004). *Genius denied: How to stop wasting our brightest young minds.* New York: Simon and Schuster.

ON BEING GIFTED AND ADOLESCENT

PART 1

On Being Gifted and Adolescent: An Overview

by Sidney M. Moon

uch of the research in the field of gifted education has focused on young children. Only a handful of researchers have focused on the needs and characteristics of gifted adolescents (Benbow, 1986; Clasen & Clasen, 1995; Coleman, 2001; Cross, Coleman, & Stewart, 1995; Lubinski & Benbow, 1994; Lubinski, Webb, Morelock, & Benbow, 2001). Existing research states that adolescence is both a time of great potential (Feldhusen, 1998; Jarvin & Subotnik, this volume; Moon, 1993; Sethna, Wickstrom, Boothe, & Stanley, 2001; Van Rossum & Gagné, this volume; VanTassel-Baska, 2001) and special vulnerability for high ability students (Clasen & Clasen; Cross, Gust-Brey, & Ball, 2002; Peterson, 2003). Being gifted and adolescent isn't easy for many reasons. These students must cope with the normal developmental issues of adolescence, and with being different because of their giftedness (Clasen & Clasen). Many of them face intense pressure from peers to deny their abilities (Cross et al., 1995; Cross, Coleman, & Terhaar-Yonkers, 1991; Steinberg, 1996). Often they do not have the opportunities they need to develop their abilities into demonstrated talents, either because their school does not have the resources to provide advanced coursework in core subject areas, such as physics or British Literature, or because they are talented in an area not emphasized in most secondary schools, such as engineering or art.

The first part of *The Handbook of Secondary Gifted Education* focuses on the students—their characteristics, needs, and individual differences. Those characteristics and needs form the foundation for services provided at the secondary level. Part I has three purposes:

- To discuss the relevance of existing conceptions of giftedness to the adolescent period and suggest a framework for secondary gifted education (Chapter 1),
- To highlight important general, developmental themes affecting all high ability adolescents (Chapters 2–3), and
- To illuminate the ways in which individual differences can influence the development of gifted and talented adolescents (Chapters 4–7).

In Chapter 1, Moon and Dixon review evolving conceptions of giftedness in the published work of four major theorists in the field of gifted education: Renzulli, Gagné, Feldhusen, and Sternberg. They conclude that all of these theorists have something to offer secondary gifted education, even though none of them developed their theories specifically for the adolescent period of development. Then, they propose a framework for secondary gifted education that builds on existing conceptions of giftedness, but suggests that secondary gifted education should place as much stress on personal and social development among high ability adolescents as it does on cognitive development.

The next two chapters illuminate some of the reasons for Moon and Dixon's stress on personal and social development. Hébert and Kelly's chapter on identity and career development highlights the importance of identity issues for adolescents and some of the unique identity issues facing gifted adolescents. Hébert and Kelly argue that career development is essential in secondary school and needs to be differentiated for gifted adolescents. Because career development is based on interests, secondary gifted educators need to assess the emerging interests of their students and help them understand how those interests can be translated into meaningful careers. Assouline and Colangelo's chapter on social-emotional development also stresses the importance of adolescence as a time of maturation and self-development in the context of teen culture. Because teen culture often emphasizes conformity, adolescence can be a difficult time for high ability youth, especially those whose talents lie in the academic areas. Assouline and Colangelo present an overview of the unique tensions experienced by gifted adolescents and provide guidance for ensuing healthy social and emotional development. Like Hébert and Kelly, they stress the importance of a focus on self-concept, identity, and career development. In addition, they provide specific guidance for furthering the development of gifted adolescents who are underachieving in school.

The final four chapters in Part I address individual differences within the gifted and talented population. It is important for secondary educators to be aware that gifted and talented students are not a homogeneous population. During adolescence, the interests of high ability youth become increasingly well-defined, their talents more and more specialized, and their levels of expertise increasingly differentiated (Gagné, 2000, 2005). In addition, factors such as gender (Chapter 4), ethnicity (Chapter 5), disabilities (Chapter 6), and differences in motivational profiles (Chapter 7) can influence their cognitive, personal, and social development. Hence, secondary gifted educators need to be aware of these individual difference factors and the ways they can influence development among high ability youth.

Reis' chapter on gender issues again stresses the importance of identity development in adolescence and defines a successful transition for gifted adolescents as "an integration of their abilities, talents, interests, personal choices, and values such that they are able to achieve at high levels and attain personal contentment" (p. 88). Gender influences every aspect of these developmental tasks. For example, researchers have found that gender influences students' attributional styles, performance on standardized tests, socialization, career aspirations, and self-concepts. Reis provides numerous strategies for parents, counselors, and teachers to use in preventing gender stereotypes from inhibiting the development of high ability adolescents, encouraging healthy gender role identities, and ensuring positive transitions through adolescence for all high ability youth.

In Chapter 5, Ford and Moore explore issues related to the additional identity-development variables of race, culture, and ethnicity. They show how these factors can inhibit or enhance talent development among gifted adolescents of color. They describe the unique psychological, socio-emotional, and academic issues faced by these high ability adolescents, stressing the need to see these students as both gifted and culturally diverse. As with the other authors in Part I, they place as much emphasis on promoting the personal and social development of these students as they do on encouraging their high cognitive abilities. They state that identity development is a central issue for culturally diverse, high ability youth, and that it is a more complex process than for other gifted adolescents. Gifted students of color must incorporate giftedness, gender, and ethnicity into their identities, often in the midst of a peer culture hostile to achievement. Ford and Moore suggest that multicultural counseling and multicultural education can help facilitate healthy development among gifted adolescents of color.

Especially challenging individual differences among gifted adolescents can stem from the presence of some type of disability. In Chapter 6, two scholars who are experts on the needs and characteristics of twice-exceptional students, Baum and Rizza, team with a twice-exceptional college student, Sara Renzulli, to provide a poignant summary of the unique challenges faced by these special individuals. The chapter authors define twice-exceptional adolescents as students with coexisting talents and deficits. These students have strengths in specific areas combined with deficits in learning, paying attention, or meeting social and emotional expectations that can impede their overall development. For example, a student who is talented in computer programming but has a co-occurring Attention Deficit Disorder would be a twice-exceptional student. Chapter 6 describes the characteristics of these students and provides suggestions on how educators can differentiate curricula for them and support their social-emotional development. Woven throughout the chapter is

Sara's story—the school experiences of one highly gifted adolescent with a learning disability who eventually learned to focus on her strengths, and compensate for her weaknesses, so she could succeed in college and life.

The final chapter in Part I focuses on motivation, a neglected area of individual differences in talented adolescents. Most conceptions of giftedness suggest motivation becomes increasingly important as gifted individuals mature and develop their talents (see Chapter 1). Patrick, Gentry, and Owen summarize research on the impact of individual differences in selected motivational constructs, such as goal orientations, on student achievement and well-being. They compare and contrast motivation research on typical students with the somewhat more limited research base on the motivational characteristics of gifted students. Chapter 7 also provides guidance on how educators can promote adaptive motivational beliefs and behaviors in all gifted adolescents.

In conclusion, Part I provides the foundation for *The Handbook of Secondary Gifted Education* by focusing attention on the unique characteristics and needs of gifted students in the adolescent period of development. Together, the chapters in Part I suggest that gifted adolescents need interventions that help them develop personally and socially, as well as academically. Perhaps the most important non-academic, developmental issue that gifted students must address in adolescence is identity development. Part I suggests that individual difference variables such as gender, race, and motivational style lend great complexity to the process of identity development among gifted adolescents. Educators and counselors need to forge strong partnerships to ensure that all of the developmental needs of gifted adolescents are met in secondary schools, and that these students have every opportunity to achieve at high levels in college and beyond.

References

Benbow, C. P. (1986). SYMP's model for teaching mathematically precocious students. In J. S. Renzulli (Ed.), *Systems and models for developing programs for the gifted and talented* (pp. 1–26). Mansfield Center, CT: Creative Learning Press.

Clasen, D. R., & Clasen, R. E. (1995). Underachievement of highly able students and the peer society. *Gifted and Talented International, 10,* 67–76.

Coleman, L. J. (2001). A "rag quilt": Social relationships among students in a special high school. *Gifted Child Quarterly, 45,* 164–173.

Cross, T. L., Coleman, L. J., & Stewart, R. A. (1995). Psychosocial diversity among gifted adolescents: An exploratory study of two groups. *Roeper Review, 17,* 181–185.

Cross, T. L., Coleman, L. J., & Terhaar-Yonkers, M. (1991). The social cognition of gifted adolescents in schools: Managing the stigma of giftedness. *Journal for the Education of the Gifted, 15,* 44–55.

Cross, T. L., Gust-Brey, K., & Ball, P. B. (2002). A psychological autopsy of the suicide of an academically gifted student: Researchers' and parents' perspectives. *Gifted Child Quarterly, 46,* 247–264.

Feldhusen, J. F. (1998). Programs and services at the secondary level. In J. VanTassel-Baska (Ed.), *Excellence in educating gifted and talented learners* (3rd ed., pp. 225–240). Denver: Love.

Gagné, F. (2000). Understanding the complex choreography of talent development. In K. A. Heller, F. J. Mönks, R. J. Sternberg, & R. F. Subotnik (Eds.), *International handbook of giftedness and talent* (pp. 67–79). Amsterdam: Elsevier.

Gagné, F. (2005). From noncompetence to exceptional talent: Exploring the range of academic achievement within and between grade levels. *Gifted Child Quarterly, 49*, 139–153.

Lubinski, D., & Benbow, C. P. (1994). The study of mathematically precocious youth: The first three decades of a planned 50-year study of intellectual talent. In R. F. Subotnik, & A. D. Arnold (Eds.), *Beyond Terman: Contemporary longitudinal studies of giftedness and talented*. Norwood, NJ: Ablex.

Lubinski, D., Webb, R., Morelock, M. J., & Benbow, C. P. (2001). Top 1 in 10,000: A 10-year follow-up of the profoundly gifted. *Journal of Applied Psychology, 86*, 718–729.

Moon, S. M. (1993). Using the Purdue three-stage model: Developing talent at the secondary level. *Journal of Secondary Gifted Education, 5*, 31–35.

Peterson, J. S. (2003). An argument for proactive attention to affective concerns of gifted adolescents. *Journal of Secondary Gifted Education, 14*, 62–71.

Sethna, B. N., Wickstrom, C. D., Boothe, D., & Stanley, C. (2001). The Advanced Academy of Georgia: Four years as a residential early college-entrance program. *Journal of Secondary Gifted Education, 13*, 11–21.

Steinberg, L. (1996). *Beyond the classroom*. New York: Simon & Schuster.

VanTassel-Baska, J. (2001). The role of Advanced Placement in talent development. *Journal of Secondary Gifted Education, 12*, 126–132.

CONCEPTIONS OF GIFTEDNESS IN ADOLESCENCE

by Sidney M. Moon
& Felicia A. Dixon

dolescence happens to gifted middle and high school students, just as it does to their nongifted peers. In fact, the adolescent period may be more prolonged among high ability youth, because their career goals may require a longer period of economic dependency during advanced schooling. How well do the conceptions of giftedness previously developed in the field of gifted education pertain to the adolescent years? Do we need conceptions of giftedness that focus specifically on adolescents? In this chapter, we provide a brief overview of the developmental tasks of adolescence. Then we review some of the conceptions of giftedness that have been developed by leaders in the field of gifted education and analyze their relevance to gifted adolescents. Finally, we offer a framework for gifted education at the secondary level that focuses on the developmental tasks facing high ability students during the adolescent period.

ADOLESCENCE

Steinberg (2005) defines adolescence as a period of transitions—biological, psychological, social, and economic. Although once thought to encompass just the teenage years, the adolescent period now has been lengthened considerably; both because young people mature earlier physically, and because so many individuals delay entering into work and marriage until their mid-20s. Often, social scientists refer to the stages of this important period as early adolescence (from about age 10–13), middle adolescence (ages 14–17), and finally late adolescence (ages 18–22). These terms seem to correspond with the school grades into which these youth fit—middle school, high school, and college. As noted above, late adolescence can extend into the mid to late 20s for youth who are pursuing careers with prolonged training, such as medicine, law, and science.

Pipher (1994) described adolescents as travelers, far from home with no native land, neither children nor adults. They are jet setters who fly from one country to another with amazing speed. Sometimes they are 4-years-old; an hour later they are 25. They don't really fit anywhere. They yearn for a place; a search for solid ground. Adolescence is a time of intense preoccupation with the self, which is growing and changing daily. Everything feels new.

Hill (1983) suggested a framework for studying the adolescent period composed of three distinct components: the fundamental changes of adolescence, the contexts of adolescence, and the psychosocial developments of adolescence. The fundamental changes of adolescence also include three elements: the onset of puberty (biological), the emergence of more advanced thinking abilities (cognitive), and the transition into new roles in society (social). These fundamental changes are universal in that all adolescents in all cultures go through them. Gifted adolescents, however, will normally progress through these changes in a different sequence from their more average ability peers. For example, advanced thinking abilities emerge earlier in gifted students and, as noted above, transitions into new societal roles may be delayed. Families, peers, schools, work, and leisure activities provide the contexts in which adolescents spend their time. Research suggests that families, peers, and schools all have a strong influence on the extent to which gifted adolescents remain committed to the talent development process (Csikszentmihalyi, Rathunde, & Whalen, 1993; Steinberg, 1996). Finally, psychosocial development includes such important dimensions as identity, autonomy, intimacy, sexuality, achievement, and the problems that arise within these areas. Adolescents are growing at rapid rates in many areas of life simultaneously. There is, perhaps, no period of the lifespan more developmentally complex than adolescence, and high ability adolescents have extra layers of complexity to navigate because of their giftedness.

Conceptions of Giftedness

How well do the conceptions of giftedness that have been developed in the field of gifted education pertain to the adolescent years? To answer this question, we provide brief descriptions of the evolving conceptions of giftedness of four theorists who have helped shape the field of gifted education: Renzulli, Gagné, Feldhusen, and Sternberg. The conceptions reviewed are the Triad Model (Renzulli); the Differentiated Model of Giftedness and Talent (DMGT; Gagné); the superior learning model and Talent Identification and Development in Education (TIDE; Feldhusen); and the triarchic theory, the development expertise theory, and the Wisdom Intelligence and Creative Synthesized (WICS) model (Sternberg). We provide a brief description of each conception of giftedness and related educational programming. Then, we analyze strengths and weaknesses of the conception as a guide for working with high ability adolescents and developing gifted education services at the secondary level. There are many other valuable conceptions of giftedness that are not reviewed here because of space limitations (see for example Gardner, 1983; Jarvin & Subotnik, this volume; Ziegler & Heller, 2000).

Joseph Renzulli

One of the most familiar conceptions of giftedness in education today was originally proposed by Renzulli (1978) and called the Triad Model. Renzulli conceptualized giftedness as having three clusters of traits: above average ability, task commitment, and creativity. These traits were selected because prior research suggested they were necessary for high levels of creative productivity and/or eminence in adults. Renzulli wrote,

> Giftedness consists of an interaction among three basic clusters of human traits—these clusters being above-average general abilities, high levels of task commitment, and high levels of creativity. Gifted and talented children are those possessing or capable of developing the composite set of traits and applying them to any potentially valuable area of human performance. Children who manifest or are capable of developing an interaction among the three clusters require a wide variety of educational opportunities and services that are not ordinarily provided through regular instructional programs. (p. 261)

The Triad model has also been called the three-ring conception of giftedness because Renzulli depicted his model as three overlapping circles, with each circle representing one of the three traits. Giftedness was defined as the area of overlap. In other words, giftedness is the co-occurrence of above-average ability, creativity, and task commitment as applied to a specific project or subject area. Renzulli called this definition an operational one since it met the criteria that enable it to be put into practice. First, this definition was derived from research studies dealing with the characteristics of gifted and talented individuals. Second, it provides guidance for the selection and/or development of instruments and procedures that can be used to design defensible identification systems. Finally, the definition provides direction for programming practices that capitalize upon the characteristics that "bring gifted youngsters to our attention as learners with special needs" (Renzulli, 1978, p. 261).

The focus on creative productivity as a hallmark of a gifted individual is clear in Renzulli's conception. He states that no single one of these three clusters makes giftedness, but rather, the interaction among the three clusters is the necessary ingredient for creative/productive accomplishment. In fact, Renzulli (1978) states that one of the major errors in identification procedures is overemphasis on superior abilities at the expense of the other two clusters of traits.

Renzulli's conception has been widely accepted in schools. His rather liberal conception of the amount of general ability needed for giftedness ("above-average intelligence") stems from his notion that more creative and productive persons come from below the 95th percentile than above it, and we may be guilty of actually discriminating against persons who have the greatest potential for high levels of accomplishment if we focus only on extremely high test scores. Task commitment is a trait found in creative and productive persons, and is a focused form of motivation. Although this is a nonintellective trait, it applies to the lives of highly productive people, and therefore is worthy of inclusion in his conception. Finally, creativity is an essential component of a gifted individual. Although measuring creativity is messy and often subjective, Renzulli found that in studying the lives of creative and productive people, a dimension of creativity was present in each.

Several school programs have been developed based on Renzulli's conception. The first model developed was the Enrichment Triad Model (Renzulli, 1977), which proposed that gifted students should experience three types of enrichment: Type I (general exploratory activities), Type II (group training activities), and Type III (individual and small group investigations of real problems). The ultimate goal of this model was to enable gifted and talented students to develop the constellation of traits needed for creative and productive giftedness. Next, the Revolving Door Identification Model was developed to provide a more flexible and inclusive approach to identification of gifted students (Renzulli, Reis, & Smith, 1981). The most recent and widely implemented model based on the Triad conceptions of giftedness is the Schoolwide Enrichment Model (SEM; Renzulli & Reis, 1985, 1997). Essentially a pull-out enrichment model, SEM offers a wide array of enrichment services for students. The model assumes that giftedness reflects behavior resulting from the interaction of the three clusters (above-average ability, task commitment, and creativity) in the three-ring conception of giftedness. Further, the model assumes that gifted behaviors can be developed, and services should be provided to any student when these behaviors are exhibited, rather than just to students who score well on standardized tests. All of these models were designed for younger children, and thus are implemented largely in elementary school contexts.

The Secondary Triad Model (Reis & Renzulli, 1986, 1989), on the other hand, was designed to implement the Enrichment Triad Model (Renzulli, 1977) at the secondary level. It is based on the three-ring conception of giftedness and provides guidance for implementing a Triad Enrichment Program with a Revolving Door Identification procedure at the secondary level. Implementation of the model begins with the formation of an interdisciplinary planning team including faculty members who volunteer to participate from each of the major academic areas. The team meets on a regular basis, and is responsible for planning and organizing the program goals and activities, curricular compacting options, and schoolwide enrichment opportunities. Prior to identifying students, the team must develop an array of enrichment services based on the Enrichment Triad Model. Once the services are in place, the team then identifies a talent pool of students representing the top 15–20% of the general population in either general ability areas or more specific areas of ability such as social studies or mathematics. After the students are selected, they are introduced to the services available to them. These services may include comprehensive assessment of student interests and learning styles, which can later be used to plan additional services related to student interests, as well as to guide students to expand their interests and learning styles. Identified students participate in Triad enrichment activities, either on a pull-out basis or through special "talent pool" classes. Eventually, they become investigators of real problems using the methods of inquiry utilized by professionals in their field of interest.

The talent pool classes can be general classes focused on group training activities, or they can be discipline-specific classes structured around the Enrichment Triad Model. In the discipline-specific classes, students enrolled in a talent pool history or science class participate in Type I activities like field trips and teacher-led discussions, Type II activities like developing research skills or learning the scientific method, and a culminating Type III activity that involves them in an independent investigation using the tools of inquiry they developed during Type II experiences. Hence, at the secondary level, the Triad enrichment model can become a curriculum framework for the development of secondary classes that emphasize the development of creative productivity.

Relative to middle schools, Renzulli (2000, 2001) proposed the establishment of Academies of Inquiry and Talent Development. Using enrichment clusters as the mode of delivery, students and teachers select the clusters in which they participate so that all students and teachers are involved. In addition, all activity is directed toward the production of a product or service, and authentic methods of professional investigators are used to pursue both the product and the service development. No predetermined lesson or unit plans govern these academies, so that the interests of the participants are truly pursued. Therefore, all students are not doing the same thing at the same time. Specially designated time blocks are established and rules of regular schooling are suspended in order for these academies to work.

In his most recent work, Renzulli has expanded his conception of giftedness to include what he calls "co-cognitive" characteristics that facilitate creative productivity (Renzulli, 2005; Renzulli & Sytsman, 2001). He calls this work "operation houndstooth" because it is an elaboration of the contextual and co-cognitive factors represented symbolically by the houndstooth background in the diagram of his original three-ring conception of giftedness (Renzulli, 1978). Through a review of the literature, Renzulli and his colleagues identified several co-cognitive factors, such as optimism, courage, passion, empathy, energy, and destiny, that facilitate talent development and creative productivity. He believes gifted programs in secondary schools should develop these co-cognitive factors in addition to the more traditional academic talents. In addition, he believes schools have a moral obligation to develop social capital by encouraging gifted students to become leaders who use their talents to enhance society. Gifted programs succeed to the extent that they develop gifted individuals who will place human concerns and the common good above material gain, ego-enhancement, and self-indulgence.

Comments on Renzulli's Conceptions and Gifted Adolescents

The Triad Model of giftedness has many strengths. It is empirically-based because it was developed after an extensive study of the traits of eminent adults from a wide variety of fields. In its original presentation, it was very easy to understand because it included only three components: above-average ability, creativity, and task commitment. The Triad Model is inclusive, especially compared to older models that set the threshold for giftedness as a score more than two standard deviations above the mean on an individual intelligence test (Terman, 1925). The typical IQ cut-off score conception of giftedness identifies only 1–2% of the population as gifted. The Triad model, on the other hand, opens the doors to gifted education to every student and actively serves at least 25–30% of the students in a school.

One of the greatest strengths of the Triad model is that it has led to very specific guidance for educational programming to foster creative productivity that spans the school years and moves into adulthood. It offers more concrete guidance than most models about how to find gifted adolescents by learning what behaviors they exhibit and developing their talents with programming that matches those traits. In offering enrichment activities that bring about creativity and productivity, the Academies of Inquiry and Talent Development and the Secondary Triad Model meet the needs of gifted adolescents who like working on self-directed projects. The Secondary Triad Model is an especially effective model for secondary students who know they have a specific talent, such as writers, scientists, artists, or actors, and want to pursue projects that further their interests. Its emphasis on exposure to a wide variety of topics, followed by independent learning of a self-selected topic is developmentally appropriate for middle school gifted students. In high school, this model can be very helpful for focused students with a project they would like to complete. In addition, the types of instructional activities recommended in the Triad model are very effective indirect methods of developing personal talent (Moon, 2003a; 2003b), and the development of personal talent is an important task for high ability adolescents.

Weaknesses of the Triad model for the secondary environment include numerous feasibility problems, especially if it is implemented through a resource room approach, with students being pulled out of regular classes in order to participate in enrichment activities. The resource room model does not map well on the structure of most secondary schools. In addition, the basic model is domain general and most secondary schools offer domain-specific curricula. This has been addressed to some extent in the Secondary Triad Model because that model recommends developing discipline-specific classes for students in the selected talent pool. However, it may be difficult to offer all of the content students need to meet state standards through talent pool classes, and it may be hard for school districts to offer talent pool classes in every subject area due to resource constraints. The Triad Model may be a better model for students in the early, exploratory stages of talent development, than for those in the middle stages (Bloom, 1985). However, many gifted adolescents are ready for middle-years interventions. The academic rigor and accelerative content of domain-specific honors or Advanced Placement classes may be a better fit for students with academic talent development at the secondary level who are in the middle stage of talent development. Finally, the Triad Model focuses on developing creative productivity; however, some gifted students lack creative or productive interests and talents. The model may not be as good a fit for students who desire to be competent professionals in fields like law, business, or medicine as it is for those who want to be groundbreaking scientists or Pulitzer prize novelists. In other words, the Triad conception of giftedness is somewhat narrow for gifted adolescents because it defines giftedness in terms of creative productivity, and not all adolescents will be interested in developing creative and productive talents.

Operation houndstooth has not yet been specifically operationalized in school settings. However, it does have implications for secondary schools. It suggests, for example, that gifted education needs to help gifted students develop attributes like courage and optimism, as well as expertise in subjects like mathematics. One way to do this would be to study biographies of individuals who exemplify one or more of the houndstooth attributes, such as Jack London, or who devoted their lives to improve society, such as Mother Theresa. It also suggests that service-learning activities should be integrated into secondary gifted education to help students develop an orientation toward community service. Since service learning offers opportunities to extend the learning context in an authentic manner, it is a good way for gifted adolescents to synthesize experiences. Finally, it suggests gifted education programs at the secondary level include character education and discussion of moral dilemmas facing high ability individuals in their curricula. Like the original Triad Model, operation houndstooth has the limitation of a priori definitions of desired outcomes for gifted adolescents. It will be a better fit for gifted adolescents who want to develop leadership talent, than for those who want to be pure academians.

Françoys Gagné

The Differentiated Model of Giftedness and Talent (DMGT; Gagné 1985, 2000; Gagné & Van Rossum, this volume) is a developmental model of giftedness that distinguishes between giftedness and talent. The model was originally presented in 1985, and has been refined by Gagné in subsequent years. Here we will emphasize the version of the model published in the *International Handbook of Giftedness and Talent* (Heller, Mönks, Sternberg, & Subotnik, 2002).

Giftedness is defined in the DMGT as natural human abilities or aptitudes. A gifted individual possesses gifts or talents that place him or her within the top 10% of his or her same aged peers. Gagné proposes that giftedness corresponds to superior performance in one or more human aptitude domains such as intellectual, creative, socio-affective, or sensorimotor. Aptitudes are conceptualized as partially controlled by genetic endowment. They are natural abilities, and are easier to observe in very young children who have had limited exposure to environmental influences and systematic learning experiences. In older children, aptitudes are best demonstrated by the ease and speed with which they acquire new knowledge and skills. Talent, on the other hand, represents high level mastery of knowledge and skills in one or more fields of human activity, including the arts, business, caring services, communication, science and technology, and sports. Talents emerge gradually over time, as the outcome of a long-term, systematic learning process. Talents emerge from aptitudes, but are more diverse and specific than aptitudes. For example, a small child with high intellectual aptitude, as measured by a traditional intelligence test, might eventually become a talented experimental physicist, history professor, or novelist.

In the DMGT, long periods of practice and training are essential for developing human aptitudes into talents. Through maturation, informal learning (i.e., those everyday tasks that shape acquired knowledge and skills), formal out-of-school learning (i.e., self-taught tasks engaged in during leisure time), and formal in-school learning, a complex, developmental process takes place that can gradually convert raw, natural aptitudes into very specific talents in areas like science and the arts.

Two categories of catalysts assist the developmental process of converting aptitudes to talents—intrapersonal and environmental. The catalysts are conceptualized as factors that either inhibit or assist the talent development process. There are five types of *intrapersonal catalysts* in Gagné's model: physical characteristics, motivation, volition, self-management, and personality. Physical characteristics include things like a person's health. Motivation and volition are psychological characteristics that help individuals set appropriate goals and persist toward those goals in the face of obstacles. Motivation is defined in the DMGT as an individual's needs, interests, and values—things that influence whether a person will initiate the process of talent development. Volition is defined as willpower, effort, and persistence. Volition enables a person to continue to strive toward his or her goals over long periods of time and to overcome setbacks on the journey. Together these two factors are very similar to task commitment, a major component of the Triad model's conceptualization of giftedness. Self-management is a related meta-construct that helps the individual structure and coordinate the talent development process. Finally, Gagné believes that an individual's personality has a strong influence on talent development, serving either to accelerate, slow down, or block learning processes.

There are four categories of *environmental catalysts* in the DMGT: milieu, persons, provisions, and events. Milieu includes various surrounding issues that influence individuals like culture, geography, family, and socio-economic status. For adolescents, the persons catalyst would include parents and other family members, teachers, coaches, and peers, among others. Provisions are where schools come into Gagné's model most closely. Schools are one of the major providers of systematic learning experiences that can either enhance or hinder the talent development process. Finally, Gagné notes that events such as accidents and receiving awards can exert an influence on talent development trajectories.

The final component of the DMGT is *chance* (Gagné, 2000). In fact, Gagné believes chance may play the greatest role of all, because it influences heritable characteristics such as aptitudes and personality traits, the opportunities available to persons to develop their talents over their lifetime, and random events, such as accidents, all of which impact the long-term talent development process. Chance is especially important in athletic talent development, where inherited physical characteristics and accidents both play a large part in the talent development process (Van Rossum & Gagné, this volume). Chance was also a major component in an earlier conceptualization of giftedness developed by Tannenbaum (1983, 1986).

Comments on the DMGT and Gifted Adolescents

Gagné's theory has direct relevance for the period of adolescence because it is developmental. His theory proposes that maturation and systematic learning experiences convert abilities to more developed talents. School, out-of-school experiences such as academic summer camps, and extracurricular activities provide catalysts for this learning and practice to take place. The theory is elegant and comprehensive. It applies to all talent areas and specifies both internal, noncognitive factors and external, environmental factors that influence whether a particular adolescent will develop his or her abilities into talents. It provides clear, operational definitions of terms that are often used interchangeably, like "gifts" and "talents." It also addresses the issue of levels of ability, stating that the top 10% in a given aptitude area should be considered gifted and the top 10% of peers with comparable learning opportunities should be considered talented. This is a somewhat more restrictive number than would be identified with Renzulli's approach, but still considerably more liberal than the older, IQ-based notion of giftedness.

Gagné's theory is complex and interesting. However, its application in the classroom for secondary teachers is not refined enough to understand what this theory means to curriculum and instruction. It tells more about the students' processes than about how to serve them. In other words, a weakness of Gagné's theory for school settings is its lack of operationalization. It was designed as a theoretical model to provide a map of the talent development terrain and to guide research on talent development processes. Although it stresses the importance of systematic learning experiences in converting aptitudes to talents, it does not provide much specific guidance for educational programming for gifted adolescents. Gagné's theory does have implications for educational programs in secondary schools, however. For example, his theory suggests that schools might want to identify adolescents for gifted and talented services by two methods: (a) aptitudes, to ensure that students with unrealized potential are identified; and (b) emerging talents, to ensure that students who are demonstrating high level expertise in a particular subject area are identified regardless of test scores. It also suggests that intrapersonal characteristics of students should be assessed and developed during adolescence to facilitate the talent development process. Finally, the model provides support for the increasing specialization of teachers and subject matter common in secondary schools. Such specialization is necessary as individuals convert their aptitudes into more specific talents. It also suggests, however, that secondary schools need to pay attention to where specific students stand on the talent development continuum so that they can be placed in courses that fit their current talent profiles, and so that they may experience coursework that provides sufficient challenge to ensure learning is taking place. The talent development process is long, even when it proceeds optimally. Secondary schools can become a hindrance to academic talent development if they provide only slow-paced instruction based on minimal competency standards.

John Feldhusen

Feldhusen's conception of giftedness derived from a focus on the characteristics and needs of children who were very able learners, rather than from a focus on the characteristics of eminent or talented adults (Feldhusen & Kolloff, 1986). Characteristics such as advanced vocabulary and quick mastery of factual information give rise to basic needs such as experiencing learning activities at an appropriate level and pace that must be met by schools if these students are to develop their potential talents to the highest level (Feldhusen & Kolloff; Feldhusen & Robinson-Wyman, 1986). Feldhusen (1983) initially conceptualized giftedness as a composite of (a) general intellectual ability, (b) positive self-concept, (c) achievement motivation, and (d) talent. Feldhusen clearly distinguished the ways giftedness manifests during adolescence from the ways it manifests in adulthood. Giftedness was seen as a psychological and physical predisposition for superior learning and performance in the formative years and high-level achievement or performance in adulthood. Because predispositions require nurturing to develop into high-level achievement, Feldhusen, like Gagné, believed chance plays a large part in the development of giftedness. Schools and families are major nurturing agencies, and both may fail at the task.

Feldhusen and Robinson-Wyman (1986) applied Feldhusen's conceptualization of giftedness to gifted adolescents. They reviewed lists of characteristics of gifted children and adolescents and found a common theme of gifted adolescents having the capacity "to absorb great amounts of information readily and to transform that information in complex and creative ways" (p. 156). Again, these characteristics led to needs which, in turn, gave rise to an eclectic programming model called the Purdue Secondary Model, which was designed to meet the needs of gifted adolescents in the typical secondary school environment. The needs that make-up the foundation of the Purdue Secondary Model are as follows (Feldhusen & Robinson-Wyman):

1. maximum achievement of basic skills and concepts;
2. learning activities at appropriate level and pace;
3. experience in creative thinking and problem solving;
4. development of convergent abilities, especially in logical deduction and convergent problem solving;
5. stimulation of imagery, imagination, and spatial abilities;
6. development of self-awareness and acceptance of own capacities, interests, and needs;
7. stimulation to pursue higher level goals and aspirations;
8. exposure to a variety of fields of study, art, and occupations;
9. development of independence, self-direction, and discipline in learning;

10. experience relating intellectually, artistically, and affectively with other gifted, creative, and talented students;
11. a large fund of information about diverse topics; and
12. access and simulation to reading.

To meet these needs, the model included a smorgasbord of provisions for talented students, including counseling services, seminars, honors and Advanced Placement classes, acceleration opportunities, foreign languages, the arts, cultural experiences, career education, vocational programs, and extra-school instruction such as summer talent development programs. The components of this model include those that are functional (i.e., counseling, vocational programs, cultural experiences) and those that are administrative (i.e., extra-school instruction, seminars, advanced classes). A student moves through the program by developing a personal growth plan consisting of both areas of strength and those of relative weaknesses that need to be remedied.

The Purdue Secondary Program Model is a comprehensive model that attends to curriculum issues, growth plans for individual students, talent development in the arts and vocational areas, as well as in the intellectual forms of giftedness. The counseling services provided to gifted students are valuable to adolescents seeking guidance to make informed decisions about plans of study and career options. Specific guidance for school districts interested in implementing programming has been provided in a book called *Identifying and Educating Gifted Students at the Secondary Level* (Feldhusen, Hoover, & Sayler, 1990). This book also includes the Purdue Academic Rating Scales, which are behavioral checklists secondary teachers can use to identify students with emerging talents in the following academic and vocational disciplines: mathematics, science, English, social studies, foreign languages, vocational agriculture, business and office, home economics, and trade and industrial fields.

Feldhusen also used the needs of gifted adolescents as the basis for a curriculum model, called the Purdue Three-Stage Model, which is uniquely suited to the learning needs of gifted and talented students (Feldhusen, 1980a, 1980b). The Purdue Three-Stage Model recommends gifted students be grouped for instruction so they can enjoy the intellectual stimulation of high ability peers as they experience fast-paced learning in an environment that encourages the development of creative and critical thinking skills, problem-solving skills, and independent learning skills. Moon (1993) has recommended this model for the development of courses for gifted and talented students at the secondary level. The model has been applied to the creation of a middle-school seminar program (Nidiffer & Moon, 1994), an honors English sequence for verbally talented 9th–12th graders (Powley & Moon, 1993), and a science research class for scientifically talented 11th and 12th graders (Whitman & Moon, 1993). More recently, the model has been promoted as being particularly effective for adolescents with talent in the STEM disciplines (science, technology, engineering, and mathematics) because it emphasizes complex problem solving and independent projects—the very types of activities professionals in the STEM disciplines utilize most often in their daily work (Moon, 2004).

Feldhusen's (1983, 1986, 1995) conception of giftedness evolved throughout his career because he was always observing, reading, and learning. He was quite open to modifying his ideas in response to new inputs. He developed the Talent Identification and Development in Education (TIDE) model to incorporate new research on the processes by which talents emerge (Feldhusen, 1995). The conception of giftedness underlying the TIDE model is more developmental than his previous conceptions, somewhat less focused on the school environment, and much more complex. It proposes that genetically determined abilities lead to precocity, which give rise to emerging aptitudes, abilities, and intelligences that can be observed by parents and teachers. These emerging abilities, in turn, interact with experiences in families and schools and emerging motivational and learning styles to develop skills such as creative insight skills, a functional knowledge base, creative skills, and metacognitive skills. These skills enable individuals to demonstrate mature talent. This model is somewhat similar to Gagné's model (1985, 2000) because it attempts to describe the process by which aptitudes are converted to talents. It is similar to Renzulli's work, because it emphasizes the importance of both motivation and creativity in the development of talent.

This developmental conceptualization of giftedness is the foundation for the TIDE programming model (Feldhusen, 1995), which is designed to highlight four talent areas particularly appropriate for development in the secondary school environment: academic/intellectual (science, math, English, social studies, language); artistic (dance, music, drama, graphics, sculpture, photography); vocational/technical (home economics, trade-industrial, business-office, agricultural, computers and technology); and interpersonal/social (leadership, care-giving, sales, human services). Again, we see the eclectic and pragmatic approach of Feldhusen to gifted education at the secondary level. The TIDE model is domain-specific and emphasizes subjects taught in most secondary schools. It is unique in highlighting the need for gifted education in the vocational/technical and interpersonal/social domains at the secondary level.

Comments on Feldhusen's Conceptualizations and Gifted Adolescents

Feldhusen's conceptualization of giftedness has the advantage of being based on research describing the observed characteristics and needs of high ability students. His list of needs can be used by secondary teachers to guide curriculum and instruction for high ability students. Feldhusen's work suggests that high ability students should be grouped together for some or all of their instruction in the secondary environment in order to meet their needs for maximum achievement, appropriately paced instruction, and opportunities to interact with other gifted and talented students. His conceptualization of giftedness is directly relevant to schools. His work led to three different application models that can guide secondary gifted education: the Purdue Secondary Model, the Purdue Three-Stage Model, and the TIDE Model. All of Feldhusen's applied work was eclectic, modular, flexible, and pragmatic, which makes it easy to implement his models in the secondary environment. Feldhusen's conceptualization of giftedness also includes affective factors, such as self-confidence and motivation, that are very important in adolescence. The TIDE conceptualization is unique in the stress it places on a large knowledge base; development of a large knowledge base is one of the functions of secondary schools.

The Purdue Secondary Model is comprehensive and has direct relevance for gifted adolescents as they move through school. The model was designed to be very pragmatic and flexible. It fits into the existing structure of most secondary schools and can be wholly or partially implemented based on the needs and resources of a particular school district. However, it is very complex, requiring many administrative functions that necessitate specialized training. In this time of inclusion in the classroom and movement away from specialized programming, there will probably be philosophical opposition to this model in some schools and communities. That said, it is relevant to adolescence, makes pragmatic use of existing programs (i.e., AP and honors classes) and seeks to enable each individual to experience appropriate educational experiences in his or her unique talent areas.

Feldhusen's initial conceptualization of giftedness was not developmental and provided little guidance for students and their families because it lacked specificity. When combined with the needs of gifted students, it did provide guidance for parents of younger high ability children advocating for appropriate services. However, this initial model was developed primarily for the elementary school environment and provided only limited guidance to adolescents and their teachers. The TIDE conception, on the other hand, is developmental and, hence, a better fit for adolescents. Indeed, it led directly to the development of a secondary programming model that includes areas often neglected in gifted education, such as technology and business education. Like the DMGT, TIDE specifies how abilities are converted to talents. However, TIDE is more limited than the DMGT. It is a model of academic talent development, not talent development in general. It also lacks the elegance of the DMGT. However, perhaps because of its specificity, it does point out some factors that are not stressed in Gagné's model, but are quite relevant to academic talent development, such as the importance of a large knowledge base and metacognition. Like Renzulli and unlike Gagné, Feldhusen places great stress on the importance of developing creative abilities. Since the development of creativity is often neglected in secondary schools, this aspect of his work serves as a reminder of the importance of creativity in the accomplishments of many talented adults and the need to focus on the development of creative skills in secondary gifted education.

Robert Sternberg

Sternberg's (1995, 1997, 2000, 2003) conceptions of giftedness have also evolved over the course of his career. He is perhaps best known for his Triarchic Theory of Intelligence. The Triarchic model is a trait model specifying the traits that distinguish gifted individuals. The Triarchic model states that one's giftedness cannot be expressed by a single IQ score, but rather is better understood through three kinds of intelligence: analytic, synthetic, and practical. Analytic intelligence is that which is necessary for most school tasks and is measured well by intelligence tests, particularly analytical reasoning and reading comprehension tasks. Synthetic intelligence is expressed best in creativity, insightfulness, intuition, and coping with novelty. Sternberg states that although these people may not score the highest on intelligence tests, good synthetic thinkers may make the greatest contributions to society because of their innovative ideas. Finally, practical intelligence involves applying both analytic and synthetic skills to practical, everyday situations. When someone needs to change a tire or follow a recipe, it does not matter what score he or she received on an intelligence test if he or she cannot perform the needed task. In his early work, Sternberg viewed giftedness as a balance among the analytic, synthetic, and practical abilities in which the gifted individual is a good mental self-manager. This model of giftedness suggests that secondary schools should be identifying students who have high levels of ability in all three of these areas of intelligence combined with good self-management skills. Schools should work with these students through special programming to further develop their abilities in the subject areas where they excel.

Sternberg (1995) provided another perspective on giftedness by suggesting an implicit theory of giftedness. In his implicit theory, there are five necessary and sufficient conditions that gifted persons have in common:

- Excellence—a person must be extremely good at something;
- Rarity—a person must exhibit a high level of an attribute uncommon in comparison to peers;
- Productivity—the superior trait must lead to productivity;
- Demonstrability—the trait must be demonstrated on one or more valid tests; and
- Value—the superior performance must be valued by society.

Sternberg suggested that such an implicit theory must be relative to culture, because different cultures behave in different ways. Implicit theories suggest their own identification systems, as well as the system of educating those identified. For example, this theory suggests that secondary schools should identify students who already excel in an area in comparison with their peers, as demonstrated by unusual performances or high scores on one or more valid tests, and then provide educational programming that enables these students to develop products that will be valued by society such as scientific discoveries, prize-winning short stories, insightful critiques, moving theatrical performances, or humanitarian policies.

Sternberg (2000) has also conceptualized giftedness as developing expertise. In this conceptualization he focuses on how individuals move from novice to expert in a given human endeavor. Hence, this is a developmental, or process model. It focuses on how giftedness develops. The developing expertise model, like Gagné's model and the Jarvin and Subotnik model in this volume, places a great deal of emphasis on the importance of focused and reflective practice by the individual. The model suggests that several characteristics of the learner, such as learning, motivation, thinking skills, knowledge, and metacognition, all have an important role to play as an individual moves from novice to expert in a given area of study. This model also acknowledges that contextual factors, such as cultural values, influence the development of expertise. In the developing expertise model secondary students are viewed as novices who are capable of becoming experts in one or more domains if they engage in appropriate deliberate practice to build their expertise.

Building on both the triarchic theory and the developing expertise theory, Sternberg (2003) has developed an even more comprehensive conceptualization he calls the WICS model of giftedness. WICS stands for Wisdom, Intelligence, and Creativity Synthesized. In his latest conceptualization, Sternberg views wisdom, intelligence, and creativity as the ingredients that must be synthesized to create a gifted individual. Hence, WICS is a trait model. Intelligence in the WICS model is conceptualized as "successful intelligence" or the ability to achieve one's goals in life by capitalizing on strengths and compensating for weaknesses in order to adapt to, shape, and select environments through a combination of analytical, creative, and practical abilities (Sternberg, 1996; Sternberg & Grigorenko, 2000, 2003). This is a much broader conceptualization of intelligence than IQ. It includes the three components of the triarchic theory of intelligence, but combines those abilities with skills from the personal domain, such as self-awareness and self-regulation, that enable individuals to achieve their goals in life.

Creativity is important in the WICS theory for the same reason it was important in the three-ring conception of giftedness—the gifted individual in the WICS theory is one who makes contributions to society and exercises effective leadership. These contributions require creativity. Sternberg believes that creative work requires applying and balancing the three intellectual abilities from the triarchic theory of intelligence—analytic, practical, and synthetic abilities. In addition, the creative individual will demonstrate the following attributes:

- the ability to redefine problems,
- questioning and analyzing of assumptions,
- willingness to "sell" his or her ideas,
- recognition of the importance of mastering the knowledge base in one's field,
- willingness to surmount obstacles,
- willingness to take sensible risks,
- tolerance of ambiguity,
- self-efficacy,
- love of what one is doing,
- willingness to delay gratification, and
- courage.

Sternberg believes that secondary schools should identify and serve students who demonstrate these attributes and work with all high ability youth to help them become more creative, so they will be able to apply their abilities in ways that will make a true difference in the world.

The final component of giftedness in the WICS theory is wisdom. Here Sternberg moves into the realm of values. Giftedness is no longer just a cognitive characteristic of individuals. Instead, the gifted individual is a highly talented person who balances self-interest with the interests of others to enhance the common good. Brilliant criminals and selfish individuals focused on accumulating material wealth are not gifted, according to WICS theory. Gifted individuals are wise leaders who use their talents to enhance the welfare of others and improve society.

Comments on Sternberg's Theories and Gifted Adolescents

Sternberg's conceptualizations of giftedness offer several useful perspectives for secondary gifted education. The Triarchic theory is one of several broadened conceptualizations of the abilities that underlie gifted performances (see also Caroll, 1993; Gardner, 1983). It is unique in its balanced emphasis on three, relatively uncorrelated sets of abilities—analytic, synthetic, and practical. Secondary schools generally place heavy emphasis on identifying and developing analytic intelligence, while virtually ignoring synthetic and practical intelligence. Because synthetic intelligence is essential for creative productive work and practical intelligence becomes increasingly important in adult life and the later stages of talent development (Jarvin & Subotnik, this volume), the Triarchic theory suggests that secondary gifted educators should place approximately equal emphasis on these three abilities, both in identifying gifted adolescents for services and in providing educational experiences for such students.

The developing expertise theory of giftedness, like Gagné's theory, is an excellent fit for the adolescent stage of development because adolescents are actively engaged in developing expertise in their potential talent area(s). There is a rule of thumb in the talent development literature that it takes approximately 10 years of focused, deliberate practice to become an expert. The process of becoming an expert was found by Bloom (1985) to occur in three distinct stages, which he termed early, middle, and late. Most high ability adolescents will be in the middle stage of academic talent development. This middle stage is extremely important because it is the stage in which students become serious about a talent area and focus on mastering the skills of the discipline. Tremendous effort is required to complete this stage of talent development successfully. Secondary schools have the potential to be major contributors to the development of expertise if they provide challenging coursework that enables students to acquire expertise rapidly and thoroughly in academic areas where they have high levels of interest and ability.

The WICS model is more focused on desired outcomes of the talent development process than on the process itself, and so may be less helpful as a guide for secondary schools. The model provides very little guidance for how it might be applied to the secondary school environment. However, the WICS model does remind secondary gifted educators that wisdom is an important component of responsible adult lives. Giftedness is a two-edged sword because it can be applied to inspiring or reprehensible deeds. WICS asks secondary educators to consider whether their strategies to educate high ability youth include developing awareness of important ethical issues and building the skills these students will need to make wise decisions for their lives and the lives of those for whom they are responsible. The WICS model may be a particularly useful framework for secondary talent development programs focused on developing leadership talent. The type of giftedness embodied in WICS (i.e., a balanced combination of intelligence, creativity, and wisdom) is especially crucial for leaders.

A Holistic, Developmental Framework

As our brief, illustrative review has demonstrated, existing conceptions of giftedness have various emphases. Some were developed to identify and explain the characteristics of gifted adults so that we could try to develop those characteristics in children (Renzulli, 1978). Others were developed to explain the talent development process (Bloom, 1985; Gagné, 1985, 2000; Jarvin & Subotnik, this volume; Sternberg, 2000). Some theories focus on specifying the traits that lead us to identify individuals as gifted, such as Terman's high IQ theory (1925), Sternberg's Triarchic Theory (1997), and Gardner's (1983) theory of multiple intelligences. Other theories are more pragmatic, focusing on identifying the characteristics of learners that suggest a need for more advanced educational experiences in schools in order to prevent the harm that can occur through inappropriate school placement and enable high-ability learners to develop their talents (Feldhusen, 1983, 1995). The outcomes promoted by the various conceptions of giftedness vary from high levels of demonstrated talent (Gagné, 2000; Sternberg, 2000), to creative productivity (Jarvin & Subotnik, this volume; Renzulli 1978), to social capital and wise leadership (Renzulli, 2005; Sternberg, 2003). However, none of the existing conceptualizations of giftedness focuses specifically and exclusively on academically gifted adolescents.

We would like to propose a holistic, developmental framework to guide secondary schools in developing gifted programming (see Figure 1). Prior to using our holistic, developmental framework, a school should develop or adopt a local definition of giftedness (for guidance on this process see Moon, in press). Once giftedness has been defined and conceptualized in a way that is consistent with local goals and values, the framework we propose in this section can be used to focus educational services on the specific developmental needs of gifted adolescents.

Our framework is holistic because it synthesizes the characteristics of high ability adolescents and the developmental tasks they face. It can be used to guide both identification and programming. It is designed to enable schools to help high-ability youth maximize their development during the adolescent years. It includes cognitive, personal, and social components. We describe each of these components and then discuss the implications of the holistic, developmental framework for secondary gifted education programs.

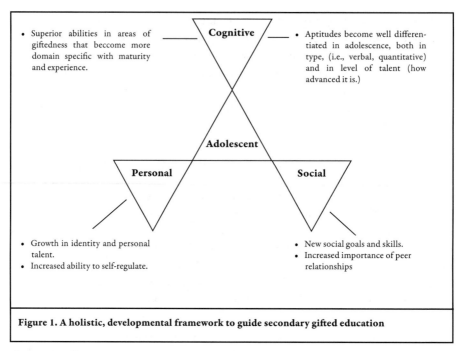

Superior abilities in areas of giftedness that beccome more domain specific with maturity and experience.

Cognitive

Aptitudes become well differentiated in adolescence, both in type, (i.e., verbal, quantitative) and in level of talent (how advanced it is.)

Adolescent

Personal

Social

- Growth in identity and personal talent.
- Increased ability to self-regulate.

- New social goals and skills.
- Increased importance of peer relationships

Figure 1. A holistic, developmental framework to guide secondary gifted education

Cognitive Components

The academically gifted adolescent will demonstrate superior cognitive abilities in his or her area(s) of giftedness. These abilities will be increasingly domain-specific as the adolescent matures. Hence, the relevance of general intelligence becomes less important over the course of adolescence, and specific aptitudes such as verbal or mathematical reasoning become more important. Like Gardner (1983) and Gagné (1985, 2000), we believe that individuals have profiles of aptitudes in different areas. Like Feldhusen (1995), Gagné (1985; 2000), and Sternberg (2000), we believe that aptitudes are converted to talents and expertise through a developmental process involving deliberate practice over a period of many years. In the academic talent areas, this conversion process usually coincides developmentally with adolescence. Hence, adolescence is a critical talent development period for academically gifted youth.

During adolescence, aptitudes become increasingly differentiated. Thus, a high-IQ child who appeared to be good at everything when she began elementary school, will have a much more distinctive pattern of cognitive strengths and weaknesses during adolescence that can predict differences in developmental trajectories and occupational pursuits (Lubinski, Webb, Morelock, & Benbow, 2001). In other words, adolescence is a period of rapidly increasing differentiation in talent profiles, both with respect to type of talent (e.g., verbal vs. quantitative) and level of talent (e.g., number of grade levels of advancement). Academically talented adolescents have the capacity for sophisticated, adult-level cognitive processes. In Piagetian terms, they are at the highest stage of cognitive development, formal operational thought. As a result, they are capable of sophisticated critical and creative thinking. They also have the capacity to master large and complex knowledge bases relatively quickly. Often these students are dialectical thinkers (Sternberg, 1998) who recognize that most real-life problems do not have a unique solution that is correct while other solutions are incorrect. Rather than closing their minds to alternatives, they propose a thesis for the solution of the problem, consider its antithesis, and look for a synthesis that somehow integrates these two opposing and often irreconcilable points of view. To fully meet these students' cognitive needs, educational experiences must incorporate open discussion and debate over issues relevant to each discipline (Dixon, this volume). Hence, their educational experiences should capitalize on these traits through challenging, information-rich coursework that furthers thinking and problem-solving abilities and produces independent learners who have mastered the foundations of each discipline and are beginning to be able to make original contributions to their areas of specialization.

Personal Components

Adolescence is also a time of personal growth for high-ability adolescents, especially in the area of identity (Hébert & Kelly, this volume). As a result, adolescence is an ideal time for academically talented students to develop personal talent (Moon & Ray, this volume). We believe it is crucial for academically talented adolescents to focus on the development of personal talent for two reasons. First, adolescence is a time of heightened personal decision making. As defined in this chapter, adolescence spans the period from middle school through the establishment of a career and/or a family. During that period, high-ability youth must make many crucial life decisions, such as where they will attend college, what fields they will study, what career they will pursue, and how they will balance their personal and professional lives. High-ability adolescents who have developed strong personal decision making skills will make better decisions than those who neglect to develop these skills. Second, self-regulation skills are increasingly important in the secondary environment because students have more choices, more opportunities, and increasingly complex work to do. Third, other skills in the personal domain, such as capitalizing on strengths and compensating for weaknesses, resisting socio-cultural stereotypes, demonstrating resilience in the face of adversity, exerting high levels of effort over long periods of time, and restoring self-confidence following poor performance, become increasingly important success factors as high ability individuals endeavor to develop very high levels of expertise (Gagné, 2000; Jarvin & Subotnik, this volume; Sternberg, 2003). Thus we believe that those high ability youth who have strong aptitude for traditional domains such as science, social studies, or creative writing, along with low to average levels of personal competence, will have difficulty converting their high aptitudes into demonstrable talents in adulthood. These students need remedial personal talent development interventions during the secondary years that will enable them to stay on track with the process of developing their gifts into talents. Similarly, adolescents with highly developed levels of personal talent will be able to achieve at higher levels in secondary school than would be predicted by purely cognitive assessments. Hence, secondary schools should consider adding personal talent assessments to their identification procedures.

Personal talent is also important for high-ability adolescents because it enables them to enhance their well-being (Moon, 2003b). In childhood, the most important influence on well-being is family functioning. Family remains very important to well-being at the beginning of adolescence, but becomes increasingly less important as adolescence progresses. Adults who live in a free and open society are responsible for creating their own well-being. Hence, adolescence becomes an important transition period between childhood, where most determinants of well-being are outside of the individual's control, to adulthood, where most determinants of well-being are under personal control. The psychological component of personal talent may be the most important component to develop in adolescents to enhance their well-being. High ability students need to understand, internalize, and exhibit the psychological dispositions that research has repeatedly demonstrated enhance well-being, such as optimism and hardiness (Moon; Moon & Ray, this volume). They also need to develop strong personal decision making skills, because the choices they make for their lives during the adolescent years will have a dramatic impact on their well-being. Finally, personal talent development is especially important for high-ability adolescents who wish to build their lives around the simultaneous achievement of multiple, competing goals. The more complex a life an adolescent wants to lead, the more important it is for him or her to develop personal talent.

Social Components

The social dimension is included in our framework because social relationships become increasingly important facilitators or inhibitors of talent development during the adolescent period. We do not believe it is necessary for all gifted adolescents to develop high levels of social talent. High levels of social talent are most essential for those adolescents whose career goals are focused on fields that have high social talent demands such as teaching and leadership (Moon & Ray, this volume). However, high ability adolescents who are able to successfully negotiate the tasks of differentiating from their family of origin and developing healthy peer relationships that promote both achievement and affiliation are likely to enjoy higher levels of well-being and success in school than their peers who experience social alienation or hide their talents in order to be accepted and popular (Clasen & Clasen, 1995; Peterson, 2002).

Because peer relationships are so important to adolescents, the social domain is an important influence on talent development trajectories in adolescence (Clasen & Clasen, 1995; Coleman, 2001; Cross, Coleman, & Stewart, 1995; Cross, Coleman, & Terhaar-Yonkers, 1991; Steinberg, 1996). In addition, as adolescence progresses, high ability adolescents are increasingly likely to want to integrate intimate relationships into their lives. Those adolescents who have superior social skills are likely to be more successful in building strong, supportive friendships and intimate relationships with persons who encourage them to fulfill their individual potential. Academically talented adolescents who participate in summer talent development programs often perceive the primary benefits of those programs to be social in nature (Enersen, 1993). In other words, these students are aware they that need, and benefit from, positive, supportive peer relationships with other students like themselves who understand them and support their achievement-orientation.

Finally, social competence is a prerequisite for success in many fields that do not require high levels of social talent. For example, engineers and scientists need to have good teamwork skills. Therefore, we believe that secondary schools must pay attention to the social dimension of students' development. It is not enough to help talented adolescents develop academic expertise. Educators must also assist them in learning skills in the social domain such as how to seek out mentors, develop collegiality, collaborate with persons from other cultures, and create support networks (Jarvin & Subotnik, this volume).

Implications for Identification and Programming

Introduction

Our holistic, developmental framework suggests school districts need to pay attention to cognitive, personal, and social characteristics in the identification process, regardless of the underlying conception of giftedness guiding programming. It is not enough to focus only on achievement when identifying gifted adolescents. Academically talented adolescents need to be assessed in three areas—cognitive, personal, and social. Profiles of student strengths and weaknesses in these three areas can guide both identification and programming. For example, some students may benefit from strength-based instruction in their talent areas and weakness-based instruction to correct personal or social skill deficits.

Programs for academically gifted adolescent students should provide direct instruction in the talent domain, as well as direct instruction in personal and social skills such as time management, personal decision-making, and conflict resolution. Instructional processes in advanced classes for academically gifted adolescents should focus on developing cognitive skills such as creative and critical thinking, enabling students to carry out projects similar to those undertaken by professionals. Advanced classes should also engage students in activities, such as role playing, simulations, and service learning, that provide opportunities to build personal and social skills. More specific guidance for identification and programming related to each of the three components of the holistic, developmental framework are provided below.

Identification and Development of Academic Talent

As a result of the increasing specificity of aptitudes as students mature, performances become more important for assessing giftedness in adolescence, especially in talent areas where few psychometrically sound assessments exist. In addition, because of the widening-gap phenomenon (Gagné, 2005), there will be greater differences in ability levels within a group of high-ability students in a given subject area in secondary school than there were in elementary school. The increasing specificity of aptitudes, combined with the widening gap phenomenon, suggests that both acceleration and grouping strategies should be utilized with high ability secondary students (Colangelo, Assouline, & Gross, 2004a; 2004b; Feldhusen & Moon, 1992; Kulik, 2003; Rogers, 1991). For example, high-ability students will benefit from access to fast-paced classes with differentiated curricula where they have an opportunity to learn alongside other students who have developed similar levels of expertise in the subject area. The cognitive characteristics of high-ability adolescents combined with their personal and social characteristics suggest that such advanced coursework should be taught in a way that will develop personal and social competencies. Curriculum models that emphasize small group problem solving and independent learning may be particularly appropriate models to guide the development of advanced coursework because they can develop personal and social competence simultaneously with academic talent. Teachers of Advanced Placement classes would benefit from considering these dimensions as they cover the necessary course material.

Identification and Development of Personal Talent

In order to develop both personal and social competence, high ability adolescents need to become skilled at identifying and expressing emotions, because both types of competence require effective emotional processing (Gardner, 1983; Mayer & Salovey, 1997; Moon & Ray, this volume). In other words, high-ability students need to develop emotional skills in adolescence to remain on positive talent development trajectories. Hence, school districts may want to include a measure of emotional intelligence in their assessment of academically talented youth (Mayer, Caruso, & Salovey, 1999; Mayer & Geher, 1996; Mayer, Perkins, Caruso, & Salovey, 2001; Salovey, Mayer & Caruso, 2002). Measuring emotional intelligence would be a first step to assessing the strengths and weaknesses of academically talented adolescents in the personal and social domains. Adolescence is a period of heightened emotions, and so it seems an ideal time for high-ability youth to focus on their emotional development.

Our framework also suggests that adolescence is an optimal time to search for students who have high levels of personal talent. The intrapersonal skills called practical intelligence (Jarvin & Subotnik, this volume), intrapersonal catalysts (Gagné, 2000; Van Rossum & Gagné, this volume), and components of personal talent (Moon, 2003b; Moon & Ray, this volume) become increasingly important in adolescence, important enough that it may be worthwhile to identify youth who have high levels of personal talent and provide them access to gifted education services. These individuals have motivational characteristics that facilitate the achievement of their goals, enabling them to derive maximum benefit from enriched and advanced coursework in their areas of interest, even when they do not score exceptionally well on traditional tests of ability (Gottfried & Gottfried, 2004; Gottfried, Gottfried, Cook, & Morris, 2005).

Both direct and indirect instructional strategies can be used to develop personal talent (Moon, 2003a; Moon & Ray, this volume). Indirect strategies can be infused into all courses targeted at high ability students. Direct strategies can be included as one component of an integrated gifted and talented program (Betts & Kercher, 1999) or a special class on personal talent development.

Identification and Development of Social Talent

Our framework suggests that adolescence is an optimal time to assess and develop talent in the social domain. Adolescents are socially oriented. They are in an opportune period of their lives to develop social skills. The more socially talented among them are eager to participate in experiences such as leadership development programs or conflict management training. Areas outside of gifted education, notably organizations like 4H and Future Farmers of America (FFA), have recognized and capitalized on the readiness of adolescents to develop social and leadership talent (Moon & Ray, this volume). Gifted education needs to do the same. Secondary gifted educators could take the lead in developing social talent assessments and programming. Identification and development of social talent is especially important when schools adopt a conception of giftedness that focuses on the development of social capital (Renzulli, 2005) or wisdom (Sternberg, 2003).

Involving Counselors in Gifted Education at the Secondary Level

Finally, our framework suggests an active role for counselors in gifted education at the secondary level (Feldhusen & Robinson-Wyman, 1986; Peterson, this volume). Counselors should intervene when an assessment reveals that a high-ability adolescent has lower emotional intelligence and/or severe personal or social deficiencies. Such deficiencies are especially common among students with dual exceptionalities or with serious family dysfunction (Moon & Hall, 1998). School counselors are trained to provide direct instruction in personal and social competencies to students who have deficiencies in these areas. They may not, however, be trained in the characteristics and needs of academically gifted adolescents or in the development of personal and social talent. Counselors who lack training in gifted education can be paired with a gifted educator to ensure that the affective needs of gifted adolescents are met in secondary schools (Peterson, this volume) to assist with the identification and development of personal and social talent (Moon & Ray, this volume), and to assist academically talented students with issues related to identity and career development (Hébert & Kelly, this volume).

CONCLUSION

In summary, we believe that conceptions of giftedness in adolescence need to focus on facilitating the processes that enable high ability students to convert raw abilities into developed talents and build satisfying lives. These include traditional talent development experiences, such as advanced coursework, mentorships, and participation in extracurricular activities in their talent domain, combined with experiences that build personal and social competencies in contexts supportive of talent development. In addition, school districts selecting a conception of giftedness to guide gifted programming at the secondary level will need to consider more pragmatic issues such as whether the proposed conception is compatible with state laws governing gifted education and consistent with local values, and whether it can be operationalized in the local context (Moon, in press; Moon & Rosselli, 2000).

REFERENCES

Betts, G., & Kercher, J. (1999). *Autonomous learner model: Optimizing ability*. Greeley, CO: ALPS.

Bloom, B. S. (Ed.). (1985). *Developing talent in young people*. New York: Ballantine.

Carroll, J. B. (1993). *Human cognitive abilities*. Cambridge, England: Cambridge University Press.

Clasen, D. R., & Clasen, R. E. (1995). Underachievement of highly able students and the peer society. *Gifted and Talented International, 10*, 67–76.

Colangelo, N., Assouline, S., & Gross, M. U. M. (2004a). *A nation deceived: How schools hold back America's brightest students* (Vol. 1). Iowa City, IA: The Connie Belin & Jacqueline N. Blank International Center for Gifted Education and Talent Development.

Colangelo, N., Assouline, S., & Gross, M. U. M. (2004b). *A nation deceived: How schools hold back America's brightest students* (Vol. 2). Iowa City, IA: The Connie Belin & Jacqueline N. Blank International Center for Gifted Education and Talent Development.

Coleman, L. J. (2001). A "rag quilt": Social relationships among students in a special high school. *Gifted Child Quarterly, 45*, 164–173.

Cross, T. L., Coleman, L. J., & Stewart, R. A. (1995). Psychosocial diversity among gifted adolescents: An exploratory study of two groups. *Roeper Review, 17*, 181–185.

Cross, T. L., Coleman, L. J., & Terhaar-Yonkers, M. (1991). The social cognition of gifted adolescents in schools: Managing the stigma of giftedness. *Journal for the Education of the Gifted, 15*, 44–55.

Csikszentmihalyi, M., Rathunde, K., & Whalen, S. (1993). *Talented teenagers*. Cambridge, England: Cambridge University Press.

Enersen, D. (1993). Summer residential programs: Academics and beyond. *Gifted Child Quarterly, 37*, 169–176.

Feldhusen, J. F. (1980a). *The three-stage model of course design*. Englewood Cliffs, NJ: Educational Technology Publications.

Feldhusen, J. F. (1980b). Using the Purdue Three-Stage Model for curriculum development in gifted education. In H. W. Singleton (Ed.), *Gifted/talented education: Perspectives on curriculum and instruction* (pp. 37–44). Toledo, OH: University of Toledo.

Feldhusen, J. F. (1983). Eclecticism: A comprehensive approach to education of the gifted. In C. P. Benbow & J. C. Stanley (Eds.), *Academic precocity: Aspects of its development* (pp. 192–204). Baltimore, MD: Johns Hopkins University Press.

Feldhusen, J. F. (1986). A conception of giftedness. In R. J. Sternberg & J. E. Davidson (Eds.), *Conceptions of giftedness* (pp. 112–127). New York: Cambridge University Press.

Feldhusen, J. F. (1995). *TIDE: Talent identification and development in education*. Sarasota, FL: Center for Creative Learning.

Feldhusen, J. F., Hoover, S. M., & Sayler, M. F. (1990). *Identifying and educating gifted students at the secondary level*. Monroe, NY: Trillium Press.

Feldhusen, J. F., & Kolloff, P. B. (1986). The Purdue Three-Stage Enrichment Model at the elementary level. In J. S. Renzulli (Ed.), *Systems and models for developing programs for the gifted and talented* (pp. 126–152). Mansfield Center, CT: Creative Learning Press.

Feldhusen, J. F., & Moon, S. M. (1992). Grouping gifted students: Issues and concerns. *Gifted Child Quarterly, 65,* 63–67.

Feldhusen, J. F., & Robinson-Wyman, A. (1986). The Purdue Secondary Model for gifted and talented education. In J. S. Renzulli (Ed.), *Systems and models for developing programs for the gifted and talented* (pp. 153–179). Mansfield Center, CT: Creative Learning Press.

Gagné, F. (1985). Giftedness and talent: Reexamining a reexamination of the definitions. *Gifted Child Quarterly, 29,*103–112.

Gagné, F. (2000). Understanding the complex choreography of talent development. In K. A. Heller, F. J. Mönks, R. J. Sternberg, & R. F. Subotnik (Eds.), *International handbook of giftedness and talent* (2nd ed., pp. 67–79). Amsterdam: Elsevier.

Gagne, F. (2005). From noncompetence to exceptional talent: Exploring the range of academic achievement within and between grade levels. *Gifted Child Quarterly, 49,* 139–153.

Gardner, H. (1983). *Frames of mind: The theory of multiple intelligences.* New York: Basic Books.

Gottfried, A. E., & Gottfried, A. W. (2004). Toward the development of a conceptualization of gifted motivation. *Gifted Child Quarterly, 48,* 121–132.

Gottfried, A. W., Gottfried, A. E., Cook, C. R., & Morris, P. E. (2005). Educational characteristics of adolescents with gifted academic intrinsic motivation: A longitudinal investigation of school entry through early adulthood. *Gifted Child Quarterly, 49,* 172–186.

Heller, A., Mönks, F. J., Sternberg, R., & Subotnik, R. (Eds.). (2002). *International handbook of giftedness and talent* (2nd ed.). New York: Elsevier Science.

Hill, J. (1983). Early adolescence: A framework. *Journal of Early Adolescence, 3,* 1–21.

Kulik, J. A. (2003). Grouping and tracking. In N. Colangelo & G. A. Davis (Eds.), *Handbook of gifted education* (pp. 268–281). Boston: Allyn & Bacon.

Lubinski, D., Webb, R., Morelock, M. J., & Benbow, C. P. (2001). Top 1 in 10,000: A 10-year follow-up of the profoundly gifted. *Journal of Applied Psychology, 86,* 718–729.

Mayer, J. D., Caruso, D. R., & Salovey, P. (1999). Emotional intelligence meets traditional standards for an intelligence. *Intelligence, 27,* 267–298.

Mayer, J. D., & Geher, G. (1996). Emotional intelligence and the identification of emotion. *Intelligence, 22,* 89–113.

Mayer, J. D., Perkins, D. M., Caruso, D. R., & Salovey, P. (2001). Emotional intelligence and giftedness. *Roeper Review, 23,* 131–137.

Mayer, J. D., & Salovey, P. (1997). What is emotional intelligence? In P. Salovey & D. Sluyter (Eds.), *Emotional development and emotional intelligence: Implications for educators.* New York: Basic Books.

Moon, S. M. (1993). Using the Purdue Three-Stage Model: Developing talent at the secondary level. *Journal of Secondary Gifted Education, 5,* 31–35.

Moon, S. M. (2003a). Developing personal talent. In F. J. Mönks & H. Wagner (Eds.), *Development of human potential: Investment into our future. Proceedings of the 8th Conference of the European Council for High Ability (ECHA). Rhodes, October 9–13, 2002* (pp. 11–21). Bad Honnef, Germany: K. H. Bock.

Moon, S. M. (2003b). Personal Talent. *High Ability Studies, 14,* 5–21.

Moon, S. M. (2004, July). *Using the Purdue Three-Stage Model to develop talent in science and technology.* Paper presented at the Asia-Pacific Conference on Giftedness, Daejeon, Korea.

Moon, S. M. (in press). Developing a definition of giftedness. In J. Purcell & R. Eckert (Eds.), *Guidebook for developing educational programs and services for highly capable students.* Thousand Oaks, CA: Corwin Press.

Moon, S. M., & Hall, A. S. (1998). Family therapy with intellectually and creatively gifted children. *Journal of Marital and Family Therapy, 24,* 59–80.

Moon, S. M., & Rosselli, H. C. (2000). Developing gifted programs. In K. Heller, F. Mönks, R. Sternberg, & R. Subotnik (Eds.), *International handbook of giftedness and talent* (2nd ed., pp. 499–521). Amsterdam: Elsevier.

Nidiffer, L. G., & Moon, S. M. (1994). Middle school seminars. *Gifted Child Today, 17*(2), 24–27, 39–41.

Peterson, J. S. (2002). A longitudinal study of post-high-school development in gifted individuals at risk for poor educational outcomes. *Journal of Secondary Gifted Education, 14*, 6–18.

Pipher, M. (1994). *Reviving Ophelia.* New York: Ballantine Books.

Powley, S. A., & Moon, S. M. (1993). Secondary English theme units: A pragmatic approach. *Gifted Child Today, 16*(4), 52–61.

Reis, S. M., & Renzulli, J. S. (1986). The secondary triad model. In J. S. Renzulli (Ed.), *Systems and models for developing programs for the gifted and talented* (pp. 267–305). Mansfield Center, CT: Creative Learning Press.

Reis, S. M., & Renzulli, J. S. (1989). The secondary triad model. *Journal for the Education of the Gifted, 13*, 55–77.

Renzulli, J. S. (1977). *The Enrichment Triad Model: A guide for developing defensible programs for the gifted and talented.* Mansfield Center, CT: Creative Learning Press.

Renzulli, J. S. (1978). What makes giftedness? Reexamining a definition. *Phi Delta Kappan, 60*, 180–184.

Renzulli, J. S. (2005, June). *Intelligences outside the normal curve: Expanding the conception of giftedness to include co-cognitive traits and to promote social capital.* Paper presented at the DISCOVER! Conference, West Lafayette, IN.

Renzulli, J. S. (2000). Academies of inquiry and talent development: Part I: Organizing exploratory curriculum. *Middle School Journal, 32*(9), 5–14.

Renzulli, J. S. (2001). Academies of inquiry and talent development: Part II: How does an AITD program get started? *Middle School Journal, 33*(3), 7–14.

Renzulli, J. S., & Reis, S. M. (1985). *The schoolwide enrichment model: A comprehensive plan for educational excellence.* Mansfield Center, CT: Creative Learning Press.

Renzulli, J. S., & Reis, S. M. (1997). *The Schoolwide Enrichment Model: A how-to guide to educational excellence.* Mansfield Center, CT: Creative Learning Press.

Renzulli, J. S., Reis, S. M., & Smith, L. H. (1981). *The revolving door identification model.* Mansfield Center, CT: Creative Learning Press.

Renzulli, J. S., & Sytsman, R. (2001, November). *Operation houndstooth: Refining concepts and examining perceptions.* Paper presented at the National Association for Gifted Children, Cincinnati, OH.

Rogers, K. B. (1991). *Relationship of grouping practices to the education of the gifted and talented learners.* Storrs, CT: The National Research Center on the Gifted and Talented.

Salovey, P., Mayer, J. D., & Caruso, D. R. (2002). The positive psychology of emotional intelligence. In C. R. Snyder & S. J. Lopez (Eds.), *Handbook of positive psychology.* Oxford: Oxford University Press.

Steinberg, L. (1996). *Beyond the classroom.* New York: Simon & Schuster.

Steinberg, L. (2005). *Adolescence* (7th ed.). New York: McGraw Hill.

Sternberg, R. J. (1995). What do we mean by giftedness? A pentagonal implicit theory. *Gifted Child Quarterly, 39*, 88–94.

Sternberg, R. J. (1997). Intelligence and lifelong learning: What's new and how can we use it? *American Psychologist, 52*, 1134–1139.

Sternberg, R. J. (1998). The dialectic as a tool for the teaching of psychology. *Teaching of Psychology, 25*, 177–180.

Sternberg, R. J. (1996). *Successful intelligence*. New York: Simon & Schuster.

Sternberg, R. J. (2000). Giftedness as developing expertise. In K. A. Heller, F. J. Mönks, R. J. Sternberg, & R. F. Subotnik (Eds.), *International handbook of giftedness and talent* (2nd ed., pp. 55–66). Amsterdam: Elsevier.

Sternberg, R. J. (2003). WICS as a model of giftedness. *High Ability Studies, 14*, 109–137.

Sternberg, R. J., & Grigorenko, E. L. (2000). *Teaching for successful intelligence*. Arlington Heights, IL: Skylight Professional Development.

Sternberg, R. J., & Grigorenko, E. (2003). Teaching for successful intelligence: Principles, procedures, and practices. *Journal for the Education of the Gifted, 27*, 207–228.

Tannenbaum, A. J. (1983). *Gifted children: Psychological and educational perspectives*. New York: Macmillan.

Tannenbaum, A. J. (1986). Giftedness: A psychological approach. In R. J. Sternberg & J. E. Edwards (Eds.), *Conceptions of giftedness* (pp. 21–52). New York: Cambridge University Press.

Terman, L. M. (1925). *Genetic studies of genius: Vol. 1. Mental and physical traits of a thousand gifted children*. Stanford, CA: Stanford University Press.

Whitman, M. W., & Moon, S. M. (1993). Bridge building: Conducting scientific research redefines the roles of teacher and student. *Gifted Child Today, 16*(5), 47–50.

Ziegler, A., & Heller, K. A. (2000). Conceptions of giftedness from a meta-theoretical perspective. In K. A. Heller, F. J. Mönks, R. J. Sternberg, & R. F. Subotnik (Eds.), *International handbook of giftedness and talent* (2nd ed., pp. 3–21). Amsterdam: Elsevier

IDENTITY AND CAREER DEVELOPMENT IN GIFTED STUDENTS

by Thomas P. Hébert
& Kevin R. Kelly

CHAPTER 2

For, indeed, in the social jungle of human existence there is no feeling of being alive without a sense of identity. (Erikson, 1968, p. 130)

The university doctoral student is delighted to learn that he has received permission from a large urban school district to conduct his dissertation research in one of the city's high schools. With this opportunity, he has access to gifted teenagers in the most culturally diverse high school in the state. In collecting his data, he spends months reviewing documents, conducting observations of students, and enjoying interviews with young people. There he finds some of the brightest and most interesting teenagers he has ever met. As a former high school teacher, he is able to appreciate the population of students he is investigating. He has an opportunity to review school records, and the participants in his study share materials such as their essays in English classes and college applications. As he reads Vaughn's college essay, he is impressed with this teenager's reflections on his character:

> Over the years, I've noticed my friends appreciating my understanding, willingness to listen, and trustworthiness. When it comes to talking to me

35

about a sensitive topic, people feel very comfortable. This is the quality I am most proud of. (Hébert, 2000a, p. 101)

Later that morning a school guidance counselor introduces him to Claire, a young African American woman with an established reputation as a serious student. He is able to interview Claire and becomes intrigued with her profound determination to succeed in life. In their conversation, Claire explains that she established her professional goals early:

I knew from second grade that I wanted to be a doctor. The sixth graders had a series of career speakers and I got to go to the sixth grade classroom to listen. I used to sit there in those classes and they used to say, "She is so little." I was focused on being a doctor! (Reis, Hébert, Diaz, Maxfield, & Ratley, 1995, p. 142)

Claire continues the conversation, explaining that she believed the television program *The Cosby Show* influenced her decision to become a pediatrician. She remained focused on her goal all through middle school, and when Claire's mother realized just how serious her daughter was, she purchased a set of medical encyclopedias for her and inscribed them with "To Dr. Claire, Love, Mother" (Hébert & Reis, 1999, p. 439).

Later that morning, Wallace, an African American scholar-athlete joins the researcher for an interview. During their conversation he describes how some of his peers do not always appreciate his academic regimentation.

A few of them will say, "You're hittin' the books too much. Why don't you ever come out with us sometimes?" I go out on weekends, but never during the week. Guys know better. They don't nag me about stuff like that. I haven't had too many problems with that. I'm not an egghead jock who's only worried about playing ball, and I'm not a nerd. Wallace the student and Wallace the athlete balance each other out. (Hébert, 1998, pp. 396–397)

The researcher wraps ups Friday afternoon in an English literature class where he has the opportunity to observe Lucio in action. The researcher is amazed as he watches Lucio in discussion about the novel *Jane Eyre,* and notices that the Latino young man is doing most of the talking as he poses many insightful questions. After class the researcher shares with Lucio how he never really appreciated *Jane Eyre* in high school and wondered how Lucio could become so excited about this literature. Lucio explains his intense involvement:

I think I resemble that little girl in the novel. That's why I'm enjoying it. She was different. I feel the same way. I never really cared about being the most noted, being class president. I never really cared for that kind of stuff. I just want to be able to be myself. (Hébert, 2000a, p. 100)

Lucio laughs as he explains, "If people don't like the way I talk or the way I think, there are a couple of adjectives I can use to describe them. I'm happy with who I am and I have friends" (Hébert, 2000a, p. 100).

The researcher leaves the high school campus that Friday afternoon with Lucio's words, "I just want to be able to be myself," reverberating in his mind. He spends the weekend transcribing his interviews, and as he does he asks himself these questions: Why is Vaughn so comfortable with his sensitive qualities? What enables Claire to feel so strongly about her plans for becoming a doctor? How has Wallace learned to maintain the role of scholar and athlete? How did Lucio gain such insight? As the transcription continues and he begins his preliminary analysis of the data, he realizes that his research may shed some understanding on the important role of identity formation in high achieving gifted students. The doctoral student is excited and is determined to pursue as much reading on identity development as he can manage to fit into his busy schedule. Inspired by what these bright teenagers are sharing with him, he's more determined than ever to gain a strong understanding of this complex phenomenon. He reaches for the work of several leading theorists as he reflects on his conversations with these students.

ERIKSON'S STAGES OF PSYCHOSOCIAL DEVELOPMENT

Erik Erikson offered a theory to explain psychosocial development. Erikson (1968) defined eight developmental stages during which human beings confront major crises in the course of a lifetime. He maintained that these crises were not problematic catastrophes, but simply significant turning points in life that presented individuals with increased vulnerability and opportunities for enhancing their potential (Santrock, 2003). Shaffer (2000) delineated Erikson's stages succinctly. They are highlighted below.

- *Trust versus Mistrust*—This stage involves the infant establishing feelings of physical comfort and minimum fear and apprehension about the future.
- *Autonomy versus Shame*—Toddlers learn to be autonomous, discovering that their behavior is their own as they begin to claim a sense of independence.
- *Initiative versus Guilt*—Preschool children try to act grown up and will attempt to take on responsibilities that are beyond their capabilities. They undertake activities that conflict with the expectations of their parents and these conflicts may have them feeling guilty.
- *Industry versus Inferiority*—Children from age 6 to puberty master important social and intellectual skills. They are enthusiastic about learning; however, they compare themselves with their peers, judging their competence and potentially developing a sense of inferiority.
- *Identity versus Identity Confusion*—Adolescents are forced to grapple with questions such as "Who am I?," "What am I all about?," and "Where am I going in life?" During this period they must craft their identity or they will remain confused about the roles they will play as adults.

- *Intimacy versus Isolation*—Individuals develop strong friendships to achieve a sense of love or companionship or a shared identity with another person.
- *Generativity versus Stagnation*—In mid-adulthood, individuals meet the challenge of becoming productive professionally and responsible for the needs of others.
- *Integrity versus Despair*—A period in which adults look back and evaluate their lives. A retrospective view of a life well lived results in integrity. If earlier life stages have not been resolved positively, despair occurs.

ERIKSON'S THEORY OF IDENTITY DEVELOPMENT

Much of our current understanding of adolescence evolved from Erikson's theory of psychosocial development. With the end of World War II, Erikson examined the struggles faced by many veterans as they made the transition back to civilian life. Through his clinical work, he came to believe that the psychological difficulties that some veterans had in transitioning from the role of soldier to that of civilian were similar to those faced by some adolescents as they left childhood and moved through adolescence to adulthood (Erikson, 1968). From his clinical work and research evolved a psychology of adolescent identity formation. He drew from his psychoanalytical thinking on ego development and proposed a definition of identity. He proposed that the ego structured a coherent personality to maintain the sameness and continuity of an individual's existence and was consistently recognized by others. Erikson explained:

> Ego identity then, in its subjective aspect, is the awareness of the fact that there is a self-sameness and continuity to the ego's synthesizing methods, the *style of one's individuality*, and that this style coincides with the sameness and continuity of one's *meaning for significant others* in the immediate community. (p. 50)

According to Erikson's view, individuals who had established an identity had a firm and coherent sense of who they were, understood where they were headed in life, and were comfortable with where they fit into society. The process for arriving at this established identity began in adolescence, and Erikson noted that multiple factors influenced its formation. Acknowledging that cross cultural variations existed in how different societies viewed adolescence, Erikson (1968) maintained that all societies offered a "psychosocial moratorium" during which a young person was expected to make "commitments for life" and to establish a firm self-definition. This moratorium was accompanied by a sense of crisis. Erikson defined crisis as a normative life event that designated "a necessary turning point, a crucial moment, when development must move one way or another, marshaling resources of growth, recovery, and further differentiation" (p. 16). This identity crisis forced a young person to struggle with making some important choices. An adolescent had to consider questions such as: Who am I as a man or woman? What religious or moral values do I hold? Which career is the best match for my talents? Just where do I fit into society? Realizing that these questions were daunting for adolescents, Erikson used the term "identity crisis" to represent the confusion and anxiety they experienced as they struggled with these questions (Shaffer, 2000). According to Erikson (1968) identity formation was the most essential challenge of adolescence, since it was necessary preparation for adulthood. During this period, teenagers had to make sense of their life experiences, their unique personality characteristics, and the beliefs they had maintained through adolescence, and combine them to form a cohesive self.

Consider the teenagers introduced earlier. Their life experiences, their unique personality characteristics, and the beliefs they held combined to shape their identities. Wallace had determined that it was cool to be academically oriented, as well as being athletically successful. Vaughn's unique personality characteristics included feeling secure enough in his masculinity to be proud of his sensitive qualities. Lucio understood what he valued in people and was comfortable with himself, and from an early age, Claire had been secure in her career plans to enter the field of medicine.

Forming a cohesive self requires hard work. Santrock (2003) indicated that identity formation involved a long messy process. He pointed out that "at bare minimum, it involves a commitment to a vocational direction, an ideological stance, and a sexual orientation" (p. 302). He captured the essence of this complex adolescent process poignantly as he explained:

> Identity development gets done in bits and pieces. Decisions are not made once and for all, but have to be made again and again. And the decisions might seem trivial at the time: whom to date, whether or not to break up, whether or not to have intercourse, whether or not to take drugs, whether or not to go to college or finish high school and get a job, which major, whether to study or to play, whether or not to be politically active, and so on. Over the years of adolescence, the decisions begin to form a core of what the individual is all about as a human being—what is called her or his identity. (p. 302)

Wallace, Vaughn, Lucio and Claire have made many of the important decisions required in adolescence. These young people have formed their identity and appear comfortable with their decisions at an early stage in their lives. Their experiences lead educators of gifted students to consider whether the process of identity development is more intense or accelerated for gifted students than for other students. Given the experiences of these urban teenagers, it is evident that intelligent young people are in charge of shaping their identity. With this understanding, teachers of gifted students may want to have their students examine the concept of identity development and reflect on how it plays out in their lives. Sharing multiple theories of identity development with gifted teenagers is helpful. Along with Erikson's work, James Marcia's theory discussed below is also enlightening to high school students.

MARCIA'S THEORY OF IDENTITY FORMATION

Inspired by the work of Erik Erikson, James Marcia (1993, 1994), a clinical psychologist and psychotherapist, posed a theory whereby individuals established identities through four distinct approaches. These could be categorized into one of four identity statuses: foreclosure, moratorium, achievement, and diffusion. These four distinct statuses were based on whether or not individuals had explored various alternatives and made firm commitments to a vocational or occupational choice; religious and political ideology; and interpersonal values such as sex role attitudes and sexuality.

Marcia (1993) examined identity development using identity status interviews to determine the degree of exploration and commitment. In doing so, he assessed the extent to which a person had genuinely examined and experimented with alternative life directions and beliefs. According to Marcia's (1993, 1994) theory, foreclosure was the identity status characterized by commitment with an absence of exploration. Individuals classified as foreclosed had committed to an identity without considering or exploring other possibilities. They preferred to be told what to do by an authority figure in their lives rather than deciding their own direction in life. They were often conformists who set high goals for themselves, and maintained the family value system. In addition, their relationships with others often lacked emotional depth. Such individuals often chose friendships with people who were much like themselves.

Individuals categorized in the Moratorium status were involved in an identity crisis, posing serious questions about life commitments, and searching for answers. They often vacillated between rebellion and conformity, and their family relationships fluctuated with their vacillation. Relationships with others were often intense and brief. They valued intimacy; however, since they were often in motion, they had difficulty maintaining committed relationships with others (Marcia, 1993, 1994).

Identity Achievement was the status to describe people who had undergone an exploratory process and had made occupational and ideological commitments. They were solid in their beliefs, having made life decisions on self-constructed values. Identity achievers were at peace with their families. These individuals had resolved their identity issues, had solid self-esteem, dealt well with stress, and were high in moral development (Marcia, 1993, 1994).

Identity Diffusion included those people who had done some searching but remained uncommitted. They had not mapped out a direction in life. Some were apathetic and socially isolated, while others sought contact almost compulsively. They were shallow in their interpersonal relationships. They struggled with stress, struggled with self-esteem, and had the lowest levels of moral development (Marcia, 1993, 1994).

Marcia's theory offers gifted teenagers much to consider as they reflect on where they are in the process of identity formation. Gifted teenagers enjoy determining whether they are foreclosed, in moratorium, achieved, or diffused. Rich discussions with students often center on whether young people today break away from their family value systems and determine their own direction in life. Some gifted students may see themselves in the moratorium stage, in which they are struggling between rebellion and conformity as they search for answers as to who they are. Some may claim to be identity achieved, while others may brush off the discussion and proudly announce that they are diffused in their search and proud to be there. Regardless of where students see themselves on Marcia's continuum, exposure to this identity development model is helpful for intelligent teenagers to consider.

IDENTITY FORMATION IN FEMALES

Having been introduced to a group of culturally diverse urban teenagers in the introduction of this chapter, we are reminded that identity development theories may speak differently to diverse populations. For example, Erik Erikson's theory, constructed upon his research with primarily White, middle class males has been criticized by a number of researchers for not being representative of women's experiences (Gilligan, 1982; Josselson, 1987). With a young African American woman like Claire, who determined her career path with the support of a loving mother, other theories of identity development may help us to better understand her experience. For this reason, educators need to consider specific theories that address identity formation in females in order to support the gifted young women in secondary classrooms.

One of the first theorists to address identity development in women was Carol Gilligan. In her seminal work, *In a Different Voice*, Gilligan (1982) maintained that women defined their identity differently from men. She began her work by asking the questions: "How is it that men in speaking of themselves and their lives, or speaking more generally about human nature, often speak as if they were not living in connection with women, as if they did not have a voice or did not experience desire?" (p. xiii). A central assumption that guided Gilligan's work was that the way people talked about their lives was important and the language they used to describe their experiences revealed a great deal about their development. Through extensive interviews, Gilligan examined individuals' conceptions of self and morality focusing on their experiences that involved conflict and choice.

In her interviews with men, Gilligan (1982) noted that men often spoke of their lives using a "language of achievement" with their stories, devoid of emotion and characterized by their measures of success and failure. Gilligan observed, "individual achievement rivets the male imagination, and great ideas or distinctive activity defines the standard of self-assessment and success" (p. 163). She explained further, "Power and separation secure the man an identity achieved through work, but they leave him at a distance from others, who seem in some sense out of his sight" (p. 163).

Gilligan's experiences interviewing women led her to understand that women saw their social reality differently from men and these differences centered on experiences of attachment and separation, important transitions that shaped their lives. When asked to describe themselves, all of the women described a "relationship depicting their identity *in* the connection of future mother, present wife, adopted child, or past lover" (p. 159).

Gilligan noted that in describing themselves, the highly successful and achieving women did not discuss their academic and professional achievements. Instead, they viewed their professional work as jeopardizing their own sense of self, and discussed how the conflict they met in choosing between achievement and relationships often left them feeling distressed. In all of the women's descriptions, identity was defined in a context of relationship and judged by standards of responsibility and care. Gilligan observed, " . . . women's sense of integrity appears to be entwined with an ethic of care, so that to see themselves as women is to see themselves in a relationship of connection" (p. 170). Gilligan (1982) concluded:

> We have come more recently to notice not only the silence of women but the difficulty of hearing what they say when they speak. Yet in the different voice of women lies the truth of an ethic of care, the tie between relationship and responsibility, and the origins of aggression in the failure of connection. The failure to see the different reality of women's lives and to hear the differences in their voices stems in part from the assumption that there is a single mode of social experience and interpretation. By positing instead two different modes, we arrive at a more complex rendition of human experience which sees the truth of separation and attachment in the lives of women and men and recognizes how these truths are carried by different modes of language and thought. (p. 174)

Carol Gilligan's work offers secondary teachers rich material to share with their students. As teenage women grapple daily with issues centered on friendships with other young women and decisions regarding dating and romantic relationships, there is no better time for them to be exposed to Gilligan's thinking on female identity formation. The secondary school experience is a period in which peer relationships play such a significant role in shaping the experiences of students, therefore it is important to have gifted young women reflect on the role relationships play in their lives and the influence such relationships may have on their life goals and career aspirations. Early exposure to Gilligan's theory in a high school classroom may influence young women's lives in powerful ways. Moreover, it is important that young men in secondary classrooms also receive the same exposure to Gilligan's work as they consider female relationships in their lives and what expectations they hold for life partnerships in their future.

Gifted secondary students appreciate debating a variety of theories; therefore educators find it helpful to also present them with the work of Ruthellen Josselson. The theory proposed by Josselson (1987) also focused on the importance women place on relationships. Through a longitudinal investigation of college women, Josselson attempted to describe the journey of identity formation in women. She saw it as a process that evolved through the entire life cycle and occurred gradually and incrementally. She maintained identity became a means by which women organized and understood their experiences and shared their understanding of life with others. According to Josselson, (1996) a woman formed her sense of self through connections with people in her life—within her family, and professional setting, and in her values and beliefs. She further explained, "Identity in women is more rooted in 'being' than in 'doing,' and a woman's life story is often centered on how she experiences herself, or wishes to experience herself, with others" (p. 32).

In her work with college women, Josselson (1987, 1996) used Marcia's interview methods to determine where the women were in forming their identities, by posing questions about four areas—occupation, religion, politics, and sexual standards—central to the understanding of identity. She evaluated whether the women had undergone a period of exploration in deciding on their values and goals in life and whether or not they had made distinct choices. Through her approach of interviewing late adolescent females about their decision-making with regard to these four areas, she was able to categorize her participants into four distinct groups that situated them in one stage or another on the path to identity formation. She provided four categories designed to be descriptive rather than evaluative and labeled them: Guardians, Pathmakers, Searchers, and Drifters.

According to Josselson (1996), Guardians had determined their identity commitments without choice, simply following life plans mapped out in childhood or designed by parents. She indicated these young women were likely to feel "This is how I am because it's how I was raised or how I've always been" (p. 35). These women knew where they were going in life without ever having considered alternatives. They had absorbed the values of their families and held onto them. "Reluctant to 'leave home' emotionally, they wanted their adult lives, as much as possible, to be a continuation of the warmth and comfort of childhood in their families" (p. 37).

Pathmakers were women who had undergone a period of exploration or crisis and then determined identity commitments on their terms. Their view was "I've tried out some things, and this is what makes sense for me" (p. 35). These independent women had undergone identity crises and were now self-confident. They had considered options, tried out alternative ways of experiencing themselves, "charted their own course" (p. 37) and designed lives that enabled them to balance work, personal interests, and significant relationships.

Searchers were women who were still involved in a period of struggle or exploration, trying to make commitments, but not finding success. They expressed their situation as, "I'm not sure about who I am or want to be, but I'm trying to figure it out" (p. 35). Josselson found these women were still in the midst of crisis and remained unsure about which path to follow in life. These young women were still in the process of exploration and experimentation, often felt guilty about having broken from the values of their childhoods, and remained fearful that they would not make the appropriate life commitments.

Drifters were without commitments and were not attempting to make them. These women either felt lost or simply were following the impulses of the day. They described their situations as, "I don't know what I will do or believe, but it doesn't matter too much right now" (p. 35). These women were neither in crisis, nor had they made commitments. Josselson (1996) described, "They were like leaves blown by the wind, living each day, sometimes happily, sometimes despairingly, but they tried to ignore the approach of the future" (p. 38).

Josselson (1996) described four groups representing "gateways to adulthood." Where a young woman was on the path to identity formation indicated how she would approach her adult years, and eventually how she would craft her life story.

She explained, "The pathway she was following at the end of college served as a portal to the future, a way of entering adulthood, with conviction and direction, with openness and flexibility, or with confusion and tentativeness" (p. 39). Reflecting on Claire's early determination to become a doctor, we might speculate why she was so secure in her plans to pursue this career path. Although she was quite young to have undergone a lengthy period of exploration and experimentation with identity, she was ready to chart her own course. What was it about this bright young woman that enabled her to do so? She appeared to be an example of an early Pathmaker. With gifted students like Claire, secondary teachers will enjoy having the young women in their classrooms reflect on whether they will be Guardians, Pathmakers, Searchers, or Drifters in life. Healthy discussions and writing activities based on Josselson's theory allow gifted secondary students the opportunity to think seriously about how they will approach their "portals to the future."

Mindful of Claire's experience as an African American female in an urban environment, secondary educators need to consider additional theories that address multilayered conceptions of identity. Since the pioneering work of Gilligan and Josselson in woman's identity development, other researchers and theorists have proposed models. Jones (1997) and Jones and McEwen (2000) indicated that identity development models for women had not addressed how an individual may simultaneously hold multiple identities. In their grounded theory research with female college students, they uncovered "intersecting social identities" (Jones & McEwen, p. 405) that included racial, ethnic, sexual, gender, social class, religious, geographic or regional, and professional identities.

Jones and McEwen (2000) provided a conceptual model of multiple dimensions of women's personal identity. In this model the researchers proposed that at the center of a woman's identity was a core sense of self. The core identity was experienced as a "personal identity" incorporating "valued personal attributes and characteristics" (Jones, 1997, p. 383). Surrounding the core identity and integrally connected to the core were the "social identities"—what women experienced as externally defined dimensions such as gender, class, race, culture, sexual orientation, and religion. These researchers indicated that contextual influences such as family background and life experiences also played important roles in shaping the multidimensional identities. Moreover, sociocultural conditions such as sexism and racism interacted with facets of identity and resulted in women developing more understanding of a particular dimension of their identity. The findings from the work of Jones and McEwen illuminated how identity in women can be understood and experienced differently and at different times in a woman's life.

IDENTITY IN RACIALLY DIVERSE POPULATIONS

In meeting Claire, Wallace, and Lucio in the introduction to this chapter, educators are reminded that the identity formation experience of culturally diverse young people may be more complex. Along with identity issues that all young people confront, ethnically diverse adolescents must also establish an ethnic identity—a personal identification with an ethnic group and the value system and traditions maintained by the group (Phinney, 1996). For some young people of color, this task may be difficult. Researchers having examined ethnic identity issues indicated that a commitment to an ethnic identity was an important component of the self-concept of culturally diverse teenagers and helped to prepare them for success in a multicultural society (Phinney, 1996).

General models of racial/ethnic identity development have been proposed (see Atkinson, Morten, & Sue, 1993; Phinney et al., 1990), as well as culture-specific models of racial/ethnic identity (see Arce, 1981; Cross, 1995; Kim, 1981). Ponterotto and Pederson (1993) examined these five models and identified commonalities across the various theories. They noted that in each of the models the cultural group underwent several stages in the process of determining a racial identity. Although Ponterotto and Pederson noted that the models differed with respect to the number of stages, they succeeded in collapsing stages across the five identity models and identified four themes that were consistent across all five theories. With these four themes, Ponterotto and Pederson proposed a four-stage integrative model.

Ponterotto and Pederson (1993) labeled the first stage "Identification with the White Majority." Individuals at this stage simply did not see the relevance of ethnic identity in their lives or they saw themselves preferring the norms and values of the dominant White culture. In the second stage of the model, "Awareness, Encounter and Search," individuals questioned their previously held beliefs, began to question their status as minorities in a racist society, and engaged in a search for their own racial identity. In stage three, "Identification and Immersion," individuals were ready to commit and immerse themselves in their own cultural values and traditions. They completely endorsed the norms, values, and customs of their own group while simultaneously rejecting the values or norms of the White majority culture. In the final stage, "Integration and Internalization," a reappraisal occurred and a bicultural or multicultural identity was eventually established. According to Ponterotto and Pederson, the emotion associated with the previous stage (negativity towards the dominant culture and positive feelings toward one's own group) became rechanneled into the development of a secure racial/ethic identity combined with an appreciation of other cultures. In this final stage, individuals had developed a strong affiliation and sense of belonging to their group and a determination to contribute to its overall well-being.

Educators of gifted culturally diverse students in middle and high schools appreciate exploring the various racial identity development models. Exposure to a theory supporting a model such as the one proposed by Ponterotto and Pederson helps teachers and students think deeply about the life experiences that have shaped their views of how they feel about themselves as gifted young people of color. Secondary educators benefit from an understanding of these models and appreciate that their gifted students may move through these stages at a faster pace. Teachers must understand that stage models are fluid, and gifted culturally diverse youngsters may fluctuate from one stage to another in unpredictable ways. Given what researchers and theorists have indicated about the heightened sensitivity of intelligent adolescents

(Piechowski, 1997) it is possible that gifted culturally diverse teenagers respond more emotionally to events that trigger movement from one stage of racial identity to another. Moreover, they also may be more deeply affected by these events. With this understanding, secondary teachers and counselors need to be prepared to provide emotional support to their culturally diverse students.

IDENTITY DEVELOPMENT IN GIFTED ADOLESCENTS

Researchers and theorists in the gifted education community have explored issues of identity development and have proposed that gifted teenagers, like all adolescents, struggle with identity development (Coleman & Cross, 2001; Coleman & Sanders, 1993). The findings of several research studies have shed light on this issue. In assessing the ego-identity formation of gifted high school students, Howard-Hamilton and Franks (1995) found that gifted adolescents scored at the adult level of identity development on the Rasmussen Ego Identity Scale (EIS; 1964) indicating that the students had successfully negotiated the psychosocial tasks Erikson believed were critical to the formation of a stable identity and were equipped with the tools they needed to develop a healthy identity. The results of this study lead us to speculate that identity formation may occur more rapidly in gifted adolescents than in other students.

Through an analysis of interview data from Lewis Terman's (1925) sample of more than 1,500 gifted children, Zuo and Tao (2001) contributed to our understanding of identity development in gifted individuals. In their examination of Terman's data, these researchers looked retrospectively for evidence of identity exploration and commitment and classified the sample into Marcia's four identity statuses. They reported conformity was seen most often in the identity foreclosure group. Subjects categorized as identity diffused displayed higher levels of inferiority and lower levels of self-confidence, persistence, and sense of purpose. Continuing this line of inquiry, Zuo and Cramond's (2001) analysis of the data indicated that the highest achieving subgroup of the participants consisted of mostly identity achievers, while the majority of the lowest achieving participants were those classified as identity diffused. These findings may help to explain one of the most important distinctions between gifted achievers and underachievers. If an intelligent young person is able to resolve the question of "Who am I?," then it seems logical that student will also be able to resolve the question of "Where do I want to go in life?" With identity in place, a gifted adolescent will more readily adopt an achievement orientation.

Coleman and Cross (2001) considered the tools behind identity formation, as well as complex issues related to how gifted students managed their identity as young people with high ability. These researchers maintained that gifted youngsters faced more conflict in their lives than other young people because their advanced development and specific talents placed them beyond societal expectations. In addition to being an adolescent, they had to be a gifted adolescent, a role they had to play that other youngsters did not have to manage. This situation made it challenging for gifted adolescents to reach a clear understanding of just who they were. Calling attention to the role that social context played in adolescent development, Coleman and Cross noted that the problem became that of " fashioning an emerging identity in the midst of conflicting social demands" (p. 187).

The conflicting social demands that Coleman and Cross (2001) referred to involved several mixed societal messages that gifted young people had to interpret. These researchers indicated that one important message gifted children received was that they are different, and "being different is problematic in that differentness prevents, or at least interferes with, full social acceptance and personal development" (p. 187). A second message gifted students had to interpret was that their differences led to being praised and criticized for their strengths. For example, the student who was so smart was also expected to be humble. A third societal message was that the young person's special gifts or talents required outstanding performance at all times. Coleman and Cross indicated that this particular message could be misinterpreted by young people in a way that led to anxiety and stress. A fourth message was that gifted students were expected to be constant achievers. A gifted adolescent could struggle to learn something difficult, but others did not understand how that the particular task could be a challenge for the gifted teenager. The student encountered disbelief on the part of others when he or she earned a low grade on a class assignment. Finally, Coleman and Cross called attention to another sensitive challenge gifted young people faced—the experience of being known for one's achievements rather than one's self. Gifted teenagers complained that others saw the label "gifted student," but did not see them as individuals, and eventually when they were successful at getting others to look more closely at them as intelligent young people, they heard messages such as "Hey! You are really are a cool kid after all!" With these complex and confusing messages, the middle and high school years involved the challenging task of managing one's identity, a far more difficult task than earlier in childhood. Coleman and Cross explained, "At this stage in life, the developmental tasks become sharply focused, the range of acceptable behaviors from peers becomes narrower, and the implications of one's ability and differentness can be grasped" (p. 191).

Pursuing another research study of gifted teenagers, Coleman and Cross (1988) explored how adolescents experience being gifted in high school. Through qualitative interviews with 15 teenagers attending a special summer science program, these researchers uncovered strong evidence supporting the hypothesis "that many (not all) gifted students do experience giftedness as a social handicap" (p. 55). As a result, the researchers maintained that "gifted students do feel stigmatized and consequently employ techniques to try to camouflage their differences" (p. 55) in order to minimize their visibility as gifted students. Coleman and Cross noted that their data suggested the past history of these teenagers and their school context played important roles in how the students experienced giftedness.

In another qualitative study examining the experiences of gifted teenagers, Hébert (2000a) also helped to shed light on the importance of healthy identity formation in gifted adolescents. In his study of six high-ability, high-achieving males in a multiethnic urban high school, Hébert identified a strong belief in self as the most important factor influencing the success of the young men. These gifted young men had constructed a solid identity that provided them with the energy, the drive, and the tools they needed to face life's challenges in an urban environment. The young men had clearly defined aspirations that were aligned with their personal qualities, strengths, and talents. They saw their aspirations as attainable, since they realized they had the motivation that kept them driven to succeed. Hébert noted that in addition to being motivated and having high aspirations, several qualities merged in these young men that assisted them in constructing their identities: sensitivity, multicultural appreciation, and an inner will. Through his data analysis, Hébert identified factors that influenced this strong belief in self. He found that relationships with supportive adults who respected the gifted males as young adults were influential. In addition, involvement in talent development opportunities such as extracurricular activities, sports, special programs, and summer school experiences appeared to reinforce their belief in self. Hébert also found that the strong identity within the young men was supported by strong emotional support from families.

In a second study of gifted males, Hébert (2000b) also uncovered a strong personal identity within a group of gifted university males pursuing elementary education careers. Hébert found that, as part of their belief in self, the gifted young men displayed empathetic qualities and comfort with their psychological androgyny. These gifted males recognized characteristics traditionally viewed as feminine within their personalities and they celebrated those traits. Their identity appeared to involve a sincere caring quality within themselves because they knew it allowed them to be better men and professionals. In addition, their empathy incorporated an appreciation for the developmental struggles faced by young children in elementary classrooms.

Identity-formation in gifted females was the focus of a study by Speirs Neumeister (2002), in which she examined factors influencing the professional achievements of three newly married, gifted young women. Speirs Neumeister found her participants attributed a significant part of their identity to their status as high-achieving females. Their identity was influenced by three factors that were instrumental in shaping and directing the high-achieving components of their identities: foundational influences, personality characteristics, and marriage as a partnership. The foundational influences included formative educational experiences, consistent high-achieving peer groups, and supportive family members and adults. Each young woman described significant educational experiences that channeled her motivation and preparation for a chosen career. Throughout high school and college, the young women consistently connected with high-achieving peers that helped to reinforce their identities as high achievers. These gifted females also acknowledged important individuals in their lives, such as parents, teachers, mentors, and extended family members who also saw them as high achievers and supported their interests, motivation, and skill development. Speirs Neumeister also found that specific attributes of their personalities, independence and nontraditional attitudes toward gender roles, enabled them to transform their drive to achieve into actual accomplishments. The three young women in the study defined their marriages as a partnership that involved communication, compromise, and support. Marriage allowed them to view their identity in relation to their spouses and create a partnership that empowered both partners to achieve their goals.

In addition to research on identity development in gifted individuals, the gifted education literature includes only one study on identity development in gifted students with learning disabilities. Dole's (2001) groundbreaking work in this area involved investigating how dual exceptionalities affected the identity formation of four gifted college students with learning disabilities. Through qualitative narrative inquiry, Dole uncovered both contextual and personal influences that shaped identities. Within the contextual influences, Dole found two themes that were integral to the identity formation of the students: support systems within family, teachers, mentors and friends, and involvement in extracurricular activities, volunteer work, and jobs. Within the personal influences, Dole uncovered three themes in identity formation: self-knowledge, self-acceptance, and self-advocacy. Dole represented identity formation within the gifted college students with learning disabilities as an ongoing, circular process. "Like a spiral that is advancing or receding, yet continuously developing, it began with self-knowledge—not only of their learning disabilities, but also of their learning abilities, talents, and strengths" (p. 122). Within these young people, Dole found that "Knowledge of self was ongoing and led to self-acceptance and self-advocacy, not necessarily in that order" (p. 122). She also noted that the students' self-acceptance and self-advocacy led them to self-determination or the setting of realistic career goals. With this self-determination, the students tapped into their strengths and interests and developed the persistence to accomplish their goals.

The researchers who have conducted these studies have stood on the shoulders of giants such as Erikson, Marcia, Gilligan, and Josselson. From that vantage point, it becomes evident that further exploration in the area is needed. Our review of literature on identity development within gifted individuals has uncovered limited research. The gifted education community is just beginning to explore this important phenomenon. Moreover, the majority of the research in this area includes qualitative studies utilizing small samples of participants, limiting the generalizability. These studies have opened the door to exploring the complexity of identity formation; however, more questions need to be raised. It is evident that researchers in gifted education need to pursue more comparative research on identity development in gifted versus nongifted students. Longitudinal studies of identity development across the lifespan of gifted individuals would also help to enlighten us. As the gifted education community continues to conduct research on identity development, educators must realize that career development occurs simultaneously. Understanding how identity and career development are interrelated is important for secondary educators if they are to work effectively in teaching and counseling gifted adolescents. To assist educators, the following discussion offers several lenses for examining vocational development in gifted adolescents, progressing from a focus on individual characteristics to a more complex view in which family and community systems and macroeconomic factors interact with individual characteristics to affect career pathways.

CAREER DEVELOPMENT OF GIFTED ADOLESCENTS

Vocational development has drawn considerable interest within the field of gifted education in large part because creative productivity in adulthood and career attainment are mature expressions of talent evident in young children. Childhood talents are captivating because of their promise. When we see great facility in mathematical calculation, are inspired by youthful poetry and writing, and observe intense scientific curiosity, we wonder "What will this child become? What will this person *do* with this talent?" Certainly educators are invested in learning for its intrinsic rewards. But, our interest in "gifted" children is compelled by a desire to see their talents expressed as "gifts" bestowed upon humanity in the practices of medicine, art, music, science, law, philosophy, and enterprise.

One of the truisms of applied psychology is that ability matters in occupational settings. Across all different types and levels of occupations, high-ability individuals will learn new skills more quickly and perform at a higher level of competence than those with lower ability levels (Hunter, 1986). General ability is the best predictor of attainment across a wide spectrum of careers (Austin & Hanisch, 1990; Ree & Earles, 1996). In general, gifted individuals are more likely than others to gain access to careers with stringent entrance requirements (e.g., medicine) and long induction periods (e.g., science), advance quickly within occupations, and establish a record of creative production.

This section of the chapter will introduce you to a number of lenses for viewing vocational development, progressing from a focus on individual characteristics to a more complex view in which family and community systems and macroeconomic factors interact with individual characteristics to affect career pathways.

Traditional Career-Relevant Individual Characteristics

The history of modern career development and counseling can be traced to Frank Parsons, an educator who provided career guidance services to immigrants and other migrants to the city during the industrial revolution. Parsons' seminal idea was to *match* individual *traits* with the *factors* required to complete various occupations (Parsons, 1909). This trait-factor approach has been the dominant career development paradigm since the early 20th century. The majority of career development research has been focused on the interests of gifted adolescents.

Career Interests

Interests predict the type of work and leisure activities that we select and find intrinsically satisfying (Lowman, 1991). Interests develop from genetic influences and social learning activities (Holland, 1997). Large-scale twin studies indicate that approximately one-third to one-half of the variance in interests is explained by heredity; the remaining variance is influenced by environmental learning (Betsworth et al., 1994; Lykken, Bouchard, McGue, & Tellegen, 1993). Heredity and a series of learning experiences in the family, school, and peer group lead to the formation of distinct preferences for activities that prove to be intrinsically rewarding.

John Holland (1997) developed a parsimonious model of career interests, which he arranged in a hexagonal model. The six interests can be described as realistic, investigative, artistic, social, enterprising, and conventional. Realistic interests include mechanical, nature/outdoors, athletic, and military activities; realistic types seek solutions to physical problems and challenges. Investigative interests include scientific and research activities; investigative types desire to seek the answers to scientific and intellectual questions. Artistic interests include musical, literary, and visual/performing art activities; creativity is the cardinal trait of the artistic personality. Social interests include helping activities such as teaching and counseling; social types seek to nurture and guide others. Enterprising interests include business, finance, and management activities; enterprising types bring together novel combinations of people and business ideas with the basic motivation to make money. Conventional interests include occupations with well-established routines and roles; the conventional type seeks the security of performing a well-defined job routine correctly.

The significance of the hexagon is twofold. First, interest types located in adjacent positions of the hexagon (Artistic-Social) are more similar than those on opposing points (Artistic-Conventional). Thus, artistic types have a greater affinity for, and more common experiences with, social types than with conventional types. Second, individuals with complex interest patterns that include strong preferences for opposing interests (e.g., realistic and social) often have difficulty finding an outlet for these competing interests in work or leisure activities. The hexagon is a heuristic device for identifying and specifying the interrelationships of interests, predicting the ease or difficulty of entry into careers, and determining the quality of *fit* among individuals and between individuals and their work environments.

With this understanding of Holland's model, educators can better understand the interests of gifted students. There are four salient facts regarding the career interests of gifted adolescents. First, there is no association between ability and specific interest types. Gifted adolescents express the whole range of human interests; one can identify examples of outstanding attainment in each interest area. Second, interests can be categorized along a concrete-abstract dimension, with realistic, enterprising, and conventional activities reflecting concrete foci and investigative and artistic activities manifesting more abstract pursuits. Individuals expressing abstract interests such as math, science, literature, and music are most readily recognized as gifted. However, extraordinary achievement can be demonstrated in realistic (e.g., Mia Hamm) and enterprising (e.g., Jeff Bezos) pursuits. Third, within the population of intellectually precocious youth, interests divide into a prevailing concern with either scientific or human/literary activities (Schmidt, Lubinski, & Benbow, 1998). That is, gifted adolescent interests can be described as primarily those of *scientists* or *humanists*—"preferences for and nonlinguistic ideation about things versus preferences for and linguistic ideation about people" (Schmidt et al., p. 446). Finally, interests begin to crystallize in early adolescence and are stable over long periods of time. Lubinski and his colleagues demonstrated that the interests of 13- and 14-year-olds in the Midwest Talent Search were predictive of their career paths 10 (Schmidt et al., 1998), 15 (Lubinski, Benbow, & Ryan, 1995), and 20 years (Lubinski, Schmidt, & Benbow, 1996) later.

There are three practical applications of this knowledge. First, we should recognize talent in all areas of interest and career pursuit. Interest in athletics, military activities, or auto mechanics is not inconsistent with intellectual precocity. Second, educators should not hesitate to administer and interpret career interest tests for young adolescents. Tests such as the Strong Interest Inventory (Harmon, Hansen, Borgen, & Hammer, 1994) have proven to be reliable and valid for this population. Third, parents, teachers, and counselors should treat adolescent interests as serious and perhaps enduring. Intense interests emerging in adolescence may be predictive of future career paths and should be validated and nurtured.

Range of Career Pursuits

Terman was the first to study the occupational fields chosen by gifted individuals. The original Terman study participants tended to choose careers in writing and teaching and were less likely to pursue business careers (Terman & Oden, 1947). Decades later Kerr and Colangelo (1988) found that gifted students expressed relatively little interest in teaching and journalism and greater interest in business. The career aspirations of gifted students are influenced by broad generational trends. For example, the tilt toward business and away from teaching and journalism in the 1980s may have reflected the economic insecurities reflected in the popular (e.g., *Bonfire of the Vanities*) and scholarly (e.g., *Decline and Fall of Great Powers)* literature of that period. More recent trends, reported in UCLA's Higher Education Research Institute (2000) annual survey of first-year college students, are of rising interest in elementary and secondary school teaching, fine arts, and the humanities. It is likely that such broad trends are reflected in the contemporary aspirations of gifted students.

Multiplicity of Interests

Multipotentiality is the ability to pursue a variety of career options (Kerr & Sodano, 2003). There have been numerous anecdotal reports of gifted children experiencing intense indecision regarding, for example, the dilemma of pursuing careers in music or science, medicine or athletics, etc. Such anecdotal reports of multipotentiality were substantiated by early studies (e.g., Fox, 1978) showing that gifted children express high interest in diverse career areas. However, more contemporary studies have shown that gifted adolescents—in general—have differentiated profiles of interests, abilities, and values (Achter, Lubinski, & Benbow, 1996; Milgram & Hong, 1999). Early reports of multipotentiality may have been due to the propensity of gifted students, particularly those chosen for inclusion in gifted programs, to express enthusiasm for and openness to a wide rage of activities. Such an enthusiastic or acquiescent response style inflates scores on interest inventories

(Prediger, 1998). The best and most recent studies indicate that multipotentiality is not a defining characteristic of gifted students (Achter & Lubinski, 2005; Achter et al., 1996). Moreover, gifted students experience little conflict about choosing from among numerous attractive career options (Hall & Kelly, 1995). Rather than being indecisive, gifted students as a whole appear to enjoy the benefits of developing crystallized interests at a relatively early age, and the freedom to pursue their primary career interests with the awareness that secondary interests can be integrated into one's leisure life.

A Systemic View of Career Development

The preceding discussion of individual traits does not represent the full complexity of career development. The following discussion will focus on the systems in which individual career development occurs.

Vocational identity does not develop in a vacuum. The individual develops within a system of interacting contexts. Vondracek, Lerner, and Schulenberg (1986) proposed a dynamic interactional model of career development. The key feature of their model is its description of the transactions among distinct systems. The family of origin system includes children, parents, siblings, and extended family. The child's extrafamilial system includes school, community, and peer networks; the adult's extrafamilial system includes work and community networks. The subsequent focus will be on the family system because it has been the subject of the majority of systems-based career development research. Three parameters of the family of origin system are related to career development: activities, relationships, and roles (Bronfenbrenner, 1979).

Family Activities

Activities are the dominant vocational, recreational, social, and spiritual pursuits of the family. We can readily recognize how the career activities of prominent parents have stimulated and facilitated children's talent and vocational identity development within music (such as the Marsalis family), film and acting (such as the Bridges and Sheen families), baseball (such as Ken Griffey Sr. and Ken Griffey Jr.), and politics (such as George H. W. and George W. Bush). Bloom's (1985) studies demonstrated the formative power of shared family activity for world-class tennis players (Monsaas, 1985), swimmers (Kalinowski, 1985), and pianists (Sosniak, 1985).

Two aspects of family activity support talent development. First, shared activity connotes the value of an activity within the family; when there is a family consensus that music, art, and sports have high intrinsic value, there is little debate about the importance of participation in a given activity when allocating children's time. Conversely, it is difficult to build or sustain excellence in a pursuit that is not valued by one's family. The second aspect is material support. Families invest considerable money and time to support music lessons and camps, summer athletic camps and traveling competitive teams, and summer classes and workshops. Direct material support gives children access to special instruction and coaching and enables them to accelerate their curve of talent development. Shared family activity is a vehicle through which early career talents are identified and developed and one's worth and standing in the family is established (Vondracek et al., 1986).

Family Relationships

If activity is the vehicle through which talents are developed, relationships fuel the vehicle. Activity describes what happens, relationships propel activities. According to Grotevant and Cooper (1985), there are two basic dimensions of parent-child relationships—support and autonomy. Relationship support is the love, affection, and encouragement that parents provide to children as they encounter developmental challenges. Whereas material support provides musical instruments and lessons, relationship support means sharing the child's frustration in struggling to master new techniques or joining their celebration after a successful recital. Relationship support involves empathy for the child and encouraging children to work through anxiety and frustration. Parental support is strongly associated with positive career development (Caldera, Robitschek, Frame, & Pannell, 2003; McWhirter, Hackett, & Bandalos, 1998; O'Brien, Friedman, Tipton, & Linn, 2000; Trusty, 2002). Adolescents with emotionally supportive families are free to explore their interests, engage in preliminary career exploration activities (Hargrove, Creagh, & Burgess, 2002), and consequently accelerate their progress in crystallizing their vocational identities (Johnson, Buboltz, & Nichols, 1999).

Autonomy is distinct from support. Parents also have the responsibility of raising children with distinct identities to function independently in the world. As they mature and make more independent decisions, children need to set their own goals, allocate their time, and learn how to resolve social, academic, and moral dilemmas. Not all challenges can be met through parental support; families also have to help children move toward functional, attitudinal, and emotional autonomy (Blustein, Walbridge, Friedlander, & Palladino, 1991; Hoffman, 1984).

Csikszentmihalyi, Rathunde, and Whalen (1993) studied support and autonomy in families of talented adolescents. They described families as primarily supportive, primarily autonomous, or complex. Supportive families were emotionally expressive, nurturing, and responsive to children's needs. Autonomous families gave children latitude to make decisions, form independent opinions, and take responsibility for meeting many of their material needs. Complex families provided high levels of both support and autonomy. The researchers found distinct outcomes associated with each type of family. Students from supportive families were most likely to receive high grades; they were rated as socially skilled and likeable by their teachers and coaches. Supportive families appear to help students develop the skills of social connection and reciprocity. Students from autonomous families were not as likely to receive high grades; however, they were more likely to be rated as talented by teachers and coaches. Autonomous students were more oriented to pursuing knowledge and skill acquisition than to getting along with others and getting good grades. Students from complex families spent the most time completing homework and practicing in their talent domain. They were most likely to be "on task" outside of school and least likely to spend time watching television.

Csikszentmihalyi et al. (1993) hypothesized that support and autonomy relate to talent development in three ways. First, supportive families help to mitigate the adverse effects of anxiety on productive engagement. Emotional support helps students to rebound from setbacks and to get back to productive activity. Second, autonomous adolescents are challenged by their families to account for their time and decisions. These students seem to be well prepared to respond to the boredom endemic in structured academic settings; autonomous students respond to boredom by creating their own challenges, which leads to higher levels of productive engagement and knowledge/skill acquisition. Third, students from complex families enjoy supportive relationships that mitigate anxiety and frustration and learn the personal skills to direct their time and focus. Thus gifted students are advantaged by family relationships that provide support and promote autonomy.

Are there family factors that inhibit talent development? Shilkret and Nigrosh (1997) used a psychoanalytic perspective in conducting a fascinating study of the academic performance of talented college women. They found two unconscious inhibitors of college student adjustment and academic performance: separation guilt and survivor guilt. Separation guilt is the unconscious belief that one's independence is dangerous or threatening to parental well-being (Shilkret & Nigrosh). Consider the child departing for college who worries that his parents will divorce now that he—the youngest child—has left the family nest. There are several nuances in separation anxiety. One concerns daughters and mothers. It is not uncommon for talented women to be concerned that their success will indict their mothers' lack of overt success in the working world. These concerns are unconscious and unavailable for free expression and articulation. Yet, they can undermine success or create failure. Parents must be not only overtly supportive of success, but also consistent in communicating that the child's autonomy is not a psychological danger to the parents.

Survivor guilt is the phenomenon of feeling undeserving of success and opportunities because close family members have not had similar opportunities (Shilkret & Nigrosh, 1997). For example, a young woman may experience survivor guilt because she earned a scholarship to attend an Ivy League college and an older sibling with similar aspirations did not succeed in doing so. A child can also experience survivor guilt because of having opportunities that were not available to his or her parents. Consider the example of the immigrant family that pools its resources to enable one child to attend college. In each of these examples, adult children experience guilt in relation to their good fortune, and unconsciously may undermine their individual success. The family must communicate that one child's success enhances the collective status of the family and of each family member. If one child's academic success proves costly to another child, this cost may unconsciously impede future attainment and success.

Individual career development occurs within a family context that attends to the psychological needs of the growing child and provides the necessary structure and expectations for the child to develop habits of productive engagement. The family is also responsible for acknowledging and celebrating various gifts and accomplishments of family members so that one member's success does not damage or diminish any other family member. Although it is powerful, the family functions within the even larger macrosystem that is described in the following section.

The Macrosystem: Social and Cultural Forces That Shape Individual Career Development

Vondracek et al. (1986) defined the macrosystem as "the overarching blueprint of culture and subcultures" (p. 62). It is the consistent form and content of familial, school, work, community, cultural, and economic systems (Bronfenbrenner, 1979). The macrosystem includes: economic conditions, social/educational policy, technological advances, job opportunities, organizational/institutional context, environmental conditions, labor laws, and sociocultural context. These broad forces can shape the course of individual careers, although they are largely unrecognized by individuals.

The impact of macrosystemic factors on the careers of gifted individuals was documented in the biographical research of the Goertzels (Goertzel & Goertzel, 1962; Goertzel, Goertzel, & Goertzel, 1978). Would Michael Dell have been an internationally famous entrepreneur if he had come of age in the 1940s, decades before the creation of the personal computer? Would he be famous if he came of age in 2004, after the market for personal computers had been established? It seems highly unlikely that his business genius would have found its full potential without the perfect alignment of his personal skills and talents with technological advances, market forces, and economic conditions. Let us briefly consider the influence of sociocultural context, economic conditions, and social/education policy on individual career development.

Sociocultural Context

Throughout history, significant cultural advances have been associated with the intermingling of distinct cultures. Participation in dual cultures, despite and perhaps because of its inherent conflicts, is associated with creative productivity. Nearly one half of the eminent contributors to American culture, industry, and science have been first- or second-generation immigrants (Goertzel & Goertzel, 1962). The intellectual stimulation of participating in two cultures, the tension between maintaining allegiance to one's native culture and assimilation into the new host culture, and the need to establish respect and recognition within the dominant culture have driven artistic, scientific, and cultural genius. In contrast, Simonton (1994) has described how politically repressive regimes have yielded few meaningful scientific or artistic contributions to the world. High levels of talent development require open political and economic conditions that give individuals of all social classes access to intellectual and monetary capital.

Economic Conditions

High levels of talent often require decades of incubation. For example, scientific innovation is preceded by an extended period of knowledge acquisition. As a result, eminent scientists tend to come from middle and upper socioeconomic levels (Goertzel et al., 1978). Most of the eminent scientists from the 1800s were supported by wealthy families who were able to provide young scientists with protection from economic reversals. Eminent scientists also tended to come from families that did not experience family trauma or early parental death or divorce. As children and adolescents, eminent scientists had the psychological and financial freedom to become absorbed in the pursuit of their interests and hobbies (Goertzel & Goertzel, 1962).

Social and Educational Policy

The response of the American government to the successful Sputnik launch by the Soviet Union is a clear example of government policy affecting individual career development. The government infused money into expanded educational opportunities within science and engineering; this policy supported the development of a whole generation of scientific talent. In another talent domain, the government passed Title IX to provide equal opportunity for women in all educational programs and activities, including athletics. Before its passage, there was limited financial support for women's athletic programs in high school and college. Since Title IX was enacted in 1972, women's participation in collegiate sports has increased from fewer than 32,000 to more than 150,000 athletes, a number displaying "proof that interest follows opportunity" (National Women's Law Center, 2005). This educational policy created opportunity for a whole generation of athletic talent that otherwise would not have found full expression: Mia Hamm, Sheryl Swoopes, and Marion Jones. The careers of these women would have followed a very different and less well-known path had it not been for the advent of this social policy.

IMPLICATIONS FOR SECONDARY EDUCATORS

Erik Erikson maintained that identity formation was the most important challenge of adolescence and necessary preparation for adulthood. We have heard the voices of Vaughn, Wallace, Claire, and Lucio, gifted urban teenagers who were well on their way to adulthood with a strong sense of personal identity. Listening to the voices of these young people, educators realize the significance of Erikson's message. From our review of theoretical and research literature we realize that identity is a complex psychological construct. In addition, we realize that identity formation may be even more complicated for gifted individuals. From this review it is clear that educators, counselors, and parents need to understand, appreciate, and support identity development in young people.

Secondary educators may want to consider a number of important questions as they work with gifted adolescents. For example, if identity development is crucial preparation for adulthood, and gifted youngsters are intellectually advanced, can we assume that their identity development may also be advanced? Reflecting on Vaughn's comfort with his sensitivity, Wallace's view of himself as a serious scholar-athlete, Lucio's strong personality, and Claire's drive to become a doctor, we might speculate that the intelligence of these gifted young people influenced the development of their strong belief in self.

Another issue is the question of whether or not identity development in gifted young people is more intense than in others. Will the search for a personal identity within a gifted student take many different directions? Experienced secondary educators reflect on former gifted students who experimented with a variety of identities within a short period of time. Teachers speak of students who arrive in high school presenting themselves as young, conservative-looking intellectuals, and within an academic year they shift to clothing and hairstyles driven by the popular culture, immersing themselves in new interests and activities that reflect an active identity search. For instance, the middle school science and math wizard may become a songwriter and poet. As teachers of gifted students and concerned parents observe these changes, they consider how "trying on many more hats" reflects the adolescent search for identity.

Our literature review provides evidence that context plays an important role in shaping the identity of gifted adolescents. Multiple researchers noted that extracurricular activities and other experiences beyond the classroom made a difference in shaping identities. Networks of high achieving peers and supportive adults and role models can also make a difference. Secondary educators who observe students gravitating to involvement in the high school band or orchestra are also going to note whether such involvement is respected or valued by the peer group. We realize that activities valued in one context may not be valued in another. In a high school environment where intellectual and athletic achievements are celebrated equally, will the culture of the school influence how gifted young people feel about who they are within that culture? As young people experiment with identities, teachers of gifted students can assist them in becoming aware of the role that school context plays in influencing decisions regarding who they want to be.

Through our literature review, we have explored a rich theoretical body of knowledge. The work of Erikson, Marcia, Gilligan, and Josselson offers us a strong theoretical foundation. The gifted education community must examine the work of these giants and consider closely how they inform our understanding of identity development within gifted young people. Cross (2004) reminds us of this challenge and highlights the significance of Erikson's work in better understanding gifted young people. He maintained that gifted children may be affected by the psychosocial crises at earlier ages than Erikson believed. Cross argues that some gifted children have the intellectual ability to understand the world ahead of their chronological age, yet with the emotional development typical of their age peers. He explained, "To take advantage of the explanatory power of Erikson's theory, one needs to interpret an individual gifted child's behavior in light of the theory and the child's idiosyncratic development and personal characteristics" (p. 29). This recommendation should be applied to the other identity development theories reviewed in this chapter. Educators must remember the idiosyncratic qualities of development in gifted teenagers when considering how their experiences may be applied to the models offered by Marcia, Gilligan, and Josselson.

From Vaughn, Wallace, Claire, and Lucio we have learned that identity is important. The challenge is now determining what can be done in our secondary schools to support that development. Secondary teachers may want to consider designing lessons that address identity issues within the curriculum. A social science teacher in a U.S. history class may have students examine Eleanor Roosevelt's life through Josselson's model. Another teacher can use identity development to frame a discussion of Harry Truman's strong sense of self and his decision to drop the atomic bomb. A literature teacher may require students to write a reflective essay drawing parallels between their emerging identities and that of a significant character from a novel. A math teacher calls attention to famous female mathematicians and facilitates a lively class discussion regarding how these women succeeded in their field given the times during which they lived. In addition to infusing identity development in the secondary curriculum, teachers and counselors may want to consider providing special class seminars or workshops with gifted teenagers in which they offer the students training in the same models reviewed in this chapter.

Brown et al. (2003) suggested four guidelines that can be used to promote career development and decision making with gifted adolescents. First, encourage students to develop written career goals with tentative implementation plans. The writing process helps to formalize goals and plans that can be shared with parents, peers, counselors, and teachers. Second, students should gather information about their career options. There is a wealth of career information available through Internet sources such as the O*NET (http://www.onetcenter.org). Students must augment this easily accessed online information with information interviews from professionals engaged in various fields. Although this can be a challenge for introverted students, the information interview invariably yields valuable informal knowledge and provides leads for further career research. Third, students should be encouraged to conduct written comparisons of their occupational options using formal criteria. Counselors can guide students in evaluating each occupational option on common criteria, such as the six values (achievement, recognition, independence, relationships, support, working conditions) assessed through the O*NET *Work Importance Profiler* (http://www.onetcenter.org/WIP.html). The process of rating options by criteria promotes self-understanding and helps students to develop more realistic and informed aspirations (Gati, 1998). Finally, students benefit from interaction with models who have successfully coped with challenges and frustrations in the career exploration and decision-making process.

From the review of research on identity development in gifted students we understand that extracurricular activities play an important role in shaping identity. Secondary educators can support gifted young people by encouraging their students to become involved in a variety of activities beyond the classroom. Teachers and counselors may encourage students to experiment with enjoying different outlets for their gifts and talents. Involvement in clubs, teams, or campaigns provides opportunities for intelligent young people to build a sense of self-efficacy and success. A strong sense of self evolves from being a member of a group noted for accomplishment. These group experiences enable teenagers to construct a positive sense of self and raise aspirations for the future. When teachers encourage their students to become involved in extracurricular activities, they are letting these young people know that their individuality is valued and their emerging identity is celebrated. As they do, they can smile to themselves and reflect on Lucio's words, "I just want to be able to be myself."

REFERENCES

Achter, J. A., & Lubinski, D. (2005). Blending promise with passion: Best practices for counseling intellectually talented youth. In S. D. Brown & R. W. Lent (Eds.), *Career development and counseling: Putting theory and research to work* (pp. 600–624). New York: Wiley.

Achter, J. A., Lubinski, D., & Benbow, C. P. (1996). Multipotentiality among the intellectually gifted: It was never there and already it's vanishing. *Journal of Counseling Psychology, 43,* 65–76.

Arce, C. A. (1981). A reconsideration of Chicano culture and identity. *Daedalus, 110,* 177–192.

Atkinson, D. R., Morten, G., & Sue, D. W. (1993). *Counseling American minorities: A cross-cultural perspective* (3rd ed.). Dubuque, IA: William C. Brown.

Austin, J. T., & Hanisch, K. A. (1990). Occupational attainment as a function of abilities and interests. A longitudinal analysis using Project TALENT data. *Journal of Applied Psychology, 39,* 77–86.

Betsworth, D. G., Bouchard, T. J., Jr., Cooper, C. R., Grotevant, H. D., Hansen, J. C., Scarr, S., et al. (1994). Genetic and environmental influences on vocational interests assessed using adoptive and biological families and twins reared apart and together. *Journal of Vocational Behavior, 44,* 263–278.

Bloom, B. S. (1985). *Developing talent in young people.* New York: Ballantine Books.

Blustein, D. L., Walbridge, M. M., Friedlander, M. L., & Palladino, D. E. (1991). Contributions of psychological separation and parental attachment to the career development process. *Journal of Counseling Psychology, 38,* 39–50.

Bronfenbrenner, U. (1979). *The ecology of human development: Experiments by nature and design.* Cambridge, MA: Harvard University Press.

Brown, S. D., Krane, N. E. R., Brecheisen, J., Castelino, P., Budisin, I., Miller, M., et al. (2003). Critical ingredients of career choice interventions: More analyses and new hypotheses. *Journal of Vocational Behavior, 62,* 411–428.

Caldera, Y. M., Robitschek, C., Frame, M., & Pannell, M. (2003). Intrapersonal, familial, and cultural factors in the commitment to a career choice of Mexican American and non-Hispanic White college women. *Journal of Counseling Psychology, 50,* 309–323.

Coleman, L. J., & Cross, T. (1988). Is being gifted a social handicap? *Journal for the Education of the Gifted, 11,* 41–56.

Coleman, L. J., & Cross, T. L. (2001). *Being gifted in school: An introduction to development, guidance, and teaching.* Waco, TX: Prufrock Press.

Coleman, L. J., & Sanders, M. D. (1993). Social needs, social choices and masking one's giftedness. *Journal of Secondary Gifted Education, 5,* 22–25.

Cross, T. L. (2004). *On the social and emotional lives of gifted children* (2nd ed.). Waco, TX: Prufrock Press.

Cross, W. E., Jr. (1995). The psychology of Nigrescence: Revising the Cross model. In J. G. Ponterotto, J. M. Casas, L. A. Suzuki, & C. M. Alexander (Eds.), *Handbook of multicultural counseling* (pp. 93–122). Thousand Oaks, CA: Sage.

Csikszentmihalyi, M., Rathunde, K., & Whalen, S. (1993). *Talented teenagers: The roots of success and failure.* Cambridge, MA: Cambridge University Press.

Dole, S. (2001). Reconciling contradictions: Identity formation in individuals with giftedness and learning disabilities. *Journal for the Education of the Gifted, 25,* 103–137.

Erikson, E. H. (1968). *Identity: Youth and crisis.* New York: W. W. Norton.

Fox, L. H. (1978). Interest correlates to differential achievement of gifted students in mathematics. *Journal for the Education of the Gifted, 1,* 24–36.

Gati, I. (1998). Using career-related aspects to elicit preferences and characterize occupations for a better person-environment fit. *Journal of Vocational Behavior, 52,* 343–356.

Gilligan, C. (1982). *In a different voice.* Cambridge, MA: Harvard University Press.

Grotevant, H. D., & Cooper, C. R. (1985). Patterns of interaction in family relationships and the development of identity exploration in adolescence. *Child Development, 56,* 415-428.

Goertzel, V., & Goertzel, M. G. (1962). *Cradles of eminence.* Boston: Little, Brown and Company.

Goertzel, M. G., & Goertzel, V., & Goertzel, T. G. (1978). *Three hundred eminent personalities.* San Francisco: Jossey-Bass.

Hall, A. S., & Kelly, K. R. (1995). Effects of academic achievement, sex, and community of residence on four types of career indecision. *Journal of Secondary Gifted Education, 7,* 293–302.

Hargrove, B. K., Creagh, M. G., & Burgess, B. L. (2002). Family interaction patterns as predictors of vocational identity and career decision-making self-efficacy. *Journal of Vocational Behavior, 61,* 185–201.

Harmon, L. W., Hansen, J. C., Borgen, F. H., & Hammer, A. B. (1994). *Applications and technical guide for the Strong Interest Inventory.* Palo Alto, CA: Consulting Psychologists Press.

Hébert, T. P. (1998). Gifted Black males in an urban high school: Factors that influence achievement and underachievement. *Journal for the Education of the Gifted, 21,* 385–414.

Hébert, T. P. (2000a). Defining belief in self: Intelligent young men in an urban high school. *Gifted Child Quarterly, 44,* 91–114.

Hébert, T. P. (2000b). Gifted males pursuing careers in elementary education. *Journal for the Education of the Gifted, 24,* 7–45.

Hébert, T. P., & Reis, S. M. (1999). Culturally diverse high-achieving students in an urban high school. *Urban Education, 34,* 428–457.

Higher Education Research Institute. (2000). *The American freshman—national norms for 1999.* Los Angeles: Author.

Hoffman, J. A. (1984). Psychological separation of late adolescents from their parents. *Journal of Counseling Psychology, 31,* 170–178.

Holland, J. L. (1997). *Making vocational choices* (3rd ed.). Odessa, FL: Psychological Assessment Resources.

Howard-Hamilton, M., & Franks, B. A. (1995). Gifted adolescents: Psychological behaviors, values, and developmental implications. *Roeper Review, 17,* 186–191.

Hunter, J. E. (1986). Cognitive ability, cognitive aptitudes, job knowledge, and job performance. *Journal of Vocational Behavior, 29,* 340–362.

Johnson, P., Buboltz, W. C., & Nichols, C. (1999). Parental divorce, family functioning, and vocational identity of college students. *Journal of Career Development, 26,* 137–146.

Jones, S. R. (1997). Voices of identity and difference: A qualitative exploration of the multiple dimensions of identity development in women college students. *Journal of College Student Development, 38,* 376–385.

Jones, S. R., & McEwen, M. K. (2000). A conceptual model of multiple dimensions of identity. *Journal of College Student Development, 41,* 405–413.

Josselson, R. (1987). *Finding herself: Pathways to identity development in women.* San Francisco: Jossey-Bass.

Josselson, R. (1996). *Revising herself.* New York: Oxford University Press.

Kalinowski, A. G. (1985). The development of Olympic swimmers. In B. S. Bloom (Ed.), *Developing talent in young people* (pp. 139–192). New York: Ballantine Books.

Kerr. B. A., & Colangelo, N. (1988). The college plans of academically talented students. *Journal of Counseling and Development, 67,* 168–186.

Kerr, B. A., & Sodano, S. (2003). Career assessment with intellectually gifted students. *Journal of Career Assessment, 11,* 168–186.

Kim, J. (1981). *Process of Asian-American identity development: A study of Japanese American women's perceptions of their struggle to achieve positive identities.* Unpublished doctoral dissertation, University of Massachusetts, Amherst.

Lowman, R. L. (1991). *The clinical practice of career assessment: Interests, abilities, and personality.* Washington, DC: American Psychological Association.

Lubinski, D., Benbow, C. P., & Ryan, J. (1995). Stability of vocational interests among the intellectually gifted from adolescence to adulthood: A 15-year longitudinal study. *Journal of Applied Psychology, 80,* 196–200.

Lubinski, D., Schmidt, D. B., & Benbow, C. P. (1996). A 20-year stability analysis of the Study of Values for intellectually gifted individuals from adolescence to adulthood. *Journal of Applied Psychology, 81,* 443–451.

Lykken, D. T., Bouchard, T. J., Jr., McGue, M., & Tellegen, A. T. (1993). The heritability of interests: A twin study. *Journal of Applied Psychology, 78,* 649–661.

Marcia, J. E. (1993). The ego identity status approach to ego identity. In J. E. Marcia, A. S. Waterman, D. R. Matteson, S. L. Archer, & J. L. Orlofsky (Eds.), *Ego identity: A handbook for psychological research* (pp. 3–21). New York: Springer-Verlag.

Marcia, J. E. (1994). The empirical study of ego identity. In H. A. Bosma, T. L. G. Graafsma, H. D. Grotevant, & D. J. de Levita (Eds.), *Identity and development* (pp. 67–80). Thousand Oaks, CA: Sage.

Monsaas, J. A. (1985). Learning to be a world-class tennis player. In B. S. Bloom (Ed.), *Developing talent in young people* (pp. 211–269). New York: Ballantine Books.

McWhirter, E. H., Hackett, G., & Bandalos, D. L. (1998). A causal model of the educational plans and career expectations of Mexican American high school girls. *Journal of Counseling Psychology, 45,* 166–181.

Milgram, R. M., & Hong, E. (1999). Multipotential abilities and vocational interests in gifted adolescents: Fact or fiction? *International Journal of Psychology, 34,* 81–93.

National Women's Law Center (2005). *Save Title IX.* Retrieved August 30, 2005, from http://www.savetitleix.com/index.html

O'Brien, K. M., Friedman, S. M., Tipton, L. C., & Linn, S. G. (2000). Attachment, separation, and women's vocational development. *Journal of Counseling Psychology, 47,* 301–315.

Parsons, F. (1909). *Choosing a vocation.* Boston: Houghton Mifflin.

Phinney, J. S. (1996). When we talk about American ethnic groups, what do we mean? *American Psychologist, 51,* 918–927.

Phinney, J. S., Lochner, B. T., & Murphy, R. (1990). Ethnic identity development and psychological adjustment in adolescence. In. A. R. Stiffman & L. E. Davis (Eds.), *Ethnic issues in adolescent mental health* (pp. 53–72). Newbury Park, CA: Sage.

Piechowski, M. M. (1997). Emotional giftedness: The measure of intrapersonal intelligence. In N. Colangelo & G. A. Davis (Eds.), *The handbook of gifted education* (2nd ed.; pp. 366–381). Boston: Allyn & Bacon.

Ponterotto, J. G., & Pedersen, P. B. (1993). *Preventing prejudice: A guide for counselors and educators.* Newbury Park, CA: Sage.

Prediger, D. J. (1998). Is interest profile level relevant to career counseling? *Journal of Counseling Psychology, 45,* 204–214.

Rasmussen, J. E. (1964). Relationship of ego identity to psychological effectiveness. *Psychological Reports, 15,* 815–825.

Ree, M. J., & Earles, J. A. (1996). Predicting occupational criteria: Not much more than *g*. In I. Denis & P. Tapsfield (Eds.), *Human abilities: Their nature and measurement* (pp. 151–165). Mahwah, NJ: Lawrence Erlbaum Associates.

Reis, S. M., Hébert, T. P., Diaz, E. I., Maxfield, L. R., & Ratley, M. E. (1995). *Case studies of talented students who achieve and underachieve in an urban high school.* [RM 95120]. Storrs, CT: National Research Center on the Gifted and Talented, University of Connecticut.

Santrock, J. W. (2003). *Adolescence* (9th ed.). Boston: McGraw-Hill.

Schmidt, D. B., Lubinski, D., & Benbow, C. P. (1998). Validity of assessing educational-vocational preference dimensions among intellectual talented 13-year olds. *Journal of Counseling Psychology, 45,* 436–453.

Shaffer, D. R. (2000). *Social and personality development* (4th ed.). Belmont, CA: Wadsworth/ Thomson Learning.

Shilkret, R., & Nigrosh, W. E. (1997). Assessing students' plans for college. *Journal of Counseling Psychology, 44,* 222–231.

Simonton, D. H. (1994). *Greatness.* New York: Guilford.

Sosniak, L. A. (1985). Learning to be a concert pianist. In B. S. Bloom (Ed.), *Developing talent in young people* (pp. 19–67). New York: Ballantine Books.

Speirs Neumeister, K. L. (2002). Shaping an identity: Factors influencing the achievement of newly married, gifted young women. *Gifted Child Quarterly, 46,* 291–305.

Terman, L. M. (1925). *Genetic studies of genius: Vol. 1. Mental and Physical traits of a thousand gifted children.* Stanford, CA: Stanford University Press.

Terman, L. M., & Oden, M. H. (1947). *The gifted child grows up.* Stanford, CA: Stanford University Press.

Trusty, J. (2002). African Americans' educational expectations: Longitudinal causal models for women and men. *Journal of Counseling and Development, 80,* 332–345.

Vondracek, F. W., Lerner, R. M., & Schulenberg, J. E. (1986). *Career development: A life-span developmental approach.* Hillsdale, NJ: Lawrence Erlbaum Associates.

Zuo, L., & Cramond, B. L. (2001). An examination of Terman's gifted children from the theory of identity. *Gifted Child Quarterly, 45,* 251–259.

Zuo, L., & Tao, L. (2001). Importance of personality in gifted children's identity formation. *Journal of Secondary Gifted Education, 12,* 212–223.

Social-Emotional Development of Gifted Adolescents

by Susan G. Assouline
& Nicholas Colangelo

Chapter 3

The North American English version of *Encarta Dictionary* gives a short definition of adolescence as the time preceding adulthood. The simplicity of these words belies the complexity of adolescent development. This is a time characterized by vibrant discovery, growth, and transformation—of mind and body—changes that appear to accelerate uncontrollably. With this development, the malleability of thought and personality patterns often manifest in fluctuating tastes in music, humor, values, philosophy of life, and commitment to education. This period of change lends to the stereotype that adolescence is a stormy time characterized by stress. We, as well as you, the reader, have lived through adolescence, and we know that the turmoil connected with this developmental period is real. There are no shortcuts through this developmental period; however, understanding the issues relevant to adolescents can help circumvent some of the turbulence.

As a developmental period, adolescence represents a time of maturation, including the establishment of self within the teenage culture. This culture becomes a dominant consideration. Our everyday language reflects our familiar experiences: Teenagers demand recognition of the right to individuality and uniqueness, as well as respect for the process of "being who they are." But, within the context of the teenage environment, the passions of the individual are often eclipsed by the needs of the group. The teenage environment is full of both spoken and unspoken mores and rules that guide adolescent behaviors and attitudes, especially in schools. The ironclad golden rules are "don't go against the group" and "do whatever it takes to be *in* rather than *out*."

Are the developmental and environmental issues mentioned above the same for the gifted adolescent? By definition, we are talking about an adolescent who has exceptional intellectual and academic ability, and therefore is already different from the typical group. Academic "gifts" tend to be unrecognized as an important characteristic in the typical teenage environment in America. The challenge to the individual adolescent, therefore, is integrating intellectual integrity within the teenage environment so that "membership" to this dubious group can be realized. This is a monumental task defined by aspects that are both obvious and nuanced. The main purpose of this chapter is to present the distinctive social-emotional issues and relationship tensions experienced by *gifted* adolescents with respect to teenage environment, self-concept, college and career counseling, multipotentiality, and underachievement.

DEFINITIONS AND BACKGROUND

For our purposes, adolescence is represented by the teen years (i.e., 13–19 and grades 6–12), and giftedness is represented by exceptional general intellectual and academic ability or academic achievement. The focus of the chapter is on the social-emotional aspects of the lives of gifted adolescents. The chapter is aimed, in particular, at school counselors and school psychologists. It is also appropriate for teachers, because often the gifted program teacher or the classroom teacher is the first to witness the social and emotional interactions of teenagers and may act as the primary adviser for many gifted adolescents.

There have been two main, and conflicting, views regarding the social-emotional development of gifted students (Neihart, 1999). One view is that gifted individuals are at least as well adjusted as any other student and may be very well adjusted because of their giftedness. From this perspective, there is little need for specialized interventions that focus on the social-emotional development of gifted adolescents.

The contrasting view is that gifted students, because of their very advanced cognitive abilities and intensity of feelings, deal with issues about themselves and others in ways that are distinct from the general population and therefore require specialized understanding. In this view, the gifted individual is not necessarily maladjusted because of the giftedness, but the giftedness uniquely organizes the social-emotional needs of adolescents (Piechowski, 1997). The assumption in this view is that, whereas the majority of gifted adolescents experience healthy growth and maturation that result in satisfactory psychological adjustment, there is a sizeable minority who are psychologically "at risk" because they are gifted (Buescher, 1991; Delisle, 1997). One of the more general risks is related to the fact that gifted students have the task of adjusting to a peer culture that is often ambiguous toward those with intellectual talent (Colangelo, 2002a). Our view is commensurate with this latter position (i.e., that gifted students do have recurring and significant counseling needs based on their special cognitive abilities). Educators need to be aware of these general issues, as well as more specific issues (e.g., underachievement and twice-exceptionality) in order to be effective in their interactions with gifted teenagers (Colangelo & Assouline, 2000).

COUNSELING AND SOCIAL-EMOTIONAL DEVELOPMENT OF GIFTED STUDENTS

Historically, there is an obvious connection between an individual's social-emotional development and the professional field of counseling. Karen St. Clair (1989) created an informative timeline of the development of the profession of counseling. In Table 1, we merge her timeline with our updated review of historical progress in understanding the social-emotional needs of gifted students.

TEENAGE ENVIRONMENT—FAMILY, FRIENDS, AND SCHOOL

Csikszentmihalyi, Rathunde, and Whalen (1993) researched three primary components of the teenage environment of the gifted adolescent—family, friends, and school. In their unique study of talented teens, Csikszentmihalyi et al. delineated family characteristics that create an environment conducive to the successful development of gifted adolescents. Their description of those families with teens who were actualizing their talent presents a dynamic model of complexity characterized by seemingly opposing relationships of integration and differentiation.

> . . . [the] connection between family members is an instance of *integration*, or the stable condition whereby the individuals feel a sense of support and consistency. *Differentiation* refers to the fact that members are encouraged to develop their individuality by seeking out new challenges and opportunities. Families that are both integrated and differentiated can be thought of as complex. (Csikszentmihalyi et al., 1993, pp. 155–156)

Csikszentmihalyi et al. (1993) reported that gifted adolescents whose families were simultaneously differentiated and integrated (or complex) experienced more positive home environments. Although we can all think of anecdotal situations in which a complex family environment, as described by Csikszentmihalyi et al., is neither necessary nor sufficient for the development of the talented teen, it is important to recognize the impact such a family environment has on the teen's social-emotional development. Complexity translates to greater efficiency in focusing attention on productive activities such as homework and study.

Teens do not pick their families; however, they do choose their friends, and the family environment can have an impact on the choice of friends, as well as on the types of activities and amount of time spent with friends. In fact, some of the

Table 1
Timeline of Social-Emotional Issues
for Gifted Students and Counseling

1. Terman's work in the early 1900s (Terman, 1925) brought recognition of the gifted student; however, Leta Hollingworth (1926, 1942) was the first to contribute evidence indicating that gifted children do have social and emotional needs that merit attention. Hollingworth also emphasized strongly that the regular school environment did not meet the educational needs of the gifted. Rather, she wrote that the typical school environment was more likely to lead to apathy about school. She anticipated some of the current emotional difficulties and peer problems. Especially noting that there is often a gap between a gifted student's intellectual and emotional development, she stated, "To have the intellect of an adult and the emotions of a child combined in a childish body is to encounter certain difficulties" (Hollingworth, 1942, p. 282).

2. Mid-century, Carl Rogers' non-directive approach to counseling and therapy (Rogers, 1951) would influence the entire counseling profession. Concurrently, the 1950s witnessed more attention to counseling gifted students and the establishment of research and guidance programs. John Rothney, a counselor educator, founded the Wisconsin Guidance Laboratory for Superior Students (University of Wisconsin-Madison), which was headed by Rothney and later by Marshall Sanborn. The Guidance Institute for Talented Students (GIFTS) was headed by Charles Pulvino, followed by Nicholas Colangelo and then by Philip Perrone (Colangelo & Zaffrann, 1979).

3. The 1960s—a time of confusion and conflict—ushered in counseling in schools and the role of the school counselor was emphasized in the development of all students with some special attention to gifted. John Curtis Gowan was a major force from the 1950s to 1970s in promoting counseling services for the gifted. Equally important in promoting counseling services for gifted students was the work of A. Harry Passow and his students Abe Tannenbaum and Miriam Goldberg; in 1954 they founded the Talented Youth Project, which had a strong counseling component.

4. The programs from the 1950s and 1960s evolved to include full-fledged programs of counseling in schools with a broad focus including counseling sessions, counseling programs, student evaluations, and research relation to school counseling. The 1960s and 1970s also witnessed increased sensitivity to the academic needs as well as the counseling needs of gifted-underrepresented groups, including females, minorities, and economically disadvantaged students.

Table 1 continued

5. The increased sensitivity to diversity, first demonstrated in the 1960s and 1970s, was fully realized in the 1980s, and included models and approaches to counseling. This decade highlighted the special issues in counseling gifted students including a focus on underachievement, females, minority students, and the impact of stress on social-emotional development. Oftentimes, one individual's actions can have a powerful impact. Such was the case for the establishment, in the 1980s, of the Supporting the Emotional Needs of Gifted (SENG) program by James T. Webb at Wright State University after the suicide of Dallas Egbert, a highly gifted 17-year-old. SENG has continued its focus on addressing the counseling and psychological needs of gifted students. The issues of depression and suicide among the gifted expanded with the work of James Delisle at Kent State University (e.g., Delisle, 1992).

6. During the 1970s and 1980s there was also considerable research and explanation on Dabrowski's theory of Positive Disintegration (e.g., Dabrowski, 1970) as a template for considering the emotional development of gifted individuals (Piechowski, 1979, 2003).

7. In 1982, Barbara Kerr established the Guidance Laboratory for Gifted and Talented at the University of Nebraska-Lincoln, to extend the work of both GIFTS and SENG (Myers & Pace, 1986). Linda Silverman (1993), a psychologist, established the Gifted Child Development Center at Denver. Silverman (2003) has written extensively on the unique academic and counseling needs of gifted students who are double labeled, e.g. gifted/learning disabled (see as example Cash, 1999).

8. In 1988, The University of Iowa established the comprehensive Connie Belin National Center for Gifted Education (renamed The Connie Belin & Jacqueline N. Blank International Center for Gifted Education and Talent Development in 1995) with Nicholas Colangelo as director. Colangelo's academic background is strongly focused on personal counseling, career guidance, and family counseling. In 1990, Susan Assouline joined the Belin-Blank Center, and is the center's associate director. As a school psychologist, Assouline added psycho-educational assessment to the center's services.

9. In 2004, the Belin-Blank Center took on a specific clinical focus with the establishment of the H. B. and Jocelyn Wallace Assessment and Counseling Clinic. Megan Foley Nicpon, a licensed psychologist, administers and supervises the clinic in association with Colangelo and Assouline. In addition to the myriad clinical services, the clinic includes research and training as components and many advanced doctoral students complete their practica and internships at the clinic (Colangelo & Assouline, 2000). In 2001, we initiated a focus on twice-exceptional students.

Table 1 continued

10. The National Association for Gifted Children (NAGC) recognized the importance of social-emotional issues of gifted students by creating the NAGC Task Force on Social-Emotional Issues for Gifted Students. This task force produced the book *Social Emotional Development of Gifted Children: What do we know?* (Neihart, Reis, Robinson, & Moon, 2002). NAGC has also established an affective curriculum task force which is developing a book that will help teachers integrate activities to promote social-emotional development into their curriculum.

As we complete this first decade of the 21st century, we anticipate future priorities for counseling gifted adolescents. These may include the integration of approaches offered by the various helping professionals, e.g., counseling psychologists, counselor educators, school psychologists, etc., so that they work together to provide for the social-emotional needs of gifted students. We also think there will be a refinement of the understanding of the academic and social-emotional needs of gifted students with disabilities even as the distinctions between students who are labeled and those who are not become more ambiguous. As a nation, we have access to copious amounts of information, which may result in more litigation between parents and schools, as parents advocate for the best services available for their students.

turbulence associated with this developmental period is the juxtaposition of differentiation and integration with respect to choices about activities with family and/or friends.

Adolescence is the time when gender and sexual roles become more pronounced, which may impact intellectual pursuits, as well as friendships. It is also a time when the peer group begins to supersede the adult figures as the main reference for acceptance. In an early discussion of the power that the desire for friendship has on the gifted student, Gross (1989) refers to a forced-choice dilemma: Does a gifted adolescent choose to acquiesce to an anti-intellectual environment in order to attain same-age friends, or does the gifted adolescent abandon the potential for friends in the pursuit of excellence? For some gifted adolescents, such a forced-choice dilemma presents an impasse that prevents them from experiencing satisfaction in either arena—academics or friendship. When viewed within the context of Silverman's (1993) observation that, "When gifted children are asked what they most desire, the answer is often 'a friend' . . . The children's experience of school is completely colored by the presence or absence of relationships with peers" (p. 72), we realize the importance of an educational environment that sustains the growth of friendships *through* the attainment of excellence.

Our interviews and surveys with gifted adolescents support these insights. In the summer of 2002, 371 gifted adolescents, who were attending residential academic programs on The University of Iowa campus, responded to an adaptation of the Rokeach Values Inventory (1973). The adaptation of the Rokeach Inventory lists 20 values, and students were asked to review the 20 values and then select their top three values. Each student's inventory was tabulated and the scores for each value were averaged. For these 371 students, friendship was the top value, followed by freedom and wisdom. We also have much anecdotal evidence, from interviews with gifted adolescents, of the importance of both friendships and the environmental setting that fosters the development of friendships. The following quote is a typical sentiment expressed by program participants: "I met a lot of new people and made a ton of new friends and learned soooo [*sic*] much over the course of these 2 weeks." From this individual's testimony, which is repeated over and over again by hundreds of gifted students who attend summer programs on university campuses throughout the United States, we see the positive effect of making new friends, especially when combined with an environment that promotes acceptance of bright individuals and engagement with challenging course work.

This student's positive description of new friends in an academically challenging setting begs additional questions. One question concerns the impact of the *typical* school environment on gifted adolescents' friendships and achievement. Given the variations in home environments, it is reasonable to assume that school represents the most common setting for adolescents, as well as a significant environment for most gifted students in terms of both talent development and social interaction. In a typical school setting, respect for intellectual ability is subsequent to athleticism, interpersonal skills, physical attraction, or other values. When things of the mind (e.g., doing well in academic classes, scoring high on standardized exams, and striving for excellent grades) are not respected, the environment is basically anti-intellectual. Thus, adolescents with a proclivity for intellectualism who find themselves in anti-intellectual environments will be in a conflicted situation. Coleman and Cross (2001) refer to this discord as a "stigma of giftedness." They acknowledge that the stigma of giftedness limits participation in many social environments due to the fact that giftedness is a positive *and* a negative factor for all adolescents. Therefore, gifted adolescents experience dissonance because they do not always know what attitudes (i.e., positive, negative, or somewhere in between) are endorsed by others, and, in addition, they cannot control the perceptions of others. If gifted adolescents feel "stigmatized" due to the discord between their intellectualism and the environment, then another question concerns the effect—if any—of this stigma on the adolescent's self-concept.

SELF-CONCEPT

The self-concept construct has deep historical roots in psychology and education, and can be viewed as a "powerful system of cognitive structures that is quite likely to mediate interpretation of and response to events and behaviors directed at or involving the individual" (Nurius, 1986, p. 435). The definition of self-concept has evolved from a "collection of self-views" (e.g., Rogers, 1951; Snygg & Combs, 1949), to general good and bad feelings about oneself (McGuire, 1984; Shavelson, Hubner, & Stanton, 1976), to recent theory and research on operationally defining the structures and contents of the self-concept (Colangelo & Assouline, 1995; Marsh, 1990; Nurius, 1986). Neihart (1999) states that self-concept is the collection of ideas that one has about oneself, an essential component of what is usually called personality.

Self-concept of gifted youngsters has received considerable attention in the past two decades (Plucker & Stocking, 2001). Neihart indicates that a number of studies have concluded that there are no differences between gifted and nongifted students; however, results from other studies have led to the conclusion that there are differences favoring gifted students particularly when measuring assessment of one's academic abilities. These studies typically have investigated:

- how gifted and average children's self-concepts compare (Hoge & Renzulli, 1993; Karnes & Wherry, 1981; Kelly & Colangelo 1984; Loeb & Jay, 1987);
- whether self-concept is a developmental construct (Harter, 1982; Hoge & McSheffrey, 1991; Hoge & Renzulli, 1993; Karnes & Wherry, 1981; Marsh, 1992, 1993); and
- how programming affects an adolescent's self-concept (Kelly & Colangelo, 1984; Loeb & Jay, 1987; Maddux, Scheiber, & Bass, 1982).

Self-concept and giftedness represent complex constructs, and the study of each is made more difficult by theoretical controversies within each field. For example, the developmental nature and processes of self-concept have been debated (Harter, 1982; Karnes & Wherry, 1981; Ketcham & Snyder, 1977). Additionally, there are concerns about the reliability and validity of measures of self-concept (Marsh, 1990, 1993, 1994; Wylie, 1989). In the area of gifted education, the question of unidimensionality versus multidimensionality has also permeated almost every aspect of the field.

Our research lends credibility to the multidimensional nature of self-concept (see also Plucker & Stocking, 2001). In a research study (Colangelo & Assouline, 1995) investigating the self-concept of 563 gifted students spanning grades 3–11, we found support for the general notion that the overall self-concept of gifted students is positive. However, there were peaks and valleys across the grade levels and various domains as measured by the Piers-Harris Children's Self-Concept Scale. Most importantly for secondary educators, including teachers, school counselors, and administrators were the following findings:

1. General self-concept scores were relatively high for elementary, middle, and high school students; however, among the three grade levels, high school students had the lowest scores. High school girls in particular had the most significant drop in self-concept scores.
2. As gifted students progress in school, they become more anxious and feel more isolated.

3. The lowest scores of the 563 students in the study were found in the domains of interpersonal skills and self-satisfaction.
4. As expected, the highest scores were in the domains of intellectual and school status.

Closely related to self-concept is the attitude that gifted students have toward their own giftedness. Three books—*On Being Gifted* (American Association for Gifted Children, 1978), *Gifted Children Speak Out* (Delisle, 1984), and *Gifted Kids Speak Out* (Delisle, 1987)—present testimonials from gifted children describing the impact of giftedness on their lives. One conclusion that can be drawn from these testimonials is that these students have mixed feelings about their giftedness. Coleman and Cross (2001), in their discussion of the "stigma of giftedness," address these concerns, and there is research that confirms the anecdotal reports of ambivalence. Colangelo and Kelly (1983) found that while gifted youngsters were positive about being labeled gifted, they perceived nongifted peers and teachers as having negative views of them. A study by Kerr, Colangelo, and Gaeth (1988) indicated that the attitude of gifted adolescents toward their own giftedness was multifaceted. Adolescents reported that being gifted was a positive with respect to their own personal growth and the effect on academics. In terms of social peer relations, however, they reported it to be a negative factor. In a partial replication of the Kerr et al. study, results from a study by Monaster, Chan, Walt, and Wiehe (1994) offer additional support for the finding that attitudes toward giftedness are multifaceted. As well, Monaster et al. found that those who knew the gifted child well had positive attitudes toward the child, and that attitudes became more negative toward 'giftedness' as respondents were removed from personal knowledge of a gifted youngster.

From 2000 to 2003, the Belin-Blank Center administered a forced-choice survey to 1,404 gifted adolescents who participated in summer residential academic programs (Belin-Blank Center, 2004). Among the items on the survey were questions about students' perceptions of their academic ability, as well as questions about students' perceptions of the ways their friends, family, and teachers felt about their academic ability. Their responses to these items (see Table 2) reinforce the conclusions noted in previous studies; specifically, gifted students generally recognize their giftedness and they are happy about it. As well, they think their family and teachers are happy about their ability. It's a different story, however, for friends; although, very few (1.4%) indicated that they thought their friends were unhappy about their ability, 41.5% indicated that their academic ability was not important to friends, and 24% indicated that they did not know how their friends felt about their academic ability. The discrepancy between an individual's self-perception and the attitudes of their peers may contribute to confusion and hesitation in the application of their abilities.

The findings from the Belin-Blank (2004) summer program participants, as well as from Kerr et al. (1988) and Monaster et al. (1994) are very relevant for secondary school counselors, psychologists, and teachers, because the issues focus on human interaction. In individual as well as group sessions, educators can discuss issues such

Table 2
Description and Perceptions of Academic Ability

How would you describe your academic ability?

Gifted = 67%   Above-average = 31%   Average = 2%

How do you feel about your academic ability?

Happy	Unhappy	Not Important	Don't know
93%	2%	4%	0%

How do you think your family feels about your academic ability?

Happy	Unhappy	Not Important	Don't know
93%	1%	2%	4%

How do you think your teachers feel about your academic ability?

Happy	Unhappy	Not Important	Don't know
78%	1%	4%	17%

How do you think your friends feel about your academic ability?

Happy	Unhappy	Not Important	Don't know
30%	2%	43%	25%

Note. Summary of unpublished raw data from the Belin-Blank Center's Parent Student Questionnaires.

as: What does it mean to be gifted? What do I like about being gifted? What do I not like about being gifted? If I were not gifted, what would be better for me? If I were not gifted, what would be worse for me? What does it mean for me to be gifted when I don't know if it matters to my friends? All these questions help students explore their understanding and feelings about self, especially as they relate to their academic ability. Betts and Kercher (1999) have organized a useful workbook of affective activities designed to foster academic ability within the context of greater understanding of the impact of the affective domain.

COLLEGE/CAREER COUNSELING WITH GIFTED STUDENTS

When gifted students are about to graduate high school and beginning to plan for college and careers, parents and educators often get involved to ensure that the student "does not waste the gift." From our experience, concerns about "wasting the gift" translate into making a decision(s) that is reasonable to the adult who is concerned about "wasting the gift." Without articulating specifics, it seems there are a number of adults who believe certain careers are worthy of a gifted student, and that other career paths are not. Careers like those of medical doctors, lawyers, engineers, and physicists typically fall into the category of worthy career goals, while being an elementary/secondary school teacher, social worker, school counselor, or nurse typically fall into a career goal category received with less enthusiasm by parents.

Career planning for high-ability students has not always been smooth (Colangelo, 2002b; Kaufmann, 1981; Kerr, 1985, 1986, 1991; Kerr & Colangelo, 1988). Gifted students do not always know what they want to do for the "rest of their lives," and while they may have the academic credentials to succeed in classes, this does not mean that they have the information to plan for a career. Ability and ambition do not always translate into planned or purposeful action.

MULTIPOTENTIALITY

A much-explored topic among educators, counselors, and psychologists working with gifted students is multipotentiality (Sajjadi, Rejskind, & Shore, 2001). As the term implies, multipotentiality refers to individuals who have diverse talents (and interests) and who could succeed at a high level in a number of different fields. The most useful definition of multipotentiality comes from Frederickson and Rothney (1972), who define it as "the ability to select and develop any number of competencies to a high level" (p. vii). Without the stipulation of developing competencies *at a very high level*, the concept of multipotentiality loses any sense of meaningfulness. The problem is, how can students make a decision or choose a path from so many realistic possibilities? For many adults, this may seem a problem one would gladly suffer; however, it is a significant problem for gifted adolescents. "Multipotentialed young people may anguish over an abundance of choices available to them during career planning unless appropriate interventions are available" (Rysiew, Shore, & Leeb, 1999, p. 423). Most educators in the field of gifted education adhere to the belief of multipotentiality (Colangelo, 2002b). While there has been some discussion that the term should be reserved for abilities and not interests (see Rysiew et al., 1999), there has been little disagreement as to the existence and importance of this concept in understanding giftedness and the need to address multipotentiality from a social-emotional perspective due to possible confusion, frustration, and ambivalence about the talent(s).

The only serious challenge to the usefulness and existence of multipotentiality has come from Achter, Lubinski, and Benbow (1996) and Achter, Benbow, and Lubinski (1997). These authors "have challenged the utility of the entire notion of multipotentiality based on their observation of widely varying patterns of specific abilities and interests in a large sample of very highly gifted adolescents, thereby challenging the ubiquity of low differentiation or high flat interest profiles" (Rysiew et al., 1999, p. 424). Also, Sajjadi et al. (2001) suggest that while multipotentiality exists with gifted students, it may not be a problem for them.

Although there is not an abundance of empirical data supporting the notion of multipotentiality, there are anecdotal and clinical reports regarding the concept (Rysiew, Shore, & Carson, 1994), and these cases continue to influence our philosophy about the need to address multipotentiality as a social-emotional issue for gifted adolescents. Polarizing the issue seems to have little use to the professional who works with gifted adolescents. It is important to acknowledge that multipotentiality may present problems or concerns, such as those outlined by Rysiew et al. (1999), especially with respect to career choices:

1. Students find it hard to narrow their focus to a career because they have so many equally viable options.
2. Multipotential students may lean toward perfectionism, thus they will look for the perfect or ideal career.
3. Students feel coerced by parents and others to make decisions based on social recognition and high earnings potential.
4. Students must make commitments that may require long-term schooling (graduate, professional) and delay financial independence or the starting of families. These long-term training investments are also difficult to change once a student has embarked for several years towards a particular career, even if there are serious doubts about the chosen career path.

Rysiew et al. (1999) review a number of writings regarding what counselors can do to help multipotential gifted students make career decisions. The recommendations include:

1. *Explore* careers as a way of life, or a lifestyle, rather than a particular job/position.
2. *Recognize* that one does not have to be limited to one career.
3. *Use* leisure activities as a way to continually develop areas of abilities and interest that are distinct from one's career.
4. *Apply* career counseling as a values-based activity, exploring broad categories of life satisfaction.
5. *Emphasize* peer discussions and group work with other multipotential youth so that students can see that they are not alone in their concerns.

Since 1988, the students selected for the Belin-Blank Center programs have had the opportunity to participate in a values-based career-counseling program. The primary purpose of this program, which incorporates the recommendations listed by Rysiew et al. (1999), is to provide a safe setting (i.e., a setting supportive of intellectualism) for students to explore their interests, personality preferences, and academic aptitudes, while also considering values relevant to them. The values-based component of this program has proven highly successful with secondary students (Kerr, 1991).

A values-based career counseling approach to working with gifted adolescents is enriched by Moon's (2003) theory of personal talent. Moon defines personal talent as "exceptional ability to select and attain difficult life goals that fit one's interests, abilities, values, and contexts" (p. 5). In a well-articulated description of personal talent as a construct, Moon distinguishes personal talent from the related constructs of motivation and personal competence. With respect to the social-emotional development of gifted adolescents, the theory of personal talent can provide insight for educators who strive to comprehend some of the puzzling phenomena associated with gifted students, including the mystery of underachievement.

UNDERACHIEVEMENT

In the Assessment and Counseling Clinic at the Belin-Blank Center, underachievement—and its associated social-emotional issues—is often a concern. The problem of underachievement is confusing because of disagreement about its definition and the inconsistency of results from interventions (Dowdall & Colangelo, 1982; Peterson & Colangelo, 1996; Reis, 1998; Whitmore, 1980).

Underachievement is usually seen as a discrepancy between assessed potential and actual performance. The discrepancy may be between two standardized measures (e.g., IQ and achievement tests), or between a standardized measure and a measure of accomplishment (e.g., an achievement test and performance on daily assignments). The label "gifted underachiever" implies a learner with a high level of potential (Reis, 1998) that does not match his or her level of achievement.

Whitmore (1980) proposed three types of underachievers: (a) aggressive, disruptor, and rebel; (b) bored, uninterested, and uninvolved; or (c) vacillator between aggressive behavior and withdrawn behavior. To a counseling professional, the discrepancy between scores is not as critical as the interpersonal dynamics involved in underachievement. Rather than looking at it as a psychometric event, counselors often see underachievement as a dysfunctional dynamic among the gifted student and teachers, parents, or peers.

Reis (1998) distinguished between chronic and temporary (situational) underachievement. Temporary underachievement is often in response to a situational stress or event (e.g., divorce, loss of a friend, problems with a teacher). A chronic underachiever is one who has a "history" and pattern of underachievement that appears to cut across a particular incident or circumstance.

For some gifted students, underachievement is a way to express either a need for attention or a need for control over a situation (Rimm, 2003). Underachievement brings considerable attention from both teachers and parents, and in extreme cases it can elicit almost doting behavior. Adults are so concerned that the gifted youngster will not make good use of his or her gifts that they (adults) give a great deal of energy and time to the student.

Counselors and psychologists often can break the attention-getting cycle by encouraging parents and teachers to avoid responding too strongly to the under-achieving behavior, or even to ignore the behavior. Adults can give attention when the child displays achievement, and minimize attention when the child is not achiev-ing well. The equation is simple; but implementation is not easy. If the child wants attention, he or she will soon learn that the attention is forthcoming only when cer-tain achieving behaviors (and attitudes) are present. The child will want to exhibit more of these kinds of behaviors, because his or her reward is the attention given to him or her.

A gifted youngster who uses underachievement as a means to gain control of a situation offers a more difficult challenge. For such youngsters, poor achievement is a way to show teachers and parents that they (the students) can do whatever they want. A typical reaction by teachers and parents to this kind of defiance is to attempt to force the student ("up the ante") to do the task and do it at levels comparable to expectation. This situation can lead to a vicious and nonproductive cycle.

The counselor or psychologist can work with teachers and parents to help break the cycle. It is likely the student will diminish the struggle if there is no one with whom to engage. Minimizing the power struggle will allow more opportunity for the student to improve performance because he or she is liberated to do so.

Often, group counseling can help gifted students better understand their behav-iors and motives and learn new patterns of interactions that are more productive (Colangelo, 2002b). In the rich atmosphere of a group of peers with a trained leader (school counselor or psychologist), a gifted youngster can explore motives and con-sequences of underachieving behavior.

Finally, it is important for the school counselors or psychologists to use school records as a source of information in understanding gifted underachievers, espe-cially at the secondary level. In a comprehensive study of 153 gifted underachievers, grades 7–12, Peterson and Colangelo (1996) found data, recorded by gender and age on attendance, tardiness, course selection, and course grades, that provided dif-ferential patterns to distinguish gifted students who had achieved from those who underachieved (i.e., those who have better attendance and were not tardy had higher achievement than those who missed multiple days and were often late). Peterson and Colangelo reported that patterns of underachievement established in junior high school, though not impossible to alter in high school, do tend to persist through high school. The school records are ubiquitous in schools and are a good resource for counselors. Records of attendance represent a simple system of tracking the impact of attendance on achievement. However, uncovering the multiple problems associ-ated with poor attendance is a complex endeavor adding to the overall enigma of underachievement. Even though the general nature of underachievement is complex and the research findings are often inconclusive and (sometimes) contradictory, Reis (1998) provides a good summary of helpful facts:

1. It appears that the beginnings of underachievement in many young people occur in elementary school.

2. Underachievement appears to be periodic and episodic, occurring some years and not others and in some classes, but not others.

3. A direct relationship seems to exist between inappropriate or unchallenging content in elementary school and underachievement in middle or high school.

4. Parental issues interact with the behaviors of some underachievers, yet no clear pattern exists about the types of parental behaviors that cause underachievement.

5. Peers can play a major role in keeping underachievement from occurring in their closest friends, making peer groups an important part of preventing and reversing underachievement.

6. Busier adolescents who are involved in clubs, extracurricular activities, sports and religious activities are less likely to underachieve in school.

7. Many similar behavioral characteristics are exhibited by bright students who achieve or underachieve in school.

8. There are some students who may underachieve as a direct result of an inappropriate and unchallenging curriculum, and before we try to "fix" the student, or punish students for their behavior, perhaps we need to advocate for drastic curriculum changes.

Are There Specific Suggestions for Teachers?

Whereas the primary role of the teacher is to teach—not counsel—teachers clearly do play a role in giving advice and counseling. Students will exhibit their difficulties in the classroom even more so than in the counselor's office. Thus, a teacher gets to "see" the problems firsthand. A teacher who lets a student know that he or she is aware the student can do better and indicates that this student matters, creates a situation that has the makings for constructive dialogue. So much of the reversal (minimizing the underachievement) is founded on constructive dialogue and on the teacher's understanding of the dynamics.

It is also important that teachers recognize that even if a counselor or psychologist is the main professional to provide the intervention, the teacher still plays an important role. By endorsing certain attitudes and behaviors, teachers can also minimize underachievement among gifted students. From our own experiences, as well as from a distillation of research and suggestions from literature, we know that it makes a difference when teachers:

- take the time to learn about the unique characteristics of gifted students so that these characteristics can be addressed in the classroom, because students are much more likely to be motivated to attend class if they feel understood and cared about;

- demonstrate passion for their subject (and teaching) since this elicits energy from students—especially the gifted students—yielding better effort and greater focus; and

- reveal a general respect for an environment that is supportive of intellectual pursuits.

This respect is primarily manifest in challenging coursework. We have seen first hand that gifted students are more likely to put forth effort in classes where success is respected and valued.

The previous discussion emphasized predominately an environmental focus, which implies that the learner has some control over both the cause and the resolution of the underachievement. Another aspect to underachievement that has been more recently recognized is the fact that some students who are not performing at a level commensurate with their ability have a specific learning disability. Silverman (2003) writes comprehensively about gifted students who have learning disabilities. In 2004, the federal Individuals with Disabilities Education Act (IDEA) was reauthorized, and Congress added gifted and talented students who have a disability to the groups of students whose needs have priority in U.S. Department of Education grants to guide research, personnel preparation, and technical assistance. For the first time, there is federal recognition that gifted students may also have disabilities that impede their achievement.

GIFTED STUDENTS WITH DISABILITIES

Although some educators and psychologists (e.g., Baum, 1990; Fox, Brody, & Tobin, 1983; Mills & Brody, 1999; Silverman, 2003) recognized the phenomenon of a gifted student with disabilities in the early 1980s, the 21st century ushered in a new awareness of dual exceptionalities to the field of gifted education, with a special emphasis on understanding how giftedness and disabilities may mask each other. Developmental exceptionalities include: autistic savant syndrome; developmental delays in speech, language, and motor coordination; disruptive behavior (including conduct and oppositional-defiant disorders); anxieties; and eating disorders (Moon & Hall, 1998). Some gifted children also have learning disorders (LD), and Attention Deficit/Hyperactivity Disorder (AD/HD; Moon & Hall; Moon, Zentall, Grskovic, Hall, & Stormont, 2001; Zentall, Moon, Hall, & Grskovic, 2001).

The most common behavior disorder in gifted children is AD/HD (Moon & Hall, 1998), which can interfere with academic and social functioning. Another important issue for gifted students as related to AD/HD concerns the use of medications to treat AD/HD (Kaufmann, Kalbfleisch, & Castellanos, 2000). For gifted students with LD or AD/HD, individualized testing will reflect patterns of inconsistency across talent areas (Moon & Hall, 1998). Multiple testing methods are typically needed to pinpoint areas of giftedness and disability (Moon & Dillon, 1995).

Twice-exceptional students are at risk for underachievement because they will have barriers to achieving at their level of giftedness. Such students can become easily frustrated (and frustrating) because their inability to perform or "behave" can bring about questions regarding their motivation and commitment. From observation, it seems dual exceptionalities are more common than most educators may think. The incongruity between educators' expectations about the rarity of twice-exceptional students and the observable fact that they exist may be accounted for by the trend of misdiagnosis (Webb et al., 2005).

There are several ways that gifted individuals may be misdiagnosed. For example, gifted students may be diagnosed as AD/HD because their gifted behaviors are misunderstood (Webb et al., 2005). It is also possible that giftedness may mask the disability and/or the disability may mask the giftedness (Baum, 1990). Another scenario is the gifted student who is misdiagnosed with a disability, for example, AD/HD, because a more accurate diagnosis, for example, Asperger's syndrome, was not available at the time of diagnosis. For example, one essential feature of Asperger's syndrome includes severe and sustained inappropriate social interactions, which has sometimes been confused with AD/HD. The *Diagnostic and Statistical Manual of Mental Disorders-IV* first recognized Asperger's syndrome in 1994, and the features were subsequently updated in the 2000 version of the *Diagnostic and Statistical Manual of Mental Disorders-IV—Text Revision*. Thus, for many teenagers in 2004, it would have been impossible for them to receive, as children, a diagnosis of Asperger's syndrome because the psychiatric community did not recognize it when their parents most likely would have taken them for an evaluation. While parents and psychologists recognized that there was a serious concern for these students, they gave them the "best" diagnosis available at the time, AD/HD.

We strongly recommend a battery of individualized tests to determine the presence of both exceptionalities—gifted and disabled—in cases where bright students are underachieving in academics and unable to function effectively in the classroom. A diagnostic battery of tests should also be considered when there is severe dysfunction with respect to social interaction.

Testing and the accurate interpretation of results are important for diagnosis, curricular programming, and social-emotional intervention. Testing is important in order to minimize misdiagnosis; yet, many advocates for testing are at a disadvantage due to the de-emphasis on IQ testing in the reauthorized IDEA. The issue of testing is also relevant for consideration of accommodations within classrooms, as well as during high-stakes testing, for example, college-entrance exams. For twice-exceptional students this may be an especially frustrating situation, as even within the professional community there is disagreement about the right to accommodations. Also, twice-exceptional adolescents may find that they have greater dependence on their parents to advocate for them because, compared to educators, parents are often in a position of having a greater understanding of both exceptionalities, possibly due to the reality that they have greater interest and concern for their child. The professional (i.e., teacher, counselor, or psychologist) must work with the parent to ensure appropriate interventions.

The teacher of the twice-exceptional student should be willing to learn more, in general, about high-ability students who have disabilities, as well as become more informed about the specific disability for which the student has been diagnosed.

Usually, it is the parent of the student who will have the most information about the child's disability, and teachers must be willing to understand that the parent has already experienced much frustration in raising the child, and has a comprehensive picture of the child's strengths and weaknesses. An understanding that the disability diagnosis is not intended to restrict the student, but rather to help the student's educators have a greater understanding of the unique learning and social-emotional needs of the student is important. As an example, a student with a very high IQ who also has Asperger's syndrome may still be relatively slow in processing information. This may be a surprise to the student's educators who would expect that students with high IQs would also process information rapidly.

Summary

Concern for the social-emotional needs of gifted students and the impact of social-emotional issues on the realization of a student's giftedness can be traced back to Leta Hollingworth's work in the first quarter of the 20th century. However, the emergence of professionals specializing in the myriad social-emotional issues related to giftedness is a relatively new phenomenon that parallels the development of newly recognized issues, for example, twice-exceptionality. Additionally, several relatively recent federal policies (e.g., No Child Left Behind and IDEA) have both direct and indirect influence on the academic and social-emotional aspects of gifted students.

Psychological assessments, as well as individual, group, or family counseling services are predicated on the assumption and evidence that youngsters with exceptional ability and talents also have unique social and emotional needs. These unique needs exist and interact in the successful or unsuccessful development of talent. Addressing social-emotional issues is a necessary component to the successful development of talent. For counselors and psychologists to be successful, they need knowledge and expertise in giftedness, as well as in psychology or counselor education. A gifted program that recognizes the social-emotional needs of gifted students will foster both the cognitive and the affective development of gifted youngsters.

References

Achter, J. A., Benbow, C. P., & Lubinski, D. (1997). Rethinking multipotentiality among the intellectually gifted: A critical review and recommendations. *Gifted Child Quarterly, 41,* 5–15.

Achter, J. A., Lubinski, D., & Benbow, C. P. (1996). Multipotentiality among the intellectually gifted: It was never there and already it's vanishing. *Journal of Counseling Psychology, 43,* 65–76.

American Association for Gifted Children (1978). *On being gifted.* New York: Walker & Company.

Baum, S. (1990). *Gifted but learning disabled: A puzzling paradox.* (ERIC EC Digest No. E479.) Retrieved December 30, 2002, from http://ericec.org/digests/e479.html

Belin-Blank Center (2004). [Descriptive statistics of responses on Parent/Student Questionnaire]. Unpublished raw data.

Betts, G. T., & Kercher, J. K. (1999). *Autonomous learner model: Optimizing ability.* Greeley, CO: ALPS Publishing.

Buescher, T. M. (1991). Gifted adolescents. In N. Colangelo & G. A. Davis (Eds.), *Handbook of gifted education* (pp. 382–401). Boston: Allyn & Bacon.

Cash, A. B. (1999). The profile of gifted individuals with autism: The twice-exceptional learners. *Roeper Review, 22*, 22–27.

Colangelo, N. (2002a, May). *Anti-intellectualism in universities, schools, and gifted education.* Paper presented at the 2002 Wallace National Research Symposium on Talent Development, The University of Iowa, Iowa City, IA.

Colangelo, N. (2002b). *Counseling gifted and talented students* (RM02150). Storrs, CT: The National Research Center on the Gifted and Talented, University of Connecticut.

Colangelo, N., & Assouline, S. G. (1995). Self-concept of gifted students: Patterns by self-concept, domain, grade level, and gender. In F. Mönks (Ed.), *Proceedings from the 1994 European council on high ability conference* (pp. 66–74). New York, Wiley.

Colangelo, N., & Assouline, S. G. (2000). Counseling gifted students. In K. A. Heller, F. J. Mönks, R. J. Sternberg, & R. F. Subotnik (Eds.), *International handbook of giftedness and talent* (2nd ed., pp. 595–607). Amsterdam: Elsevier.

Colangelo, N., & Kelly, K. R. (1983). A study of student, parent, and teacher attitudes towards gifted programs and gifted students. *Gifted Child Quarterly, 27*, 107–110.

Colangelo, N., & Peterson, J. S., (1993). Group counseling with gifted students. In L. S. Silverman (Ed.), *Counseling the gifted and talented* (pp. 111–129). Denver: Love.

Colangelo, N., & Zaffrann, R. T. (Eds.). (1979). *New voices in counseling the gifted.* Dubuque, IA: Kendall Hunt.

Coleman, L. J., & Cross, T. L. (2001). *Being gifted in school: An introduction to development, guidance, and teaching.* Waco, TX: Prufrock Press.

Csikszentmihalyi, M., Rathunde, K., & Whalen, S. (1993). *Talented teenagers: The roots of success and failure.* New York: Cambridge University Press.

Dabrowski, K. (1970). *Mental growth through positive disintegration.* London: Gryf.

Delisle, J. R. (1984). *Gifted children speak out.* New York: Walker.

Delisle, J. R. (1987). *Gifted kids speak out.* Minneapolis: Free Spirit.

Delisle, J. R. (1992). *Guiding the social and emotional development of gifted youth.* New York: Longman.

Delisle, J. R. (1997). Gifted adolescents: Five steps toward understanding and acceptance. In N. Colangelo & G. A. Davis (Eds.), *Handbook of gifted education* (2nd ed., pp. 475–482). Boston: Allyn & Bacon.

Dowdall, C. B., & Colangelo, N. (1982). Underachieving gifted students: Review and implications. *Gifted Child Quarterly, 26*, 179–184.

Fox, L., Brody, L., & Tobin, D. (Eds.). (1983). *Learning disabled gifted children: Identification and programming.* Austin, TX: ProEd.

Frederickson, R. H, & Rothney, J. W. M. (Eds.). (1972). *Recognizing and assisting multipotential youth.* Columbus, OH: Merrill

Gross, M. U. M. (1989). The pursuit of excellence or the search for intimacy? The forced-choice dilemma of gifted youth. *Roeper Review, 11,* 189–194.

Harter, S. (1982). The perceived competence scale for children. *Child Development, 53,* 87–97.

Hoge, R. D., & McSheffrey, R. (1991). An investigation of self-concept in gifted children. *Exceptional Children, 57,* 238–245.

Hoge, R. D., & Renzulli, J. S. (1993). Exploring the link between giftedness and self-concept. *Review of Educational Research, 63,* 449–465.

Hollingworth, L. S. (1926). *Gifted children: Their nature and nurture.* New York: Macmillan.

Hollingworth, L. S. (1942). *Children above 180 IQ.* New York: World Book.

Karnes, F. A., & Wherry, J. N. (1981). Self-concepts of gifted students as measured by the Piers-Harris Children's Self-Concept Scale. *Psychological Reports, 49,* 903–906.

Kaufmann, F. A. (1981). The 1964–1968 Presidential Scholars: A follow-up study. *Exceptional Children, 48,* 164–169.

Kaufmann, F. A., Kalbfleisch, M. L., & Castellanos, F. X. (2000). *Attention deficit disorders and gifted students: What do we really know?* (RM00146). Storrs, CT: The National Research Center on the Gifted and Talented, University of Connecticut.

Kelly, K. R., & Colangelo, N. (1984). Academic and social self-concepts of gifted, general, and special students. *Exceptional Children, 50,* 551–554.

Kerr, B. A. (1985*). Smart girls; gifted women.* Columbus, OH: Ohio Psychology Publications.

Kerr, B. A. (1986). Career counseling for the gifted: Assessments and interventions. *Journal of Counseling and Development, 64,* 602–604.

Kerr, B. A. (1991). *Handbook for counseling the gifted and talented.* Alexandria, VA: AACD Press.

Kerr, B. A., & Colangelo, N. (1988). The college plans of academically talented students. *Journal of Counseling and Development, 67,* 42–48.

Kerr, B. A., Colangelo, N., & Gaeth, J. (1988). Gifted adolescents' attitudes toward their giftedness. *Gifted Child Quarterly, 32,* 245–247.

Ketcham, B., & Snyder, R. T. (1977). Self-attitudes of the intellectually and socially advantaged student: Normative study of the Piers-Harris Children's Self-concept Scale. *Psychological Reports, 40,* 111–116.

Loeb, R. C., & Jay, G. (1987). Self-concept in gifted children: Differential impact in boys and girls. *Gifted Child Quarterly, 1,* 9–14.

Maddux, C. D., Scheiber, L. M., & Bass, J. E. (1982). Self-concept and social distance in gifted children. *Gifted Child Quarterly, 26,* 77–81.

Marsh, H. W. (1990). A multidimensional, hierarchical model of self-concept: Theoretical and empirical justification. *Educational Psychology Review, 2,* 77–172.

Marsh, H. W. (1992). Content specificity of relations between academic achievement and academic self-concept. *Journal of Educational Psychology, 84,* 35–42.

Marsh, H. W. (1993). The multidimensional structure of academic self-concept: Invariance over gender and age. *American Educational Research Journal, 30,* 841–860.

Marsh, H. W. (1994). Using the national longitudinal study of 1988 to evaluate theoretical models of self-concept: The self-description questionnaire. *Journal of Educational Psychology, 86,* 439–456.

McGuire, W. J. (1984). Search for self: Going beyond self-esteem and reactive self. In R. A. Zucher, J. Arnoff, & A. I. Rubin (Eds.), *Personality and the prediction of behavior* (pp. 73–120). New York: Academic Press.

Mills, C. J., & Brody, L. E. (1999). Overlooked and unchallenged: Gifted students with learning disabilities. *Knowledge Quest, 27*(5), 36–40.

Monaster, G. J., Chan, J. C., Walt, C., & Wiehe, J. (1994). Gifted adolescents' attitudes toward their giftedness: A partial replication. *Gifted Child Quarterly, 38,* 176–178.

Moon, S. M. (2003). Personal talent. *High Ability Studies, 14* (1), 5–22

Moon, S. M., & Dillon, D. R. (1995). Multiple exceptionalities: A case study. *Journal for the Education of the Gifted, 18,* 111–130.

Moon, S. M., & Hall, A. S. (1998). Family therapy with intellectually and creatively gifted children. *Journal of Marital and Family Therapy, 24,* 59–80.

Moon, S. M., Zentall, S. S., Grskovic, J. A., Hall, A., & Stormont, M. (2001). Emotional and social characteristics of boys with AD/HD and giftedness: A comparative case study. *Journal for the Education of the Gifted 24,* 207–247.

Myers, R. S., & Pace, T. M. (1986). Counseling gifted and talented students: Historical perspectives and contemporary issues. *Journal of Counseling and Development, 64,* 548–551.

Neihart, M. (1999). The importance of giftedness and psychological well-being: What does the empirical literature say? *Roeper Review,* 22, 10–17.

Neihart, M., Reis, S. M., Robinson, N. M., & Moon, S. M (2002). *The social and emotional development of gifted children: What do we know?* Washington, DC: National Association for Gifted Children.

Nurius, P. S. (1986). Reappraisal of the self-concept and implications for counseling. *Journal of Counseling Psychology, 33,* 429–438.

Peterson, J. S., & Colangelo, N. (1996). Gifted achievers and underachievers: A comparison of patterns found in school files. *Journal of Counseling and Development, 74,* 399–407.

Plucker, J. A., & Stocking, V. B. (2001). Looking outside and inside: Self-concept development of gifted adolescents. *Exceptional Children, 67,* 535–548.

Piechowski, M. M. (1979). Developmental potential. In N. Colangelo & R. T. Zaffrann (Eds.), *New voices in counseling the gifted* (pp. 25–57). Dubuque, IA: Kendall/Hunt.

Piechowski, M. M. (1997). Emotional giftedness: The measure of interpersonal intelligence. In N. Colangelo & G. A. Davis (Eds.), *Handbook of gifted education* (2nd ed., pp. 366–381). Boston: Allyn & Bacon.

Piechowski, M. M. (2003). Emotional and spiritual giftedness. In N. Colangelo & G. A. Davis (Eds.), *Handbook of gifted education* (3rd ed., pp. 403–416). Boston: Allyn & Bacon.

Reis, S. (1998, Winter). Underachieving for some: Dropping out with dignity for others. *Communicator* 29(1), 19–24.

Rimm, S. B. (2003). Underachievement: A national epidemic. In N. Colangelo, & G. A. Davis (Eds.), *Handbook of gifted education* (3rd ed., pp. 424–443). Boston: Allyn & Bacon.

Rogers, C. R., (1951). *Client-centered therapy.* Boston: Houghton-Mifflin.

Rokeach, M. (1973). *The nature of human values.* New York: Free Press.

Rysiew, K. J., Shore, B. M., & Carson, A. D. (1994). Multipotentiality and overchoice syndrome: Clarifying common usage. *Gifted and Talent International, 9*(2), 41–46.

Rysiew, K. J., Shore, B. M., & Leeb, R. T. (1999) Multipotentiality, giftedness and career choices: A review. *Journal of Counseling and Development,* 77, 423–430.

Sajjadi, S. H., Rejskind, F. G., & Shore, B. M. (2001). Is multipotentiality a problem or not? A new look at the data. *High Ability Studies, 12*(1), 27–43.

Shavelson, R. J., Hubner, J. J., & Stanton, G. C. (1976). Validation of construct interpretations. *Review of Educational Research, 46,* 407–441.

Silverman, L. K. (Ed.). (1993). *Counseling the gifted & talented.* Denver: Love.

Silverman, L. K. (2003). Gifted children with learning disabilities. In N. Colangelo & G. A. Davis (Eds.), *Handbook of gifted education* (3rd ed., pp. 533–543). Boston: Allyn & Bacon.

Snygg, D., & Combs, A. W. (1949). *Individual behaviors: A perceptual approach to behavior* (Rev. ed.). New York: Harper.

St. Clair, K. L., (1989). Counseling gifted students: A historical review. *Roeper Review, 12,* 98–102.

Terman, L. M. (1925). *Genetic studies of genius Vol. 1: Mental and physical traits of a thousand gifted children.* Stanford, CA: Stanford University Press.

Webb, J. T., Amend, E. R., Webb, N. E., Goerss, J., Beljan, P., & Olenchak. F. R. (2005). *Misdiagnosis and dual diagnoses of gifted children and adults: ADHD, Bipolar, OCD, Asperger's, depression, and other disorders.* Scottsdale, AZ: Great Potential Press.

Whitmore, J. (1980). *Giftedness, conflict, and underachievement.* Boston: Allyn & Bacon.

Wylie, R.C. (1989). *Measures of self-concept.* Lincoln: University of Nebraska Press.

Zentall, S. S., Moon, S. M., Hall, A. M., & Grskovic, J. A. (2001). Learning and motivational characteristics of boys with AD/HD and/or giftedness. *The Council for Exceptional Children, 67,* 499–519.

GENDER, ADOLESCENCE, AND GIFTEDNESS

CHAPTER 4

by Sally M. Reis

For the last two decades, an increasing number of educators have shown interest in gifted and talented students and the reasons they may underachieve or excel in school. While the body of research on this population has grown, comparatively little has focused on the adolescent period of these students, during which time identities further develop and many academically talented students begin to either achieve at high levels or to underachieve (Reis, 1998; Reis & McCoach, 2000). In this chapter, research from the last two decades concerning gifted and talented male and female adolescents is summarized, with particular attention paid to how gender, giftedness, and adolescence interact. *Research* here is defined as quantitative or qualitative data-based studies of male and female adolescents who have been identified as academically talented, high achieving, or gifted. The focus on research stems from the observation that, although much has been written about gender differences in gifted students, few of the suggestions and strategies offered in the literature are supported by data-based studies. In this chapter, current research is summarized about academically talented adolescents in areas such as test differences; abilities and beliefs about abilities; the effects of stereotyping; peer, parent, and teacher influ-

ences; and career choices. Some prior conclusions are reaffirmed, present contradictory research evidence is discussed; older findings are reviewed in light of new
information; questions are raised about the importance, significance, and broader
applicability of prior conclusions; and future research is suggested about the interaction of gender, adolescence, and giftedness.

Adolescence is the period in which children search for their identities. A successful transition between adolescence and adulthood is characterized by the distillation
of the self into a consistent image of one's beliefs, preferences, values, commitments,
abilities, and choices about work and identity (Marcia, 1980, 1987; Reis, 1998). In
terms of identity formation, adolescence marks the shift away from family influence
to peer influence on self-definition. In addition, other changes to one's view of self,
belief in self, and the emerging understandings of one's role in life (including the
ability to achieve at high levels in school and beyond) occur in adolescence. I define
a successful transition for gifted adolescents as an integration of their abilities and
talents, interests, personal choices, and values, such that they are able to achieve at
high levels and attain personal contentment.

Research suggests a useful theoretical framework with which to explore the
interaction of gender, ability, and adolescence (Marcia, 1980, 1987) by extending the seminal work of Erik Erikson (1968). Erikson's adolescent stage is appropriately known as *identity versus role confusion*. This stage is characterized by
the importance of peer relationships and can be summarized as the teenager's
quest to achieve identity in gender role, behaviors, values, politics, religion,
and career. James Marcia and his associates suggest that most adolescents move
in one of four directions as they undertake this quest. First, adolescents may
realize *identity achievement*, a direction in which choices appear clear and their
identity emerges well formed. Marcia suggests that this occurrence is on the
decline for adolescents today, particularly for those who are college-bound, and
therefore exposed to a wider array of choices. The second alternative, *identity
foreclosure*, occurs when adolescents do not consider a range of identities and
goals, but rather simply adopt or agree to the values and lifestyles of their parents or significant others in their lives. The third alternative, *identity diffusion*,
occurs when adolescents struggle to make choices, or avoid making any definitive choice. This occurs with some academically talented students who have
multiple interests and talents and cannot or do not focus their energies. The
last alternative for adolescents is *identity moratorium* (Erikson, 1968, 1980) in
which teenagers delay making firm choices about the directions their lives will
take. Erikson initially regarded this period as a temporary identity crisis characterized by confusion, but more recent theorists consider this purposeful delay
healthy (Marcia, 1980). In our contemporary society, this moratorium period
may provide opportunities for adolescents, particularly gifted adolescents with
many choices, to better understand and explore their abilities, interests, preferences, styles, choices, careers, and values before they commit to choices that may
limit future opportunities.

GENDER ROLE IDENTITY ISSUES

The word *gender* usually refers to judgments about masculinity and femininity based on culture and context (Deaux, 1993). Gender role identity usually refers to the image that each person has about his/her masculine and feminine characteristics. Most individuals regard themselves as either having feminine or masculine characteristics, but some regard themselves as more androgynous, that is, they believe they have both feminine and masculine characteristics. Both socialization and aptitude influence gender identity and the formation of gender schemas, also known as organized networks of knowledge about what it means to be male or female (Woolfolk, 2004).

One of the most critical truths about gender role identity is that males and females differ in fundamental ways. Feingold (1994) summarized decades of personality research in suggesting that on average, men are more assertive and have higher self-esteem than women, while women are more extroverted, anxious, and trusting. Little comprehensive research, however, has addressed gender differences in the development of talent in adolescence, with the exception of Csikszentmihalyi, Rathunde, and Whalen (1993) who suggest that the 208 male and female academically talented adolescents they studied were "equally likely to continue in or become disengaged from the domain of the area of their talent by the end of high school" (p. 207).

GENDER, ADOLESCENCE, AND GIFTEDNESS

Ability, Achievement, and Belief in Self

Effort, ability, and belief in self are the reasons that most students either achieve or underachieve in school (Good & Brophy, 1986). Attribution theory suggests that students attribute their academic successes and failures largely to ability, effort, task difficulty, and luck, and it is commonly believed that how students implement these four constructs affects achievement outcomes. Higher-achieving students tend to attribute their successes to a combination of ability and effort, and their failures to lack of effort (Franken, 1988; Good & Brophy). Students who underachieve, however, often attribute their successes to external factors such as luck, and their failures to lack of ability (Ames, 1978; Reis, 1987, 1998; Siegle & Reis, 1998).

Current research indicates that gender plays a role in attribution. Researchers have found academically talented boys more often attribute their successes to ability and their failures to lack of effort (Hébert, 2001), while academically talented girls often attribute their successes to luck or effort and their failures to lack of ability (Rimm, 1999; Reis, 1987, 1998). Nicholls' (1975) study found that boys enhance academic efficacy in times of success by assigning responsibility for their achievements to native ability, while maintaining efficacy during failures by owning that talent would have prevailed if not for poor effort. However, the same may not be true for adolescent females, who frequently choose the second, less effective attribution strategy where they credit success to effort and failure to lack of ability. In effect, they are accepting responsibility for failure, but not success (Reis, 1998). Reinforcing girls' use of this less effective attribution style is the fact that, although research has consistently found that girls earn higher grades in both elementary and secondary school, previously recorded achievement test scores largely favor academically talented boys (American College Testing Program, 1989; Coleman, 1961; Davis, 1964; Kimball, 1989). Girls' attainment of higher grades, when contrasted with their lower scores on some standardized tests may contribute to talented female adolescents' beliefs that they are not as "bright" as boys and can only succeed by working harder.

Recent research by Reis and Park (2001) emphasized this link between self-concept, locus of control, and standardized test scores. Utilizing data from the National Education Longitudinal Study, two subsamples were selected representing the highest achieving students in math and in science. Results indicate that there were more males than females in both subsamples of high achieving students in math and science, and that the best predictor for distinguishing between mathematically high achieving males and females was locus of control. Moreover, high achieving males had both higher self-concept and higher standardized math test scores than high achieving females. In contrast, female students were more influenced by teachers and more likely than the male students to regard "hard work" as more important in their life than "chance or luck."

It is important that students establish self-belief early in their academic careers, because "by the end of elementary school, children's [perceptions] ... of ability begin to exert an influence on achievement processes independent of any objective measures of ability" (Meece, Blumenfeld, & Hoyle, 1988, p. 521). The results described above suggest that while work remains in encouraging all talented students to succeed, talented female adolescents continue to lag behind their male counterparts.

Gender and Standardized Tests

Rosser (1989) proposed that sex bias against girls on standardized tests is expressed in four ways. First, the test content he studied often referred to men more than women. When women were referred to or depicted, Rosser found, they are typically shown in lower status situations. Second, he believed test contexts place questions in settings and experiences more familiar to males. Third, he proposed that test validity underpredicts women's academic capabilities while men's are overpredicted, and last, he believed test use limits women's access to educational opportunities reliant on test scores that underpredict their abilities.

Other differences in standardized tests favor high-school-aged males who score at the highest levels on these measures. Halpern (1989) found that "large and consistent differences favoring male students are still found among the upper levels of mathematics aptitude on the PSAT and the SAT" (p. 1156). In 1989, for example, the population of girls taking the Scholastic Aptitude Test (SAT) averaged 46 points lower than boys on the math section of the SAT (Educational Testing Service, 1989).

At the score of 750 or higher on the math portion of the SAT administered in 1989, sex differences were even more pronounced. In 1989, girls also scored lower on the PSAT/NMSQ, used by the National Merit Scholarship Corporation for awarding scholarships to promising college students (Rosser, 1989). On the 2001 SAT test, males not only scored 35 points higher in math, but also 7 points higher on the verbal section (Educational Testing Service, 2003). The trend for lower SAT scores for girls has continued, but girls have made significant gains in SAT scores over the last decade. In 2003, females' math scores were averaged at 503 points, while males were averaged at 537 points (College Board, 2003). However, these scores reflected a gain of 19 points on females' math scores since 1993, and a gain of only 13 points on males' math scores. In addition, of the 1.4 million students taking the SAT in 2003, 54% of test takers were female (College Board, 2003). The most recent performances of female students on the SAT have yet to be tabulated, but in March 2005, College Board officials began administering a new, more difficult SAT, with a writing section, critical reading section, and an expanded math section (College Board, 2002) that will surely affect both boys' and girls' scores on future SAT tests.

Becker and Forsyth (1990) studied gender differences on the Iowa Tests of Basic Skills (ITBS) and found that males performed significantly better at the upper percentiles (90th and 75th) in vocabulary and mathematics problem solving across all grade levels, and at the 90th percentile, "males consistently scored higher than females in vocabulary at the upper percentiles of the score distribution across all grades" (p. 7). Martin and Hoover (1987) found that males in grades 3–8 scored higher on ITBS subtests of Visual Materials, Mathematics Concepts, and Mathematics Problem Solving, and that the largest differences in these areas occurred at the upper portion of the score scales. And, a widely cited and disseminated American Association of University Women (AAUW; 1991) report concluded "all differences in math performance between girls and boys at ages eleven and fifteen could be accounted for by differences among those scoring in the top ten to twenty percent" (p. 25).

Unfortunately, there are significant ramifications for these differential scores, including fewer opportunities for selective colleges and programs for the gifted and talented—particularly at the secondary level. Worse yet, test scores may have even more detrimental effects on gifted females than previously believed. Rosser (1989) found that both boys and girls estimate their math and English abilities closer to their SAT scores than to their grades, suggesting that girls underestimate their own abilities. Rosser also found that "girls planned to go to slightly less prestigious colleges than boys with equivalent GPAs" (p. iv). This finding, in conjunction with the findings of Boyer (1987), where 62% of students questioned said they lowered their expectations after receiving their SAT or ACT scores, suggests detrimental effects for academically talented females, especially those in high school. If girls' SAT scores are lower, they may lower their expectations and apply for admission at less prestigious colleges.

Lower scores may also have a detrimental impact on girls' selection of careers (Reis, 1998; Sadker & Sadker, 1994), and the damage is not limited to the topics addressed on the general SAT or PSAT. Selection of majors, academic interests, and vocation can be affected by the achievement tests that many young people take. For example, in 1990, boys scored higher on 11 of 14 achievement tests, with European history representing the largest gap (60 points) between boys and girls. In 1991, the largest point gap was in physics (62 points).

While the overall news is generally positive about the gains made by girls in test scores in general, and in math and some areas of science specifically in the last decade, little progress has been made in the areas of technology and engineering. In fact, a recent National Science Foundation (NSF) report (2000) details the problem clearly, stating that "at all levels of education and in employment, women are less likely than men to choose science and engineering fields" (p. xi). Although the number of women receiving degrees has increased in some areas of science and math, bachelor's degrees granted to women in computer science have actually decreased from 37% in 1984 to 28% in 1996 (NSF).

Research by Siegle and Reis (1994) suggests that both male and female adolescents fail to see science and math as female domains. Male gifted students indicated they had higher ability than females in mathematics, science, and social studies, while adolescent female gifted students indicated they had higher ability than males in language arts only. High school females still take fewer higher level math and science classes, and data from the 2003 SAT test indicates that only 18% of those who expressed an interest in pursuing engineering, and only 16% of those interested in computer or information sciences were female (Educational Testing Service, 2003). This means that many female mathematics and technology students may have less interest in or encouragement to pursue technology, math, or science than their male counterparts. The problem may be worse for academically talented girls who often fail to perform at levels that match their potential (Reis, 1998), particularly after they leave high school.

Social and Emotional Factors and Gender

Research suggests that talented adolescent females begin to lose self-confidence in elementary school and continue to do so throughout their academic careers (AAUW, 1991; Arnold, 1993). Kline and Short (1991) and Reis (1998) summarized research on gifted girls' social and emotional development, concluding that self-confidence and self-perceived abilities steadily decreased through high school. As gifted girls reach adolescence, they often remain competitive and perfectionistic, but value their own personal achievements less. Therefore, adolescence may affect the achievement and the self-confidence of gifted females. For example, in a qualitative study of five gifted adolescents, not one participant attributed her success in school to extraordinary ability (Callahan, Cunningham, & Plucker, 1994).

Identification as gifted and acceptance of gifts and talents may be problematic for both female and male adolescents because of adverse social consequences (Alvino, 1991; Buescher, Olszewski, and Higham, 1987; Callahan et al., 1994; Eccles, Midgley, & Adler, 1984; Hébert, 2000, 2001; Kramer, 1991; Reis, 1998). Kramer, for example, found that gifted girls deliberately underestimated their abilities in order to avoid being seen as physically unattractive or lacking in social competence. In one data-based study, the gifted female adolescents studied by Swiatek (2001) sacrificed giftedness for acceptance and also denied their giftedness. Eccles et al. (1984) found a "general increase in negativism toward academic achievement . . . is even characteristic of the better students in junior and senior high school" (p. 291). Buescher et al. (1987) found that gifted boys and girls were more alike than peers not identified as gifted, except in the critical area of the recognition and acceptance of their own level of ability. Callahan et al. (1994) found that middle school gifted females avoided displays of outstanding intellectual ability and work to conform to the norm of the peer group. Alvino (1991), summarizing the sparse research available on gifted adolescent males, suggested that needs and problems of preadolescent and adolescent gifted boys emerged as a direct function of their giftedness and gender. He summarized the challenges facing gifted boys thematically in terms of cultural conditioning, sexuality and success-orientation, and ego development.

In a study by Klein and Zehms (1996), the self-concept scores of gifted girls declined significantly between grades 3–8 and grades 5–8. Eighth grade gifted girls had a much more negative sense of self in the cluster areas of behavior, intellectual, and school status and popularity than girls of average to below average abilities in the same grade. Kline and Short (1991) studied gifted boys during their elementary and secondary school experiences, and found significantly higher levels of discouragement and feelings of hopelessness for adolescent gifted boys as compared with senior high school gifted boys. During junior high, gifted boys had increased feelings of depression, worry, and loneliness, and were more vulnerable, requiring special attention and understanding from adults and teachers. Heiss (1995) also studied the personality differences and interests of adolescent gifted girls and boys, finding that the alienation and loneliness experienced by many gifted boys put them at risk for social problems and even antisocial behavior.

Underachievement also differentially affects adolescent boys and girls, as more academically talented boys are identified as underachievers than girls (Reis & McCoach, 2000). Hébert (2001) studied gifted underachieving young men in urban classrooms and identified several problems that contributed to their underachievement, including inappropriate curricular and counseling experiences, problematic family issues, a negative peer group, negative environmental influences, and discipline problems. In particular, he found that the lack of belief in self contributed to underachievement in high-potential males. In an attempt to synthesize his research with adolescent boys over the last decade, Hébert identified six issues contributing to a failure to achieve in this population: image management, self-inflicted pressure, being labeled "different," the need for male bonding, cultural expectations, and gender role conflict.

Some academically gifted and promising students begin to underachieve during adolescence (Reis & McCoach, 2000). Research with both academically talented male and female students has suggested that a number of personality factors, personal priorities, and social-emotional issues are contributing to many adolescents not realizing their potential. Not all gifted adolescents experience the same issues, but a synthesis of current research suggests a combination of the following contributing reasons: dilemmas about abilities and talents, personal decisions about family, peer pressures, ambivalence of parents and teachers toward developing high levels of potential, absence of self-regulation, social issues about labeling and about being perceived as too smart, and choices about personal decisions and sacrifices necessary to develop one's abilities (Reis & McCoach, 2000). It is interesting to note that while current research suggests that more adolescent boys than girls underachieve in school, some researchers believe that girls, who usually receive higher grades in schools, tend to underachieve in professional accomplishments in life (Reis, 1987, 1998; Reis & McCoach).

Some high-ability adolescents do view their abilities and talents positively. For example, Ford (1992) studied gender differences in the American achievement ideology among 148 gifted and nonidentified African American male and female adolescents, exploring perceptions of social, cultural, and psychological determinants of achievement and underachievement. In this study, both male and female gifted students expressed the greatest support for the achievement ideology, and gifted females believed they had the highest teacher feedback on their efforts. Reis and Callahan (1994) studied gifted adolescents, focusing on their attitudes and beliefs about achievement and personal choices related to abilities and talents and found gender differences. Both male and female gifted adolescents had positive views about both school and achievement, but they found boys believed they were more often encouraged to pursue specific careers.

In a longitudinal study of 35 academically talented adolescents in an urban high school (Reis, Hébert, Díaz, Maxfield, & Ratley, 1995), the majority of high-achieving culturally diverse students were proud of their abilities and did not minimize their intelligence. The high-achieving gifted girls avoided dating, focused on academic work, and achieved at high levels academically, enabling them to pursue their interests and abilities in school.

Gender Differences and Socialization

Jeanne Block (1982) believed that a fundamental task of the developing individual is the mediation between internal biological impulses and external cultural forces as they coexist in a person's life space and life span (p. 2). She further believed that the socialization process, defined as internalization of values, appears to have differential effects on the personality development of males and females. Socialization, Block asserted, narrows females' options while broadening males' options (p. 220). Unfortunately, as girls get older, many of them learn that their perception of reality differs from the life experiences they encounter with their families, teachers, and friends, in school and life experiences in general. Whether socialization more positively or negatively affects male or female adolescents is unclear, but some recent work about gifted adolescents offers some interesting findings. Reis and Callahan (1994) identified differences in the perceptions of young gifted males and females relative to career opportunities for females after marriage and children. While both males and females have high career goals, gender differences emerge on how these career goals will be met. Reis and Callahan found the adolescent males they studied often indicated that they wanted their wives to stay home with their children and postpone or delay their careers until their children are grown. It is apparent that the girls, whose perceptions and beliefs are quite different, may have to address these traditional views of some young males with whom they may eventually raise families.

Parental Influences and Gender

Research has established the importance of parents' attitudes and beliefs about the academic self-perceptions and achievement of their adolescent children (Hess, Holloway, Dickson, & Price, 1984; McGillicuddy-De Lisi, 1985; Parsons, Adler, & Kaczala, 1982; Stevenson & Newman, 1986). In some studies, parents' beliefs about children's abilities had an even greater effect on children's self-perceptions than did previous performance (Parsons et al., 1982). Phillips (1987) confirmed this finding in her study of high-ability students. A study of parental influence on math self-concept with gifted female adolescents found consistently significant correlations between parental expectations and student math self-concept (Dickens, 1990). Reis (1995, 1998) found that memories of negative parental comments continue to negatively affect gifted and talented women decades after they left home. Hébert (2002) found that gifted Black males were positively influenced by their mothers, the recognition of their giftedness, and by support given by significant teachers and mentors. Parental opinions matter greatly to adolescents, and the messages sent by subtle and obvious verbal and nonverbal interactions may encourage or discourage gifted adolescents throughout their lives.

Parental interaction can affect students positively, as well. Reis, Hébert, Díaz, Maxfield, and Ratley (1995) compared culturally diverse, high-achieving, males and females attending a low socio-economic high school to a group of high ability females who underachieved in school for a period of 3 years. The young, high-achieving women who participated in the study were extremely determined to be independent, as several said they wanted a different life from that of their mothers. Many had mothers who had dropped out of school and struggled financially. The female achievers consistently echoed their determination to be different and to succeed, and many explained that their parents' lives and experiences had helped instill their determination to succeed. The high-achieving female students studied said they rarely dated or became romantically involved; were extremely supportive of other high-achieving girls; pursued multiple activities; and were independent, resilient, and dedicated to higher education, graduate school, and a professional career.

TEACHER ATTITUDES AND GENDER

Teachers can also contribute to students' beliefs. As early as first grade, teachers tend to attribute causation of boys' successes and failures to ability and girls' successes and failures to effort (Fennema, Peterson, Carpenter, & Lubinski, 1990). Pintrich and Blumenfeld (1985) found that "teachers' feedback about work was a better predictor for children's self perceptions about their ability and effort than were other types of interactions with the teacher or with peers" (p. 654). Schunk (1984) found that successful students who received feedback complimenting their ability, rather than focusing on their effort, developed higher self-efficacy and learned more than students who received feedback complimenting their effort. Siegle and Reis (1998) also found that teachers' instructional practices affect student self-efficacy.

Kramer (1985) found that the teachers she studied were usually able to identify gifted boys, but were often surprised to learn that a girl was considered smart. The gifted girls she studied were very successful at hiding their intelligence and in silencing their voices. In another analysis of research about adult perceptions of girls' intelligence, Sadker and Sadker (1994) summarized their findings regarding gender differences and teachers and parents, explaining, "study after study has shown that adults, both teachers and parents, underestimate the intelligence of girls" (p. 95). Kissane (1986) found that teachers are less accurate in pinpointing girls who are likely to do well on the quantitative subtest of the SAT, than they were in naming boys who were likely to achieve a high score. Cooley, Chauvin, and Karnes (1984) found that both male and female teachers regarded smart boys as more competent than gifted girls in critical and logical thinking skills and in creative problem-solving abilities, while they thought smart girls were more competent in creative writing. The male teachers they studied viewed female students in a more traditional manner than did female teachers, perceiving bright girls to be more emotional, more high strung, more gullible, less imaginative, less curious, less inventive, less individualistic, and less impulsive than males.

Teachers have been found to believe and reinforce one of the most prevalent sex stereotypes—that males have more innate ability, while females must work harder. Fennema (1990), commenting on the role of teacher beliefs on mathematics performance, reported that in a study she conducted with Peterson, Carpenter, and Lubinski, teachers selected ability as the cause of their most capable males' success 58% of the time, and the cause of their best females' success only 33% of the time. They also concluded that even though teachers did not tend to engage in sex-role stereotyping in general, they did stereotype males as their best students in the area of mathematics and attributed characteristics such as volunteering answers, enjoyment of mathematics, and independence to males.

Teachers can make a positive difference, that is, they can implement specific strategies to help academically talented adolescents to succeed in all content areas. In particular, if they address areas that have been ignored in the past, differences can occur. For example, girls in upper elementary or middle school grades are at a critical point in their scientific, mathematical, and technical development. When teachers create nurturing and encouraging environments, they offer support and confidence to girls who may be interested in advanced opportunities in math, science, and technology (National Council of Teachers of Mathematics, 2000). Teachers play a critical role in encouraging girls in mathematics, science, and technology, by acting as role models and creating a "psychologically safe" environment conducive to all students' learning. For example, Rogers (1990) found that teachers who made significant progress in attracting talented females to higher-level mathematics courses created open and supportive classroom environments for all students. Gavin (1996) found that almost half of the female mathematics majors at a very competitive college attributed their decision to major in mathematics to the influence of a high school teacher, specifically, someone who maintained a personal relationship with their students throughout their college years.

Gender Differences in Loss of Belief in Abilities and Self-Confidence

Previous research has found that some gifted girls lose, to varying degrees, their enthusiasm for learning and their courage to speak out and display their abilities. Some research and reviews of research (Bell, 1989; Cramer, 1989; Hany, 1994; Kramer, 1991; Leroux, 1988; Perleth & Heller, 1994; Reis & Callahan, 1989; Subotnik, 1988) have indicated that some gifted females begin to lose self-confidence in elementary school and continue this loss through college and graduate school. These girls may grow to increasingly doubt their intellectual competence, perceive themselves as less capable than they actually are, and believe that boys can rely on innate ability, while they must work harder to succeed. Some research also indicates that girls try to avoid competition in order to preserve relationships, even if that means that they don't have an opportunity to use their skills (Rizza & Reis, 2001).

Bell (1989) identified several dilemmas facing gifted girls that may contribute to personality development issues later in adolescence. She found that gifted girls often perceive achievement and affiliation as opposite issues, because to girls, competition means that someone wins and someone loses. The gifted girls Bell studied encountered great difficulty with comparisons and downplayed their own accomplishments. The girls also feared social isolation as a consequence of their success.

Kline and Short (1991) found that the self-confidence and self-perceived abilities of gifted girls steadily decreased from elementary grades through high school. Buescher et al. (1987) found gifted boys and girls were more alike than their peers not identified as gifted except in one critical area—the recognition and acceptance of their own level of ability. Interviews with middle school gifted females revealed that they avoided displays of outstanding intellectual ability and searched for ways to better conform to the norm of the peer group (Callahan et al. 1994).

Gender Differences in Education, Career, and Family

Hébert (2000) studied the lives of six gifted male undergraduate students to understand how their life experiences influenced their decision to pursue elementary education as a career, finding that gifted males had a strong belief in self, incorporating empathy and psychological androgyny. Participants identified the following factors influencing this strong belief in self: formative experiences with difficult issues during childhood, adolescence, and early adulthood; exposure to male teachers as appropriate career models; and open-minded parents who provided emotional support.

In research about gifted female adolescents as compared to gifted male adolescents, Reis and Callahan (1994) found that more than twice the percentage of gifted adolescent boys mentioned a specific career goal than did adolescent girls. When asked what they would be doing after they graduated from college, boys were more likely to name a specific job or career. Altogether, their research found that 46.4% of the boys and only 27.1% of the girls mentioned a specific job or career. At the time, 65% of the boys they surveyed and 25% of the girls thought women should not work after they had children. Some girls still thought they would need to support the family (19%), but fewer boys thought that support was important (11%). In addition, only a very small number of the boys (5%) as compared to the majority of the girls Reis and Callahan studied said they expected both partners to work and for them both to share the childcare.

RESEARCH ABOUT GENDER, GIFTEDNESS, AND ADOLESCENCE

Too little research has addressed the area of gender, giftedness, and adolescence. Three areas of research could provide critical information about the interaction of gender differences and talent development in adolescents, and it is hoped that future research will be conducted about each of these areas.

Self-Regulated Learning Strategies

Academic self-regulation refers to the process by which students activate and sustain cognitions, behaviors, and affections that are systematically oriented toward the attainment of goals (Zimmerman, 1989). According to Zimmerman's social cognitive perspective, the construct of self-regulation refers "to the degree that individuals are metacognitively, motivationally, and behaviorally active participants in their own learning process" (p. 329). Zimmerman identified the hallmarks of academic self-regulation to include academic time management, practice, and mastery of learning methods; goal-directedness; and a sense of self-efficacy. A major component of academic self-regulation is the ability to acquire self-regulated learning (SRL) strategies defined by Zimmerman as "actions and processes directed at acquiring information or skills that involve agency, purpose, and instrumentality perceptions by the learners" (p. 329). Zimmerman and Martinez-Pons (1986), using interviews with adolescents, found evidence of 14 types of self-regulated learning strategies, including methods such as organizing and transforming information, seeking information, and rehearsing and using memory aids. Students' use of these strategies was highly correlated with their achievement and with teachers' ratings of their self-regulation in a class setting. In fact, students' reports of their use of these self-regulated learning strategies predicted their achievement track in school with 93% accuracy, and 13 of the 14 strategies discriminated significantly between students from the upper achievement track and students from lower tracks. The three classes of strategies that students can use to improve self-regulation include: (a) personal functioning, (b) academic behavioral performance and use of processing strategies, and (c) learning environment (Bandura, 1986; Zimmerman, 1989). A strong relationship exists between academic achievement and the use of self-regulated learning strategies by low- and high-achieving students (Pintrich, Anderman, & Klobucar, 1994; Zimmerman & Martinez-Pons, 1986). Research about self-regulated learning models might provide insight into gender differences in academically successful adolescents and help address some the higher incidence of underachievement noted in boys (Pintrich & Garcia, 1991; Reis & McCoach, 2000). A fascinating area of research would encompass teaching academically talented students self-regulation skills at a young enough age to enable them to achieve at high levels throughout high school and college.

Schoolhouse Giftedness and Creative Productive Giftedness

Renzulli (1986) defines schoolhouse giftedness as test-taking, lesson-learning, or academic giftedness or talents. Individuals who fall into this category generally score well on more traditional intellectual or cognitive assessments and perform well in school. He defines creative/productive giftedness and talent as individuals who have the potential to become producers (rather than consumers) of original knowledge, materials, or products, and who employ thought processes that tend to be inductive, integrated, and problem oriented (Renzulli). However, few studies have examined similarly talented adolescents who may have the potential for high levels of creative productive work (Bloom, 1985; Csikszentmihalyi et al., 1993; Winner, 1996; Winner & Martino, 1993). A consistent finding from adolescent studies is that several characteristics, personality traits, and environmental factors facilitate the subsequent development of high levels of creativity and creative productive giftedness in young people and adolescents, but little is known about gender differences in creativity and creative productivity (Csikszentmihalyi et al., 1993; Gardner, 1983; Reis, 1998; Renzulli, 1986; Sternberg & Lubart, 1993). In research by Reis (2001) and Kirschenbaum and Reis (1997), it appears that there is less encouragement for or interest in creative productivity on the part of girls than boys.

Several researchers also suggest that certain environments can help nurture high levels of creative potential (Amabile, 1989; Csikszentmihalyi, 1990; Torrance, 1978). For instance, families with moderate levels of stress may promote creativity in children because children learn to tolerate tension and ambiguity, and are less pressured to conform (Torrance). Yet, the creative adolescent also needs support. For example, MacKinnon (1978) concluded that creative talent requires a need for understanding from others to convey confidence in abilities. This reinforcement and affirmation of one's abilities seems to address the anxieties that may be associated with creative ideas, but it does not belittle the intensity nor dismiss the reality of creative ideas. Runco (1992) also found that creativity requires an environment that nurtures and then actively supports independence of judgment. Runco also found that creative individuals tend to be self-evaluative by nature, but this self-evaluation cannot be sustained without external support systems. When support is unavailable, frustration may develop.

Torrance (1978) determined that the creative personality requires a variety of social and emotional support mechanisms and that denial of those needs would likely result in both physiological and psychological illnesses. These needs include parental support and understanding of frustration as it develops and the need for reinforcing experimentation. In other words, creatively gifted adolescents are more likely to thrive in environments where risk taking is valued and promoted, and where there is less pressure to conform to prescribed conventions (Wildauer, 1984). These needs do not end with adolescence, but continue throughout life (Willings, 1983). In studies of talented adolescents, Bloom (1985) points to the important influence of gifted peers who match or surpass a student's abilities, and share the motivation needed for persistent effort over a prolonged period. Access to a group of peers with similar passions and abilities prepares creatively gifted adolescents to cope with the realities of the intense competition and stardom that characterize some creative careers later in life.

Csikszentmihalyi's (1996) research on creative adolescents suggests that the pursuit of high creative achievement among this group is likely to result in reduced popularity and perhaps increased marginalization or alienation from peers. Creatively gifted persons may appear particularly odd to peers when they have interests and passions that differ from the mainstream, and a proclivity for unique thinking and self-expression. Development of creative talent often necessitates that gifted students spend more time alone than average teens do, and the amount of time allocated to mental play appears to inhibit sexual awareness and independence. Research is needed about how to encourage and help creatively gifted adolescents. In particular, studying gender differences in creatively gifted students would provide more information about a critical area of need in our society; that is, the importance of creative expression and creative productivity in male and female gifted adolescents who can use their creativity to address problems to be faced in our complex world.

Talent Development and Goal Theory

Csikszentmihalyi et al. (1993) studied 208 talented teenagers with exceptional talent in art, athletics, mathematics, music, and/or science to identify the aspects of talent-related experience and activity that contribute to the cultivation of talent over time. They were especially interested in studying personality, goals, and daily living that enables the integration of talent into future choices. Goal theory suggests that important relationships exist among goals, expectations, attributions, conceptions of ability, motivational orientations, social and self comparisons, and achievement behaviors (Blumenfeld, 1992; Pintrich, 2000). Dweck (1986) suggests that one's goal orientation relate to one's beliefs about ability, and proposed two theories of intelligence: entity and incremental. People who hold an entity theory believe intelligence is relatively fixed, stable, and unchanging, and only effort will help you reach your limit. Those who hold an incremental theory equate intelligence with learning. Intelligence can change and increase with experience, effort, and learning. Students with an incremental view of intelligence are likely to believe that learning can enhance ability. The research conducted by Csikszentmihalyi et al. (1993) suggested that when talented students experienced flow while working on their talent, the likelihood they would continue to develop their gift increased significantly. Their research strongly suggested that the education of talented adolescents needs to become more intrinsically motivating to enable students to develop personality traits conducive to concentration, enjoyment of learning and openness to experience. Future research should examine the process of goal orientations and how these are linked with conceptions of ability, particularly in light of gender differences in this area, to better understand how the beliefs of male and female adolescents influence their achievement motivation. Of particular interest would be how gifted program experiences influence students' beliefs in abilities, goal acquisition, and motivation.

Ziegler and Heller (2003) have also found that female middle school students who have participated in a 10-week attribution-training program in physics significantly improved their performance in physics. The program also favorably affected their motivation and self-cognition skills. The intervention, an attribution retraining program, was conducted in conjunction with regular physics classes by the girls' physics teachers, who had been trained in two attribution retraining techniques. The study was conducted in Europe, and replication of such a study for an American population could provide insights into whether a similar intervention or approach might positively affect American adolescent girls. Bandura (1986) views motivation as goal directed behavior instigated and sustained by people's expectations concerning the anticipated outcomes of their actions and their self-efficacy for performing those actions. Attributions influence motivation in part through goals and expectations, and little research has addressed gender differences in these areas.

IMPLICATIONS FOR PARENTS, TEACHERS, AND COUNSELORS RELATED TO GENDER AND ADOLESCENCE

The work of Marcia (1980) also offers a useful framework of the roles parents and teachers can play in the development of gifts and talents. It would appear that few gifted adolescents reach the stage of identity achievement in which their choices appear clear and their identities emerge as well formed. Gifted boys may struggle with cultural conditioning, sexuality, success-orientation, and ego development, and thus face a number of problems resulting from the interaction of their gender and giftedness (Alvino, 1991; Kerr & Cohn, 2001). Gifted girls face some of the same challenges, and a host of others unique to their gender and gifts and talents (Reis, 1998). Fewer adolescents today achieve well-formed identity achievement due to the wide array of choices regarding interests and careers. In fact, some very successful gifted program options provide the rationale for consistent exposure to new topics, issues, ideas, and disciplines (Feldhusen & Kolloff, 1986; Renzulli & Reis, 1985, 1997). It may be that the broader array of choices that are part of organized gifted program opportunities may actually delay well-formed choices and clear understanding of identities. Indeed, with opportunities for travel abroad, enriched educational experiences, and the broader access to enrichment and knowledge available on the Web, more options are presented on a regular basis. The other key issue to consider is that more androgynous opportunities exist today for gifted girls and boys. Talented adolescent girls are less often held back by the cultural and gender stereotyping that in the past might have affected their career options, college majors, and choices. With fewer restrictions of choice, more gifted adolescents may experience a longer delay in clear identity achievement. Parents, counselors, and teachers can help overcome the gender and cultural stereotyping that often affects gifted and talented adolescents. Table 1 provides a list of recommendations for parents, teachers, and counselors.

The second alternative choice, identity foreclosure, occurs when adolescents do not consider a range of options of identities and goals, but rather simply adopt or agree to the values and lifestyles of their parents or significant others in their lives. Gifted male and female adolescents may agree to live the lifestyles espoused by their parents less frequently in the future. Gifted girls, who have been more often influenced by their parents and teachers, may increasingly become less afraid to follow their own interests and desires. They may also be less afraid of disappointing or losing those they love if it means giving up an interest or a career. Gifted boys may increasingly become more willing to choose careers in the helping professions or the arts. As more gifted women enter and select full-time careers, more gifted males may have to worry less about finances and supporting their family, and find themselves able to make choices that provide them with a vehicle for their talents, regardless of the financial benefits or losses that ensue from these choices.

Marcia's (1980) phase of identity diffusion occurs when adolescents make no definitive decisions, struggle to make choices, or avoid making any choice whatsoever. With talented adolescents, this may occur when students have multiple interests and talents and cannot focus their interests or talents; this is sometimes described as multipotentiality. Adolescents may also encounter an identity moratorium (Erikson, 1968, 1980) in which teenagers delay making firm choices about the directions their lives will take.

This purposeful delay may be considered healthy for talented and gifted adolescents, as research by Moon (2003) and Reis (1998, 2005) suggests that the desire to develop one's talents emerges over time. Moon (2003) defines personal talent as the exceptional ability to select and attain difficult life goals that fit one's interests, abilities, values, and contexts, and discusses the importance of goal selection to identify interests, abilities, and values. The stages of identity diffusion and moratorium can be considered a positive alternative for gifted adolescents, as these stages enable them to have the time to pursue their interests, consider alternative choices, and reflect on various careers and work they may believe is important at different stages in their lives.

Time for growth and reflection may be critical for both male and female talented adolescents, as many older talented individuals reflect back on their choices with regret for chances not taken and opportunities lost (Reis, 1998). Reis (2005)

Table 1
Parent, Counselor, and Teacher Recommendations **to Encourage Gifted Adolescent Girls and Boys**

School, Classroom and Home Strategies

- Provide numerous enrichment opportunities for talented adolescents to expose them to multiple areas of interest and enrichment.
- Encourage adolescents to become involved in many different types of activities and provide exposure to travel opportunities, clubs, and sports.
- Expose students to gifted male and female adult role models through direct and curricular experiences—field trips, guest speakers, seminars, books, videotapes, articles, and movies.
- Form task forces to advocate for various levels of programming and equal opportunities.
- Provide appropriate treatment in nonstereotypical environments (e.g., ensure equal access to technology and computers in classes).
- Encourage both boys and girls to take the full range of Advanced Placement and honors classes in all areas of interest; carefully ensure that girls continue taking advanced math/science courses and that boys are reinforced in areas such as the arts and literature. Support successes in these and all areas of endeavor for talented students.
- Help gifted adolescents to appreciate and understand healthy competition by encouraging active involvement in leadership, athletics, and academic competitions.
- Encourage advanced summer enrichment and acceleration opportunities with other academically gifted and talented adolescents.
- Spotlight the academic achievements of gifted boys and girls in a variety of different areas.
- Provide educational opportunities compatible with advanced cognitive development and individualized styles of learning.
- Establish equity in classroom interactions.

Strategies to Promote Healthy Social and Emotional Development

- Show sensitivity to the different nonverbal ways girls and boys express themselves and watch carefully if they begin to deny their abilities or hide their talents.
- Understand some of the external and internal barriers that may impede girls' and boys' successes.
- Encourage relationships among gifted adolescents who want to achieve and help the high achieving peer groups to be developed and maintained.

Table 1 continued

- Consistently point out options for careers and encourage future choices and help students to focus on specific careers.
- Stress self-reliance, independence, decision making, humor, and safe risk taking, and encourage inclination for creative action.
- Provide individualized, goals-oriented post-secondary and career counseling.
- Enable students to learn various communication styles.
- Express a positive attitude about talents and provide an unequivocal source of support, avoiding criticism as much as possible.
- Consciously discuss and actively challenge obstacles and barriers to success by pointing out negative stereotypes.
- Help to foster a secure sense of self by helping talented adolescents to understand and develop a belief in self and an understanding of their talents and ability.
- Encourage personality characteristics such as independence, smart risk taking, and self-confidence, self-reliance, and decision making.
- Accept differences and encourage diverse interests, styles, and choices.
- Encourage parental awareness of the special needs of gifted and talented adolescents.
- Develop an awareness of personal dilemmas and personality differences.
- Discuss the importance of peers and loved ones who support students' aspirations.

Implications for Parents

- Become assertive advocates for the development of interests and talents.
- Provide career encouragement and planning.
- Provide extensive experiences in museums, travel, and interaction with adults.
- Help your child to develop independence and an inclination for creative action.
- Encourage humor and positive risk taking.
- Encourage independent decision making and allow daughters to make their own decisions.
- Encourage participation in sports, competition, summer enrichment, and extracurricular activities that support talent development.
- Monitor television viewing and media exposure and the use of free time.
- Help support friendships with other high-achieving students.

Implications for Teachers

- Provide equal treatment in a non-stereotyped environment and in particular, provide encouragement for advanced coursework.

Table 1 continued

- Reduce sexism and stereotyping in classrooms and establish equity in classroom interactions.
- Help gifted adolescents understand healthy competition.
- Group gifted students homogeneously in separate classes or in clusters with heterogeneous classrooms.
- Expose gifted adolescents to other gifted adults who can act as role models through direct and curricular experiences—field trips, guest speakers, seminars, books, videotapes, articles, and movies.
- Provide educational interventions compatible with cognitive development and styles of learning (independent study projects, small group learning opportunities, etc.).
- Use a variety of authentic assessment tools such as projects and learning centers in addition to tests.

Implications for Counselors

- Provide individualized, goal-oriented career counseling and maintain an interest in talented adolescents with high potential who need help to develop their talents.
- Provide group counseling sessions for gifted and talented adolescents to address issues such as multipotentiality, underachievement, or absence of belief in ability.
- Encourage participation in honors and Advanced Placement courses, and in extracurricular activities and summer and out-of school programs such as college science and math classes.
- Sponsor conferences, workshops, and symposiums for and about gifted women for talented girls and their parents.
- Provide bibliotherapy and videotherapy in small group sessions; provide readings in a wide variety of excellent resources and view films such as *The Joy Luck Club* about the struggle of talented individuals.
- Establish support groups with a network of same-sex peers; encourage use of role models and mentors with gifted adolescents in careers and leadership positions.
- Contact and involve parents when gifted adolescents begin to underachieve or seem confused about abilities, aspirations, or careers.
- Provide a variety of career counseling and exposure opportunities.
- Provide information about societies, Web pages, and resources that encourage and support gifted adolescents.

defines the process of talent development in women as occurring when women with high intellectual, creative, artistic, or leadership ability or potential achieve in an area of choice, and when they make contributions that they consider meaningful to society. Over a decade of research in this area led to a preliminary conception of talent realization in women (Reis, 1995, 1998) that was further refined in subsequent years (Reis, 2005). The factors that contribute to this conception include: abilities (intelligence and special talents), personality traits, environmental factors, and personal perceptions, such as the social importance of the use of one's talents to make a positive difference in the world. Each of these factors contributes to what Gruber (1986) called "self-mobilization" (p. 258), characterized in the women Reis studied by the development of belief in self, their fervent desire to develop their own talents, and a sense of destiny enabling them to make conscious decisions to develop their talents, often with little support and against many obstacles. These talents emerged over many years and were constructed using earlier varied life experiences that served as valuable backdrops to prepare them for future accomplishments.

Based on these newer conceptions of giftedness (Moon, 2003; Reis, 1998, 2005) the identity moratorium stage may provide an appropriate phase to enable gifted adolescents the gift of time to pursue interests, become involved in increasingly challenging work, and develop their own sense of interests and passions.

REFERENCES

Alvino, J. (1991). An investigation into the needs of gifted boys. *Roeper Review, 13*, 174–180.

Amabile, T. M. (1989). *Growing up creative: Nurturing a lifetime of creativity.* Williston, VT: Crown House Publishing Limited.

American Association of University Women (AAUW). (1991). *Shortchanging girls, shortchanging America: A call to action.* Washington, DC: The American Association of University Women Educational Foundation.

American College Testing Program. (1989). *State and national trend data for students who take the ACT Assessment.* Iowa City, IA: Author.

Ames, C. (1978). Children's achievement attributions and self-reinforcement: Effects of self-concept and competitive reward structure. *Journal of Educational Psychology, 70*, 345–355.

Arnold, K. D. (1993). Academically talented women in the 1980s: The Illinois valedictorian project. In K. Hulbert & D. Schuster (Eds.), *Women's lives through time: Educated American women of the twentieth century* (pp. 393–414). San Francisco: Jossey-Bass.

Bandura, A. (1986). *Social foundations of thought and action: A social cognitive theory.* Englewood Cliffs, NJ: Prentice-Hall.

Becker, D. F., & Forsyth, R. A. (1990, April). *Gender differences in grades 3 through 12: A longitudinal analysis.* Paper presented at the meeting of the American Educational Research Association, Boston.

Bell, L. A. (1989). Something's wrong here and it's not me: Challenging the dilemmas that block girls' success. *Journal for the Education of the Gifted, 12,* 118–130.

Block, J. H. (1982). *Sex role identity and ego development.* San Francisco: Jossey-Bass.

Bloom, B. (Ed.). (1985). *Developing talent in young people.* New York: Ballantine Books.

Blumenfeld, P. C. (1992). Classroom learning and motivation: Clarifying and expanding goal theory. *Journal of Educational Psychology, 84,* 272–281.

Boyer, E. L. (1987). *College: The undergraduate experience in America.* New York: Harper & Row.

Buescher, T. M., Olszewski, P., & Higham, S. J. (1987, April). *Influences on strategies adolescents use to cope with their own recognized talents* (Report No. EC 200755). Paper presented at the biennial meeting of the Society for Research in Child Development, Baltimore, MD.

Callahan, C. M., Cunningham, C. M., & Plucker, J. A. (1994). Foundations for the future: The socio-emotional development of gifted, adolescent women. *Roeper Review, 17,* 99–105.

Coleman, J. (1961). *The adolescent society.* New York: Free Press.

College Board. (2002, June 27). *The College Board announces a new SAT.* Retrieved July 26, 2005, from http://www.collegeboard.com/press/article/0,3183,11147,00.html

College Board. (2003, August 26). *SAT verbal and math scores up significantly as a record-breaking number of students take the test.* Retrieved July 26, 2005, from http://www.collegeboard.com/press/article/0,3183,26858,00.html

Cooley, D., Chauvin, J., & Karnes, F. (1984). Gifted females: A comparison of attitudes by male and female teachers. *Roeper Review, 6,* 164–167.

Cramer, R. H. (1989). Attitudes of gifted boys and girls towards math: A qualitative study. *Roeper Review, 11,* 128–133.

Csikszentmihalyi, M. (1990). *Flow: The psychology of optimal experience.* New York: Harper & Row.

Csikszentmihalyi, M. (1996). *Creativity: Flow and the psychology of discovery and invention.* New York: HarperCollins Publishers.

Csikszentmihalyi, M., Rathunde, K., & Whalen, S. (1993). *Talented teenagers.* New York: Cambridge University Press.

Davis, J. A. (1964). *Great aspirations: The school plans of America's college seniors.* Chicago: Aldine.

Deaux, K. (1993). Commentary. Sorry, wrong number: A reply to Gentile's call. *Psychological Science, 4,* 125–126.

Dickens, M. N. (1990). *Parental influences on the mathematics self-concept of high achieving adolescent girls.* Unpublished doctoral dissertation, University of Virginia, Charlottesville.

Dweck, C. S. (1986). Motivation processes affecting learning. *American Psychologist, 41,* 1040–1048.

Eccles, J. S., Midgley, C., & Adler, T. F. (1984). Grade-related changes in the school environment: Effects on achievement motivation. In J. Nicholls (Ed.), *Advances in motivation and achievement* (Vol. 3, pp. 283–331). Greenwich, CT: JAI Press.

Educational Testing Service. (1989). *1989 profile of SAT and achievement test takers.* Princeton, NJ: Author.

Educational Testing Service. (2003). *2003 college-bound seniors: A profile of SAT program test takers.* Princeton, NJ: Author.

Erikson, E. (1968). *Identity, youth, and crisis.* New York: Norton.

Erikson, E. (1980). *Identity and the life cycle* (2nd ed.). New York: Norton.

Feingold, A. (1994). Gender differences in personality: A meta-analysis. *Psychological Bulletin, 116,* 429–456.

Feldhusen, J., & Kolloff, P. B. (1986). The Purdue three-stage enrichment model for gifted education at the elementary level. In J. S. Renzulli (Ed.), *Systems and models for developing programs for the gifted and talented* (pp. 126–152). Mansfield Center, CT: Creative Learning Press.

Fennema, E. (1990). Teachers' beliefs and gender differences in mathematics. In E. Fennema & G. Leder (Eds.), *Mathematics and gender* (pp. 1–9). New York: Teachers College Press.

Fennema, E., Peterson, P. L., Carpenter, T. P., & Lubinski, C. A. (1990). Teachers' attributions and beliefs about girls, boys and mathematics. *Educational Studies in Mathematics, 21,* 55–69.

Ford, D. Y. (1992). The American achievement ideology as perceived by urban African-American students. *Urban Education, 27,* 196–211.

Franken, R. E. (1988). *Human motivation* (2nd ed.). Pacific Grove, CA: Brooks/Cole Publishing.

Gardner, H. (1983). *Frames of mind: The theory of multiple intelligences.* New York: Basic Books

Gavin, M. K. (1996). The development of math talent: Influences on students at a women's college. *Journal of Secondary Education, 2,* 476–485.

Good, T. L., & Brophy, J. E. (1986). *Educational psychology: A realistic approach* (3rd ed.). New York: Longman.

Gruber, H. E. (1986). The self construction of the extraordinary. In R. J. Sternberg & J. E. Davidson (Eds.), *Conceptions of giftedness* (pp. 247–260). New York: Cambridge University Press.

Halpern, D. (1989). The disappearance of cognitive gender differences: What you see depends on where you look. *American Psychologist, 44,* 1156–1158.

Hany, E. A. (1994). The development of basic cognitive components of technical creativity: A longitudinal comparison of children and youth with high and average intelligence. In R. F. Subotnik & K. D. Arnold (Eds.), *Beyond Terman: Contemporary longitudinal studies of giftedness and talent* (pp. 115–154). Norwood, NJ: Ablex.

Hébert, T. P. (2000). Gifted males pursuing careers in elementary education: Factors that influence a belief in self. *Journal of Secondary Gifted Education, 24,* 7–45.

Hébert, T. P. (2001). "If I had a new notebook, I know things would change": Bright underachieving young men in urban classrooms. *Gifted Child Quarterly, 45,* 174–194.

Hébert, T. P. (2002). Gifted Black males in a predominately White university: Portraits of high achievement. *Journal for the Education of the Gifted, 26,* 25–64.

Heiss, R. H. (1995). *Personality and interests of gifted adolescents: Differences by gender and domain.* Unpublished doctoral dissertation, Iowa State University.

Hess, R. D., Holloway, S. D., Dickson, W. P., & Price, G. G. (1984). Maternal variables as predictors of children's school readiness and later achievement in vocabulary and mathematics in sixth grade. *Child Development, 55,* 1902–1912.

Kerr, B. A. & Cohn, S. J. (2001) *Smart boys: Talent, manhood, and the search for meaning.* Scottsdale, AZ: Great Potential Press.

Kimball, M. M. (1989). A new perspective on women's math achievement. *Psychological Bulletin, 105,* 198–214.

Kirschenbaum, R. J., & Reis, S. M. (1997). Conflicts in creativity: Talented female artists. *Creativity Research Journal, 10,* 251–263.

Kissane, B. V. (1986). Selection of mathematically talented students. *Educational Studies in Mathematics, 17,* 221–241.

Klein, A. G., & Zehms, D. (1996). Self-concept and gifted girls: A cross sectional study of intellectually gifted females in grades 3, 5, and 8. *Roeper Review, 19,* 30–33

Kline, B. E., & Short, E. B. (1991). Changes in emotional resilience: Gifted adolescent boys. *Roeper Review, 13,* 184–187.

Kramer, L. R. (1985, April). *Social interaction and perceptions of ability: A study of gifted adolescent females.* Paper presented at the annual meeting of the American Educational Research Association, Chicago.

Kramer, L. R. (1991). The social construction of ability perceptions: An ethnographic study of gifted adolescent girls. *Journal of Early Adolescence, 11,* 340–362.

Leroux, J. A. (1988). Voices from the classroom: Academic and social self-concepts of gifted adolescents. *Journal for the Education of the Gifted, 11,* 3–18.

Marcia, J. (1980). Ego identity development. In J. Adelson (Ed.), *The handbook of adolescent psychology* (pp. 159–187). New York: Wiley.

Marcia, J. (1987). The identity status approach to the study of ego identity development. In T. Honess & K. Yardley (Eds.), *Self and identity: Perspectives across the lifespan* (pp. 161–171). London: Routledge & Kagan Paul.

Martin, D. J., & Hoover, H. D. (1987). Sex differences in educational achievement: A longitudinal study. *Journal of Early Adolescence, 7*, 65–83.

MacKinnon, D. W. (1978). *In search of human effectiveness.* Buffalo, NY: Creative Education Foundation.

McGillicuddy-De Lisi, A. V. (1985). The relationship between parental beliefs and children's cognitive level. In R. Sigel (Ed.), *Parental belief systems* (pp. 7–24). Hillsdale, NJ: Erlbaum.

Meece, J. L., Blumenfeld, P. C., & Hoyle, R. H. (1988). Students' goal orientations and cognitive engagement in classroom activities. *Journal of Educational Psychology, 80*, 514–523.

Moon, S. M. (2003). Personal talent. *High Ability Studies, 14*, 5–21.

National Council of Teachers of Mathematics (2000). *Principles and standards for schools mathematics.* Reston, VA: Author.

National Science Foundation. (2000). *Shaping the future.* Washington, DC: Author.

Nicholls, J. G. (1975). Causal attributions and other achievement-related cognitions: Effects of task outcome, attainment value and sex. *Journal of Personality and Social Psychology, 31*, 379–389.

Parsons, J. E., Adler, T. F., & Kaczala, C. (1982). Socialization of achievement attitudes and beliefs: Parental influences. *Child Development, 53*, 310–321.

Perleth, C., & Heller, K. A. (1994). The Munich longitudinal study of giftedness. In R. F. Subotnik, & K. K. Arnold (Eds.), *Beyond Terman: Contemporary longitudinal studies of giftedness and talent* (pp. 77–114). Norwood, NJ: Ablex

Phillips, D. A. (1987). Socialization of perceived academic competence among highly competent children. *Child Development, 58*, 1308–1320.

Pintrich, P. R. (2000). Issues in self-regulation theory and research. *Journal of Mind and Behavior, 21*, 213–219.

Pintrich, P. R., Anderman, E. M., & Klobucar, C. (1994). Intraindividual differences in motivation and cognition in students with and without learning disabilities. *Journal of Learning Disabilities, 27*, 360–370.

Pintrich, P. R., & Blumenfeld, P. C. (1985). Classroom experience and children's self-perceptions of ability, effort, and conduct. *Journal of Educational Psychology, 77*, 646–657.

Pintrich, P. R., & Garcia, T. (1991). Students goal orientation and self-regulation in the college classroom. *Advances in Motivation and Achievement, 7*, 371–402.

Reis, S. M. (1987). We can't change what we don't recognize: Understanding the special needs of gifted females. *Gifted Child Quarterly, 31*, 83–88.

Reis, S. M. (1995). Talent ignored, talent diverted: The cultural context underlying giftedness in females. *Gifted Child Quarterly, 39*, 162–170.

Reis, S. M. (1998). *Work left undone: Compromises and challenges of talented females.* Mansfield Center, CT: Creative Learning Press.

Reis, S. M. (2001). Toward a theory of creativity in diverse creative women. In M. Bloom & T. Gullotta (Eds.), *Promoting creativity across the life span* (pp. 231–276). Washington, DC: CWLA.

Reis, S. M. (2005). Feminist perspectives on talent development: A research based conception of giftedness in women. In R. J. Sternberg & J. Davidson (Eds.), *Conceptions of giftedness* (2nd ed.). New York: Cambridge University Press.

Reis, S. M., & Callahan, C. M. (1989). Gifted females: They've come a long way—or have they? *Journal for the Education of the Gifted, 12*, 99–117.

Reis, S. M., & Callahan, C. M. (1994). Attitudes of adolescent gifted girls and boys toward education, achievement, and the future. *Gifted Education International, 9*, 144–151.

Reis, S. M., Hébert, T. P., Díaz, E. I., Maxfield, L. R., & Ratley, M. E. (1995). *Case studies of talented students who achieve and underachieve in an urban high school* (RM 95120). Storrs, CT: The National Research Center on the Gifted and Talented, University of Connecticut.

Reis, S. M., & McCoach, D. B. (2000). The underachievement of gifted students: What do we know and where do we go? *Gifted Child Quarterly, 44*, 152–170.

Reis, S. M., & Park, S. (2001). Gender differences in high-achieving students in math and science. *Journal for the Education of the Gifted, 25*, 52–73.

Renzulli, J. S. (1986). The three ring conception of giftedness: A developmental model for creative productivity. In R. J. Sternberg & J. E. Davidson (Eds.), *Conceptions of giftedness* (pp. 53–92). New York: Cambridge University Press.

Renzulli, J. S., & Reis, S. M. (1985). *The schoolwide enrichment model: A comprehensive plan for educational excellence.* Mansfield Center, CT: Creative Learning Press.

Renzulli, J. S., & Reis, S. M. (1997). *The schoolwide enrichment model: A how to guide for educational excellence.* Mansfield Center, CT: Creative Learning Press.

Rimm, S. (1999). *See Jane win.* New York: Random House.

Rizza, M. G., & Reis, S. M. (2001). Comparing and contrasting: Stories of competition. *Gifted Child Quarterly, 45*, 54–62.

Rogers, P. (1990). Thoughts on power and pedagogy. In L. Burton (Ed.), *Gender and mathematics: An international perspective* (pp. 38–46). London: Cassell.

Rosser, P. (1989). *Sex bias in college admissions tests: Why women lose out.* Cambridge, MA: National Center for Fair and Open Testing.

Runco, M. A. (1992). The evaluative and divergent thinking of children. *Journal of Creative Behavior, 25*, 311–319.

Sadker, M., & Sadker, D. (1994). *Failing at fairness: How America's schools cheat girls.* New York: Charles Scribner's Sons.

Schunk, D. H. (1984). Sequential attributional feedback and children's achievement behaviors. *Journal of Educational Psychology, 75*, 511–518.

Siegle, D., & Reis, S. M. (1994). Gender differences in teacher and student perceptions of students' ability and effort. *Journal of Secondary Gifted Education, 6*, 86–92.

Siegle, D., & Reis, S. M. (1998). Gender differences in teacher and student perceptions of students' ability and effort. *Gifted Child Quarterly, 42*, 39–47.

Sternberg, R. J., & Lubart, T. (1993). Creative giftedness: A multivariate investment approach. *Gifted Child Quarterly, 37*, 7–15.

Stevenson, H. W., & Newman, R. S. (1986). Long-term prediction of achievement in mathematics and reading. *Child Development, 57*, 646–659.

Subotnik, R. (1988). The motivation to experiment: A study of gifted adolescents' attitudes toward scientific research. *Journal for the Education of the Gifted, 11*, 19–35.

Swiatek, M. A. (2001). Social coping among gifted high school students and its relationship to self-concept. *Journal of Youth and Adolescence, 30*, 19–39.

Torrance, E. P. (1978). Healing qualities of creative behavior. *Creative Child and Adult Quarterly, 3*, 146–158.

Wildauer, C. A. (1984). *Identification and nurturance of the intellectually gifted young child within the regular classroom: Case histories.* Washington, DC: U.S. Department of Education, Educational Information Center. (ERIC Document No. ED254041)

Willings, D. (1983). *The gifted child grows up.* Washington, DC: U.S. Department of Education, Educational Information Center. (ERIC Document No. ED252038)

Winner, E. (1996). *Gifted children: Myths and realities.* New York: Basic Books.

Winner, E., & Martino, G. (1993). Giftedness in the visual arts and music. In K. A. Heller, F. J. Mönks, & A. H. Passow (Eds.), *International handbook of research and development of giftedness and talent* (pp. 253–281). New York: Pergamon Press.

Woolfolk, A. E. (2004). *Educational psychology.* Boston: Allyn & Bacon.

Ziegler, A. & Heller, K.A. (2003). Effects of an attribution retraining with female students gifted in physics. *Journal for the Education of the Gifted, 23,* 217–243.

Zimmerman, B. J. (1989). A social cognitive view of self-regulated academic learning. *Journal of Educational Psychology, 81,* 329–339.

Zimmerman, B. J., & Martinez-Pons, M. (1986). Development of a structured interview for assessing student use of self-regulated learning strategies. *American Educational Research Journal, 23,* 614–628.

Being Gifted and Adolescent: Issues and Needs of Students of Color

by Donna Y. Ford
& James L. Moore III

Background and Definitions

Over the years, educators (e.g., teachers, counselors, and administrators) and parents have expressed serious concerns about the psychological and socio-emotional needs of gifted students, particularly as they impact students' school achievement. Specifically, studies have examined issues centered on self-esteem, self-concept, and other identity-related variables (e.g., race, gender, etc.) for gifted students and how the issues may differ for students identified as gifted versus those not identified as gifted. Educational researchers have also explored issues such as the effects of labeling on gifted students' self-image and their feelings about being gifted, as well the quality of peer and sibling relationships for students identified as gifted. Many of these studies have rendered findings that have helped teachers, counselors, administrators, and parents to increase their understanding of the specific and, perhaps, unique academic, psychological, and socio-emotional needs and development of gifted students. Although there is an established body of literature that focuses on the psychological and socio-emotional needs of gifted students, it fails to differentiate or address the unique needs and development of gifted students of color, defined in this chapter as African American, Hispanic American, Native American, and Asian American students[1].

In this chapter, we attempt to fill the gaps in the literature by exploring psychological, socio-emotional, and academic (i.e., achievement) issues of gifted students of color. The model we use to explore these various issues is rather simple, but is best illustrated using a Venn diagram (see Figure 1). This model urges educators working with gifted students of color to consider the needs of these students as gifted individuals and as culturally diverse individuals. For example, gifted adolescents of color are confronted with challenges similar to all other gifted students, as well as issues unique to adolescents of color. Like other gifted students, students of color often possess perfectionist characteristics, experience difficulties finding and establishing relationships with peers, struggle with identity issues, and suffer uneven cognitive and social development (Ford & Moore, 2004; Moore, Ford, & Milner, 2005). Ford (1995, 1996) and Fordham and Ogbu (1986) maintain that social needs and issues may be different for students of color in comparison to White students. In particular, these educational researchers pinpoint the consistent pattern of high-achieving African American students facing negative peer pressures. Many high-achieving or gifted African American students, especially adolescents, are accused of "acting White[2]," when they do well academically and/or participate in gifted classes and Advanced Placement (AP) courses. Such accusations often negatively impact these students' academic performance because many succumb to the negative social and psychological pressures of their peers. Therefore, we urge educators to focus on: (a) how self-esteem and self-concept affect diverse students' school outcomes *and* (b) how racial identity affects their achievement. These issues are discussed in more detail below.

Textbooks in gifted education often give cursory or tangential attention to culturally diverse students; that is, they typically contain one chapter on culturally diverse populations, while other chapters virtually ignore these students. Hence, a chapter focusing on identifying gifted students may not even mention culturally diverse students and is otherwise trivial; likewise, a chapter on teaching gifted students may not address culturally different ways of learning or multicultural curriculum. As a result, educators—teachers, counselors, and administrators—learn little about cultural diversity in gifted education. The implications for such colorblind training (e.g., Ford, Moore, & Milner, 2005) are clear but mind-boggling. Educators are allowed to see cultural diversity as a separate issue—a topic that is not central to their goals of learning to teach, counsel, or conduct research. Unfortunately, educa-

---

1   In this chapter, we use "culturally diverse," "minority," and "students of color" interchangeably.

2   The overwhelming majority of literature on negative peer pressures has been conducted with African American students. Less often has research focused on other groups of color, especially when it comes to being accused of "acting White." However, we believe that Hispanic Americans (more than Asian Americans and Native Americans) also experience this form of peer pressure at high rates. So little has been written about Native American students, especially gifted ones, that we do not have a picture—even a faint one—of peer pressures. Finally, as discussed later, Asian Americans often face positive peer pressures, as well as positive stereotypes and expectations; this is unlike other diverse students, and creates unique challenges.

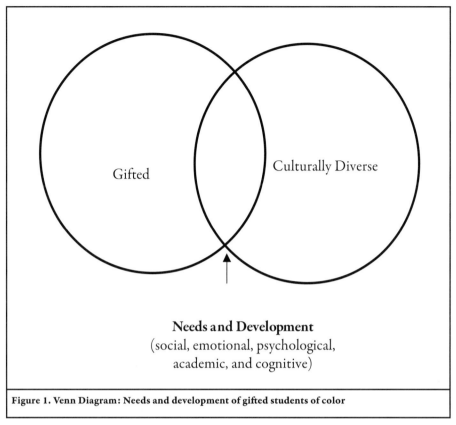

Needs and Development
(social, emotional, psychological,
academic, and cognitive)

Figure 1. Venn Diagram: Needs and development of gifted students of color

tors often make the mistake of viewing gifted students as a homogeneous group. In turn, the development, characteristics, and needs of gifted students of color are inadequately addressed or go unmet.

In this chapter, we begin with a brief overview of our definitions and views. We start by defining the concept of "culture." Next, some of the socio-emotional issues confronting gifted ethnic minority students are examined. Special attention is given to peer pressures faced by students of color, although we recognize that many social ills exert their toll on the lives of diverse populations[3]. Third, we discuss psychological issues with specific attention to the topic of racial identity using a widely researched theory of racial identity development (Cross, 1971, 1995; Cross & Vandiver, 2001). The chapter concludes with suggestions for interventions appropriate for use with culturally diverse gifted students. Five major questions guide this chapter: (a) How do students achieve when they are culturally different? (b) What issues and needs must educators have familiarity with regarding gifted students of color? (c) How do socio-emotional issues affect gifted students of color? (d) How do psychological needs impact gifted students of color? and (e) What interventions have the poten-

---

3   By social ills, we are referring to low teacher expectations of students of color, stereotypes, prejudices, racism, and the like. Space limitations do not allow us to delve into these issues; readers are referred to the large body of work on these issues in educational, sociology, counseling, and multicultural-based journals.

tial for helping gifted students of color to achieve academically and to become socio-emotionally and psychologically "healthy" individuals?

CULTURE: A BRIEF OVERVIEW

Since the 1980s, there has been an increase in research and scholarship on students of color. This body of knowledge, targeting researchers, practitioners, and policy makers, has attempted to change the negative perceptions professionals—including educators—hold of gifted students of color. Much of this work argues that the notion of racial and cultural deprivation is negative and educationally harmful to students and society at-large. To be culturally deprived implies that one does not have a culture; to be culturally disadvantaged implies that one (and one's) culture is inferior to another. Instead, it is more proactive and advantageous for students if educators and other professionals believe that students are culturally "different" and culturally "diverse" (rather than culturally disadvantaged or deficient; Ford et al., 2005).

Why is a chapter on gifted students of color necessary or even important? Despite the exponential growth in student diversity in recent decades, educators still enter classrooms lacking substantive multicultural preparation; that is, they seldom have significant formal training about and with students from different cultural backgrounds (Banks, 1999; Milner, 2002). Consequently, many of these educators often lack the competencies to address the academic, cognitive, socio-emotional, psychological, and cultural needs of diverse students, including gifted students of color. When educators do not understand the cultural backgrounds of students and the experiences that diverse students bring into the classroom, it is often difficult for them to understand, teach, counsel, and promote academic achievement among diverse students. Toward that end, many educators have never attended schools themselves with individuals of a different culture or lived in cross-cultural neighborhoods and, as a result, their knowledge and understanding of students of color are negatively skewed because they rely on negative stereotypes gathered from popular media and other uninformed sources (Ford, 1996; Ford, Harris, Tyson, & Frazier Trotman, 2002; Milner, 2002). Unfortunately, these stereotypical beliefs, whether consciously or unconsciously present, often force educators to make different curricular decisions and use deficit-thinking models to teach students of color. In turn, these students are presented with a set of obstacles beyond those experienced at home or with peers.

Because educators serve a critical role in the lives of gifted students of color, especially those who are adolescents, it is important to note that they are not exempt from needing formal and substantive training/preparation to work with these students. While it is logical to assume that teachers, counselors, and administrators who pursue coursework or professional development in gifted education will learn about the characteristics of gifted students, it is not safe to assume that they will learn about the characteristics and classroom experiences of students of color and the affective, psychological, cultural, and social issues often associated with these students. Where do we go from here? The first step is for educators to adopt a definition of culture, and then to proceed on an aggressive and proactive journey toward becoming culturally competent educational professionals.

Culture: A Definition

Many definitions of culture can be found in the literature. In this chapter, *culture* is defined as beliefs, values, dispositions, traditions, customs, and habits that are shared among a group of people. These beliefs, values, traditions, and so forth, serve as a filter through which a group of people view and respond to the world (thus, informing a person's paradigmatic thinking). For example, in the "teen culture," one finds shared values, beliefs, and so forth that are thought to characterize the period of adolescence (e.g., increased concerns for popularity, heightened need for affiliation, anxiety about physical characteristics, temperament, thirst for independence, experimentation with the unknown, high risk taking, etc.). The cultural characteristics for each group represent modal characteristics, common patterns, and generalizations, but it is important that they are not used to produce stereotypes, especially negative stereotypes.

More specifically, cultural characteristics have two dimensions—visible and invisible (see Figure 2). Borrowing from the analogy of an iceberg, much of culture is deeply rooted because it is beneath the surface and out of conscious awareness. For example, visible or obvious characteristics include foods, holidays, dress, and music preference shared by a cultural group. Less visible cultural characteristics ("deep culture") relate to such variables as attitudes, beliefs, values, and ways of perceiving and thinking. That is, different groups have different beliefs and values about cooperation versus competition, about matriarchal versus patriarchal households, about nuclear versus extended family structures, about communicating verbally versus nonverbally, and so forth. Individuals from different cultural backgrounds may have different beliefs about a number of issues, including showing respect to elders or those in authority, showing emotions, asking questions or asking for help, handling conflict, solving problems, touching, time, and personal space (Shade, Kelly, & Oberg, 1998; Storti, 1991, 1998). Figure 3 presents an overview of how groups from four different cultural backgrounds may differ in culture at the both the deep level and on the surface. While no one chart or model can capture all of the characteristics and nuances associated with different groups and their culture, Figure 3 is a beginning. It offers several examples designed to show only a few differences among four groups. These differences carry profound implications for identification and assessment, curriculum and instruction, as well as counseling. A few scenarios will be used to illustrate this point[4].

- Two years ago, Maria and her family immigrated to the U.S. from Puerto Rico. Her parents brought with them the belief that females do not need as much of an education as males given that their primary role is to take care of the family.

---

4   For other scenarios between diverse students and their teachers, see Ford et al., 2005.

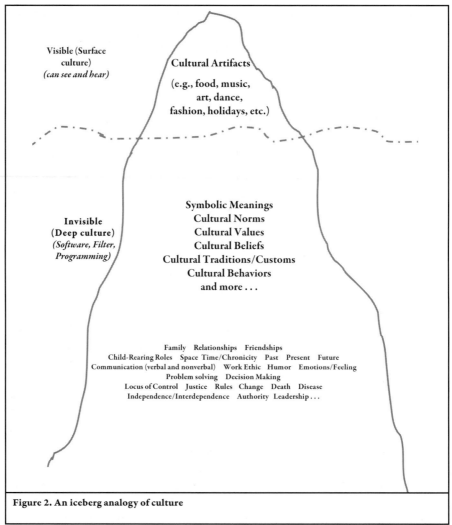

Figure 2. An iceberg analogy of culture

Thus, they are not buying into the idea that their daughter needs to be recognized as gifted; nor does she need to participate in AP classes. Maria agrees.

- Lee, a Japanese student, has been identified as gifted in the visual arts, with teachers wanting him to have more challenge in arts. His parents are not enthusiastic about this because they are more concerned about his development in the "academic" or "core" subject areas. Rather than openly share their views, however, they have been more indirect by frequently finding excuses for him to miss school-related art events and activities when his grades are not affected.

- Kim, a Korean student, is having difficulty in her AP English class and honors courses. However, she is not willing to share this with Ms. Robinson, her teacher. To do so would suggest that Ms. Robinson is not a good teacher. This would be disrespectful.

- Terrance, an African American male, has been identified as gifted and participates in AP chemistry and calculus. He is one of a few students of color in

Style	Very Little	Little	Medium Average	Much	Very Much
Animated; Emotionally expressive	Asian Native American	Hispanic	White		Black
Gestures	Asian Native American		White	Hispanic	Black
Speech volume	Asian	Hispanic	Native American	White	Black
Directness of questions	Native American Asian	Hispanic			Black White
Directness of answers	Native American Asian	Hispanic			Black White
Blunt, gets to the point	Asian	Hispanic Native American		White	Black
Directness of eye contact	Asian Native American	Hispanic			Black White
Firm, long handshake	Native American Asian		Hispanic	Black	White
Touching	Native American Asian		White		Black Hispanic
Monochronic	Native American Hispanic	Black		Asian	White
Task more important than relationships	Native American Asian Hispanic	Black			White
Individualism	Native American	Hispanic Asian Black			White
Large personal space	Native American Asian	White			Black Hispanic

Figure 3. Cross-cultural comparison chart: Potential similarities and differences among Asian American, Hispanic American, Native American, White, and Black students

Style	Very Little	Little	Medium Average	Much	Very Much
Writing preferred over speaking	Native American Hispanic Black			Asian	White
Speaks when others are speaking; ignores taking turns	Native American Asian	Hispanic		White	Black
Automatic deference to authority	Native American Black		Hispanic White		Asian
Spiritual elements often considered	White	Asian Hispanic			Native American Black
Speed of response	Native American		Hispanic Asian		Black White

Figure 3 continued

Note. This chart is not comprehensive; it represents modal characteristics of each cultural group, and serves as a starting point from which to begin understanding and working with culturally different groups.

these AP classes, along with a Chinese student and Mexican American student. Terrance has complained often about feeling isolated from classmates; he wants to take honors or lower level classes with his friends. His parents are torn between meeting his academic needs and his socio-emotional needs[5].

- Marlene is multiracial (African American and White American). She is taking three honors courses, but complains that she is there to serve as a "token." As an outspoken, direct student, Marlene believes inequities should be addressed rather than ignored. She often interrupts lessons and finds other ways to share her views. Teachers are not pleased; her parents are proud of her.

Clearly, understanding how one's culture operates and the relation of that culture to an individual's orientations and choices can help us to understand how culturally different students approach learning, achievement, and social relationships (with other students and teachers, counselors and administrators).

---

5   This topic of minority parents feeling conflicted is given more consideration by Ford (2004) in *Gifted Child Today*.

According to Frasier and colleagues (1995), even views about "giftedness" are culturally bound—the belief in "giftedness" and manifestations of characteristics associated with giftedness may be different in culturally diverse students; the example of Maria and Lee in the above scenarios are two such examples. To repeat, without on-going and substantive cross-cultural or multicultural training, educators may not recognize giftedness in culturally diverse students. This lack of recognition can manifest itself in several ways: (a) educators—teachers, counselors, and administrators—may not refer these students for gifted education screening, so students may go unchallenged and become bored in school; and (b) educators may not understand the learning and cultural styles of students from different cultural backgrounds; thus, students' learning styles and educators' teaching styles may not match. In both instances, gifted diverse students may underachieve or feel alienated from students from other backgrounds, as well as teachers and other educators. This issue of cultural mismatch is presented in Figure 4, along with potential impacts. In terms of the iceberg analogy (Figure 2), imagine the iceberg of one student (his/her deep cultural values and beliefs) clashing with the iceberg of another student; imagine the values and beliefs of a student and teacher clashing. These differences cannot be taken lightly or trivialized in any way.

In the next section, we begin to unravel some of the special issues facing gifted students of color, beginning with a discussion of socio-emotional issues.

SOCIO-EMOTIONAL ISSUES FACING
GIFTED STUDENTS OF COLOR

All individuals and groups contend with social and emotional issues, particularly adolescents. During this developmental period, allegiance issues and peer relationships reign supreme. For adolescents of color, it seems that pressures have a particularly powerful influence (Steinberg, Brown, & Dornbusch, 1996). African Americans, seemingly more than other students, have a strong need for affiliation, which contributes to a high value placed on peer acceptance. Conversely, Asian Americans are less likely to succumb to negative peer pressures, and have one of the highest needs for achievement of all groups. Findings on these two issues—need for achievement versus need for affiliation—are inconclusive for Hispanic American students, and little is known about Native American students due to sparse research. Most research focuses on negative rather than positive peer pressures, perhaps due to the increased amount of antiachievement sentiments that appear among adolescents. In our work with African Americans, we often see students of color facing conflict relative to supporting the beliefs, values, and norms of the different peer groups in their schools and communities. On the one hand, gifted students of color can associate with other gifted students in their courses; these students are likely to be White given the underrepresentation of students of color in gifted education, honors, and AP courses. Frequently, gifted students of color can associate with other diverse students (e.g., students with disabilities, etc.), too few of whom are likely to be identified as gifted. In too many cases,

Variable	Teacher	Minority Student Response or Outcome	Family Response or Minority Student Response or Outcome
Learning Environment	(1) Teacher adopts a colorblind philosophy—makes a conscious effort to not notice differences in students' cultural background, needs, values, traditions, etc. (2) Teacher does not accept or respect (i.e., rejects, disregards) the students' culture, including values, traditions, etc.	(1) Student feels invisible, insignificant, and/or unimportant in the classroom. (2) Student feels resentful, angry, offended because his or her culture is not addressed and/or affirmed. (3) Student does not feel like a member of the classroom; student feels like an outsider or intruder.	(1) Family perceives schools as hostile; feels devalued and unwelcome; family involvement decreases; options for family involvement are diminished (e.g., family may not wish to visit classrooms to discuss his or her culture during programmed events, etc.). (2) Family wants school to increase teacher diversity so that students have more cultural advocates and minority role models.
Curriculum and Instruction	(1) Teacher provides a monocultural, ethnocentric curriculum—the curriculum is devoid of a multicultural orientation. (2) Attempts to infuse multicultural content into the curriculum are low. (3) Diverse learning styles are not recognized or are recognized but not valued.	(1) Student is disinterested or disengaged; the curriculum seems irrelevant and meaningless (e.g., student wants to know "When I am going to use this?" "What does this have to do with me?"), uncomfortable (e.g., ashamed) with stereotypes and one perspective being presented. (2) Student fells angry and resentful about being silenced and/or stereotyped.	(1) School lacks a multicultural focus, but may consider it disrespectful to "tell the teacher how to do his or her job." (2) Family finds other means of ensuring the child has strong sense of culture (e.g., participates in culture events, etc.)
Student-Teacher-Family Relationship	(1) Teacher does not place much value on getting to know students; emphasis is placed on teaching his or her subject matter.	(1) Student values teachers who care. (2) Student wants teachers to get to know him or her personally.	(1) Family has little to no interaction with schools; may not confront teachers about concerns for fear of reprisals. (2) May elect to not have children participate in gifted programs; may place social needs of child over academic needs (e.g., wants child to be happy).
Expectations	(1) Teacher holds lower expectations for minority students (e.g., may not push a minority student to exert more effort on assignment); teacher may not refer minority students for gifted education screening	(1) Student self-expectations may decrease, including lowered aspirations, decreased motivation, and/or increased apathy. (2) Student may disidentify with academics. (3) Students may refuse to participate in gifted education opportunities.	(1) Family may resist or refuse to have their child participate in gifted services.

Figure 4. Components of cultural mismatch and possible outcomes
Note. Compiled from Elliott, Adams, & Sockalingam (1999); Ford (1999); Foster (2000); Maker (1989); Shade, Kelly, & Oberg (1999); and Storti (1989, 1998).

gifted students of color struggle to fit in with both groups; ultimately, they epitomize what W. E. B. DuBois (1970) described as "double consciousness"—the ongoing psychological struggle of trying to fit in two worlds—in this case, one's racial group and mainstream society. Leanita McClain, the first African American female elected to the Board of Directors of the *Chicago Tribune*, was subsequently perceived by many as acting White. She described the dilemma of bicultural stress most poignantly in her newspaper column, entitled "The Middle Class African American's Burden":

> I run a gauntlet between two worlds, and I am cursed and blessed by both. I travel, observe and take part in both; I can also be used by both. I am a rope in a tug of war. If I am a token in my downtown office, so am I at my cousin's tea. I assuage White guilt . . . I have a foot in each world, but I cannot fool myself about either . . . Whites won't believe that I remain culturally different; African Americans won't believe that I remain culturally the same. (McClain, 1986, p. 14)

McClain (1986) described this identity issue as "hellish confusion" whereby successful African Americans feel guilty and stressed about their success. Nevertheless, it sometimes leads African Americans to ask themselves, as did McClain, "I have made it, but where?" (Campbell, 1984, p. 74). McClain eventually committed suicide. This frustration, confusion and anger were more recently discussed in Ellis Cose's (1993) *Rage of a Privileged Class*. It appears that success does not come without a price for many persons of color.

Not surprisingly, then, many educators have noted a significant change in the aspirations of students of color toward academic achievement and social mobility (Moore, Madison-Colmore, & Smith, 2003; Ogbu, 2003; Ogbu & Simmons, 1998). In their work, Ogbu and Simmons distinguished between voluntary minorities and involuntary minorities. Briefly, he illustrated that voluntary minorities are individuals who *choose*—consciously and intentionally—to come to the United States in search of a better life and/or the "American dream." They, therefore, are open to the idea of assimilating and doing what is necessary to fit in and, of course, be successful. Many scholars have noted that Asian students and their families—voluntary minorities—epitomize what can happen when coming to the U.S. in search of the American dream. These groups are especially effective at assimilating and taking on the attitudes and behaviors that will improve their academic success. In examining achievement, attitudes, and behavioral differences (e.g., effort, studying, choosing academic-oriented friends) among African American, Asian, White and Hispanic adolescents in a large, longitudinal study, Steinberg et al. (1996) reported that Black students have the highest need for affiliation compared to all other groups. At the opposite end of this were Asian students, most of whom had the highest need for achievement and exerted effort to ensure high grades and test scores. This finding also appeared in the work of Mickelson (1990) and Ford (1992) who studied abstract and concrete ideals and ideas about achievement among different cultural groups. Both found that while African American students express high levels of belief in the value of school and doing well (abstract beliefs), they do not follow through this belief with concrete behaviors, such as studying, spending time on homework and so forth. Both authors also found that when pressed to delve into their beliefs, African American students are not as optimistic about the actual payoffs of working hard in school. And Steinberg et al.'s larger study found similar disturbing findings. Hence, while Asian Americans, Hispanic Americans, Native Americans, and African Americans are all considered "students of color," their different histories and experiences in the U.S. have contributed to different beliefs and needs. The most visible example of these differences is that Asian American students are the only group of students who are well-represented in gifted programs—the only group of color for whom stereotypes tend to be positive, and the only group with peer support for achievement.

Ogbu argued that many involuntary minority groups (especially African Americans and Native Americans) are not as eager or willing to assimilate. In most cases, these individuals did not *choose* to come to the United States. As a result, many involuntary minorities have developed, over time, an attitude of resistance to assimilation and any behavior that may lead one to believe that they have "sold out" and are "acting White" when they achieve (Corwin, 2001; Fordham, 1988; Suskind, 1998). For instance, to reinforce the belief that they are still legitimate members of their respective communities, many involuntary minorities may disengage psychologically from the academic process or channel their energies on non-academic things or activities that reflect their perceived cultural identity. With this anti-achievement ethic, many students of color from involuntary groups may underachieve, drop out, refuse to participate in gifted and AP courses, refuse to accept certain positions, and otherwise fail to reach their academic potential in school and life (Corwin, 2001; Ford, 1996; Fordham, 1988; Steinberg et al., 1996; Suskind, 1998). In sum, while all adolescents struggle with social acceptance, the struggle seems to be intensified among students of color who are members of involuntary minority groups. These students appear to be especially vulnerable to peer pressures and allegiance issues.

PSYCHOLOGICAL ISSUES FACING GIFTED STUDENTS OF COLOR: AFRICAN AMERICANS AS A CASE IN POINT

In 1996, Ford argued that people of color have been shortchanged in theories of self-concept because these theories have failed to consider racial identity in the context of self-concept, self-esteem, and overall self-perceptions. Attention to racial identity among students of color dates back to the early work of Kenneth Clark (1940) who used African American and White dolls to examine the extent to which African American children recognized themselves as racial or ethnic beings, and how they felt about being African American. Since then, countless studies have examined have been conducted examining racial identity issues for people of color, as well as Whites. Many of these studies postulate that students of color, such as African Americans, are more likely than their White counterparts to encounter psychological barriers to healthy racial identity development (Helms, 1989; Parham, 1989; Parham & Helms, 1985; Smith, 1989; Spencer & Markstrom-Adams, 1990). Racial identity concerns the extent to which people of color are aware of, understand, and value their racial background and heritage. A central question is: "Do students of color recognize and value their racial background and appearance?"

Individuals often define themselves in terms of racial membership in a particular group (Smith, 1989). Smith contends that a healthy regard for one's racial status is psychologically important for people of color. Race affects one's social-emotional and psychological health in significant ways because the complexity of racial identity development increases as a function of color and physical features. Smith also maintained that racial identity development is a process of coming to terms with one's racial group membership as a salient reference group. Aligned with this notion, Rotheram and Phinney (1987) defined self-identification as the accurate and consistent use of an ethnic label, based on the perception and conception of belonging to an ethnic group

Ford, Harris, and Schuerger (1993), Smith (1989), and others (Moore et al., 2005) have proposed that, for diverse adolescents, racial identity has a significant impact on achievement, motivation, and attitudes toward school. For example, in the earlier stages of racial identity development, described in the next section, adolescents of color may deliberately underachieve and choose not to participate in gifted programs to avoid peer pressures and accusations that they are "acting White," or they may camouflage their abilities to be accepted socially by their peers (Fordham, 1988, 1991, 1996; Ogbu, 2003; Ogbu & Simmons, 1998).

The issue of race may be more salient for students of color than for White students. For instance, White Americans are much less likely to experience the chronic stress and psychological problems associated with race because the color of their skin is not viewed with a deficit orientation and, thus, are not a barrier to academic and social success. Furthermore, racial oppression and discrimination can negatively affect the extent to which adolescents of color identify with their racial background and heritage; it can hinder their racial pride. As with self-concept and self-esteem, racial identity influences students' motivation, persistence, achievement, and relationships (Ford, 1996; Ford & Moore, 2004; Moore et al., 2005). Theories of racial identity exist for every major cultural group (see Ponterotto, Casas, Suzuki, & Alexander, 1995 or Ponterotto & Pedersen, 1994, for an overview of each theory); however, in this chapter, we focus on the most widely researched theory (Cross, 1971, 1995; Cross & Vandiver, 2001; Worrell, Cross, & Vandiver, 2001).

Racial Identity Among African Americans: A Case in Point

In his revised model of racial identity, entitled Nigrescence Theory and also referred to as the process of becoming Black, Cross and colleagues (Cross & Vandiver, 2001; Worrell et al., 2001) present eight identity types clustered into three major stages: (a) pre-encounter; (b) immersion-emersion; and (c) internalization. *Pre-encounter assimilation* describes the individual whose social identity is organized around his or her sense of being an American and an individual. Such individuals place little emphasis on racial group identity, affiliation, or salience. Consequently, the individual is not engaged in his or her respective community and culture. *Pre-encounter miseducation* depicts an individual who accepts without question, the negative images, stereotypes, and historical misinformation about his or her culture or community. This person commonly sees little strength in his or her culture and hesitates to engage in solving or resolving issues in his or her respective community. Furthermore, the individual often holds the attitude . . . "That's the way *they* act, but

I am different." The final pre-encounter type is called *pre-encounter racial self-hatred.* This individual often harbors negative feelings and experiences severe self-loathing as a result of his or her racial-ethnic membership. Cross and Vandiver (2001) contend that this dysfunction and group hatred limit the person's positive engagement with others assigned to the racial-ethnic group.

The next stage of identity, immersion-emersion, is characterized by two identity types. In *immersion-emersion anti-White*, the individual is nearly consumed with hatred of members of the majority group (e.g., Whites), and all that it represents. Frequently, he or she engages in social redemptive activities for the advancement of his or her racial-ethnic group, but is frequently full of fury and pent-up rage. In *immersion-emersion intense Black involvement*, the person often holds a simplistic, romanticized, and obsessive dedication to all things Black or other people of color. For example, a Black person engages in race-conscious activities in nearly a cult-like fashion and is subject to competitive yet insecure-related "Blacker-than-thou" social interactions with other Blacks.

The final racial identity stage, internalization, is comprised of three identity types. In *internalization nationalist*, the individual, particularly African American, stresses an Africentric perspective about him- or herself, other African Americans, and the world. Without question, this individual engages in the African American community and African American social struggles. *Internalization biculturalist* is an individual who gives equal importance to being a person of color and American. For example, an African American person is able to celebrate being both Black and an American, and is able to engage in both cultures without identity conflicts, doubt, and self-questioning. Finally, *internalization multiculturalist* is an exemplar of a Black person whose identity fuses between two or more social categories or frames of reference. The person is frequently interested in resolving issues that address multiple oppressions and is confident and comfortable in multiple groups.

Although a stage model, Cross and Vandiver (2001) acknowledged that individuals can regress or get stuck at any particular time as he or she progresses through the different stages. Whether a person regresses, progresses, or becomes stuck during the racial identity process depends, in large part on the individual's personality, support base, resources, and personal experiences. For example, African American adolescents in predominantly White settings (like gifted programs and AP classes) may experience more negative encounters based on race than those in predominantly African American settings. Those who are identified as gifted may also experience such encounters at an earlier age than students not identified as gifted and than students in predominantly African American settings. Relative to gifted African American adolescents, their perceptiveness, insightfulness, and keen sense of justice may push them through the racial identity stages at an earlier age and faster pace (Ford, 1996; Moore, 2001). The achievement of diverse students, including those identified as gifted, in the first five stages of identity is in jeopardy as these students grapple with their uncertain identity, allegiance issues, anger issues, and working within mainstream classrooms, gifted and AP classrooms, and the larger society (Ford & Moore, 2005).

Little, if any, age limitations were placed on the racial identity theory (Cross, 1971, 1995; Cross & Vandiver, 2001; Worrell et al., 2001). For example, one can experience a negative racial encounter at the age of 4, 14, or 40. Noteworthy, African Americans in predominantly White settings may experience more negative racial encounters than those in predominantly African American settings (Smith, 1989). Gifted African Americans in predominately White settings also may experience such encounters at an earlier age than African Americans in predominantly Black settings. Further, because of characteristics often associated with giftedness (insight-fulness, intuitiveness, sensitivity, keen sense of justice, etc.), gifted African American students may be especially aware of and sensitive to racial injustices and feelings of rejection and isolation.

One's stage of racial identity may also be related to achievement (Ford et al., 1993). Specifically, there may be a curvilinear relationship between racial identity and achievement, with those in the earliest stage (pre-encounter) and those in the last stage (internalization) having the highest achievement orientation. Achievement orientations and academic performance may be similar between those in the different stages (earliest vs. latest), but the extent to which the individual is perceived as "acting White" or "selling out" is different. Pre-encounter individuals, because of their low-salience or anti-Black attitudes, are likely to be rejected by the Black community; immersion-emersion and internalization individuals, because of their strong and positive racial identification, bicultural stance, and pluralistic perspectives, are more likely to be accepted by members of the Black community. Individuals in the middle stages of racial identity appear so subsumed with finding their identity that academic achievement may have low significance in their lives.

In addition to understanding the power and impact of racial identity in the lives of students of color, Steele (1997) maintains that they must be familiar with another issue—stereotype threat.

Stereotype Threat

Stereotype threat is a "situational threat"—a threat in the air—that, in general form, can affect the members of a group about whom a negative stereotype exists. Where African Americans are concerned, stereotype threat is a "social psychological predicament rooted in the prevailing image of African Americans as intellectually inferior" (Aronson, Fried, & Good, 2002). The idea here is that when stereotyped individuals are in situations where the stereotype applies, they bear an extra emotional, psychological, and cognitive burden. The burden that African Americans face concerns the possibility of confirming the stereotype in the eyes of others or themselves. Similarly, when females are asked to solve complicated mathematics problems, for example, they are at risk of confirming widely held stereotypes that females are inferior to boys in mathematics. It is not necessary that the individual even believes the stereotypes him- or herself. All that matters is that the person is aware of the stereotype and cares about performing well enough to disprove its unflattering implications (Aronson et al., 1999; Moore et al., 2003).

The most immediate effect of stereotype threat can be anxiety that under-mines performance (Osborne, 2001). In a series of experiments, Claude Steele, Josh Aronson, and their colleagues demonstrated that when African American or Latino college students are put in situations that induce stereotype threat, their performance suffers (Steele & Aronson, 1995). For example, African American and White undergraduate students in an experiment at Stanford University were told that the test they were about to take would precisely measure their verbal ability. A similar group of students was told that the pur-pose of the test was to understand the psychology of verbal problem solving and not to assess individual ability. When the test was presented as diagnostic of verbal ability, the African American students solved about half as many problems as the White students. In the non-threat situation, the two groups solved about the same number of problems. Anxiety and distraction were the main problems cited. The African American students were more likely to be thinking about the stereotypes as they tried to work (Osborne; Steele, 1997; Steele & Aronson). Thus, gifted students and culturally diverse students in general may operate in classrooms where they are concerned about confirming stereotypes. Psychologically, students carry the burden of "being a representa-tive" of "their" group. Attempting to demystify or change negative stereotypes also carries enormous burdens for students.

In summary, students of color encounter more barriers to racial identity development than White students (Helms, 1989; Parham, 1989; Parham & Helms, 1985; Smith, 1989; Spencer & Markstrom-Adams, 1990). Moreover, gifted students of color may have unique psychological and emotional stress-ors (Ford, 1996). In essence, Lindstrom and San Vant (1986) argued that gifted minority children find themselves in a dilemma in which they must choose between academic success and social acceptance. They quoted one gifted Black student who said, "I had to fight to be gifted and then I had to fight because I am gifted" (p. 584). In some situations, gifted or high-achiev-ing minority students may perceive academic achievement as a pyrrhic victory (Fordham, 1988; Ogbu, 2003). They win in one respect—academically, but lose in another respect—socially. Feelings of loneliness, isolation, and rejection increase, and the need for affiliation begins to outweigh the need for achieve-ment (Ford, 1996). When caught in this psychological and social tug-of-war, some African American students attempt to sabotage their achievement (e.g., procrastinating, failing to do assignments, exerting little effort, refusing to be in gifted education and advanced level classes; Ford, 1996; Ogbu; Ogbu & Simmons, 1998). Efforts are reprioritized, with energy devoted to seeking and securing social acceptance. Because of the many problems that can influence the psychological well-being of Black students, and because of our limited understanding of these problems, attention to racial identity development in educational settings is critical.

IMPLICATIONS AND RECOMMENDATIONS
FOR EDUCATORS AND PARENTS

In this section, we provide recommendations for educators and parents of gifted students of color. Our recommendations relate to not only counseling interventions, but educational interventions, as well.

Multicultural Counseling

Students of color experiencing racial identity difficulties and/or conflicts can profit from multicultural counseling. They need opportunities to share their concerns with other students who are gifted and come from diverse backgrounds. At minimal, the school counselor should have two goals: improving students' relationships and coping skills, and improving students' racial identities.

Social Experiences Focus

School personnel, such as school counselors, can also use small group and cooperative learning experiences to facilitate sharing and communication among students (Ford & Moore, 2004). Sessions may focus on such topics as coping with peer pressures and gaining conflict resolution skills and strategies. These strategies provide students of color with opportunities to establish friendships with White students and other diverse peers and to decrease feelings of isolation and alienation (Ford, 1996). Diverse students should also be encouraged to participate in extracurricular activities that promote social interaction and leadership. In essence, social and group experiences will give students of color an opportunity to talk about their lives and concerns as racial and cultural beings: To whom can students of color, such as African Americans, Latinos, and Native Americans, turn to for psychological, socio-emotional, and academic support? How do they feel about being identified and placed in a gifted program? How difficult is it to make friends and to share needs and concerns with others?

Racial Identity Focus

Counseling strategies and initiatives need to be designed to assist gifted students of color with poor racial identities (e.g., being in the pre-encounter, encounter, and immersion-emersion stages of identity) so that they may understand and appreciate their dual identities of being both gifted and diverse or "different." More specifically, White educators—teachers, counselors, and administrators—need to also understand that students in the encounter and immersion-emersion stages of racial identity may reject their help. These students may generalize negative perceptions of Whites in general to White counselors and educators (Bailey & Moore, 2004; Exum & Colangelo, 1981; Madison-Colmore & Moore, 2002; Moore, 2000). Therefore, educational professionals need to be patient and persistent in earning the trust of these students. On this note, a mentor or role model may be helpful in pushing diverse students in the pre-encounter, encounter, or immersion-emersion stages into higher and more positive stages of racial identities (ideally, the multicultural stage) (Moore et al., 2005). A mentor or role model can also help students in the higher racial identity stages to maintain their positive, healthy, balanced self-perception. Furthermore, Ford and Harris (1999) and Ford and Moore (2004) offered an extensive list of resources, particularly multicultural literature, as a way to enhance and nurture the racial identities of gifted diverse students.

Multicultural Education

It is essential that school personnel are cognizant of their biases and learned prejudices. Therefore, it is important that they evaluate the extent to which their curriculum and instruction affirm students of color's racial identities, while increasing all students' knowledge and acceptance of the nation's multicultural heritage (see Ford & Harris, 1999). How does the curriculum promote negative or positive images of students of color? Does the curriculum (e.g., topics and books) promote racial pride in students of color? Do students of color feel connected to the subject matter? Do they see themselves in the lesson plans and textbooks?

According to Banks and Banks (1995), few schools infuse multicultural content into the curricula, thereby leaving students of color often feeling disconnected to the subject matter and, at times, the school in general. When students—regardless of their racial background—do not see the curricula as personally relevant, they often become disinterested and unmotivated, and begin to underachieve (Ford & Harris, 1999). To improve school outcomes, Banks and Banks advised school personnel to focus less on the contributions and additive approaches and more on the transformation and social action approaches, as described in Figure 5. This advice is even more relevant for gifted students who excel in their capacity for autonomous learning and understanding of complex ideas.

Building Relationships

Multicultural education is more than just the curriculum. It is also about relationships and an atmosphere of mutual respect. Mutual understanding and respect between White students and culturally diverse students and between White school personnel and students of color are the ideals of multicultural education. In order to build such relationships, educators—teachers, counselors, and administrators—need to spend ample time getting to know students of color in regard to their dreams, values, and cultural traditions. Suggestions for providing students with a multicultural education, building positive relationships between minority and White students, and building positive student-teacher relationships are described by Ford (1996), Ford and Harris (1999), Ponterotto and Pedersen (1993), and in most multicultural books and articles (e.g., Banks & Banks, 1995; Lee, 1997; Ponterotto et al., 1995; Sue & Sue, 1990).

LEVEL 4
THE SOCIAL ACTION APPROACH

Students make decisions on important social issues and take actions to help solve them. Students become empowered to make meaningful contributions to the resolution of social and cultural issues/problems.

LEVEL 3
THE TRANSFORMATION APPROACH

The structure of the curriculum is changed to enable students to view concepts, issues, events, and themes from the perspectives of diverse racial and cultural groups. Students become more empathetic, culturally sensitive and aware. Educators are active and proactive in seeking training and experience with ethnically and culturally diverse groups.

LEVEL 2
THE ADDITIVE APPROACH

Content, concepts, themes, and perspectives are added to the curriculum without changing its structure. Students fail to understand how the predominant culture interacts with and is related to ethnically and culturally diverse groups.

LEVEL 1
THE CONTRIBUTIONS APPROACH

Focuses on heroes, holidays, and discrete cultural elements. Students acquire a superficial understanding of ethnically and culturally diverse groups. Students acquire stereotypes and misperceptions of diverse groups.

Figure 5. Levels of integration of multicultural content into curriculum

---

Multicultural Training for School Personnel

Thus far, our recommendations have focused on how educators can help gifted students of color. In this section, we offer a different set of recommendations that target educational professionals themselves. Ultimately, to work effectively with gifted students of color, educators, such as teachers and school counselors, require multicultural training. Such training is available through more than 700 ethnic studies and multicultural programs at colleges and universities around the country (Banks & Banks, 1995). School counselors require an understanding of self-perceptions that goes beyond self-esteem and self-concept when working with racially and culturally diverse students. Several professional counseling associations (e.g., American Counseling Association, Association for Multicultural Counseling and Development, American Psychological Association) have guidelines and position statements regarding multicultural competencies. School counselors wishing to build a positive and trusting relationship with ethnic minority students can take multicultural counseling courses offered at colleges and universities, attend multicultural workshops and conferences offered by professional associations, seek internships in urban communities, and subscribe to publications that address issues of diversity (Flowers, Milner & Moore, 2003).

Research Agenda

Compared to research on issues facing gifted students in general, research on gifted students of color is scant. For example, Ford (1996) reported that less than 2% of articles on gifted students focused on gifted diverse students. This lack of research and literature results in a dearth of knowledge from which to draw upon when seeking to work effectively with gifted students from diverse backgrounds. Simply put, we need gifted students of color to be the focus of more research. We need more research on all issues that threaten the psychological, social, academic, and cognitive well-being of gifted diverse students.

Parent Education

While the majority of this article has focused on the role of school personnel in promoting strong racial identities among students, the role of families cannot be overlooked (Herndon & Moore, 2002; Moore, 2001; Yan, 2000). Few parents or families have formal education and training in self-concept and racial identity theories. While some parents may be aware of the need to develop their children's self-concept, they may not know that the focus on self-concept must include racial identity. School counselors who have multicultural training are in the best position to provide training to minority families on this topic (Flowers et al., 2003). For instance, families can be taught how to: (a) discuss prejudice and discrimination with their children, (b) discuss negative peer pressures and resolving conflicts with their children, and (c) how to select books and movies that promote strong racial pride (see Ford & Harris, 1999 for a list).

SUMMARY

In the final analysis, culturally diverse adolescents live in a world and learn in schools that seldom affirm their cultural and scholar identities. Many adolescents of color, like adults, struggle to develop a healthy sense of self. This struggle seems especially difficult for diverse students who are identified as gifted. These adolescents frequently face negative peer pressures relative to doing well in school; they are often accused of "acting White"; and they are frequently alienated and isolated from their diverse peer group and White students alike (Ford & Moore, 2004; Moore et al., 2005). We believe, without questions, that when students of color develop healthy racial identities (namely, the internalization and internalization-commitment stages), they are freer to focus on the need to achieve; and when they develop healthy racial identities, these adolescents are less likely to succumb to negative peer pressures (Ford, 1996; Moore et al., 2005).

People are not born with both a self-concept and racial identity; these perceptions of self are developed over time, as we interact with others. Racial identities are formed at home, by the media, and in day cares, preschools, and throughout the educational pipeline (i.e., elementary, secondary, and postsecondary education) (Herndon & Moore, 2001; Moore, 2001). Thus, school personnel—teachers, school counselors, and administrators—must be aggressive and assertive about understanding the powerful influence that self-perception has on students' achievement and motivation (Flowers et al., 2003; Moore, Flowers, Guion, Yhang, & Staten, 2004).

REFERENCES

Aronson, J., Fried, C., & Good, C. (2002). Reducing the effects of stereotype threat on African American college students by shaping theories of intelligence. *Journal of Experimental Social Psychology, 38,* 113–125.

Aronson, J., Lustina, M. J., Good, C., Keough, K., Steele, C. M., & Brown, J. (1999). When White men can't do math: Necessary and sufficient factors in stereotype threat. *Journal of Experimental Social Psychology, 35,* 29–46.

Bailey, D. F., & Moore, J. L., III. (2004). Emotional isolation, depression, and suicide among African American men: Reasons for concern. In C. Rabin (Ed.), *Linking lives across borders: Gender-sensitive practice in international perspective* (pp. 186–207). Pacific Grove, CA: Brooks/Cole.

Banks, J. A. (1999). *Introduction to multicultural education* (2nd ed.). Boston: Allyn & Bacon.

Banks, J. A., & Banks, C. A. M. (Eds.). (1995). *Handbook of research on multicultural education.* New York: Simon & Schuster Macmillan.

Campbell, B. M. (1984, December). To be Black, gifted, and alone. *Savvy,* 67–24.

Clark, K. B., & Clark, M. K. (1940). Skin color as a factor in racial identification of Negro preschool children. *Journal of Social Psychology, 11,* 159–167.

Corwin, M. (2001). *And still we rise: The trials and triumphs of twelve gifted inner city students.* New York: Perennial.

Cose, E. (1993). *The rage of a privileged class.* New York: HarperCollins.

Cross, W. E., Jr. (1971). Toward a psychology of Black liberation: The Negro-to-Black conversion experience. *Black World, 20,* 13–27.

Cross, W. E., Jr. (1995). The psychology of Nigrescence: Revising the Cross model. In J. G. Ponterotto, J. M. Casas, L. A. Suzuki, & C. M. Alexander (Eds.), *Handbook of multicultural counseling* (pp. 93–122). Thousand Oaks, CA: Sage.

Cross, W. E., Jr., & Vandiver, B. J. (2001). Nigrescence theory and measurement: Introducing the Cross Racial Identity Scale (CRIS). In J. G. Ponterotto, J. M. Casas, L. A. Suzuki, & C. M. Alexander (Eds.), *Handbook of multicultural counseling* (2nd ed., pp. 371–393). Thousand Oaks, CA: Sage.

Dubois, W. E. B. (1970). *The souls of Black folk.* Greenwich, CT: Fawcett. (Original work published in 1903)

Elliott, C., Adams, R. J., & Sockalingam, S. (1999). *Multicultural toolkit.* Retrieved July 26, 2005, from http://www.awesomelibrary.org

Exum, H. A., & Colangelo, N. (1981). Culturally diverse gifted: The need for ethnic identity development. *Roeper Review, 3,* 15–17.

Flowers, L. A., Milner, H. R., & Moore, J. L., III. (2003). Effects of locus of control on African American high school seniors' educational aspirations: Implications for preservice and inservice high school teachers and counselors. *The High School Journal, 87,* 39–50.

Ford, D. Y. (1992). Determinants of underachievement as perceived by gifted, above-average, and average Black students. *Roeper Review, 14,* 130–136.

Ford, D. Y. (1995). *A study of achievement and underachievement among gifted, potentially gifted, and average African-American students.* Storrs, CT: The National Research on the Gifted and Talented.

Ford, D. Y. (1996). *Reversing underachievement among gifted Black students: Promising practices and programs.* New York: Educators College Press.

Ford, D. Y., & Harris, J. J., III. (1999). *Multicultural gifted education.* New York: Educators College Press.

Ford, D. Y., Harris, J. J., III, & Schuerger, J. M. (1993). Racial identity development among gifted Black students: Counseling issues and concerns. *Journal of Counseling and Development, 71,* 409–417.

Ford, D. Y., Harris, J. J., III, Tyson, C. A., & Frazier Trotman, M. (2002). Beyond deficit thinking: Providing access for gifted African American students. *Roeper Review, 24,* 52–58.

Ford, D. Y., & Moore, J. L., III. (2004). The achievement gap and gifted students of color. *Understanding Our Gifted, 16,* 3–7.

Ford, D. Y., Moore, J. L., III, & Milner, H. R. (2005). Beyond cultureblindness: A model of culture with implications for gifted education. *Roeper Review, 27,* 97–103.

Fordham, S. (1988). Racelessness as a factor in Black students' school success: Pragmatic strategy or pyrrhic victory? *Harvard Educational Review, 58,* 54–84.

Fordham, S. (1991). Peer-proofing academic competition among Black adolescents: "Acting White" Black American style. In C. E. Sleeter (Ed.), *Empowerment through multicultural education* (pp. 69–93). Albany, NY: State University of New York Press.

Fordham, S. (1996). *Blacked out: Dilemmas of race, identity, and success at Capital High.* Chicago: The University of Chicago Press.

Fordham, S., & Ogbu, J. U. (1986). Black students' school success: Coping with the burden of acting White. *The Urban Review, 18,* 1–31.

Frasier, M. M., Garcia, J. H., & Passow, A. H. (1995). *A review of assessment issues in gifted education and their implications for identifying gifted minority students.* Storrs, CT: The National Research Center on the Gifted and Talented.

Helms, J. E. (1989). Considering some methodological issues in racial identity counseling research. *The Counseling Psychologist, 17,* 227–252.

Herndon, M. K., & Moore, J. L., III. (2002). African American factors for students success: Implications for families and counselors. *The Family Journal: Counseling and Therapy for Couples and Families, 10,* 322–327.

Lee, C. C. (Ed.). (1997). *Multicultural issues in counseling: New approaches to diversity* (2nd ed.). Alexandria, VA: American Counseling Association.

Lindstrom, R. R., & San Vant, S. (1986). Special issues in working with gifted minority adolescents. *Journal of Counseling and Development, 64,* 583–586.

Madison-Colmore, O., & Moore, J. L., III. (2002). Using the H. I. S. model in counseling African-American men. *The Journal of Men's Studies, 10,* 197–208.

Maker, J. (1989). *Critical issues in gifted education: Defensible programs for cultural and ethnic minorities.* Austin, TX: Pro-Ed.

McClain, L. (1986). *A foot in each world: Essays and articles.* Evanston, IL: Northwestern University Press.

Mickelson, R. (1990). The attitude-achievement paradox among Black adolescents. *Sociology of Education, 63,* 44–61.

Milner, H. R. (2002). Affective and social issues among high-achieving African American students: Recommendations for teachers and teacher education. *Action in Teacher Education, 24,* 81–89.

Moore, J. L., III. (2000). Counseling African American men back to health. In L. Jones (Ed.), *Brothers of the Academy: Up and coming Black scholars earning our way in higher education* (pp. 248–261). Herndon, VA: Stylus.

Moore, J. L., III. (2001). Developing academic warriors: Things that parents, administrators, and faculty should know. In L. Jones (Ed.), *Retaining African-American faculty, administrators, and students in the 21st century and beyond* (pp. 77–90). Herndon, VA: Stylus.

Moore, J. L., III, Flowers, L. A., Guion, L. A., Zhang, Y., & Staten, D. L. (2004). Investigating nonpersistent African-American male students' experiences in engineering: Implications for success. *National Association of Student Affairs Professionals Journal, 7*, 105–120.

Moore, J. L., III, Ford, D. Y., & Milner, E. (2005). Recruitment is not enough: Retaining African-American students in gifted education. *Gifted Child Quarterly, 49*, 51–67.

Moore, J. L., III, Madison-Colmore, O., & Smith, D. M. (2003). The prove-them-wrong syndrome: Voices from unheard African-American males in engineering disciplines. *The Journal of Men's Studies, 12*, 61–73.

Ogbu, J. U. (2003). *Black students in an affluent suburb: A study of academic disengagement.* New York: Lawrence Erlbaum.

Ogbu, J. U., & Simmons, H. D. (1998). Voluntary and involuntary minorities: A cultural-ecological theory of school performance with some implications for education. *Anthropology and Education Quarterly, 29*, 155–188.

Osborne, J. W. (2001). Testing stereotype threat: Does anxiety explain race and gender differences in achievement? *Contemporary Educational Psychology, 26*, 291–310

Parham, T. A. (1989). Cycles of psychological Nigrescence. *The Counseling Psychologist, 17*, 187–226.

Parham, T. A., & Helms, J. E. (1985). Relation of racial identity attitudes to self-actualization and affective states of Black students. *Journal of Counseling Psychology, 32*, 431–440.

Ponterotto, J. G., Casas, J. M., Suzuki, L. A., & Alexander, C. M. (Eds.). (1995). *Handbook of multicultural counseling.* Newbury Park, CA: Sage.

Ponterotto, J. G., & Pedersen, P. B. (1994). *Preventing prejudice: A guide for counselors and educators.* Newbury Park, CA: Sage.

Reis, S. M., & Callahan, C. M. (1989). Gifted females: They've come a long way—or have they? *Journal for the Education of the Gifted, 12*, 99–117.

Rotheram, M. J., & Phinney, J. S. (1987). Introduction: Definitions and perspectives in the custody of children's ethnic socialization. In J. S. Phinney & M. J. Rotheram (Eds.), *Children's ethnic socialization.* Newbury Park, CA: Sage.

Shade, B. J., Kelly, C., & Oberg, M. (1997). *Culturally responsive teaching.* Washington, DC: American Psychological Association.

Smith, E. M. J. (1989). Black racial identity development. *The Counseling Psychologist, 17*, 277–288.

Spencer, M. B., & Markstrom-Adams, C. (1990). Identity processes among racial and ethnic children in America. *Child Development, 61*, 290–310.

Steele, C. M. (1997). A threat in the air: How stereotypes shape the intellectual identities and performance of women and African Americans. *American Psychologist, 52*, 613–629.

Steele, C. M., & Aronson, J. (1995). Stereotype threat and the intellectual test performance of African-Americans. *Journal of Personality and Social Psychology, 69*, 797–811.

Steinberg, L., Brown, B. B., & Dornbusch, S. M. (1996). *Beyond the classroom: Why school reform has failed and what parents need to do.* New York: Simon & Schuster.

Storti, C. (1991). *The art of crossing cultures.* Yarmouth, ME: Intercultural Press.

Storti, C. (1998). *Figuring foreigners out.* Yarmouth, ME: Intercultural Press.

Sue, W., & Sue, D. (1990). *Counseling the culturally different: Theory and practice* (2nd ed.). New York: Wiley.

Suskind, R. (1998). *A hope in the unseen: An American odyssey from the inner city to the Ivy League.* New York: Broadway Books.

Worrell, F. C., Cross, W. E., Jr., & Vandiver, B. J. (2001). Nigrescence theory: Current status and challenges for the future. *Journal of Multicultural Counseling and Development, 29,* 201–213.

Yan, W. (2000). Successful African American students: The role of parental involvement. *Journal of Negro Education, 68,* 5–22.

TWICE-EXCEPTIONAL ADOLESCENTS

Who Are They?
What Do They Need?

by Susan M. Baum, Mary G. Rizza, & Sara Renzulli

CHAPTER 6

y fear of getting sick began to take over and increasingly get in the way. I could sense my relationships crumbling, and I felt entirely out of control to stop the process. It was like my life had become a movie. And I was watching it fall apart, but I was powerless to do anything about it, I was no longer in control of the action. Like all seventh graders I wanted to be liked and accepted. But my anxiety and my shame about that fear got in the way. Even when I was confronted about my isolating antisocial behavior, I was unable to admit the truth. I chose to lose friends rather than own up to my fears. (Abeel, 2003, pp. 65–66).

Samantha Abeel, a highly gifted writer, was diagnosed with a learning disability in seventh grade. She had pronounced difficulty telling time and counting money, and had problems with language arts skills such as spelling and punctuation. By the time she was identified with a learning disability, she was under severe stress. Persistent questions haunted her. She wondered how she could be smart and still have debilitating weaknesses in those simple things her peers could perform with no effort. There were many trips to the doctor for stomach aches, and panic and anxiety attacks began to surface.

In truth, her academic and learning issues paled in comparison to the social and emotional concomitants of being considered a twice-exceptional student.

WHO ARE TWICE-EXCEPTIONAL STUDENTS?

The term *twice-exceptional* refers to students who have or show potential for remarkable gifts and talents in specific areas, but whose deficits and difficulties in learning, paying attention, or meeting social and emotional expectations impede their development. For too many practitioners, however, the terms *deficits* and *giftedness* are incompatible, therefore being twice-exceptional is an impossible phenomenon. In fact, many youngsters who are bright, but who have been diagnosed with some sort of disability are more likely to receive special education services than talent development opportunities. Likewise some gifted students use their talents to mask their learning difficulties and struggle in school to compensate for undiagnosed problems, thus obscuring their need for special education support. These students are often seen as lazy or over anxious, and are expected to "shape-up," as in the case of Samantha (Baum & Owen, 2003; Davis and Rimm, 2004; Reis, McGuire, & Neu, 2000).

Twice-exceptional students do exist and have a unique set of academic, social, and emotional needs. The very dichotomy of abilities and disabilities that comprise their dual diagnosis sets them apart from their peers who are identified as gifted and from those who receive special education services (Baum & Owen, 2003; Brody & Mills, 1997; Lovecky, 2004; Neihart, 2000; Olenchak & Reis, 2002). In fact, twice-exceptional students require dual differentiation in order to meet their often-contradictory sets of needs (Baum, Cooper, & Neu; 2001). We will discuss these unique needs later in the chapter and describe how developmental needs of adolescence exacerbate the issues.

A Closer Look at Exceptionalities

Some still deny that students with special needs can also be gifted. Uneasiness about the apparent contradiction stems primarily from faulty ideas and stereotypical images associated with the notion of giftedness and disabilities. If professionals associate giftedness with high achievement, superior IQ scores, and profound verbal abilities, they may have difficulty believing that some gifted students may not be able to read, spell, attend to tasks, or relate well with others. These biases often exclude bright students from learning support and/or prevent students with learning disabilities, attention deficit, or Asperger's syndrome from being identified as gifted (Coleman & Gallagher, 1995; Davis and Rimm, 2004; Neihart, 2000). There is evidence that an increasing number of gifted students also struggle with learning and behavioral challenges such as: Attention Deficit Disorder, a specific learning disability, behavior disorders, or social issues relating to autism or Asperger's syndrome. (Baum & Olenchak, 2002; Kaufman, Kalbfleisch, & Castellanos, 2000; Neihart, 2000; Neu, 2003). Most of these students are dramatically underserved or misunderstood (Baldwin & Valle, 1999; Webb et al., 2005).

Table 1
Characteristics of Psychological Diagnoses

Attention Deficit Disorder (AD/HD)	Conduct Disorders (Oppositional Defiant Disorder; ODD)	Specific Learning Disabilities (SLD)	Asperger's Disorder (AD)
Fidgets, squirms, is restless; Has difficulty remaining seated	Argumentative, has temper tantrums	Speaks well, but reads poorly; Confuses similar letters and words May have problems reading the social context (nonverbal learning disability) Has difficulty understanding or following directions	Quantitative impairment in social interactions (manifests at least two); Lack of nonverbal behaviors Failure to develop peer relation-ships; Lack of spontaneous seeking to share interests, joy, or achievement; Lack of social or emotional reci-procity Restricted repetitive and stereo-typed patterns of behavior, inter-ests, and activities; Preoccupation with one or more stereotyped and restricted patterns of interest abnormal in either intensity or focus;
Difficulty following directions and finishing tasks	Irritable, cruel fights	Has difficulty in expressing or organizing thoughts verbally or in writing Has difficulty functioning when there is no structure or predictabil-ity; (nonverbal learning disability)	Apparently inflexible adherence to specific nonfunctional routines or rituals; Stereotyped or repetitive motor mannerisms Persistent preoccupation with parts of objects
Easily distracted	Hyperactive and distractable	Short attention span, easily dis-tracted, is overactive or inactive	No delay in cognitive development
Often interrupts or intrudes on others	Impulsive	Is clumsy	No delay in language
Often engages in physically danger-ous activities without considering possible consequences (not for purpose of thrill-seeking) e.g. runs into street without looking	Poor peer relations, teases, shows off	Is impulsive, cannot wait, cannot foresee circumstances	Clearly significant impairment in social, occupational, or other important areas of functioning
Blurts out answers to questions	Demanding, stubborn, moody	Difficulty with math; Has trouble understanding time and distance	

Note. Compiled from *Diagnostic and Statistical Manual of Mental Disorders IV-TR*, by American Psychiatric Association, 2000, Washington, DC: Author. Copyright© 2000 by American Psychiatric Association.

To be twice-exceptional, then, is to demonstrate gifted behaviors or traits at cer-tain times, under certain circumstances, in certain areas (Gardner, 1999; Renzulli, 1999; Sternberg, 1997; U.S. Department of Education, 1993), but simultaneously experience problematic weaknesses in other areas. Consider Nelson Rockefeller, whose outstanding leadership potential is well known, but who was also dyslexic. His reading, writing, and spelling skills were highly deficient. David Neeleman, the founder of Jet Blue airlines was diagnosed with AD/HD, and Temple Grandin, a researcher in the field of animal science, has autism.

Bright students with learning or behavior challenges may have a dual diagnosis that combines giftedness with one or more of the following psychological diagno-ses: Attention Deficit/Hyperactivity Disorder (AD/HD), conduct disorders such as Oppositional Defiant Disorder (ODD), specific learning disabilities (SLD), or Asperger's syndrome (AS). To become more familiar with these psychological cat-egories, we provide a table of salient behavioral characteristics as described in the Diagnostic and Statistical Manual IV-TR (APA, 2000) in Table 1.

An examination of these behaviors reveals an overlap in behaviors across diagnostic categories. Diagnosis, therefore, becomes complicated, as one category may take precedence and the nuances of a dual diagnosis may be missed. In fact, many of these students are classified with multiple labels. For instance, a high percentage of gifted students with AD/HD have also been found to have a learning disability (Lovecky, 2004; M. Cherkes, personal communication, April 4, 2003). The question then becomes which of the labels is the underlying cause of the problem and which is an outcome of the disability area. Sometimes this multiple labeling stems from faulty diagnosis, inappropriate interventions, or a lack of understanding of the complex interactions between giftedness and learning differences (Baum & Olenchak, 2002; Webb et al., 2005). Misdiagnosis also occurs because there is a lack of awareness or attention given to the unique needs of gifted students. When bright students are forced to complete work that is inappropriate, they can exhibit characteristics that are oppositional-defiant. When bright students can't read because of a learning disability, they can have a difficult time paying attention. Some students are gifted in spatial areas, but have difficulty attending to and processing verbal information (Gardner, 1999; Silverman, 2002; West, 1997). For the purpose of this chapter, we choose to use the term twice-exceptional to avoid being caught up in a specific label that may or may not be accurate. Instead we can focus on the general issues that are involved when bright students learn and behave differently than their gifted peers due to some sort of disability (Webb et al., 2005).

What Is it Like to Be Twice-Exceptional?

To gain a better understanding of and a sensitivity for the academic and emotional frustrations faced by twice-exceptional students, the third author of this chapter shares her own story—one with which many twice-exceptional students can identify. Through her words, we can relive her experiences and identify the issues facing twice-exceptional students. Her experiences serve as a platform for discussing the issues both theoretically and practically.

Sara's Story: Part One

Where I am today and where I started 18 years ago are two very different places. Today I am about to enter my sophomore year at Union College in Schenectady, NY, where I plan to major in history and minor in political science. I hope to get my master's degree in public history and eventually make historical documentaries for public television.

I enrolled in kindergarten when I was 5, but within 2 weeks was moved up to first grade because I could not deal with the excessive amount of noise in the room. In addition, I was bored. The curriculum was far too easy. I had already learned the colors, numbers, and the alphabet at home. The 2 weeks that I did spend in kindergarten found me in the corner crying. I could not focus or relax with so much activity and noise taking place in one room. The overstimulation made my brain hurt.

Skipping kindergarten and going directly to first grade created an unanticipated problem. I wasn't able to read or write even though I seemed to have the readiness skills. At 6-years-old I began to develop strategies to keep my inabilities a secret. All through elementary school I would just try to go unnoticed. I thought that if I could be invisible and keep my teachers and peers in the dark about what I couldn't do, I could escape the embarrassment. My inability to read when all my other classmates could was devastating. Luckily, I had a wonderful memory and was able to memorize several books that my parents had read to me at home. I actually knew what word my finger should be under and when I should turn the page. When it came to writing, I used another trick. Whenever we had to hand in writing samples to the teacher, I would use the same method. I actually memorized paragraphs. Yes, I created all of these techniques to mask "my problem." Sadly, the teachers found out and promptly placed me in remedial reading, math, and writing programs beginning in the third grade. I was devastated to be in those programs, because it was now clear to my whole class that I was one of the stupid kids. None of my friends were in "those" classes, why did I have to be? I was just like them in gym and art, why was I so different in the regular classroom? These were questions that continued to plague me throughout my educational experience.

THE PROBLEM

The Elementary Years

The major issues confronting twice-exceptional students during the elementary years are the initial awareness of the problem and how to cope with the evolving discrepancies between what they can and cannot do. Without appropriate diagnosis and effective programming, these students become confused and depressed and doubt their academic abilities (Brody & Mills, 1997; Whitmore, 1985). In many ways, Sara's story typifies the experiences of twice-exceptional students as they begin to be challenged by the requirements of school. Heretofore, many of these students, like their gifted peers, appear advanced in their development in terms of knowledge, vocabulary, and interests (Kingore, 1998). The idea that there could be a problem is alarming. Entering school with its demands for sitting still, following directions, focusing, and learning to read and write brings to light, often for the first time, the uneven profiles manifested by twice-exceptional students, exposing their weaknesses. For Sara, it centered on reading; for Samantha it was math. Other bright youngsters find difficulties paying attention, putting their ideas in writing, getting along with peers, or following routines. The discrepancies between gifts and talents and problematic weaknesses can cause twice-exceptional children to feel like failures, lowering their academic self-efficacy (Baum & Owen, 2003). Identification and access to appropriate programming become essential. The longer it takes to identify students and provide them with accommodations, the more problematic it is for students, parents, and teachers to cope with the inconsistencies in performance and behavior, as described by Sara.

In Sara's case we see that her early years are marked by dichotomies. She knows she is bright; in fact, she skipped kindergarten. How then can she reconcile the fact that she is smart with the fact that she can't read like her classmates? Like most gifted students with academic challenges, coping with the reality of academic inconsistencies became an ongoing frustration for Sara (Baum & Olenchak, 2002; Reis et al., 2000). Even in their early years, gifted students try to hide their deficits. To reveal a weakness would be akin to admitting failure. Sara's tactic to "just try to go unnoticed" is a common reaction to the confusion experienced because of the mixed messages about talent and learning problems. For students who are first identified as gifted, the realization that there might be a problem is unfathomable. Their entire self-worth is based in their ability to be smart, or at least to appear that way. When problems in school start to arise, the first reaction is often to withdraw, as we see in Sarah's case. Her horror at being placed in remedial classes reinforced her feelings of "being dumb" and her academic self-efficacy worsened.

There are many strategies used by twice-exceptional students to fit in or compensate for their academic difficulties, some appropriate and some highly problematic (Baum & Owen, 2003; Moon, 2003; Whitmore, 1985). Many twice-exceptional students develop strategies on their own and are able to elude detection far longer than their counterparts who are not gifted. As we see in Sara's case, memory played an important role in helping to appear successful. Reading problems are especially difficult to identify early because students are able to memorize words and passages or get enough information from auditory stimuli to maintain the façade of reading. Many twice-exceptional students, like Sara, are able to elude detection until middle school; some because of successful coping strategies and others because their abilities mask their disability areas. The ability for these students to mask or compensate for weaknesses places them at risk for appropriate diagnosis. Their gifts may hide the disability as the advanced abilities of these students often distract professionals from discovering the gaps in skills. For instance, in the case of students with Asperger's syndrome, their advanced knowledge precludes consideration for a disability (Neihart, 2000). In Sara's case, the school was reluctant to believe she had a disability as she remained on grade level in many areas due to her ability to compensate for her weaknesses and her willingness to put forth extraordinary efforts to achieve. Some twice-exceptional students are at risk for not having their gift identified. Students who fail to learn their letters, decode words, or memorize simple math are flagged much earlier for educational assessment. Once identified as having a special need, little or no attention is given to recognizing or identifying any gifted potential. Much evidence documents the resistance of schools to look for or to develop gifts and talents among classified students receiving special education services (Baum & Owen, 2003; Cline & Hegeman, 2001; Coleman, Gallagher & Foster, 1994).

Part Two of Sara's story describes her middle school years, where she was identified as having a learning disability, but never received the kind of programming that would eventually help her to compensate for her weaknesses and develop her gifts and talents, as well. Her increasing feelings of failure compounded by issues of adolescence negatively impacted her attempts at success and happiness.

Sara's Story: Part Two

By the fifth grade (which was my first year of middle school), I was still having trouble reading, and was reading mainly by memory. My parents constantly told me that everyone was good at different things. So maybe reading was not "my thing," but I still had to read to make it through middle school. From the time I was 3-years-old, I had participated in a premature infant study conducted by researchers at the University of Connecticut where they annually tested my IQ, which was around 130. With such high potential, it was difficult to understand why I could not read. This was incredibly frustrating to me. At this point in my life I had two conflicting situations taking place. At home each night my parents would reteach material and I felt smart, but at school I felt dumb because no one understood how I learned, and no one could help me. With the enormous help of my parents, who read to me for hours and hours every night, and my younger sister, who began reading at the age of three and was always willing to help me, I slowly began to read. A major turning point in my learning how to read was finding books that related to hobbies that I had. The Saddle Club was the first series of books I read on my own. I even began to enjoy reading because it related to my real passion at the time, horseback riding.

In fifth grade I moved from my small elementary school to a larger middle school. The transition was a hard one for me; there were so many new kids and my group of elementary friends was split up. I did not enjoy going to school at all and could not wait to get home every day. Academically, I was struggling. The workload was heavier, and because I was still very slow at reading and writing, it took me a long time to do my assignments. During the early years of middle school, my parents continually questioned my teachers about the discrepancy between my performance on school achievement tests, which were in the 2nd percentile, when my verbal IQ score was at the 99th percentile. My fifth grade math teacher, Mrs. P., noticed that I got every single math problem wrong because I copied the material incorrectly from the board. It was then that I was referred for testing and it was confirmed that I had a learning disability. Being identified as having a learning disability was a relief to me, and I felt as if a large weight had been taken off my shoulders. As soon as I was identified, I began working during free periods with an LD specialist who helped me understand my disability. At that point I began the long process of trying out a variety of compensation strategies. I was identified with dyslexia, an auditory processing problem, and Attention Deficit Disorder.

I completed fifth grade and things looked like they were improving academically and socially. For the first marking period of sixth grade I traveled with my parents who were taking sabbatical. I received individual tutoring, and when I returned to school, I felt on level with the rest of my classmates for the first time. I even found pleasure in reading. This new sense of academic confidence spread outside the classroom. I found the courage to go out for recreational basketball. There I found a whole new group of friends, who are still my best friends to this day.

I left sixth grade feeling good about myself and my ability to be successful in school, but seventh and eighth grade were turbulent times. Not only was I in the heart of adolescence, but I was also in with the popular crowd at school and did not want to have anything wrong with me. I was extremely embarrassed about my learning disability and would go to great lengths to hide it from my peers. Fearing that they would not understand, I decided it was better to avoid talking about it than to explain it. Although I received accommodations for my disabilities, I was reluctant to use them or discuss them. I did not want to be different. I would pretend to not hear kids ask me where I was during the test, or why I left the class to go to "that" room. However, pretending it did not exist was nearly impossible because the curriculum was getting much harder and my methods of dealing with my learning disability were not yet developed. Rather than type everything on a computer to make up for my spelling, I just rushed through any writing I had to do, purposely writing in a messy way so the teacher might overlook the spelling errors. Rather than take notes in class, I would zone out, look out the window, and watch the second hand on the clock tick on.

Concurrent with these feelings of academic inadequacy were tremendous feelings of guilt when I received a good grade. I somehow felt I was cheating because of my accommodations. On one occasion, when I received a good science grade, a fellow student told me that the only reason I got the grade was because I had taken the test in a different room, and the adults answered everything for me. These insensitive remarks had a long lasting effect on my fragile sense of self. Each one caused my spirits to plummet. In fact, I continue to this day to feel guilty about receiving accommodations for my disability. I cannot pinpoint where this guilty feeling comes from inside of me, but it probably has to do with not wanting to be different from my friends.

The Middle School Years

Once identified, Sara received assistance from the LD specialists and tutors to help her with her academics. This was a temporary reprieve for her, as she finally understood why she experienced difficulty on certain academic tasks, and she began to work with the learning specialist to develop appropriate compensation strategies. By chance, Sara also was afforded high levels of enrichment as she traveled with her parents during the first semester of sixth grade. Experiential learning within a non-competitive environment allowed her to learn in ways appropriate to her style. In short, Sara's problem was identified; she was receiving academic support, and had educational enrichment as well—all essential ingredients in twice-exceptional programming (Brody & Mills, 1997; Olenchak & Reis, 2002). Unfortunately, seventh and eighth grade reversed her feelings of academic self-efficacy and self worth. As academic challenges increased, so did her needs for accommodation. Each day she felt alienated from her classmates and marginalized—a term used by Cline and Hegeman (2001) to explain how these students participate in two different cultures—that of the gifted child and that of the disabled. Indeed, what was Sara's identity? How could she preserve the concept of being a highly able and capable young woman, when she felt different and frustrated?

Adolescence and Identity

As these students continue their educational journey through middle and high school, the challenges of being twice-exceptional become more complicated and may have dire social, academic, and emotional implications if not addressed. Contributing factors relate to the predictable stressors of adolescence, the issues of being gifted, and the learning problems caused by the specific disability. Each of these factors exerts pressure on the student and confounds development in general.

As is commonly acknowledged, identity issues define adolescence. Knowing who you are and where you fit is the main task of this developmental stage (Erikson, 1968). Normal development requires exploration and flexible boundaries with regard to role taking and behavior. Gifted students may have difficulties with this stage, because their abilities set them apart from their peers (Coleman & Sanders, 1993). According to Coleman & Cross (2001) gifted students manage their identity in three different ways:

- becoming highly visible (often seen as school leaders, contest winners, and enthusiastic participants in many activities);
- becoming invisible by hiding or camouflaging their talents to appear normal; and
- disidentifying with gifted peers by demonstrating or adopting the behaviors of a more desirable group.

For the twice-exceptional student, the conflict of adolescence is compounded by the possibility that they may not be seen as gifted, normal, or disabled, thus not fitting into any group. Which behaviors they hide and which they assume align to their individual personalities. For Sara, it was identifying with the popular group in school (most of those students were also bright). To do this she tried to hide her disability. However, hiding the disability is an ineffective strategy because it becomes increasingly difficult as schoolwork becomes more challenging. Due to twice-exceptional students' lack of prowess in the academic curriculum, peers and teachers don't regard these students as having gifts and talents. Some peers and teachers take the attitude that any high grade must be attributed to the use of learning accommodations, an experience Sara faced. These setbacks were difficult for Sara as she struggled to identify with the popular students and chose to hide her learning disability, believing her friends would never understand it.

Indeed the maturity needed to believe it is OK to have learning and behavior challenges, specific gifts and talents, and still fit in socially is usually not present during middle school years. These students often go to great lengths to mask those behaviors that make them seem different and less able. For instance, a dyslexic student who was a highly intelligent and talented artist would not let her peers know she couldn't read for fear of being laughed at or disrespected (Baum & Owen, 2003). Another youngster, who was extremely bright but autistic, was purposely obnoxious to her middle school peers as a protection against being rejected (Olenchak, personal communication, July, 1995). A gifted middle school boy whose grades dropped terribly in middle school due to an undiagnosed learning disability became the class clown and playground bully to divert attention from his lack of school success. (Baum, Renzulli, & Hébert, 1995).

Academically, other confusions abound. Some twice-exceptional students may be placed in remedial programs or in classes with fewer challenges and intellectual peers. In this setting, twice-exceptional students may also feel disconnected from the group because of the lack of commonality they share with more average students. In short, twice-exceptional students will simultaneously feel less capable than their gifted peers and more capable than their peers in special education, thus causing them to question who they are. This lack of group identity influences the successful navigation of the school's social scene. Twice-exceptional students, by virtue of their unique learning profiles, may be misunderstood by their peers. Other students cannot make the leap in understanding that someone who is able to succeed in one area may need assistance in another. Many people, adults included, still find it a difficult concept to comprehend.

Twice-exceptional students may react to this misunderstanding by either withdrawing from their peers or acting out. Their acute sensitivity and painful awareness of the lack of congruence between academic potential, school achievement, and social competence can cause many of these students to become extremely depressed and require counseling and/or medication to deal with their frustration over discrepancies between what they can and cannot do. Part Three of Sara's story depicts how these issues punctuated her adolescent existence in high school.

Sara's Story: Part Three

I started high school in this highly-charged emotional state. I had little self-confidence and was not prepared for the social or academic issues that would confront me in this new setting. The high school was much bigger than the middle school and highly academic in its philosophy. On my first day of high school, I walked into my honors biology class where the teacher welcomed us to our new world by lecturing us in what seemed to me to be a foreign language. The scientific vocabulary she used seemed suitable for a Ph.D. seminar!

This honors biology class proved to be my worst nightmare in ninth grade. Because I failed most of the tests, the teacher agreed to try an alternate form of the test, but she used language in the questions that even my LD specialists could not understand. My grade went from D- to a D. I had no idea how to study or take notes in this class. I would sit and listen to the lecture and begin writing something down, but was easily distracted as the lesson went too quickly, with few concrete examples or visual organizers. My notes were useless, the text, incomprehensible. I was completely lost. I had to do something. Making the decision to switch from advanced biology to average level biology was the first of many changes I made to my schedule.

After receiving a number of failing grades on tests in other subjects, including English and keyboarding, the school team counselor decided to move me down to average level classes because they thought I was not smart enough to handle the material. In their minds, if I could not pass the written test, I did not understand the material.

In keyboarding class, we were expected to copy from a textbook onto a Word document with a wood box over our hands to see how proficient we became at typing; however, what proved to be a major issue for me is that they would not let me use spell check. After several meetings with the teacher about this, an agreement was finally reached where I could type my document, print it out and then go to the resource room and have someone edit it by hand. After a few weeks of doing this, the keyboarding teacher lashed out at me in front of the whole class after I asked if I could go upstairs to edit something. She quipped, "Edit your work here, you don't need to go upstairs."

I was humiliated, mortified, embarrassed, and distraught after this incident. I am someone who prefers to understate things rather then overstate them. I prefer private conversations to discuss my additional needs and subtle procedures when using accommodations. My mother spoke with the teacher, attempting to explain that a severely dyslexic student should be allowed to use spell check on all documents. To this the teacher responded, "I once had dyslexia, but I got over it." I wanted to scream at the woman. She embarrassed me in front of my peers. I wanted to pose this question to her: "Do you think I wanted to have dyslexia? Do you think I asked for this, just like I would ask for a Christmas present?"

After this event took place in my freshman year, I became even more introverted. I did not want to approach my teachers at all, fearing that a similar situation would occur. I preferred to do everything through my LD teacher. That one single action by a teacher really shook me up, and it took me a very long time to get over. This one incident was a major step backwards in my attempt to become more independent and advocate for myself. I felt that all my teachers thought that it was a problem to have me in their classroom. I felt like the teachers should receive extra compensation to have students like me in their classrooms; after all, I was a burden that they had no time or energy to handle.

Even with the constant reassurance of my parents that I was smart, I still felt dumb. The few teachers who bothered to really get to know me in the regular level classes noticed right away that I was smart and not challenged in these classes. They saw me as a "fish out of water." Yet, even with these statements, which were reassuring in some small way, my grades continued to be poor because I could not take traditional tests. I couldn't help wondering why, if I were as smart as everyone was telling me, I could not get good grades in these non-challenging classes.

My one saving grace in public school was the law class I took sophomore year. This class tapped into all of my best attributes. My excellent verbal skills and critical thinking abilities served me well in this class. I was excelling in this class, and my teacher became one of my biggest advocates at the school. He insisted on attending all of my IEP meetings and helping me to plan a future in law. Law class allowed me to combine my passion for history with the law when examining Supreme Court cases. The class introduced me to the world of public speaking. That same year I joined the state mock trial team and took on twice as much work as everyone else. It was worth it as I preformed wonderfully at the competitions. At least I had one shining moment in this otherwise dismal high school existence. I was doing well and had another adult advocate who was more than willing to speak up for me and guide me through the rest of my days there.

My unhappiness in high school was not confined to the classroom. I was separated from all of my middle school friends, mainly because they were all in honors classes. I hardly ever saw any of them, even in the hallway. I was also extremely shy and did not feel comfortable enough to go and introduce myself to all of these new strangers. Instead of trying to make new friends, I spent most of my free time in the special education room getting to know the people there. Spending time in the resource room was my refuge from the stressors around each corner. It became my favorite place to be during the day.

My unhappiness was not limited to the hours of school either; I was still depressed after I got off the bus at night. My parents tried everything to lessen my worsening state of depression—getting me a second dog, taking me to the mall countless times, and sending me to a therapist. The dog is still a joy in all of our lives, and the mall was greatly appreciated, but the therapist did not help, in my opinion. Rather than understanding my misery at school and supporting my ideas of leaving the public school in favor of a private institution, she looked at the situation as if it was a torn piece of paper that could be fixed with the right amount of tape. I felt that, if the therapist did not understand what I was going through, no one else would.

Even wonderful support of my LD specialist and my law teacher was not enough to keep me at the school; there were just too many depressing situations that I went through daily. When I was not in law class or in my LD room, I often felt like I was in a jungle with people out to devour me, bit by bit. Not all of the awful aspects were because of the teachers. Noise from building construction, bomb threats, and crowded hallways all became distracters and began to eat away at me. When there was little left to bite off, I made the decision to look at private schools.

The High School Years

Sara's transition to high school illustrates many of the issues faced by twice-exceptional students in similar situations. Being successful at the high school level demands intellectual fortitude and self-regulation, especially if students elect to, or are selected to, participate in rigorous academic programs such as honors and AP courses or the International Baccalaureate program. These classes usually demand proficiency in—and expect lots of—reading, listening, and note taking. Students are expected to complete long written assignments involving synthesis and organization of information. They are also expected to work at higher levels with little acknowledgement of differences in learning needs. All too often, teachers of high ability students expect these students to take responsibility for their own learning, without adequately preparing them for the task.

This was the attitude Sara encountered when she entered high school. Although she qualified for the honors classes, Sara needed accommodations to succeed. Some of her teachers seemed to resent such assistance and showed little empathy for her situation. Humiliating comments and low expectations by teachers and peers, increased demands for student self-regulation, and ongoing failure to perform well on traditional measures chipped away at Sara's identity as a gifted learner. For Sara and students like her, there is a fine line between understanding and accepting differences, which could mean refusing accommodations in order to fit in. Adults, and specifically teachers, play an important role in fostering self-efficacy and overall functioning in school (Deci & Ryan, 2002; Ryan, Stiller, & Lynch, 1994). Among the components that place a student at risk during high school are their perceptions of their own competency, autonomy, and relatedness (Ryan & Deci, 2000). When schools fail to promote these important factors, the student suffers. Without the support and understanding of her teachers, Sara began to question her abilities and entertained feelings of stupidity. These feelings diminished when she was able to spend time with adults who believed in her abilities—her law teacher and the learning disabilities specialist. In their presence, Sara felt capable and valued. These adults focused on her gifts and provided support for her learning difficulties. Continued frustrations with meeting expectations of self and others, however, ultimately caused her to withdraw academically and socially, and to become deeply depressed.

Depression is a common by-product of adolescence (Neihart, 2002) and may be a risk factor especially among high-ability children (Altman, 1983; Webb, Meckstroth & Tolan, 1982). Factors relating to the characteristics of gifted students, such as asynchronous development, perfectionism, social isolation, and sensitivity, may cause them to be more susceptible to depression (Neihart, 2002). For twice-exceptional students the stressors are magnified. Like Sara, these students' reality is coping daily with the discrepancy between what they can and cannot do. Their perfectionism prevents them from viewing achievement with accommodations as success experiences. They have difficulty finding a peer group with whom to identify, and extreme sensitivity makes twice-exceptional students acutely aware of their plight. Due to these factors it is not surprising that many twice-exceptional adolescents take medication for depression (Baum & Owen, 2003; Olenchak & Reis, 2002) and lose their motivation to achieve. At this juncture counselors can help students to accept their differences, to identify what they need to be successful and to advocate for their own needs. Reversing the downward spiral will most often require creating more appropriate learning environments for these students. In Sara's case, she chose to attend a private school.

Sara's Story: Part Four

I chose to attend a highly reputable private school in New England. Looking back on the experience, I don't think I knew what I was getting into; the only thing I knew was that I was going to a different place—I did not understand the magnitude of the change that would take place in my life. I would gain a new family with friends and acquaintances from all places and walks of life. I would be facing the most rigorous academic challenges. The transition was eased by the enormous support of the school community of caring teachers, advisers, dorm parents, and classmates. Academic adjustment was my first goal. I had just gotten a test back for which I really studied hard. I rejoiced in my score of 80 until a classmate commented, "Oh, that's too bad, there is always the next one to improve on." I had always thought a grade of 80 was reputable and knew it surpassed my usual scores in the 60s. The school staff was not accustomed to working with students who had a learning disability, but were willing to try to accommodate my learning needs. I took mostly English and history classes during my time there, taking advantage of the wide variety offered. The classes were small, usually under 10 people, and mostly discussion based, which was wonderful for me, because it was another way to show the teacher that I knew what I was talking about. Having the smaller classes also made me interact with the teachers, and within a month into the academic year, I was very comfortable with talking to my teachers about my special needs once again. It was incredibly reassuring knowing that, if I made the effort to go talk to teachers, they would equally make the effort to help me do the best that I could in their class. These teachers were committed to having all their students be successful, and it showed every day.

My performance in the classroom required extensive work outside of the classroom. Because, as I mentioned earlier, I took mainly history and English classes, I had enormous amounts of nightly reading. I developed a strategy for taking notes on what I read that helped me to understand classroom discussions. Not all of the girls worked as hard as I did, and I was jealous of the ones who did not have to. But, I firmly believed that someday all of my work would pay off. My strategies for reading all the material continually developed into methods that worked for me. For example, I read all of my history textbooks by section, highlighting and taking notes on that section before moving on to the next one. This allowed me to have all the material that was purposely put together in my head at one time, then down on paper together without ideas or facts from other sections possibly interfering. I also realized that for extensive note taking typing was the best method, because I could take advantage of various outline forms. I found that when I put information into these outlines I understood it in a much easier way, possibly because it was organized. After realizing this, I began taking the notes I had taken in class and putting them into an outline format, complete with bullets and color-coding. After I became very comfortable with this format, I began to implement it in class. In many ways I began to hear a teacher's lecture differently, and much more effectively. Naturally, the more organized the teacher was, the better and easier it was for me. This system of outlining has proved very effective for me as a method of absorbing information.

Taking obsessive notes forced me to stay very focused in class. In AP art history, for example, I photocopied all of the images we studied and shrunk them to half their size or less and put a copy of the image in my notes and another copy on a note card to study from. Yes, it was a lot of work, and my binder looked more like a textbook than anything else. But, it was what I had to do to be successful, and it was the only way I knew I could make myself successful in that situation.

The greatest challenges and most rewarding academic experiences came from my independent study and Advanced Placement classes in high school. In these classes I was able to shine and show everyone including the teachers, administrators, and peers that I was smart and passionate about schoolwork. I actually began tutoring most of my classmates before tests and helping them plan their papers. Being able to help my peers in the AP classes was so gratifying and so different from previous situations and positions I had been in. I finally was feeling competent and smart.

Social adjustment at the new high school took awhile. At first, I avoided big social interactions with all the girls that knew each other in favor of interacting with my advisee group or just a few "new juniors." At the beginning of junior year I also started taking Zoloft, which is an anti-anxiety medication. I think it helps me feel more comfortable in social situations, as well as more comfortable with test anxiety and other potential stressors. It also gave me courage to engage socially and participate in school activities. After much convincing on the part of my parents, I tried out for the debate team, and even more surprisingly I made it. The coach was a strict taskmaster who was known for pushing the debaters to their limits and making many of them cry in practice. For my first few weeks on the team, I laid low, preferring to learn all the tactics and be more involved as a researcher. But lo and behold, the day before a tournament someone dropped out and I was the replacement. After having to redo everything myself and memorize the eight minute constructive, I was convinced that if I just got through the tournament alive I could quit the team the following Monday. I could claim that I was just not "debate material." Contrary to my prediction, my partner and I ended up winning the team award and taking the two top slots for individual speaking. After that win, my confidence soared. One of the top debaters on the renowned high school team and others on campus commented on my accomplishments. I continued to excel at debate and attended the top program in the country that summer at Northwestern University with my debating partner. The two of us went on to be cocaptains of the team and had much success together in competitions. I met many of my closest friends through debate. It is a talent that I am blessed to have.

The friends that I made at my private high school are a second family to me; they are the people I look forward to seeing the most when on vacation, and often the people I want to tell big news to first. I believe I was able to make these friends because I became comfortable with who I was. A large part of that was figuring out on my own how to deal with my learning disability and be as successful as I could possibly become. My friends know I have a learning disability, but it is not how they define me. They define me by all my weird, quirky traits that make up my character. In public school I was defined by my learning disability; often, teachers would come up to me and say "your reputation precedes you," but in a negative way. They viewed me as the special ed kid with tough parents. At my private high school, the only reputation that preceded me was my love of history and my superior public speaking skills. That positive restart freed me from the negative bonds that held me captive and played havoc with my self-esteem.

MEETING THE NEEDS
OF TWICE-EXCEPTIONAL ADOLESCENT STUDENTS

Sara's journey, while unique, articulates important issues that confront many twice-exceptional students as they grapple with making sense of their world—academically, emotionally, and socially. These issues include:

- Finding appropriate academic challenge and talent development opportunities (Baum & Owen, 2003; Brody & Mills, 1997; Kaufman et al., 2000; Lovecky, 2004; Olenchak & Reis, 2002).
- Offering a learning environment that aligns to how these students learn (Baum & Olenchak, 2002; Baum, Olenchak, & Owen, 1998; Lovecky, 2004; Silverman, 1989).
- Discovering individual compensation strategies to regulate learning and behavior, including metacognitive strategies, appropriate medication as indicated, and academic accommodations (Kaufman et al., 2000; Neihart, 2002; Reis et al., 2000; Weinfeld, Barnes-Robinson, Jeweler, & Shevitz, 2002).
- Learning how to balance academic and social needs (Baum & Owen, 2003; Lovecky, 2004; Reis et al., 2000).

How these issues play out in the lives of twice-exceptional students is idiosyncratic to their individual personalities, family values, and school opportunities (Moon, 2003; Neihart, 2000; Olenchak & Reis, 2002). Looking back at Sara's story confirms that she had difficulty trying to satisfy her cognitive and social needs until she entered private school. She struggled with the need for challenge and the need for an appropriate learning environment. Feeling that she couldn't compete in the most rigorous classes with her high achieving friends, she placed herself in lower level classes. However, her need for challenge and her intellectual curiosity played havoc with her fitting in socially with students who were less motivated. Like many gifted students, Sara was highly perfectionistic (Olenchak, 1994). She set high standards for herself and often refused to accept accommodations that she felt gave her an advantage. To meet her own expectations for achievement she chose instead to expend considerable time and effort to her academics. Driven by their need, some choose to abandon social life and extracurricular activities and spend many hours completing assignments. Others may do the opposite and give up trying. To fail because one didn't hand in an assignment is preferable to struggling with it and receiving a low grade (Baum & Owen, 2003). In either case, these students become discouraged and depressed during the high school years.

Sara's solution was to enter private school where she attended small classes along with her intellectual peers. The small class placement helped her to deal with her auditory processing problems, and the high level discussion enhanced her ability to attend to curricula. The school encouraged her to participate in activities that nurtured her interests. In Sara's case, the debate team provided her with an effective talent development opportunity. Her high motivation to succeed required her to develop cognitive strategies to compensate for her difficulties with attention, auditory processing, organization, and memory. Her particular strategies aligned with both her sequential learning style and her perfectionistic personality. Residing with others facilitated more social engagement. All of these factors helped Sara to correct the causes of her depression. Successfully competing with non-disabled but talented debaters enhanced her self-worth and reinforced her feelings that she was smart and capable. Sara also began accepting the fact that she is twice-exceptional, while focusing on her gifts as she plans for her future.

What Can We Learn From Sara's Experience?

Most students will not have the luxury of attending private schools, but some public schools can provide many of the same accommodations Sara found in a private setting. Programs for these students in the public sector have offered flexible opportunities in class placement, and instruction, as well as talent development opportunities (Baldwin, 1995; Nelson, 2000; Weinfeld et al., 2002). Indeed, research on successful kinds of interventions (although sparse and usually focused on gifted students with learning disabilities) does offer evidence of the need to focus on strengths and talents (Baum, 1985; Cooper, Baum & Neu, 2004; Lovecky, 2004; Moon, 2003; Neihart, 2002). As Neihart (2002) explains,

> Effective interventions are always those that are tailored to the unique strengths and needs of the individual. There is wide agreement in the literature on gifted children with learning problems that, as a general strategy, interventions should focus on developing the talent while attending to the disability. Keeping the focus on the talent appears to yield more positive outcomes and to minimize problems of social and emotional adjustment. (p. 3)

Indeed, traditional remedial practices such as making tasks simpler, providing less stimulation, and proceeding at a slower pace can result in more frustration and inattention, especially for gifted AD/HD students (Moon, 2002).

Schools need to design educational programs that consider the whole student. For typically developing gifted students, academics pose few problems (Davis & Rimm, 2004). Likewise, gifted students without disabilities tend to have high academic efficacy, positive self-esteem, and well-honed social skills as compared to their nongifted peers (Field et al., 1998). Advanced classes and talent development opportunities can meet their need for challenge, stimulating teachers, and opportunities for higher-level thinking. Unfortunately, the case is quite different for twice-exceptional students. They, too, require challenging opportunities, but in an environment that is both stimulating and accommodating.

THE COMPREHENSIVE PLAN

A comprehensive educational plan for these students needs to address the issues of talent development, the least restrictive learning environment, appropriate curriculum and instruction, and social and emotional support in order to address the issues mentioned previously (see Table 2). The challenge we face is that most individual educational plans focus on student deficits. Even parents may be reluctant to push talent development when the students struggle with the core subjects. However, selective attention to only some of these elements greatly compromises the effectiveness of programs designed to nurture individual development of twice-exceptional students.

An Appropriate Identification System

Comprehensive programs begin with appropriate diagnosis. As mentioned earlier, identification of twice-exceptional students remains a great challenge (Coleman et al., 1994; Johnson, Karnes, & Carr, 1997; Webb et al., 2005). The disability may be obscured because the student is not falling below grade level. To identify learning problems, it is necessary to examine discrepancies between potential and performance. Subtest scores on intelligence tests, time and support necessary for the students to complete assignments, and classroom performance all provide important information (Baum & Owen, 2003). Classroom performance and test scores can prevent appropriate identification if a student has learning or behavioral difficulties. Likewise, conservative and rigid identification procedures complicate the identification of students' abilities and gifts. Rather, to identify students' gifts, schools should analyze individual subtest scores and patterns on tests of intelligence, as well as emphasize authentic assessment of talent within specific domains using student products, auditions, and interviews (Baum & Owen).

Table 2
Essential Program Components

An appropriate identification system
- Identification of giftedness
- Evidence and description of academic performance discrepancies

Attention to the student's gifts
- College courses
- AP classes
- Honors Programs
- Online courses
- Mentorships and internships
- Specialized programs and competitions

Placement in, and assurance of, the least restrictive supportive environment(s) (Continuum of Services)
- Regular classroom with support
- Resource room support
- Special classes for gifted
- Special classes for twice-exceptional
- Special schools for twice-exceptional

Classroom intervention strategies
- Alternate approaches to curriculum and instruction for all students
- Accommodations and modifications allowed for all students
- Self-regulation and compensation strategies provided
- Remedial support as needed

Social and emotional support
- Group counseling
- Family counseling
- Individual counseling

Note. From *To Be Gifted and Learning Disabled: Strategies for Helping Bright Students With LD, ADHD, and More,* by S. Baum and S. Owen, 2003. Copyright ©2003 by Creative Learning Press. Adapted with permission.

Attention to Students' Gifts

Twice-exceptional students require opportunities to display and develop specific gifts or talents. Attention to the development of students' gifts has many advantages. First, talent development has resulted in dramatic growth in the twice-exceptional students' self-regulation, perceptions of ability, and academic achievement (Baum & Owen, 2003; Birely, 1991; Cooper, Baum & Neu, 2004; Neihart, 2000; Neilson, 2002). Talent development also allows these students to find their individual niche so that they can have a productive and rich life. Documentation of students' extraordinary accomplishments in a talent area provides evidence of achievement necessary to the continuance of education at the appropriate institutions of higher learning. Last, but perhaps most important, are the current views on what constitutes happiness and satisfaction in life. Recent research suggests that the happiest people make life and career decisions that align with their individual strengths, interests, and passions (Gardner, 1999; Goleman, 1995; Sternberg, 1997). By making sure twice-exceptional students appreciate and develop their unique gifts, we can furnish them with self-knowledge and skills that will promote their self-actualization.

For the adolescent especially, talent development offers another benefit—the opportunity to meet others with similar gifts and interests. Such common attributes form the basis for socialization, friendships, and identity. Opportunities for talent development for twice-exceptional students include special classes, internships and mentorships, college classes, competitions, and clubs and activities (Olenchak & Reis, 2002; Weinfeld et al., 2002).

Placement in, and Assurance of, the Least Restrictive Supportive Environment(s)

The setting that offers twice-exceptional students their finest chance for success depends on various factors, including the severity of the disability, the nature of the gift, and the age of the student. The regular classroom environment, coupled with time in the resource room for academic support and time in a talent development program, can work effectively for many of these students, especially if the learning environments value individual differences and provide options for how students acquire information and express what they have learned. However, if these gifted students' reading levels are considerably below grade level and their ability to write is greatly impaired, or if attention problems demand settings with fewer students, success in the regular classroom is doubtful, especially as the students get older and reading and writing dominates the academic setting. Particularly problematic is the fact that these students are sensitive about their disabilities and may prefer to hide their differences. They may be unwilling to accept a particular accommodation if they feel it makes them look stupid or disabled in the eyes of their peers. For these students, special classes, special schools, or varied opportunities for individualized learning may be best. Some students simply need a small class size in a seminar-like setting where they are more comfortable asking questions and actively engaging in the curriculum. Others may elect to take online courses where the challenge, pace, and environment can so easily be controlled.

Albuquerque, NM, and Montgomery County, MD, boast two highly successful programs for twice-exceptional students (Neilson, 2002; Weinfeld et al., 2002). Both these programs offer a continuum of services based on the severity of the needs of the individual students. These services range from inclusion to self-contained special classes for gifted students with learning or attention difficulties. Schools that try to find ways to accommodate the needs of twice-exceptional students fare much better than those that insist that the students fit into traditional offerings (Davis & Rimm, 2004). Samantha (the student mentioned at the start of this chapter) attended public high school. She was enrolled in honors classes except for mathematics, her area of her disability. She enrolled in general math courses and was tutored in math by the special education teacher during middle school and high school. Her English teacher became her writing mentor to help Samantha publish a book of poetry, *Reach for the Moon* (Abeel & Murphy, 1993), while still in high school. Samantha then began giving talks to elementary students about what it was like to have a learning disability. Her success with writing gave her the confidence she needed to work effectively with others and to put forth time and energy to conquer her math challenges.

Bill, a student with learning and attention challenges, also attended public high school. This school provides a special seminar program for twice-exceptional students conducted by a guidance counselor. During these group sessions, students receive social, emotional, and academic support. This counselor works with the students and their families to create a viable program that works for the individual student. When Bill failed ninth grade biology, he was encouraged to take a summer AP course in biology instead and earned an A+. This fast-paced class, with the majority of sessions spent in the laboratory, aligned perfectly to Bill's learning strengths. Learning by doing was much preferred over listening to a lecture. Bill also was overwhelmed by the amount of homework required in typical classes. Thus, he chose to complete high school in 5 years so that he could proceed at his own pace. Bill attended some honors courses in math and enrolled in an online course in English because his attention was much improved when using technology. Taking the online course also allowed him to adjust his own pace of learning. To earn additional high school credit in science, he took an independent study with his chemistry teacher and served as a lab assistant during his senior year. Bill and a friend used their summer to produce an award-winning international science fair entry.

Creative solutions that allow these students to learn in ways that align to their strengths while providing them with the skills they need to be successful are essential elements in providing appropriate learning opportunities for twice-exceptional students.

Classroom Intervention Strategies

Twice-exceptional students need dually differentiated curriculum and instruction (Baum, Cooper, & Neu, 2001). Strategies used in the classroom must take into account the advanced cognitive abilities of gifted students while simultaneously addressing the academic and social challenges caused by the specific disability. In short, curriculum and instruction must afford the students the opportunity to develop their skills and talents in ways that accommodate for problematic weaknesses. Table 3 illustrates the idea of dual differentiation as it summarizes a sample of characteristics of gifted learners and some academic and social challenges facing the twice-exceptional learner. The final column provides the dual differentiation. The characteristics and suggestions are based on research focusing on learning traits and successful practices for the targeted populations.

Providing a dually differentiated curriculum provides embedded accommodations into curriculum and instruction. In their study of successful high ability college students with learning disabilities, researchers found that these students had learned how to study and take notes, developed unique strategies for achievement based on their learning styles and talents, and could advocate for accommodations they needed to be successful such as the use of technology and additional time for

Table 3
Fundamentals of the Dually Differentiated Curriculum

Characteristics of Gifted Students	Problems Arising from the Disability (Including learning disability, AD/HD, Asperger's syndrome)	Curricular Accommodations
(Baum, Renzulli, & Hebert, 1995; Cramond, 1994; Emerick, 1992; Rimm, 2002; Rogers, 2002; Schuler, 2002; Silverman, 2003, 1989)	(Abeel, 2003; Baum, Olenchak, & Owen, 1998; Baum & Owen, 2003; Brody & Mills, 1997; Kaufman, Kalbfleisch, and Castellanos, 2000; Lovecky, 2004; Moon, 2002; Mooney & Cole, 2000; Neihart, 2002; Reis et al., 2000; Zental et al, 2001)	(Baum, Cooper, & Neu, 2001; Baum & Owen, 2003; Cooper, Baum, & Neu, 2004; Gentry & Neu, 1998; Kaufman, Kalbfleisch, and Castellanos, 2000; Lovecky, 2004; Moon, 2002; Nelson, 2000; Olenchak & Reis; 2002; Weinfeld et al., 2002; West, 1997; Zental et al., 2001)
Propensity for advanced-level content to accommodate the gift or talent.	Limited skills in reading and math.	Alternate means to access advanced information.
Producers of new knowledge through authentic products.	Difficulty with spelling and handwriting.	Alternate means to express ideas and create products; unlimited use of technology.
Creative and spatial learning styles.	Poor organization.	Visual organization schemes (e.g., timelines, flow charts, webbing).
Intellectual challenge based on individual talents and interests.	Problems with sustaining attention and focus.	Interest-based authentic curriculum; high stimulation; more time for tasks.
Need to identify with others of similar talents and interests.	Inappropriate social interaction; Immaturity; Often interact better with individuals younger or older.	Group identity based on talent or ability; multi-aged groupings.
Heightened sensitivity to failure.	Low self-efficacy and esteem.	Recognition for accomplishment.

test taking (Brody & Mills, 1997; Moon, 2002; Nelson, 2000; Olenchak & Reis, 2002; Reis et al., 2000; Weinfeld et al., 2002).

Social and Emotional Support

For twice-exceptional adolescents, social and emotional support is a high priority (Baum & Owen, 2003; Brody & Mills, 1997; Nelson, 2000). Several studies looking at the emotional needs of gifted students with learning disabilities found these students had more extensive feelings of failure (Baum, 1985), deep frustrations over the discrepancies of what they can and cannot do (Schiff, Kaufman, & Kaufman, 1981), and the need for counseling as they dealt with mild depression to contemplation of suicide (Reis et al., 2000). According to Olenchak (1994), ongoing stress of living through school-related frustration may require in-depth individual support to help twice-exceptional youngsters deal with their duality of traits.

New challenges and difficulties offer mixed messages about perceived ability and projections for the future. Students need opportunities to talk about their feelings, to learn how to advocate for themselves, and to set goals that align to their gifts and talents. Counseling can help them deal with depression and anger that they may feel as they struggle with the inconsistencies in their performance. Group, family, and individual counseling all offer promise in assisting these special youngsters to develop strategies for coping with their dual exceptionality. In addition, counseling should help these youngsters to gain an acceptance of being twice-exceptional.

When twice-exceptional students are placed in an appropriate learning environment where their gifts are honored and accommodations are made, these students begin to excel. For some like Sara, support included medication (her doctor did prescribe an antidepressant) and a more appropriate setting as opposed to formal counseling. Her success in this educational setting contributed to her ability to cope with being both gifted and learning disabled.

CONCLUSION

School for the twice-exceptional student is rarely a positive experience, but for the adolescent learner, it can be a nightmare. On the one hand, these students have remarkable gifts and talents that need development. When these students are so engaged, their efficacy soars. We see these students apply extraordinary energy to accomplish goals and engage productively in academic challenges. On the other hand, these youngsters struggle with simple tasks like organization, writing, spelling, reading, or paying attention. In those times, students find themselves in survival mode fighting to stay afloat. This Jekyll and Hyde profile was evident throughout Sara's story. We saw her blossom when involved in classes that tapped her talents and respected her intelligence, and wilt when deprived of the nurturance needed. Unfortunately, most educational settings focus on the deficit areas of students, often without consideration for their intellectual, social, and emotional needs. Under those conditions, twice-exceptional students become trapped in mediocrity resulting in diminished self-efficacy and motivation.

As discussed, the primary need for students during adolescence is the development of a positive identity. Adolescents need to know who they are and what they can achieve. They need to associate with others who are like them in an environment where they feel productive and valued. Because of the learning difficulties faced by twice-exceptional learners, they often find themselves in situations where they are not competitive and cannot perform simple tasks. When identity is tied into academic competence, twice-exceptional students may be at a disadvantage because of the disparate nature of their abilities. It may be difficult for them to completely understand where they fit in. In addition, this confusion can impede the development of a healthy sense of self. Poor sense of self also thwarts the development of social relationships and may lead to a sense of alienation.

When the disability area is emphasized in his or her schoolwork, the student may form an identity that is tied to what he or she cannot do. If the work is perceived as too easy, the student may form the opinion that he or she is incapable or unworthy. When expectations are low, students may also perceive themselves as working to their potential because that is what is expected of them. In either case, the student's motivation is at risk and the possibility for underachievement is great.

To combat these issues we suggested a comprehensive educational plan consisting of five critical elements:

- identification of disabilities and gifts;
- opportunities for talent development;
- placement in the least restrictive environment where physical, intellectual, and emotional needs can be met;
- provision of a dually differentiated curriculum providing challenge, appropriate instruction, accommodations for problematic weaknesses, and compensation strategies; and
- social and emotional support.

Sara found a school that had challenging courses and unique ways of delivering the curricula. The small-sized classes, high expectations, and opportunities to excel on the debate team were exactly what she needed to build her confidence and to develop a strong identity as a debater, writer, and friend. With this newly found confidence, Sara is tackling the challenge of college. We conclude with Sara's final reflection:

> After the many different experiences under my belt, I've often thought: If I could take any of them back, would I? Absolutely not. While I went through a good amount of depression, embarrassment, and unhappiness, it was all of those emotions and bad experiences that make me realize how good things have become and how to keep the good in place. One of the biggest lessons I've learned is not to make the main focus of my life my disability, but rather to focus on what I am good at and what I love to do. It is with that knowledge that I am going forth into my sophomore year at Union College.

REFERENCES

Abeel, S. (2003). *My thirteenth winter: A memoir.* NY: Orchard Books.

Abeel, S., & Murphy, C. R. (1994). *Reach for the moon.* Duluth, MN: Pfeifer-Hamilton Publishers.

Altman, R. (1983). Social and emotional development of gifted children and adolescents: A research model. *Roeper Review, 6,* 65–67.

American Psychiatric Association (2000). *Diagnostic and statistical manual of mental disorders* (4th ed., text revision). Washington, DC: Author.

Baldwin, L. (1995). *Portraits of gifted learning disabled students: A longitudinal study.* Unpublished doctoral dissertation, Teachers College, Colombia University, NY.

Baldwin, A., & Valle, W. (1999). *The many faces of giftedness: Lifting the mask.* Ontario: Wadsworth Publishing.

Baum, S. (1985). *Learning disabled students with superior cognitive abilities: A validation study of description behaviors.* Unpublished doctoral dissertation, University of Connecticut, Storrs, CT.

Baum, S. M., Cooper, C. R., & Neu, T. W. (2001). Dual differentiation: An approach for meeting the curricular needs of gifted students with learning disabilities. *Psychology in the Schools, 38,* 477–490.

Baum, S., & Olenchak, F. (2002). The alphabet children: GT, ADHD and more. *Exceptionality, 10,* 77–91.

Baum, S., Olenchak, F., & Owen, S. (1998). Gifted students with attention deficits: Fact and/or fiction? Or, can we see the forest for the trees? *Gifted Child Quarterly, 42,* 96–104.

Baum, S., & Owen, S. (2003) *To be gifted and learning disabled: Strategies for helping bright students with LD, ADHD, and more.* Mansfield Center, CT: Creative Learning Press

Baum, S., Renzulli, J. S., & Hébert, T. (1995). *The prism metaphor: A new paradigm for reversing underachievement.* Storrs, CT: The National Research Center on the Gifted and Talented.

Birely, M. (1991). The paradoxical needs of the disabled gifted. In M. Birely & J. Gensheft (Eds.), *Understanding the gifted adolescent: Educational, developmental, and multicultural issues* (pp. 163–175). New York: Teachers College Press.

Brody, L. E., & Mills, C. J. (1997). Gifted children with learning disabilities: A review of the issues. *Journal of Learning Disabilities, 30,* 282–296.

Cline, S., & Hegeman, K. (2001). Gifted children with disabilities. *Gifted Child Today, 24*(3), 16.

Coleman, L. J., & Cross, T. L. (2001). *Being gifted in school: An introduction to development, guidance, and teaching.* Waco, TX: Prufrock Press.

Coleman, L. J., & Sanders, M. D. (1993). Understanding the needs of gifted students: Social needs, social choices and masking one's giftedness. *Journal of Secondary Gifted Education, 5,* 22–25.

Coleman, M. R., & Gallagher, J. J. (1995). State identification policies: Gifted students from special populations. *Roeper Review, 17,* 268–275.

Coleman, M. R., Gallagher, J. J., & Foster, A. (1994). *Updated report on state policies related to the identification of gifted students.* Chapel Hill, NC: University of North Carolina.

Cooper, C., Baum, S., & Neu, T. (2004). Developing scientific talent in students with special needs: An alternative model for identification, curriculum, and assessment. *Journal of Secondary Gifted Education, 15,* 162–169.

Davis, G. A., & Rimm, S. B. (2004). *Education of the gifted and talented* (5th ed.). Needham Heights, MA: Allyn & Bacon.

Deci, E. L., & Ryan, R. M. (2002). The paradox of achievement: The harder you push, the worse it gets. In J. Aronson (Ed.) *Improving academic achievement: Contributions of social psychology* (pp. 59–85). New York: Academic Press.

Cramond, B. (1994). Attention Deficit Hyperactivity Disorder and creativity: what is the connection? *Journal of Creative Behavior, 28,* 193-209.

Emerick, L. (1992). Academic underachievement among the gifted: Students' perceptions of factors that reverse the pattern. *Gifted Child Quarterly, 36(3),* 140–146.

Erikson, E. (1968). *Identity: Youth and Crisis.* London: Faber & Faber.

Field, T., Harding, J., Yando, R., Gonzalez, K. Lasko, D., Bendell, D., et al. (1998). Feelings and attitudes of gifted students. *Adolescence, 33,* 331–342.

Gardner, H. (1999). *Intelligence reframed: Multiple intelligences for the 21st century.* New York: Basic Books.

Gentry, M., & Neu, T. (1998). Project High Hope's summer institute: Curriculum for developing talents in students with special needs. *Roeper Review, 20,* 291–296.

Goleman, D. (1995). *Emotional Intelligence.* New York: Bantam.

Johnson, L. J., Karnes, M. B., & Carr. V. W. (1997). Providing services to children with gifts and disabilities: A critical need. In N. Colangelo & G. A. Davis (Eds.), *Handbook of gifted education* (2nd ed., pp. 516–527). Needham Heights, MA: Allyn & Bacon.

Kaufman, F., Kalbfleisch, M. L., & Castellanos, F. X. (2000). *Attention Deficit Disorders and gifted students: What do we really know?* Storrs, CT: The National Research Center on the Gifted and Talented.

Kingore, B. (1998). Seeking advanced potentials: Developmentally appropriate procedures for iden- tification. In J. Smutny (Ed.), *The young gifted child: Potential and promise, an anthology* (pp. 31–51). Cresskill, NJ: Hampton.

Lovecky, D. V. (2004). *Different minds.* Philadelphia: Jessica Kingsley.

Moon, S. M. (2002). Gifted children with Attention Deficit/Hyperactivity Disorder. In M. Neihart, S. Reis, N. Robinson, & S. Moon (Eds.), *The social and emotional needs of gifted students: What do we know?* (pp. 193–204). Waco, TX: Prufrock Press.

Moon, S. M. (2003). Personal talent. *High Ability Studies, 14,* 5–21.

Mooney, J., & Cole, D. (2000). *Learning outside the lines.* New York: Simon and Schuster.

Neihart, M. (2000). Gifted children with Asperger's syndrome. *Gifted Child Quarterly, 44,* 222–230.

Neihart, M. (2002). Gifted children and depression. In M. Neihart, S. Reis, N. Robinson, & S. Moon (Eds.), *The social and emotional needs of gifted students: What do we know?* (pp. 93–102). Waco, TX: Prufrock Press.

Nelson, C. M. (2000). Educating students with emotional and behavioral disabilities in the 21st century: Looking through windows, opening doors. *Education and Treatment of Children 23,* 204–222.

Neilson, E. (2002). Gifted students with learning disabilities. *Exceptionality 10,* 93–112.

Neu, T. (2003). When gifts are camouflaged by disabilities: Identifying and developing talent in gifted students with disabilities. In J. Castellano (Ed.), *Special populations in gifted education: Working with diverse gifted learners* (pp. 151–162). Boston: Allyn & Bacon.

Olenchak, F. R. (1994). Talent development: Accommodating the social and emotional needs of sec- ondary gifted/learning disabled students. *Journal of Secondary Gifted Education, 5,* 40–52.

Olenchak, F. R., & Reis, S. M. (2002). Gifted students with learning disabilities. In M. Neihart, S. Reis, N. Robinson, & S. Moon (Eds.), *The social and emotional needs of gifted students: What do we know?* (pp. 177–192). Waco, TX: Prufrock Press.

Reis, S. M., McGuire, J. M., & Neu, T. W. (2000). Compensation strategies used by high-ability stu- dents with learning disabilities who succeed in college. *Gifted Child Quarterly, 44,* 123–144.

Renzulli, J. S. (1999). What is this thing called giftedness, and how do we develop it? A twenty-five year perspective. *Journal for the Education of the Gifted, 23,* 3–54.

Rimm, S. (2002). Peer pressures and social acceptance of gifted students. In M. Neihart, S. Reis, N. Robinson, & S. Moon (Eds.), *The social and emotional needs of gifted students: What do we know?* (pp. 13–19). Waco, TX: Prufrock Press.

Rogers, K. (2002). Effects of acceleration on gifted learners. In M. Neihart, S. Reis, N. Robinson, & S. Moon (Eds.), *The social and emotional needs of gifted students: What do we know?* (pp. 3–13). Waco, TX: Prufrock Press.

Ryan, R. M., & Deci, E. L. (2000). Self-determination theory and the facilitation of intrinsic motiva- tion, social development, and well-being. *American Psychologist, 55,* 68–78.

Ryan, R. M., Stiller, J., & Lynch, J. H. (1994). Representations of relationships to teachers, parents, and friends as predictors of academic motivation and self-esteem. *Journal of Early Adolescence, 14,* 226–249.

Schiff, M. M., Kaufman, A. S., & Kaufman, N. L. (1981) Scatter analysis of WISC-R profiles for learn- ing disabled children with superior intelligence. *Journal of Learning Disabilities, 22,* 469–486.

Schuler, P. (2002). Perfectionism in gifted children and adolescents. In M. Neihart, S. Reis, N. Robinson, & S. Moon (Eds.), *The social and emotional needs of gifted students: What do we know?* (pp. 71–80). Waco, TX: Prufrock Press.

Silverman, L. K. (1989). Invisible gifts, invisible handicaps. *Roper Review, 12,* 37–41.

Silverman, L. K. (2002). *Upside-down brilliance: The visual-spatial learner.* Denver: DeLeon Publishing.

Sternberg, R. (1997). *Successful intelligence.* New York: Simon and Schuster.

U.S. Department of Education. (1993). *National excellence: A case for developing America's talent.* Washington, DC: U.S. Government Printing Office.

Webb, J. T., Meckstroth, E., & Tolan, S. (1982). *Guiding the gifted child: A practical source for parents and teachers.* Columbus, OH: Ohio Psychology Publishing Company.

Webb, J. T., Amend, E. R., Webb, N. E., Goerss, J., Beljan, P., & Olenchak, F. R. (2005). *Misdiagnosis and dual diagnosis of gifted children and adults.* Scottsdale, AZ: Great Potential Press.

Weinfeld, R., Barnes-Robinson, L., Jeweler, S., & Shevitz, B. (2002). Academic programs for gifted and talented/learning disabled students. *Roper Review 24,* 226–233.

West, T. (1997). *In the mind's eye: Visual thinkers, gifted people with dyslexia and other learning difficulties, computer images and the ironies of creativity* (Rev. ed.). New York: Prometheus Books.

Whitmore, J. R. (1985). *Underachieving gifted students.* Reston, VA: ERIC Clearinghouse on Handicapped and Gifted Children. (ERIC Document Reproduction Service No. ED262526)

Zental, S., Moon, S., Hall, A., & Grskovic, J. (2001), Learning and motivational characteristics of boys with giftedness and/or Attention Deficit/Hyperactivity Disorder. *Exceptional Children, 67,* 499–519.

MOTIVATION AND GIFTED ADOLESCENTS

by Helen Patrick, Marcia Gentry, & Steven V. Owen

MOTIVATED AND GIFTED ADOLESCENTS

I t is easy to assume that gifted students will be successful at school, because—by definition—they learn and understand things more quickly and more easily than their age-mates do. But, school accomplishment is no guarantee; motivation plays a critical role in success (Robinson, Zigler, & Gallagher, 2000). Because motivation is so complex, there are various routes to enhance or stifle it, and teachers, parents, and peers travel many of those routes. In this chapter we focus on understanding gifted students' motivation, and address what others can do to promote these students' adaptive motivation, with an emphasis on the middle- and high-school grades. We take the approach that gifted adolescents are characterized by high ability in one or more areas of human endeavor, but vary dramatically in their motivational profiles, showing patterns of motivation that range from optimal to maladaptive. This perspective allows us to consider underachieving gifted students who exhibit maladaptive motivational patterns. It is also consistent with dynamic and incremental approaches to viewing giftedness, such as creative productive giftedness (Renzulli, 1978), successful intelligence (Sternberg, 1997), and theories of personal talent (Moon, 2003).

In the best situation, gifted students are focused on enhancing their knowledge and abilities, so they can develop their potential most fully and be poised to make the kinds of contributions that society wants and needs. And the best situations are not that rare. Many gifted students are eager to develop their competencies, embrace challenge and opportunities for growth, and seek to realize their academic and personal potential. For example, adolescents identified as gifted also demonstrated, on average, superior academic intrinsic motivation, compared to nongifted peers (Gottfried & Gottfried, 1996). But, giftedness does not automatically confer self-regulation skills and strong confidence about learning new skills. Gifted students are at risk for developing a set of maladaptive motivational beliefs and behaviors (Whitmore, 1986). Gifted students, whether they are identified as such or not, can be content with "coasting" and mediocrity. Even though they may appear to be successful, in that they perform acceptably in school, by adolescence some gifted students have developed motivational beliefs that undermine achievement. They may be primed for, if not already begun on, a trajectory of underachievement. Gifted students' underachievement often begins during adolescence (Reis & McCoach, 2000). When a talented student underperforms, there are two likely reasons. First, she may be gifted *and* learning disabled (see Chapter 6) or she may have maladaptive motivational beliefs that need attention. Thus, students' motivational beliefs are the theme of this chapter.

The Direction of Motivation, not Just Amount, Is Important

Classroom folk wisdom suggests that the two boys in the back of the room—one dozing, and the other staring out the window—are unmotivated. That is an incorrect belief. Humans are consistently motivated for some kind of outcome. The two boys are indeed motivated, but they likely are not motivated to do what teachers, or parents, want them to do. They may manifest this in a number of ways—by remaining passive, by actively resisting, or by distracting the attention of the class, to cite only a few. So it is more accurate, and more educationally useful, to consider *what* students are motivated for. We can make inferences about the direction of students' motivation by considering aspects of their behavior (Pintrich & Schunk, 2002). Key indicators of motivation include:

- *Activity choices*, including what students choose to do and how much challenge is involved. Do students select tasks from which they are most likely to learn, or do they choose overly simple tasks to ensure an easy A? Do they engage in school work when not monitored closely, or do they jump to other activities?
- *Activity level*, or the amount of energy expended. Do students engage in tasks enthusiastically, or superficially, or reluctantly, procrastinating and searching for ways to avoid work?
- *Engagement behaviors*, including the type and quality of behaviors. Do students use effective, active, and effortful strategies, such as monitoring their own

understanding and self-correcting, or do they use superficial strategies that get them to the end of the assignment, but do not promote real understanding and remembering? Do they seek help with school tasks when they need it, or skip over tasks or copy mindlessly from others?

- *Persistence*, or the extent that students stick with tasks. Do students persevere when the activity becomes difficult or success is not immediate, or do they stop working?
- *Continuing motivation*, or the extent that students show continued interest and go beyond what is expected at school. Do students do more than the minimum, and continue to think about content outside school or after the unit of study has finished (e.g., check out library books to read more about a subject, think how content connects to the world outside of school)?

These behavioral indicators can be explained and understood by social cognitive theories (Pintrich & Schunk, 2002). The social aspects of such theories point out that most learning and behavior occurs in a social context, observing and interacting with others. Even a recluse is involved in a social world, when he or she reads a novel or a newspaper, watches television, or even thinks about others. Social observations and transactions fuel learning and behavior. The cognitive part of these theories emphasizes students' thoughts, beliefs, and perceptions—about themselves, about the activity or subject, and about the context or situation (Pintrich & Schunk). Theories involve how students evaluate and respond to questions such as: Why do I want to engage in the activity? Can I succeed? Why do I want to succeed? What will it cost me to succeed? What will count as success? Why did I succeed (or fail)?

Motivational theories differ in the sorts of questions that they are most suited for addressing. We can understand students' motivation best, therefore, when we consider their responses to a number of such questions by drawing from a range of motivational theories. In this chapter we discuss four different, but complementary, types of motivational beliefs—self-efficacy, values, goal orientations, and attributions. However, we first briefly discuss developmental issues that are most relevant to gifted students' motivation in middle and high school, because individuals' beliefs are understood best in relation to their development. This will serve as a backdrop for the subsequent discussion of motivation during adolescence.

DEVELOPMENTAL ISSUES OF ADOLESCENCE

Many changes occur during adolescence, involving both the individual and how others relate to him or her. Because developments in individuals' cognitive abilities, identity perceptions, and social relationships have broad implications for their motivational beliefs and behaviors, we give a brief overview of predominant issues of development here. We focus specifically on early and middle adolescence, highlighting how giftedness relates to each of these aspects of development.

Cognitive Development

Adolescence is characterized by steady improvement in a range of distinct cognitive abilities. This is related to biological and neurological maturing, but cognitive development is also affected strongly by experience. Adolescents process information increasingly more quickly and more efficiently, and their memory improves. In addition to improved control of and coordination among different cognitive processes, better information processing assists other aspects of thinking. Adolescents become more self-aware and more skilled at metacognition, that is, able to reflect on, and steer, their thinking and performance. They become increasingly able to engage in complex thinking, reasoning, decision making, and problem solving, although their performance is much better when they apply their thinking to things they already have some knowledge about, rather than thinking about tasks with unfamiliar or abstract content. Adolescents also become better at appreciating others' perspectives. The integration of these capabilities is responsible for adolescents' cognitive superiority compared to earlier periods. In addition to coordinating different aspects of cognition, adolescents become better at coordinating their thinking, emotions, and behavior (Byrnes, 2003; Keating, 2004).

Gifted adolescents, by their very nature, are distinguished from their peers by more advanced cognition; this is often apparent from early childhood (Davis & Rimm, 2003; Gross, 1999). Cognitive capabilities that are just emerging for their adolescent peers have often been practiced for many years by gifted students. Gifted students think more abstractly than their nongifted peers, and they learn more material faster. They are often concerned with nuances surrounding topics of study, and with ideas that do not interest their age-peers. For example, many gifted preteens see a much wider perspective than the daily routine of school, family, and friends; some grow overly worried about war, politics, the effects of automobile emissions on air quality and consequently our reliance on fossil fuels, death, or the "why" of the human condition. Most checklists of characteristics of gifted children include superior analytic ability; superior reasoning and problem solving; abstract, complex, logical, and insightful thinking; greater metacognition; and emotional sensitivity (Davis & Rimm). So, although all adolescents are changing and developing, gifted adolescents' superior cognitive abilities create a capacity for powerful learning as they navigate their secondary school experiences (Csikszentmihalyi, Rathunde, & Whalen, 1993; Davis & Rimm; Neihart, Reis, Robinson, & Moon, 2002). Often, adolescence is a time in which gifted students' interests, talents, and insights intensify; these areas may or may not be related to what goes on at school. Obviously, when a student's interests and talents are different from the school menu, he or she may be spending less motivational energy on school tasks.

Changes in adolescents' cognitive abilities are related to other developmental changes, particularly those that involve identity and social relationships. That is, the ability to think more deeply and in new ways enables adolescents to think more abstractly about who they are and how they relate to others.

Identity Development

Identity encompasses a sense of who one is, in terms of physical, cognitive, and psychological characteristics and features (Erikson, 1968; Kroger, 2003), and involves a commitment to chosen beliefs, goals, and actions (Bosma & Kunnen, 2001). Thus, establishing an identity involves the process of exploring and embarking on commitments (both emotionally, and in terms of time and resources) to particular paths and desired outcomes. Adaptively, individuals come to settle on a sense of self after a period of some exploration and "trying on" roles. Because adolescents become able to consider future possibilities and situations that are different from reality, they can ponder issues such as who they are and who they would like to become (Harter, 1990). This can be a preoccupying concern for adolescents, at least in Western cultures. Adolescents' identity is related closely to many decisions they make, especially involving educational and occupational choices, and therefore it shapes the trajectories they launch. Although identity continues to grow through adulthood (Bosma & Kunnen), identity development is especially important during adolescence, because issues involving identity during this time shape future opportunities and experiences. Because Hébert and Kelly (this volume) discuss issues specific to gifted students' identity development, we do not repeat that information here. We do want to speak, though, about how the social environment influences adolescent identity.

Social Relationships

One of the most dramatic changes associated with the onset of adolescence is the increased importance of peer relationships, compared to earlier periods of development (Furman & Buhrmester, 1992). As children move into adolescence, they spend an increasing amount of time with peers compared to time spent with family members or on their own (Csikszentmihalyi & Larson, 1984). Peer relationships become more intense and close, and involve more self-disclosure (Buhrmester & Furman, 1987). These changes are facilitated by cognitive development, which enables thinking abstractly about values, friendship, and identity.

In addition to changes in friendships, changes in students' broader peer group surface during early adolescence. Sharply distinct peer groups, with different identifying characteristics, reputations, and status hierarchies, emerge and become increasingly important to adolescents (Brown, 1990; Brown, Eicher, & Petrie, 1986). Associated with this emergence of cliques and crowds is the concern about how a student is viewed by others. A desire to "fit in" and be like others is especially strong for early adolescents, who around this time pay particularly close attention to their peers' behaviors. Adolescents' growing ability to reflect on how they are seen by others often gives rise to increased self-consciousness, concern about one's social image, and use of image-management strategies (Elkind, 1967; Juvonen, 2000; Keating, 1990).

These issues may also affect gifted adolescents. Research on the social development of gifted youth shows conflicting results (Neihart et al., 2002). Some researchers (e.g., Gross, 1993; Silverman, 1993) have argued that gifted adolescents are at risk for serious social adjustment problems, whereas others (e.g., Bain & Bell, 2004; Kelly & Colangelo, 1984) have found evidence that gifted youth are at least as well adjusted, on average, as their nongifted peers. These contrary findings reinforce that gifted youth are not homogeneous, but rather diverse in their social adjustment and development. Those who are well adjusted socially often prefer to work alone even though they get along well with peers, and they may defer romantic relationships in favor of some area of study that they love. They also seek out small peer groups with similar interests and abilities, and tend to be influenced less by broader peer fashions and trends (Csikszentmihalyi et al., 1993; Dai, Moon, & Feldhusen, 1998). At the same time, gifted youth are sometimes so worried about their social standing that they adopt strategies that contribute to school underachievement. For example, there have been suggestions (Betts & Neihart, 1988) that gifted children "go underground," or hide their abilities so they appear more like their age-mates or like "regular" teens. This may occur because gifted adolescents, like their nongifted age-mates, also experience self-conscious pressures to fit with their peers, and at the same time, distance themselves from authority—all this against a backdrop of high intellectual abilities and sharp social awareness, which add to the pressures of simply being an adolescent. So Suzie, who always excelled intellectually in elementary school and showed keen interest in learning, may now sense that she doesn't fit into the social scene. As an adaptive pose, she may appear apathetic about school work, hide her abilities, and "try on" a new image that involves being more like the popular girls she observes. Such situations can be very frustrating for parents and teachers alike. It may also prove exasperating for Suzie if her would-be friends reject her overtures; dismissing schoolwork or being dismissed by peers will probably spin off more emotional turmoil and unsettle Suzie's sense of self.

Changes in adolescents' cognitive abilities and social relationships influence adolescents' unfolding perceptions of themselves—who they are, what they are good or not good at, what they value or devalue, what they aspire to do or be and what they shun, and where they want to invest resources. These types of perceptions and beliefs help to explain motivated behavior. In the next section, we take a more focused view of four areas of personal beliefs that have vital sway over motivation: self-efficacy expectations ("Can I succeed?"), value beliefs ("Why do I want to succeed?" and "What would it cost me to succeed?"), goal orientations ("Why am I doing these behaviors?" and "What counts as success?"), and causal attributions ("Why was I successful [or not]?").

UNDERSTANDING AND EXPLAINING MOTIVATION: THEORIES AND RESEARCH

Can I Succeed? Self-Efficacy Beliefs

People make judgments about whether they can succeed at a particular task or goal. Bandura (1977, 1997) termed such judgments *self-efficacy*, and he has claimed that efficacy beliefs form a central factor in understanding motivated behavior and performance. Self-efficacy appraisals refer to specific skills, behaviors, and situations. For example, a gifted student may be abundantly confident about balancing redox reactions for her chemistry homework (high self-efficacy), but feel uncertain about doing the same problems under the pressure of competition (low self-efficacy). Or, she may feel efficacious about doing any sort of redox problem, but lack self-efficacy about predicting formulas of ionic compounds. Self-efficacy can have strong influence on behavior, and, fortunately for our chemistry student, it can develop rapidly and is reasonably alterable. It is notably different, therefore, from other types of self-perceptions, such as self-concept. Self-concept involves a broad assessment of an individual and his or her competence. It is constructed slowly, is relatively stable, and does not influence behavior clearly. Bong and Skaalvik (2003) provide an extended discussion of similarities and differences between self-efficacy and self-concept.

Self-efficacy beliefs are related to students' achievement. When students feel confident they can learn, they tend to show greater effort and persistence, use more—and more effective—self-regulatory strategies, and experience less stress and anxiety (Pajares, 1996b; Zimmerman, 2000), all factors that facilitate learning. Although self-efficacy is related to previous academic success, in that students who have experienced greater achievement are more likely to feel confident they will be successful again, there is considerable variation in self-efficacy among students with similar levels of achievement. When students' previous achievement histories are equivalent, those with higher self-efficacy generally experience greater achievement than do students with lower self-efficacy (Pajares).

Self-efficacy research, across all age groups and many cultural groups, in schools, health care settings, industry, and sports, has produced some important principles. Perhaps the strongest principle is that behavior outcomes and self-efficacy feed each other. Task success strengthens efficacy beliefs, and stronger efficacy beliefs make it more likely that a person will be interested in, and choose, that task; spend energy and persistence in mastering it; and seek strategies to make success happen. Gains in proficiency are also accompanied by increased personal value for the task. In short, someone with robust self-efficacy shows behavior very much like the indicators of motivation we outlined at the beginning of this chapter. When these indicators are present, the odds of success improve dramatically. A reverse spiral is just as predictable: Failure weakens self-efficacy, which in turn makes it more likely that a person will not persevere, but will stop or choose to do something else. When Cisco stumbles—again—on his weekly geometry quiz, he will feel less inclined to study the very material that he needs to pass the next quiz. During the quiz itself, a sense of discouragement and ineptitude may hinder his reading the questions thoroughly, and prompt him to answer with sloppy guesses or even give up and not answer. Even though giving up guarantees failure, Covington (2000) argued that it is a face-saving response for adolescents, because failure can be blamed on a lack of effort, rather than low ability (we expand on this line of reasoning in the later section on student attributions).

A second important influence on self-efficacy beliefs is whether peers are observed succeeding or failing. People continually watch others to make social comparisons. When Brecca sees other students in her Advanced Placement French class fumble and stumble with their oral translations, she receives efficacy information. If these other capable kids are bombing, she may think, then maybe I will have trouble, too. Of course, if Brecca considers herself *more* talented at translating than her peers are, their observed failures will have little effect on Brecca's efficacy expectations. In other words, learners with plenty of experience put less weight on others' performance when they make self-appraisals of competence. For the inexperienced learner, observing the successes of others like her works in the expected direction. When her peers are showing seamless translations, the implication for Brecca is that she, like her classmates, should be able to master this.

Researchers have studied individual differences between groups in students' self-efficacy for different subjects. Gender differences have been examined most often. In general, girls tend to underestimate their abilities more than boys do. For example, although girls in high school tend to be better writers than boys, their self-efficacy is not higher (Pajares & Valiante, 1999). The same has been found for efficacy for mathematics; whereas girls' grades tend to be higher than boys', their efficacy is no different (Kenney-Benson, Pomerantz, Ryan, & Patrick, in press). There has also been some attention to self-efficacy among students with different racial or ethnic backgrounds. One persistent finding is that African American students' self-efficacy tends to be higher than that of White students (Freeman, Gutman, & Midgley, 2002) and more discrepant with their achievement (Pajares & Kranzler, 1995). There is disagreement among researchers about whether processes associated with self-efficacy differ for students of different ethnicities; some evidence supports this view (e.g., Klassen, 2004). On the other hand, Bandura (1997) argues that, although there may be cultural differences in magnitude, the development and operations of self-efficacy are universal. Plainly, more research with students of color is needed to understand this issue better.

Gifted Students' Self-Efficacy Beliefs

There has been a little research on self-efficacy with gifted students. Pajares (1996a) found that gifted students' efficacy beliefs about math skills were not only higher, but were somewhat more accurate (i.e., less inflated) than those of regular students. He also found gender differences: Although gifted girls outperformed the boys' in math, they had equivalent efficacy beliefs. Other studies have found a pattern similar to that of their nongifted peers—with gifted girls having, on average, math achievement equal to that of boys, but efficacy beliefs significantly lower than boys' (Junge & Dretzke, 1995; Malpass, O'Neil, & Hocevar, 1999). Gender differences in self-efficacy may be developmental. Pajares (2002) pointed out that until middle school girls and boys have about equal self-efficacy for various school skills, but as they advance through high school boys pull ahead in perceptions but not performance. Cultural expectations may play a role in growing self-efficacy differences between males and females. Despite huge pressures from the feminist movement since the 1970s, females are stereotypically expected to be as modest as males are cocky. Even highly talented females have lower career and salary aspirations than their male companions. Early adolescence is a prime time for gender role expectations to be formed, and gifted youth seem every bit as vulnerable as their peers to absorbing cultural myths about who should do what. Not surprisingly, females attending single-sex schools, where social comparisons do not include males, resist the downward expectations and show higher aspirations (Watson, Quatman, & Endler, 2002).

Despite the strong role that self-efficacy beliefs play, it is only one of a constellation of motivating perceptions that should have implications for teaching and learning. For example, imagine the situation where a gifted adolescent feels confident about learning a specific skill or topic, but does not value it and is not interested in it, we would expect her motivation to falter. Conversely, an adolescent may have self-doubts about his ability, but if he puts high value on the topic, he may out-persist and eventually out-perform his classmates. In the next sections, we consider other kinds of students' motivational beliefs, such as values.

Do I Want to Succeed? What Would it Cost Me to Succeed? Value Beliefs

Eccles (Eccles, 1983; Wigfield & Eccles, 1992) has identified four different types of value beliefs. *Importance* refers to the attainment value or personal significance of a task; *intrinsic value* is the enjoyment and interest experienced during the activity; *utility value* concerns the usefulness of the activity for the individual with respect to future goals; and *cost* refers to perceptions of negative aspects of involvement in the activity (e.g., possible failures, too much time or energy spent, other opportunities missed).

Students tend to respond similarly to questions about importance, intrinsic value, and utility value within a particular subject, and so those three aspects of value are often examined together (e.g., Anderman et al., 2001; Jacobs, Lanza, Osgood, Eccles, & Wigfield, 2002). From about the midway point of elementary school, students' value beliefs for different subjects come to be influenced by their previous achievement and their beliefs that they will be successful in the future (Wigfield, 1994). However, value is also affected by teachers' practices. For example, Anderman and his colleagues found that the students of teachers who emphasized competition and "besting" others showed a significant drop in value for math and for reading, compared to the values they expressed the previous year. This is likely because competition usually has an extrinsic, public emphasis, which detracts from students' existing intrinsic feelings such as interest and pleasure (Ryan & Deci, 2000).

Students' values are related to how they engage in academics. When students value learning about a subject, they pay attention more and use effortful cognitive and regulatory learning strategies (Pintrich & De Groot, 1990; Pokay & Blumenfeld, 1990). Not surprisingly, all these factors (valuing the activity, paying careful attention, using deep learning strategies) are associated positively with achievement (Pintrich & De Groot; Schiefele, Krapp, & Winteler, 1992). Value beliefs also influence educational decisions, such as choices about which classes to enroll in and which to avoid. Interestingly, longitudinal research has shown that value beliefs are better predictors of future choices than are expectancy (similar to self-efficacy) beliefs (Eccles & Wigfield, 2002).

Value beliefs are a significant explanation for the tendency of girls who had been successful in math to *not* continue with advanced math classes; despite valuing mathematics, they tend to value other subjects more (Eccles, 1994; Eccles, Adler, & Meece, 1984). Although an increasing numbers of girls are enrolled in advanced math classes (American Association of University Women, 1999), sharp gender differences in the perceived value of various subjects seems to account for the low numbers of females whose college majors include math and physical science.

Although different value beliefs are sometimes considered as a whole, students from late elementary school onward respond differently to the various aspects of value (Wigfield & Eccles, 1992). Students can distinguish importance from interest in various subjects (Fredricks & Eccles, 2004). Students who were surveyed from 3rd to 12th grades reported on all occasions that, on average, math was more important than interesting. Their interest in math decreased gradually throughout the years. The importance they gave to math similarly decreased until 10th grade, at which time students began to see it as increasingly more important. By contrast, students reported that sport was more interesting than important. Interest in sports declined slightly throughout the 10 years, and its perceived importance declined markedly after elementary school.

Both importance and interest involve valuing activities or subjects for intrinsic reasons, whereas utility value involves a more extrinsic emphasis, focusing on what a person can get as a result of the accomplishment. Teachers sometimes exhort students to work harder by emphasizing that new learning will open future doors (e.g., getting into college, earning a scholarship). But, research shows that when students are already interested in learning the material, emphasizing its later utility can undermine motivation by way of increasing stress, lowering test scores, and making students less persistent with the activity (Vansteenkiste et al., 2004). This finding is congruent with a larger group of studies showing that giving rewards for activities students already find interesting is associated with decreases in their future interest and motivation (Ryan & Deci, 2000). Therefore, when Juan shows a keen interest in science, it is fitting to respond to his interests with genuine learning opportunities and acknowledge his accomplishments in the subject. But, he can do so without nagging reminders that science is needed for entry to high-paying careers such as medicine or engineering.

Researchers have examined perceived costs less often than they have considered importance, interest, and utility. Costs are associated negatively with college students' intentions for future education, but the other three value beliefs are related more strongly, and positively, to future plans (Battle & Wigfield, 2003).

Gifted Students' Value Beliefs

Considering perceived value provides a very useful way to think about gifted students' school-related choices, and their engagement in classes once they have made those choices. There has been very little research focused specifically on gifted students' value beliefs. Despite limited evidence, it appears that the value gifted students have for a subject is related to career preferences, similar to findings with non-gifted students. Among female high school students identified as talented in science, intrinsic value or interest in science was related to preferences for careers that involve science (Jacobs, Finken, Griffin, & Wright, 1998). Interest in biology was related to preferences for jobs in health professions and in human services, whereas interest in physical science was related to preferences for jobs involving physical science.

A value perspective can explain why students opt out of a subject they are extremely good at and feel efficacious about. It can also highlight dilemmas students face with selecting some options over others, particularly when they are accomplished students in many areas. Choices are rarely as simple as high value versus low value; several valued options may be pitted against each other. Although values influence current choices, they also have implications for future experiences. Will students have sufficient tenacity to persist at something they believe will be important in the future, but which they currently find uninteresting? Will the quality of their efforts be high if their interest or enjoyment is low? What about feelings of satisfaction or enthusiasm, or their creativity? If students begin with initial high utility value and experience success, will interest follow? There are many unanswered research questions.

Gifted students who value doing well academically may nevertheless place greater value on other domains, such as forming and maintaining peer relationships, having approval from peers, or developing expertise in nonacademic subjects, such as sports or music (Eccles, 1985). Choices about time and effort may thus favor other activities, perhaps to the detriment of schoolwork. This can account for some gifted students' underachievement. Students may generally value learning, but be turned off by teacher-assigned tasks if they are perceived as busywork or "hoop-jumping." As adolescents move through high school, they need and want to practice autonomy and self-direction, and so may resist the role of a compliant student who trudges obediently through meaningless tasks. Although they may show signs of high value and motivation *in the same subject matter* outside of school, rote classroom activities usually lead to low effort and perhaps to underachievement. This should lead educators to consider carefully how to enhance the quality and meaningfulness of schoolwork, thus increasing its potential value to gifted students. One 10th grader we know, Maria, usually aced her biology tests, but hated her biology assignments. So her course grade suffered because she consistently got docked points for missing homework. When her teacher asked her why she didn't do her homework, Maria explained that she found the work easy but boring busywork, and she learned more biology in her out-of-class volunteer work on local environmental issues. Maria's attentive teacher responded by substituting assignments with others that helped mesh Maria's values in environmental work with the class objectives.

It is also relevant to consider perceived costs. Although there has been very little research about the perceived costs that students (gifted or otherwise) associate with selecting particular classes, participating actively, and being successful academically, this is an important issue that warrants attention. It seems especially significant when gifted students' enjoyment of school and academic success are burdened by perceived social costs. There is considerable concern that gifted adolescents—particularly girls—try to hide their abilities and accomplishments from their nongifted peers to appear less different from them, and many are vulnerable to adopting self-handicapping strategies that forecast underachievement (Rimm, 2002). Students of color are also likely to be affected by competing value beliefs. For example, middle-school boys were asked which students they most admired, respected, and wanted to be like. Whereas African Americans and Latinos named low-achieving boys most often, White boys more often named high-achieving students (Graham, Taylor, & Hudley, 1998). Such apparent differences in cultural values likely have important influences on the motivation of gifted students of color. Unfortunately, despite the obvious importance of cultural differences in school-related values, there is very little research that has addressed these differences.

Why Am I Doing the Tasks? What Counts as Success? Goal Orientations

Another useful way to consider students' motivation is to focus on the reasons that students engage in school work and academics, and the meanings they give to that behavior. That is, *why* do students engage in academic tasks? And how do they define success? These questions are addressed by goal orientation theory (Ames, 1992; Nicholls, 1989).

Researchers have focused on two different goal orientations, or reasons for engaging in school work; these are called *mastery* and *performance goal orientations* (Ames, 1992; Pintrich, 2000). A mastery goal orientation focuses on developing competence. For example, Simon is fascinated about how machines work, and his primary aim in physics class is to learn about how mechanical and electrical forces operate in machinery. A performance goal orientation focuses on displaying one's competence publicly, and a concern with how well she or he "stacks up" in the hierarchy of ability. Within a performance orientation, people can have an *approach* focus, where the goal is to look better or smarter than others, or an *avoidance* focus, where the goal is to not appear less competent than others. Aggy wants to do well in all of her courses, by which she means getting the highest scores; she would really like to be class valedictorian (performance-approach). Kimi is in most of the same courses, but is far more concerned about what others in the psychology class think about her ability, and her focus is on not looking like the dumbest student in the class (performance-avoid). These goal orientations are not independent of each other; people may hold them in different combinations or patterns. Randall, for example, enjoys not only the satisfaction of understanding more about American history (mastery orientation), but also letting others know when he aces a history exam (performance-approach orientation). Students may be oriented to just one primary goal, or several simultaneously, or not appear to be oriented to any. Furthermore, students' goal orientations can vary across different situations or for different subjects, and these patterns may change over time. Different goal orientations are associated with different patterns of thoughts, emotions, and achievement behaviors.

A mastery goal orientation involves wanting to develop competence by increasing understanding, insight, or skill. Students with a mastery orientation value learning as an end in itself, rather than just as a means to an end. They monitor their progress in mastering new skills and content. Success is gauged in terms of their own improvement, and not by comparison to other students. Students with a mastery orientation are more likely to engage in tasks in ways that maximize opportunities to learn. Specifically, when students apply this collection of beliefs to their work they are also likely to choose tasks they will learn from, use effective learning strategies, persist, show interest, seek help with school tasks when they need it, and feel positively about school and themselves as learners (see Kaplan, Middleton, Urdan, & Midgley, 2002, for a recent review). Predictably, students who hold a mastery orientation also show strong academic self-efficacy. Earl, 16, but already a gifted writer, works with a mentor to discuss writing strategies, language, editing, and revision. He pays attention to different styles and tries out many of them in his column for the local paper. Earl listens eagerly to comments others make about his writing, and tries to incorporate feedback into subsequent columns and assignments.

A performance goal orientation involves wanting to demonstrate competence, either by performing better than others (performance-approach) or by not looking worse than others (performance-avoid). Students with a performance orientation view academic tasks as a route to an end or an opportunity to look successful. They concentrate on how well they do relative to others, and gauge their success in terms of normative comparisons.

A performance-avoid goal orientation is maladaptive in terms of learning and achievement, because, faced with new learning challenges, those students are likely to avoid activities at which they may not look competent. By spending energy on image management, they miss opportunities to learn and improve. Focusing on avoiding an aura of incompetence means that resources and strategies are devoted to saving face and protecting self-esteem (Covington, 1992). A performance-avoid orientation is linked to self-handicapping (i.e., purposefully withdrawing effort, so that poor results can be attributed to low effort rather than low ability), and students avoiding seeking needed help (Urdan, Ryan, Anderman, & Gheen, 2002). It is also associated with anxiety, taking a disorganized approach to studying, using superficial and expedient learning strategies (e.g., skimming, rushing through, asking others to tell them the answers), low use of deep processing strategies, poor persistence, and lower exam performance (Elliot, McGregor, & Gable, 1999; Middleton & Midgley, 1997). Nathan, for example, wants his teacher and peers to see him as good at math, but he is worried that fumbling on some hard upcoming units will detract from this impression. Before the remaining quizzes, he spends time memorizing answers from previous class tests, writes crib notes on the label of his water bottle, and tells anyone within earshot about how working at his part-time job meant he didn't have time to study.

Research on performance-approach goal orientation does not provide as clear a picture for achievement-related processes as is found with mastery and performance-avoid goal orientations. There seems to be both the potential for adaptive and maladaptive achievement-related processes. On one hand, a performance-approach orientation has been linked with extra effort and persistence while studying for an exam, and higher exam scores, at least for undergraduates (Elliot et al., 1999). On the other hand, some of the extra effort and persistence is wasted on taking a disorganized approach to studying, and using superficial learning strategies such as rote memorization (Elliot et al.; Middleton & Midgley, 1997). Researchers disagree about whether or not a performance-approach orientation to school work can be adaptive. Some (e.g., Harackiewicz, Barron, Pintrich, Elliot, & Thrash, 2002) argue that focusing on wanting to improve one's understanding (mastery orientation) *and* trying to beat out others (performance-approach orientation) is adaptive, although research supporting this view comes primarily from college students. Other researchers (e.g., Midgley, Kaplan, & Middleton, 2001) noted that there is little evidence of positive outcomes associated with middle- and high-school students having a performance-approach focus, and expressed concern that adolescents' mastery orientation will be diluted or strangled by a focus on doing better than others.

In addition to considering various goal orientations, it is important to observe how students' orientations change over time. In particular, there has been concern about the long-term outcomes for students who experience success *and* look competent, and for whom striving to be the best does not seem to foster negative outcomes (Midgley et al., 2001). What happens when these students move to new learning environments, particularly those that seem to have more, or more competent, students (e.g., moving to a larger school, or a class with more advanced content or more high-achieving students)? One possibility is that students accustomed to out-performing others and being viewed that way by other people, but who are not confident about maintaining their rank, will move to an avoidance focus (see Gibbons & Benbow, 1994). This was exactly what Middleton and colleagues (2004) found among middle school students. Sixth graders' performance-approach orientation predicted a performance-avoidance orientation in seventh grade, but, interestingly, only for students with high self-efficacy in sixth grade. That is, students who felt confident of their abilities and were concerned with scoring higher than others were more likely, as they progressed in middle school, to become focused on protecting their image and have distracting concerns of not looking incompetent compared to other students.

Gifted Students' Goal Orientations

The limited research on gifted students' goal orientations has shown outcomes similar to those found within the general student population. Gifted adolescents' mastery orientation predicts choosing challenging tasks that involve uncertain success over easy tasks, expending effort, persisting in the face of obstacles, and using adaptive cognitive and self-regulatory strategies (Dai, 2000; Malpass et al., 1999). Additionally, a performance-approach orientation is associated with a preference for challenging tasks, whereas a performance-avoid orientation is linked to preferring easy tasks to challenging ones and lowering persistence (Dai).

Middleton et al.'s (2004) research, showing that students with high self-efficacy and a performance-approach orientation tended to become more performance-avoidant, has important implications for talented youth. Gifted students, at least those in regular classes, tend to find schoolwork easier than their classmates, and can become accustomed to out-performing others. They probably also get attention or encouragement from others—especially teachers and parents—that reinforces this drive to score higher than others. Superficially, their situation appears positive. However, educational transitions often create much larger "ponds" with many more "big fish." If students entering a larger pond—such as college—feel uncertain about whether they can maintain their relative standing, and it is important to them that they do, they may switch to a maladaptive performance-avoid orientation. As we saw, by trying to protect one's image as a "high achiever," students squelch opportunities for growth and improvement.

How students perceive and explain their successes and failures has important implications for their ongoing achievement motivation. The final motivational theory we will address in this chapter involves the reasons that students give for different outcomes, or their attributions.

Why Was I Successful (or not Successful)? Attributions

Individuals hold beliefs about why they were successful, or not, in any activity. The more valued the activity, the more important these personal explanations become. For example, Rosemarie believes she did well on her economics assignment because she worked really hard on it, whereas Jerome believes his poor grade was due to the teacher not grading it fairly. We don't usually do a deep search for reasons for all our outcomes, but individuals can typically do so if asked, and are especially likely to do so when the result is unexpected (e.g., we do poorly when we thought we would do well), negative, or important. Causal attributions, or the kinds of reasons we give, have implications for future motivation, such as how likely we are to expend effort on future tasks.

According to attribution theory (Weiner, 1986), three dimensions comprise every reason or attribution: *locus*, *control*, and *stability*. Locus refers to whether the cause is seen as *internal* to the person (i.e., something about me or what I did) or *external* (i.e., outside of me). Control refers to beliefs about personal responsibility for, or control over, the outcome; an outcome may be attributed to a *controllable* or *uncontrollable* factor. And stability refers to the beliefs about the predictability of the outcome; attributions may be *stable* (i.e., this outcome will likely always happen) or *unstable* (i.e., the outcome may be different next time). As we mentioned, each reason involves all three dimensions. For example, Rosemarie, who worked long and hard on her economics project, attributed her success to internal, controllable, and unstable factors; that is, her effort came from within her, was in her control, and open to change. Jerome, who perceived teacher bias, attributed his failure to external and uncontrollable factors; that is, the teacher's unfairness was external to him and out of his control. We don't know whether he views the teacher as *always* unfair to him (stable) or whether he believes this was an unusual occurrence (unstable).

The causal attributions students make have significant implications for their later motivational beliefs and behaviors. Although success builds students' confidence in their abilities and skills, this is so only when they see themselves as the reasons for their success (i.e., their attributions are internal). Therefore, success due to the task being easy, or the teacher giving a lot of help, does not tend to promote self-efficacy. Additionally, if students see their failures as due to uncontrollable and stable factors, such as "having my mother's genes for being bad at math," they will act as though there is little they can do to prevent future failure. Over time, this can lead to a helpless pattern, whereby students give up—with the mentality of "why waste effort if you 'know' you won't be successful?"

For motivation, it is best when students view their failures as being due to unstable, controllable, and, at least in part, internal causes. These reasons may include not having good work habits, using inappropriate learning strategies, or having poor test-taking strategies. With such attributions, students may potentially exert control and effect change by improving strategic behaviors. With causal attributions that are stable, controllable, and external, however, there is little to encourage a student to try to effect change, and thus little hope for future success. Accordingly, students may reason that it makes no sense for them to persist on the task, and, in the extreme, a pattern of helpless responses may follow (Dweck, 1986).

It is good for students to take credit for their successes (i.e., make internal attribution); successes viewed as resulting from an easy assignment or the teacher's leniency (external attributions) do not enhance self-efficacy (Bandura, 1997). Although both ability and effort are internal attributions, motivational researchers (e.g., Pintrich & Schunk, 2002) recommend that students be encouraged to attribute successes at least in part to effort. This is because effort is controllable, whereas ability is usually seen as relatively stable and therefore not controllable. Therefore, when the inevitable occurs and students experience failure, they will be used to linking achievement with effort.

There are persistent gender differences in attributions. Compared to boys, girls are less likely to attribute success to stable internal factors, such as high ability, and more likely to attribute success to unstable factors, such as luck (Eisenberg, Martin, & Fabes, 1996; Ziegler, Heller, & Broome, 1996). Girls tend to attribute their failures to low ability more often than boys do (Eisenberg et al., 1996). These gender differences can be related to socialization factors, such as tendencies for teachers and parents to interact differently with boys and girls (Ruble & Martin, 1998).

There has been less research concerning differences in students' attributions associated with race or ethnicity. It is likely that the general process is similar for all individuals, but that specifics differ (Weiner, 2004). This includes cultural differences in beliefs about the relative impact that effort, versus ability, has in influencing achievement. For example, people in the United States are more likely to view ability as being most responsible for high achievement, whereas Japanese individuals are more likely to credit high effort than high ability. The types of factors seen as responsible for successes and failures also vary between different groups. For example, African American students are more likely to perceive discrimination (an external factor) as a cause of failure (Graham & Hudley, 2005), compared to White students.

Gifted Students' Attributions

There have been few studies that have compared the attributional patterns of gifted students with those of nongifted students. Chan (1996) found that gifted and nongifted high school students had different patterns of attributions for success and failure. Gifted students were more likely to attribute success to effort, and rarely believed that luck was responsible for either success or failure. Further, gifted students were prone to blame failure on lack of trying rather than on low ability.

Just like with regular students, there is also evidence of gender differences in attributions with gifted students (see Robinson, 2002a). Gifted girls were more likely than gifted boys to attribute their successes and failures in math, science, and English to effort and strategy use (Li & Adamson, 1995); that is, they take both more credit and more blame for their academic performances. Ziegler (e.g., Heller & Ziegler, 1996) has argued that the tendency for girls to view failure as internal, stable, and uncontrollable places them at risk for learned helplessness, a debilitating set of beliefs where students give up trying because they don't believe they can be successful (Dweck, 1986). To counter this, he and his colleagues have developed and evaluated relatively brief interventions that involve receiving specific types of teacher feedback or watching a short video. These programs have been successful in changing gifted girls' maladaptive attributional patterns about their performance in physics and chemistry (Ziegler & Heller, 2000; Ziegler & Stoeger, 2004).

GIFTED STUDENTS' MOTIVATIONAL BELIEFS AND IMPLICATIONS OF THOSE BELIEFS

Optimally, gifted students' identity includes a commitment to continually develop their competence and understanding. They are mastery-oriented and have high (but not exaggerated) self-efficacy. Their sense of self and worth does not rest heavily on being the best, or achieving high status in a hierarchy of rankings. They hold strong intrinsic value and importance beliefs that are not overshadowed by utility value and cost perceptions, at least for some academic subjects. Their thoughts during learning situations are focused on problem solving, being strategic, and monitoring their progress, and are not diverted to how they appear to others or whether they can better their peers. They are not afraid or embarrassed to ask the teacher or peers for help (because needing help does not imply insufficient ability). Neither are these students hesitant about giving help to others, because others' successes do not detract from their own. They do not fret about possible social consequences, or better, do not experience negative consequences for being enthusiastic about particular academic subjects or types of activities. It is with this focus that they are likely to enjoy challenging tasks, and to feel good about being challenged, which is to say that challenge itself is motivating. They are likely to be resilient to setbacks, and develop the persistence and tenacity needed for future, more difficult, accomplishments. With new personal accomplishments, they set even higher goals for the future (Bandura, 1997). In other words, they will be exhibiting personal talent (Moon, 2003). And, overwhelmingly, they are most likely to experience significant learning and achievement.

This best-case scenario does not always play out, however. Gifted students are at risk for developing less adaptive patterns of beliefs and behaviors, and for failure to develop personal talent in spite of having abundant prerequisite abilities. This is especially so for highly academically gifted students, who are used to learning almost effortlessly, to being very successful with very little effort, to scoring high marks without having to develop learning or self-regulatory strategies, and to consistently out-performing others. Students who regularly experience considerable academic success and attention from others may come to gain an inflated level of personal validation or esteem from beating others, and perceive that outranking others is a central part of their identity. That is, a major part of their personal identity involves scoring at or near the top of their class or having a perfect GPA. This can lead to a number of maladaptive outcomes (see Urdan et al., 2002, for a review). Such students may experience excessive anxiety, especially if they are not confident of the outcome. Having a strong push to out-perform others can also lead to low levels of risk taking in the future. Their identity development may also be constrained, so that exploration is limited because only easy or "safe" classes or topics are chosen. If it is allowed in their school, such students may drop a class after the first test or assignment if they did not score an A. Given choices about assignments, students may opt for things they already know about, in order to assure success, and in extreme situations, they may recycle previous work (their own or someone else's) that has scored well. In such situations, students experience limited opportunities to develop self-regulatory strategies and to develop their skills. They also avoid sticking with a problem or persisting on a task despite initial difficulties, and thus lack resilience to initial setbacks. These outcomes undermine new learning and or even prevent it. For example, John, the top student in his elementary school, is now a middle school student who demands precisely clear instructions from his teachers, and then creates exactly what they require, nothing more. He takes no risks, answers every question with the answer he thinks the teacher is looking for, and defines learning as finishing-the-assignments. For very readable and compelling, but distressing, illustrations of many of these situations, see Pope's (2001) descriptions of high achievers and model high school students (as nominated by school personnel), and their strategies for "doing school." To accrue high grades and favorable teacher perceptions, these "model" students work to "beat the system" by engaging in practices such as manipulating teachers, doing homework for another class while faking attention to the current lesson, hiding academic opportunities from classmates to prevent them from excelling, copying homework, being absent during tests and talking to classmates before retaking them, and ducking courses that may result in subpar performance.

Promoting *Adaptive Motivational Beliefs and Behaviors: Implications for Educators and Parents*

Obviously, it is desirable for students to approach academic work with confidence and a focus on mastery, effort, and personal improvement. Although there will always be individual differences among students, research has shown clearly that teachers can, and do, influence their students' motivational beliefs and behaviors (e.g., Anderman et al., 2001; Patrick, Turner, Meyer, & Midgley, 2003). How can classroom teachers purposely promote adaptive beliefs and behaviors with their students? It is primarily through the explicit and implicit messages teachers send via their comments and instructional decisions they make. These instructional decisions include the types of tasks that are assigned or made available. Providing talented students with meaningful academic work and opportunities can go a long way toward fostering learning for learning's sake. Providing students with relevant and honest feedback concerning their work and their efforts can develop confidence, risk taking, and understanding. Other decisions, such as the participation structures used (e.g., whole class or group discussions, or individual work) and practices involving providing feedback and recognition, play important roles (Ames, 1992).

Changing Self-Beliefs About Competence

Enhancing academic self-efficacy sounds straightforward—just create lots of success opportunities. But, it is not so simple. For one thing, there is no absolute definition of success. What a teacher (or parent) considers success can differ sharply from a gifted student's thinking (Baum & Owen, 2004). In most cultures, high grades are evidence of successful academic work. However, if Zach's grade of A in his chemistry class came about from boring memorization and too-easy lab assignments, Zach is unlikely to treat that grade as a realistic marker of accomplishment, and attribute the A to external factors. For most gifted students, authentic successes come from activities that are personally meaningful and interesting. It is even better if those activities are challenging but attainable (Bandura, 1997). Self-efficacy is strengthened when students think that accomplishment flows from a combination of ability *and* effort, skill *and* will. These conditions are more likely when students can negotiate self-chosen tasks and personal goals. When teachers set academic goals, they can be way off the mark for students, as far as challenge and interest are concerned (Gentry & Owen, 2004). In a highly structured secondary classroom environment, where a single academic menu is offered to all 27 youngsters in the class, gifted students are far less likely to discover meaningful, interesting, challenging, and personal successes. Although talented high school students will likely complete their highly structured courses with good marks, they may find little value or interest in the experience or the subject matter.

Providing Challenges

Gifted students thrive in situations where they have appropriate challenges, regardless of whether they are in a gifted or regular class. When Ling has sufficient challenge in her school work, she learns to work hard, to experience—and get over—frustration, and to welcome additional challenges without fear of failure, because her successes with previous challenges have prepared her for later ones. Neihart et al. (2002) suggested that consistent, appropriate academic challenges and intellectual peer groups are the two most important factors in healthy social and emotional adjustment for gifted youth. However, research has shown repeatedly that much of the curriculum content is too easy for these students (Colangelo, Assouline, & Gross, 2004; Reis et al., 1993). Insufficient challenge is most likely to occur when teachers use a one-size-fits-all curriculum. Classroom teachers, then, must adjust curricula and instruction so that it provides optimal challenge for gifted students (Tomlinson, 2003; USOE, 1993).

Secondary teachers can manage the delivery of appropriately challenging curricula and instructions through the use of flexible instructional groups based on student skills (Gentry & Ferriss, 1999). Challenging tasks must be accompanied with opportunities for scaffolded learning, or the provision of an appropriate amount and type of support (Turner & Meyer, 1999). Providing optimal challenge is accomplished best by adjusting the tasks assigned to students, so that the material is difficult enough to stretch the students' minds, but not so difficult as to frustrate them. If tasks are too simple, students will likely experience boredom and feel little sense of accomplishment from their completion, but tasks that are too difficult generally elicit anxiety and risk student failure (Csikszentmihalyi & Rathunde, 1993). Neither of these situations promotes efficacy beliefs or importance and intrinsic values. For example, challenge for a talented math student might be arranged through acceleration over content and connecting with a math mentor. In language arts, teachers might provide advanced opportunities for writing and publishing, or literature groups in which advanced works are read and discussed. In science, students might work with their teachers to compact the basic curriculum and, working with content experts, design original inquiry projects based on community problems, as students did in the program described by Gentry and Ferriss. In these situations, students can tackle challenging tasks with the support that will allow for success and allay anxiety, so they will experience the feelings of accomplishment that foster self-efficacy. On the other hand, however, challenge can be overdone; students do not need to be stretched with every daily activity, and it is good for students to occasionally repeat tasks that they can do more effortlessly. This solidifies competencies, and fosters positive feelings abut one's abilities and the task or subject (Turner & Meyer).

Educators should be willing to substitute (not add) appropriately challenging curricula in areas where gifted students demonstrate high levels of ability or interest. This can be done through a combination of enrichment and acceleration. In middle and high schools, a complement of advanced, honors, Advanced Placement, independent and International Baccalaureate courses, dual enrollment in college courses, and curricular adjustments can provide appropriate challenges and intellectual peer groups for gifted students (Gentry & Owen, 2004; Renzulli, 1994). Other programs, such as Betts' (1985) Autonomous Learner Model, have shown promise with secondary students. Working to ensure meaningfulness and relevance of study topics to students' lives will also increase the likelihood that students will engage in the learning for authentic purposes, thus increasing optimal patterns of learning-related motivational beliefs and learning behaviors (Dai, 2000).

Providing Task Variety

Having a range of task options allows for students to select those that will provide optimal challenge (Tomlinson, 2003). When students work on tasks that are very different from those their classmates are engaged in, it is harder for students to make social comparisons (e.g., about speed, which is often taken as a signal of relative ability). Further, having variety contributes to a classroom environment where individualizing activities, making exceptions, assigning different things to different students, and offering choices are commonplace and not exceptional (Gentry, Rizza, & Owen, 2002). This type of environment negates the "It's not fair" or "Why does he/she get to do that?" comparison tendencies that occur in classrooms where exceptions are rare occurrences. Offering a variety of tasks can also serve to reduce competitive pressures and emphasize the need to consider one's own progress relative to objective and self-referenced criteria (i.e., a mastery focus). A primary consideration to providing task variety involves ensuring that tasks of varying degrees of difficulty are seen by students as important, interesting, and worth doing (Tomlinson, 2003). In other words, students who are challenged by the "grade level" curriculum should be provided with alternatives that are not deficit-based and remedial, but that are interesting, high quality, and challenging but attainable, thereby facilitating growth and learning. In doing so one avoids the remedial approach of reteaching difficult content more slowly and more loudly, which implies to the student that he or she cannot do the work. Conversely, students for whom the grade level curriculum is easy should not be offered more of the same, but given different, extended, or accelerated curricula, with opportunities for self-study in a related area of interest. In offering such accommodations, educators begin to allow for the depth and complexity that gifted students crave and can handle (Reis et al., 1993). Such modifications can form the basis for self-motivated learning in areas of intense interest and meaningful learning.

Providing Student Choices

Offering options to students is a serious and important consideration that can enhance their motivation (Eccles & Midgley, 1989; Renzulli, Gentry, & Reis, 2003). For example, Csikszentmihalyi and his colleagues (1993) found that gifted and talented teenagers' perceptions of choice were crucial in realizing the intrinsic rewards of schooling. Further, through the provision of choices (e.g., what they do, or how or when), students rehearse the fundamental skills of making wise choices and choosing problems and projects that develop their creativity, interests, and personal talent (Moon, 2003; Sternberg, 1997). However, our research has shown that students in middle school report having significantly fewer choices than students in elementary grades. And, although middle school students reported dependably lower levels of choice, interest, enjoyment, and challenge compared to elementary children, their perceptions of choice were markedly lower than the other types of classroom perceptions (Gentry & Gable, 2002). It is telling that, although teachers seem to know that choice is important, and claim to make choices available, their students generally do not perceive these choices (Gentry et al., 2002).

Providing students with meaningful choices is probably the simplest modification teachers can make to increase motivation and learning in the classroom, and choices are especially important for adolescent students as they develop identity and test authority. Offering choices regarding the order of curriculum, specific content, audiences, and relevant homework, group members (if any), and types of assessments are some not-too-difficult means of integrating choice into the classroom.

Teacher Enthusiasm

Teachers' enthusiasm for the subjects and the students they teach is a powerful factor in fostering positive motivated behavior (Brophy, 2004; Patrick et al., 2003). When teachers with the most adaptive classroom motivational environments talk about academics, they convey their own high level of interest and enthusiasm. Further, their enthusiasm centers around enjoyment of the process of learning in its own right; they emphasize intrinsic and enjoyable aspects of engaging in tasks, and in achieving competence in them. Their teaching rests on positive expectations, such that students want to learn and are lucky to have the opportunities to do so. Teachers in maladaptive motivational environments assume that students do not want to do a task, will find it boring, or would rather be elsewhere (Patrick et al.). And the situation becomes a self-fulfilling trap when those same teachers show little enthusiasm for the topics they teach or for teaching in general. Effective teachers of gifted students connect with their students in personally meaningful ways, and serve more as guides and mentors and less as lecturers and deliverers of content. They inspire, respect, and expect great things from their students, and their students respond in kind (Feldhusen, 1997).

Feedback to Students

Effective feedback, including praise, needs to be contingent, specific, accurate, and informational so that it builds self-efficacy and facilitates a mastery orientation (Brophy, 1981; Patrick, Anderman, Ryan, Edelin, & Midgley, 2001). Students need to know what specifically they did well, and how they can improve in the future. General, nonspecific feedback (e.g., "Good job!", "Way to go!") may assist with a positive classroom environment, but is not very helpful for the learning process and does not strengthen self-efficacy (Pintrich & Schunk, 2001). Feedback should also be referenced to students' previous efforts and accomplishments, and not involve comparisons with other students. This promotes a mastery orientation among students, and does not encourage a performance orientation. Teachers who are developers of talent can help guide their students to heights they might not have imagined were possible. This guidance can take many forms, including career counseling, arranging for mentoring in an area of talent, or providing students with resources in their particular interest area. Such teachers often recognize potential and facilitate growth by making exceptions, compacting curricula, offering special independent study opportunities, and advocating for the student (Renzulli, 1994).

Downplay Competition and Emphasize Individual
Improvement, Effort, and Adaptive Strategies

A mastery orientation is clearly the most adaptive for students at all levels of ability. This suggests that teachers focus on objective criteria of success, and students' personal improvement relative to those criteria. Despite popular belief to the contrary, and even though gifted students usually come out on top in competitions, a competitive, norm-referenced focus tends to affect highly gifted students in negative ways, particularly with respect to important and long-term educational goals (Clinkenbeard, 1989; Schneider & Udvari, 2000). For example, a competitive (compared to individualistic) environment has been associated with students perceiving less satisfaction from learning, lower importance of effort relative to ability, lower continuing motivation, and greater probability of choosing an easy but uninteresting project over a difficult but highly interesting project (Clinkenbeard, 1989). Surprisingly, Clinkenbeard discovered perceived negative effects in gifted students who performed well under competitive circumstances and who claimed to enjoy competition. Thus, there is clear evidence that educators and parents (and others) should downplay competition among students, and avoid emphasizing students' performance relative to each other. Obviously, some students do score higher than others; although it is reasonable to acknowledge this, it should be communicated with messages that everyone's performance is affected by factors that are open to change (e.g., strategy use, effort), and that what really matters is that students learn more than they knew yesterday and do better than they did previously. We need to be wary of long-term motivational outcomes for students—especially those near the top of achievement hierarchies—whose identity depends on doing better than others. The motivation to engage in academics primarily to beat others, rather than to improve one's personal best, is antithetical to healthy classroom behaviors and optimal development of personal potential. Gifted students, and perhaps their family members, may need guidance to develop healthy views of competition with personal improvement as the goal.

Positive and Supportive Teacher-Student Relationships

The quality and nature of teachers' relationships with their students play a strong role in facilitating adaptive motivational beliefs. Teachers need to communicate support, clearly and unequivocally, for *both* students' learning and for them as persons (Patrick et al., 2001; Wentzel, 1997). Capable teachers convey two crucial messages: They care about students' learning and want to, can, and will help them learn; and they care about their students at a personal, socio-emotional level. Students need to be assured of both forms of caring.

Entire school cultures also affect student motivation, through their policies and what is emphasized at the school level, in much the same way that teachers and their instructional practices do (Maehr & Anderman, 1993; Roeser, Midgley, & Urdan,

1996). Schools in which students report significantly more adaptive motivational behavior are places where they feel connected to teachers, and believe that individual improvement and mastery of content is valued, while comparisons among students' achievement are not accentuated. These larger adaptive environments also build *collective* self-efficacy (Bandura, 1997), where students and teachers root for and help one another. Such schools foster pride and a "can-do" attitude among teachers, administrators, parents, and even maintenance workers.

In summary, although gifted students need positive motivation in order to realize the promise of their gifts, that motivation can be helped or hindered by the actions of others, including peers, teachers, school administrators, and parents. Adolescent peers have enough to keep them busy, but school personnel and parents are expected to create an environment in which gifted students will develop strong self-efficacy, a mastery orientation, and value for academics. This includes offering content and tasks that are meaningful and worthy of pursuit, providing choices, and creating contexts where challenge, risk taking, and learning from mistakes converge. When that happens, it is not just the participants, but society in general, who will profit.

Although there is considerable understanding of some aspects of student motivation, our knowledge is still patchy. This is particularly so when we consider gifted students' motivation. In the final section of this chapter, therefore, we outline some of the most pressing issues (in our opinions) that need to be addressed by researchers and educators concerned with gifted adolescents.

ISSUES AND DIRECTIONS FOR FUTURE RESEARCH

The research addressing gifted adolescents' motivation has been predominantly comparative, looking at gifted versus nongifted students. As Dai et al. (1998) noted, such comparisons imply that gifted students are a fairly homogeneous group with shared characteristics. This approach to research masks important individual differences among gifted students. Person-centered statistical approaches (e.g., cluster analyses), in contrast to variable-centered approaches (e.g., regressions), can identify different typologies or profiles of students (see Clinkenbeard, 1996). Research on students within these different clusters will undoubtedly be crucial to understanding potential differences in motivational patterns and different trajectories of achievement.

There is also a great need for researchers to focus on *processes* by which factors affect gifted adolescents' motivation, and their subsequent beliefs and behaviors. For example, *how* and *why* do different educational outcomes (e.g., achievement) and affective outcomes (e.g., liking school, losing interest in, or developing apathy for school) come about over time? What are the mechanisms that produce highly resilient talented youth, those who rise far beyond their impoverished environments?

Targeted intervention efforts for gifted students have been called for (e.g., Robinson, 2002b), but in order to carry out such interventions, educators need more individualized information. Research that examines different outcomes and processes for different kinds of gifted students will surely help educators organize more facilitative kinds of educational options.

Although longitudinal study is probably the most difficult form of research, there is a dire need for such research on gifted students (e.g., Gottfried & Gottfried, 1996; Richardson & Benbow, 1990), so that we can understand how different motivational patterns play out over time. What, for example, are the long-term implications of students receiving extrinsic rewards for high achievement, or for being very focused on being the best? Avoidance beliefs or extrinsic/utility value beliefs may take considerable time to manifest in maladaptive ways, so that what at one glance appears benign, or even positive, may devolve into negative behaviors many years later.

It is clear that there has been very little attention paid to cultural variations in motivation and learning. In one respect this is understandable—students of color are particularly underrepresented in the pool of students identified as gifted. However, it is imperative that researchers extend their focus past those students who are most visible and most easily accessed. Again, too, we need much more information than group mean differences. For example, we already know—and it is not that informative—that African American students generally report significantly higher self-efficacy than do White students, and that this high efficacy is typically inconsistent with their current performance. What we do not know is what these beliefs mean to those students, in the context of their lives and larger world beliefs. Thus, a focus on processes—how motivation and achievement play out against the background of students' experiences and environments—will provide the most meaningful and usable information.

REFERENCES

American Association of University Women Educational Foundation. (1999). *Gender gaps: Where schools still fail our children.* New York: Marlow and Company.

Ames, C. (1992). Classrooms: Goals, structures, and student motivation. *Journal of Educational Psychology, 84,* 261–271.

Anderman, E. M., Eccles, J. S., Yoon, K. S., Roeser, R., Wigfield, A., & Blumenfeld, P. (2001). Learning to value mathematics and reading: Relations to mastery and performance-oriented instructional practices. *Contemporary Educational Psychology, 26,* 76–95.

Bain, S. K., & Bell, S. M. (2004). Social self-concept, social attributions, and peer relationships in fourth, fifth, and sixth graders who are gifted compared to high achievers. *Gifted Child Quarterly, 48,* 167–178.

Bandura, A. (1977). Self-efficacy: Toward a unifying theory of behavioral change. *Psychological Review, 84,* 191–215.

Bandura, A. (1997). *Self-efficacy: The exercise of control.* New York: Freeman.

Battle, A., & Wigfield, A. (2003). College women's value orientations toward family, career, and graduate school. *Journal of Vocational Behavior, 62,* 56–75.

Baum, S. M., & Owen, S. V. (2004). *To be gifted and learning disabled: Strategies for helping bright students with LD, ADHD, and more* (2nd ed.). Mansfield Center, CT: Creative Learning Press.

Betts, G. T. (1985). *Autonomous learner model for the gifted and talented.* Greeley, CO: Autonomous Learning Publications and Specialists.

Betts, G. T., & Neihart, M. (1988). Profiles of the gifted and talented. *Gifted Child Quarterly, 32,* 248–253.

Bong, M., & Skaalvik, E. M. (2003). Academic self-concept and self-efficacy: How different are they really? *Educational Psychology Review, 15,* 1–40.

Bosma, H. A., & Kunnen, E. S. (2001). Determinants and mechanisms in ego identity development: A review and synthesis. *Developmental Review, 21,* 39–66.

Brophy, J. (1981). Teacher praise: A functional analysis. *Review of Educational Research, 51,* 5–32.

Brophy, J. (2004). *Motivating students to learn* (2nd ed.). Mahwah, NJ: Lawrence Erlbaum.

Brown, B. B. (1990). Peer groups and peer cultures. In S. S. Feldman & G. R. Elliott (Eds.), *At the threshold: The developing adolescent* (pp. 171–196). Cambridge, MA: Harvard University Press.

Brown, B. B., Eicher, S. A., & Petrie, S. D. (1986). The importance of peer group ("crowd") affiliation in adolescence. *Journal of Adolescence, 9,* 73–96.

Buhrmester, D., & Furman, W. (1987). The development of companionship and intimacy. *Child Development, 58,* 1101–1113.

Byrnes, J. P. (2003). Cognitive development during adolescence. In G. R. Adams & M. D. Berzonsky (Eds.), *Blackwell handbook of adolescence* (pp. 225–246). Malden, MA: Blackwell Publishing.

Chan, L. K. S. (1996). Motivational orientations and metacognitive abilities of intellectually gifted students. *Gifted Child Quarterly, 40,* 184–193.

Clinkenbeard, P. R. (1989). The motivation to win: Negative aspects of success at competition. *Journal for the Education for the Gifted, 12,* 293–305.

Clinkenbeard, P. R. (1996). Research on motivation and the gifted: Implications for identification, programming, and evaluation. *Gifted Child Quarterly, 40,* 220–221.

Colangelo, N., Assouline, S. G., & Gross, M. U. M. (2004). *A nation deceived: How schools hold back America's brightest students.* Retrieved February 18, 2005, from http://nationdeceived.org/download.html

Covington, M. V. (1992). *Making the grade: A self-worth perspective on motivation and school reform.* Cambridge, England: Cambridge University Press.

Covington, M. V. (2000). Goal theory, motivation, and school achievement: An integrative review. *Annual Review of Psychology, 51,* 171–200.

Csikszentmihalyi, M., & Larson, R. (1984). *Being adolescent.* New York: Basic Books.

Csikszentmihalyi, M., & Rathunde, K. (1993). The measurement of flow in everyday life: Toward a theory of emergent motivation. In J. Jacobs (Ed.), *Developmental perspectives on motivation: Nebraska Symposium on Motivation* (pp. 57–97). Lincoln, NE: University of Nebraska Press.

Csikszentmihalyi, M., Rathunde, K., & Whalen, S. (1993). *Talented teenagers: The roots of success and failure.* New York: Cambridge University Press.

Dai, D. Y. (2000). To be or not to be (challenged), that is the question: Task and ego orientations among high-ability, high-achieving adolescents. *The Journal of Experimental Education, 68,* 311–330.

Dai, D. Y., Moon, S. M., & Feldhusen, J. F. (1998). Achievement motivation and gifted students: A social cognitive perspective. *Educational Psychologist, 33,* 45–63.

Davis, G. A., & Rimm, S. B. (2003). *Education of the gifted and talented.* Boston: Allyn & Bacon.

Dweck, C. S. (1986). Motivational processes affecting learning. *American Psychologist, 41,* 1040–1048.

Eccles, J. S. (1983). Expectancies, values and academic behaviors. In J. T. Spence (Ed.), *Achievement and achievement motives* (pp. 75–146). San Francisco: Freeman.

Eccles, J. S. (1985). Why doesn't Jane run? Sex differences in educational and occupational patterns. In F. D. Horowitz & M. O'Brien (Eds.), *The gifted and talented: Developmental perspectives* (pp. 251–295). Washington, DC: American Psychological Association.

Eccles, J. S. (1994). Understanding women's educational and occupational choices: Applying the Eccles et al. model of achievement-related choices. *Psychology of Women Quarterly, 18,* 585–609.

Eccles (Parsons), J. S., Adler, T., & Meece, J. L. (1984). Sex differences in achievement: A test of alternate theories. *Journal of Personality and Social Psychology, 46,* 26–43.

Eccles, J. S., & Midgley, C. (1989). Stage-environment fit: Developmentally appropriate classrooms for young adolescents. In C. Ames & R. Ames (Eds.), *Research on motivation in education: Vol. 3, Goals and cognitions* (pp. 13–44). New York: Academic.

Eccles, J. S., & Wigfield, A. (2002). Motivational beliefs, values, and goals. *Annual Review of Psychology, 53,* 109–132.

Eisenberg, N., Martin, C. L., & Fabes, R. A. (1996). Gender development and gender effects. In D. C. Berliner & R. C. Calfee (Eds.), *Handbook of educational psychology* (pp. 358–396). New York: Simon & Schuster Macmillan.

Elkind, D. (1967). Egocentrism in adolescence. *Child Development, 38,* 1025–1034.

Elliot, A. J., McGregor, H. A., & Gable, S. (1999). Achievement goals, study strategies, and exam performance: A mediational analysis. *Journal of Educational Psychology, 91,* 549–563.

Erikson, E. H. (1968). *Identity: Youth and crisis.* New York: Norton.

Feldhusen, J. F. (1997). Educating teachers for work with talented youth. In N. Colangelo & G. A. Davis (Eds.), *Handbook of gifted education* (2nd ed., pp. 547–552). Boston: Allyn & Bacon.

Fredricks, J. A., & Eccles, J. S. (2004). Children's competence and value beliefs from childhood through adolescence: Growth trajectories in two male sex-typed domains. *Developmental Psychology, 38,* 519–533.

Freeman, K. E., Gutman, L. M., & Midgley, C. (2002). Can achievement goal theory enhance our understanding of the motivation and performance of African American young adolescents? In C. Midgley (Ed.), *Goals, goal structures, and patterns of adaptive learning* (pp. 175–204). Mahwah, NJ: Erlbaum.

Furman, W., & Buhrmester, D. (1992). Age and sex differences in perceptions of networks of personal relationships. *Child Development, 63,* 103–115.

Gentry, M., & Ferriss, S. (1999). StATS: A model of collaboration to develop science talent among rural middle school students. *Roeper Review, 21,* 316–320.

Gentry, M., & Gable, R. K. (2002). Students' perceptions of classrooms activities: Are there grade level and gender differences? *Journal of Educational Psychology, 94,* 539–544.

Gentry, M., & Owen, S. V. (2004). Student perceptions of classroom quality: Differences between honors, AP, and advanced students and students in general classes. *Journal of Secondary Gifted Education, 16,* 20–29.

Gentry, M., Rizza, M. G., & Owen, S. V. (2002). Examining perceptions of challenge and choice in classrooms: The relationship between teachers and their students and comparison between gifted students and other students. *Gifted Child Quarterly, 46,* 145–155.

Gibbons, F. X., & Benbow, C. P. (1994). From top dog to bottom half: Social comparison strategies in response to poor performance. *Journal of Personality and Social Psychology, 67,* 638–652.

Gottfried, A. E., & Gottfried, A. W. (1996). A longitudinal study of academic intrinsic motivation in intellectually gifted children: Childhood through early adolescence. *Gifted Child Quarterly, 40,* 179–183.

Graham, S., & Hudley, C. (2005). Race and ethnicity in the study of motivation and competence. In A. J. Elliot & C. S. Dweck (Eds.), *Handbook of competence and motivation* (pp. 392–413). New York: Guilford Press.

Graham, S., Taylor, A., & Hudley, C. (1998). Percentage of female classmates nominated as valued by female nominators in three ethnic groups, as a function of ethnicity and achievement level of nominee. *Journal of Educational Psychology, 90,* 606–620.

Gross, M. U. M. (1993). *Exceptionally gifted children.* London: Routledge.

Gross, M. U. M. (1999). Small poppies: Highly gifted children in the early years. *Roeper Review, 21,* 207–214.

Harackiewicz, J. M., Barron, K. E., Pintrich, P. R., Elliot, A. J., & Thrash, T. M. (2002). Revision of achievement goal theory: Necessary and illuminating. *Journal of Educational Psychology, 94,* 638–645.

Harter, S. (1990). Self and identity development. In S. S. Feldman & G. R. Elliot (Eds.), *At the threshold: The developing adolescent* (pp. 352–387). Cambridge, MA: Harvard University Press.

Heller, K. A., & Ziegler, A. (1996). Gender differences in mathematics and the sciences: Can attributional retraining improve the performance of gifted females? *Gifted Child Quarterly, 40,* 200–210.

Jacobs, J. E., Finken, L. L., Griffin, N. L., & Wright, J. D. (1998). The career plans of science-talented rural adolescent girls. *American Educational Research Journal, 35,* 681–704.

Jacobs, J. E., Lanza, S., Osgood, D. W., Eccles, J. S., & Wigfield, A. (2002). Changes in children's self-competence and values: Gender and domain differences across grades one through twelve. *Child Development, 73,* 509–527.

Junge, M. E., & Dretzke, B. J. (1995). Mathematical self-efficacy gender differences in gifted/talented adolescents. *Gifted Child Quarterly, 39,* 22–28.

Juvonen, J. (2000). The social functions of attributional face-saving tactics among early adolescents. *Educational Psychology Review, 12,* 15–32.

Kaplan, A., Middleton, M. J., Urdan, T., & Midgley, C. (2002). Achievement goals and goal structures. In C. Midgley (Ed.), *Goals, goal structures, and patterns of adaptive learning* (pp. 21–53). Mahwah, NJ: Erlbaum.

Keating, D. P. (1990). Adolescent thinking. In S. S. Feldman & G. R. Elliot (Eds.), *At the threshold: The developing adolescent* (pp. 54–89). Cambridge, MA: Harvard University Press.

Keating, D. P. (2004). Cognitive and brain development. In R. M. Lerner & L. Steinberg (Eds.), *Handbook of adolescent psychology* (2nd ed., pp. 45–84). Hoboken, NJ: Wiley.

Kelly, K. R., & Colangelo, N. (1984). Academic and social self-concepts of gifted, general, and special students. *Exceptional Children, 50,* 551–554.

Kenney-Benson, G. A., Pomerantz, E. M., Ryan, A. M., & Patrick, H. (in press). Sex differences in math performance: The role of children's approach to schoolwork. *Developmental Psychology.*

Klassen, R. M. (2004). A cross-cultural investigation of the efficacy beliefs of South Asian immigrant and Anglo Canadian nonimmigrant early adolescents. *Journal of Educational Psychology, 96,* 731–742.

Kroger, J. (2003). Identity development during adolescence. In G. R. Adams & M. D. Berzonsky (Eds.), *Blackwell handbook of adolescence* (pp. 205–226). Malden, MA: Blackwell Publishing.

Li, A. K. F., & Adamson, G. (1995). Motivational patterns related to gifted students' learning of mathematics, science and English: An examination of gender differences. *Journal for the Education of the Gifted, 18,* 284–297.

Maehr, M. L., & Anderman, E. M. (1993). Reinventing schools for early adolescents: Emphasizing task goals. *Elementary School Journal, 93,* 593–610.

Malpass, J. R., O'Neil, H. F., & Hocevar, D. (1999). Self-regulation, goal orientation, self-efficacy, worry, and high-stakes math achievement for mathematically gifted high-school students. *Roeper Review, 21,* 281–288.

Middleton, M. J., Kaplan, A., & Midgley, C. (2004). The change in middle school students' achievement goals in mathematics over time. *Social Psychology of Education, 7,* 289–311.

Middleton, M., & Midgley, C. (1997). Avoiding the demonstration of lack of ability: An underexplored aspect of goal theory. *Journal of Educational Psychology, 89,* 710–718.

Midgley, C., Kaplan, A., & Middleton, M. (2001). Performance-approach goals: Good for what, for whom, under what circumstances, and at what cost? *Journal of Educational Psychology, 93,* 77–86.

Moon, S. M. (2003). Personal talent. *High Ability Students, 14,* 5–21.

Neihart, M., Reis, S. M., Robinson, N. M., & Moon, S. M. (2002). *The social and emotional development of gifted children: What do we know?* Waco, TX: Prufrock Press.

Nicholls, J. G. (1989). *The competitive ethos and democratic education.* Cambridge, MA: Harvard University Press.

Pajares, F. (1996a). Self-efficacy beliefs and mathematical problem-solving of gifted students. *Contemporary Educational Psychology, 21,* 325–344.

Pajares, F. (1996b). Self-efficacy beliefs in academic settings. *Review of Educational Research, 66,* 543–578.

Pajares, F. (2002). Gender and perceived self-efficacy in self-regulated learning. *Theory Into Practice, 41,* 116–125.

Pajares, F., & Kranzler, J. (1995). Self-efficacy beliefs and general mental ability in mathematical problem-solving. *Contemporary Educational Psychology, 20,* 426–443.

Pajares, F., & Valiante, G. (1999). Grade level and gender differences in the writing self-beliefs of middle school students. *Contemporary Educational Psychology, 24,* 390–405.

Patrick, H., Anderman, L. H., Ryan, A. M., Edelin, K., & Midgley, C. (2001). Teachers' communication of goal orientations in four fifth-grade classrooms. *The Elementary School Journal, 102,* 35–58.

Patrick, H., Turner, J. C., Meyer, D. K., & Midgley, C. (2003). How teachers establish psychological environments during the first days of school: Associations with avoidance in mathematics. *Teachers College Record, 105,* 1521–1558.

Pintrich, P. R. (2000). The role of goal orientation in self-regulated learning. In M. Boekaerts, P. Pintrich, & M. Zeidner, (Eds.), *Handbook of self-regulation.* San Diego: Academic Press.

Pintrich, P. R., & De Groot, E. V. (1990). Motivational and self-regulated learning components of classroom academic performance. *Journal of Educational Psychology, 82,* 33–40.

Pintrich, P. R., & Schunk, D. H. (2002). *Motivation in education: Theory, research, and applications* (2nd ed.). Englewood Cliffs, NJ: Prentice-Hall.

Pokay, P., & Blumenfeld, P. C. (1990). Predicting achievement early and late in the semester: The role of motivation and use of learning strategies. *Journal of Educational Psychology, 82,* 41–50.

Pope, D. C. (2001). *Doing school: How we are creating a generation of stressed out, materialistic, and miseducated students.* New Haven, CT: Yale University Press.

Reis, S. M., & McCoach D. B. (2000). The underachievement of gifted students: What do we know and where do we go? *Gifted Child Quarterly, 44,* 152–170.

Reis, S. M., Westberg, K. L., Kulikowich, J., Caillard, F., Hébert, T., Plucker, J., et al. (1993). *Why not let high ability students start school in January? The curriculum compacting study.* Storrs, CT: The National Research Center on the Gifted and Talented.

Renzulli, J. S. (1978). What makes giftedness? Reexamining a definition. *Phi Delta Kappan, 60,* 180–184, 261.

Renzulli, J. S. (1994). *Schools for talent development: A practical plan for total school improvement.* Mansfield Center, CT: Creative Learning Press.

Renzulli, J. S., Gentry, M., & Reis, S. M. (2003) *Enrichment clusters: A practical plan for real-world, student-driven learning.* Mansfield Center, CT: Creative Learning Press.

Richardson, T. M., & Benbow, C. P. (1990). Long-term effects of acceleration on the social-emotional adjustment of mathematically precocious youths. *Journal of Educational Psychology, 82,* 464–470.

Rimm, S. (2002). Peer pressures and social acceptance of gifted students. In M. Neihart, S. M. Reis, N. M. Robinson, & S. M. Moon (Eds.), *The social and emotional development of gifted children: What do we know?* (pp. 13–18). Waco, TX: Prufrock Press.

Robinson, N. M. (2002a). Individual differences in gifted students' attributions for academic performances. In M. Neihart, S. M. Reis, N. M. Robinson, & S. M. Moon (Eds.), *The social and emotional development of gifted children: What do we know?* (pp. 61–69). Waco, TX: Prufrock Press.

Robinson, N. M. (2002b). Introduction. In M. Neihart, S. M. Reis, N. M. Robinson, & S. M. Moon (Eds.), *The social and emotional development of gifted children: What do we know?* (pp. xi–xxiv). Waco, TX: Prufrock Press.

Robinson, N. M., Zigler, E., & Gallagher, J. J. (2000). Two ends of the normal curve: Similarities and differences in the study of mental retardation and giftedness. *American Psychologist, 55,* 1413–1424.

Roeser, R. W., Midgley, C., & Urdan, T. C. (1996). Perceptions of the school psychological environment and early adolescents' psychological and behavioral functioning in school: The mediating role of goals and belonging. *Journal of Educational Psychology, 88,* 408–422.

Ruble, D. N., & Martin, C. L. (1998). Gender development. In W. Damon & N. Eisenberg (Eds.), *The handbook of child psychology. Volume 3: Social, emotional, and personality development* (5th ed., pp. 933–1016). New York: John Wiley.

Ryan, R. M., & Deci, E. L. (2000). When rewards compete with nature: The undermining of intrinsic motivation and self-regulation. In C. Sansone & J. M. Harackiewicz (Eds.), *Intrinsic and extrinsic motivation: The search for optimal motivation and performance* (pp. 13–54). San Diego, CA: Academic Press.

Schiefele, U., Krapp, A., & Winteler, A. (1992). Interest as a predictor of academic achievement: A meta-analysis of research. In K. A. Renninger, S. Hidi, & A. Krapp (Eds.), *The role of interest in learning and development* (pp. 183–212). Hillsdale, NJ: Erlbaum.

Schneider, B. H., & Udvari, S. J. (2000). Competition and the adjustment of gifted children: A matter of motivation. *Roeper Review, 22,* 212–216.

Silverman, L. (1993). *Counseling the gifted and talented.* Denver: Love.

Sternberg, R. J. (1997). *Successful intelligence.* New York: Plume.

Tomlinson, C. A. (2003). *Fulfilling the promise of the differentiated classroom: Strategies and tools for responsive teaching.* Alexandria, VA: Association for Supervision and Curriculum Development.

Turner, J. C., & Meyer, D. K. (1999). Integrating classroom context into motivation theory and research: Rationales, methods, and implications. In T. Urdan (Ed.), *Advances in motivation and achievement, volume 11. The role of context* (pp. 87–121). Stamford, CT: JAI Press.

Urdan, T. C., Ryan, A. M., Anderman, E. M., & Gheen, M. (2002). Goals, goal structures, and avoidance behaviors. In C. Midgley (Ed.), *Goals, goal structures, and patterns of adaptive learning* (pp. 55–83). Mahwah, NJ: Lawrence Erlbaum.

U.S. Department of Education, Office of Educational Research and Improvement. (1993). *National excellence: A case for developing America's talent.* Washington, DC: U.S. Government Printing Office.

Vansteenkiste, M., Simons, J., Lens, W., Soenens, B., Matos, L., & Lacante, M. (2004). Less is sometimes more: Goal content matters. *Journal of Educational Psychology, 96,* 755–764.

Watson, C. M., Quatman, T., & Endler, E. (2002). Career aspirations of adolescent girls: Effects of achievement level, grade, and single-sex school environment. *Sex Roles: A Journal of Research, 46,* 323–335.

Weiner, B. (1986). *An attributional theory of motivation and emotion.* New York: Springer-Verlag.

Weiner, B. (2004). Attribution theory revisited: Transforming cultural plurality into theoretical unity. In D. M. McInerney & S. Van Etten (Eds.), *Big theories revisited: Volume 4. Research on sociocultural influences on motivation and learning* (pp. 13–29). Greenwich, CT: Information Age Publishing.

Wentzel, K. R. (1997). Student motivation in middle school: The role of perceived pedagogical caring. *Journal of Educational Psychology, 89,* 411–419.

Whitmore, J. R. (1986). Preventing severe underachievement and developing achievement motivation. *Journal of Children in Contemporary Society, 18,* 119–133.

Wigfield, A. (1994). Expectancy-value theory of achievement motivation: A developmental perspective. *Educational Psychology Review, 6,* 49–78.

Wigfield, A., & Eccles, J. (1992). The development of achievement task values: A theoretical analysis. *Developmental Review, 12,* 265–310.

Ziegler, A., & Heller, K. A. (2000). Effects of an attributional retraining with female students gifted in physics. *Journal for the Education of the Gifted, 23,* 217–243.

Ziegler, A., Heller, K. A., & Broome, P. (1996). Motivational preconditions for girls gifted and highly gifted in physics. *High Ability Studies, 7,* 129–143.

Ziegler, A., & Stoeger, H. (2004). Evaluation of an attributional retraining (modeling technique) to reduce gender differences in chemistry instruction. *High Ability Studies, 15,* 63–83.

Zimmerman, B. J. (2000). Self efficacy: An essential motive to learn. *Contemporary Educational Psychology, 25,* 82–91.

TALENT DEVELOPMENT IN ADOLESCENCE

Talent Development in Adolescence: An Overview

by Sidney M. Moon

*T*he purpose of Part II of this book is to give educators a sense of the complete talent development process in several different domains: academic, visual arts, personal, social, and sports. Adolescence is a critical period for developing talent in all of these domains. Those who have studied the process of developing talent to high levels agree that the process takes a long time and requires intense involvement (Bloom, 1985; Ericsson, Krampe, & Tesch-Romer, 1993; Gagné, 2000). In general, it takes at least 10 years of dedication and practice in a specialized talent area to reach the top levels of a field. In some fields, such as science, it may take much longer. Doctors, for example, spend at least 7 years in training before they begin to practice medicine, and then require many more years of practice before they rise to the level of nationally recognized specialists. Research neurologists may have an even longer apprenticeship before they reach the top of their field (Bloom). In sports, on the other hand, young people can generally reach Olympic-level performance with 10 years of making a serious commitment to a particular sport such as tennis or soccer (Van Rossum & Gagné, this volume). The field of music also allows for relatively fast progress from novice to expert (Bloom).

Individuals peak at different ages in different fields (Simonton, 1994). In sports, peak performance generally occurs quite young, in a person's 20s or 30s. On the other hand, in the STEM disciplines (science, technology, engineering, and mathematics), the age at which an individual makes his or her best contribution ranges from an average of late 30s in mathematics to early 40s in medicine. In politics, Simonton reported that only 13% of illustrious leaders attained power before the age of 40. In other words, the average age for peak performance varies considerably by discipline, occurring early in sports, in mid-life in the sciences, and in later life in politics.

In a study of persons who had reached world-class status in six different fields at a relatively young age, Bloom (1985) and his colleagues discovered that all of these individuals moved through three quite distinct stages of talent development. In the *early years* they experienced playful, fun activities with immediate rewards. Their teachers were warm, affectionate, and encouraging. This stage tended to coincide with the preschool and elementary school years, although there was some variation in timing based on discipline and students' prior experiences. As the students moved into the *middle years*, things changed dramatically. They became committed to excelling in their chosen discipline and willing to work long and hard to master that discipline. The bond between the students and their teachers shifted from one of love to one of respect. They developed the ability to practice monotonous or boring tasks in order to improve their skills. They no longer needed learning to be fun in order to stay motivated. Instead, they seemed motivated by an intrinsic desire for mastery, and began building a sense of identity around their competencies in their chosen field. Eventually, usually after high school, these talented young people moved on to the *later stages* of learning. The later stages often involved moving across the country to work with a world-class teacher or coach who enabled the students to begin to push the boundaries of their fields and/or make original contributions. Teachers at this stage were exacting taskmasters with very high standards. They expected total dedication from their students. This stage tended to occur at the end of adolescence or the beginning of adulthood. For scientists, this stage occurred in graduate school. For musicians, it occurred in college.

Some middle/high school students will be in the early stages of talent development. For example, Bloom (1985) found that most students talented in the visual arts were still in the early years of talent development in high school, because there were few opportunities for them to develop artistic talent earlier in their schooling. On the other hand, adolescents who were talented in sports and striving to qualify for the Olympics were often at the end of the middle years of talent development, or even the beginning of the later years, by the end of high school; these students faced severe challenges in balancing the demands of regular schooling with their athletic training programs (Bloom; Van Rossum & Gagné, this volume).

In addition, high-ability middle and high school students in the same classroom can be in different stages of the talent development process. Some will still need the warm, fun classroom environment of the early years, while others will be ready for the more rigorous and mastery-oriented environment of the middle years. One of the challenges facing secondary teachers is how to accommodate students who are in different stages of the academic talent development process. Another is how to support students whose primary talent discipline lies in another area. For example, how does a history teacher support a student who is an Olympic hopeful in swimming? And how does that support differ from the support a history teacher might provide for a student who is seriously considering a career in medieval history and already knows more about medieval history than the teacher?

This brief review of talent development trajectories suggests that secondary teachers need to know their students well if they are to design appropriate talent development experiences for students with different degrees of commitment to their talent, and those who are in different stages of talent development in the discipline. That conclusion is also supported by one of the most ambitious studies of gifted adolescents ever conducted, *Talented Teenagers* (Csikszentmihalyi, Rathunde, & Whalen, 1993). This study of more than 200 teenagers who were talented in several domains provides some guidance for secondary teachers who want to help students develop talent in mathematics, science, music, art, and athletics. The purpose of the study was to determine why some gifted teens developed their abilities while others dropped out of the talent pipeline. The study provided partial support for the Differentiated Model of Giftedness and Talent (DMGT; Gagné, 2000; Van Rossum & Gagné, this volume) because it suggested that both intrapersonal and environmental catalysts were important influences on the talent development trajectories of gifted adolescents during the teen years. The primary finding of the study with respect to schooling was that it was essential for teachers to provide skilled students with challenging instruction. Skilled students experiencing unchallenging learning environments quickly became unmotivated and uninvolved.

The individual chapters in Part II of *The Handbook of Secondary Gifted Education* can help secondary teachers understand the talent development process and how they can assist with that process. In Chapter 8, Jarvin and Subotnik explicate the SP/A model of talent development. This model is designed to show how individuals rise to the level of artistry and/or scholarly productivity in a given field. In other words, it is a creative-productive model of talent development (see also Renzulli, 1978; Moon & Dixon, this volume). The model was originally developed by studying how musicians moved from high-ability novices to world-class creative artists. It is applied here to the development of academic talent. Like Bloom (1985), Jarvin & Subotnik conceptualize three stages of talent development, each characterized by a different type of learning opportunity. In stage one, students convert their raw abilities into competence as they experience instruction with emphasis on exposure to content knowledge and guided skill practice. As they develop their competence into expertise during stage two, they need instruction focused on creative problem finding and solving. In the final stage, they are socialized into their field with the assistance of master teachers. This stage usually occurs after high school in the academic disciplines. Most of the mediating variables Jarvin and Subotnik emphasize are intrapersonal, that is, they are characteristics of students rather than of their environments. High intrinsic motivation facilitates talent development in all three stages. Students become increasingly autonomous as they move through the stages. For example, in stage one, teachers assess student strengths and weaknesses, while in stage two students are expected to know their own strengths and weaknesses. The model also suggests that practical intelligence is increasingly important as students become more skilled and committed. The model provides support for the emphasis on personal and social development in the framework for secondary gifted education provided in Chapter 1 (Moon & Dixon, this volume).

The development of visual arts talent at the secondary level is the focus of Chapter 9. Sabol provides a comprehensive look at the factors that secondary schools need to consider in developing discipline-based art education (DBAE) programs. In addition, he addresses definitional issues, the characteristics of secondary students with talent in the visual arts, and factors that enhance or inhibit the development of artistic talent. He notes that many arts educators prefer not to distinguish between gifts and talents because they feel such distinctions place too much emphasis on cognitive skills and not enough on expressive ones, relegating the arts to second-class status. Perhaps in part because of Western society's devaluing of the arts, he stresses that good visual arts programming at the secondary level is a critical factor in identifying and nurturing students who have artistic potential. His review of the literature indicates that artistic students of both genders have unique challenges with identity development because the development of their talent requires focusing on uniqueness and originality at a time in life when their peer culture emphasizes conformity. Supportive parents and/or networks of artistic peers can help artistically talented adolescents develop healthy identities as artists.

In Chapter 10, Moon and Ray discuss the importance of personal and social talent development in adolescence from several perspectives. First, they state that secondary schools should help all gifted adolescents develop personal and social skills because, as noted above, these skills become increasingly important to success as students increase their expertise in a domain and/or begin making original contributions to a domain. Personal and social competence is also vitally important to the well-being of adults. Adolescence is an ideal time to work on skill development in the personal and social domain, because identity development and relationship building are key tasks for students in this period of life (Moon & Dixon, this volume).

Second, Moon and Ray argue that secondary schools should identify students with high levels of expertise in the personal domain because these students may be able to achieve at exceptionally high levels due to their advanced goal setting and self-regulation skills. Finally, they suggest that the identification of social talent in adolescence would facilitate early identification of students likely to be strong leaders, effective teachers, and/or skilled therapists. In other words, many adult professions require highly developed social talents, and these talents can and should be identified in adolescence so they can be developed either *indirectly* through social skill development activities that are infused into gifted and talented courses in different subject areas or *directly* in classes designed to teach social and/or leadership skills. Providing for direct instruction in personal and social skills is particularly important for school districts that adopt a social capital conception of giftedness (Moon & Dixon, this volume).

The final chapter in Part II discusses talent development in the domain of sports using the DMGT as the framework for the analysis. This chapter is more research-based that the preceding chapters because more research has been conducted on adolescents who have athletic talent, than on students in the other talent domains. In addition, sports provide a relatively "pure" environment to observe talent development processes because, as Gagné and Van Rossum stress, participation in sport is voluntary, not compulsory, and because the competitive nature of sports enables very clear distinctions between individuals with regard to the outcomes of the talent development process. At a relatively young age, athletes can be divided into those who merely have developed regional levels of talent versus those who have achieved at the national or international levels. Chapter 11 provides an extended example of the way the DMGT can be used to analyze the talent development process of athletes in adolescence and many research-based suggestions for how coaches can assist adolescents with athletic talent development.

In summary, Part II provides an overview of the talent development process in different domains during adolescence. The authors of the four chapters in Part II focus on talent development from the perspective of the individual adolescent who is in the midst of a long and difficult process of mastering, or transforming, a domain that most of his or her peers understand dimly, if at all. This complements the more cross-sectional emphasis of Part III on the things teachers can do in specific classes to aid academically talented adolescents in developing expertise in a specific domain like science or mathematics. Themes from Part II that teachers need to keep in mind when working with talented teenagers are (a) the importance of appropriately challenging learning experiences; (b) the need for talented individuals to develop strong personal skills such as self-confidence and self-regulation; and (c) the importance of supportive families and/or peer networks.

REFERENCES

Bloom, B. S. (Ed.). (1985). *Developing talent in young people.* New York: Ballantine.

Csikszentmihalyi, M., Rathunde, K., & Whalen, S. (1993). *Talented teenagers.* Cambridge, England: Cambridge University Press.

Ericsson, K. A., Krampe, R. T., & Tesch-Romer, C. (1993). The role of deliberate practice in the acquisition of expert performance. *Psychological Review, 100,* 363–406.

Gagné, F. (2000). Understanding the complex choreography of talent development. In K. A. Heller, F. J. Mönks, R. J. Sternberg, & R. F. Subotnik (Eds.), *International handbook of giftedness and talent* (pp. 67–79). Amsterdam: Elsevier.

Renzulli, J. S. (1978). What makes giftedness? Re-examining a definition. *Phi Delta Kappan, 60,* 180–184.

Simonton, D. K. (1994). *Greatness: Who makes history and why.* New York: Guilford.

UNDERSTANDING ELITE TALENT IN ACADEMIC DOMAINS

CHAPTER 8

A Developmental Trajectory From Basic Abilities to Scholarly Productivity/Artistry

by Linda Jarvin & Rena Subotnik

INTRODUCTION TO THE ACADEMIC TALENT DOMAIN

Overview

*I*n this chapter we discuss the characteristics that facilitate or inhibit elite talent development in academic domains, with a special focus on adolescence. Our aim is to present transitional stages of gifted development, rather than to focus on curriculum and instruction (see Part III of this volume) or on teacher education (see Part IV). We present here the SP/A model of academic talent development, whose components change in importance over time. We argue that this model, like others described in the literature review that follows, is applicable within and outside of academic disciplines and fields. We also argue that highly able adolescents, even the most accomplished, may or may not reach the third stage in the model, *scholarly productivity or artistry* (SP/A), because different factors gain importance during the transition from expertise, the second stage of talent development, to SP/A. Thus, only some adolescents who achieve expertise will create transformative ideas that mark the pinnacle of the SP/A talent development model.

Literature

Traditionally, abilities, competencies, and expertise have been viewed as separate and largely distinct constructs and research areas within the broader field of psychology. In this view, abilities are regarded as largely innate capabilities, competencies are acquired basic skills, and expertise reflects high-level mastery of skills. We believe that the three constructs are inextricably linked, and that abilities are to be measured as developing competencies, which in turn can be transformed into various forms of developing expertise, and at the final stage, into scholarly productivity or artistry (SP/A). Abilities, then, are nascent forms of developing expertise. As a result, abilities, as well as the competencies and expertise that develop from them, are flexible and modifiable in nature. We argue that in the domain of academic talent, giftedness, in its early manifestation, is defined by the efficient yet comprehensive development of ability into competence in a domain. During the middle stage, competence is transformed by the gifted individual with the help of his or her teachers into precocious achievement of expertise in creative problem finding and solving. Finally, we view giftedness in adulthood as SP/A, taking the form of unique contributions to a field or domain.

The general theoretical framework for our research is Sternberg's (1997) theory of successful intelligence. We hypothesize that success is associated with analytical, creative, and practical intelligence. Young scholars need *analytical* skills to understand the basic content and procedures associated with their discipline, as well as important interdisciplinary connections. As they become experts in their discipline, these rising stars employ *creativity* to generate new, useful, and elegant questions and solutions to projects they pursue. They also need *practical* intelligence, particularly in the transition from expertise to SP/A, to know what kinds of creative innovations are likely to be well received by the public and what kinds are not. The constructs of analytical, creative, and practical intelligence are not hierarchical per se. That is, analytical intelligence is not limited to the "transition to competence stage," nor is practical intelligence confined to the "transition to expertise stage." One can, however, note that the respective weights of these three constructs change over time. As detailed in Figure 1, practical intelligence and creativity increase in importance in the transitions from competence to expertise, and from expertise to SP/A.

Specifically, this work rests on two theoretical premises: (1) abilities are forms of developing expertise (Sternberg, 1998, 2000), and (2) beyond expertise exists the realm of elite talent (Subotnik, 2000). According to our view, abilities have interactive genetic and environmental components, yet are modifiable to some degree and capable of being flexibly deployed. An important educational implication of this view is that competence, expertise, and scholarly productivity or artistry cannot be developed without appropriate supports and guidance from teachers and mentors. For example, an adolescent with an affinity for chemistry will not be able to fully develop her potential if she is not provided access to the necessary physical support (e.g., laboratory equipment, books, and computers) and teacher guidance. Competencies are acquired skills, such as reading for comprehension, writing for communication, and computing for data analysis. Each of these competencies, when mastered, allows for deeper understanding and pursuit of an academic discipline.

Expertise involves using one's abilities to acquire, store, and use explicit knowledge of a *domain* (a knowledge base; Sternberg, Wagner, Williams, & Horvath, 1995) and implicit or tacit knowledge of a *field* (the social organization of that knowledge base; Csikszentmihalyi, 1988, 1996) that can potentially be used to find and solve important problems.

Explicit knowledge is knowledge of the facts, formulas, principles, and major ideas of a domain of inquiry, for example, the periodic table, attribution theory, or $E=MC^2$. Implicit, or tacit, knowledge is what one needs to attain success in a field, but that usually is not overtly or formally taught. Some programs, such as the Science Outreach program at Rockefeller University, help young scientists assimilate the values of biomedical research, as well as the skills of technical writing for publication—in other words, tacit knowledge made explicit.

In sum, an individual might take a given ability, nurture it into a competence, and then into an expertise. Expertise, however, is a relatively passive enterprise. To move beyond expertise to achieve SP/A, one needs to exhibit intellectual, creative, or pioneering leadership that extends a field beyond its current boundaries. Scholarly productivity or artistry is the ultimate goal of talent development, one that adolescents are not yet expected to reach. We nevertheless include the SP/A stage to present the direction in which the stages are headed and to provide a comprehensive overview of the trajectory of talent development.

This chapter is divided into five parts: Following this introduction, we provide a summary of various talent development models that have helped inform our perspective. Next, we describe the domain-specific characteristics of academically gifted adolescents. Then, we discuss talent facilitators and talent inhibitors. In the last section, we briefly review talent development opportunities.

Models of Talent Development

The models of talent development that have most informed our perspective include, but are not limited to, those of Bloom (1985), Tannenbaum (1983), and Gagné (2003). Bloom outlines stages of instruction on the part of expert teachers outside traditional school settings. Tannenbaum provides us with the key variables that enhance or impede talent development. Gagné frames the transformation of gifts into talents as a developmental process. We describe these models to give the reader a clear understanding of how they enhance and differ from the SP/A model.

Bloom and his colleagues (1985) explored eminence and elite talent in a retrospective study of six fields (two in sports, two in the arts, and two in academics). Their aim was to unearth the elements of talent development across fields, as well as the characteristic elements unique to each field. Bloom's model is comprised of three stages. The first stage is distinguished by its informal, recreational involvement with a domain often highly valued by families or communities. Teachers, brought into the picture by family or communities, characterize students with ability as fast learners, and motivate them with praise and opportunities to display their abilities. The second stage of Bloom's model is marked by a focus on acquisition of technique, content knowledge, and rules guided by expert teachers. In this stage, parental roles in teaching decrease and teachers' influence expands. As students progress, they become socialized into the values of the domain and identify themselves as members of a community—as swimmers, scientists, musicians, etc. As they become more capable, talented individuals become their own critics, which can lead to first-time feelings of self-doubt.

Once a learner has acquired sufficient expertise to pursue the third stage, he or she would study under a third-level master teacher. Such masters expect total commitment from the student as they focus on the learner's unique qualities as a scholar or performer who has the potential to contribute to the field or domain. Students at this stage seek out and capitalize on opportunities to exercise their developed abilities.

This three-stage model is developmental, aspires to SP/A, and emphasizes that various attributes or variables play important roles at different points in time. Although the Bloom model addresses catalysts such as quality instruction and peer and family support, it downplays factors such as personality or social interaction in achieving SP/A. Additionally, the model minimizes the role of abilities as a source of elite talent.

Tannenbaum (1983) proposed that if (a) *giftedness* (defined as high levels of g) were channeled into a specific talent domain, (b) personality characteristics such as motivation and persistence were developed, (c) recognition and support were received from some important stakeholder(s), and (d) an individual capitalized on being in the right place at the right time, giftedness in childhood would translate into critically acclaimed performance or production of great ideas (corresponding to SP/A) in adulthood. Tannenbaum qualifies that g need not be equally high in every domain to achieve greatness. For example, according to Tannenbaum, an outstanding physicist needs a higher IQ than an outstanding teacher. Correspondingly, personality variables may determine one's ability to fulfill one's potential, depending on the domain. Although a teacher and a physicist both need motivation and persistence to achieve excellence, a teacher may need to be more extroverted and gregarious than does a physicist.

In many ways, Tannenbaum's theory is consistent with the SP/A model we propose in this chapter: It is domain specific, identifies outstanding performance or the generation of great ideas as a desired outcome, and highlights the importance of supportive teachers, family, and peers. The model also stresses the roles played by personality and an individual's capitalization on opportunity.

Our model diverges from Tannenbaum's in two ways: We substitute *abilities* for g because the general factor of intelligence does not describe the foundational *ability* associated with great performance or idea generation, as does acuity with language or mathematics. Second, Tannenbaum does not frame his model in developmental terms. He identifies those variables that augment or hamper the transformation of *g* to outstanding performance or great ideas, but he does not address the transformation of abilities to SP/A.

Gagné's (2003) theory of talent development is also multifaceted and domain specific, and thus we find it especially elegant. The model begins with abilities (which Gagné calls *giftedness* or *aptitude domains*), which are transformed either positively or negatively by four catalysts: (a) intrapersonal variables including motivation and personality; (b) environmental conditions (surroundings, people, activities, and events); (c) developmental processes (learning, training, and practicing); and (d) chance factors.

Our research supports the key roles of these four catalysts. However, unlike Gagné, we weigh the importance of each variable at each developmental level. Finally, we pursue eminence or SP/A as our outcome, whereas Gagné focuses on the transformation of giftedness or abilities into high-level expertise.

The model of academic talent development that we present in this chapter derives from our model of musical talent development, which in turn stems from empirical research with highly gifted and successful classical musicians and "gatekeepers" of the music world (Subotnik, & Jarvin, 2005; Subotnik, Jarvin, Moga, & Sternberg, 2003). The model defines giftedness as a transitional process in which different characteristics contribute to the transformation of abilities into competencies and expertise, and in exceptional cases, into scholarly productivity or artistry. This transformation is made possible through the interaction of innate abilities and context, as specified at each stage. We believe that insofar as high-level achievement can be viewed as performance (e.g., high academic achievement is a form of performance), this model is a useful explanatory framework for talent development in any domain.

DOMAIN-SPECIFIC CHARACTERISTICS OF ACADEMICALLY TALENTED ADOLESCENTS: COMPONENTS OF A DEVELOPMENTAL TRAJECTORY MODEL

Figure 1 describes our SP/A model of academic giftedness, adapted from our model of musical giftedness. The middle stage of the model is most closely associated with adolescence and is the stage most relevant to secondary school educators. In preparation for this stage, gifted young people must transform their abilities into competencies through instruction with an emphasis on content knowledge and guided skill practice. Examples include basic principles and concepts in mathematics or science, or the knowledge needed to perform effective computer searches or write a structured essay. Once competence is achieved, the student can progress toward expertise through further instruction that emphasizes mastery of skills and knowledge applied to creative problem finding and solving. For example, at this level, students should be able to define their own research paper topics or develop original interpretations of literary or art works, or design ways to test why a laboratory procedure was not successful. The SP/A model demonstrates that expertise is not necessarily the endpoint for a gifted adolescent's aspirations. He or she will need a different balance of skills, knowledge, and mentoring to transform this expertise into SP/A.

At each stage of the model we review the factors that respectively facilitate and inhibit the development of elite academic talent. We summarize these inhibitory and facilitating factors after the full description of the model. Our SP/A model defines giftedness as a transitional process in which different characteristics contribute to the transformation of abilities into competencies and expertise, and in exceptional cases, into scholarly productivity or artistry.

Abilities

We refer to *abilities* as those interactive genetic and environmental components that anchor the model. They comprise traditional abilities and personality factors, and include (a) acuity in language, mathematics, or spatial reasoning; (b) intrinsic motivation; and (c) charisma. The first two abilities are important throughout the talent development process. Charisma becomes important during the third stage in the transition from expertise to SP/A.

Domain-specific acuity is demonstrated by intuitive understanding of the basic structures and patterns of language, mathematics, or visual/spatial phenomena (Winner, 1996). Let us illustrate this activity with an anecdote. A kindergarten student in an elementary school for gifted students offered the word *millennium* when his teacher asked the class to brainstorm words associated with time. When asked to explain the meaning of the word, the student reasoned aloud: "Well, I learned in Spanish that *mil* is a thousand, so is it a thousand years?" Another example is a child's voluntary attempts to draw two-dimensional representations of the three-dimensional objects that surround her.

Intrinsic motivation is associated with a powerful love of learning and exploring intellectual domains (Renzulli, 1986; Subotnik, 2003; Winner, 1996). Without intrinsic motivation, a young person will not persist through failure on tests, competitions, challenging material, or classes. Learning to master laboratory techniques or conversational Spanish takes practice and a desire to be successful.

Charisma refers to the ability to draw colleagues and reviewers to one's ideas and work products, either through the communicative elegance of the work itself or through the force of one's personality (Riggio, 1998; Riggio, 2004). Charisma plays a significant role in the third level of the talent development process. Gifted individuals with sparkling personalities or notable ideas usually draw mentors, patrons, and opportunities toward them. With training, charm can be enhanced, but creative ideas that provide substance for the charming communication are more difficult to account for through instruction.

From Abilities to Competencies

Notably, each academic domain has its own trajectory. In mathematics, gifted individuals progress through the stages more rapidly than do philosophers or psy-

Analytic, Creative and Practical Intelligence Constructs	TRANSITION FROM ABILITY TO COMPETENCY — *Opportunity for instruction with emphasis on exposure to content knowledge, and guided skill practice.* Mediating variables:	Analytic, Creative and Practical Intelligence Constructs	TRANSITION FROM COMPETENCY TO EXPERTISE — *Opportunity for instruction with emphasis on moving beyond mastery of skills and knowledge to exercising creative problem finding and solving* Mediating variables:	Analytic, Creative and Practical Intelligence Constructs	TRANSITION FROM EXPERTISE TO SP/A — *Opportunity for socialization into the field and networking guided by master teachers, agents, and other gatekeepers.* Mediating variables:
A	Fast learner				
A	Proficient with application of skills and knowledge	C	Proficiency in creative problem finding and solving		
P	Parental support or pressure	P	Parental support		
A	Teachability	C	Teachability (beginning of differentiation)		
A	Teacher assesses student strengths and weaknesses	A	Knowing one's own strengths and weaknesses	P	Capitalizing on strengths
P	External rewards; recognition, battling perceived lack of abilities ("I'll show you")	P	External rewards: Recognition, opportunity to compete or publish, ("I'll show you")	P	External rewards: Recognition, opportunity to compete, publish, financial independence, ("I'll show you")
P	Persistence in good and bad times	P	Persistence in good and bad times	P	Persistence in good and bad times
P	Intrinsic motivation	P	Intrinsic motivation	P	Intrinsic motivation
A	Acuity in language, mathematics, or spatial reasoning	A	Acuity in language, mathematics, or spatial reasoning	A	Acuity in language, mathematics, or spatial reasoning
		P	Self promotion by seeking mentors	P	Promotion of self through a mentor
		P	Learning how to play the game	P	Mastering the game
		P	Social skills: collegiality	P	Social skills: collegiality and engaging patrons
		P	Restoring self confidence	P	Exuding self confidence
				C	Risk taking
				C	Charisma

Figure 1. Scholarly production/artistry (SP/A) model

Note. Domain affects the age at which each stage of the process takes place. A, C, P indicates the intelligence construct (analytical, creative, practical) that plays the greatest role. In each case, however, the construct rarely operates independently.

chologists. Content area expertise is important at an early age to nurture talent in a young mathematician (see Feldman's explanation of why prodigies can only exist in certain fields, Feldman, 1986).

During the elementary and early secondary school years, abilities are transformed into competencies by way of exposure to the skills and concepts of the academic disciplines. This progression takes place mostly in school by exposing students to knowledge. The high-quality teacher is one who can use assessment to determine students' ability levels and then provide them with challenging material. Optimal instruction constantly challenges a child's zone of proximal development (Vygotsky, 1978) and helps the child transition from one step to the next. With high-quality instruction, a child can develop domain-specific abilities into competencies. The effectiveness of this instruction is mediated by:

- how fast students can learn,
- the proficiency with which students can analyze and apply the skills and knowledge they learn,
- parental support or pressure,
- students' teachability (i.e., willingness and openness to being taught),
- quality of the student–teacher relationship and the teacher's ability to assess students' strengths and weaknesses,
- availability of external rewards such as praise and recognition, and
- persistence through good and bad times.

The more quickly and thoroughly students can move through the academic curriculum, the more they benefit from exposure to great ideas. For this reason, *speed of learning* is especially helpful in the first stage of talent development (e.g., reading many facts about the Civil War), whereas during later stages, speed is replaced in importance by deep acquisition and creative exploration of a domain (e.g., analyzing and understanding the effects of the Civil War on all segments of modern-day American society). Teachers can facilitate a student's development by providing a wide array of resources (e.g., texts of various difficulty levels and from different perspectives or eras in history) in classrooms.

The *proficiency with which students can analyze and apply the skills and knowledge they learn* will depend on the quality of instruction they receive and their commitment to study and mastery. For example, a student in a school where laboratory equipment cannot be accessed outside of instructional time will not achieve the same mastery as a student who can go into a laboratory to practice or experiment during study hall. Schools and individual teachers can contribute to student development by increasing access to resources.

At this stage, *parental involvement* can be either negative (e.g., nagging, restricting freedom of choice, or turning an initially pleasurable experience into a constraint) or positive involvement (Olszewski, Kulieke, & Buescher, 1987; Subotnik, Olszewski-Kubilius, & Arnold, 2003). Positive parental involvement can take the form of initial pressure or support. By insisting on serious attention to academic pursuits, parents help transform abilities into competencies. Negative parental involvement can take the form of mixed messages. On the one hand, parents are pleased that their children are academically able, considering it a form of status. On the other hand, parents may not want their children to specialize or to give up their social lives in favor of academic pursuits alone.

Children's *teachability*, that is, their willingness and openness to being taught, is considered an attractive quality in a student, and leads to more enthusiastic instruction. If students seem resistant to instruction, they will not be viewed as a good investment for their teachers' efforts (Subotnik et al., 2003), when compared with those students who are prepared and actively participate in classroom discussions. The teacher can contribute to a classroom atmosphere in which all students are encouraged to participate actively and present their work to their peers.

The likelihood that acuity and intrinsic motivation will be directed productively is related to the quality of the student–school relationship. Talented young scholars and their families hope for a rigorous curriculum and high expectations and will take necessary steps to find an environment that matches these expectations. Starting in middle school, teachers will guide students toward opportunities to test their strengths and weaknesses through honors classes rather than regular classes. More specifically, outstanding teachers help young scholars *recognize their strengths and address their weaknesses*. By helping students recognize their strengths, teachers can also orient students toward additional development opportunities outside the classroom (e.g., readings, after-school programs, specialized summer camps, etc.).

Although a child can derive much pleasure from early school experience, for most individuals (even the most gifted), studying and persistence need to be buttressed by positive reinforcement from parents and teachers (Bloom, 1985). Recognition for one's exceptional talent is an important *external reward* for young scholars. Recognition can also serve to fulfill the talented individual's need to disprove a perceived lack of ability on the part of family or teachers (Ochse, 1990). Classroom teachers can support the gifted student by offering recognition in the form of praise or nominations for schoolwide awards. *Persistence through good and bad times*, supported by positive reinforcement, genuine curricular challenge, and parental pressure, prepares young scholars for handling the rejections or failures that are part of the growth process in talent development (Subotnik, 2003).

From Competency to Expertise

Most academically gifted youngsters enter secondary school highly competent in at least one domain. To transform their competence into expertise in that domain, they must move beyond mastery of skills and knowledge to exercising strategies of creative problem finding and solving. For this reason, elite talent development occurs less often in secondary schools where teachers have difficulty providing individual attention, except in special classes, clubs, or after-school programs. Speed of learning is no longer as important to the development of expertise as is pursuit of the deep structure of the discipline and its connections to other disciplines.

The mediating variables at this transitional stage are proficiency in creative problem finding and solving, parental support, teachability, knowing one's strengths and weaknesses, availability of external rewards, persistence through good and bad times, intrinsic motivation, and acuity. Parental support remains important, but parental pressure at this stage of talent development can be counterproductive and lead to resistance on the part of the student. Although teachability remains an attractive quality for teachers, the best instructors expect their students to "bite back" rather than regurgitate, and prefer that students insist on cultivating their own voices or ideas at the secondary level (Subotnik & Jarvin, 2005). Teachers can promote this in their students by encouraging the expression of personal views, arguments, and assessments.

Persistence through good and bad times becomes increasingly important as the adolescent approaches adulthood and is faced with key life choices and gains independence from her or his parents. Further, during the transition from competence to expertise, teachers expect students to analyze and manage their own profiles of strengths and weaknesses and approach their studies accordingly. For example, a student who is weak in written communication but strong in scientific reasoning is expected to acknowledge this discrepancy and to seek help and additional instruction in technical writing. We view the self-knowledge of strengths and weaknesses as an important competence at this stage. Other authors (e.g., Moon, 2003) would place this competence within the domain of personal talent.

Although recognition on the part of teachers, parents, and now peers remains an important external reward in this transitional stage, talented adolescents enjoy opportunities to compete with others and to publish their own work. Opportunities for publication or competition are forms of performance that allow individuals to test their mettle and reinforce their identities as developing experts (Subotnik, Maurer, & Steiner, 2001). Teachers and mentors use these opportunities to help talented students refine problem finding and solving skills, and the thrill of participation at high levels such as Olympiads and science talent searches, or publication in *Concord Review*, becomes the central expressive outlet for the young scholar's life. Teachers and parents will find a nonexhaustive list of such opportunities at the end of this chapter.

At this stage, the gifted student must also rely more on his or her personal skills (Moon, 2003). These variables include self-promotion, learning how to play the game, social skills, and restoring self-confidence.

Self-promotion is necessary for success in any field. Work that is hidden from view is not open to critiques that, although difficult, are critical for growth. Teachers provide the tacit knowledge students need to *play the game* by suggesting programs to attend, people to meet, contests to enter, and ways to approach potential mentors. Most students recognize the necessity of self-promotion and playing the game, but find the notions repulsive. With reluctance, young scholars learn from their peers and teachers that there are challenges beyond the expertise they have acquired—for example, establishing a notable résumé, connecting with a respected mentor, and honing their proverbial connections. Teachers can encourage and help their students by guiding them toward after-school opportunities or by working with the school's guidance counselor to create an information bank of available resources.

Teachers at this stage also play an important role in promoting *social skills* such as arriving on time, being well prepared and courteous, and learning to accept success gracefully and failure with resilience. Mentors at out-of-school laboratories and cultural institutions begin to socialize students into the value systems of the discipline.

Most students enter secondary school confident in their abilities. As in all transitions to more competitive environments, many will temporarily question their abilities as they witness the competence of their new peers (Marsh, Hau, Craven, 2004). If talented, they will attend more and more selective institutions—or classes within institutions (e.g., a special research class or seminar class vs. regular curriculum). Students need the resources (both internal and external, in the form of adult support) to work through this challenge to *restore their self-confidence.*

From Expertise to SP/A

Although most gifted adolescents will not achieve SP/A, we provide further description of the outcome stage of the model. This last transition from expertise to scholarly productivity or artistry (SP/A) relies more exclusively on the opportunity for mentors and other gatekeepers to impart to their protégées their tacit knowledge and ability to network. Content and skill proficiency (because it is assumed), parental support, and teachability play a diminished role in the talent development process at this level. Whereas young gifted children achieve competence with the help of teachers who identify strengths and weaknesses, and adolescent scholars gain expertise when they can identify their own strengths and weaknesses, at the transition to SP/A level, the gifted individual capitalizes more exclusively on his or her strengths.

Mediating variables at this transition include the availability of external rewards, persistence through good and bad times, intrinsic motivation, acuity, promotion by a mentor, mastering the game, social skills, and exuding self confidence.

Eminently gifted adult intellectuals and scholars still seek external rewards for their efforts, including recognition, competition, publication, and *financial independence.* Lack of financial reward can drive some of the most talented experts away from scholarship to professional fields. Once promising scientists leave the laboratory for a medical practice, they will have far less time for large-scale innovation.

Another transition takes place in the realm of *self-promotion.* Young scholars can now count on their mentors and developing bodies of work to serve as agents for their careers. Because successful protégées bring status to mentors, mentors are motivated to get their mentees' ideas widely noticed and reviewed (Zuckerman, 1996).

Rising stars have also learned to play the networking game well. Those who have achieved SP/A can be said to have *mastered the game. Social skills* continue to be important in engaging grants, mentors, and others who will help one's ideas to be widely noticed and reviewed.

As reported earlier, a cornerstone of the second stage of our model is the restoration of shaken self-confidence on the part of rising stars. The individual who achieves SP/A must *exude self-confidence* in his or her mastery of the domain (e.g., as a mathematician), especially in areas where debate over outcomes is heated and pointed. Self-confidence is derived from the thoroughness of their expertise and a creative view of the domain.

Additional characteristics at this stage include *risk taking* and *charisma* (Subotnik et al., 2001). The concept of risk taking involves the notion of investing one's time and effort in one endeavor, sometimes to the sacrifice of a "balanced" life and possibly more lucrative professional pursuits. More centrally, risk taking, supported by self-confidence, is an important factor in any creative endeavor, insofar as one needs to "defy the crowd" (Sternberg & Lubart, 1995) to present and promote novel ideas. By virtue of their novelty, these ideas will not elicit popular support. In the academic domain risk taking might be, for example, to present a new interpretation of historical facts, develop a new economic model, or suggest a different route for solving a yet unsolved mathematical problem.

DOMAIN-SPECIFIC TALENT FACILITATORS

To summarize, the development of abilities into competencies relies on interactive genetic and environmental components, including intrinsic motivation and acuity in language, mathematics, or spatial reasoning. With high-quality instruction, a child can develop these abilities into competencies. The instruction should emphasize exposure to and guided practice in the skills and knowledge of the domain. The effectiveness of this instruction is mediated by a number of factors, including how fast the student can learn, the proficiency the student can attain in the application of skills and knowledge, parental support or pressure, the student's teachability (i.e., willingness and openness to being taught), the quality of the student's experience in school, the match between the student's and school's expectations, the teacher's ability to identify strengths and weaknesses and provide students with appropriately challenging classes, the availability of external rewards such as praise and recognition, and the student's persistence through good and bad times.

At the second stage, typically experienced during adolescence or early adulthood, competency develops into expertise through continued opportunity for instruction, with an emphasis on moving beyond mastery of skills and knowledge to exercising creative problem finding and solving. New mediating variables at this stage are responsibility for managing one's strengths and weaknesses, self-promotion, learning how to play the game, social skills, and restoring self-confidence.

The last transition in our model is from expertise to scholarly productivity or artistry (SP/A), which is facilitated in the academic world by the opportunity for socialization into the field and networking guided by mentors and other gatekeepers. New mediating variables at this stage are a willingness to take risks and charisma.

DOMAIN-SPECIFIC TALENT INHIBITORS

The model described above depicts the mediating variables that enable the gifted adolescent to move from one stage of talent development to the next. If these mediating variables are missing, development will be inhibited, explaining why few gifted youngsters grow to become gifted adults (see also Subotnik & Arnold, 1994; Winner, 2000a).

Each stage of the development process presents its challenges. When students transition from abilities to competencies and beyond, intrinsic motivation and acuity for language, mathematics, or spatial/visual reasoning remain important factors. What happens, however, if a student with acuity and intrinsic motivation does not have sufficient support either at home or at school? This situation is tragically common. However, if instruction improves sufficiently and students apply their ability to learn quickly and proficiently, the transition from abilities to competencies, which often takes place during childhood, can extend into adolescence (Subotnik, 2003).

Achieving expertise, the second stage of the model and the one most closely associated with adolescence, is virtually impossible without resources, instruction, support, social skills, tacit knowledge, and deep commitment. Exceptional talent does not develop in a vacuum, and the gifted adolescent's chances to thrive and reach the level of SP/A will depend in part on the sociocultural environment in which he or she grows up (Feldman, 2000). Exposure and training are not enough; being in the right place at the right time matters, as does a willingness to seize opportunities when they present themselves, and to risk creative setbacks, financial loss, and dwindling support from friends and patrons.

DOMAIN-SPECIFIC TALENT
DEVELOPMENT OPPORTUNITIES

Two important points must be noted. The first is that many gifted adolescents have uneven profiles; that is, they can demonstrate gifts in one area but low competence or even a lack of ability in another area (Newman & Sternberg, 2004; Winner, 2000b). For example, some students have great acuity in language but none in spatial reasoning.

The second point is that each subject area of discipline has its own trajectory, and that the passage from one stage to the next will not take place at the same age in all areas (Simonton, 1989, 1991a, 1991b). For example, music and mathematics abilities reveal themselves early (Feldman, 1986). Further, even within a discipline there exist variations. In the domain of music, the stages at which one develops from competent to expert are different for violinists and singers (the former bloom before the latter). In the academic domain, the accumulated knowledge necessary to produce a historical novel makes for later success than does creative short-story writing.

As described in our model, it is essential for gifted adolescents to benefit from high-quality teaching to continue to develop their gifts, and the academically gifted are often under challenged in regular classrooms (Winner, 1997). There exist a multitude of residential and day programs for academically gifted children, and it is estimated that 15,000 students attend summer programs for the gifted each year (Bilger, 2004). A noncomprehensive sample of Web sites for residential and day programs for gifted adolescents are listed in Appendix A.

Schooling is usually not sufficient to support talent development unless the school has specialized curricula and selection processes through research, seminar, or apprenticeship programs. At the higher stages of talent development, almost all further progress in talent development happens after school and in the summers. Talented adolescents can begin with fast-paced and expertly taught classes offered by talent searches, Olympiads, and other college-based programs. A list of Internet resources for such programs can be found in Appendix A.

Once a passion for a domain or field becomes apparent, summers and after-school hours should be devoted to special focus on this work guided by a professional or scholar. Examples of such programs are also included in Appendix A.

More generally, gifted adolescents seeking additional expertise and guidance can approach science laboratories at local universities, hospitals, or research centers, as well as state and city academies of science. Those interested in other domains should consider internships at museums, associations such as the American Psychological Association, nonprofits, and congressional offices. Other listings of available programs can be found on the Internet, either directly or by consulting one of the national interest groups for gifted students and their parents, such as the National Association for Gifted Children (http://www.nagc.org), the Davidson Institute for Talent Development (http://www.ditd.org), the National Research Center on the Gifted and Talented (http://www.gifted.uconn.edu/nrcgt.html), or the Center for Gifted Education Policy at the American Psychological Association (www.apa.org/ed/cgep.html).

In our search for sample programs on the Web, we noted that most programs designated for elite talent development are in the domain of sports and are not located in the U.S.

CONCLUSION

We have presented a model of academic giftedness that describes the transitional nature of talent development and details what will favor or inhibit the expression of elite talent. The model focuses on academic talent, but the general developmental framework is adapted from our work on musical talent, and we believe that the model holds promise to describe the developmental trajectories in other achievement domains, as well.

The stages of talent development are the successive transformations of abilities into competencies, into expertise, and finally into scholarly productivity or artistry. The progression from one stage to the next will result from an interaction of personal and environmental factors, and, although the age at which one reaches each stage is domain-specific, the middle stage, which represents a "make it or break it" point, will typically take place in adolescence.

APPENDIX A: INTERNET RESOURCES

Residential and day programs for gifted students:

http://www.advancedacademy.org
http://www.clarkson.edu/tcs
http://depts.washington.edu/cscy
http://www.roeper.org
http://www.simons-rock.edu
http://www.buacademy.org
http://www.bard.edu/bhsec
http://www.calstatela.edu/academic/eep
http://www.mbc.edu/peg (for women only)
http://www.earlycollegeonline.org/
http://dept.lamar.edu/taolith
http://www.tams.unt.edu
http://www.education.uiowa.edu/belinblank/programs/naase
http://www.nwmissouri.edu/MASMC
http://web2.mgc.edu/natsci/games/gameshome.html
http://www.giftedschool.org
http://www.bsu.edu/web/academy
http://www.educationaladvancement.org/resources/search/schools_overview.php
http://www.ncssm.edu
http://www.pen.k12.va.us/VDOE/Instruction/Govschools

Talent searches and other college-based programs:

http://www-2.cs.cmu.edu/~leap
http://www.ctd.northwestern.edu
http://www.tip.duke.edu
http://www.jhu.edu/gifted
http://www.giftedstudy.com
http://www.themathcircle.org
http://www.giftedstudy.com
http://www.themathcircle.org
http://www.sea.edu
http://ysp.ucdavis.edu
http://www.summerscience.org
http://www.internaldrive.com
http://www.challengecamps.com
http://www.ivyleaguekids.com/www/Explore
http://www.explorebeyondschool.com
http://youthprograms.mtu.edu
http://edweb.csus.edu/Projects/ATS
http://www.education.uiowa.edu/belinblank

http://www.cmu.edu/cmites
http://www.geri.soe.purdue.edu/youth/default.html
http://www.usm.edu/gifted/Sum_Gifted_Studies.html
http://www.wku.edu/gifted
http://ucollege.wustl.edu/hssp
http://www.du.edu/education/ces/rmts.html
http://www-epgy.stanford.edu/epgy
http://cfge.wm.edu/precollegiate.php

Olympiads:

http://www.cee.org/usabo
http://www.unl.edu/amc/e-exams/e8-usamo/usamo.html
http://www.chemistry.org
http://www.jyu.fi/tdk/kastdk/olympiads
http://www.moems.org
http://www.soinc.org
http://www.scienceolympiad.com
http://www.olympiad.org.za
http://www.ibo-info.org

Other programs:

http://www.claymath.org
http://www.promys.org
http://www.rockefeller.edu/outreach
http://www.math.ohio-state.edu/ross
http://www.sciserv.org
http://www.weizmann.ac.il/diff_angle
http://www.cee.org/rsi
http://www.pen.k12.va.us/VDOE/Instruction/Govschools/summerres.html
http://www.gifted.uconn.edu/mentoruc.html
http://www.jsa.org/summer/summer/js.html
http://wtp.mit.edu

REFERENCES

Bilger, B. (2004). Kid geniuses. *The New Yorker Online.* Retrieved September 19, 2005, from http://www.newyorker.com

Bloom, B. (1985). *Developing talent in young people.* New York: Ballantine.

Csikszentmihalyi, M. (1988). Society, culture, and person: A systems view of creativity. In R. J. Sternberg (Ed.), *The nature of creativity* (pp. 325–339). New York: Cambridge University Press.

Csikszentmihalyi, M. (1996). *Creativity: Flow and the psychology of discovery and invention.* New York: HarperCollins.

Feldman, D. H. (1986). *Nature's gambit: Child prodigies and the development of human potential.* New York: Basic Books.

Feldman, D. H. (2000). Was Mozart at risk? A developmentalist looks at extreme talent. In R. C. Friedman, & B. M. Shore (Eds.), *Talents unfolding: Cognition and development*. Washington, DC: American Psychological Association.

Gagné, F. (2003). Transforming gifts into talents: The DMGT as a developmental theory. In N. Colangelo & G. A. Davis (Eds.), *Handbook of gifted education* (3rd ed., pp. 60–74.) Boston: Allyn & Bacon.

Marsh, H. W., Hau, K. T., & Craven, R. (2004). The big-fish-little-pond effect stands up to scrutiny. *American Psychologist, 59*, 269–271.

Moon, S. M. (2003). Personal talent. *High Ability Studies, 14*, 5–21.

Newman, T., & Sternberg, R. J. (Eds.). (2004). *Students with both gifts and learning disabilities*. Boston: Kluwer Academic Publishers.

Ochse, R. (1990). *Before the gates of excellence: Determinants of creative genius*. New York: Cambridge University Press.

Olszewski, P., Kulieke, M. J., & Buescher, T. (1987). The influence of the family environment on the development of talent: A literature review. *Journal for the Education of the Gifted, 11*, 6–28.

Renzulli, J. S. (1986). The three-ring conception of giftedness: A developmental model for creative productivity. In R. J. Sternberg & J. E. Davidson (Eds.), *Conceptions of giftedness* (pp. 53–92). New York: Cambridge University Press.

Riggio, R. E. (1998). Charisma. In H. S. Friedman (Ed.), *Encyclopedia of mental health* (pp. 387–396). San Diego, CA: Academic Press.

Riggio, R. E (2004). Charisma. In J. M. Burns, W. Goethals, & G. Sorenson (Eds.), *Encyclopedia of Leadership* (Vol. 1, pp. 158–162). Great Barrington, MA: Berkshire Publishing.

Simonton, D. K. (1989). Age and creative productivity: Nonlinear estimation of an information-processing model. *International Journal of Aging and Human Development, 29*, 23–37.

Simonton, D. K. (1991a). Career landmarks in science: Individual differences and interdisciplinary contrasts. *Developmental Psychology, 27*, 119–130.

Simonton, D. K. (1991b). Creative productivity through the adult years. *Generations, 15*(2), 13–16.

Sternberg, R. J. (1997*). Successful intelligence*. New York: Plume.

Sternberg, R. J. (1998). Abilities are forms of developing expertise. *Educational Researcher, 27*, 11–20.

Sternberg, R. J. (2000) Giftedness as developing expertise. In K. A. Heller & F. J. Mönks (Eds.), *International handbook of giftedness and talent* (2nd ed., pp. 55-66). New York: Elsevier.

Sternberg, R. J., & Lubart, T. I. (1995). *Defying the crowd: Cultivating creativity in a culture of conformity*. New York: Free Press.

Sternberg, R. J., Wagner, R. K., Williams, W. M., & Horvath, J. A. (1995). Testing common sense. *American Psychologist, 50*, 912–927.

Subotnik, R. F. (2000) Developing young adolescent performers at Juilliard: An educational prototype for elite level talent development in the arts and sciences. In C. F. Van Lieshout & P. G. Heymans (Eds.), *Talent, resilience, and wisdom across the lifespan* (pp. 249–276). Hove, UK: Psychology Press.

Subotnik, R. F. (2003). A developmental view of giftedness: From being to doing. *Roeper Review, 26*, 14–15.

Subotnik, R. F., & Arnold, K. (1994). *Beyond Terman: Contemporary longitudinal studies of giftedness and talent*. Westport, CT: Ablex Publishing.

Subotnik, R. F., & Jarvin, L. (2005). Beyond expertise: Conceptions of giftedness as great performance. In R. J. Sternberg & J. E. Davidson, (Eds.), *Conceptions of giftedness* (2nd ed., pp. 343-357). New York: Cambridge University Press.

Subotnik, R. F., Jarvin, L., Moga, E., & Sternberg, R. J. (2003). Wisdom from gate-keepers: Secrets of success in music performance. *Bulletin of Psychology and the Arts, 4*(1), 5–9.

Subotnik, R. F., Maurer, K., & Steiner, C. L. (2001). Tracking the next generation of the scientific elite. *Journal of Secondary Gifted Education, 13,* 33–43.

Subotnik, R. F., Olszewski-Kubilius, P., & Arnold, K. (2003). Beyond Bloom: Revisiting environmental factors that enhance or impeded talent development. In J. Borland (Ed.), *Rethinking gifted education* (pp. 227–238). New York: Teachers College Press.

Tannenbaum, A. J. (1983). *Gifted children: Psychological and educational perspectives.* New York: McMillan.

Vygotsky, L. S. (1978). *Mind and society: The development of higher mental processes.* Cambridge, MA: Harvard University Press.

Winner, E. (1996). *Gifted children: Myths and realities.* New York: Basic Books.

Winner, E. (1997). Exceptionally high intelligence and schooling. *American Psychologist, 52,* 1070–1081.

Winner, E. (2000a). The origins and ends of giftedness. *American Psychologist, 55,* 159–169.

Winner, E. (2000b). Giftedness: Current theory and research. *Current Directions in Psychological Science, 9,* 153–156.

Zuckerman, H. (1996). *Scientific elite: Nobel laureates in the United States.* New Brunswick, NJ: Transaction Publishers.

AUTHOR NOTE

Preparation of this chapter was supported by a grant under the Javits Act Program (Grant No. R206R000001) as administered by the Institute of Educational Sciences, formerly the Office of Educational Research and Improvement, U.S. Department of Education. Grantees undertaking such projects are encouraged to express freely their professional judgment. This article, therefore, does not necessarily represent the position or policies of the Institute of Educational Sciences or the U.S. Department of Education, and no official endorsement should be inferred. The authors would like to thank Lindsey Vance for her research on Internet resources.

DEVELOPMENT OF VISUAL ARTS TALENT IN ADOLESCENCE

by F. Robert Sabol

INTRODUCTION TO TALENT IN THE VISUAL ARTS

ducation in the visual arts has gone through remarkable reform in the past two decades. Keeping pace with educational reforms in other disciplines, reforms in art education have reflected new understanding of the functions and purposes of education in the visual arts and provided for demonstrations of accountability in them. As reforms progressed, many issues and concerns emerged for the education of gifted secondary visual arts students. A brief overview of some of these follows.

Publications such as *A Nation at Risk* (National Commission on Excellence in Education, 1983), *Toward Civilization* (National Endowment for the Arts, 1988), *America 2000*, (U.S. Department of Education, 1991), *Goals 2000* (U.S. Department of Education, 1994), the No Child Left Behind Act (2001), and other national and state initiatives launched numerous national education reforms. Although these publications focused principally on reform of general education, repercussions were felt in gifted visual arts education, as well.

Much of the reform effort in general education during the 1980s and 1990s focused on the creation of curriculum standards. The standards movement in visual arts education was fueled by the fact that art educators and other stakeholders had little agreement about content central to the education of students in the visual arts. Not only was the structure of curricula within the visual arts disciplines disputed (Clark & Zimmerman, 1983; Sabol, 1994, 1998a, 2004a, 2004b), but also fundamental curricula content lacked agreement (Dorn, Madeja, & Sabol, 2004; Sabol, 2004a, 2004b).

This same lack of agreement abounded in art education programs for gifted and talented students. At the time, a wide range of visual arts gifted education program types and content existed (Clark & Zimmerman, 1984, 2004; Hurwitz, 1983). The movement to create standards for art education culminated in the publication of *National Standards for Arts Education: What Every American Should Know and Be Able to Do in the Arts* (Music Educators National Conference, 1994). Unfortunately, similar standards for specific curricula in gifted art education programming have not resulted. Often, content in such programs is modeled after the national visual arts standards, with modifications designed to be compatible with local resources and art teachers' knowledge and skills and to meet the varying needs of gifted secondary students in art.

Defining Talent in the Visual Arts

In the late 1980s, discipline-based arts education (DBAE) emerged as a new curriculum model for art education (Clark, Day, & Greer, 1987). The rise of the DBAE model led to a broadening of the structure of content for education in the visual arts. The new model consisted of: (a) aesthetics, including study of the philosophical nature of art; (b) art criticism, consisting of viewing works of art and responding to them; (c) art history, involving learning about the historical and contextual records of art; and (d) production, focusing on making works of art.

This pivotal emergence of DBAE included a number of imbedded questions related to the education of gifted secondary visual arts students. Traditionally, the emphasis of art education programs at the secondary level was on studio production. Ostensibly, this was the case in secondary gifted education programs in the visual arts, as well. With the rise of DBAE, art education curricula in secondary schools increasingly reflected knowledge, skills, processes, and methods of inquiry used by aestheticians, art critics, and art historians, as well as artists (Clark & Zimmerman, 1978; Sabol 1994, 1998a). Because of the widespread impact of DBAE, new curricula and definitions of giftedness and talent in the visual arts were recommended (Sabol, 1998b). Definitions of giftedness in the visual arts needed to be radically expanded beyond the focus of art production to include the disciplines of aesthetics, art criticism, and art history. The distinct possibility of whole populations of gifted secondary visual arts students, unconsidered in the past, who may or may not be gifted in studio production, but who have high ability in the disciplines of art criticism, art history, and aesthetics, existed. Related questions arose about appropriate methods to identify these students, expansion of curricula and assessments, and non-studio-based products demonstrating giftedness in these areas.

Not only was expanding the definition of high-ability students in the visual arts a concern, but also disagreement about what term or terms should be used to identify such students is ongoing. There are no agreed-upon definitions of *gifted, talented, high ability,* or *talent development* in the visual arts (Clark & Zimmerman, 2004; Csikszentmihalyi, 1988; Feldhusen, 1992; Gardner, 1983, 1996; Hoffer, 1990; Kleinman, 1990; Pariser, 1997; Winner, 1996; Winner & Martino, 2000). Clark and Zimmerman discussed the problems of gifted and talented nomenclature. They suggested that:

> The term *gifted* frequently refers to students with superior intellectual abilities, while *talented* has come to mean possessing superior abilities in a single subject, including mathematics, language arts, science, or fine arts. The term *gifted and talented,* in some contexts has been replaced by *talent development,* driven by an emphasis on processes of developing talents rather than working with predetermined gifts. (p. 20)

Clark and Zimmerman (2004) also suggested that visual arts talents are manifested in many ways in arts media, processes, products or performances, problem-solving skills, creative expression, abilities to produce adult-like products, or personality characteristics and values, and that a conclusive definition of talent in the arts, to be used to identify students for school programs, is not possible or even desirable.

There are those who argue against distinguishing between terms such as gifted and talented, high ability, and other widely used terms (Eisner, 1990; Winner & Martino, 2000). Eisner argued that dividing students into either gifted or talented categories contributes to discrimination in favor of cognitive development at the expense of students whose abilities lie in the fine arts. He asserted that talent in the sciences, which is associated with abstract thinking, is given higher status and considered more worthwhile than talent in painting, drawing, sculpture, and the like. Such artificial divisions, he claimed, also contribute to the notion that the visual arts are not as rigorous or cognitively challenging and do not involve the full range of higher order thinking skills as other disciplines.

Winner and Martino (2000) argued that children with high ability in art are similar to academically gifted children in three respects. They suggested that gifted visual arts students master the first steps in their domain at an earlier than average age and learn more rapidly in that domain. They continued by arguing that gifted visual arts students also have the "rage to master" (p. 95), that is to say they are intensely interested in making sense of their domain and have an obsessive interest and ability to focus sharply in their area of ability. Finally, they argued that those of high ability in the visual arts learn differently than others. They virtually learn on their own, requiring minimum adult scaffolding while solving problems in their domain in novel or idiosyncratic ways.

The ongoing debate about how to define or categorize students who have extraordinary ability in the visual arts is likely to continue. The purpose of this discussion was not to propose such a definition, but to merely demonstrate the perplexing problem of defining giftedness in the visual arts and the problem of meeting the needs of art education.

Another issue of central importance for the education of secondary gifted students in the visual arts is the problem of creating programs with accelerated or enriched curricula. The Marland Report (Marland, 1972) stated that high-ability students require differentiated educational programs and services not ordinarily provided by schools in order to develop their abilities fully. The report did not specify how these specialized programs should be differentiated or how curricula in these programs should be structured. Calls for specialized programming and services in secondary gifted art education continue to be made (Clark & Zimmerman, 1984, 2004; Eisner, 1966; Sabol, 1998b; Salome, 1974). A problem arises when art teachers are faced with the decision of whether to develop accelerated or enriched visual arts curricula. To date, no significant research has been done in the field of gifted visual arts education to determine the efficacy of either approach. Either approach may yield beneficial results based on a wide variety of variables that may influence the degree of talent development coming from the selected approach. Suffice it to say that the nature of the students' needs and interests should be the determining factor in selecting one approach over the other, coupled with the knowledge, skills, and training of art teachers and local and state resources.

The preceding discussion of a sample of central developments and issues in art education and the related implications for secondary gifted and talented students in art education plays a significant role in providing a context for the following discussions pertaining to the characteristics of gifted individuals in the visual arts and of the products they create. The previous discussion merely provides an introduction to essential questions art teachers, parents, administrators, and policymakers concerned with secondary education of gifted students in the visual arts should consider.

CHARACTERISTICS OF ADOLESCENTS TALENTED IN THE VISUAL ARTS

Wechsler (1958) and Guilford (1967) reported that intelligence is normally distributed and that individual intelligence test scores will fall somewhere on a normal curve. Research has been done to establish that art talent also is a normally distributed trait, dependent upon societal norms and subject to cultural interpretation (Clark 1984; Clark & Zimmerman, 2004). Valid and reliable instruments, such as Clark's Drawing Abilities Test have demonstrated that everyone has some artistic talent and that some will have little, average, or superior art ability. Clark and Zimmerman (1978, 1983, 1984) suggested a continuum to describe how art talent develops. The model suggested that art talent progresses from the naïve or undeveloped stage, to sophisticated or highly developed ability with the majority of individuals attaining intermediate levels of development, thus suggesting the normal curve.

In order to identify art talent, characteristics of such talent need to be specified. The literature of art education reveals fascinating and often contradictory points of view. It is commonly believed that artistically talented students and their work can be easily identified in classrooms. However, Clark (1984), Dorn et al. (2004), Sloane and Sosniak (1985), Wilson and Wilson (1976), and Winner and Martino (2000) suggested that many students exhibit their talents in activities outside the classroom and art teachers are often unaware of the strength of students' expression outside the art classroom. Dorn et al. (2004) reported that adolescent students who make art at home do so for reasons that differ from those used for making art in school. Further, they reported that the criteria used by these students for judging the quality of works of art made at home differ significantly from those used to evaluate artwork made in school. Clark and Zimmerman (2004) reported that many adolescent students mask their art abilities because such ability is often misunderstood or considered strange by fellow students and teachers. Students who conform to classroom expectations and perform well in art are frequently judged as talented. Additional students may be unrecognized because their school performance is inconsistent with art teachers' expectations (Gallagher, 1985), while others only demonstrate their superior abilities in extracurricular activities they perceive as less threatening and more rewarding (Dorn et al.; Fine, 1970). This is not to say that talented art students do not need instruction or specialized programming to meet their needs. Feldman (1979) and Zimmerman (1995) reported that their studies of artistically talented students revealed that directive instruction is essential to the development of superior abilities.

Characteristics of visual arts talent generally are divided into two categories, including observable student behaviors and characteristics of students' art products. It is widely agreed upon that multiple characteristics should be used to identify gifted secondary visual arts students and their products (Clark & Zimmerman, 1984, 2004; Hurwitz & Day, 2001; Renzulli & Reis, 1985; Sabol, 1998b; Winner, 2000).

Observable Characteristics of Gifted Adolescents

Schmitz and Galbraith (1985) reported that virtually all highly gifted students know they are different from their peers by the time they are 5 or 6 years old. Sloane and Sosniak (1985) found that secondary students gifted in the visual arts made average grades in secondary school and they became increasingly involved with art making and networking with other students with similar interests for emotional support. Not surprisingly, they also were identified by other adolescents as having artistic talent. Widely varying criteria have been suggested to identify secondary students gifted in the visual arts by Boston (1987); Clark and Zimmerman (1984, 1997, 2004); Csikszentmihalyi, Rathunde, and Whalen (1993); Hurwitz and Day (2001); Pariser (1997); Richert (1987); Sabol (1998b); Sloane and Sosniak; Winner (2000); Winner and Martino (2000); and others. Observable characteristics of gifted visual arts adolescents may include *predispositional characteristics* and *observable process characteristics*.

Clark and Zimmerman (1984) identified a range of predispositional characteristics and observable process characteristics based on an extensive review of the lit-

---

Table 1
Predispositional Characteristics for Gifted Adolescents

Superior manual skill
Independence of ideas
Adherence to rules and regulations
Superior energy level
Desire to work alone
Compulsion to organize to satisfy desire for precision
High adaptability
High potential for leadership
Good concentration
Intuitive dynamic imagination
Unusual penchant for imagery and fantasy
Intense desire to fill extra time with art activities
High interest in drawing representationally
Sustained interest
Desire to improve their artwork
Persistence
Willingness to explore
Ambitious for an art career
Easy visual recall
Skills of visual perception
Planning of art products prior to production
Above-average IQ
Does well in other subjects
Display mature high quality behaviors for their age
Display individuality

---

erature in gifted visual arts education. They defined predispositional characteristics as "Behaviors that are observable in a student, independent of the creation of an art product" (p. 51). Predispositional characteristics they identified include, but are not limited to, those listed on Table 1.

Clark and Zimmerman (1984) also identified observable process characteristics for gifted adolescents in the visual arts. They defined observable process characteristics as "Observable behaviors of students during the processes of making or criticizing art" (p. 51). Process characteristics or behaviors they identified are listed on Table 2.

Giftedness is often associated with high intelligence, and many programs for gifted adolescents examine intelligence as a variable for identifying gifted students. Because superior intelligence and superior art talent are clearly independent, not all children with a high IQ will possess art talent. However, researchers have found that most children with superior art talent did possess a higher than average IQ (Clark & Zimmerman, 1984; Hollingworth, 1926; Luca & Allen, 1974; Manuel, 1919; Schubert, 1973). A higher than average IQ has been described as a necessary condition, by several of the researchers cited previously, for acquir-

---

Table 2
Process Characteristics of Gifted Adolescents

Originality and idiosyncratic depictions of content

Completion of specific ideas

Subtle and more varied graphic vocabulary

Flexibility with ideas

Confidence and comfort with art media and tasks

Purposefulness for art making

Directness of expression

Enjoy working with their hands

Clear understanding of structure and sense of the interrelationships of parts in artwork

Gives less personal and more objective reasons for critical judgments of the work of others

Genuine interest in the art work of others

Can appreciate and learn from the work of others

Applies critical insight to own work

---

ing the advanced techniques and skills required for superior art work (Clark & Zimmerman, 1984, 2004).

Products of Gifted Adolescents

Works of art and other products created by gifted secondary students in the visual arts traditionally have been the focus of defining high ability in the visual arts. It is widely agreed upon that such works of art have identifiable characteristics that distinguish them from works of art created by individuals with lesser artistic ability (Clark & Zimmerman, 1984, 2004; Hurwitz, 1983; Hurwitz & Day, 2001; Karpati, 1997; Sabol, 1993). However, identifying characteristics of exceptional works of art created by gifted secondary students is a thorny issue. There is little agreement among art educators and researchers about how to define high ability in the visual arts or how to adequately characterize artistic products of gifted individuals in the visual arts. The problem is compounded by the variety of studio products secondary gifted students in the visual arts may produce. An entirely new range of criteria is needed to judge types of products created by secondary students gifted in aesthetics, art criticism, and art history. In these disciplines, studio products rarely are produced. More traditional written or language-based products typically result, such as reports, papers, discussions, critiques, and other vehicles that allow the students to demonstrate the extent of their talents in these areas through forms of communication involving the use of language.

A Few Problems With Art Products Created by Gifted Adolescents

A caveat must be offered at this point in the discussion. Identifying a set of characteristics to describe works of art produced by gifted secondary visual arts students raises a number of perplexing problems. Characteristics of artwork for various stages of artistic development have been identified (Hurwitz & Day, 2001; Kellogg, 1969; Kindler, 1997); however, standard images to which responses can be compared have not been commonly accepted. In seeking a standard image to which responses can be compared, the assumption is that such an example exists and is capable of being manufactured by individuals or groups of individuals. This assumption is suspect. With all the subtlety, variety, personal expression, and complexity involved in creation of works of art, is it possible for a singular work or a set of works of art to represent such a standard?

This problem raises a more fundamental question for gifted visual arts education. Responses on standardized tests generally are evaluated by their degrees of "correctness" when compared to a standard. An answer is either correct or not. Items on these tests generally require students to produce a singular convergent response. However, art production by its very nature implies the creation of diverse responses in works of art. In fact, atypical works of art are often given higher evaluations by art teachers than typical ones due to creativity, risk taking, novelty, originality, or other factors that contribute to their unique quality (Dorn et al., 2004; Sabol, 1993). In identifying a production standard or list of criteria for such products, the assumption is made that a "correct" or "incorrect" response can be produced or that a "gifted style" exists in artwork. Creation of such standards is questionable in light of implications associated with it. Labeling artwork as "gifted" demands identification of standards for comparison and raises all of the associated problems of such standards. However, identification of a set of characteristics for this purpose holds merit. If such standards or characteristics are broad and fluid and do not establish rigid boundaries in which to make judgments about the character or merits of the works, creative and original responses will be permitted and encouraged instead of being eliminated because they do not conform to the predetermined set. To illustrate this point, Sabol suggested that art created by gifted secondary visual arts students may not simply be a question of superior quality in the technical aspects of the work involving the uses of art media, but also may involve the sophistication of ideas and meaning of the work independent of students' technical skills with media. Some gifted visual arts students may be highly skilled technically but lack sophistication in the generation of ideas and themes, while other may be highly facile in identifying and interpreting themes and ideas for works of art while lacking the technical skills to sufficiently portray them with art media.

Further, Gardner (1993) and Winner and Martino (2000) suggested that for giftedness to progress from adolescence into adulthood, gifted visual arts students must make the transition from technical perfection to innovation and domain creativity. They contended that merely attaining technical perfection without doing anything innovative will ultimately lead to fading interest and to decreasing development of visual arts talent. However, the degree of technical skill in childhood cannot by itself predict later creative eminence; nor can early detection or the best and most rigorous course of training (Winner and Martino, 2000). Without innovative creative development of works of art, the highly able individual is likely to fade from public view. This leap of innovation and creative development is essential for adolescents to become successful adult artists.

Some Characteristics of Studio Art Products Created by Gifted Adolescents

Products of artists have historically provided the foundation for the study of the visual arts and a focus for identifying adolescents gifted in the visual arts. A broad variety of criteria to identify gifted visual arts studio products have been recommended by various researchers in the field. This list does not suggest "necessary" properties of each work of art, but rather functions as a "menu" of possible characteristics works of art made by gifted secondary visual arts students may exhibit. The criteria are listed in Table 3.

Some Characteristics of Other Products Created by Gifted Adolescents

With the pervasive curricular emphasis on discipline-based art education, language-based products, such as reports and critiques that exemplify giftedness in the disciplines of aesthetics, art criticism, and art history also need a set of characteristics to properly identify good work. Sabol (1998b) suggested that observable characteristics of such products in written or oral forms include, but are not limited to:

- insightful or unique interpretations or judgments of works of art;
- identification and use of sophisticated criteria for classification or grouping of works of art;
- sophisticated knowledge of artists, works of art, and the era or culture in which they were created;
- unique analysis, synthesis, or evaluation of knowledge of philosophical questions related to the study of art;
- sophisticated knowledge of the impact of works of art during the era in which they were created, throughout the history of art, or in contemporary society;
- identification and in-depth explanation of themes and functions of art and their universal applications to art and artifacts from a broad spectrum of cultures; and
- sophisticated knowledge of the impact of the era or context on the lives of artists or on works of art from the era or context.

It is clear that there are many ways to describe and categorize superior visual arts talent in adolescent students. It must be understood, however, that no single set of

Table 3
Characteristics of Studio Art Products Created by Gifted Adolescents

Well-developed drawing ability (Clark & Zimmerman, 1984; Golomb, 1992; Hurwitz, 1983; Hurwitz & Day, 2001; Sabol, 1998b)

Bold use of the elements of art and the principles of design (Clark & Zimmerman, 1984; Golomb, 1992, 1995; Hurwitz, 1983; Hurwitz & Day, 2001; Sabol, 1998b)

Skillful composition (Clark & Zimmerman, 1984; Golomb, 1995; Hurwitz, 1983; Lark-Horovitz, Lewis, & Luca, 1967; Sabol, 1998b)

Coherent designs (Karpati, 1997; Lark-Horovitz et al., 1967; Sabol, 1998b)

Purposeful asymmetrical arrangement (Clark & Zimmerman, 1984; Lark-Horovitz et al., 1967; Sabol, 1993)

Complex compositions (Clark & Zimmerman, 1984; Golomb, 1992; Hurwitz, 1983; Hurwitz & Day, 2001; Lark-Horovitz et al., 1967)

Elaboration and depiction of details (Clark & Zimmerman, 1984; Golomb, 1992, 1995; Hurwitz, 1993; Hurwitz & Day, 2001; Karpati, 1997; Lark-Horovitz et al., 1967; Sabol, 1998b)

Well-organized and deliberate use of colors (Clark & Zimmerman, 1984; Lark-Horovitz et al., 1967; Sabol, 1998b)

Subtle blending of colors (Hurwitz & Day, 2001; Kough & DeHaan, 1955)

Bold use of line (Clark & Zimmerman, 1984; Sabol, 1993, 1998b; Wilson & Wilson, 1976)

Subtle use of line (Clark & Zimmerman, 1984; Kough & DeHaan, 1955; Sabol, 1993, 1998b)

Predominant use of vertical lines and forms (Sabol, 1998b; Wilson & Wilson, 1976)

Accurate depiction of light and shadow (Clark & Zimmerman, 1984; Sabol, 1993, 1998b; Wilson & Wilson, 1976)

Intentional use of haziness and indefinite shapes (Clark & Zimmerman, 1984; Lark-Horovitz et al., 1967)

Excellence in the use of color, form, grouping, or movement (Clark & Zimmerman, 1984; Golomb, 1995; Hurwitz & Day, 2001; Sabol, 1993, 1998b)

Adept depiction of movement (Clark & Zimmerman, 1984; Golomb, 1995; Lark-Horovitz et al., 1967; Sabol, 1993, 1998b)

True to appearance representation (Clark & Zimmerman, 1984; Golomb, 1992; Hurwitz & Day, 2001; Karpati, 1997; Sabol, 1993, 1998b)

Accurate depiction of depth or perspective (Clark & Zimmerman, 1984; Golomb, 1995; Kough & DeHaan, 1955; Sabol, 1998b)

Highly imaginative quality of work (Clark & Zimmerman, 1984; Golomb, 1992, 1995; Sabol, 1993, 1998b; Wilson & Wilson, 1976)

Good use of proportion (Clark & Zimmerman, 1984; Kough & DeHaan, 1955; Sabol, 1993)

Effective innovative use of media (Clark & Zimmerman, 1984; Sabol 1998b)

Skillful use of a variety of media (Clark & Zimmerman, 1984; Hurwitz & Day, 2001)

Visual narratives used for self-expression (Clark & Zimmerman, 1984; Golomb, 1995; Hurwitz, 1983; Hurwitz & Day, 2001; Sabol, 1993, 1998b; Wilson & Wilson, 1976)

Experimentation or risk taking (Clark & Zimmerman, 1984; Golomb, 1992, 1995; Hurwitz & Day, 2001; Karpati, 1997)

Sophistication of theme or idea (Clark & Zimmerman, 1984; Hurwitz & Day, 2001; Karpati, 1997; Sabol, 1993)

Development of a personal style (Clark & Zimmerman, 1984; Sabol, 1993, 1998b)

Creativity (Clark & Zimmerman, 1984; Karpati, 1997; Sabol, 1993)

Maximum use of black and white contrast (Sabol, 1998b; Wilson & Wilson, 1976)

Skilled use of action and movement (Clark & Zimmerman, 1984; Sabol, 1993, 1998b)

Specialization in one subject (Clark & Zimmerman, 1984; Lark-Horovitz et al., 1967; Sabol, 1998b)

Use of a wide variety of subject matter (Clark & Zimmerman, 1984; Golomb, 1995; Hurwitz & Day, 2001; Sabol, 1998b) characteristics will completely capture the complexity or scope of gifted individuals or the products they create in the visual arts.

VISUAL ARTS TALENT FACILITATORS

For talent in the visual arts to develop, a number of factors are necessary and these factors may contribute to talent development in various ways. Tan (1993), Feldman and Goldsmith (1986), Winner (2000), and Zimmerman (1992) stressed that talent development was dependent upon the following factors:
- a strong innate affinity for the medium and the domain,
- an insatiable hunger for mastery of the cultural forms,
- instruction about art forms that can be communicated effectively within the culture,
- access to a symbol system and a domain of knowledge valued by the culture,
- access to like-minded peers, and
- access to specialized programming in the discipline.

Csikszentmihalyi (1996), Feist (1999), and Pariser and Zimmerman (2004) reported that in order for talent development to occur conditions consisting of training, expectations, resources, recognition, hope, opportunity, and both extrinsic and intrinsic rewards must be available to the gifted secondary visual arts student.

The above factors facilitate talent development in gifted secondary visual arts students, but the interplay of a group of individuals in the life of these students also fosters talent development in essential ways. This group of individuals includes family members, teachers, mentors, and other stakeholders from the community.

Bloom and Sosniak (1981), Clark and Zimmerman (1984, 1995, 2004), Csikszentmihalyi et al.(1993), Davis and Rimm (1985), Freeman (1979), Sloane and Sosniak (1985), VanTassel-Baska (1989), and Winner (2000) identified multiple roles families play in facilitating development of visual arts talent. They found that families of those gifted in the visual arts:
- are supportive,
- play a positive role,
- allow the child access to teachers or trainers capable of developing talent,
- are least directive,
- hold high levels of expectations for the child,
- provide enriched family environments with a high level of artistic stimulation,
- are child-centered,
- often totally focused on the child's needs,
- provide art materials,
- display artwork around the home, and
- exemplify role models of the personality and life-style of artists.

It should be understood that although families play an important role in facilitating talent development in adolescents, the research does not support the conclusion that particular family characteristics play a causal role in developing giftedness (Winner, 2000). However, Sloane and Sosniak (1985) suggested that parents of students gifted in the visual arts were knowledgeable about the arts. Clark and Zimmerman (1984, 2004), Davis and Rimm (1985), Feldman (1979), Winner (2000), and others have grappled with the "nature versus nurture" question of whether gifted students are born with innate gifts in the visual arts or whether the environment, including the influences of families, contribute to the development of visual arts talent. No definitive answer to this question can be provided and discussion of this perplexing question will, in all likelihood, continue indefinitely.

The Role of Art Teachers in Development of Talent in Gifted Adolescents

Teachers make up another group of individuals central to development of talent in gifted secondary visual arts students. Clark and Zimmerman (1984, 2004), Feldman (1980), and Hurwitz (1983), have described contributions art teachers make in the ongoing development of gifted secondary visual arts students. They identified a number of traits art teachers of gifted secondary visual arts students have. Reviews of lists of desired teacher characteristics simply describe desirable traits of teachers of all students. Traits of teachers of the gifted may be distinguishable from good teachers by differences in degree, not kind. The art teacher of gifted secondary visual arts students frequently possesses the characteristics listed on Table 4.

Hurwitz and Day (2001) reported that art teachers must make every attempt to challenge gifted students to improve their art products by improving their skill and mastery with art media, making more penetrating insights, discovering facts or techniques for themselves, providing access to fine works of art, and suggesting outstanding works of art for them to study.

Clark and Zimmerman (2004) and Feldman (1980) concluded that progress in learning in the visual arts among gifted adolescents is linked to intensive and prolonged instruction. Art teachers play significant roles in such development through their ability to communicate instruction effectively, and by selecting learning experiences that lead their students to attain challenging and advanced levels of achievement.

Another group of individuals who can contribute to the facilitation of visual arts talent in secondary students includes community members. This group consists of mentors, such as artists, art historians, art critics, aestheticians, art collectors, gallery owners, art museum personnel, art related business owners, and others in the community who have knowledge of the visual arts. People in this group can be enlisted to work with individuals or groups of gifted secondary visual arts students. They may provide unique insights, experiences, and knowledge that can be used to successfully mentor gifted secondary visual arts students. They can participate in talent development by providing financial and material resources, experiences, educational opportunities, flexible scheduling, contacts in the community, space or facilities, access to works of art, and through other essential forms of mentorship.

Table 4
Characteristics of Teachers of Gifted Adolescents

Proven teaching ability (Clark & Zimmerman, 1984)

Considerate (Gallagher, 1985)

Exceptionally well-versed in subject matter (Clark & Zimmerman, 2004; Gallagher, 1985; Hurwitz & Day, 2001)

Creative (Clark & Zimmerman, 1984, 2004; Hurwitz & Day, 2001)

High intelligence (Clark & Zimmerman, 1984; Maker, 1976)

Knowledgeable about a wide array of general topics (Hurwitz, 1983)

Knowledgeable about pedagogy (Clark & Zimmerman, 2004)

Enthusiastic (Clark & Zimmerman, 2004; Hurwitz, 1983)

Humorous (Clark & Zimmerman, 1984, 2004; Hurwitz & Day, 2001)

Empathetic (Clark & Zimmerman, 2004)

Charismatic (Clark & Zimmerman, 2004)

Well-organized (Clark & Zimmerman, 2004; Hurwitz, 1983)

Promotes goal achieving behaviors (Clark & Zimmerman, 2004; Feldman, 1980)

Provides feelings of belonging (Clark & Zimmerman, 2004)

Relates to students (Clark & Zimmerman, 1984; Hurwitz & Day, 2001)

Possesses favorable attitudes toward gifted and talented adolescents (Hurwitz, 1983; Maker, 1976)

Allows students to work on their own (Clark & Zimmerman, 2004; Drews, 1964; Hurwitz, 1983; Hurwitz & Day, 2001)

Accepts the widest possible set of solutions to problems (Hurwitz, 1983; Hurwitz & Day, 2001)

Encourages students to become engaged in art issues (Pariser & Zimmerman, 2004)

Encourages students to think reflectively about the content of their work (Pariser & Zimmerman, 2004)

Makes courses interesting and stimulating (Clark & Zimmerman, 1984, 2004; Hurwitz, 1983)

Creates a stimulating physical classroom environment (Hurwitz, 1983)

Firm and consistent (Clark & Zimmerman, 1984)

Challenges gifted students to work to their highest capability (Feldman, 1980; Hurwitz & Day, 2001)

Provides extra attention (Clark & Zimmerman, 2004)

Willing to give of their time (Hurwitz, 1983)

Provides access to peers of equal talent (Clark & Zimmerman, 1984, 2004)

Willing to develop advanced programming such as Advanced Placement and International Baccalaureate (Clark & Zimmerman, 2004; Pariser & Zimmerman, 2004)

Encourages students to participate in competitions and exhibits (Clark & Zimmerman, 2004)

VISUAL AND PERFORMING ARTS TALENT INHIBITORS

It is commonly believed that because certain individuals are gifted or talented they will automatically develop their talents. This is far from true. A wide range of factors and circumstances inhibit, or may actually prevent, talent development. These factors may be part of the personality or psychological make-up of the talented individual or of the school, home, economic, social, or cultural environments in which they live. Others may be related to gender, race, and disabilities. Still others may be related to the lack of role models and misperceptions about employment and stereotypes relating to gifted individuals in the area.

Gifted students (Schmitz & Galbraith, 1985) have reported a number of factors that have complicated or inhibited the development of their talent. They included:

- no one explained what being gifted is all about;
- school is too easy and too boring;
- parents, teachers, and friends expect them to be perfect all the time;
- friends who really understand them are few and far between;
- other students often tease them about being smart;
- they feel overwhelmed by the number of things they can do in life;
- they feel different or alienated; and
- they worry about the world's problems and feel helpless to do anything about them.

Combinations of any of these factors may contribute to inhibiting the development of talent in gifted students. Educators, family members, and others concerned about developing visual arts talent in secondary students must be aware of these and additional factors and make efforts to help gifted visual arts students and visual arts education programs for the gifted overcome as many of them as possible.

Personality or Psychological Factors That Inhibit Talent Development

Clark and Zimmerman (2004) reported that adult artists are often caricatured in the United States as social misfits, nonconformists, or loners; children with superior art abilities often suffer from similar caricatures by adults, although these caricatures often are false. There also are false stereotypes of gifted children as socially inept, physically immature, or emotionally unstable. Studies (Clark, 1979; Guskin, Zimmerman, Okola, & Peng, 1986; Tuttle & Becker, 1980) have shown talented students to be social and intellectual leaders, physically superior to their peers, and emotionally well adjusted. Often, talented secondary visual arts students' misperceptions of being unusual or negative stereotypes such as those listed above contribute to their lack of interest in developing their artistic talent.

Educators and parents must deal with the emotional lives of their talented students and children, not just their intellectual needs. Schmitz and Galbraith (1985) suggested that like members of an ethnic minority group, gifted secondary students might feel insecure just because they are different from the norm. Unfortunately, gifted secondary visual arts students frequently are perceived as geeks or nerds by their peers (Clark & Zimmerman, 2004). Teenagers and preteens in particular want desperately to be like everyone else and any differences, whether positive or negative, are cause for anxiety. They suggested that the nonconforming nature of highly creative individuals is in direct conflict with the extreme conformity demanded by adolescents in groups. For this reason, many gifted secondary visual arts students may hide their talents or feel they contribute to a lack of acceptance by their peers

(Winner, 2000). As a result, they may shun opportunities and experiences that could help develop their talent.

Adderholdt-Elliott (1987), Clark and Zimmerman (1984, 2004), Kerr (1987), and Schmitz and Galbraith (1985) reported that perfectionism is another factor that may contribute to inhibiting talent development. Gifted secondary visual arts students may perceive this trait as a character or personality flaw, and they may try to ignore or deny their perfectionist tendencies as a reason for not developing their talents. They may be disturbed by the perceptions that their artwork is not at the level of quality they desire and become frustrated in their efforts to develop their abilities because of these perceptions.

Some talented adolescents lack motivation to develop their talent. They may not want the attention it could bring to them, both positive and negative, or they may feel no obligation to use their talents to make meaningful contributions to society. Schmitz and Galbraith (1985) contended that all gifted students need special amounts of acceptance and approval *as people*, particularly if all their self-worth is tied to accomplishments, performances, and products. This perception can contribute to a decreased motivation to develop their talents and lowered self-esteem because they may feel other people value them only for the superior artwork they produce, whereas, other students are loved simply for being alive or for being who they are as individuals.

Schmitz and Galbraith (1985) and Winner (2000) cited a number of behaviors that may indicate serious problems, many of which contribute to inhibiting the development of talent. They suggested that talented adolescents frequently:

- are introverted and gain more stimulation from themselves than from others;
- are desirous of contacts with like-minded peers;
- drop out of school;
- brag;
- tease or put others down;
- avoid responsibility, and generally display poor attitudes;
- have low self esteem and display aggression, rage, depression, or suicidal tendencies;
- are narcissistic;
- display fascination with violence;
- have eating disorders such as bulimia and anorexia;
- abuse chemicals and other substances; and
- display other rigidly compulsive disorders.

Any of these personality or psychological factors and others may contribute to inhibiting artistic talent development in secondary students.

School, Home, Economic, Social, and Cultural Factors That Inhibit Talent Development

Talented secondary visual arts students live in a number of complex overlapping environments. This mixture of school, home, economic, social, and cultural environments can support or interfere with the development of their talents. Often, conflicting messages are received from these environments and gifted secondary visual arts students are faced with the problems of blending or segregating these messages in the quest to develop their talents. Frequently, such conflicting messages contribute to inhibiting talent development.

The school environment must deal with its responsibility of adequately preparing students to meet the economic, social, and political needs of society, while accommodating the needs of all students at the same time. The realities of this responsibility frequently force decision-makers to inadequately meet the needs of talented students in the visual arts. Often educators feel that specialized programming is not needed to assist these students in their development. Those holding this opinion may feel that talented students will develop their talent without the assistance of specialized programming. Others believe there are insufficient numbers of talented secondary visual arts students to warrant the creation of specialized programming or the spending of funds to support them and that such programming is elitist (Winner, 2000). Other considerations prevent gifted program development in secondary schools. Among these considerations are insufficient funding, lack of interest or specialized training in gifted education among art teachers, lack of classroom space, lack of time in the schedule, lack of administrative support, and insufficient resources (Sabol, 1998c, 2001).

Factors present in the home can play a significant role in inhibiting the development of visual arts talent. Supportive parents are an essential component of talent development (Clark & Zimmerman, 1984, 2004; Hurwitz and Day, 2001; Pariser & Zimmerman, 2004; Winner 2000). Parents who are sympathetic to their children's talent development and who have provided their children an environment that supports the development of visual arts talent by encouraging risk taking, providing art materials at a young age, exposing children to works of art, museums, art exhibits, and other art-related experiences, have aided their children in developing their talents (Pariser & Zimmerman). In some cases, families have moved to allow their children access to teachers, artists, or programs that would foster talent development. Lack of such parental support significantly limits talent development. The economic standing of the family can also inhibit talent development in some secondary students. Impoverished families may not be able to support talent development due to the lack of money needed to provide art materials, experiences, and access to training. Lack of support from the home in any of these aspects may lead to the delay or prevention of talent development in the visual arts. Despite such limitations, numbers of gifted secondary students have succeeded in developing their talent.

American society traditionally has not highly valued the visual arts. The visual arts are not perceived as playing a central role in the historic traditions of our country. Most Americans are unaware of the extraordinary impact the arts play in our economy and the role visual arts play in their daily lives (Americans for the Arts, 2002). They do not view a new car, clothing, or home designs as being the products of visual artists. They fail to understand the power of imagery created by graphic designers in influencing decisions, attitudes, and judgments in their lives. They lack quality art education that teaches them about art and its role in improving the quality of their lives. In short, society has not placed significant value on works of art, or on those who create them. Gifted secondary visual arts students, aware of American society's lack of emphasis on the visual arts, often do not see an enticement to develop their talents. Even fewer see it as their responsibility to enrich American society with the products they may create.

Cultural environments play a significant role in how gifted secondary visual arts students perceive themselves, and thus how they are motivated to develop their talents. For example, in certain cultures, drawing attention to oneself is considered inappropriate and taboo. Students from such cultures are less likely to pursue their talent development because of the contradiction it may impose on their cultural values and traditions (Pariser & Zimmerman, 2004). In other cultures art production is not valued as a worthwhile pursuit because of the unsavory stereotypes and lifestyles of some who practice the visual arts (Winner, 2000). Clark and Zimmerman (2004) raised the issue of teachers' sensitivity to cultural stereotyping in their choices of subject matter and media when developing learning activities for students from various cultural backgrounds. Further, they contend that teachers must consider local cultural contexts and global popular culture and the role these cultural concerns play in fostering talent development in gifted visual arts education at the secondary level.

Gender, Racial, and Disabilities Factors That Inhibit Talent Development

Society's expectations have contributed to conflicts in talent development in males and females. Studies of gifted visual arts students (Clark & Zimmerman, 2004; Gardner, 1983; Reis, 1991; Winner, 2000; Zimmerman, 1995) revealed a number of talent inhibitors. Gender issues have provided a number of obstacles that have inhibited development of visual arts talent. Factors that inhibit visual arts talent development among adolescent girls include:

- negative feelings about the adequacy of their ability;
- lack of confidence and creativity about displays of their talent in front of boys, who may interpret such displays as unfeminine;
- complaints about not conforming to teacher expectations and standards;
- lack of acknowledgement of their talent or lack of interest in developing it;
- lack of self-esteem;
- lack of time to do artwork because of school commitments;
- inability to attend after-school classes because they were needed at home;
- encouragement to marry, have children, stay in their communities, and follow traditional ways of conducting their lives; and
- the lack of female role models in art.

Gifted adolescent boys have similar concerns that inhibit their talent development. Clark and Zimmerman (1984, 2004) identified visual arts talent development inhibitors common to adolescent boys. They reported that gifted adolescent boys are:

- not concerned about making good grades and obtaining achievement through conventional means;
- concerned about art careers that would lead to job security and high earnings;
- not concerned about being well-behaved;
- not admired by their teachers and peers;
- not interested in mathematics and do not perform well in math classes;
- not encouraged to pursue development of their talent by parents;
- unable to find peers with similar artistic interests and abilities;
- unable to take art classes because of tight scheduling of academic classes; and
- criticized by their art teachers and others for subject matter contained in their artwork.

Among gifted secondary visual arts students who come from minorities other factors may inhibit development of their talent. Schmitz and Galbraith (1985) found that for some gifted students, there are feelings of being trapped between theirs and the White culture, and their success may be interpreted by some from their racial group as "selling out" to the White culture. For others, perceptions of being different from their parents, family, or ethnic community may cause guilt or anxiety, causing them to refrain from developing their talent. Occasionally, students from ethnic minorities possess talent that is recognized within their ethnic group, but not by Western society. Further, gifted students from minorities whose principal language is not English may test below their ability levels on tests and other forms of identification traditionally used in gifted education programs, thereby denying these students access to gifted education programming.

Gifted handicapped students are an unseen minority. Rarely does the image of a gifted person include someone who is handicapped. Yet, research finds high-ability individuals in all handicapped areas, including the visual arts (Clark, 1979; Schmitz & Galbraith, 1985; Winner, 2000). However, a problem arises when traditional identification measures are used to identify handicapped students. It is a frequent misunderstanding that people with handicaps who cannot perform a task are associated with not being able to think or understand. Others, including art teachers, may automatically lower their standards and expectations for people with handicaps because of low expectations gifted people may have for themselves or that others have for them. Finally, isolation imposed by handicaps may lower self-esteem among people with handicaps and lowered self-esteem may contribute to inhibiting talent development among gifted secondary visual arts students with handicaps.

Lack of Role Models, Misperceptions About Employment, and Stereotypes That Inhibit Talent Development

A final group of factors contribute to inhibiting the development of visual arts talent in secondary students. These factors consist mainly of misperceptions on the part of these students and their families. For nearly all groups of gifted visual arts students, the lack of role models is a significant factor in preventing these students from developing their talents. They and their parents or guardians may not be able to identify with the commonly accepted role models or may view them as suspect or objectionable for a variety of reasons. Positive role models exist, but students may be unaware of them. Educators need to make particular efforts to introduce these models to gifted visual arts students as early as possible.

The field of the visual arts is fraught with many stereotypes about artists and others who are engaged in the world of art. Often, the public associates artists and the culture of artists or the art world with substance abuse, questionable life styles, transience, unacceptable values and ethics, unstable living conditions, deviant sexual practices, limited economic potential, high costs of art materials, and a host of other associations that may be unsavory to most people (Sabol, 1993). Parents are justifiably concerned about the ability of their children to earn a living capable of supporting themselves. Gifted secondary visual arts students may feel it is necessary to leave their communities in order to earn a living or to be fully immersed in the art world. They may not have ample opportunities to receive adequate art education in their communities, and they may see their community's values opposing those of the art world. In some cases, these perceptions may be born out of facts; however, these same misperceptions can be held about individuals in many other disciplines, as well. Such misperceptions can significantly contribute to attitudes that restrict or prohibit talent development among gifted adolescents in the visual arts.

In spite of the myriad of factors that can conceivably restrict development of talent in the visual arts, educators and others interested in such development must make continual efforts to assist gifted secondary visual arts students in developing their talent. Parents and art educators must vocalize their support of developing programs for this purpose and for providing educational programming that will meet the individual needs of gifted secondary visual arts students. Students must be proactive in seeking these programs, and they must continue to try to understand the nature of their talent and to strive to develop it.

VISUAL ARTS TALENT DEVELOPMENT OPPORTUNITIES

Gifted secondary visual arts students must have opportunities to develop their talent. Such opportunities may come in a variety of forms and present an even wider variety of experiences gifted secondary visual arts students need. Availability of such programming will vary from community to community and from school to school. Art educators, students, parents or guardians, and members of the community need to band together to create and support ongoing programming that facilitates talent development in the visual arts.

Gifted Visual Arts Education Programs in Schools

Schools are the most common source of programming for gifted secondary visual arts students. In order for these programs to be successful, a number of factors must be considered.

Creating and sustaining gifted visual arts programs demands support from the local school district's administration. Such support comes not only in the form of agreement about the need for such programs, but also by providing funding for materials, instructors, and any other financial needs of the programming. Administrators must also include time within the school schedule or annual calendar for these programs. If time is not available in the daily or weekly class schedule, alternative times may be acceptable, including before or after regular school hours, on Saturdays, or during summer breaks. Occasionally, gifted programming has been run concurrently with other courses so that classes containing both regular and gifted students meet simultaneously with special assignments or areas of study specially focused for the gifted visual arts student. Another arrangement could include independent study, in which the student and instructor collaborate to design the scope and nature of assignments or experiences that will contribute to each gifted secondary student's needs.

Program designers should also consider available resources in the community. Individuals in the community such as artists, art historians, art critics, gallery owners, people in business, and others may be able to assist in teaching or provide resources to facilitate talent development (Dorn et al., 2004). Community resources also may exist in the form of materials, space, or financial support. These and other community resources must be surveyed and utilized when possible.

Identifying Gifted Adolescents in the Visual Arts

A critical aspect of designing gifted programming is being sure that students have access to such opportunities. Art educators must be conscientious in their efforts to recognize students who have talent in the visual arts and to encourage these students to pursue development of their talents. Art educators must develop procedures for identifying talented students that involve use of multiple means and instruments (Clark & Zimmerman, 1984; Hurwitz, 1983). A full range of measures exists including, but not limited to, intelligence and achievement tests; aptitude tests; creativity tests; Clark's Drawing Abilities test (CDAT) and other standardized art talent identification tests; questionnaires; interviews; peer, parent, and teacher nominations; work sample portfolios; checklists; rating scales; puzzles; and games (Clark & Zimmerman, 2004, 1984, Hurwitz, 1983). No single measure will adequately serve to identify talent in the visual arts, while specific combinations may be successful in one locale and not in another. It is up to art educators to evaluate the effectiveness of each measure and to decide which combinations are most effective for identifying talent in their schools.

Professional-Grade Materials and Development of Visual Arts Talent

Talent development at the secondary level requires that talented students have access to professional-grade art materials. Differences in the quality between school-grade and professional-grade art materials can significantly play a role in talent development. Inferior materials prohibit talented students from fully exploring the potential of their talents. Experimentation with and mastery of professional quality materials typically leads to heightened quality in the students' products and increased personal expression (Sabol, 1998c, 2001). The expense of providing these materials is an important concern and may be seen as elitist by some; however, the limitations imposed by inferior materials can limit or halt talent development in gifted secondary visual arts students and steps must be taken to provide professional quality materials at all times.

Other Factors That Contribute to Effectiveness of School Programs for Gifted Adolescents

Art educators need to pursue specialized training in the education of students talented in the visual arts. Many colleges and universities provide specialized training and programming in gifted visual arts education. A number of states offer gifted and talented teaching license endorsements. Art educators must take advantage of such training in order to more effectively meet the needs of their talented students. Often art teachers feel they can easily identify talent and that they can create adequate gifted programming based on their knowledge of the general field of art. This is a common misunderstanding. Art teachers need to learn about the nature of giftedness in the visual arts, development of curricula for the gifted, identification techniques, the nature of gifted students, and how to evaluate products and programs for the gifted.

Schools provide the most easily accessible setting for the education of those talented in the visual arts. Art educators must be creative and persistent in their efforts to create, seek, support, and improve gifted programming for students in their schools. Art educators should investigate and study gifted education programs in other schools and elicit input from those who teach and direct these programs. Observations of and collaborations with such programs can assist art educators in launching similar programs in their schools.

Finally, art educators and administrators should be mindful that the needs of gifted secondary students are in a constant state of flux. Established programs for gifted students need to be routinely reevaluated to examine their effectiveness in meeting students' needs and to determine if the structure of the program supports ongoing identification, development, and support of students' talent (Sabol, 1998c, 2001). Revisions of gifted programs should be routinely made and changes should be evaluated for effectiveness.

Community-Based Gifted Visual Arts Education Programs

Programs designed to meet the needs of gifted secondary visual arts students frequently exist outside schools in the local community, within the state, or in the country. Art educators and administrators should keep informed about such programs and inform students and parents about them. In many cases such programs offer unique opportunities or resources that schools may not be able to provide. Often gifted students feel more at ease or challenged in programs that include peers with similar talents and are removed from the school setting (Dorn et al., 2004). Programs of this sort may exist in art museums, colleges or universities, local art centers, galleries, businesses, churches, libraries, with individuals, and in other common local settings. They may be offered during the summer, on weekends, or before or after school hours. Gifted students and their parents or guardians should be encouraged to take advantage of such programs when they exist.

Program and Curriculum Content in Community-Based Programs

An important concern for such programming is to ensure that the nature and content of the program is appropriate for gifted students at the secondary level. Often, programs in community settings are geared for elementary students or for students with passing interest in talent development. Decision-makers for these programs are often faced with offering programming that has the best chance to draw high numbers of participants in order to sustain them. Requests from art educators, gifted students, and their families for secondary programs or collaborations between art educators and people from the community may lead to such program offerings. Those creating, teaching, or administering such programs ought to consider whether their program meets the needs of secondary students and shape their programs to be compatible with those of gifted students.

In deciding what kinds of programming to offer for gifted visual arts students, community-based programs should consider providing a broad variety of courses. Drawing, painting, and craft courses are among those most commonly provided. There is sufficient justification for these offerings; however, limited course offerings may not be appealing to students who find their interests and gifts lie in other areas, such as in art history, aesthetics, and art criticism or in other production areas such as jewelry, textiles, printmaking, photography, computer graphics, and so on. Rotating offerings in these areas will contribute to encouraging students' access to them. Course content should be reflective of providing quality education about the content of the discipline, but it must also account for the individual interests of students. Collaborating with gifted students to sample their interests and to encourage their input has proven to be highly successful by providing a sense of input and direction gifted visual arts students seek (Clark & Zimmerman, 2004). Further, sequencing courses so that students can continue to advance their development through increasingly complex content will significantly contribute to development of visual arts talent in secondary students. Working with individual instructors for extended periods of time, as in the apprentice system artists have utilized for centuries, holds extraordinary potential for helping students develop their talents. In order for this model to succeed, community-based programs must be committed to maintaining programs and courses over extended periods of time. Changes in personnel, facilities, equipment, and funding may create challenges for sustaining programs and courses. Program directors should anticipate such change and initiate steps to keep pace with them.

Access to Community-Based Programs

Access to gifted visual arts programs in the community requires that students have the means to attend them. Often these programs are in remote locations and require transportation in order for students to participate. Parents or guardians generally have provided transportation, but a number of circumstances may prevent them from doing so. Secondary students may be able to transport themselves or have other means of attending; however, community-based programs should be aware that lack of transportation could prohibit some students from accessing their programs. If possible, community-based gifted art education programs should make arrangements for safely transporting students to and from their programs.

Community-based art education programs incur costs that often are off set by charging tuition or program fees. High fees for such programs can restrict students from attending them. Program teachers and administrators should seek sources of outside funding in the form of grants, endowments, gifts, scholarships, and any other forms of support available from individuals and local, state, and national agencies. Resourcefulness in obtaining needed personnel, materials, space, and equipment can significantly reduce fees. Keeping fees as low as possible or eliminating them can facilitate growth of the program and enable gifted students to participate in them.

Teachers in Community-Based Programs

Ideally, individuals who have in-depth knowledge of the visual arts and of teaching should lead community-based programs. Working with young people and successfully helping them develop their talents requires ability and skill beyond simple knowledge of the discipline. The interactions between students and teachers are essential components in the successful development of artistic talent. These interactions may be in the form of challenges to students, assistance in problem identification and problem solving, instruction, counseling, and numerous other forms of mentoring that require specialized training and experience. Community-based art education programs may access local art teachers, professors, artists, and others with teaching experience to act as instructors.

Community-based art education programs designed to meet the needs of gifted secondary visual arts students have played a significant role in talent development. Developers of these programs have unique concerns, restrictions and problems that must be overcome. Furthermore, they can provide unique opportunities, experiences, and training many schools may not be able to give students. Meeting the specialized needs of gifted visual arts students depends on combined efforts from schools and communities.

Conclusion

Gifted secondary visual arts students have unique needs and characteristics, as do the works of art they create. Successfully contributing to development of visual arts talent demands knowledge, training, experience, commitment, resources, and a broad base of support from art teachers, administrators, parents or guardians, and others in the community. Indeed, gifted visual arts students must make commitments to developing their talents and persist in that development, as well. Because the visual arts play such an important role in the daily lives of all people in our society, ongoing commitment to developing the talents of gifted students in our secondary schools and communities is warranted. If, as Thomas Jefferson, a renown artist, architect, musician, *and* politician, suggested, the purpose of schooling is to develop the individual talents of people to their utmost in order for them to contribute to the growth and preservation of our society, then schools and those who teach in them, and communities and all who live in them, have an obligation and the responsibility for educating the future generations of artists, art historians, art critics, and aestheticians. With the assistance of quality education, our young people gifted in the visual arts will develop their talents and create artistic products that will contribute to the rich artistic tradition that exists in the United States.

References

Adderholdt-Elliott, M. (1987). *Perfectionism: What's bad about being too good?* Minneapolis, MN: Free Spirit Publishing.

Americans for the Arts (2002). *Arts and economic prosperity.* Washington, DC: Author.

Bloom, B. S., & Sosniak, L. A. (1981). Talent development vs. schooling. *Educational Leadership, 39*(2), 86–94.

Boston, N. E. (1987). *Determining giftedness in elementary visual arts students.* South Bend, IN: Indiana University. (ERIC Document Reproduction Service No. ED301025)

Clark, B. (1979). *Growing up gifted: Developing potential of children at home and at school.* Columbus, OH: Merrill.

Clark, G. (1984). Establishing reliability of a newly designed visual concept generalization test for the visual arts. *Visual Arts Research, 10,* 73–78.

Clark, G., Day, M., & Greer, W. D. (1987). Discipline-based art education: Becoming students of art. *Journal of Aesthetic Education, 21,* 129–193.

Clark, G., & Zimmerman, E. (1978). A walk in the right direction: A model for visual arts education. *Studies in Art Education, 19*(2), 34–49.

Clark, G., & Zimmerman, E. (1983). Toward establishing first class, unimpeachable art curricula prior to implementation. *Studies in Art Education, 24*(2), 77–85.

Clark, G., & Zimmerman, E. (1984). *Educating artistically talented students.* Syracuse, NY: Syracuse University Press.

Clark, G., & Zimmerman, E. (1995). You can't just scribble: Art talent development. *The Educational Forum, 59,* 400–408.

Clark, G., & Zimmerman, E. (1997). The influence of theoretical frameworks on Clark and Zimmerman's research about art talent development. *The Journal of Aesthetic Education, 31*(4), 49–63.

Clark, G., & Zimmerman, E. (2004). *Teaching talented art students: Principles and practices.* New York: Teachers College Press.

Csikszentmihalyi, M. (1988). Society, culture, and person: A systems view of creativity. In R. Sternberg (Ed.), *The nature of creativity: Contemporary psychological perspectives* (pp. 325–340). New York: Cambridge University Press.

Csikszentmihalyi, M. (1996). *Creativity: Flow and the psychology of discovery and invention.* New York: HarperCollins.

Csikszentmihalyi, M., Rathunde, K., & Whalen, S. (1993). *Talented teenagers: The roots of success and failure.* New York: Cambridge University Press.

Davis, G. A., & Rimm, S. B. (1985). *Education of the gifted and talented.* Englewood Cliffs, NJ: Prentice-Hall.

Dorn, C. M., Madeja, S. S., & Sabol, F. R. (2004). *Assessing expressive learning.* Mahwah, NJ: Erlbaum.

Drews, E. M. (1964). *The creative intellectual style in gifted adolescents.* East Lansing, MI: Michigan State University.

Eisner, E. (1966). Arts curricula for the gifted. *Teachers College Record, 67,* 492–501.

Eisner, E. (1990). Implications of artistic intelligences for education. In W. J. Moody (Ed.), *Artistic intelligences: Implications for education* (pp. 31–42). New York: Teachers College Press.

Feist, J. (1999). The influence of personality on artistic and scientific creativity. In R. J. Sternberg (Ed.), *Handbook of creativity* (pp. 273–296). Cambridge: Cambridge University Press.

Feldhusen, J. F. (1992). *Talent identification and development in education (TIDE).* Sarasota, FL: Center for Creative Learning.

Feldman, D. H. (1979). The mysterious case of extreme giftedness. In A. H. Passow (Ed.), *The gifted and the talented: Their education and development* (pp. 335–351). Chicago: University of Chicago Press.

Feldman, D. H. (1980). *Beyond universals in cognitive development.* Norwood, NJ: Ablex.

Feldman, D. H., & Goldsmith, L. (1986). Transgenerational influences on the development of early prodigious behavior: A case study approach. In W. Fowler (Ed.), *Early experience and the development of competencies.* San Francisco: Jossey-Bass.

Fine, M. J. (1970). Facilitating parent-child relationships for creativity. *Gifted Child Quarterly, 21,* 487–500.

Freeman, J. (1979). *Gifted children: Their identification and development in a social context.* Baltimore, MD: University Park Press.

Gallagher, J. J. (1985). *Teaching the gifted child* (3rd ed.). Boston: Allyn & Bacon.

Gardner, H. (1980). *Artful scribbles: The significance of children's drawings.* New York: Basic Books.

Gardner, H. (1983). *Frames of mind: The theory of multiple intelligences.* New York: Basic Books.

Gardner, H. (1993). *Creating minds: An anatomy of creativity seen through the lives of Freud, Einstein, Picasso, Stravinsky, Eliot, Graham, and Gandhi.* New York: Basic Books

Gardner, H. (1996). The creator's patterns. In M. A. Boden (Ed.), *Dimensions of creativity* (pp. 143–158). Cambridge, MA: MIT Press.

Golomb, C. (1992). *The child's creation of the pictorial world.* Berkeley, CA: University of California Press.

Golomb, C. (1995). *The development of artistically gifted children: Selected case studies.* Hillsdale, NJ: Erlbaum.

Guilford, J. P. (1967). *The nature of human intelligence.* New York: McGraw-Hill.

Guskin, S., Zimmerman, E., Okola, C., & Peng, J. (1986). Being labeled gifted or talented: Meaning and effects perceived by students in special programs. *Gifted Child Quarterly, 30,* 41–50.

Hoffer, C. R. (1990). Artistic intelligences and music education. In W. J. Moody (Ed.), *Artistic intelligences: Implications for education* (pp. 135–140). New York: Teachers College Press.

Hollingworth, L. S. (1926). *Gifted children: Their nature and nurture.* New York: Macmillan.

Hurwitz, A. (1983). *The gifted and talented in art: A guide to program planning.* Worcester, MA: Davis.

Hurwitz, A., & Day, M. (2001). *Children and their art: Methods for the elementary school* (7th ed.). San Diego, CA: Harcourt, Brace, Javanovich.

Karpati, A. (1997). Detection and development of visual talent. *The Journal of Aesthetic Education, 31*(4), 79–93.

Kellogg, R. (1969). *Analyzing children's art.* Palo Alto, CA: National Press Books.

Kerr, B. A. (1987). *Smart girls, gifted women.* Columbus, OH: Ohio Psychology Publishing.

Kindler, A. M. (1997). *Child development in art.* Reston, VA: National Art Education Association.

Kleinman, S. (1990). Intelligent kinesthetic expression. In W. J. Moody (ed.), *Artistic intelligences: Implications for education* (pp. 123–129). New York: Teachers College Press.

Kough, J., & DeHaan, R. (1955). *Teacher's guidance handbook, elementary school edition, volume I: Identifying children with special needs.* Chicago: Science Research Associates.

Lark-Horovitz, B., Lewis, H., & Luca, M. (1967). *Understanding children's art for better teaching.* Columbus, OH: Merrill.

Luca, M., & Allen, B. (1974). *Teaching gifted children art in grades one through three.* Sacramento, CA: California State Department of Education. (ERIC Document Reproductions Service No. ED082433)

Maker, J. C. (1976). *Training teachers of the gifted and talented: A comparison of models.* Reston, VA: Council for Exceptional Children.

Manuel, H. T. (1919). *A study of talent in drawing.* Bloomington, IL: Public School Publishing.

Marland, S. P. (1972) *Education of the gifted and talented. Reports to the Congress of the United States by the U. S. Commissioner of Education and background papers submitted to the U.S. Office of Education,* 2 vols. Washington, DC: U.S. Government Printing Office. (Government Documents, Y4.L 11/2: G36).

Music Educators National Conference. (1994). *National standards for arts education: What every young American should know and be able to do in the arts.* Reston, VA: Author.

National Commission on Excellence in Education. (1983). *A nation at risk.* Washington, DC: U.S. Government Printing Office.

National Endowment for the Arts. (1988). *Toward civilization: Overview from the report on arts education.* Washington, DC: Author.

No Child Left Behind Act, 20 U. S. C. § 6301 (2001).

Pariser, D. (1997). Conceptions of children's artistic giftedness from modern and postmodern perspectives. *The Journal of Aesthetic Education, 31*(4), 35–47.

Pariser, D., & Zimmerman, E. (2004). Learning in the visual arts: Characteristics of gifted and talented individuals. In E. Eisner & M. Day (Eds.), *Handbook of research and policy in art education* (pp. 379–405). Mahwah, NJ: Erlbaum.

Reis, S. M. (1991). The need for clarification on research designed to examine gender differences in achievement and accomplishment. *Roeper Review, 13,* 193–202.

Renzulli, J. S., & Reis, S. M. (1985). *The Schoolwide Enrichment Model: A comprehensive plan for educational excellence.* Mansfield Center, CT: Creative Learning.

Richert, E. S. (1987). Rampant problems and promising practices on the identification of disadvantaged gifted students. *Gifted Child Quarterly, 31,* 149–154.

Sabol, F. R. (1993, May). Characteristics of high ability visual arts students' drawings on Clark's drawing abilities test. Paper presented at the national convention of the National Art Education Association, Phoenix, AZ.

Sabol, F. R. (1994). A critical examination of visual arts achievement tests from state departments of education in the United States. *Dissertation Abstracts International, 56* (2A), 9518525. (UMI No. 5602A)

Sabol, F. R. (1998a). What are we testing?: Content analysis of state visual arts achievement tests. *Visual Arts Research, 24*(1), 1–12.

Sabol, F. R. (1998b). Assessing visual arts ability. In J. Adams-Byers (Ed.), *Assessing high ability students* (pp. 57–65). Indianapolis, IN: Indiana State Department of Education Gifted/Talented Unit.

Sabol, F. R. (1998c). *Needs assessment and identification of urban art teachers in the western region of the national art education association.* Reston, VA: The National Art Education Foundation.

Sabol, F. R. (2001). *Reaching out to rural and urban art teachers in the western region of the national art education association: Needs assessment and identification of new members.* Reston, VA: National Art Education Foundation.

Sabol, F. R. (2004a). The assessment context: Part one. *Arts Education Policy Review, 105*(3), 3–10.

Sabol, F. R. (2004b). The assessment context: Part two. *Arts Education Policy Review, 105*(4), 3–8.

Salome, R. A. (1974). Identifying and instructing the gifted in art. *Art Education, 27*(3), 16–19.

Schmitz, C. C., & Galbraith, J. (1985). *Managing the social and emotional needs of the gifted: A teacher's survival guide.* Minneapolis, MN: Free Spirit Publishing.

Schubert, D. S. P. (1973). Intelligence as necessary but not sufficient for creativity. *Journal of Genetic Psychology, 122,* 45–47.

Sloane, K. D., & Sosniak, L. A. (1985). The development of accomplished sculptors. In B. S. Bloom (Ed.), *Developing talent in young people* (pp. 90–138). New York: Ballantine Books.

Tan, L. (1993). *A case study of an artistically gifted Chinese girl: Wang Yani.* Unpublished master's thesis, Concordia University, Montreal.

Tuttle, F., & Becker, L. (1980). *Characteristics and identification of gifted and talented students.* Washington, DC: National Education Association.

U.S. Department of Education (1991). *America 2000: An education strategy.* Washington, DC: U.S. Government Printing Office.

U.S. Department of Education (1994). *Goals 2000: Educate America Act.* Washington, DC: U.S. Government Printing Office.

VanTassel-Baska, J. (1989). Characteristics of the development path of eminent and gifted adults. In J. VanTassel-Baska & P. Olszewski-Kubilius (Eds.), *Patterns of influence on gifted learners: The home, the self, and the school* (pp. 146–162). New York: Teachers College Press.

Wechsler, D. (1958). *The measurement and appraisal of adult intelligence* (4th ed.). Baltimore, MD: Williams and Wilkins.

Wilson, B., & Wilson, M. (1976). Visual narrative and the artistically gifted. *Gifted Child Quarterly, 20,* 432–447.

Winner, E. (1996). *Gifted children: Myths and realities.* New York: Basic Books.

Winner, E. (2000). The origins and ends of giftedness. *American Psychologist, 55,* 159–169.

Winner, E., & Martino, G. (2000). Giftedness in non-academic domains: The case of the visual arts and music. In K. A. Heller, F. J. Mönks, R. J. Sternberg, & R. F. Subotnik (Eds.), *International handbook of giftedness and talent* (pp. 95–110). Oxford, United Kingdom: Elsevier Science Ltd.

Zimmerman, E. (1992). Factors influencing the graphic development of a talented young artist. *Studies in Art Education, 5,* 295–311.

Zimmerman, E. (1995). It was an incredible experience: The impact of educational opportunities on a talented student's art development. In C. Golomb (Ed.), *The development of artistically gifted children: Selected case studies* (pp. 135–170). Hillside, NJ: Erlbaum.

PERSONAL AND SOCIAL TALENT DEVELOPMENT

by Sidney M. Moon
& Karen Ray

*W*hat are personal and social talents? What do they have in common? How do they differ? Recently, many scholars have been focusing on these questions (Gardner, 1983; Goleman, 1995; Kelly & Moon, 1998; Sternberg, 1996; Zins, Bloodworth, Weissberg, & Walberg, 2004). For example, in his seminal book *Frames of Mind,* Howard Gardner included the "personal intelligences" as two of seven intelligences in his original multiple intelligence framework. He divided the personal intelligences into two related types. *Intrapersonal intelligence* involved access to one's own feelings and awareness of one's internal beliefs and values. *Interpersonal intelligence,* on the other hand, focused outward, with the core capacity being the ability to notice and make distinctions among other people. In this chapter, intrapersonal intelligence is conceptualized as a building block of personal talent, and interpersonal intelligence is conceptualized as a key component of social talent. Personal and social talents are both related to people and require effective processing of emotions. They are different because one is related to the self, while the other turns outward and focuses on relationships or social systems. Although they are facilitated by cognitive abilities, they are not exclusively cognitive. Indeed, as noted above, emotional intelligence (Mayer, Caruso, & Salovey, 1999) is a key building block of both types of talent.

Recently, several groups of scholars have developed models to organize the many personal and social competencies into a single framework. One such framework groups these competencies into five categories: self-awareness, social awareness, responsible decision making, self-management, and relationship management (Zins et al., 2004). In this chapter, the personal-social distinction has been selected as the primary organizing framework for personal and social competencies, because it provides a parsimonious, two-pronged focus for talent identification and development. In the personal-social framework, skills in self-awareness, decision making, and self-management from the Zins et al. model are discussed as components of personal talent, while skills in social awareness and relationship management are considered markers of social talent.

Western societies tend to focus on the development of academic, artistic, and athletic talents and neglect the development of personal and social talents. Secondary schools reflect this neglect. Most secondary schools do not provide any specific coursework in the personal and social domains. The middle school movement has encouraged middle schools to pay attention to the affective needs of middle school students, but has done so primarily through restructuring their environments, rather than through developing subject matter courses in the personal and social domains. Therefore, personal and social talents are harder to identify and develop in secondary school environments than talents in more traditional domains such as math, English, history, biology, music, and the visual arts.

This is unfortunate for gifted students. Personal and social competencies are important building blocks of successful and happy adult lives for talented individuals. And, personal and social talents can facilitate the development of high-level expertise in demanding career fields such as medicine, law, science, politics, and the arts. In addition, some domains, such as teaching, leadership, and family counseling, require practitioners with high levels of personal and social talent. If students are not introduced to these fields in secondary schools, they may be less aware that such socially oriented fields are a good fit for their interests, values, and abilities. They will also be less likely to develop the readiness skills needed for success in college programs in these domains, many of which have a substantial experiential component that requires mastery of prerequisite personal and social skills for successful participation.

However, there are many strategies that can be used in secondary schools by teachers and counselors to identify and promote the development of personal and social talents. The first purpose of this chapter is to help education personnel understand the characteristics of individuals with personal and social talents and identify students with these talents. The second purpose of the chapter is to help educators develop a variety of direct and indirect strategies to develop these talents through activities infused into their regular curricula. *Direct* instructional strategies develop personal and social talent by explicit teaching of knowledge and/or skills in the personal or social domains. For example, a unit on time management provides direct instruction in a key area of the personal domain and a mediation training program provides direct instruction in the social skill of conflict management. *Indirect* strategies provide experiential opportunities for students to practice personal or social skills. For example, a social studies simulation of the development of a national constitution provides numerous opportunities for students to practice decision making and negotiation skills. Because personal and social talents are conceptualized here as distinct but correlated domains, they will be addressed in separate sections, beginning with personal talent.

PERSONAL TALENT

Personal talent is exceptional ability to select and attain difficult life goals that fit one's interest, abilities, values, and contexts (Moon, 2003b). To develop personal talent, one needs to build a knowledge base in three areas: (a) self-knowledge and awareness; (b) environmental and contextual knowledge, which includes traditional academic domains, as well as tacit knowledge of specific contexts in which the individual is living; and (c) psychological knowledge related to dispositions and behaviors that facilitate goal selection, goal attainment, and personal well-being. But, knowledge is not enough. The individual with personal talent also must develop high-level skills in two areas: (a) personal decision making and (b) self-regulation or self-management.

Assessing Personal Talent

The construct of personal talent raises two separate issues for talent identification. First, how do we identify the relative strength of personal abilities among students who have high levels of talent in a traditional domain such as science? This is important because highly talented scientists, artists, writers, and computer programmers are more likely to make good career and life choices and be successful in accomplishing their goals if they have developed personal talent (Jarvin & Subotnik, this volume). The second issue is a more typical talent identification issue, that is, how do we identify students whose exceptionally high levels of personal talent may allow them to accomplish more in a traditional domain than might be predicted from their academic or standardized test performance? We know that this can happen from research on some of the components of personal talent such as intrinsic motivation. Students with high levels of intrinsic motivation for academic tasks have been shown to be able to outperform many students with higher levels of measured intelligence on a number of relevant variables, including school achievement (Gottfried & Gottfried, 2004a, 2004b). It is also important to identify students with high levels of personal talent because these students will be more likely to build a complex life that balances multiple roles effectively. Managing complexity is increasingly important in modern life and is especially important for talent development among gifted females (Arnold, 1995; Noble, 1996; Reis, 1998, 2002). As adults, gifted females are more likely than males to want to pursue multiple goals in different spheres of life simultaneously. They often struggle to achieve balance between work, family, and time spent alone. In addition, gifted females may deny or downplay their talents in adolescence if they perceive that achievement and social acceptance are mutually exclusive pursuits instead of complementary ones (Clasen & Clasen, 1995; Reis, 2002). They may engage in conditional life planning, which can lower their career aspirations and make it difficult for them to pursue careers with long apprenticeship periods (Arnold, 1995).

There are no standardized instruments available to assess personal talent, although a few researchers have developed instruments that measure related abilities such as emotional intelligence (Mayer et al., 1999; Salovey, Mayer, & Caruso, 2002) and practical intelligence (Sternberg, 1993; Sternberg et al., 2000; Sternberg & Wagner, 1986; Williams et al., 2002). Therefore, secondary teachers will need to rely on personal observations of classroom performances to assess levels of personal talent among their students. The same methods and activities that assess individual differences in the personal competencies of gifted students can also be used to identify students whose high levels of personal talent may allow them to accomplish goals that seem to be beyond their academic, artistic, or athletic capabilities. Suggestions for teachers who want to assess the five personal competencies that comprise personal talent are given below.

Assessing Personal Talent Knowledge

The knowledge components of personal talent include knowledge of self, the environment, and psychology. Students who are strong in *self-knowledge* are aware of their cognitive, affective, and motivational strengths and weaknesses. Affective activities that require students to rate their satisfaction with different areas of their lives, compare themselves to characters in a novel or experts in content domains, list their goals, describe their abilities in multiple domains, share their opinions on world events, or reflect on their feelings about specific events or performances can assist teachers in assessing individual differences in students' self-knowledge. Secondary teachers who use the Parallel Curriculum Model can use the curriculum of identity to both assess and develop student self-knowledge (Tomlinson et al., 2002). The Parallel Curriculum Model is a guide for developing differentiated curriculum for gifted students. It has four strands; one of which is "the curriculum of identity," which helps students understand their interests, strengths, and weaknesses in relation to specific subject matter content. It is also important that students develop self-understanding in the cultural context of their lives.

Knowledge of the environment has several components, with factual or declarative knowledge being the easiest to assess. Here the goal is to find out whether students have a large knowledge base of information about the world in which they live. Much of this knowledge base is transmitted in typical Pre-K–12 courses, so secondary teachers are in an excellent position to assess the knowledge of gifted students in the domains they teach. Discipline-specific standardized achievement tests can also be used to assess this aspect of student knowledge. Such factual knowledge of a discipline is essential to the development of academic talent.

In order to develop personal talent, however, other types of knowledge are also important. For example, personally talented students are skilled at developing tacit knowledge of specific contexts through direct experience; in other words, they have high levels of practical intelligence. Tacit knowledge is untaught knowledge about how a system or environment works (Sternberg, Wagner, & Okagaki, 1993; Wagner & Sternberg, 1985). Since students have spent much of their lives in school, secondary teachers can measure individual differences in gifted students' tacit knowledge abilities by assessing their understanding of the tacit rules of their current school setting or classroom environment (Williams et al., 2002). Experiential learning activities such as simulations, mentorships, and problem-based learning (PBL) activities enable teachers to see differences in their students' abilities to rapidly acquire tacit knowledge about a new context or system.

To develop personal talent, students also need to be sensitive to the ways in which their own socio-cultural conditioning limits their perceptions and options. For example, stereotypes may prevent males from pursuing careers as elementary school teachers, or females from pursuing careers as engineers unless teachers intervene to make students aware of the ways cultural patterns, media images, and textbook stereotypes can influence career decision making. Activities for assessing this type of knowledge include classroom discussions, group counseling focused on socio-cultural issues, and units focused on cultural and/or cross-cultural issues.

Assessing the *psychological component* of personal talent knowledge is much more difficult for secondary teachers. Knowledge of scientific advances in psychology is usually only a minimal part of the training of secondary teachers. In addition, the psychological knowledge base needed to develop expertise in the personal domain is quite large and often takes years to master. Therefore, the assessment of this component of personal talent may need to be carried out by people with psychological training such as school counselors or school psychologists. A comprehensive assessment of the psychological component of students' personal talent knowledge base would include, but not be limited to, the assessment of their knowledge of the following areas of psychology:

- human abilities, personality traits, and values;
- effective goal selection strategies;
- attribution theory;
- adaptive and maladaptive perfectionism;
- theories of identity and career development;
- theories of talent development; and
- research on factors that contribute to well-being among adults in different cultures.

These are just a sampling of the aspects of psychological knowledge that would need to be assessed in order to identify students with high levels of expertise in the personal domain. If assessment shows that few gifted students possess the psychological knowledge needed to develop high levels of personal talent, secondary schools might consider adding a positive psychology course to their curriculum.

There is a close relationship between assessment and the development of expertise in the personal domain. In general, classroom activities that develop personal talent knowledge bases can also later be used to assess the status of those knowledge bases.

Assessing Personal Talent Skills

The core personal talent skills of decision making and self-regulation are self-referenced and best assessed by the individual. Given the self-referenced nature of these skills, secondary teachers can assess them in their students by designing and implementing student self-assessment activities. For example, secondary teachers in any domain might ask students to make a decision about a free choice assignment by a certain date, develop a written rationale for their decision, and, after the assignment has been graded, reflect on the quality of their decision and what they would do differently the next time. Frequent assignments of this type would allow teachers to assess student growth in decision making skills and facilitate the development of self-assessment skills.

Teachers can also measure personal talent skills through observing student behaviors. Observational assessments will be more accurate if the classroom environment is designed to require decision making and self-regulation. Teachers using traditional lecture techniques will not be in a good position to observe these skills in their students. On the other hand, secondary teachers who create complex classrooms that allow students choices over many aspects of their learning, involve them in complex problem solving and/or independent study, and are responsive to student input will be able to observe and assess decision making and self-regulation skills and to identify students who have high levels of personal talent. Personal talent skills can also be observed effectively in extracurricular activities. These activities provide students with opportunities to make choices and develop the self-regulation skills required for effective participation.

Unfortunately, even teachers who create complex and responsive classrooms can not fully assess personal talent skills in their students. Personal talent is about life management. A comprehensive assessment of student personal talent skills needs to examine students' management of their whole life, both in and out of school, over a long period of time. Comprehensive assessments can be accomplished by using a combination of methods such as asking students to respond to periodic surveys designed to assess personal talent skills, clinical interviews conducted by school counselors or psychologists, and case conferences, where the informal observations of a number of adults who see the student in a variety of contexts are shared and combined.

Personal Talent Development

For most of human history, personal talent development has been left to chance. For centuries, no programs of study existed to help individuals develop personal talent. Instead, those who developed personal talent did so because they were adept at learning through experience. Often, these individuals were especially skilled at what Sternberg calls "practical intelligence," or the ability to build tacit knowledge without direct instruction (Sternberg & Wagner, 1986; Sternberg et al., 1993; Williams, Blythe, White, Sternberg, & Gardner, 1996). When these individuals had fully developed personal talent, they were called astute or wise or successful.

However, one of the main tenets of personal talent theory is that personal talent can be developed through systematic instruction (Moon, 2003b). This implies that educators can develop instructional strategies and curricula that will help students develop personal talent. Based on our previous discussion of personal talent characteristics, two types of curriculum and instruction are needed. First, we need methods that will help adolescents who have been identified as having high levels of personal talent continue to develop their talent. Second, we need methods differentiated for gifted students that can help those adolescents who have deficiencies in the personal domain remediate those deficiencies as efficiently as possible so they can realize their academic, artistic, and/or athletic potential. Finally, we need to be aware of specific facilitators and inhibitors of personal talent development. These issues are the focus of the next section of this chapter.

Facilitators and Inhibitors of Personal Talent

The theory of personal talent is based on almost a century of research on factors that seem to facilitate good personal decision making and goal attainment (Moon, 2003b). This literature suggests there are many factors that can facilitate or inhibit the development of personal talent knowledge and skills among gifted adolescents. We will discuss these factors at four levels: Socio-cultural, school, family, and individual.

Socio-cultural. Personal talent development is facilitated by cultures that allow individuals considerable freedom of choice in selecting life goals and by those that provide multiple avenues for goal attainment. In other words, free, democratic societies facilitate the development of personal talent, especially with respect to goal selection skills. Cultures that celebrate individual differences, provide effective social structures through equitable laws, and refuse to tolerate discrimination in any form provide the ideal support for the development of personal talent. Gifted adolescents are more likely to develop personal talent when they grow up in a culture that provides them with the freedom to explore, envision, and discover as much as they can about themselves and the world in which they live. Such cultures promote the development of self-regulation rather than conformity to societal norms, and provide multiple low-risk opportunities for adolescents to learn to make sound personal decisions on a daily basis.

The influence of culture can also be seen on goal attainment skills. For example, most Eastern cultures emphasize effort over ability when explaining the reasons for achievement, while Western cultures do just the opposite (Hseuh & Moon, 1997; Stevenson, 1994, 1998). The Eastern perspective appears to facilitate more positive attributional styles, greater persistence in the face of challenges, and a stronger work ethic than is typically the case in Western cultures like the United States.

Unfortunately, there are also places that provide only minimal support for personal talent development. In cultures where the basic needs of life are not met because of poverty or lawlessness, survival needs take precedence over self-actualization and curtail personal talent development. Antiachievement peer cultures, such as those that exist in many urban areas in the United States, may make it difficult for gifted adolescents in those areas to develop personal talent. At the very least, antiachievement peer cultures require gifted adolescents to make difficult choices between support (friends) and autonomy (achievement) at a stage in their life cycle when they may not be equipped to make the best choices for their long-term development. Similarly, it is hard to explore all aspects of one's self if some aspects are inhibited by the surrounding culture. In cultures that suppress the rights of women, it is difficult for them to develop personal talent. Too many of their choices are foreclosed by cultural stereotypes. Hence, culture has a tremendous influence on the development of personal talent and can both facilitate and inhibit its development.

School. Schools have cultures just as societies do. School cultures that promote personal talent are similar to the societal cultures that facilitate personal talent. They respect the dignity of every student in the school, celebrate and encourage individual differences, and scaffold the development of personal decision making skills. For example, classrooms that encourage differentiation of instruction in response to student readiness, interest, and learning profiles, as recommended by Tomlinson (Tomlinson, 1995; Tomlinson et al., 2003) are more effective in developing personal talent than classrooms that provide one-size-fits-all instruction.

Both direct and indirect strategies can be used to help gifted students build the knowledge, skills, and psychological dispositions that comprise personal talent (Moon, 2003a). Schools and teachers help adolescents develop personal talent *indirectly* when they provide student-centered learning environments that balance challenge with support. Personal talent is also indirectly developed when teachers model skills such as adaptive attributions for success and failure or effective time management. Many of the instructional strategies recommended for gifted adolescents, such as problem-based learning in social studies (Gallagher, 1997), model eliciting activities in mathematics (Chamberlin & Moon, 2004), and independent research in science (Moon, Feldhusen, Powley, Nidiffer, & Whitman, 1993; Whitman & Moon, 1993) are also good, indirect strategies for the development of personal talent, because they involve gifted students in making choices, solving complex problems, and self-regulation.

One of the best secondary gifted education models for personal talent development is the Autonomous Learner Model or ALM (Betts & Kercher, 1999).

This model focuses on optimizing ability through integrating individual development with enrichment, seminars, and in-depth study of self-selected topics. All components of this model facilitate the development of personal talent. Similarly, the principles of teaching successful intelligence (Sternberg & Grigorenko, 2003) provide good guidance for teachers who want to use indirect methods to develop personal talent.

In order to help adolescents develop personal talent *directly*, scholars in the field of gifted and talented education need to develop differentiated, sequenced personal talent curricula that can teach gifted adolescents all aspects of personal talent. Such curricula should promote individual awareness of strengths, weaknesses, and personality traits. Educators must provide instruction about how socio-cultural influences affect goal selection and attainment; for example, how gender stereotypes and perceptions about work vary by culture. Personal talent curricula can provide explicit instruction on how to build positive psychological dispositions, such as adaptive attributional styles (Kobasa, 1979; Oulette, 1993; Ziegler & Heller, 1997, 2000), hardiness (Kobasa; Kobasa, Maddi, Puccetti, & Zola, 1985; Oulette), and hope (Curry, Snyder, Cook, Ruby, & Rehm, 1997; Snyder, 1994; Snyder et al., 1995) through strategies such as monitoring self-talk, building visualization skills, and seeking the assistance of a therapist. Finally, a comprehensive personal talent curriculum provides direct, experiential instruction in personal decision making and self-regulation skills.

An example of a partial personal talent curriculum can be found in Betts's guidebook for the Autonomous Learner Model (Betts & Kercher, 1999). The guidebook includes numerous exercises to help students develop self-awareness by identifying their interests, abilities, and values. For example, the Learner Orientation Questionnaire has 23 creative prompts to help students identify their learning characteristics, the Multiple Intelligences Checklist provides students with a rough assessment of their abilities with regard to Gardner's eight intelligences, the Journey Into Self exercise asks student to identify qualities they like about themselves and qualities they want to improve about themselves, and I AM Poems ask students to use a structured format to create a poem describing themselves. Gifted students who complete these activities and share them with peers learn a great deal about themselves and others. The ALM manual also includes units on aspiration development and organizational skills.

There are a few other resources available to help adolescents learn specific personal talent skills such as time management. For example, *Organizing From the Inside Out for Teens* (Morgenstern & Morgenstern-Colon, 2002) provides easily accessible guidance from one of America's top time management experts and her daughter. The authors of this chapter are unaware of any curricula written specifically to help gifted adolescents learn the psychological knowledge and skills necessary for personal talent development. In general, there is a lack of preexisting personal talent curricula designed for adolescents. Such curricula need to be developed if teachers are to become more effective at direct methods of personal talent development.

Family. There is strong evidence from both the general child development literature (Baumrind, 1989; Collins, Macoby, Steinberg, Heatherington, & Bornstein, 2000) and the literature on adolescent talent development (Csikszentmihalyi, Rathunde, & Whalen, 1993; Moon, Jurich, & Feldhusen, 1998; Rathunde, 1988, 1996) that families who provide an appropriate balance of support and challenge, closeness and independence, are more likely to produce adaptive children than families that are either too permissive or too authoritarian. The same family factors that foster healthy identity development (Hébert & Kelly, this volume) foster the development of personal talent, because one aspect of personal talent is a healthy identity. Complex families that encourage individual exploration and talent development while providing teens with emotional support can assist them in developing personal talent if the environment provides sufficient challenges for teens to develop resilience and sufficient options for them to fully explore their interests and potentials.

It is also true, however, that in certain exceptional cases very negative family environments can promote personal talent development in resilient individuals (Masten, 2001; Masten & Coatsworth, 1988; Masten & Marie-Gabrielle, 2002). Indeed, one irony of personal talent development is that it is sometimes honed best in adverse circumstances, because adversity can encourage individuals to "dig deep" into their coping repertoire as they seek to overcome their adverse circumstances. This is one reason why many eminent individuals, especially in the arts, come from unhappy or dysfunctional families (Goertzel & Goertzel, 1962). The same dynamic can promote personal talent development in adolescents with disabilities. The adversity route to personal talent development is a high risk one and not to be encouraged. However, knowledge of this pathway provides a potential avenue for teachers and counselors to use with gifted adolescents who are facing difficult circumstances of any kind. If these students can be counseled to see the adversity as an opportunity to become stronger, to develop resilience, and to hone their motivation and character, their experiences can become building blocks of personal talent.

Individual. Personal talent is an intrapersonal talent domain, therefore, individual factors are hypothesized to be the most important factors in facilitating or inhibiting the development of personal talent. Acquisition of the psychological knowledge and dispositions required for the development of personal talent are influenced by personality, creativity, and both emotional and cognitive intelligence. Emotional intelligence is an individual difference factor that influences the extent to which a gifted individual will be able to develop personal talent, with individuals who have higher levels of emotional intelligence finding it easier to develop certain components of personal talent, especially self-awareness and skills in decision making and self-regulation (Moon, 2003b).

It has been shown that certain individuals are able to thrive in external circumstances that would crush others. Individual characteristics associated with resilience also promote the development of personal talent (Bland, Sowa, & Callahan, 1994;

Masten & Marie-Gabrielle, 2002; Neihart, 2002). These factors include intelligence, curiosity, high self-efficacy, optimism, a sense of humor, flexibility, and problem-solving ability. Hardiness has been identified as one of several personality traits that buffers the effects of stress in adults, creating resilience in times of change (Kobasa, 1979; Kobasa, Maddi, & Kahn, 1982; Maddi & Kobasa, 1984). Hardy adults exhibit the three C's in the face of stressful circumstances: challenge, control, and commitment. They view stressful events as a challenge and opportunity, rather than an overwhelming problem. They maintain a sense of control in the face of changing circumstances by focusing on the aspects of the situation in which they have choices. They also have the ability to remain committed to their goals when faced with set-backs. For adolescents, hardiness has been found to have four components: control, challenge, commitment to school, and commitment to self (Morissey & Hannah, 1987). Gifted adolescents with high levels of hardiness will exhibit higher levels of personal talent.

There is more information available about the individual characteristics associated with personal talent than there is about how to develop those characteristics. It seems reasonable to assume that they could be nurtured through gifted and talented programs that provide training in creative problem solving, self-awareness, and self-regulation. However, no studies have been conducted to determine the extent to which these characteristics, or other aspects of personal talent, can be developed among gifted adolescents and, if they can, what is the best way to do so. Gifted adolescents, by definition, probably have the threshold levels of intelligence required for developing resilience. So, the individual difference characteristics that facilitate or inhibit the development of personal talent among intellectually gifted adolescents probably lie in areas such as temperament, executive processing abilities, and learned psychological traits. Temperament seems to play a part in the development of resilience and appears to be relatively stable over an individual's lifetime. Similarly, the Big Five personality traits of neuroticism, extraversion, openness, agreeableness, and conscientiousness are relatively stable characteristics of individuals (Costa & McCrae, 1990). At the same time, research on psychological dispositions associated with personal talent, such as optimism and hardiness, suggests that these characteristics can be modified through intervention (Dweck, 1999; Kobasa et al., 1985; Moon, 2003b; Seligman, 1998; Seligman & Csikszentmihalyi, 2000). Hence, an important area for future research on personal talent is the malleability of personality. Can gifted adolescents learn a positive explanatory style? Can they develop hardiness through direct instruction and coached practice? Future research is also needed to determine the potential of gifted adolescents with deficits in intrapersonal intelligence, emotional intelligence, and/or executive abilities, such as selective attention, to develop personal talent. For example, can gifted adolescents with AD/HD develop personal talent through specific compensation strategies in spite of their cognitive and affective weaknesses? The answers to such questions await the findings of future research.

Opportunities for Personal Talent Development

Within-School Opportunities

Personal talent is different from other talent domains in that there currently is no place in the secondary curriculum where students are exposed to direct instruction in personal talent. Students who are talented in science, creative writing, music, or the arts have at least some direct opportunities to develop their talents in the secondary school setting through specific coursework. Personal talent development, on the other hand, is currently informal and unstructured. Secondary schools that are serious about promoting the development of personal talent might encourage their teachers and counselors to work in teams to create personal talent curricula focused on topics such as self-awareness, socio-cultural conditioning, coping with stress and adversity, combating negative peer pressure, setting goals, and managing time effectively.

Professional development of teachers is also a key to personal talent development at the secondary level. Secondary schools that want to encourage personal talent development need to work with all of their teachers to ensure that the instruction for talented adolescents is challenging, interesting, and provides opportunities for student choice. Challenging curricula also provide opportunities for developing hardiness. As students struggle with problems that require high levels of persistence and effort to solve, teachers can provide feedback and modeling that encourages students to view hard problems as opportunities to develop the three C's—challenge, commitment, and control. For example, they can encourage students to see hard problems as enjoyable challenges, to remain committed to both the assignment and their own learning by persisting in the face of initial difficulties, and to focus on developing problem-solving strategies that are under their control. Challenging curricula also require students to prioritize their time outside of school to ensure that they complete their assignments. However, challenging curricula must be delivered by teachers who are trained in modeling adaptive self-talk and giving feedback that promotes adaptive attitudes toward subject matter, so that students will not develop learned helplessness in the face of the challenge, but instead will increase their self-confidence as they rise to the challenges embedded in their coursework (Ziegler & Heller, 1997, 2000). Teachers need to learn how to provide the appropriate balance of support and challenge for their gifted adolescents if they are to help them develop personal talent in addition to achievement in the subject area. Secondary schools that provide career development interventions for their gifted adolescents could expand these interventions to include other aspects of personal talent development, such as developing dispositions like hardiness that are known to facilitate both achievement and personal well-being under stressful conditions.

Out-of-School Opportunities

More indirect ways for secondary schools to promote personal talent include encouraging students to participate in extracurricular activities such as clubs and sports. Such extracurricular activities provide talented adolescents with experience in making choices, regulating their emotions in unstructured situations, and persisting toward self-selected goals, all building blocks of personal talent. This may be one reason why participation in extracurricular activities is more predictive of life success, especially in creative endeavors, than school grades (Milgram & Hong, 1999). Service learning programs, mentorships, and jobs can also be excellent vehicles for indirect development of personal talent.

Secondary schools can encourage gifted adolescents to build personal talent by making constructive choices about how to spend their summers. University-based talent development programs provide students with opportunities to explore their academic interests, interact with an international gifted peer group, and experience the freedom and responsibility inherent in living in a residential environment on a college campus (Enersen, 1993; Goldstein & Wagner, 1993; Olszewski-Kubilius, 1989, 2003). By definition, these camps provide challenging academic curricula in a supportive context with similar peers, facilitating the development of a healthy gifted identity and building skills in self-regulation, time management, and decision making. Students who are building personal talent eschew passive activities like watching television for active learning experiences such as participating in a community theatre, creating a business enterprise, going on a church mission trip to an impoverished country, or joining a scientific lab as a research intern. The key to developing personal talent through out-of-school activities is active, experiential learning. Gifted adolescents can benefit from both formal and informal learning experiences if they are chosen by the student and there is an opportunity for reflection afterward.

SOCIAL TALENT DEVELOPMENT

History and Issues

Psychologists have studied social intelligence since the 1920s. Thorndike (1920) postulated an overall intellectual capacity composed of three intelligences: abstract, mechanical, and social. The social component involved "the ability to understand and manage people" (p. 228). Although he expressed concerns about the difficulty of measuring an intelligence that was vivid in naturalistic settings but hard to describe precisely, one of his contemporaries devised the George Washington Social Intelligence Test (GWIST; Hunt, 1928). Using subtests of (a) judgment in social situations, (b) memory for names and faces, (c) observation of human behavior, (d) recognition of mental states behind words, and (e) recognition of mental states from facial expressions, he found that social intelligence correlated highly with general intelligence. This compromised claims that social intelligence was a different factor than general intelligence, which in turn led to a decline in interest in and use of this instrument and the construct of social intelligence.

Interest in social intelligence was renewed in the 1960s following Guilford's (1967) development of his Structure of the Intellect model. This rather complicated system included four categories of content (figural, symbolic, semantic, and behavioral); five classes of operations (cognition, memory, divergent production, convergent production, and evaluation); and six categories of products (units, classes, relations, systems, transformations, and implications). These components resulted in Guilford's prediction of at least 120 intellectual abilities based on varying combinations of content, operations, and products. Social intelligence is placed within the behavioral domain (five operations times six products). O'Sullivan, Guilford, and Demille (1965) initially found research support for a six factor model related to cognitive social intelligence. After structural equation modeling was developed, Romney and Pyryt (1999) used it to reanalyze the data and concluded that a single factor more accurately described O'Sullivan, Guilford, and Demille's data. To Romney and Pyryt, finding a single factor underlying social intelligence made the measurement of this intelligence easier.

Walker and Foley (1973) proposed that social intelligence consisted of two elements: cognitive skill in understanding social interactions and competent social behavior based on that understanding. Similarly, Ford and Tisak (1983) found that academic and social intelligence could be separated when social intelligence was measured as behavioral effectiveness, rather than with verbal instruments. By the early 1980s there was agreement that social intelligence existed, and that it was a separate construct from academic intelligence (Kelly & Moon, 1998).

Interventions addressing social skills and behaviors began with a focus on remediation. Over time, there has been a progression from a remediation perspective to a growth perspective (Durlak & Wells, 1997). Spaulding and Balch (1983) describe the historical progression of mental health movements starting with the mental hygiene movement, early child guidance clinics, the eugenics movement, federal government involvement, and more recent research efforts. Behavioral psychology, humanistic psychology, and family systems therapy provided resources to assist in the remediation of social problems. As problems with legal and illegal drug use and dependency increased, communities and organizations began adopting and implementing drug education programs. Prior to the 1990s there was little intervention research focused on developing social talent.

Current Theories

Gardner's (1983) theory of multiple intelligences stimulated renewed interest in interpersonal skills. As noted in the introduction to this chapter, Gardner called social intelligence "interpersonal intelligence." He defined interpersonal intelligence as an exceptional capacity for communication and relationships, being good at communicating, and having a sense of other people's feelings and motives. He offered Lyndon B. Johnson as an exemplar of interpersonal intelligence.

More recently, Salovey and Mayer have studied the emotional abilities underlying social intelligence (Mayer et al., 1999; Mayer & Salovey, 1993, 1997; Salovey et al., 2002). They defined emotional intelligence as a subset of social intelligence having five domains: self-awareness, managing emotions, motivating one's self, empathy, and managing relationships (Mayer & Salovey, 1993). They postulated that emotional intelligence incorporated both of Gardner's (1983) interpersonal and intrapersonal intelligences.

Kelly & Moon (1998) reviewed the research on personal and social talents and found more research on social talent than personal talent. For example, researchers have concluded that socially talented people have complex declarative knowledge about people and social situations and are able to respond quickly in social arenas by using their extensive base of procedural knowledge with conditional observations to guide their behavior. These theoretical conceptualizations and the empirical social/emotional research literature have considerable overlap and seem to be addressing similar underlying phenomena.

Issues

The majority of existing literature approaches social development from a remediation perspective. There is clear evidence that deficits in social development lead to problems such as delinquency, early and unplanned pregnancy, school truancy, and aggressive behavior (Catalano, Berglund, Ryan, Lonczak, & Hawkins, 2004). There is less understanding that social talent can be developed purposively. That perspective may be changing as groups such as the Center for Social and Emotional Education (CSEE; see http://www.csee.net) and the Collaborative for Academic, Social, and Emotional Learning (CASEL; see http://www.casel.org) work to establish curricula models and share information. By the late 1900s, several of these movements began contributing to the rise of school-based health centers that provided prevention and treatment services. These prevention programs, in turn, led to a focus on resiliency. Later, the positive psychology movement focused on factors that contribute to success and happiness in life (Seligman & Csikszentmihalyi, 2000; Snyder & Lopez, 2002). This progression has set the stage for examining social talent from a high functioning perspective rather than a remediation perspective.

Even with these positive developments, however, there has been little focus on identifying and developing exceptional levels of social talent. There are also questions about why anyone should be concerned with higher levels of social talent development. The authors suggest that many occupations (e.g., business, politics, and the helping professions) rely on high levels of social talent and even more occupations benefit from it. Many lives are influenced positively by people with high levels of social development. For example, researchers have found that physiological responses to stress are mitigated by improved social relationships (Sachser, Durschlag, & Hirzel, 1998) and health improves when social relations are positive (Berkman, 1995). Thus, it seems important to increase the focus of secondary schools on this area of talent development.

Yet another complication in this area is that social talent appears to be very complex. It is composed of a large number of related subskills, some of which overlap with the personal talent skills described in the previous section. For example, in a major review of programs seeking to enhance social development, Catalano and col-

Table 1
Social Intelligence Competencies

Self-Awareness	Self-Management	Responsible Decision Making	Social Awareness	Relationship Management
Identifying and recognizing emotions	Impulse control and stress management	Problem identification and situation analysis	Perspective taking	Communication, social engagement, and building relationships
Accurate self-perception	Self-motivation and discipline	Problem solving	Empathy	Working cooperatively
Recognizing strengths, needs and values	Goal setting and organizational skills	Evaluation and reflection	Appreciating diversity	Negotiation, refusal, and conflict management
Self-efficacy		Personal, moral, and ethical responsibility	Respect for others	Help seeking and providing
Spirituality				

Note. Adapted from "The Scientific Base Linking Social and Emotional Learning to School Success," by J. E. Zins, M. E. Bloodworth, R. P. Weissberg, and H. J. Walberg, 2004, in *Building Academic Success on Social and Emotional Learning: What Does the Research Say?* (p. 7), New York: Teachers College Press. Copyright ©2004 by Teachers College Press. Reprinted with permission.

leagues (2004) found some common denominators among empirical studies that identified successful programs. Several kinds of competence mattered: social, emotional, cognitive, and moral. Self-determination, self-efficacy, and having a clear and positive identity contributed to improvement in social development. Possessing prosocial norms, being recognized for positive behavior, and having opportunities for recognition and reinforcement of prosocial behavior were also influential in social development. Additionally, resilience, spirituality, and belief in the future contributed to social development. Even this lengthy list doesn't capture what it means to be gifted socially, but does point out again the complexity and intercorrelation between personal and social talent.

Elias and colleagues (1997) categorize social and emotional skills as follows: (a) self-awareness related to emotions and their origins, (b) self-regulation of emotions including coping, managing, and mobilizing positive feelings, (c) self-monitoring of performance, (d) empathy with listening and perspective taking components, and (e) social skills in relationships. At first glance, the skills of self-awareness, self-regulation, and self-monitoring may seem unconnected with social skills, but many scholars have suggested that they are as crucial for social talent development as they are for personal talent development. These skills seem to have the greatest overlap between the two talent areas. They are all self-oriented, which suggests that some of the inner-directed personal talent skills may be prerequisites for the development of social talent. The framework of Zins et al. (2004) mentioned in the introduction (see Table 1) provides further support for this view. In summary, there appear to be multiple facets to social talent including self-knowledge; skills in emotional regulation and self-care; competence in social skills such as assertiveness, communication, empathy, persuasiveness, and conflict negotiation; and moral competence.

Strategies for Identification

Although there are few measures of this complex and broad talent domain, it is possible to recognize secondary students who demonstrate exceptional social talent. Individuals exhibiting talent in social areas are able to understand other people and use this knowledge to guide others to mutually satisfying outcomes (Kelly & Moon, 1998). Socially talented individuals have a solid knowledge of self, coupled with the ability to manage their emotions in healthy ways. They are well connected with their family, peers, school, and community. They manage and guide those connections, even at a young age, through judicious use of interpersonal skills such as assertiveness, communication, and conflict negotiation. Their relationships are mutually satisfying and reciprocal. Socially talented adolescents may have mentors who provide support and encouragement (Kaufman, Harrel, Milam, Woolverton, & Miller, 1986). They possess exceptional empathy and a strong moral sense. Cognitive, affective, and behavioral components interact in social talent. Although there is no adequate assessment system, the secondary teacher can recognize individuals who demonstrate these behaviors through astute observation, as was the case for personal talent.

Social Talent Development

Both personal and social talents have a skill-based component that can be taught. Additionally, taking the time to establish and execute programs to teach skills related to social and emotional intelligence can improve academic achievement (Elias et al., 1997). Currently, some programs already exist that capitalize on the skills of socially talented students, that is, peer mediation (Smith, Daunic, Miller, & Robinson, 2002), prevention (Black, Tobler, & Sciacca, 1998), leadership training (Matthews, 2004) and mentoring experiences (Casey, 2000). Those programs involve identifying individuals who already have exceptional poise and ability to interact with peers and adults and provide training to further hone their proficiency. This suggests that it is possible to deliberately develop exceptional social talent through purposeful educational activities.

Facilitators and Inhibitors of Social Talent

Culture. Little is know about the specific cultural influences that best promote the development of social talent. Cultural influences on social talent development are extensive and complex. Socialization is one of the purposes of culture, and takes numerous forms across cultures. Even when similar social behavior can be identified across cultures, the meaning of that behavior is often different. For example, shyness can be identified in both Western and Chinese cultures. It is seen as a disadvantage in individualistic Western cultures, but the same behavior is not seen as maladaptive in Chinese cultures (Rubin, 1998). "Indeed, inhibited children are viewed as interactively competent and perhaps because they are viewed as achievement oriented, independent, and academically accomplished, they develop positive relationships with their peers" (p. 612). Social competence in American majority culture is highly valued and prepares students for adult roles in an individualist society (Schneider, 1998). Thus, social talent at a gifted level may ease the transition to adulthood in these societies. However, that leads to independence in decision making about social relationships, sometimes leading to a pattern of teenage alienation. In collectivistic cultures, there tends to be more reliance on parental judgment about social relationships with an accompanying concern for general harmony and attention to the effect of behavior on others. The latter is a hallmark of social awareness, which is seen as a part of social talent. These examples are relatively straightforward, however, cultural influences on social talent development are likely to reflect many layers of meaning, within the individual, within the interaction between individuals, within the relationship, and within group factors (Rubin, 1998). It is reasonable to expect that individual temperament affects social talent development, as does interaction between individuals. There are anecdotal examples of gifted individuals whose social behavior is admired by one teacher as novel and valued, while the same behavior is rejected and considered by another teacher to be abrasive and arrogant. As interactions accumulate, relationships develop with their history and expectations. Individuals, interactions, and relationships function within what Bronfenbrenner (1989, 1994) terms the *macrosystem*. The influence of the macrosystem may be subtle, but it is also pervasive and influential, especially in regards to social roles. Although all of these cultural influences on social talent development have been extensively studied, this is such a complex area that scholars are only beginning to ascertain the influences that lead to high levels of social talent.

More is known about the ways that culture inhibits social talent identification and development. For example, cultural differences may complicate the identification of social talent. Baldwin (2002) writes about the drawbacks of using established criteria to identify diverse students for gifted programming, and many of her cautions apply to identifying diverse students who have social talent. She notes that giftedness can be expressed in many behaviors (some of which may not be familiar to the examiner). Because there are gifted individuals in all cultures, training for educators is needed so they know how to recognize cultural expressions of giftedness. This is especially important when considering social talent, because social interactions and behaviors are heavily context-laden.

Another class of cultural inhibitors of social talent development for gifted youth relates to uncertainty about the relationship between giftedness and social skills. Hollingworth (1926, 1942) described highly gifted students (intelligent quotients over 180) as having problems with social and emotional adjustment. On the other hand, Terman and his colleagues (Terman, 1925; Terman & Oden, 1959) found that gifted students were better adjusted than nongifted children. This debate has continued to the present day with experts on both sides of the issue weighing in (Gross, 1993; Karnes & Wherry, 1981; Neihart, Reis, Robinson, & Moon, 2002; Tannenbaum, 1983).

Among intellectually gifted students, negative and limiting stereotypes related to giftedness can inhibit social talent development (Ray, 2004). Images of the nerdy science student and geeky band member are common in the media, as are other derogatory perceptions. Historically, the United States has had an anti-intellectual culture (Hofstadter, 1966), and appears to be continuing in that path (Winner, 1997). Socially talented students may be adept at avoiding some of the repercussions of those stereotypes because of their greater social skills. However, students who are intellectually gifted and socially average may not have the grace to deflect or defuse the results of stereotypes and prejudice.

School. There are programs to build social and emotional skills for secondary students with roots in education, the mental health movement, and societal social action movements. Dewey (1897) and other progressive educators in the late 19th century developed ideas about reflective education, which emphasized the whole child. As other scholars implemented and elaborated on Dewey's ideas, they conducted peace studies, service learning, and affective education in the mid-20th century. Cooperative learning and conflict resolution programs led to the character education movement. All of these strands culminate in social and emotional education. If leadership training, or, for that matter, any of these programs, is offered at schools, students who are poor or have transportation difficulties can participate in them more easily (Karnes, Lewis, & Stephens, 1999). Even without such programs in place, school itself may be a facilitator of social talent development because it draws together students and adults and provides an opportunity for considerable social interaction.

There is a small amount of research regarding gifted students and social talent development. Culross and Jenkins-Friedman (1988) warned against using a problem-focused model to develop affective skills in gifted students. Instead, their program focused on providing information about giftedness and coping skills. Reis, Colbert, and Hébert (2004) conducted a longitudinal study of urban, economically disadvantaged, academically talented high school students. They found that peer, family, and school support networks acted as protective factors to help students maintain high achievement. Similarly, negative interactions with teachers became a risk factor, decreasing student achievement. Sowa and May (1997) studied stress and coping paradigms among 20 gifted 9- to 14-year-olds. They concluded that parents and teachers of gifted students needed to foster a balance between achievement adjustment (using behavioral coping strategies to adjust to the environment, e.g., meditation) and process adjustment (using cognitive coping strategies to cope with the environment, e.g., reframing negative events in a positive light) in order to achieve optimal social and emotional growth. Elmore and Zenus (1994) created a 12-week social development program for gifted students in an accelerated mathematics class based on the principles of cooperative learning. Social-emotional skills were taught to facilitate math learning, so this was an indirect and minimalist approach regarding social-emotional skills. Nonetheless, they found positive changes in self-esteem in addition to gains in mathematics achievement. On the other hand, it may be possible to be too minimalist. Clark and Dixon (1997) conducted a communication workshop with four gifted students and found no increase in academic or social self-concept. However, their procedure was limited in time and emphasized low level skills (e.g., how to greet a new person). Perhaps the brevity of the workshop, the low level of skills presented, and the small number of participants resulted in an intervention that lacked potency.

As mentioned in the section on personal talent, the Autonomous Learner Model (Betts & Kercher, 1999) includes interpersonal and intrapersonal skill development. Although not the primary focus of the model, social skills are an intrinsic part of it, and are carried out through the same explorations, investigations, cultural activities, service, and adventure trips advocated for other content areas. Betts believes social development needs to occur early in the learning process so the learner is prepared to work with others in content domains. Because this model frequently uses individualized and independent work, it allows students to work at their own level while in the company of intellectual peers. Overall, the existing research about gifted students and social relationships indicates the importance of social development.

Multiple programs are available that can be used in schools to promote social and emotional competence, increase academic success, and reduce problem behaviors such as school dropouts, low attendance, and conduct problems (Zins et al., 2004). Early intervention (grades 1–6) through a social development model has produced positive changes in school attachment and commitment in high school (Catalano et al., 2004). A strong bond to school has been found to serve as a protective factor against antisocial behavior. However, few studies exist that explore the development of social talent in students who are socially gifted. Likewise, little research examines the effectiveness of the participation of gifted and talented students in social and emotional development programs designed for general education.

Research has shown that lack of access to similar peers can inhibit the social development of academically gifted students (Gross, 2000; Neihart, Reis, Robinson, & Moon, 2002). It is possible that an overemphasis on academic learning in competitive and individualistic contexts might inhibit or delay the development of social talent. The pervasive neglect of social skills curricula is a barrier to social talent development in the secondary setting. Few schools currently have a strong, focused curricular emphasis on social talent development. Even if such programs are implemented, it takes a strong commitment to maintain them, especially in educational environments that emphasize minimal competency testing. Hence, the programs are often short-lived experiments. The widespread lack of systematic social talent development programs is undoubtedly inhibiting the identification and development of socially talented individuals at the expense of both the talented persons and society. Another inhibitor is the tendency of schools to function on their own, detached from parents and local communities. Because the best results stem from broad models that integrate services between school, family, and community, the lack of coordination is an inhibitor. Lastly, insofar as a socially talented student is also academically talented, curriculum choices at an appropriate level and with an appropriate pace facilitate social development, and the lack of such academic services inhibit it. When the need for intellectual stimulation is not met, students spend time and psychological energy coping with the resulting boredom rather than being able to grow socially.

Family. Family influence is complex, reciprocal, and based on both genetics and environment (Collins et al., 2000). Families influence the development of social talent directly, through teaching and experiences in the family, and indirectly through behavioral modeling and by influencing the selection of peers and goals. Parents who use induction, explaining how their child's actions have affected someone else rather than punishment or behavioral reinforcement, raise children who are better able to understand another person's perspective (Eisenberg & Fabes, 1998). This is especially helpful for gifted youth who, because they differ from the majority of students, may have more need to understand differing points of view.

Interaction with schools provides another complicated layer to family influence. Giftedness complicates relationships between parents and schools. Parental advocacy in school settings influences social and emotional adjustment (May, 1994). Parents' interactions with schools are affected by their own experiences in secondary schools, pressures from work, and other responsibilities. The focus in this section is on how teachers can influence parents. It is important for students' success that schools and parents work together; however, that becomes difficult at the secondary level, as parents' contact with and involvement in schools decreases (Elias, Bryan, Patrikakou, & Weissberg, 2003). One basic intervention is simple—finding common ground with the parents. While educators are experts in curriculum and teaching, parents are experts on their children. It is vital that school personnel engage that expertise rather than alienate it. Part of this is providing a respectful, understanding climate when interacting with parents at conferences, meetings, and school events.

It is difficult to say with certainty how families might inhibit social development. As with other adolescents, family dysfunction can prevent optimal development. In addition, there are some family issues specific to families with gifted adolescents. For example, parents may have difficulty dealing with giftedness in females or have problems discerning when their child's problems are related to giftedness or are those typical of the adolescent stage of development (Fornia & Frame, 2001). Giftedness may be a stressor itself or part of a constellation of concerns related to the expression of giftedness (Colangelo, 1988, 1997, 2003). Little is known about how a socially gifted son or daughter affects family dynamics, although scholars have speculated that the influence is reciprocal, with the giftedness being influenced by and influencing the family (West, Hosie, & Matthews, 1989). The extra level of social competency might be a welcome asset to the family and actually improve functioning, or it might be viewed as a threat, resulting in deterioration of family functioning.

Individual. Individual predispositions leading to high levels of social talent have not been identified. Several socially talented individuals who were also intellectually gifted were interviewed to elicit input regarding personal factors (S. Goetz, E. P. Frisch, T. C. Hagman, K. Laughlin, & C. Rhoads, personal communication, January, 2005). Several common themes emerged from their responses. Factors cited as facilitating social talent development included respect for other people, establishing and maintaining a purpose to communicate well, and responding to others' communications sensitively. These themes reflect components of perspective taking, assertiveness, and empathy, which are all part of social awareness. Interviewees mentioned being taught how to interact in social situations either in formal educational situations or by someone who worked with them on an individual level.

Other factors contribute to high levels of social development at an individual level. First, if educators want students to develop social talent, they must have an opportunity to practice and rehearse the necessary component skills. Feedback from skilled adults is important. Students need time to reflect and ponder on themselves, their relationships, and the dynamic interplay between them.

> In almost every school, who gets the most practice? Those performing with the band or chorus, on sports teams, or on the stage. They come to school early, stay late, and work on their own on weekends. Why? Because this is how skills are learned. (Elias et al., 1997, p. 52)

Developing social talent does take time, as do most worthwhile endeavors, and time is a valuable commodity in school settings where conflicting demands clamor for attention.

However, these skills can be integrated and practiced during classroom work, at least some of the time. Students studying the American Civil War can gather information about a number of historical figures. Then the students can complete an analysis of which figure they are most like and explain why (J. D'Lamater, personal communication, March, 2001). Students in a literature class can write about the feelings and motives of characters, or they can write different endings for novels and short stories using prompts from the teacher to design prosocial, argumentative, or unassertive (passive) interactions. Mathematics students can examine the costs of stress-related illness and project financial savings for stress reduction programs. Science students can compare the physiology of human endocrine responses to isolation versus companionship or altruism versus selfishness. Students can use interdisciplinary approaches to suggest solutions to real-world social problems such as homelessness.

Inhibitors at the individual level occur in varied forms. Specific social and emotional issues for gifted students may include emotional sensitivity, intensity, perfectionism, underachievement, and asynchrony, that is, being different from chronological peers or having varying levels of abilities within the self (Fornia & Frame, 2001). Not all of these attributes are present in every gifted child. One example illustrates how these might interact with high levels of social development or prevent the development of social talent. A student who is chronologically 14 years old but intellectually 20 has little in common with other 14-year-olds (Gross, 1993). This asynchrony forces an unusual division between otherwise similar peers and makes finding common ground difficult, inhibiting the social development of gifted children. To reverse the damage, schools need to provide opportunities for highly intellectually gifted children to interact with mental age peers. For example, the talented 14-year-old might attend classes at a local college for part of the day.

Twice-exceptional students may also experience inhibitors to the development of social talent and/or social competence (Baum, 1994; Moon, Zentall, Grskovic, Hall, & Stormont, 2001; Olenchak & Reis, 2001; Reis, Neu, & McGuire, 1997). Twice-exceptional refers to students who are gifted with a concomitant disability. Some disabilities, such as autism, Asperger's syndrome, and AD/HD, directly impair some or all of the abilities required for social talent development. Other disabilities, such as learning or physical disabilities, distance the twice-exceptional student from both average and high-ability peers and can contribute to victimization in the form of harassment, bullying, or rejection. The pressures of the disability itself can cause delays in social talent development or interfere with programs designed to develop social talent. Adaptations in social development programs for these students are needed to maximize the benefit from the program and reduce the interference of the disability. These students may need the support of a small group to integrate new skills. Expert assistance is almost always necessary in these situations. It is important to find clinicians who have skill in working with gifted students, the students' families, and the disability in question (Moon & Hall, 1998).

Opportunities for Social Talent Development

In-school. Opportunities for social talent development need to be integrated into the school day for three reasons: developing social talent improves achievement across a broad range of academic content areas, integrating learning across multiple disciplines is simply good teaching, and developing social talent makes classroom management easier. Catalano et al. (2004) describe several programs available for implementation in the school. Most of these are situated in elementary schools with follow-up measurements indicating that gains from the programs continue through later years. Catalano and colleagues did find one program designed to use direct instruction in social skills at the middle school level, the Social Competence Program for Young Adolescents. This program resulted in reductions in minor delinquency, increases in positive behavior, involvement with peers, and social acceptance. Another approach that is more labor intensive is mentoring, which has been advocated for gifted students because it allows schools and communities to match gifted youth with competent adults who share specific interests (Hébert, 2002). Additionally, the mentor is able to influence students socially and even mitigate the effects of some socio-economic barriers (Stormont, Stebbins, & Holliday, 2001). Mentoring is an example of a direct instruction program in a content area and an indirect program in social skills.

As in other content areas, a planned curriculum integrated on a school wide basis is most effective. If that is not possible, individual teachers can adapt programs for use in their classrooms. A curriculum in social talent development should have sufficient scope to allow growth for all students, including those who already have high levels of social talent. It is not appropriate to use socially talented students as tutors for other students with behavior deficits, because those who are socially talented deserve an opportunity to further develop socially with planned activities and training.

As noted previously, the Autonomous Learner Model (Betts & Kercher, 1999) for gifted education programs can be effective in promoting social and personal talent development among academically gifted students. This model has five dimensions: orientation, individual development, enrichment, seminars, and in-depth study. The focus in the orientation and individual development sections is on assessing and understanding one's self, as well as cultivating strengths and skills for use in content areas. The orientation activities provide direct instruction about self, giftedness, and social interaction. The enrichment activities (exploration, investigation, cultural activities, service, and adventure training) may be conducted at the individual or group level. When performed in groups, they provide opportunities for students to practice social skills in conjunction with their academic work, an example of indirect instruction in social talent development. Likewise, the seminar dimension uses social skills extensively to work with higher order thinking skills in various topic areas.

Out-of-school. Out-of-school activities to develop social talent in secondary students can be thought of at the individual, family, or societal level. Gifted students can identify individuals who have the time and skills to be an example in social talent development. Although this is somewhat of a hit-and-miss approach, there are certainly students who have benefited from specific relationships with specific people. Parents can arrange activities for their children involving social experiences with a broad range of people. The ability to interact with people in various circumstances builds self-confidence, as well as open-mindedness. Participation in summer academic programming for gifted students can help develop social talent (Olszewski-Kubilius, 2003). Through contact with intellectual peers and satisfaction of deep needs for intellectual stimulation, students' social needs are indirectly met (Enersen, 1993). Additionally, leisure activities that are not academically oriented (e.g., hobbies, sports, cultural events, and visiting with family and friends) may improve psychosocial skills (Munson & Savickas, 1998).

There are numerous programs related to developing leadership in diverse organizations as such as 4-H, Future Farmers of America, and Girl Scouts and Boy Scouts (Dormody & Seevers, 1994; Karnes & Stephens, 1999; Seevers & Dormody, 1994). Freeman (2002) surveyed out-of-school gifted education programs and found a number that seek to develop leadership skills in addition to providing education programs in the United States, the former Soviet Union, Hong Kong, India, and Taiwan. These programs rely on didactic and experiential education, seeking to give students direct practice in using the leadership skills being taught. The pervasiveness of these programs indicates that leadership is a trait valued by people working with gifted students. It does seem logical to expect high-ability students to be able to take on leadership roles. Leadership is often seen as a component of social talent. Barker (1997) describes leadership as involving the traits of the leader and the process between leaders and followers, and sensitivity to the goals of all participants. Leadership is also reciprocal in nature. In this sense, leadership and social talent would coexist. It is possible to have high levels of social talent without being a leader. Still, leadership development programs almost always provide some emphasis on the identification and development of social talent. For example, Smith and Smith (1991) examined the effect of the Superintendent's Leadership Conference, a one-week summer residential event using cognitive, affective, and physical challenge components to develop talents of adolescents already gifted in leadership. Smith and Smith determined that the students became more willing to respond to other group members, increased their ability to influence others, and demonstrated more assertiveness, participation, better decision making, and more self-confidence.

Other extracurricular activities can provide outlets for socially gifted students. Volunteer opportunities for socially significant service abound. For example, gifted adolescents can serve as volunteers at local hospitals or participate in programs, like Habitat for Humanity, that build homes and improve urban neighborhoods. Socially gifted youth may also created their own volunteer opportunities, as in the case of Ryan Hreljac (Livingston, 2004). He's known as the "water boy," because he has turned his concern for people without clean water into his mission, raising more than $1 million to provide wells and sanitation projects in eight developing countries. (For more information about Ryan see his Web site at http://www.ryanswell.ca).

CONCLUSION

In summary, personal and social talents draw on some similar abilities, such as emotional intelligence, awareness of self and others, and self- and relationship-management skills. Both talent domains have high significance for the individual and society and are vitally important in adult life. These talents can facilitate mastery of content areas such as science that require strong time management and/or teamwork. They are essential skills in professions such as teaching, business, nursing, family therapy, social work, and politics. In addition, personal and social talents tend to facilitate happiness and help individuals build a satisfying personal life and positive relationships with family and friends.

Secondary schools currently de-emphasize these talent areas in favor of more traditional academic areas like mathematics, English, biology, and economics. Because personal and social talents are so important, secondary school teachers need to consider ways to integrate personal and social talent development activities into their instruction. School administrators need to consider adopting social/emotional development programs, such as mediation training for talented teens. Finally, school counselors need to be easily accessible when teens and their families experience social/emotional difficulties or traumatic stressors. A greater emphasis on personal and social skill development in secondary schools will assist in identifying students with talents in these areas and in raising the general competencies of all students in the personal and social domains.

REFERENCES

Arnold, K. D. (1995). *Lives of promise: What becomes of high school valedictorians? A 14-year study of achievement and life choices.* San Francisco: Jossey-Bass.

Baldwin, A. Y. (2002). Culturally diverse students who are gifted. *Exceptionality, 10*, 139–147.

Barker, R. A. (1997). How can we train leaders if we do not know what leadership is? *Human Relations, 50*, 343–362.

Baum, S. M. (1994). Meeting the needs of gifted/learning disabled students. *Journal of Secondary Gifted Education, 5*, 6–22.

Baumrind, D. (1989). Rearing competent children. In W. Damon (Ed.), *Child development today and tomorrow*. San Francisco: Jossey-Bass.

Berkman, L. F. (1995). The role of social relations in health promotion. *Psychosomatic Medicine, 3*, 245–254.

Betts, G., & Kercher, J. (1999). *Autonomous learner model: Optimizing ability*. Greeley, CO: ALPS.

Black, D. R., Tobler, N. S., & Sciacca, J. P. (1988). Peer helping/involvement: An efficacious way to meet the challenge of reducing alcohol, tobacco, and other drug use among youth? *The Journal of School Health, 68*, 87–93.

Bland, L. C., Sowa, C. J., & Callahan, C. M. (1994). An overview of resilience in gifted children. *Roeper Review, 17*, 77–80.

Bronfenbrenner, U. (1989). Ecological systems theory. In R. Vasta (Ed.), *Annals of child development* (Vol. 6, pp. 189–250). Greenwich, CT: JAI.

Bronfenbrenner, U. (1994). Ecological models of human development. In T. N. Postlethwaite & T. Husen (Eds.), *International Encyclopedia of Education* (2nd ed., Vol. 3, pp. 1643–1647). Oxford: Pergamon Press.

Casey, K. M. A. (2000). Mentors' contributions to gifted adolescents' affective, social, and vocational development. *Roeper Review, 22*, 227–230.

Catalano, R. F., Berglund, M. L., Ryan, J. A. M., Lonczak, H. S., & Hawkins, J. D. (2004). Positive youth development in the United States: Research findings on evaluations of positive youth development programs. *Prevention and Treatment, 5*, 1–111.

Chamberlin, S., & Moon, S. M. (2004). *Analysis of interest during and after model eliciting activities: A comparison of gifted and general population students*. Unpublished manuscript.

Clark, J. J., & Dixon, D. N. (1997). The impact of social skills training on the self-concepts of gifted high school students. *Journal of Secondary Gifted Education, 8*, 179–188.

Clasen, D. R., & Clasen, R. E. (1995). Underachievement of highly able students and the peer society. *Gifted and Talented International, 10*, 67–76.

Colangelo, N. (1988). Families of gifted children: The next ten years. *Roeper Review, 11*, 16–18.

Colangelo, N. (1997). Counseling gifted students: Issues and practices. In N. Colangelo & G. A. Davis (Eds.), *Handbook of gifted education* (pp. 353–365). Boston: Allyn & Bacon.

Colangelo, N. (2003). Counseling gifted students. In N. Colangelo & G. A. Davis (Eds.), *Handbook of gifted education* (pp. 373–387). Boston: Allyn & Bacon.

Collins, W. A., Macoby, E. E., Steinberg, L., Heatherington, E. M., & Bornstein, M. H. (2000). Contemporary research on parenting: The case for nature and nurture. *American Psychologist, 55*, 218–232.

Costa, P. T. J., & McCrae, R. R. (1990). *Revised NEO Personality Inventory (NEO-PI-R) and NEO Five-Factor Inventory (NEO-FFI) professional manual*. Odessa, FL: Psychological Assessment Resources.

Csikszentmihalyi, M., Rathunde, K., & Whalen, S. (1993). *Talented Teenagers*. Cambridge, England: Cambridge University Press.

Culross, R. R., & Jenkins-Friedman, R. (1988). On coping and defending: Applying Bruner's personal growth principles to working with gifted-talented students. *Gifted Child Quarterly, 32*, 261–266.

Curry, L. A., Snyder, C. R., Cook, D. L., Ruby, B. C., & Rehm, M. (1997). The role of hope in academic sport and achievement. *Journal of Personality and Social Psychology, 73*, 1257–1267.

Dewey, J. (1897). My pedagogic creed. *The School Journal, 54*(3), 77–80.

Dormody, T. J., & Seevers, B. S. (1994). Predicting youth leadership life skills development among FFA members in Arizona, Colorado, and New Mexico. *Journal of Agricultural Education, 35*, 65–71.

Durlak, J. A., & Wells, A. M. (1997). Primary prevention mental health programs for children and adolescents: A meta-analytic review. *American Journal of Community Psychology, 25*, 115–152.

Dweck, C. S. (1999). *Self-theories: Their role in motivation, personality, and development.* Philadelphia, PA: Psychology Press.

Eisenberg, N., & Fabes, R. A. (1998). Prosocial development. In W. Damon & N. Eisenberg (Eds.), *Handbook of child psychology* (5th ed., Vol. 3, pp. 721–778). New York: Wiley.

Elias, M. J., Bryan, K., Patrikakou, E. N., & Weissberg, R. P. (2003). Challenges in creating effective home-school partnerships in adolescence: Promising paths for collaboration. *School Community Journal, 13*, 133–153.

Elias, M. J., Zins, J. E., Weissberg, R. P., Frey, K. S., Greenberg, M. T., Haynes, N. M., et al., (1997). *Promoting social and emotional learning: Guidelines for educators.* Alexandria, VA: Association for Supervision and Curriculum Development.

Elmore, R. F., & Zenus, V. (1994). Enhancing social-emotional development of middle school gifted students. *Roeper Review, 16*, 182–185.

Enersen, D. (1993). Summer residential programs: Academics and beyond. *Gifted Child Quarterly, 37*, 169–176.

Ford, M. E., & Tisak, M. S. (1983). A further search for social intelligence. *Journal of Educational Psychology, 75*, 196–206.

Fornia, G. L., & Frame, M. W. (2001). The social and emotional needs of gifted children: Implications for family counseling. *The Family Journal: Counseling and Therapy for Couples and Families, 9*, 384-390.

Freeman, J. (2002, June). *Out of school educational provision for the gifted around the world.* Retrieved March 3, 2005, from http://www.joanfreeman.com/mainpages/freepapers.htm

Gallagher, S. A. (1997). Problem-based learning: Where did it come from, what does it do, and where is it going? *Journal for the Education of the Gifted, 20*, 332–362.

Gardner, H. (1983). *Frames of mind: The theory of multiple intelligences.* New York: Basic Books.

Goertzel, V., & Goertzel, M. G. (1962). *Cradles of eminence.* Boston: Little, Brown & Company.

Goldstein, D., & Wagner, H. (1993). After school programs, competitions, school olympics, and summer programs. In K. A. Heller, F. J. Mönks, & A. H. Passow (Eds.), *International handbook of research and development of giftedness and talent* (pp. 593–604). Oxford, England: Pergamon.

Goleman, D. (1995). *Emotional Intelligence.* New York: Bantam.

Gottfried, A. E., & Gottfried, A. W. (2004a). Toward the development of a conceptualization of gifted motivation. *Gifted Child Quarterly, 48*, 121–132.

Gottfried, A. E., & Gottfried, A. (2004b, November). *Gifted motivation: Theory, research, student identification, program evaluation.* Paper presented at the National Association for Gifted Children convention, Salt Lake City, UT.

Gross, M. U. M. (1993). *Exceptionally gifted children.* London: Routledge.

Gross, M. U. M. (2000, May). *From "play partner" to "sure shelter": How do conceptions of friendship differ between average-ability, moderately gifted, and highly gifted children?* Paper presented at the 5th Biennial Henry B. and Jocelyn Wallace National Research Symposium on Talent Development, Iowa City, IA.

Guilford, J. P. (1967). *The nature of intelligence.* New York: McGraw-Hill.

Hébert, T. P. (2002). Educating gifted children from low socioeconomic backgrounds: Creating visions of a hopeful future. *Exceptionality, 10*, 127–138.

Hofstadter, R. (1966). *Anti-intellectualism in American life.* New York: Vintage.

Hollingworth, L. (1926). *Gifted children.* New York: World Press.

Hollingworth, L. S. (1942). *Children above 180 IQ.* New York: World Book.

Hseuh, W. C., & Moon, S. M. (1997, August). *Family characteristics of gifted children in Taiwan and the United States: A comparative review of the literature.* Paper presented at the World Conference of the World Council for Gifted and Talented Children, Seattle, WA.

Hunt, T. (1928). The measurement of social intelligence. *Journal of Applied Psychology, 12*, 317–334.

Karnes, F. A., & Stephens, K. R. (1999). Planning for the future: leadership education in the schools. *Educational Horizons, 77, 89–94.*

Karnes, F. A., Lewis, J. D., & Stephens, K. R. (1999). Parents and teachers working together for advocacy through public relations. *Gifted Child Today, 22*(1), 14–18.

Karnes, F. A., & Wherry, J. N. (1981). Self-concepts of gifted students as measured by the Piers-Harris Children's Self-Concept Scale. *Psychological Reports, 49*, 903–906.

Kaufman, F. A., Harrel, G., Milam, C. P., Woolverton, N., & Miller, J. (1986). The nature, role, and influence of mentors in the lives of gifted adults. *Journal of Counseling and Development, 64*, 576–578.

Kelly, K. R., & Moon, S. M. (1998). Personal and social talents. *Phi Delta Kappan, 79*, 743–746.

Kobasa, S. C. (1979). Stressful life events, personality, and health: An inquiry into hardiness. *Journal of Personality and Social Psychology, 37*, 1–11.

Kobasa, S. C., Maddi, S., & Kahn, S. (1982). Hardiness and health: A prospective study. *Journal of Personality and Social Psychology, 42*, 168–177.

Kobasa, S. C., Maddi, S. R., Puccetti, M. C., & Zola, M. A. (1985). Effectiveness of hardiness, exercise, and social support as resources against illness. *Journal of Psychosomatic Research, 29*, 525–533.

Livingston, G. (2004, April 1). Weir, 12-year-old among honorees. *London Free Press*, p. C8.

Maddi, S. R., & Kobasa, S. C. (1984). *The hardy executive: Health under stress.* Homewood, IL: Dow Jones-Irwin.

Masten, A. S. (2001). Ordinary magic: Resilience processes in development. *American Psychologist, 56*, 227–238.

Masten, A. S., & Coatsworth, J. D. (1988). The development of competence in favorable and unfavorable environments: Lessons from research on successful children. *American Psychologist, 53*, 205–220.

Masten, A. S., & Marie-Gabrielle, J. (2002). Resilience in development. In C. R. Snyder (Ed.), *Handbook of positive psychology* (pp. 74–88). London: Oxford University Press.

Matthews, M. S. (2004). Leadership education for gifted and talented youth: A review of the literature. *Journal for the Education of the Gifted, 28*, 77–113.

May, K. M. (1994). A developmental view of a gifted child's social and emotional adjustment. *Roeper Review, 17,* 105–109.

Mayer, J. D., Caruso, D. R., & Salovey, P. (1999). Emotional intelligence meets traditional standards for an intelligence. *Intelligence, 27*, 267–298.

Mayer, J. D., & Salovey, P. (1993). The intelligence of emotional intelligence. *Intelligence, 17*, 433–442.

Mayer, J. D., & Salovey, P. (1997). What is emotional intelligence? In P. Salovey & D. Sluyter (Eds.), *Emotional development and emotional intelligence: Implications for educators.* New York: Basic Books.

Milgram, R. M., & Hong, E. (1999). Creative out-of-school activities in intellectually gifted adolescents as predictors of their life accomplishments in young adults: A longitudinal study. *Creativity Research Journal, 12*, 77–87.

Moon, S. M. (2003a). Developing personal talent. In F. J. Mönks, & H. Wagner (Eds.), *Development of human potential: Investment into our future. Proceedings of the 8th Conference of the European Council for High Ability (ECHA). Rhodes, October 9–13, 2002* (pp. 11–21). Bad Honnef, Germany: K.H. Bock.

Moon, S. M. (2003b). Personal Talent. *High Ability Studies, 14,* 5–21.

Moon, S. M., Feldhusen, J. F., Powley, S., Nidiffer, L., & Whitman, M. (1993). Secondary applications of the Purdue Three-Stage Model. *Gifted Child Today, 16*(3), 2–9.

Moon, S. M., & Hall, A. S. (1998). Family therapy with intellectually and creatively gifted children. *Journal of Marital and Family Therapy, 24,* 59–80.

Moon, S. M., Jurich, J. A., & Feldhusen, J. F. (1998). Families of gifted children: Cradles of development. In R. C. Friedman & K. B. Rogers (Eds.), *Talent in context: Historical and social perspectives on giftedness* (pp. 81–99). Washington, DC: American Psychological Association.

Moon, S. M., Zentall, S. S., Grskovic, J. A., Hall, A., & Stormont, M. (2001). Emotional and social characteristics of boys with AD/HD and/or giftedness: A comparative case study. *Journal for the Education of the Gifted, 24,* 207–247.

Morgenstern, J., & Morgenstern-Colon, J. (2002). *Organizing from the inside out for teens.* New York: Henry Holt.

Morissey, C., & Hannah, T. E. (1987). Measurement of psychological hardiness in adolescents. *Journal of Genetic Psychology, 148,* 393–397.

Munson, W. W., & Savickas, M. L., (1998). Relation between leisure and career development of college students. *Journal of Vocational Behavior, 53,* 243–253.

Neihart, M. (2002). Risk and resilience in gifted children: A conceptual framework. In M. Neihart, S. M. Reis, N. M. Robinson & S. M. Moon (Eds.), *The social and emotional development of gifted children: What do we know?* (pp. 113–122). Waco, TX: Prufrock.

Neihart, M., Reis, S., Robinson, N., & Moon, S. M. (Eds.). (2002). *The social and emotional development of gifted children. What do we know?* Waco, TX: Prufrock.

Noble, K. D. (1996). Resilience, resistance, and responsibility: Resolving the dilemma of the gifted woman. In K. D. Arnold, K. D. Noble, & R. F. Subotnik (Eds.), *Remarkable women: Perspectives on female talent development* (pp. 413–426). Cresskill, NJ: Hampton Press.

O'Sullivan, M., Guilford, J. P., & Demille, R. (1965). *The measurement of social intelligence.* Los Angeles, CA: University of Southern California.

Olenchak, F. R., & Reis, S. M. (2001). Gifted students with learning disabilities. In M. Neihart, S. M. Reis, N. M. Robinson, & S. M. Moon (Eds.), *The social and emotional development of gifted children* (pp. 267–289). Waco, TX: Prufrock Press.

Olszewski-Kubilius, P. (1989). The development of academic talent: The role of summer programs. In J. VanTassel-Baska & P. Olszewski-Kubilius (Eds.), *Patterns of influence on gifted learners* (pp. 214–230). New York: Teachers College Press.

Olszewski-Kubilius, P. (2003). Special summer and Saturday programs for gifted students. In N. Colangelo & G. A. Davis (Eds.), *Handbook of gifted education* (pp. 219–228). Boston: Allyn & Bacon.

Oulette, S. C. (1993). Inquiries into hardiness. In L. Goldberger & S. Breznitz (Eds.), *Handbook of stress: Theoretical and clinical aspects* (2nd ed., pp. 77–100). New York: Free Press.

Rathunde, K. (1988). Optimal experience and the family context. In M. Csikszentmihalyi & I. S. Csikszentmihalyi (Eds.), *Optimal experience: Psychological studies of flow in consciousness.* New York: Cambridge University Press.

Rathunde, K. (1996). Family context and talented adolescents' optimal experience in school-related activities. *Journal of Research on Adolescence, 6,* 605–628.

Ray, K. E. (2004). *A research proposal to explore perceptions about gifted award winners.* Unpublished manuscript.

Reis, S. M. (1998). *Work left undone: Choices and compromises of talented females.* Mansfield Center, CT: Creative Learning Press.

Reis, S. M. (2002). Gifted females in elementary and secondary school. In M. Neihart, S. M. Reis, N. M. Robinson, & S. M. Moon (Eds.), *The social and emotional development of gifted children: What do we know?* (pp. 125–135). Waco, TX: Prufrock.

Reis, S. M., Colbert, R. D., & Hébert, T. P. (2004). Understanding resilience in diverse, talented students in an urban high school. *Roeper Review, 27*, 110–120.

Reis, S. M., Neu, T. W., & McGuire, J. M. (1997). Case studies of high ability students with learning disabilities who have achieved. *Exceptional Children, 63*, 463–479.

Romney, D. M., & Pyryt, M. C. (1999). Guilford's concept of social intelligence revisited. *High Ability Studies, 10*, 137–142.

Rubin, K. H. (1998). Social and emotional development from a cultural perspective. *Developmental Psychology, 34*, 611–615.

Sachser, N., Durschlag, M., & Hirzel, D. (1998). Social relationships and the management of stress. *Psychoneuroendocrinology, 23*, 891–904.

Salovey, P., Mayer, J. D., & Caruso, D. R. (2002). The positive psychology of emotional intelligence. In C. R. Synder & S. J. Lopez (Eds.), *Handbook of positive psychology*. Oxford, England: Oxford University Press.

Schneider, B. H. (1998). Cross-cultural comparison as a doorkeeper in research on the social and emotional adjustment of children and adolescents. *Developmental Psychology, 34*, 793–797.

Seevers, B. S., & Dormody, T. J. (1994). 4-H participation in leadership development activities: A three state study. *Journal of Agricultural Education, 35*, 49–54.

Seligman, M. E. P. (1998). *Learned optimism.* New York: Pocket Books.

Seligman, M. E. P., & Csikszentmihalyi, M. (2000). Positive psychology: An introduction. *American Psychologist, 55*, 5–14.

Smith, S. W., Daunic, A. P., Miller, M. D., & Robinson, T. R. (2002). Conflict resolution and peer mediation in middle schools: Extending the process and outcome knowledge base. *Journal of Social Psychology, 142*, 567–586.

Smith, D. L., & Smith, L. (1991). Exploring the development of leadership giftedness. *Roeper Review, 14*, 7–12.

Snyder, C. R. (1994). *The psychology of hope.* New York: The Free Press.

Snyder, C. R., & Lopez, S. J. (Eds.). (2002). *Handbook of positive psychology*. Oxford, England: Oxford University Press.

Snyder, C. R., Rapoff, M., Ware, L., Hoza, B., Pelham, W. E., Samuelson, B., et al. (1995, August). *The children's hope scale.* Paper presented at the American Psychological Association, New York City.

Sowa, C. J., & May, K. M. (1997). Expanding Lazarus and Folkman's paradigm to the social and emotional adjustment of gifted children. *Gifted Child Quarterly, 41*, 36–43.

Spaulding, J., & Balch, P. (1983). A brief history of primary prevention in the twentieth century: 1908–1980. *American Journal of Community Psychology, 11*, 59–80.

Sternberg, R. J. (1993). *Sternberg Triarchic Abilities Test.* Unpublished manuscript.

Sternberg, R. J. (1996). *Successful intelligence.* New York: Simon & Schuster.

Sternberg, R. J., Forstythe, G. B., Hedlund, J., Horvath, J. A., Wagner, R. K., Williams, W. M., et al. (2000). *Practical intelligence in everyday life.* Cambridge, England: Cambridge University Press.

Sternberg, R. J., & Grigorenko, E. L. (2003). Teaching for successful intelligence: Principles, procedures, and practices. *Journal for the Education of the Gifted, 27*, 207–228.

Sternberg, R. J., & Wagner, R. K. (1986). *Practical intelligence: Nature and origins of competence in the everyday world.* Cambridge, England: Cambridge University Press.

Sternberg, R. J., Wagner, R. K., & Okagaki, L. (1993). Practical intelligence: The nature and role of tacit knowledge in work and at school. In H. Reese & J. Puckett (Eds.), *Advances in lifespan development* (pp. 205–227). Hillsdale, NJ: Erlbaum.

Stevenson, H. W. (1994). Education of gifted and talented students in mainland China, Taiwan, and Japan. *Journal for the Education of the Gifted, 17,* 104–130.

Stevenson, H. W. (1998). Cultural interpretations of giftedness: The case of East Asia. In R. C. Friedman & K. B. Rogers (Eds.), *Talent in context: Historical and social perspectives on giftedness* (pp. 61–77). Washington, DC: American Psychological Association.

Stormont, M., Stebbins, M. S., & Holliday, G. (2001). Characteristics and educational support needs of underrepresented gifted adolescents. *Psychology in the Schools, 38,* 413–423.

Tannenbaum, A. J. (1983). *Gifted children: Psychological and educational perspectives.* New York: Macmillan.

Terman, L. M. (1925). *Genetic studies of genius: Vol. 1. Mental and physical traits of a thousand gifted children.* Stanford: Stanford University Press.

Terman, L. M., & Oden, M. H. (1959). *Genetic studies of genius: Vol. 5. The gifted group at mid-life: Thirty-five years' follow-up of the superior child.* Stanford: Stanford University Press.

Thorndike, E. L. (1920). Intelligence and its uses. *Harper's Magazine, 140,* 227–235.

Tomlinson, C. (1995). *How to differentiate instruction in mixed ability classrooms.* Alexandria, VA: Association for Supervision and Curriculum Development.

Tomlinson, C. A., Kaplan, S. N., Renzulli, J. S., Purcell, J., Leppien, J., & Burns, D. (2002). *The parallel curriculum: A design to develop high potential and challenge high ability learners.* Thousand Oaks, CA: Corwin Press.

Tomlinson, C. A., Brighton, D., Hertberg, H., Callahan, C. M., Moon, T. R., Brimijoin, K., et al. (2003). Differentiating instruction in response to student readiness, interest, and learning profile in academically diverse classrooms: A review of the literature. *Journal for the Education of the Gifted, 27,* 119–145.

Wagner, R. K., & Sternberg, R. J. (1985). Practical intelligence in real-world pursuits: The role of tacit knowledge. *Journal of Personality and Social Psychology, 49,* 436–458.

Walker, R. E., & Foley, J. M. (1973). Social intelligence: Its history and measurement. *Psychological Reports, 33,* 839–864.

West, J. D., Hosie, T. W., & Matthews, F. N. (1989). Families of academically gifted children: Adaptability and cohesion. *The School Counselors, 37,* 121–127.

Whitman, M. W., & Moon, S. M. (1993). Bridge building: Conducting scientific research redefines the roles of teacher and student. *Gifted Child Today, 16*(5), 47–50.

Williams, W., Blythe, T., White, N., Sternberg, R., & Gardner, H. (1996). *Practical intelligence for school.* New York: Harper Collins.

Williams, W. M., Blythe, T., White, N., Brown, J. L., Gardner, H., & Sternberg, R. J. (2002). Practical intelligence for school: Developing metacognitive sources of achievement in adolescence. *Developmental Review, 22,* 162–210.

Winner, E. (1997). Giftedness vs. creativity in the visual arts. *Gifted and Talented International, 12,* 18–26.

Ziegler, A., & Heller, K. A. (1997). Attribution retraining for self-related cognitions among women. *Gifted and Talented International, 12,* 36–41.

Ziegler, A., & Heller, K. A. (2000). Effects of an attribution retraining with female students gifted in physics. *Journal for the Education of the Gifted, 23,* 217–243.

Zins, J. E., Bloodworth, M. E., Weissberg, R. P., & Walberg, H. J. (2004). The scientific base linking social and emotional learning to school success. In J. E. Zins, R. P. Weissberg, M. C. Want, & H. J. Walberg (Eds.), *Building academic success on social and emotional learning: What does the research say?* (pp. 3–22). New York: Teachers College Press.

TALENT DEVELOPMENT IN SPORTS

CHAPTER 11

by Jacques H. A. van Rossum
& Françoys Gagné

*H*ow do young promising athletes become top-level performers in their chosen sport? Can we find clear indications in research that would help predict which young athletes have much better chances of reaching national or international eminence in a given sport? Can these studies offer parents, coaches, or the athletes themselves some precise guidelines to better structure their training process? Alas, although the prediction of excellence in sports is a worthy and important goal, science is still unable to answer such questions very clearly; at best it can offer moderate probabilities: "This young athlete has a much better chance than these others to emerge among the best in his or her field." Still, reducing the level of chance in our predictions of future success means that some utopian dreams will be scaled down earlier, and that scarce training money will be spent more effectively.

Although the information presented here will cover the total development process, from initial identification as a promising young athlete to emergence among top performers, we will try to respect the general theme of this book by focusing on the adolescent years of these young athletes. Unfortunately, the scientific literature on talent development in sports during that specific period is limited; the major database of sports publications, called SPORTDISCUS, yielded only 40 documents on the subject, all of them published since 1990. Talent development in sports differs from academic talent development in one major way: free entry and exit. As opposed to schooling, where laws require all children to attend until they reach some predetermined age, no one is forced to participate in a competitive training program in any sport; moreover, athletes who participate in a training program can drop out at any time if their interest wanes or their achievements do not reach expectations.

The potential causes of talent emergence in sports are numerous: bodily characteristics (such as height in basketball), physiological attributes (such as cardiovascular endurance in cross-country skiing or triathlon), psychological characteristics (such as the will power needed to train for hours day after day), or environmental influences (such as parental support, financial support, or adequate training facilities). In order to look at these in a well-organized way, we have adopted a model developed by Gagné (1985, 2003, 2005a), called the Differentiated Model of Giftedness and Talent (DMGT).

THE DIFFERENTIATED MODEL OF GIFTEDNESS AND TALENT

The DMGT grew out of its author's frustration with the ambiguity surrounding the definition of the two central concepts used to describe individuals with outstanding abilities and/or skills, namely the concepts of *giftedness* and *talent*. In fact, these terms are used synonymously most of the time, as in "the gifted and talented are . . ." One will occasionally find a distinction between the two concepts; unfortunately, these distinctions vary from one author to the next. Although this judgment applies especially well to the gifted education literature, the ambiguity can also be observed in sports publications. For instance, in a recent glossary of sport terms (Cashmore, 2002), the following description is found under the entry for talent:

> Talent is conventionally defined as a possession of special desirable gifts, faculties or aptitude (for music, for art, etc.). Athletes are frequently described as "talented" or even "multi-talented", meaning they are highly proficient in a particular skill or set of skills. (p. 255)

Note that in the first sentence talent is defined as gifts and aptitudes, whereas it becomes a sign of skilled proficiency in the next one.

Those involved in the field of athletics (e.g., athletes, coaches, managers, journalists, parents) often associate the term "talent" with aptitude or potential. However, within the context of scientific research, talent is often defined in terms of outstanding performance; it identifies athletes whose achievements are extraordinary for their age, or athletes selected for a national team. But, underlying this ambiguity, we observe in many definitions, explicitly or implicitly, a distinction between outstanding natural physical abilities (the "potential") and their development into out-

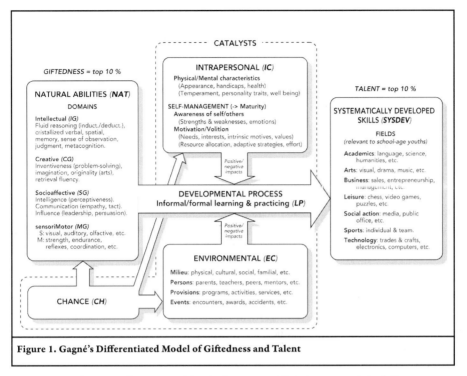

Figure 1. Gagné's Differentiated Model of Giftedness and Talent

standing athletic performance (the "achievement"). The DMGT's differentiation between the two concepts rests on that well-accepted distinction between potential and achievement.

Overview of the DMGT

In the DMGT, *giftedness* designates the possession and use of high natural abilities (called aptitudes) in at least one of four ability domains (see Figure 1), so that the level of performance places the person among the top 10% of same-age peers. *Talent* is the demonstration of systematically developed and trained abilities in any field of human activity at a level such that the individual belongs to the top 10% of peers having had equivalent training. The six components of the DMGT bring together in a dynamic way all the recognized determinants of talent emergence in any field of human activity.

Natural abilities, which have a partial genetic origin, can be observed more directly in young children because environmental inputs and systematic learning have exerted their moderating influence in a more limited way. However, they still manifest themselves in older children, even in adults, through the *ease and speed* with which they acquire new skills. The easier or faster the learning process, the greater the gifts. Many laypersons call these gifts "natural talent." Talents progressively emerge from the transformation of high aptitudes into the well-trained and systematically developed skills typical of a particular field of human activity. Thus, natural abilities act as the raw materials or *constituent elements* of talents: Except for borderline cases, one cannot become talented without being gifted. However, the converse is not true: It is possible for outstanding natural abilities not to be translated into talents, for instance when intellectually gifted children achieve poorly in school.

The process of talent development manifests itself when the individual engages in systematic *learning and practicing* (courses, music conservatories, competitive teams, etc.); the higher the level of talent sought, the more intensive these activities will be. This process can be facilitated or hindered by two types of *catalysts*—intrapersonal and environmental. Among the *intrapersonal* catalysts, motivation and volition (or persistence, see Corno and Kanfer, 1993) play a crucial role in initiating the process of talent development, guiding it, and sustaining it through obstacles, boredom, and occasional failure. Genetic predispositions to behave in certain ways (temperament), as well as acquired personality traits and attitudes, also contribute significantly to the talent development process. The *environment* manifests its significant impact through four agents, either physical or social (see Figure 1). *Chance* appears in the model as a fifth causal factor; it affects the others in different ways (e.g., the randomness of the genetic endowment for abilities or temperament, the chance of having good parents, accidents, etc.). In summary, talent emerges progressively from natural gifts thanks to a complex choreography between numerous causal influences.

How Many Are There?

Giftedness and talent are *normative* concepts. Such concepts define populations that are different from the norm (e.g., obesity, poverty). Good definitions of normative concepts must specify to what extent the target population differs from the norm and what it means in terms of their prevalence. In the DMGT, the threshold for both the giftedness and talent concepts is placed at the 90th percentile (Gagné, 1998). That threshold applies to *each* giftedness domain or talent field; thus, the *total* percentage of gifted and talented persons probably exceeds 30%. This generous minimum threshold is counterbalanced by a system of levels of giftedness and talent. Within the top 10% of "mildly" gifted or talented persons, the DMGT recognizes four increasingly selective subgroups, respectively labeled "moderately" (top 1:100), "highly" (top 1:1,000), "exceptionally" (top 1:10,000), and "extremely" (top 1:100,000). Applied to intellectual giftedness, these five levels would have the following IQ thresholds: ≥ 120 for mildly, ≥ 135 for moderately, ≥ 145 for highly, ≥ 155 for exceptionally, and ≥ 165 for extremely (or profoundly).

To apply these intensity labels most accurately in a specific sport, we would need to know how many youngsters begin practicing that sport, the percentage of these beginners who enter a competitive training program, the percentage who move to the next level of competition, and so forth. These successive percentages would tell us when to switch from one label to the next. As an approximate analogy, we could associate the lowest level (mild talent) with participation in an elite baseball team excelling in a town league, the next level with excellence in a regional team, high talent with excellence at the state level, exceptional talent with excellence at the national level, and extreme talent with international eminence.

Structure of the Chapter

The DMGT can serve as a framework to organize information about talent development in sports, indeed in any field of human activity. For instance, research on parental involvement would be classified under environmental influences; studies of motivational issues would appear within the intrapersonal catalysts; discussions of the impact of amount of training would belong to the developmental process; and so forth. This chapter will present information in sections identified with the major components of the DMGT. The six components will be grouped into two trios: the talent development trio and the trio of catalysts. These two trios will constitute the backbone of this chapter (second and third sections). The last section of this chapter will address the most crucial question for athletes and trainers: "What makes the difference between reaching high level talent and remaining among the virtually unknown within a given sport?"

THE TALENT DEVELOPMENT TRIO

The first trio of components includes physical gifts as basic building blocks, talents as the outstanding skills developed in a particular sport, and the talent development process itself that transforms natural abilities into sporting skills.

Giftedness and Sports

When Greg Louganis, Olympic and world championship diver, was only 18 months old, he accompanied his mother to his older sister's dance class. During this short visit he showed a great sense of balance and a precocious mastery of muscular control by learning to do a headstand and a somersault. (Michelmore, 1988, p. 164)

In Romania, tots are singled out as young as age 4 for training at one of the country's elite sports schools. To gain admission, the tumbling tykes not only have to excel at tests that demonstrate speed, flexibility, and abdominal strength, but they must also convince coaches that they possess that unquantifiable drive that makes for champions. (Smolowe, 1988, p. 56)

Showing exceptional physical coordination before age 2 or being identified as a promising high-level gymnast at age 4 are examples of outstanding precocity. And precocity, which is the demonstration of abilities typical of much older individuals, is a trademark of high natural abilities (the giftedness in the DMGT). An unlimited number of similar examples could be given of athletes who were identified very early through exceptional natural abilities or unusually precocious achievements.

Inventory of Natural Physical Abilities

Human fitness and performance can be analyzed through a set of five major components (Bouchard & Shepard, 1994). Two of them directly refer to our common sense understanding of "natural" physical abilities: the muscular component, expressed in power, strength, and endurance, and the motor component, manifested in agility, balance, coordination, and speed. The three other components act as morphological (e.g., body mass index, body composition and measurements, bone density, flexibility); physiological (e.g., maximum aerobic power, heart and lung functions); and metabolic (e.g., glucose tolerance and insulin sensitivity) underpinnings of phenotypic ability measures. Readers will easily associate the above characteristics with specific sports, like tall stature with basketball, flexibility and balance with gymnastics, speed with running, coordination with pole-vaulting, and so forth.

Natural abilities can be measured at a very early age, usually in the first year of elementary school, well before most children have begun any specific training in a sport. Physical education teachers regularly assess some of these abilities more or less formally during their fitness work with young students. More systematic assessments also exist. For instance, in the United States, the President's Council on Physical Fitness and Sports (2001) makes available to school districts complex batteries of tests to assess the physical fitness of children in elementary or junior high schools. Similarly, the Australian Institute of Sports has put together an extensive battery of basic physical exercises used in high school to identify youngsters with exceptional natural abilities who could, after appropriate training, excel in a sport (Australian Sports Commission, 1994). The comparison norms prepared for these ability batteries show huge individual differences among very young children. For example, very slow 5-year-old boys (bottom 5% threshold) cover 600 yards in a 9-minute race, whereas their very fast peers (top 5% threshold) cover 1760 yards, almost three times as much. Every type of basic motor exercise (e.g., sit-ups, push-ups, vertical jump, weight-lifting) similarly produces very large differences between very poor and very good performers.

The Genetics of Natural Abilities

Why are marathon runners so often from Ethiopia? Why are there so many African Americans in basketball or football? Why are most Olympic events subdivided by sex? These are just a few of the questions brought to mind when thinking of the possible action of genes on human physical performances. Let us first point out that individual differences in the level of natural physical abilities are not directly hereditary; all human abilities do need appropriate maturation of the body, as well as some degree of nonsystematic exercise to develop. But, having said that, it remains that amount of exercise does not totally account for observed differences in physical ability; a significant percentage of these differences have been shown to possess genetic roots, especially when we look at the three underlying components (morphologic, physiological, metabolic) mentioned above. The complexity of research on the genetics of human behavior precludes looking at it in detail here. Thankfully, others have done so. Bouchard, Malina, and Pérusse (1997) surveyed in detail the literature on the genetics of each of the five components—and subcomponents—of physical performance. They point out that "the knowledge base about the genetic and molecular foundations of human sport performance is embryonic" (p. 366). Maintaining the typical caution of scholars, they still propose two main conclusions.

> First, the elite athlete is probably an individual with a favorable profile in terms of the morphological, physiological, metabolic, motor, perceptual, bio-mechanical, and personality determinants of the relevant sport. Second, the elite athlete is a highly responsive individual to regular training and practice. (p. 366)

The second conclusion is particularly important, because it indicates that some individuals are innately more reactive to systematic training programs, whereas others remain almost impervious to such training.

To what extents do these natural abilities and their underpinning characteristics make a difference in the emergence of highly talented athletes? That question will be dealt with in the last part of the chapter, after we have looked at all the other DMGT components of athletic excellence.

Talent in Sports

In the DMGT, the concept of talent refers to systematically developed skills in a particular field of human endeavor. In the case of sports and athletics, the fields correspond to any sporting discipline, either broadly defined or more specifically circumscribed. Talent is performance assessed *normatively*, which means by comparison with age peers who have been training for a similar amount of time. The label "talented" is strictly based on measures of performance; no other qualities are required, either in terms of personality, motivation, or intensity of training. Some athletes are the envy of their peers because they progress much more easily and rapidly than most. Very young athletes can be labeled talented, even highly talented (1:1,000), as long as the reference group is a fair one, namely other youngsters who have had a chance to train for an equivalent period of time. In very rare cases, that of prodigies, athletes will achieve international ranking at a much younger age than most peers. But, because of the requirements of body maturation, sport prodigies are a much less common phenomenon than music or chess prodigies.

Talent in sports is easier to measure than in any other field. Indeed, measurement is intrinsic to any normative assessment of performance. Time is the most common measurement index used, for instance, in running (short and long distance), swimming, bicycling, cross-country skiing, speed skating, and so forth. Weight will, of course, be the measure in weightlifting; height will serve to compare individuals in pole vaulting, while distance covered is measured in sport tasks like javelin throwing, shot putting, and the long jump. In most team sports, but also in some individual sports (e.g., judo, table tennis), the number of points scored or games won will determine the level of excellence within a league or division. In the case of team sports, assessment of individual performances is not as easy; still, most team sports rank individual players according to goals scored or similar measures, and the all-around best become famous stars (e.g., Pelé in football/soccer, Wayne Gretsky in hockey, Barry Bonds in baseball, or Michael Jordan in basketball). In some cases, performance assessment will require judges, like in figure skating, diving, or gymnastics; this unavoidably introduces an element of subjectivity. In summary, it is usually very easy to discriminate athletes in terms of their performance level. Even during the training years, every sport offers its athletes clear goals to aim for if they want to improve their standing, and get a chance to be selected for a regional, state, or national team.

The Talent Development Process

The educational system tightly oversees the academic talent development process: Everyone begins in kindergarten, and then successively attends elementary school, middle school, and high school. Fewer will go to college, and just a small percentage will reach graduate school. Academic acceleration is not a common occurrence; most students advance in a lockstep fashion, and reach each major new step at about the same age. Such is not the case in sports. First, the beginning of competitive training varies a lot from one sport to another. Second, because coaches adjust the training program to each person's natural aptitudes, the pace of progress may differ markedly from one individual to the next. Third, some individuals begin training in one sport, and then switch to another, using part of their earlier training to advance more rapidly in the new sport. Finally, sports careers are usually much shorter than academic or professional careers, showing a positive trend toward a peak, usually followed by a slow decline until the athlete stops competing. Various surveys have shown that, as a rule of thumb, a career in athletics takes more or less 10 years to reach peak level. Let us survey some markers of the talent development process in sports.

The First Competitive Steps

It used to be quite common to enter sports competition as late as adolescence or even early adulthood. Nowadays, the trend is toward athlete's early entrance into the competitive world. A large-scale United Kingdom survey of elite and pre-elite athletes in 12 sports revealed the athlete's average starting age was 11.5 years, but with large differences between sports. Swimmers and judo competitors were the youngest beginners (fewer than 9 years old), and female rowers and female rugby players were the eldest beginners (on average more than 16 years old; English Sports Council, 1998). In another English study, the TOYA study (Training of Young Athletes; e.g., Baxter-Jones & Helms, 1996; Rowley, 1995), a large group of talented young athletes in four sports (soccer, gymnastics, swimming, and tennis) was followed for 4 years. Its results suggest it is not the age one starts to participate that is important, but that the age at which systematic practice (or intensive training) begins is most relevant (Rowley, 1992).

In the United States, as well as in many other developed countries, one can see 3-year-olds enrolled in swimming and gymnastics clubs; by age 5, others will be seen in track-and-field, wrestling, and baseball matches (Martens, 1988). These early competitive opportunities offer coaches a chance to assess precocious achievements, as well as natural physical gifts. Local, regional, and national programs of talent development regularly offer similar detection opportunities. This early identification process has both advantages and drawbacks. On the bright side, young athletes begin earlier to accumulate the thousands of practice hours necessary to achieve very high performance levels and increase their chances of being selected for international competition. On the other hand, some fear that it can lead to a too early specialization in one sport. The dangers of moving away from a more general education in athletics at an early age seem especially relevant if school authorities decide to cut down on the time devoted to physical education in elementary and secondary schools (see Baker, Horton, Robertson-Wilson, & Wall, 2003).

Major Developmental Phases

The decade of pre-peak training typical of athletic careers can be subdivided in phases or stages. Benjamin Bloom (1985) proposed a three-level system based on intensive interviews with 120 internationally renowned individuals from six fields: concert pianists and sculptors in arts, mathematicians and neurologists in academia, and tennis players and swimmers in sports. Bloom labeled these three developmental phases "the early years," "the middle years," and "the later years." Salmela (1994) suggested more descriptive labels for sports: the *Initiation* phase, the *Development* phase, and the *Mastery* phase. The first phase, which usually occurs before adolescence, corresponds to playful and nonsystematic exercise, with a loose role for the coach. The second stage, usually covering most of adolescence, marks a clear commitment to excellence from the young athlete; the coaching becomes more demanding, and the parents must expect important sacrifices to help the young athlete's progress. The third and last stage, often attained at the end or after adolescence, marks the access to high-level performance, with more autonomy and responsibility from the athlete, more respect for the coach, and a reduced, more distant role for the parents.

Bloom's system looks at talent development from the inside. But, most athletes and trainers measure progress with external markers, more specifically geographical ones, like local, regional, or national eminence. To respect that common practice, researchers at the Australian Institute of Sports (Oldenziel, Gagné, & Gulbin, 2003) created a four-level system of developmental phases called the Athlete Development Triangle (see Figure 2). It offers a junior and senior pathway, and its four levels (basic, advanced, pre-elite, elite) are directly associated with geographical degrees of emergence (local, regional, state, national). A large Australian survey revealed that, on average, young athletes enter basic junior competition at age 10, they reach senior competition at age 15, and move to the elite level at age 20. But, these averages must be used with caution, since the standard deviations hover around 3 years; in other words, although about two thirds of athletes begin competing between the ages of 7 and 13, the other third enter basic competition either before or after that 6-year span. Similar large ranges apply to all other achievement levels; of course, the ages mentioned also vary between sport fields.

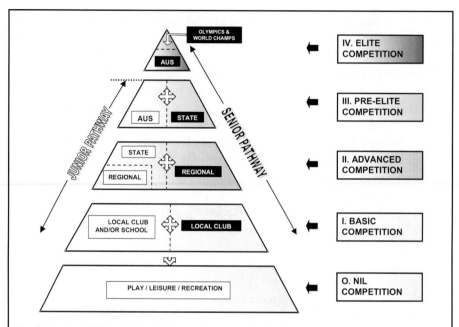

From the triangle model (Figure 2), junior level competition was considered to be age restricted (e.g., Under 23, U19, U14, etc.), while senior level competition was defined as having no age restrictions. With respect to competition progression or movement within the triangle, it is understood that athletes could move from junior to senior competition within the level (i.e., left to right across the triangle) before moving up to the next level. Some might progress directly up one side of the triangle only, while others may zig-zag up and down the triangle.

Figure 2. The Athlete Development Triangle

Note. From *How Do Elite Athletes Develop? A Look Through the 'Rear-View Mirror'* (p. 19), by K. Oldenziel, F. Gagné, and J. Gulbin, 2003, Canberra: Australian Institute of Sport, Australian Sports Commission. Copyright ©2003 by Australian Sports Commission. Reprinted with permission from the Australian Sports Commission.

The Role of Practice

One word summarizes the daily life of an athlete: practice, and more practice, thousands of repetitions of the same movements until perfection is reached. This is one major area of difference between sports and regular high school; because of the unchallenging curricula offered to the brightest students, they need very little "practice"—beyond listening to the teacher—to maintain their top rank academically. Sports practice can be examined quantitatively (amount) and qualitatively (types of activities). We have already mentioned a first quantitative yardstick—the 10-year rule representing the average span of time between initial competitive training and peak performance. There is a second yardstick called the 10,000-hour rule, which represents the average time investment of an athlete over that decade of training. Ten thousand hours is a lot of time, about 20 hours per week for every week of those 10 years! And, this practice is in addition to all those weekly hours of regular school and family activities. However, that total is not distributed equally over the 10-year span. The weekly practice regimen is smaller at first, and then increases, year after year, as the athlete reaches higher performance levels.

Qualitatively, practice will vary a lot from sport to sport, as well as from novice level to expert level. Within the context of the study of expertise, these hours of training have been termed *deliberate practice* (Ericsson, 1998; Starkes, Deakin, Allard, Hodges, & Hayes, 1996). In this context, some researchers have examined in detail the training activities of athletes. In one case, members of the U.S. junior and senior figure skating team used four criteria (relevance, effort required, concentration required, and enjoyment) to assess the quality of various components of their training (weight training, stretching, jogging, cycling, lessons with coach, choreography, on-ice training, mental training, and video feedback; Starkes et al., 1996). Of course, the skaters gave on-ice training as well as lessons with the coach the highest ratings. Deliberate practice is a combination of all of these elements. The skating illustration shows that practice or training should not be considered identical to physical exercise, nor should it be limited to sport-specific physical exercise. In top-level athletics, practice includes a diversity of components, which vary from sport to sport, and also depend partly on the competitive or age level of the athlete. Interestingly, components judged highly relevant were also assessed as highly enjoyable by the athletes (Starkes et al.; see also Deakin & Cobley, 2003). This result contrasts sharply with earlier findings from a study with talented musicians, who regarded highly relevant components (such as practicing alone) as not very enjoyable (Ericsson, Krampe, & Tesch-Römer, 1993).

THE TRIO OF CATALYSTS

The second trio of components includes both the intrapersonal and environmental catalysts, as well as chance factors. Two reasons explain their treatment as a separate subgroup. First, they are not "intrinsic" parts of the talent development process, as defined and described in the preceding section. Second, the three of them play a similar role as *modulators* of that process, just as chemical catalysts do with regard to chemical processes.

Intrapersonal Catalysts

The list of potentially influential intrapersonal catalysts is almost endless. As shown in Figure 1, it includes stable human characteristics, both physical and mental, as well as the numerous components associated with the complex process of self-management. Among that large inventory of influential moderators of talent development, some have been studied much more than others. We will focus here on two groups of them, namely motivation and personality, which are well recognized by most researchers to play a significant facilitating—or inhibiting—role in talent development, especially when athletes reach high levels of performance.

The field of study most people identify as "motivation" can be subdivided into two distinct areas, the first one concerned with the identification of the proper goal(s) to pursue, and the second one concerned with the activities performed to reach this/these goal(s). Some scholars (e.g., Corno, 1993) have associated the terms motivation and volition (will power) respectively to these two sequential steps in the global motivational process. Moon (2003) recently introduced a similar distinction in her definition of a construct called *personal talent*. Much confusion remains in the use of the terms motivation and volition by both scholars and lay people, with the term motivation often covering both phases of the total goal reaching process. For instance, the intensity of motivation is often measured with questions dealing with energy to overcome obstacles, to resist the boredom of repetitive daily practice, to put extra effort in reaching a short-term goal, and so forth. In spite of the ambiguous usage, we will try here to address these two concepts separately.

Motivation

Research on the motivational aspects of athletic talent development has followed many parallel paths, and borrowed instruments and concepts from many partially related areas of study. Think of terms like intrinsic/extrinsic motivation, task and ego orientation, achievement motivation, competitiveness, desire to win, and so forth. In the context of sport, the term *achievement motivation* probably best summarizes the main focus of interest. Its study was facilitated by the construction of the Sport Orientation Questionnaire or SOQ (Gill & Deeter, 1988). Thanks to this instrument, two different facets of achievement motivation were identified, called *win orientation* and *competitiveness*. In a nutshell, win orientation means battling for superiority with an opponent (a normative—me-against-others—perspective), while competitiveness means trying to improve one's own past performance and becoming the best one can be (an ipsative—me-against-myself—perspective). In recent years, these two components of positive achievement motivation have been relabeled *ego* orientation and *task* orientation (Hanrahan & Biddle, 2002).

The distinction has played a central role in sport psychology research over the last two decades (e.g., Gill, 1993). Among other things, it helps understand long-term commitment in an athletic career. Research shows that higher scores on competitiveness are related to a more intense involvement in the improvement of one's own performance (Gill; Smith & Smoll, 1996; Smoll & Smith, 2001); it also helps predict who among young promising athletes will reach international eminence. This was demonstrated in two longitudinal studies with young tennis players, one in Germany (Schneider, Bös, & Rieder, 1993), and the other in Poland (Unierzyski, 2003). Moreover, as observed in a study of young professional Dutch soccer players (Van Yperen & Duda, 1999), a positive relationship appeared to exist between win orientation (ego orientation) and the belief that innate talent is a major determinant of athletic success; in contrast, task orientation or competitiveness was related to the belief that effort, team play, and parental support are the major contributors to athletic success. On the negative side, athletes who drop out tend to be more win oriented than those who maintain their participation (Brustad, 1993; Petlichkoff, 1994; Whitehead, 1986). But, the two SOQ scales are not negatively correlated, nor independent. Although the scores on the win and competitiveness scales usually entertain low correlations, Van Rossum & Vergouwen (2003) found that they were more strongly correlated in an international sample of top-level field hockey players (members of the Australian, Dutch, or South African national teams). This result suggests that for adult elite players both the ipsative (task) and normative (ego) aspects of sport achievement motivation are judged important.

In most comparative studies, one of the recurring methodological problems is that authors do not specify the competitive level of the athletes involved. It has to be assumed, therefore, that the subjects of these studies are athletes of mediocre caliber, probably not even mildly talented. There is, however, some empirical evidence that talented young athletes differ from "normal" adolescents. In a recently completed 8-year longitudinal study (Van Rossum, 2005) a sample of talented track-and-field and volleyball athletes ($N=178$) scored higher on the task-orientation scale of sport achievement motivation, compared to a control group of "normal" athletes of similar age and gender ($N=174$). However, the two groups did not differ on the ego scale. Interestingly, the group of 23 athletes in the original sample of talented athletes ($N = 178$) who had reached (inter-) national-level eminence at the end of the longitudinal study, was found to have a significantly higher score on both the task and ego scales compared to those who were considered talented 8 years before but turned out not to be successful (Van Rossum). Thus, even within a sample of talented athletes, differences in certain psychological characteristics are apparent.

Early studies on the phenomenon of achievement motivation revealed that any goal-oriented behavior activates two basic needs: the need to reach success and the need to avoid failure. The fear of failure component did attract much research attention during the 1970s (e.g., Martens, 1977). This component, named competitive anxiety, is probably the best-known concept in sport psychology. A scale, called the Sport Competition Anxiety Test (SCAT) was built to measure the phenomenon (Smith, Smoll, & Wiechman, 1998). More recently, research has shown that the construct is multidimensional, having both a physiological component ("somatic anxiety") and a mental one ("cognitive anxiety"; Martens, Vealey, & Burton, 1990). A similar distinction has been found with regard to students' reactions to tests and exams (Anastasi & Urbina, 1997).

Logically, most studies about motivational issues belong to the section on intrapersonal catalysts in the DMGT. But, a few of them have looked at the motivational characteristics of the immediate environment of the athlete, called the *motivational climate* (e.g., Kavussanu & Roberts, 1996; Ntoumanis & Biddle, 1998). Unsurprisingly, both the coach and the parents play an active role in creating a specific climate. Scholars have identified the two same orientations, namely task and ego. In a task- or mastery-oriented climate, athletes are encouraged to focus on the learning process, on their personal improvement, and on effort and participation; in a result- or ego-oriented climate, we observe much more normative feedback, public evaluation, and comparisons between athletes. From Bloom's (1985) description of athletic careers, it appears that an ego climate is detrimental to progress; moreover, recent research suggests that a task or mastery climate is preferable, even for top-level athletes (Van Rossum, 2004a).

Volition (Will-Power)

Because of the usual lumping of goal-defining and goal-reaching activities under the umbrella label of motivation, it is not easy to pinpoint studies focusing on the volitional aspects of the talent development process, as Gagné & St. Père (2002) did in the case of academic achievement. A search for psychological measures of concepts synonymous with volition (e.g., perseverance, persistence, endurance, will power, determination) was unsuccessful. However, more qualitative data suggest that perseverance and determination play a crucial role in talent development in sports. For instance, in a nationwide survey of top-level Dutch athletes, conducted by a well-known Dutch sports magazine, 95% of the respondents judged "perseverance" a good personal characteristic, and 65% identified it as *the* most important characteristic (Sport International, 1995). These figures put "perseverance" by far at the top of the list, according to these athletes. Similarly, when asked to identify characteristics that discriminate between those who reach the top from those who don't, young preprofessional Dutch dancers gave persistence a high ranking (Mariën & Van Pelt, 1998).

Personality Factors

In the presentation of the DMGT, we mentioned a distinction between genetic predispositions to behave in certain ways (temperament) and acquired personality traits and attitudes. The scientific study of temperamental traits has been a well-accepted area for some decades, especially in the context of Eysenck's (1955) theory on introversion-extraversion and neuroticism (e.g., Hardman, 1973; Geron, Furst, & Rothstein, 1986), however, research with adolescent athletes remains limited. Two recent studies used a Dutch questionnaire that measures four temperament factors (Feij & Kuiper, 1984): neuroticism, or *emotional instability* (or the extent to which someone tends to have feelings of worry, fear, debt and shame, be anxious about things and brood), *extraversion* (or the extent to which someone makes social contacts and expresses his or her feelings easily, and is talkative and frank), *impulsivity* (or the extent to which someone has little control over their own behavior, has little doubt when making decisions in insecure situations, and is often impatient) and *sensation seeking* (or when someone often searches for new, strongly varied experiences, is hungry for new, exciting, and dangerous situations, and is looking for risky and adventurous physical experiences). The first study involved male and female adolescent field hockey players, all members of national Dutch junior teams (Van Rossum & Vergouwen, 2003); in the second study, the subjects belonged to the Dutch national volleyball school (Douma & Companjen, 2003). In both studies, a majority of these adolescents differed from their nonathletic age peers on two characteristics: They obtained significantly higher scores on extraversion, and significantly lower scores on neuroticism, implying good emotional stability. These findings with adolescent talented athletes can be considered supportive of Eysenck's theory (cf. Eysenck, Nias, & Cox, 1982; Kremer & Scully, 1994; Woods, 1998).

With respect to personality characteristics, there is evidence that they manifest a specific pattern of mood states, called an "iceberg profile." This profile shows low scores on variables of tension, depression, anger, fatigue, and confusion, and a high score on vigor. Further, elite athletes have more self-confidence, and differ from the average athlete on some specific anxiety, motivation and cognitive variables (Van den Auweele, De Cuyper, Van Mele, & Rzewnicki, 1993). In a more recent review on this issue (Van den Auweele, Nys, Rzewnicki, & Van Mele, 2001), the authors questioned the existence of a unique set of characteristics for high-level athletes across all sports. Highlen and Bennett (1983) had earlier argued that the converse assumption, namely that each sport requires its own unique set of characteristics, seemed equally untenable. They proposed a typological hypothesis that there are types of sports in which athletes are similar to each other on psychological features. One might consider the difference between athletes in open- and closed-skill sports (e.g., tennis vs. golf), or make a distinction between athletes in contact versus non-contact sports (e.g., soccer vs. volleyball), or between athletes in sports that require different types of motor coordination (e.g., speed skating vs. rowing). The relative paucity of solid empirical evidence on psychological characteristics of elite athletes is surprising, given the often-voiced argument that "top level athletes in a specific sport are, to a great extent, homogeneous with regard to physiological, technical, and tactical parameters. Therefore, differentiation in performance might be attributed mostly to psychological factors" (Van den Auweele et al., 2001, p. 247).

Environmental Catalysts

In the DMGT, environmental catalysts take many forms: locations, people, activities, provisions, and so forth. Space limitations have forced us to focus on environmental elements that have been found to play a more significant role in the talent development of adolescent athletes. Consequently, we will look more closely at two groups of significant individuals in the lives of young athletes: their parents and coaches. With regard to developmental programs, we will examine typical in-school and out-of-school training programs. Finally, because of its major role during adolescence, we will discuss in some detail the sometimes-conflicting relationship between athletic and academic activities.

Coaches

This section does not discuss the activities of coaches in noncompetitive athletic activities; in most cases, these coaches are volunteers with minimal training. Yet, they often play a vital role by spotting the outstanding natural abilities of young athletes under their guidance. When asked who discovered their athletic potential, a majority of successful athletes say it was the coach (Bloom, 1985; Van Rossum, 1992). During their K–12 education, students will be "coached" by dozens of teachers, from one per year in elementary school to one per subject in high school. Sport coaching offers much more stability; athletes will often keep the same coach for many years as they move from one talent development phase to the next. Still, athletes will rarely keep the same coach throughout their career, as they move from local to national or international competition. If the athletes (or their parents) fail to recognize the necessity to change coaches, it could easily delay their athletic career, or even stop its progression.

Most athletes acknowledge the importance of their coach, and attribute them a significant role in their success. Coaches are not pivotal just in the early phases of an athletic career; they become an even more central person in later phases of the career; for instance, 91% of a sample of 192 members of Dutch national-level athletes in four Olympic sports mentioned the high significance of their coach (Van Rossum, 1992, 1995). Even when athletes keep the same coach for long periods of time, his or her role will change from one developmental phase to the next (Bloom, 1985). To examine coaching behavior, Chelladurai and his colleagues (Chelladurai & Saleh, 1980) constructed a multidimensional scale, called the Leadership Scale of Sport (LSS). One of its five subscales covers the instrumental tasks of the coach (training and instruction), two are concerned with motivation (positive feedback, social support), and two explore the decision-making process (democratic behavior, autocratic behavior; Chelladurai & Riemer, 1998; Chelladurai & Saleh, 1980). From its administration to various samples of athletes, it was found that the three most important dimensions of the ideal coach were, in this order, instrumental tasks, positive feedback, and social support; these judgments remained the same for low-level and high-level athletes in various sports, as well as for men and women (Chelladurai, 1993; Van Rossum, 1997).

Another issue regarding coaches is their effectiveness. Effectiveness can be defined either in terms of athlete performance or training climate. This last perspective was examined by Smith and Smoll (see Smith & Smoll, 1996; Smoll & Smith, 2001), who defined effectiveness as higher athlete self-esteem, higher team cohesion, more enjoyment, less anxiety, and fewer athletes dropping out of their sport. Although decades of research have made it clear that a positive orientation (rewards coupled with relevant feedback) is much more effective than a negative one (based on punishment and intimidation), Smith and Smoll's work did not show any differences between effective and less effective coaches in their win-loss record. One of their intriguing findings was the following comment: "coaches were, for the most part, blissfully unaware of how they behaved" (Smoll & Smith, 2001, p. 381).

Parents

Most people have probably read magazine articles on the extremely active parenting roles played by Richard Williams, father of international tennis players Venus and Serena, and Earl Woods, father of golf "genius" Tiger. In discussing the sport parent, Cashmore (2002) describes the influence of these two fathers as follows:

> Richard Williams was not a sportsman, but pushed his daughters Venus and Serena into tennis at an early age and encouraged them to follow a strict training regime. His authoritarian approach stemmed from his own experiences as a boy in Louisiana, where he was racially abused (he and his mother were made to flee to Compton, Los Angeles). The rationale behind his maneuvers was to prevent his daughters from enduring similar experi-

ences. By contrast, Earl Woods believed he was acting out a divine plan when his propelled his son Eldrick into golf. "The Almighty entrusted this precious child to me," wrote Earl in his book *Training a Tiger: A father's guide to training a winner in both golf and life*. (Cashmore, 2002, p. 190)

But, that type of parental involvement remains the exception; parents usually stay in the background, especially as their child's career progresses during adolescence. In their review of parental involvement, Woolgar and Power (1993) identified four types of roles parents can play: (a) emotional support; (b) tangible support (e.g., money, transportation); (c) role modeling associated with motivational, volitional, and ethical behavior; and (d) career advising, with the proviso that they will not confound their own (unsatisfied) dreams with those of their children. One can find books and brochures of advice to parents on the best ways to "play" each of these roles (American Sport Education Program 1994; Rotella & Bunker, 1998; Smoll & Smith, 1999). Much of the contents of these publications overlap advice commonly given to parents of academically talented students.

Do parents remain equally active during the whole of an athlete's career? According to a common view, the respective roles of parents and coaches are inversely proportional; as the career of an athlete progresses, the initial, very active role of parents decreases to be replaced by more direct involvement of the coach. In his seminal work, Bloom (1985) could describe active parental roles during the first two phases of the talent development process, but considered them almost absent during the third "mastery" phase of that process. But, others disagree with that view. For example, Van Rossum (1992, 1995) found that parents played a leading part in the background of top-level Dutch athletes; 89% of a large sample of them gave a "most important" rating to their parents. Similarly, in the Heidelberg Longitudinal Study of top-level tennis players (Bös & Schneider, 1997), the researchers found that successful players received more parental support during their adolescent years than those who did not reach international competition.

Do all parents play a positive and influential role in the growth of their children's career in sports, or is there a dark side to parent involvement? We often hear, for instance, of meddling, troublesome, and difficult-to-handle parents who sometimes act violently in sports arenas or confront coaches. In other cases, when parents live vicariously through their child's talent, caring more about their child's achievements than their emotional life, they are likely to end up with a bitter dropout. A talented individual might become the focus and central person within a family, and this could easily lead to the destruction of the whole family. Hellstedt (1995) discusses how such a process typically unfolds and how it might be remedied; his chapter offers good advice to coaches and parents who enter a developmental process whose consequences for their talented child and the rest of the family they can't easily estimate. To ensure an optimal talent development climate, the relationship between the talented athlete, the coach, and the parents is of decisive importance. Every talented adolescent goes through hard times: playing badly, getting a serious injury, sitting on the bench, or sometimes being judged unfit to remain on a team. Parents can make the difference in such circumstances; their unconditional support can help the adolescent athlete handle such difficulties. However, coaches are not always anxious to actively involve parents; they are often afraid that parents, especially fathers, will try to take on some of their coaching tasks. For this reason, Smoll (1993) took the parents' defense, and proposed organizing meetings with parents, not just to talk about auxiliary services (such as transportation and money), but also to discuss the coach's training philosophy and rules.

Special Programs

Talent development programs in sport can take many forms. Most of those we examined from a large number of countries can be categorized under three major formats: (a) programs appended to the regular school curriculum; (b) special high schools devoted to helping hopeful athletes pursue their sport career and their regular education simultaneously; and (c) out-of-school programs, usually administered by state or national sport organizations. In a kaleidoscopic view of talent development programs, a special issue of *Coaching Focus* (1996) surveyed 10 programs from various sports and countries. These included the Australian National Talent Search Program (Hoare, 1996), three distinct models successfully used in Germany (Kozel, 1996), the Canadian Sport Schools (Bales, 1996) similar to the Dutch sport-oriented LOOT schools (see below), and a few others, each devoted to a specific sport (such as cricket, golf, gymnastics, rugby, soccer, and squash).

Schools cannot be dismissed or ignored in any talent development program, because the quality of basic motor skills depends to some extent on schools' physical education classes. Schools often offer the building blocks on which further sport-specific development is based. But, physical education programs in schools, being oriented toward the health of all children and adolescents, are not structured to foster talent development in sports. Theoretically, "Phys. Ed." teachers could play a very useful role in the identification of physically gifted individuals. Unfortunately, as Kane (1986) pointed out, the reality is not always that idyllic:

> The school physical education program would seem to represent the best developmental influence and opportunity for the emergence of talent where it exists, but many programs, being geared to the "average" pupil, or incorporating a wide range of sports activities, fail to identify the gifted performers. (p. 189)

Moreover, physical education activities do not seem to play a direct role in the development of athletic talent. Their potential role, during adolescence, corresponds to the first format mentioned above: offering adjustments to the regular school schedule so that young high-level athletes will be able to replace regular courses with personal study, reschedule exams when they conflict with competitions, and so forth. School administrators will offer these accommodations on a case-by-case basis. Sometimes, a sport organization will arrange for their young players to leave school in the afternoon for practice, and they will provide opportunities for supervised homework at the playground. It seems that most school administrators show openness toward the scheduling problems of promising athletes, whatever their sport discipline.

But, a new trend involves creating special high schools that offer an integrated academic and athletic curriculum. Such special schools have been popping up in many countries around the world. In the Netherlands, 14 sport-oriented high schools (so-called "LOOT" schools) are presently active regionally. Talented athletes from various sport disciplines are admitted to the "sport stream," provided their talent has been recognized by a sports association, and confirmed by the Dutch Olympic Committee. Being in a sport stream provides adolescent athletes with extra opportunities for practice during school hours, and opportunities to adjust the academic schedule to the demands of athletic training and competition. An evaluation of these experimental sport schools in Finland (Suomalainen, Telama, Kemppainen, & Pulkkanen, 1990) revealed that simply organizing flexible teaching arrangements (the first format) does not automatically yield more practice hours in the sport domain. Indeed, athletically talented boys attending the special sport high schools had about twice as many practice hours as talented boys attending regular high schools. Interestingly, this difference was not observed for girls attending these two types of high schools.

Although the concept of special high schools for high-level athletes spreads slowly within and across countries, in most countries around the world, a majority of athletic activities are still held within a sports club. Many professional sport organizations, for example, baseball and ice hockey in North America, and soccer in Europe, offer opportunities for adolescents to develop their capacities and find out whether a professional sport career is possible. Such programs are part of the club's organization, although the program might be geographically located elsewhere, as is the case in U.S. minor league baseball, or in satellite soccer clubs (e.g., Ajax Amsterdam is tied to Ajax Cape Town in South Africa). In youth sport, programs appear to exist at a national level in many countries (De Knop, Engström, & Skirstad, 1996); such programs are described and documented in North and South America (Canada, United States, and Brazil), and in most countries of Western Europe, Asia (Israel, Japan, and China), and Oceania (Australia and New Zealand). In some sports, private enterprises help national associations. For example, in England, both structures collaborated to organize a team of experts in squash (Milton, 1996), as well as create the Yorkshire Cricket School (Middlebrook, 1996). These two initiatives aimed to facilitate the transition from recreational to competitive athlete, then to a full-time professional athlete.

A Frequent Dilemma: Sport vs. School

For most young athletes, the talent development process is pursued parallel to schooling, especially during the adolescent years. And, because athletics will occupy only a short period of a person's total life, most young athletes will continue their schooling at the college level to prepare for a career that will also be pursued parallel to their athletic career, or just after abandoning competition. Adolescence is a crucial period in the athletic career, and the combination of sport and school education can create major problems for the talented athlete. The provision of a sport-oriented facility will not in itself solve the problem. Even if school is an institution most athletically talented adolescents have to come to terms with, parents and teachers might attach more importance to the school progress than do the talented athletes themselves.

In two separate studies (Mariën & van Pelt, 1998; Van de Langemheen & De Wit, 2003), talented Dutch adolescents from three domains (athletics, dance, music) were asked to assess the importance of school with regard to seven other important aspects in their life (e.g., career plans, friends, leisure, family activities). The respondent had to distribute 50 points according to the relative importance they gave each life area. The young dancers allotted 43% of their points to dance and only 19% to academics; in music, the respective percentages were 31 and 17%; and in athletics, the two percentages were much more balanced, namely 27 and 26%. Obviously, in addition to their preferred activity other things do also matter in the life of talented adolescents. It is clear, then, that school is not considered that important, especially for those talented individuals in dance or music. As a tentative conclusion, one can say that school is not as important to talented adolescents as parents and teachers might want it to be. For them, the next game or performance is often of more value and interest than the next examination in science or an English essay. Parents and teachers, on the other hand, know all too well that among those who start out as talented and promising athletes, aiming for top-level sports, most will not attain the desired goal. Some will quit sports altogether, others will continue at a less ambitious level. Against that background, it seems wise, at least from the perspective of a parent or a schoolteacher, not to put all one's eggs in one basket, that is, to invest all efforts into the athletic career. Many professional teams do keep these problems in mind. For instance, as a constant reminder to its young athletes, the professional soccer club Ajax Amsterdam informs the adolescents in their youth teams that if they don't maintain their school work at an adequate level, they will be kept off the team until it is satisfactory; and if that takes too long, they risk being expelled from the club's soccer education program at the end of the season. Many questions still remain unanswered between the sometimes-conflicting demands of the professional and athletic careers. For many athletically talented adolescents, however, these questions may be of the utmost importance; during their high school years, most sports demand much more practice hours than before, as well as a high level of commitment to the chosen sport. There is a distinct risk that many youngsters will not be able to handle equally well their academic and athletic duties, and will then give up or start to fail in either domain or in both.

Chance Factors

As shown in Figure 1, chance plays an important role in the DMGT. Beyond the fact that nature accounts for a significant part of chance's importance, other significant factors can make talent development a probabilistic enterprise. Just think that being raised in a family whose income is close to poverty level, a totally uncontrollable event for an athletically gifted child, may make the whole difference between being able or not to pursue one's training in some sports (e.g., figure skating, ice hockey, alpine skiing). But, when we think of uncontrollable events in sports, the first thing that comes to mind is injuries—a major accident may mean the brutal end of a promising athletic career.

Injuries occur often in youth sport participation. Research on the frequency of injuries indicates large differences between sport disciplines. According to a recent U.S. survey, between 40 and 61% of athletes in football are injured each year; the percentage varies between 40 and 46% in wrestling and gymnastics; between 31 and 37% in basketball; and between 7 and 18% in volleyball, baseball, soccer, cross country skiing, softball, and track-and-field (Adirim & Cheng, 2003). Generally, no distinction is made between levels of participation. This is unfortunate, since more practice hours and more games or tournaments could increase the risk of injuries, whereas better equipment, higher awareness by the athlete, and better coaching, as well as better medical and paramedical care could lower the risk of injuries. Injuries are mentioned relatively often by athletes as one of their reasons for quitting competitive training in sports.

Two types of injuries are commonly distinguished: acute and overuse injuries. Acute injuries occur suddenly, and often appear as a result of uncontrolled circumstances. In addition to fractures, so-called soft tissue injuries (sprains and contusions) belong to this category. Acute injuries also result from aggressions between players, especially during games. In a recent study with athletically active adolescents and young adults in Canadian high schools and universities, between 12 and 79%—depending on the sport—admitted having been tempted to physically injure opponents at least once per game (Widmeyer, Dorsch, Bray & McGuire, 2002); there were of course many more males than females confessing to such temptations. Overuse injuries, also known as chronic injuries, take time to develop. When small injuries that usually require a couple of days of rest are neglected, they can lead easily to a chronic problem. In chronic injuries, elements of coaching (high pressure, the idea that one should always be prepared to give 100%) often coincide with a macho climate (ideas that one should not complain about a little pain and the pain belongs to practice). Athletes who fear being put on the bench or not being selected for an elite team often decide to conceal a small injury. On the other hand, a chronic injury can also result from multiple repetitions of similar movements (e.g., pitching in baseball). This type of injury occurs frequently in sport disciplines where, even with young athletes, high intensity and lots of repetitions during practice is considered normal, such as in gymnastics and swimming.

Family income constitutes another chance factor closely associated with sports. In a survey of a large sample of British elite and pre-elite athletes from 12 sports (English Sports Council, 1998), it was found that the main source of financing came from parents and even among elite performers, 40% were mainly supported by their family. One might also consider the quality of athletic coaching as a chance factor, that is, a factor the adolescent athlete has no control over. Nor does the talented athlete have control over the existence of a solid athletic program for the development of athletic talent in his local club or in his regional or national association. Chance manifests itself in the genetic make-up of the athlete. A few years ago, Howe, Davidson and Sloboda (1998) debated the controversy over talent as an inborn quality (nature) as opposed to the result of intensive training (nurture). While they themselves clearly adopted an environmentalist position, they acknowledged that "there is no conclusive support for either account, and it is doubtful that talent could be explained exclusively by one of them" (p. 141). In a review on the development of talent in sport, Durand-Bush & Salmela (2001) came to a similar conclusion: "Regardless of the amount of research that will be conducted in the near future, the nature-nurture debate will not be resolved any time soon" (p. 285). Nevertheless, there appears to be consensus about the strong genetic foundation of some qualities that are highly relevant ingredients for specific athletic tasks, such as VO_2max (maximum oxygen intake; a high level is needed for endurance tasks like middle- and long-distance running), and muscle fiber composition (e.g., a large amount of "fast twitch" fibers is a definite advantage in sprinting).

WHAT MAKES THE DIFFERENCE?

The above sections have allowed us to examine studies showing the relevance of causal factors associated with each component of the DMGT. Physical giftedness appears important as a basis for talent development, as do motivation, persistence and dedication, parental support, coach expertise, financial support, and countless other factors. But, as suggested by this section's title, is it possible to identify one, or a limited set of influences that, *on average*, play a determining role on the emergence of high talent in sports? There is no lack of professional opinion on that question. It is easy to find in the scientific literature strong defenders for each of the major components in the DMGT. For instance, some scholars consider natural abilities to be the key ingredient (Régnier, Salmela, & Russell, 1993); others argue that the key to talent is mostly the amount of practice (Starkes et al., 1996; Ericsson et al., 1993); still others will insist that environmental support (parents, trainers) will determine who achieves at high levels (Bloom, 1985). But, as we will see, very few studies have systematically examined many distinct causal factors simultaneously in order to assess their relative impact on talent development in sports.

The qualifier "on average" is very important, insofar as no single causal factor can be expected to be *the* most significant influence in every talent development situation. Moreover, it is doubtful that talent development could be reduced to the role of a single causal influence; the best we could hope for is to identify a limited set of causal influences that appear again and again to discriminate high-level athletes from less achieving ones. This is what the "what makes the difference" (WMD) question refers to. As mentioned at the beginning of this chapter, this is the question is the most practical application for those in charge of identifying young athletes with the best chances of achieving the highest performances, either at the very beginning of the training process, or at different intermediate steps in their talent development process. In this section, the WMD question will be examined from different perspectives, some of them more indirect and subjective than others.

Indirect Responses

We consider as indirect responses to the WMD question any information or study results that rely on opinion, even expert opinion. We have placed under this heading three sets of information: (a) the implicit judgment of experts as deduced from what characteristics they mainly look for when implementing large-scale identification programs, (b) what can be summarized from systematic interviews with high-level athletes discussing their past talent development activities, and (c) more systematic assessment of WMD through rankings of causal factors made by athletes and coaches.

Identification Practices

When putting together a talent identification program, most coaches or sport organizations borrow heavily from both the published scientific literature and their long-term experience. What do these procedures show us about the most significant characteristics to look for when searching for those youth considered as professional "hopefuls"? The very first published overview of talent identification in sports was included in the first edition of the *Handbook of Research on Sport Psychology* (Régnier et al., 1993). In that chapter, nine earlier published models of talent detection were described. Interestingly, most of these models put strong emphasis on anthropometrical, physical, and physiological characteristics. Let us examine one concrete example of a talent identification procedure.

More than a decade ago, the Australian Institute of Sport started a countrywide talent search program, based heavily on measures of natural abilities and physiological characteristics (Hoare, 1996). They invited all secondary schools to administer a battery of tests to large numbers of young (11- to 15-year-old) adolescents. These tests assessed general physical and physiological characteristics, what we could call physical giftedness. They invited those with very high scores (within the top 2% on any of the tests) for a more detailed regional measurement session. The regional high achievers were then invited to the national centre for even more advanced measurements in their laboratories. Those who obtained high scores in the lab tests were offered a subsidized high-level talent development program, supervised by state and national sports associations. In one case, a 16-year-old girl who had never heard of rowing was discovered, through the testing, to be a "physically suitable" candidate (Dale & Cameron, 1994). Within 3 years, she was participating in her first Olympic final (at the Barcelona 1992 Olympics). In a report about the program, Hoare (1996) noted that 40% of all invited schools across Australia did participate, implying that more than 100,000 high school students had been tested. About 10% of these tested adolescents were invited for more specific testing at the regional level. Of these, again about 1,000 athletes had joined a talent development program in a specific sport. The program can be considered as very successful, since it has produced many junior world medalists (Hoare, 1998).

Interview Studies

These studies, essentially qualitative in nature, usually target exceptionally talented athletes. The questions attempt to pinpoint not only the major events in their talent development process, but also what these athletes consider to have been key ingredients in the emergence of their talent. The main limit of such studies is their lack of a comparison group of persons who did not reach similar eminence in their field; because of that, it is not as easy to be sure about "what makes a difference." Among many available examples, here are two well-known studies.

Hemery (1986), himself an Olympic-level athlete in track-and-field, interviewed extensively more than 60 athletes who had reached international eminence in their sport. These athletes came from 22 sports and 12 different countries. The question he asked was: "What makes a sporting champion?," and he aimed for common factors that separated the highest achievers from all other competitors. He asked more than 80 questions, covering the athletes' childhood and upbringing, their athletic specialization, the coaching they received, how they coped with pressure and stress, and the physical, social, psychological and moral factors they considered relevant for their athletic success. Since it is difficult to summarize his findings, the following sentences can be taken as illustrations of the various themes addressed in the study.

> Very few of the group saw themselves as aggressive outside of the competitive arena. . . . Almost universally, their upbringing was stable, secure, happy and predictable. They were all well nurtured. . . . Their parents had not attempted to live through them; encouragement and support were given in every area of interest, but they were not pushed. The obvious advantage was that the athletes' bodies and minds were allowed to mature. Specialization could take place when the athlete was ready to make his or her commitment to their sport. If the personal desire did not come from inside the athlete, no amount of external pushing was going to help. . . . These athletes developed their abilities over *years* of consistent training and competition. . . . Those who were late developers would have often struggled to prove that there was more to them than others saw on the surface. . . . Almost all of these achievers found humour an invaluable part of life, seeing it as a tension reliever. . . . Another characteristic of these achievers was their determination not to give up. . . . Having the right support systems for their individual needs provided these achievers with the opportunity to progress. . . . Most of the achievers believed, to a large extent, that they controlled their own destiny. This is reflected in the fact that they took responsibility for their actions. A physical example of this is that they would usually keep themselves away from distraction prior to important competitions. (pp. 200–203)

In the most widely cited interview study, Benjamin Bloom and his collaborators (1985) interviewed about 20 internationally renowned individuals in each of six fields, a total of 120 talented persons: music and sculpture in arts, mathematics and neurology in science, and tennis and swimming in sports. Bloom expressed his environmental leanings from the beginning in that credo: "It is likely that some combinations of the home, the teachers, the schools, and the society may in large part determine what portions of this potential pool of talent become developed" (p. 5). In the final chapter, he reiterated that credo, but added two major ingredients. First, he mentioned three important personal characteristics, namely a strong commitment to the chosen talent field, a very high achievement motivation, and a willingness to put in great amounts of time and effort. Second, he acknowledged the role of giftedness: "Another general quality that was noted in each of the talent fields was the *ability to learn rapidly and well*" (p. 545).

Athlete and Coach Rankings

The basic idea behind this group of studies is to create a list of characteristics (e.g., natural abilities, motivation, effort, parental support) and ask target groups to rank them in terms of their perceived relative importance as causes of talent emergence. These target groups of athletes or coaches express their own views about the WMD question. Because of their unique position, athletes and coaches have a chance to observe phenomena that outside researchers have little chance to observe. It is not easy to summarize this area of study: the survey instruments and techniques differ a lot, the target athletes vary, the level of talent varies from local to international, and so forth. Here are a few examples. German national coaches from 30 different sports were asked to rate a long list of characteristics (anthropometric, physical abilities, physiological, and psychological) in terms of their importance to describe the top-level athletes they trained. These coaches did agree that a few of them were important in all sports; most of these belonged to the psychological domain, namely persistence, goal-directed determination, ability to resist stress, and readiness to give a maximum effort during competition. In the case of physical or anthropomorphic characteristics (e.g., strength, speed, tallness, long limbs) each appeared associated with a small group of sports (Gabler & Ruoff, 1979).

In a more recent pair of studies (Van Rossum, 2004b; Van Rossum & Gagné, 1994), the authors asked approximately 200 coaches of top-level Dutch athletes in six different disciplines (field hockey, golf, track-and-field, cycling, badminton, and tennis) to distribute 100 points among 10 different characteristics according to their relative contribution to excellence in their sport. The top three factors (mental fitness, natural endowment, physical fitness) received 16–17 points on average; the average then dropped to 10–11 points for other factors (e.g., amount of training, specific motor skills, tactical ability). It indicates that no single factor emerged above all others.

Gagné, Blanchard, & Bégin (1998) used a slightly different methodological approach to query hundreds of athletes and coaches about the "what makes a difference" question. They gave them a list of nine different characteristics (level of interest, perseverance and tenacity, level of aptitudes, personal qualities, parental supervision and encouragement, sport-centered family environment, amount of practice, quality of coaching, and chance factors), asking them to choose two (ranked 1 and 2) that best distinguished very successful athletes (national or international eminence) from unsuccessful ones (regional excellence), as well as two others (ranked 8 and 9) that least distinguished them. Perseverance came well ahead of all others with an average ranking of 2.79, followed by three almost equally important factors: aptitudes (3.83), practice (3.89), and personality (4.04). The three environmental catalysts, as well as chance factors, were judged least important. Schader (2001) replicated that methodology with a large group of U.S. female Olympians, and obtained very similar results.

Direct Responses

We have grouped under this heading three distinct empirical perspectives that can shed some light on the major difference(s) between those who attain high performance levels in sports and those who remain at lower achievement levels or never embark on a systematic talent development process. First, we will look at the reasons given by those who decide (or are forced) to drop out of a training program. Then, we will examine the major results of empirical studies aimed at comparing high achievers and low achievers in sports on various dimensions measured simultaneously. They will be grouped within two different types of methodologies: cross-sectional and longitudinal studies.

Dropping Out

Every talent development program focuses primarily on the most successful athletes. But, unsuccessful athletes by far outnumber successful ones, especially as we look at higher levels of performance. As opposed to general education, the field of sports allows athletes to quit at any point; no law forces young athletes to keep practicing a given sport until a certain age. The dropout rates vary a lot from one sport to the next, and from one performance level to the next; a majority will move from local to regional teams, but very few of them will achieve national eminence (Van den Auweele, Van Parijs & Vankerckhoven, 1988; Whyte, 1993).

Attention to such "casualties" should be part of the regular duties of every training program; unfortunately, they are overlooked more often than not. In most cases, dropping out of talent development programs results from other peoples' decisions, such as when athletes who are not talented enough are not chosen to become members of more advanced competitive teams. What do we know about the causes of such lack of progress? As mentioned earlier, injuries account for a large number of dropouts. In three independent surveys of sports dropouts, one with talented Scottish adolescent athletes (Whyte, 1993), the two others with Dutch young athletes (Van Santbrink, 1988; Van Rossum, 2005), 26% of the Scottish, and 24 and 28% of the Dutch dropouts identified injuries as an important reason. In a German study with female track-and-field athletes (Bussman & Alfermann, 1994), the authors found a high incidence of injury-related withdrawals.

But, other reasons are invoked. For instance, Csikszentmihalyi, Rathunde, and Whalen (1993) assembled a sample of adolescents from five talent fields (science, mathematics, arts, music, and athletics), and examined their reasons for continuing or quitting. Strong similarities were observed among the five fields—dropping out turned out to result mainly from lack of intrinsic motivation and extrinsic motives (e.g., popularity, traveling, money, status) played no significant role. In short, the "staying on the way" of a talented adolescent is heavily dependent upon maintaining one's intrinsic motivation.

Cross-Sectional Studies

Cross-sectional studies usually compare two groups, one of which will be made up of talented athletes, and the other might comprise lower level competitive athletes, amateur athletes, and even individuals who do not practice any sport. When these studies include a fair number of causal variables, they can be used to answer the WMD question. The sports literature includes a large number of such studies; of course, none includes as many variables as those mentioned in the DMGT. Space requirements allow mentioning just a few examples of this category. Here is a first example from a group of studies in which just a few variables were measured. In a study with 17-year-old elite male and female Czech triathletes (Bunc, Heller, Horcic, & Novotny, 1996), maximal oxygen intake (VO_2max, a measure of endurance) was measured and compared to that of elite swimmers, elite cyclists, and elite middle-distance runners. The physiological characteristics of triathletes were found to be most similar to those of middle-distance runners.

Spamer & Coetzee (2002; see also Nieuwenhuis, Spamer, & Van Rossum, 2002) gathered large samples of very talented and less talented young adolescent players in five studies in four different sports (field hockey, rugby, netball, soccer). In each study they measured a large number of variables from various scientific disciplines. For example, in the field hockey study no less than 41 distinct variables were measured: 16 anthropometric measures, 9 motor abilities (field hockey skills), 7 physiological characteristics, and 9 psychological attributes. Spamer and Coetzee (2002), using the statistical tool of discriminant analysis, found in each study that they could reliably distinguish the groups of talented and less talented athletes with just a small number of these measures, usually less than 10, but at least one from each of the four domains. More detailed inspection by the present author of the results of the five studies indicates that two kinanthropometric variables repeatedly appear in the prediction function: circumference of the femur (upper arm) and circumference of the humerus (upper leg). Two other variables are often, but not always present, namely speed (a run over a short distance of 20 or 40 meters) and agility (a run over a short distance with changes in direction). The combination of these variables suggests that explosive strength and anaerobic capacity are important variables for the discrimination between higher and lower levels of achievement in these sports. This finding fits well with a commonly shared notion that natural physical abilities and anthropometric qualities are very important in the athletic domain.

Here are two final examples, both with samples of talented adolescents in individual sports. In a German study on the detection of early talent in track-and-field sports, Heck, Mayer, and Wasmund-Bodenstedt (1995, 1997) found that performance on the 20-meter run best discriminated between three samples of school children (8.5 to 10.5 years old): a talented group ($n = 69$), an average group ($n = 289$), and a group of poor performers ($n = 19$). In an Australian study on tennis talent development, Elliott, Ackland, Blanksby, and Bloomfield (1990) found that the performance on a 40-meter run and on an agility run (switching directions, slaloming) were the best discriminators at ages 11, 13, and 15 between three groups: talented tennis players, less talented ones, and athletically inactive peers.

Longitudinal Studies

Longitudinal studies represent the best methodological approach to answering the WMD question. Here is how it works. A large group of young athletes are followed for some years, with many variables being measured at regular intervals. No comparison group is necessary since there will be enough variation in performance within the group to see what makes a difference between the best and worst performers, or between those who advance to higher levels and those who quit competitive training. In one of the early studies in sports on the individual qualities of top-level achievers, Carlson (1988) attempted to reconstruct the emergence of Swedish professional tennis players of international caliber. In 1985, five male and five female top-15 players were compared to those individuals of the original sample who had played tennis at national level during their adolescent years, but who had not been successful at the international level. Information was gathered retrospectively from the athletes themselves, their parents, and their coaches. Searching for an answer to the question of what made the difference between the successful and unsuccessful tennis players, Carlson concluded: "The results clearly indicate that it is not possible to predict who will develop into a world-class tennis player based on individual talent alone" (p. 241).

Several years later, the same question was differently answered in the Heidelberg Longitudinal Study, a German study on tennis talent development (Bös & Schneider, 1997; Schneider et al., 1993). This study constitutes an excellent example of a longitudinal study on the WMD question. The sample included all the adolescent tennis players (73 boys, 34 girls) selected for the national junior teams for a period of 5 successive years (1978–1982). Each year, the researchers gathered a large set of measures from various domains, including motor abilities, physical, physiological and psychological characteristics, a detailed developmental history, as well as medical and orthopedic examinations during the adolescent years of the athletes. Several years later, the collected data were used to predict international tennis ranking, based on tournament results, between 1985 and 1992. In a reanalysis of the data, two groups were distinguished: a talented group (18 professional players with ATP-ranking, including Boris Becker and Steffi Graf) and a control group of 27 players who did not attain professional status.

In a concise overview of the results of the study, Schneider (2000, p. 172) summarized the results as follows: "parents' support, the amount and intensity of practice, as well as the level of achievement motivation significantly predicted children's tennis rankings several years later." He added, however, that the importance of natural motor abilities should not be overlooked:

> Although tennis-specific skills and the amount and intensity of practice accounted for most of the variance in children's tennis rankings several years later, the effects of basic motor abilities on tennis performance could not be ignored. That is, when the basic ability construct was omitted from the model, the model no longer fitted the data. Although individual differences in basic motor abilities were not large in this highly selected sample,

they made a difference when it came to predicting individual tennis performance. (Schneider, 2000, p. 172)

In short, this study reveals that variables from several domains contribute to a good prediction that athletic achievement at the world level is based on variables from several scientific disciplines: parental support and achievement motivation from the social sciences, tennis-specific motor skills (e.g., accuracy of forehand, service), and basic motor skills (e.g., sprinting speed, flexibility) from the sport and movement sciences, as well as amount of training. Although the Heidelberg Study covered a large set of potentially relevant factors, it remains a single study and should suggest only tentative conclusions. Additional similar studies could, in time, provide solid information about the most relevant variables to predict top-level athletic achievement for almost every sport.

Summing Up

So, what makes a difference? From the above survey of all kinds of methodological approaches to answering that crucial question, it appears that we are still far from a clear response. No doubt that natural abilities differ a lot among young boys and girls, and that they contribute to bringing some to competitive training in sports. Also, personal characteristics, especially those associated with high intrinsic motivation, the rage to achieve and conquer, and long-term perseverance and tenacity, seem to distinguish those who reach the highest levels from those who fall to the sidelines. Finally, some environmental support, from both the family and the coach, will help growing athletes maintain their drive towards excellence. As Gagné (2000) explained, talent in any field results from a complex choreography between all the components of the DMGT. Their relative importance will change not only from one person to the next or from one field of sport to the next, but also over time as the athlete moves from lower to higher levels of excellence.

CONCLUSION

We have tried in this chapter to survey the scientific literature of the past few decades on the process of talent development in sports. We structured that overview around Gagné's (2003) Differentiated Model of Giftedness and Talent. We examined separately the relevant literature associated with each of the DMGT's five causal components: (a) natural abilities or gifts, (b) the developmental process itself, (c) intrapersonal catalysts, (d) environmental catalysts, and (e) chance factors. This survey brought us to a crucial integrative question: What makes the difference between reaching and not reaching high levels of talent in sports? We had to acknowledge that there was not yet a very clear and final answer to that complex question, and that the best way to summarize the existing literature was to speak of complex interactions between the components, acting differently from one athlete to the next, and from one stage to the next in a sports career. The metaphor of individual choreographies probably best represents our present knowledge.

The "What Makes the Difference" discussion points to the fact that top-level achievements in sports spring from a combination of relevant characteristics—which is exactly why one of the main reasons making predictions of long-term athletic performance is as difficult as it is. The compensation phenomenon is considered a central obstacle for solid predictions on the basis of personal characteristics of an athlete (Régnier et al., 1993). Further, the athlete's individual characteristics are to be matched to the environment, that is, to the quality of the athletic program. Here, one of the most relevant ingredients is the quality of the coaching staff, in terms of both knowledge and skills. Therefore, the process of the development of athletic talent should not be oriented toward (early) selection, but would be best advanced by giving prominence to what Régnier et al. (1993) call "talent surveillance," a process similar to job counseling within an industrial setting.

Of what use can this chapter be to educators in schools? What suggestions can the field of sports offer to teachers of gifted and talented children, and to the professionals and school administrators responsible for planning, funding, and implementing enrichment programs in the school system? Two major observations come to mind.

First, it seems clear that the vast majority of trainers and coaches in sports readily recognize the large breadth of individual differences in natural physical abilities; this is why they invest much time and energy in identification instruments and procedures, as evidenced by one showcase example described earlier, the Australian Talent Search Program. The fact that active participation in sports is not compulsory, as schooling is, no doubt increases the importance of actively searching for those few who manifest the high natural abilities that will be, in the DMGT's terms, the *building blocks* of future talent in sports. By contrast, educators give much less importance to individual differences in academic aptitudes; most of them defend a position whose environmentalist leanings emphasize the capacity of the school environment to nullify, or at least strongly reduce the large individual differences in school achievement observed as early as the first grades of elementary school (Gagné, 2005b). This does not mean that most educators ignore the existence of individual differences in natural cognitive abilities, as measured by IQ tests; but, not only do they question the "naturalness" of these abilities, they also tend to give only lip service to the research showing the power of these measures as predictors of academic achievement (Gagné & St. Père, 2002).

The second observation concerns the way professionals in sports foster the talent development process. Two key concepts, familiar to educators, could summarize typical programming activities in sports: ability grouping and accelerative enrichment. Ability grouping means that young athletes with exceptional natural abilities or precocious high achievements are rapidly invited to join competitive teams that bring together similarly gifted peers. Accelerative enrichment means that the pace of the talent development activities closely follows each individual's learning aptitudes. Young athletes who master more easily the skills of their sport will be the ones who will soon move to the next training level—this is how the most talented athletes reach national or international competition well before adulthood. By contrast, both ability grouping and accelerative enrichment remain very controversial—and rarely used—administrative options in school districts. In the first case, administrators massively favor heterogeneous grouping at all levels of the K–12 curricula. They refuse to admit that (a) the vast majority of teachers cannot cope with the demands of the classic mainstreamed classroom (Gagné, in press), and that (b) those whose educational needs get "forgotten" in the process are the high achievers. In the case of academic acceleration options, although their value has been demonstrated through hundreds of evaluative studies (Colangelo, Assouline, & Gross, 2004), they face similar resistance from teachers and school administrators. Instead of adapting the teaching pace to the more rapid learning pace of academically talented students, most schools force their brightest students to progress at the same slow pace as their average and below average peers. Julian Stanley, one of the most eminent scholars in the field of gifted education, derisively called that approach the "age-grade lockstep" (Stanley, 1979).

Other disparities could be discussed (e.g., disparities in funding for talented athletes as opposed to talented scholars). But, if just the two observations mentioned in the preceding paragraphs were adopted in schools, the changes would be immense and the benefits to the talented students incommensurable.

REFERENCES

Adirim, T. A., & Cheng, T. L. (2003). Overview of injuries in the young athlete. *Sports Medicine, 33*, 75–81.

American Sport Education Program (1994). *Sport parent survival guide*. Champaign, IL: Human Kinetics.

Anastasi, A., & Urbina, S. (1997). *Psychological testing* (7th ed.). Upper Saddle River, NJ: Prentice-Hall.

Australian Sports Commission (1994). *The search is over: Norms for sport related fitness tests in Australian students aged 12–17 years*. Canberra, Australia: Author.

Baker, J., Horton, S., Robertson-Wilson, J., & Wall, M. (2003). Nurturing sport expertise: Factors influencing the development of the elite athlete. *Journal of Sports Science and Medicine, 2*, 1–9.

Bales, J. (1996). The Canadian sport schools. *Coaching Focus, 31*, 7–8.

Baxter-Jones, A. D. G., & Helms, P. J. (1996). Effects of training at a young age: A review of the training of young athletes (TOYA) Study. *Pediatric Exercise Science, 8*, 310–327.

Bloom, B. S. (Ed.). (1985). *Developing talent in young people*. New York: Ballantine Books.

Bös, K., & Schneider, W. (1997). *Vom Tennistalent zum Spitzenspieler: Eine Reanalyse von Längsschnittdaten zur Leistungsprognose im Tennis* [From talented tennis player to top-level player: A re-analysis of longitudinal data regarding the prognosis of tennis performance]. Hamburg: Czwalina Verlag.

Bouchard, C., & Shepard, R. J. (1994). Physical activity, fitness, and health: The model and key concepts. In C. Bouchard, R. J. Shepard, and T. Stephens (Eds.), *Physical activity, fitness, and health* (pp. 77–88). Champaign, IL: Human Kinetics.

Bouchard, C., Malina, R. M., & Pérusse, L. (1997). *Genetics of fitness and physical performance*. Champaign, IL: Human Kinetics.

Brustad, R.J. (1993). Youth in sport: Psychological considerations. In R. N. Singer, M. Murphy, & L. K. Tennant (Eds.), *Handbook of research on sport psychology* (pp. 695–717). New York: Macmillan.

Bussmann, G., & Alfermann, D. (1994). Drop out and the female athlete—A study with track and field athletes. In D. Hackfort (Ed.), *Psycho-social issues and interventions in elite sports* (pp. 89–128). Frankfurt am Main: Peter Lang.

Bunc, V., Heller, J., Horcic, J., & Novotny, J. (1996). Physiological profile of best Czech male and female young triathletes. *The Journal of Sports Medicine and Physical Fitness, 36*, 265–270.

Carlson, R. (1988). The socialization of elite tennis players in Sweden: An analysis of the players' backgrounds and development. *Sociology of Sport Journal, 5*, 241–256.

Cashmore, E. (2002). *Sport psychology: The key concepts.* London: Routledge.

Chelladurai, P. (1993). Leadership. In R. N. Singer, M. Murphey, & L. K. Tennant (Eds.), *Handbook of research on sport psychology* (pp. 647–671). New York: Macmillan.

Chelladurai, P., & Riemer, H.A. (1998). Measurement of leadership in sport. In J. L. Duda (Ed.), *Advances in sport and exercise psychology measurement* (pp. 227–253). Morgantown, WV: Fitness Information Technology.

Chelladurai, P., & Saleh, S.D. (1980). Dimensions of leader behavior in sports: Development of a leadership scale. *Journal of Sport Psychology, 2*, 34–45.

Colangelo, N., Assouline, S., & Gross, M. U. M. (2004). *A nation deceived: How schools hold back America's brightest students* (Vol. I). Iowa City, IA: The Connie Belin & Jacqueline N. Blank International Center for Gifted Education and Talent Development.

Corno, L. (1993). The best-laid plans: Modern conceptions of volition and educational research. *Educational Researcher, 22*, 14–22.

Corno, L., & Kanfer, R. (1993). The role of volition in learning and performance. In L. Darling-Hammond (Ed.), *Review of research in education* (Vol. 19, pp. 301–341). Washington, DC: American Educational Research Association.

Csikszentmihalyi, M., Rathunde, K., & Whalen, S. (1993). *Talented teenagers: The roots of success and failure.* Cambridge: Cambridge University Press.

Dale, R., & Cameron, C. (1994). *The contenders.* London: Boxtree.

De Knop, P., Engström, L. M., & Skirstad, B. (1996). Worldwide trends in youth sport. In P. De Knop, L. M. Engström, B. Skirstad, & M. R. Weiss (Eds.), *Worldwide trends in youth sport* (pp. 276–281). Champaign, IL: Human Kinetics.

Deakin, J. M., & Cobley, S. (2003). A search for deliberate practice: An examination of the practice environments in figure skating and volleyball. In J. L. Starkes & K. A. Ericsson (Eds.), *Expert performance in sports: Advances in research on sport expertise* (pp. 115–135). Champaign, IL: Human Kinetics.

Douma, J., & Companjen, T. (2003). *Eigenschappen van talentvolle volleyballers van de NeVoBo volleybalschool* [Characteristics of talented athletes in volleyball, selected for the Dutch Volleyball Association volleyball school]. Unpublished master's thesis, Vrije Universiteit, Amsterdam, Netherlands.

Durand-Bush, N., & Salmela, J.H. (2001). The development of talent in sport. In R. N. Singer, H. A. Hausenblas, & C.M. Janelle (Eds.), *Handbook of sport psychology* (2nd ed., pp. 269–289). New York: Wiley.

Elliott, B. C., Ackland, T. R., Blanksby, B. A., & Bloomfield, J. (1990). A prospective study of physiological and kinanthropometric indicators of junior tennis performance. *The Australian Journal of Science and Medicine in Sport, 22*, 87–92.

English Sports Council (1998). *The development of sporting talent 1997: An examination of the current practices for talent development in English sport.* London: English Sports Council.

Ericsson, K. A. (1998). The scientific study of expert levels of performance: General implications for optimal learning and creativity. *High Ability Studies, 9*, 75–100.

Ericsson, K. A., Krampe, R.T. & Tesch-Römer, C. (1993). The role of deliberate practice in the acquisition of expert performance. *Psychological Review, 100*, 363–406.

Eysenck, H. J. (1955). Cortical inhibition, figural after-effects and theory of personality. *Journal of Abnormal and Social Psychology, 51*, 94–106.

Eysenck, H. J., Nias, D. K. B., & Cox, D. N. (1982). Sport and personality. *Advances in Behavioral Research and Therapy, 4*, 1–56.

Feij, J. A. & Kuiper, C. M. (1984). *ATL, Adolescenten Temperament Lijst: Handleiding* [Temperament questionnaire for adolescents: Manual]. Lisse: Swets & Zeitlinger.

Gabler, H., & Ruoff, B. A. (1979). Zum Problem der Talentbestimmung im Sport [Regarding the problem of the destination of talent in sports]. *Sportwissenschaft, 9*, 164–180.

Gagné, F. (1985). Giftedness and talent: Reexamining a reexamination of the definitions. *Gifted Child Quarterly, 29*, 103–112.

Gagné, F. (1998). A proposal for subcategories within the gifted or talented populations. *Gifted Child Quarterly, 42*, 87–95.

Gagné, F. (2000). Understanding the complex choreography of talent development through DMGT-based analysis. In K. A. Heller, F. J. Mönks, R. J. Sternberg, & R. F. Subotnik (Eds.), *International handbook of giftedness and talent* (2nd ed., pp. 67–79). Amsterdam: Elsevier.

Gagné, F. (2003). Transforming gifts into talents: The DMGT as a developmental theory. In N. Colangelo & G. A. Davis (Eds.), *Handbook of gifted education* (3rd ed., pp. 60–74). Boston: Allyn & Bacon.

Gagné, F. (2005a). From gifts to talents: The DMGT as a developmental model. In R. J. Sternberg, and J. E. Davidson (Eds.), *Conceptions of giftedness* (2nd ed., pp. 98–119). New York: Cambridge University Press.

Gagné, F. (2005b). From noncompetence to exceptional talent: Exploring the range of academic achievement within and between grade levels. *Gifted Child Quarterly, 42*, 139–153.

Gagné, F. (in press). Ten commandments for academic talent development. *Gifted Child Quarterly.*

Gagné, F., & St. Père, F. (2002). When IQ is controlled, does motivation still predict achievement? *Intelligence, 30*, 71–100.

Gagné, F., Blanchard, D., & Bégin, J. (1998). *Beliefs of trainers, athletes, professors and students in physical education, concerning the major determinants of talent in sports.* Unpublished research report. Université du Québec à Montréal, Département de Psychologie, Montreal, Canada.

Geron, D., Furst, P., & Rotstein, P. (1986). Personality of athletes participating in various sports. *International Journal of Sport Psychology, 17*, 120–135.

Gill, D.L. (1993). Competitiveness and competitive orientation in sport. In R. N. Singer, M. Murphey & L. K. Tennant (Eds.), *Handbook of research on sport psychology* (pp. 314–327). New York: Macmillan.

Gill, D. L., & Deeter, T. E. (1988). Development of the sport orientation questionnaire. *Research Quarterly for Exercise and Sport, 59*, 191–202.

Hanrahan, S. J., & Biddle, S. J. H. (2002). Measurement of achievement orientations: Psychometric measures, gender, and sport differences. *European Journal of Sport Science, 2*(5), 1–12.

Hardman, K. (1973). A dual approach to the study of personality and performance in sport. In H. T. A. Whiting, K. Hardman, L. B. Hendry, & M. G. Jones (Eds.), *Personality and performance in physical education and sport* (pp. 77–121). London: Henry Kimpton.

Heck, E., Mayer, D., & Wasmund-Bodenstedt, U. (1995). Längsschnittstudie zur Identifikation von Sporttalenten. Teil I: Methodologische Probleme [Longitudinal research on the identification of athletic talent. Part 1: Methodological problems]. *Sportonomics, 1*(2), 71–75.

Heck, E., Mayer, D., & Wasmund-Bodenstedt, U. (1997). Längsschnittstudie zur Identifikation von Sporttalenten. Teil II: Anwendung von Cluster-und Diskriminanzanalysen [Longitudinal research on the identification of athletic talent. Part 2: The use of cluster and discriminant analysis]. *Sportonomics, 3*(1), 43–46.

Hellstedt, J. C. (1995). Invisible players: A family systems model. In S. H. Murphy (Ed.), *Sport psychology interventions* (pp. 117–146). Champaign, IL: Human Kinetics.

Hemery, D. (1986). *The pursuit of sporting excellence: A study of sport's highest achievers.* London: Willow Books.

Highlen, P. S., & Bennett, B. B. (1983). Elite divers and wrestlers: A comparison between open- and closed-skill athletes. *Journal of Sport Psychology, 5*, 390–409.

Hoare, D. (1996). The Australian national talent search program. *Coaching Focus, 31*, 3–4.

Hoare, D. (1998, Spring). Talent search: A review and update. *Sports Coach, Spring*, pp. 32–33.

Howe, M. J. A., Davidson, J. W., & Sloboda, J. A. (1998). Innate talents: reality or myth? *Behavior and Brain Sciences, 21*, 399–442.

Kane, J. E. (1986). Giftedness in sport. In G. Gleeson (Ed.), *The growing child in competitive sport* (pp. 184–204). London: Hodder and Stoughton.

Kavussanu, M., & Roberts, G.C. (1996). Motivation in physical activity context: The relationship of perceived motivational climate to intrinsic motivation and efficacy. *Journal of Sport and Exercise Psychology, 5*, 168–176.

Kozel, J. (1996) Talent identification and development in Germany. *Coaching Focus, 31*, 5–6.

Kremer, J., & Scully, D. (1994). *Psychology in sport.* London: Taylor & Francis.

Mariën, S. E. J. M., & Van Pelt, J. (1998). *Klassieke en moderne dansers in vooropleiding* [Classical and modern dancers in their pre-professional training]. Unpublished master's thesis, Vrije Universiteit, Amsterdam.

Martens, R. (1977). *Sport competition anxiety test.* Champaign, IL: Human Kinetics.

Martens, R. (1988). Youth sport in the USA. In F. L. Smoll, R. A. Magill, & M. J. Ash (Eds.), *Children in sport* (3rd ed., pp. 17–23). Champaign, IL: Human Kinetics.

Martens, R., Vealey, R. S., & Burton, D. (1990). *Competitive anxiety in sport.* Champaign, IL: Human Kinetics.

Michelmore, P. (1988, June). Greg Louganis: High diver with a heart. *Reader's Digest*, 163–170.

Middlebrook, R. (1996). The Yorkshire cricket school. *Coaching Focus, 31*, 18.

Milton, J. (1996) Prospects squash management. *Coaching Focus, 31*, 14–15.

Moon, S. (2003). Personal talent. *High Ability Studies, 14*, 5–21.

Nieuwenhuis, C. F., Spamer, E. J., & Van Rossum, J. H. A. (2002). A prediction function for identifying talent in 14- to 15-year-old female field hockey players. *High Ability Studies, 13*, 21–33.

Ntoumanis, N., & Biddle, S. J. H. (1998). The relationship between competitive anxiety, achievement goals, and motivational climates. *Research Quarterly for Exercise and Sport, 69*, 176–187.

Oldenziel, K., Gagné, F., & Gulbin, J. (2003). *How do elite athletes develop? A look through the 'rear-view mirror.'* Canberra: Australian Institute of Sport, Australian Sports Commission.

Petlichkoff, L. M. (1994). Dropping out of sport: Speculation versus reality. In D. Hackfort (Ed.), *Psycho-social issues and interventions in elite sports* (pp. 59–87). Frankfurt am Main: Peter Lang.

President's Council on Physical Fitness and Sports (2001). *President's challenge: Physical fitness program packet.* Retrieved September 7, 2005, from http://www.fitness.gov/challenge/challenge.html

Régnier, G., Salmela, J., & Russell, S. J. (1993). Talent detection and development in sport. In R. N. Singer, M. Murphey, & L. K. Tennant (Eds.), *Handbook of research on sport psychology* (pp. 290–313). New York: Macmillan.

Rotella, B., & Bunker, L. K. (1998). *Parenting your superstar: How to help your child balance achievement and happiness.* Chicago: Triumph Books.

Rowley, S. (1992). *The Training of Young Athletes Study (TOYA): Identification of talent.* London: English Sports Council.

Rowley, S. (1995). Identification and development of talent in young athletes. In J. Freeman, P. Span, & H. Wagner (Eds.), *Actualizing talent: A lifelong challenge* (pp. 128–143). London: Cassell.

Salmela, J. H. (1994). Phases and transitions across sport careers. In D. Hackfort (Ed.), *Psycho-social issues and interventions in elite sports* (pp. 11–28). Frankfurt am Main: Peter Lang.

Schader, R. M. (2001). *Perceptions of elite female athletes regarding success attributions and the role of parental influence on talent development.* Unpublished doctoral dissertation, University of Connecticut, Storrs.

Schneider, W. (2000). Giftedness, expertise, and (exceptional) performance: A developmental perspective. In K. A. Heller, F. J. Mönks, R. J. Sternberg, & R. F. Subotnik (Eds.), *International handbook of giftedness and talent* (2nd ed., pp. 165–177). Oxford: Elsevier Science/Pergamon.

Schneider, W., Bös, K., & Rieder, H. (1993). Leistungsprognose bei jugentliche Spitzensportler [Prediction of achievement in young elite athletes]. In J. Beckmann, H. Strang, & E. Hahn (Eds.), *Aufmerksamkeit und Energetisierung; Facetten von Konzentration und Leistung* (pp. 277–299). Göttingen: Hogrefe.

Smith, R. E., & Smoll, F. L. (1996). The coach as a focus of research and intervention in youth sports. In F. L. Smoll & R. E. Smith (Eds.), *Children and youth in sport: A biopsychosocial perspective* (pp. 125–141). Madison: Brown & Benchmark.

Smith, R. E., Smoll, F. L., & Wiechman, S. A. (1998). Measurement of trait anxiety in sport. In J. L. Duda (Ed.), *Advances in sport and exercise psychology measurement* (pp. 105–127). Morgantown, WV: Fitness Information Technology.

Smoll, F. L. (1993). Enhancing coach-parent relationships in youth sports. In J. M. Williams (Ed.), *Applied sport psychology* (2nd ed., pp. 58–67). Mountain View, CA: Mayfield.

Smoll, F. L., & Smith, R. E. (1999). *Sports and your child: A 50-minute guide for parents.* Portola Valley, CA: Warde Publishers.

Smoll, F. L., & Smith, R. E. (2001). Conducting sport psychology training programs for coaches: Cognitive-behavioral principles and techniques. In J. M. Williams (Ed.), *Applied sport psychology: Personal growth to peak performance* (4th ed., pp. 378–400). Mountain View, CA: Mayfield Publishing Company.

Smolowe, J. (1988, September 19). Sprite fight: Which of the extraordinary tumbling pixies will become the Seoul sweetheart? *Time, 132*, 56–57.

Spamer, E. J., & Coetzee, M. (2002). Variables which distinguish between talented and less talented participants in youth sport—A comparative study. *Kinesiology, 34*, 141–152.

Sport International (1995). *Topsporters 1995: Een onderzoek van Sport International* [Top-level athletes: A study by Sport International]. Amsterdam: Weekbladpers.

Stanley, J. C. (1979). Educational non-acceleration: An international tragedy. In J. J. Gallagher (Ed.), *Gifted children: Reaching their potential* (pp. 16–43). Jerusalem: Kollek & sons.

Starkes, J. L., Deakin, J. M., Allard, F., Hodges, N. J., & Hayes, A. (1996). Deliberate practice in sports: What is it anyway? In K. A. Ericsson (Ed.), *The road to excellence: The acquisition of expert performance in the arts and sciences, sports and games* (pp. 81–106). Mahwah, NJ: Lawrence Erlbaum.

Suomalainen, M., Telama, R., Kemppainen, A., & Pulkkanen, A. (1990). Time budget and life-style of athletes at ordinary high schools and at special sport high schools. In R. Telama, L. Laakso, M. Pieron, I. Ruoppila, & V. Vihko (Eds.), *Physical education and life-long physical activity* (pp. 592–599). Jyvaskyla, Finland: Reports of Physical Culture and Health 73.

Unierzyski, P. (2003). Level of achievement motivation of young tennis players and their future progress. *Journal of Sports Science and Medicine, 2*, 184–186.

Van de Langemheen, H., & De Wit, A. (2003). *Tijdsbesteding, motivatie en betrokkenheid van jonge getalenteerde sporters en musici* [Time spending, motivation and commitment of young talented athletes and musicians]. Unpublished master's thesis, Vrije Universiteit, Amsterdam.

Van den Auweele, Y., De Cuyper, B., Van Mele, V., & Rzewnicki, R. (1993). Elite performance and personality: From prescription and prediction to diagnosis and intervention. In R. N. Singer, M. Murphey, & L. K. Tennant (Eds.), *Handbook of research on sport psychology* (pp. 257–289). New York: Macmillan.

Van den Auweele, Y., Nys, K., Rzewnicki, R., & Van Mele, V. (2001). Personality and the athlete. In R. N. Singer, H. A. Hausenblas, & C. M. Janelle (Eds.), *Handbook of sport psychology* (2nd ed., pp. 239–268). New York: Wiley.

Van den Auweele, Y., Van Parijs, M., & Vankerckhoven, G. (1988). Topsport, hoe kom je er (niet) toe? Studie van het carrièreverloop van jonge talenten [Top-level sports, what is helping or hindering? A study on the career of young talents]. *Sport, 30,* 19–26.

Van Rossum, J. H. A. (1992). *Talent-ontwikkeling: Loopbaan en kenmerken van topsporters. Een onderzoek bij de nederlandse selecties van vier olympische takken van sport* [Talent development: Career and characteristics of top-level athletes. A study with Dutch squads of four Olympic sports]. Arnhem: NOC*NSF.

Van Rossum, J. H. A. (1995). Talent in sport: Significant others in the career of top-level Dutch athletes. In M. W. Katzko & F. J. Mönks (Eds.), *Nurturing talent: Individual needs and social ability* (p. 43-57). Assen: Van Gorcum.

Van Rossum, J. H. A. (1997). Leiderschap in de sport: De trainer/coach [Leadership in sports: The coach]. *Richting Sport-Gericht,* 51, 321–328.

Van Rossum, J. H. A. (2004a). Coaches who never lose—a valid approach even in top-level sports? In E. Van Praagh & J. Coudert (Eds.), *Book of abstracts* (CD-ROM; Proceedings of 9th Annual Congress of the ECSS). Clermont-Ferrand, France: European College of Sport Science.

Van Rossum, J. H. A. (2004b). Perceptions of determining factors in athletic achievement: An addendum to Hyllegard, et al. (2003). *Perceptual and Motor Skills, 98,* 81–86.

Van Rossum, J. H. A. (2005). *Volhouden of afhaken: Een longitudinaal onderzoek naar talent-ontwikkeling in de sport, met aandacht voor dropouts en toppers* [Carry on or pull out: A longitudinal study on the development of talent in sports, considering both dropouts and top-class athletes]. Amsterdam: Stichting HQ&P.

Van Rossum, J. H. A., & Gagné, F. (1994). Rankings of predictors of athletic performance by top level coaches. *European Journal for High Ability, 5,* 68–78.

Van Rossum, J. H. A., & Vergouwen, P. C. J. (2003). *De jeugdige getalenteerde hockeyer: Een beeld vanuit medisch, psychologisch en inspanningsfysiologisch perspectief* [The talented young field hockey player: A medical, psychological and exercise physiological view]. Arnhem: NOC*NSF.

Van Santbrink, A. J. (1988). *Dropout onder jeugdige atletiektalenten in Oost* [Dropout among young talented track-and-field athletes in the eastern provinces of the Netherlands]. Velp: Gelderse Sport Federatie.

Van Yperen, N. W., & Duda, J. L. (1999), Goal orientations, beliefs about success, and performance improvement among young elite Dutch soccer players. *Scandinavian Journal of Medicine & Science in Sports, 9,* 358–364.

Whitehead, J. (1986). Achievement goals and drop-out in youth sports. In G. Gleeson (Ed.), *The growing child in competitive sport* (pp. 240–247). London: Hodder and Stoughton.

Whyte, I. (1993). *Scottish elite young performers in selected sports: Motives for dropping out.* Edinburgh: The Scottish Sports Council.

Widmeyer, W. N., Dorsch, K. D., Bray, S. R., & McGuire, E. J. (2002). The nature, prevalence, and consequences of aggression in sport. In J. M. Silva & D. E. Stevens (Eds.), *Psychological foundations of sport* (pp. 328–351). Boston: Allyn & Bacon.

Woods, B. (1998). *Applying psychology to sport.* London: Hodder & Stoughton.

Woolgar, C., & Power, T. G. (1993). Parent and sport socialization: Views from the achievement literature. *Journal of Sport Behavior, 16,* 171–189.

WHAT SCHOOLS CAN DO

Curriculum and Instruction: An Overview

by Felicia A. Dixon

 ppropriate curriculum for gifted students and the instructional strategies employed to transmit the curriculum are the educational responses to the unique learner characteristics of talented adolescents. For adolescents in middle and high school, this response has not been as clearly defined or as considerate of their uniqueness as it has been for the elementary gifted student. VanTassel-Baska (2004) writes that curriculum designed for the gifted must "... provide students a rigorous, high quality experience that readies them to successfully traverse the next level of educational challenge in a selective university as well as ground them in self-learning and social learning of the moment" (p. xxxii).

The purpose of Part III is to give educators guidelines for what needs to be done within schools and classrooms for secondary gifted adolescents. Consistent with Parts I and II, the adolescent's unique qualities set the context for the educational interventions that are the focus of these chapters. Hence, these 10 chapters focus on critical and creative thinking skills, affective issues that impact curriculum, extracurricular activities that augment school programs, models that meet adolescent needs, schools that offer choices in scheduling and concentration especially designed for gifted adolescents, and domain-specific courses that offer both rigorous content and appropriate strategies to address the students' need for both breadth and depth of content.

Part III authors followed three guidelines that serve as organizing features: (a) to provide a theoretical rationale for the topic's relevance to gifted adolescents; (b) to review the current empirical literature on the chapter topic as it exists in gifted education relative to gifted adolescents; and (c) to offer curricular materials, strategies, and appropriate assessments suitable for meeting the needs of gifted adolescents. As others have stated in this book (see Chapter 24), secondary education for the gifted is largely a domain-specific issue for most schools. Part III seeks to cut across the domain-specific lines, offering instructional strategies that are pertinent to all disciplines (see Chapters 12, 13, and 18) and programs that concentrate on the unique learner characteristics of gifted adolescents (see Chapters 19, 20, and 21). In addition, the distinct disciplines are addressed (see Chapters 14, 15, 16, and 17), with a definite emphasis on ways of teaching within the specific discipline that take into account the cognitive and affective needs of students and offer these adolescents choices.

According to Passow (2004),

> Curriculum for the gifted and talented at the secondary level involves more than deciding whether to accelerate or enrich, to group or not, to offer an honors program or an advanced seminar, or to offer advanced placement courses. Rather, it consists of the total learning environment and encompasses the general education, specialized education, co-curricular, and education in non-school settings, together with the climate which is created in the school and classroom for pursuit of excellence. (p. 103)

Passow argued that gifted adolescents at the secondary level have a sound general education that provides opportunities to engage in appropriate learning experiences in disciplines and subject areas that contribute to a mastery of the cultural heritage and nurture these students as creative participants and productive contributors to that culture. In addition, it is important that gifted secondary students have opportunities to develop their particular areas of specialized talents, recognizing that in most areas, the talents will not be fully nurtured in secondary school (i.e., these students will not be accomplished scientists, mathematicians, writers, or historians at this point). Passow also stated that affective goals, as well as cognitive and academic goals must be attended to in the curriculum and program offerings for gifted secondary students.

The individual chapters in Part III of *The Handbook of Secondary Gifted Education* seek to address these curricular issues. In Chapter 12, Dixon sets the context for challenging curriculum that cuts across the disciplines by arguing for the importance of a critical thinking emphasis in all lessons designed for gifted secondary students. Dixon reviews the literature on critical thinking and argues that because gifted secondary students think critically when they enter secondary schools, teachers must teach to their pre-existing thinking levels. Several instructional strategies are offered for embedding critical thinking in activities. Dixon's focus on a process for critical thinking derived from the Hegelian Dialectic presents a unique strategy that addresses dialectical thinking, which may describe the rich cognitive processing that characterizes many secondary gifted adolescents.

Adams and Pierce offer interesting suggestions for interjecting creative thinking strategies across disciplines in Chapter 13. They caution that from all indications, creativity does not hold a place of importance in the secondary classroom. However, they assert that creativity can be used as a means of expanding and enriching any content area and it will empower gifted adolescents to tap into new realms of thinking. They review past definitions of creativity and offer their own useful applications to secondary classrooms. Especially meaningful to secondary teachers of all disciplines are their points concerning exactly how to teach the creative process, integrating creativity into all parts of the learning environment: content, process, product, affect, and the learning environment itself. Adams and Pierce are seasoned consultants and presenters who understand teachers, and their understanding comes through meaningfully in this important chapter.

Chapters 14–17 are devoted to the all-important content domains. As secondary education is much more content-focused than elementary education, these chapters are very important to the context of this book. Dixon's chapter, "Secondary English for High-ability Students," relies upon her years of teaching gifted students in the classroom to set the context for the theoretical rationale and strategies that follow. Dixon suggests that the key to meeting the needs of gifted students in secondary English classes is for teachers to understand the needs of high-ability students and then appropriately differentiate the classes to meet those needs. Even in AP classes, differentiation must occur if students are to work to their potential. Dixon suggests that challenging content sets the context for processes focused on vocabulary development, grammar study, writing assignments, and literary discussions. All of these essential factors meet the needs of these students because they continually offer choices and challenge. Dixon's focus is on academic rigor, and the last part of the chapter offers specific examples of tests, discussion questions, and project ideas that include appropriate assessment suggestions, as well as comments on why they are effective and what cautions she would suggest.

In Chapter 15, Stepien and Stepien offer a clear rationale for the teaching of social studies and history to high-ability secondary students. In this chapter, the authors argue that students, especially gifted and talented adolescents, can achieve significant subject matter outcomes and find motivation when social studies and history curricula reflect national standards, activate and nourish the talents of gifted students, and are delivered through constructivist methodologies, such as *problem-based learning* (PBL). Indeed, their expertise with problem-based learning and constructivist strategies are evident throughout this chapter. Stepien and Stepien use the metaphor of "pulling the cat's tail" to describe how teachers of social studies and history must engage students in the active pursuit of knowledge in order to meaningfully integrate the content, process, and products of social studies and history classes for secondary gifted students. Their specific strategies and lesson plans illustrate the theoretical rationale they present.

Science courses are essentially the major focus of secondary education for many gifted and talented students. These students view physical science, biology, chemistry, and physics as foundational for a strong background for their pursuit of high level careers after college graduation. Gifted students choose special schools early on in order to concentrate on the sciences. Gallagher understands science for secondary students, and Chapter 16 presents a clear view of what is necessary in science classes for high-ability secondary students. Gallagher focuses on issues and strategies that help define what it takes to be considered an expert scientist in today's society. Her theoretical rationale offers three perspectives that contribute a unique set of attributes for an approach to science education for gifted students: (1) the actual practice of modern science will provide information about skills and tools, (2) the source of new ideas in science will help establish behavior qualities of the expert, and (3) the framework of beliefs that guide scientific activity will reveal an important philosophical underpinning. Gallagher asserts that this approach will ensure that gifted students are not only prepared to work, but are also able to experience "the exhilaration of discovery." She offers strategies and suggestions that are helpful in all science classes for gifted students.

The final chapter in the content section is Chapter 17, "Mathematics for High-ability Students." Chamberlin offers a rationale for teaching mathematics to adolescents, reviews the current empirical literature concerning secondary mathematics for gifted students, discusses teaching strategies appropriate for secondary classes in mathematics, presents challenging curricula, and addresses appropriate assessment. Chamberlin's view is that curricula for the gifted secondary mathematician should engage the student both in acceleration and enrichment activities. Problem solving must be implicit in all curricula, and authentic assessment should be used in coordination with norm- and criterion-referenced tests. Chamberlin asserts that real-life problems lend themselves to real-life assessment, which is very possible in the mathematics classroom. Chamberlin suggests a sequence of courses appropriate for secondary mathematics, arguing that all students are entitled to a challenging curriculum, and for the mathematically gifted, a challenging curriculum may be more necessary than for other students because much of the ordinary curriculum may seem mundane. The mathematically gifted can move through the curriculum more quickly than peers, but still appreciate the beauty and aesthetics of mathematics.

In Chapter 18, VanTassel-Baska brings her wealth of knowledge across all curriculum in gifted education to focus on the need for an affective curriculum at the secondary level. She argues that both curriculum and instructional approaches matter in addressing the affective needs of secondary gifted students. Concentrating on the Integrated Curriculum Model as a framework to tap into an understanding of emotional intelligence at the level of curriculum interventions, VanTassel-Baska offers lesson modules for easy implementation by facilitators who may be teachers or counselors.

VanTassel-Baska's chapter is important for curriculum for the gifted at the secondary level, and she states that addressing affective issues should be a major way to reach gifted adolescents, help them create meaning in their lives, relieve their anxieties about being gifted, and contribute to the development of strong peer networks for them.

In Chapter 19, Callahan outlines the strengths and weaknesses of program options for the gifted secondary student. Her understanding of programming options, her work with evaluation of gifted programs, and her research on both AP and IB for secondary students make Callahan's chapter a major contribution to this section of *The Handbook of Secondary Gifted Education.* Callahan begins by cautioning that the wide variations in conceptions of giftedness underlying each model and the differing goals and objectives of the models suggest that decisions about the appropriateness of a given program's options for secondary level gifted students must be based on the context of the school, the accepted beliefs about giftedness, and the values and goals of gifted education. Callahan suggests that in planning for gifted students at this level, educators must ask two questions, (1) What types of giftedness are accepted and valued by the community? and (2) What are the goals we have for providing educational programs to gifted students? Chapter 19 outlines a variety of program options available at the secondary level. In addition, Callahan urges that the most critical concern of all schools should be to evaluate the outcomes of the options that are offered.

In Chapter 20, "Extracurricular Activities," Calvert and Cleveland present evidence that extracurricular activities provide essential options and skills for gifted students at the secondary level in a variety of settings. Providing training opportunities in specific talent areas in an environment where achievement is generally valued, extracurricular activities may also provide a set of "metaskills" that enables talent to develop. Essential metaskills include the development of attention management, emotional self-regulation, and intrinsic enjoyment of work and activities related to the student's talent (Csikszentmihalyi, Rathunde, & Whalen, 1993). Calvert and Cleveland suggest that the benefits of extracurricular activities may be both direct and indirect in a gifted adolescent's life. The lists of extracurricular activities, the individual focus of types of activities, and Web sites and resources available for finding more information make this chapter useful for educators and students alike. Calvert and Cleveland offer practical information but do state that more research is needed on the effects of participation in extracurricular activities on gifted youth. For many gifted students at the secondary level, extracurricular activities provide the context that makes school bearable.

The final chapter in Part III of *The Handbook of Secondary Gifted Education,* Chapter 21, is Michael Sayler's chapter entitled, "Special Schools for the Gifted and Talented." Sayler's experience with gifted adolescents at the secondary level and his clear understanding of special schools make this chapter relevant and necessary to Part III. Sayler asserts that while schools address the needs of many students, most schools are unable to offer the diversity of courses and depth of learning necessary for those students whose needs exceed even the gifted program options. This chapter focuses on these special schools for the gifted, which have grown out of the advanced needs of some students; some because their potential or current performance exceeds that of other gifted students, others because their advanced needs are in areas that the local school does not or cannot address easily. Sayler reviews many of these schools, citing why they fill the needs of gifted students who are not easily served in regular high schools.

In sum, Part III is the longest part in this book. The chapters focus on the schooling options for gifted adolescents at the secondary level. Feldhusen (1997) stated that talented youth need the stimulation that can only come with advanced and enriched instruction, highly knowledgeable teachers, and equally talented/precocious peers. These issues are addressed in the chapters in Part III. Although certainly not exhaustive, the topics covered are essential for a book that focuses on the secondary gifted adolescent. Further, the practical suggestions for lessons that focus on the cognitive, personal, and social aspects of the adolescent (Moon & Dixon; see Chapter 1) are embedded in many of the chapters. One always wishes that a section could be longer, and in this section, it would have been good to include a chapter on the importance of foreign languages. However, the chapters included provide clear theoretical rationales, review empirical evidence, and offer practical suggestions. These are important elements of the life of a gifted adolescent at the secondary level and are worthy of our in-depth consideration.

REFERENCES

Csikszentmihalyi, M., Rathunde, K., & Whalen, S. (1993). *Talented teenagers: The roots of success and failure*. New York: Cambridge University Press.

Feldhusen, J. F. (1997). Secondary services, opportunities, and activities for talented youth. In N. Colangelo and G. Davis (Eds.), *Handbook of gifted education* (2nd ed., pp. 189–197). Boston: Allyn & Bacon.

Passow, A. H. (2004). Curriculum for the gifted and talented at the secondary level. In J. VanTassel-Baska (Ed.), *Curriculum for gifted and talented students* (pp. 103–113). Washington, DC: National Association for Gifted Children.

VanTassel-Baska, J. (2004). Introduction to curriculum for gifted and talented students: A 25-year retrospective and prospective. In J. VanTassel-Baska (Ed.), *Curriculum for gifted and talented students* (pp. xxiii–xxxii). Washington, DC: National Association for Gifted Children.

CRITICAL THINKING

CHAPTER 12

*A Foundation
for Challenging Content*

by Felicia A. Dixon

onsider the following vignettes from former students, as well as a renowned scholar:

> I discovered J. D. Salinger the other day and in the course of a week read all his novels. No doubt they are some of the best I have come across. I've also been trying to expose myself to a number of literary styles, reading Japanese and South American novels in translation. You often hear about the way in which Japanese wood block prints, etc. influenced visual artists in Europe, but rarely of the same in the literary world. I think it is pretty clear these influences did occur, though perhaps much later—50s or so. More than likely, I've just never heard it vocalized. —Seth

> I just wanted to let you know what has happened to me since graduation. I went to university for one year and then quit school. I moved in with my boyfriend and moved away. I actually began to get along with my parents after I moved out of their house. I do wish I hadn't quit school. But,

some things have to happen for other things to happen. A pretty vague philosophy, huh?

Now I'm working in an office, and it's boring. I was just thinking the other day, that in *Songs of Innocence* when he talks about the things that take away the innocence of childhood, he really means things like this dumb job. Tedious is the word I am thinking of. —Jenna

Maybe you don't remember me, but I graduated from the Academy in [1998] and took your literature courses all four semesters I was there. I went to Indiana University on a Wells Scholarship, did a journalism BA, and lived in India for a year after that. Now I am living in Texas and will be married this summer. I have just finished my first collection of short stories—not yet published, but I am working on that! Basically, I am writing to you because I want to continue sharing my writing with you. To this day, I base my knowledge and understanding of writing on what I learned and read in your courses. I especially keep close to my heart *Jane Eyre* and would like to send you a copy of my book, my homemade version thus far, and for that I just need to get your postal address. Hope you are doing well, and it'd be wonderful to hear from you. —Sadiyya

Today my history professor said in class that books had changed his life, and when I asked him after his lecture which books, he said that was private and refused to tell me. That seemed a strange attitude for a humanities teacher, but I guess it's not strange for a Harvard professor, sadly. I haven't had time to do much reading outside of classes, but I am writing (probably very bad, but oh well) fiction of my own, and volunteering in a battered women's shelter, which is the part of my life here that seems the most real to me. Also, I go to the art museum to see films, which I love. —Kate

The striking feature of Nash's paper is not its difficulty, or its depth, or even its elegance and generality, but rather that it provides an answer to an important problem. Reading Nash's paper today, one is struck most by its originality. The ideas seem to come out of the blue. There is some basis for this impression. Nash arrived at his essential idea—the notion that the bargain depended on a combination of the negotiators' back-up alternatives and the potential benefits of striking a deal—as an undergraduate at Carnegie Tech before he came to Princeton, before he started attending Tucker's game theory seminar, and before he had read von Neumann and Morgenstern's book. It occurred to him while he was sitting in the only economics course he would ever attend. —(Nasar, 1998, p. 90)

These glimpses of gifted adolescents, whether former students or renowned scholar John Forbes Nash, are interesting in the variety of issues they showcase.

While variability exists among the accounts, there is also a certain amount of consistency found in each. In examining characteristics of gifted adolescents, their obvious abilities suggest the types of activities that would provide academic experiences to match their cognitive ability. These students are unique, and yet they also share some interesting commonalities:

1. *Strong ability to analyze situations.* All of the gifted students in the vignettes above analyzed a situation of some sort. Seth analyzed his response to literary styles, while Jenna assessed her work situation. Both Sadiyya and Kate analyzed experiences in classes, and John Forbes Nash examined the thoughts behind his own essential idea. Whether in casual letters or in a description of a scholar in a class, analysis was a natural event.

2. *Synthesis leading to new ideas as a hallmark of their comments.* These vignettes clearly depict synthesis in action, as students combined a variety of sources to arrive at a novel idea of their own. Seth synthesized Japanese wood block prints and literary styles, concluding that clearly there was a definite influence, probably present after the 1950s. Jenna synthesized her tedious job with an idea suggested in Blake's *Songs of Innocence*, and Sadiyya synthesized her own experiences in a literature class and their influence on her own writing. Kate, an avid reader, sought to connect the history professor's comments about books changing his life with the life changes she was experiencing. Nash's synthesis of material he learned in his one economics class with his own ideas were clearly represented in Sylvia Nasar's account.

3. *Need to give the "big picture."* Most obvious concerning the idea of the "big picture" were the accounts of lived experiences—both good and bad. Kate's discouragement with her class was offset by her presentation of meaningful experiences, such as working at the battered women's shelter. Jenna's experiences and her disappointment with quitting school were offset by the realization that her parents were really OK, and Nasar's description of an eminent scholar's experience in an undergraduate class as the instigator of his award-winning theory were especially evident of accounts that provided a two-sided story.

4. *Admiration for high level challenge and assignments that are not busy work.* Seth's self-assignments, especially his completion of J. D. Salinger's works, and his pride in the accomplishment clearly showcased the power of challenge in academic work. Jenna's memory of *Songs of Innocence* reveals her appreciation of challenging work, while Sadiyya spoke of the influence she experienced in classes that challenged her to think. Nash was clearly impacted by ideas presented in his undergraduate economics class and what they meant to his own ideas.

5. *Ability to offer new perspectives on situations.* Seth's perspectives on art, both visual and literary, were refreshing and "new." Jenna's ideas about the loss of innocence in her own life offered a rather novel approach to her situation. Sadiyya, a journalist and world traveler, was most impressed with *Jane Eyre*, and Kate's ideas about a professor's public proclamations in a classroom and refusal to share experiences with students privately offered a new take on a familiar experience.

6. *Struggles in life and sensitivity to situations.* Jenna clearly struggled in her life choices and experienced some anxious moments as a result of quitting school and coping with a tedious job. Kate was very sensitive to the situation presented in her history class, and Sadiyya wanted to publish her book and hoped it would happen.

7. *Ability to cope with problems.* All of the students coped with problems and indicated their ability to do so. The most obvious was Kate, who had to return to class and deal with the professor's response to her after she had asked him to share his influential books. Jenna had to cope with the problem of being a very overqualified person in a nonchallenging job because she had decided to quit school. Seth contended with the problem of seeking to understand questions about literature in translation, and Nash coped with sorting through ideas presented in one class early on in his career and then applying these ideas later on when he needed them.

8. *Self-efficacy.* To accomplish the difficult tasks that confronted them, these gifted individuals had to believe they had the ability to do it. Clearly, to read Salinger in one week and challenge himself to think about the influence of wood block prints on literary style, Seth had to believe in his own capabilities to think through issues. Jenna knew she was overqualified and should not be working at the menial job in which she found herself, while Kate was efficacious in her volunteering for a battered women's shelter, knowing she could make a difference. Nash did not doubt his ability to combine ideas even at the beginning of his career, and Sadiyya knew she could write a book.

These vignettes present pictures of gifted individuals who were good critical thinkers. Their thinking was evident in the way they described their lives and their experiences. This chapter is about critical thinking and why it is essential in secondary gifted education. Students like the five presented here have the right to be in classes in which they are challenged to think.

THEORETICAL RATIONALE

Students who have high ability, that is, those whose cognitive performance exceeds the norm for their age group, must be challenged at their cognitive level for maximum educational value to be achieved. In this era of advanced technology, of greater expectations than ever before for performance accountability, and of post-Sept. 11 expectations for new ideas to solve different issues, schools must be vigilant in developing student talent. High-ability students are a natural resource. If these students who have clearly demonstrated their ability to go beyond the regular curricular expectations of all students are not given a different type of curriculum, they may languish in boredom in school and fail to develop their talent.

This situation can be prevented if teachers provide challenging and worthwhile tasks that foster maximum engagement and provide cognitive rigor. In observing students' out-of-school behavior, it is obvious that they engage in numerous activities from passively watching television, to actively participating in sports, to choosing challenging volunteer or work situations (Csikszentmihalyi, Rathunde, & Whalen, 1993). They may engage in a variety of extracurricular activities from early on in their educational careers. Their lives are not characterized by a one-size-fits-all paradigm. Rather, although patterns emerge that may describe a large subset of students, many often exhibit unique characteristics and seek activities that allow their uniqueness to grow and flourish. Gifted students are interested in different ideas, in different books, and in different ways of exploring ideas. Schools must foster this individual uniqueness, as well as attend to individual differences and provide differentiation in curriculum. Further, teachers must be chosen appropriately to teach these students and must understand their characteristics and be able to tailor assignments to their unique needs. Critical thinking is one of those unique characteristics of gifted students that must be understood and used both in the design of activities and in the choice of appropriate content for all courses (Dixon et al., 2004).

THE ADOLESCENT EXPERIENCE AND THINKING

This book is explicitly focused on the education of gifted adolescents, a group that is usually taken for granted educationally. Adolescents are expected to move through school and graduate. If they are "smart," they are expected to go on to a college or university and get on with their lives as productive citizens. If they are gifted, they are expected to do whatever they want and succeed. Although gifted students share some experiences with other adolescents, they are also unique in their advanced cognitive development.

In addition, being gifted does not ensure an easy and successful life, as was evident in some of the vignettes presented at the beginning of this chapter. The following general description of adolescence is a good point of departure:

> Adolescence is one of the most fascinating and complex transitions in the life span: a time of accelerated growth and change second only to infancy; a time of expanding horizons, self-discovery, and emerging independence; a time of metamorphosis from childhood to adulthood. The events of this crucially formative phase can shape an individual's life course, and thus the future of the whole society. (Carnegie Council on Adolescent Development, 1995, p. 7)

Regardless of advanced cognitive development, adolescence is a constant for middle and high school students. However, because the general assumption that everyone goes through the same events at the same time does not hold true for gifted students, school may not be an easy place for growth to occur.

Piaget's stage theory approach for cognitive development must be touched upon in light of gifted adolescents and their departure from the norm. In the late 1950s, Inhelder and Piaget (1958) found that, while adolescents could perform tests of reasoning skills (e.g., proportional reasoning, hypothetical reasoning, correlational reasoning, and systematic combination of items in a set), preadolescents could not. Inhelder and Piaget concluded that adolescents use formal operations (i.e., generalized abstract schemas or blueprints that enable them to solve abstract or hypothetical problems independent of their content). Before adolescence, students use concrete operations in which reasoning is tied to actual objects and their representations. For example, to combine chemicals to find a particular reaction, concrete thinkers use trial and error rather than devise a system. When they get a reaction, they stop, failing to consider the possibility that another combination might also produce the reaction (Kurfiss, 1988).

In contrast to average students, gifted students seem to move through these stages more rapidly, often demonstrating formal operational thinking at early ages (Sternberg & Williams, 2002). For example, Kanevsky (1992) compared young, high IQ children (in elementary school) matched in mental age with an older, average IQ group on the Tower of Hanoi game. Her study showed that the high IQ students were not only more efficient in the task, but were more likely to engage in strategies in which they imposed additional challenges on themselves by changing the rules of the exercise. In seeking to become more efficient problem solvers, these students improved their tactical skills in the course of solving the problem. Kanevsky's study indicates evidence that bright children possess distinct behaviors in the process of learning. Subsequently, Shore and Kanevsky (1993) provided a literature review in which they reported that gifted children, defined on the basis of IQ and high achievement, know more, know more about what they know, and know how to interconnect their accumulating knowledge better than do less able children. Not only do they know more, but they also have more strategies for applying what they know. Clearly, these students are engaging in formal operational thought. Maker (1982) suggested that gifted learners acquire more knowledge without much practice and are proficient at using information at higher levels.

Some argue that Piaget's stage theory stops short of the full picture of human thought; that there is a fifth stage, dialectical thinking, that better describes the mature thinker (Labouvie-Vief, 1980; Pascual-Leone, 1984; Riegel, 1973). This group of Neo-Piagetian scholars states that, as students mature through adolescence and into early adulthood, they recognize that most real-life problems do not have a unique solution that is correct while other solutions are incorrect. Rather, thinking evolves as individuals propose a thesis as a solution to a problem. Often someone else counters with an antithesis that directly contradicts the proposed thesis. Subsequently someone may propose a synthesis that integrates what had appeared to be two opposing and even irreconcilable points of view (Sternberg & Williams, 2002).

The dialectical system of reasoning dates back to the German philosopher, George Frederick Hegel. Hegel created a system of philosophy regarded as "unquestionably one of the most influential systems of thought in the nineteenth century" (Aiken, 1962, p. 271). He offered the dialectic, not only as a useful tool for thought, but also as a means for understanding history. Indeed, Hegel regards all change as historical and history itself as the dialectic employed in time. As such, it is, in effect, a great waltz-like movement, from thesis through antithesis to synthesis, with each step representing a still higher stage in the self-development of the absolute. Each historical movement, in negating its antecedent, at the same time takes up whatever is significant in it and preserves it as the aspect of a richer, more comprehensive social reality.

Hegel's system demands the study of contradictions, and this examination fits well with mature thought. As one person pronounces a judgment, he or she externalizes a standard that will direct and modify another person's judgment, which, once it too has been pronounced, will produce further modifications. Thus, these interactions form a process in which continuous fluctuation occurs and which only temporarily rests at the moments in which a pronouncement takes place.

According to Klaus Riegel (1973), such a process of evaluation and reevaluation characterizes the thoughts and judgments of mature persons. A commitment to Hegel enables people to reinterpret Piaget's theory with due consideration to mature and critical thinking. Because gifted adolescents are advanced in many of their operations (Colangelo, Assouline, & Gross, 2004; Davidson, Davidson, & Vanderkam, 2004), this fifth stage of thinking may appropriately describe how they process information. Indeed, they may be ready to develop dialectical thinking in adolescence, in advance of their average ability peers. However, Neo-Piagetians suggest that people might reach dialectical maturity without ever having passed through the period of formal operations or even through that of concrete operations. This provision for gifted adolescents addresses asynchronous development, as well as interindividual variation at the individual level of maturity.

Finally, in their study of talented teenagers, Csikszentmihalyi et al. (1993) wrote, "It is during adolescence and young adulthood that many individuals who seem destined for great futures in the arts or the sciences seem to lose interest and settle for careers that require average skills" (p. 1). These authors suggest that how a person invests the limited time at his or her disposal is an important question. Equally important, however, is how a person experiences the events of daily life. For adolescents, most of the year is spent in school. If school means unresponsive classes that are unconcerned with differentiation for gifted teens, gifted students are left with two choices: create one's own challenges or languish in boredom in school.

REVIEW OF CURRENT EMPIRICAL LITERATURE

Definitions of Critical Thinking

Part of the problem with a discussion of critical thinking is defining the term. Many people have embraced a program as a definition. In other words, as elementary students, gifted children have been exposed to TAG or some other popular name for a gifted program in which they are pulled out of their class to do "critical thinking" activities. An actual definition of what they are doing is often not available. In addition, they may be "doing Bloom's" on Friday, which usually signifies that they are concentrating on analysis, synthesis, and evaluation activities. But, the definition of what constitutes analysis, synthesis, and evaluation activities is nebulous at best. Critical thinking activities in pullout enrichment programs often are accomplished through worksheets that may be reproduced easily for quick use (Cox, Daniel, & Boston, 1985). In fact, Reis and Burns (1991) state that "many thinking skills activities in academically talented education programs seem to suffer from an abundance of puzzles, games, and worksheets, and a shortage of teaching, transfer, and relevance" (p. 72).

Explicit definitions of critical thinking do exist. Ennis (1985) wrote that critical thinking is reasonable and reflective thinking that is focused on deciding what to believe or do. His definition gives both behaviors (reasoning, reflecting, and deciding) and outcomes (beliefs and actions) that result. Paul and Elder (2001) state that critical thinking is comprised of three phases: the ability to analyze thinking, the ability to assess thinking, and the ability to improve thinking. Therefore, when an individual thinks critically, he or she is analyzing, evaluating, and being creative. Critical thinking is described here as clear steps that seem to occur progressively. Indeed, both Ennis and Paul and Elder have emphasized that a major facet of critical thinking involves examining assumptions that underlie thought and action.

John Dewey (1933) coined the term "critical thinking," defining it as "active, persistent, and careful consideration of any belief or supposed form of knowledge in the light of the grounds that support it and the further conclusions to which it tends" (p. 9). Dewey preferred to call this form of thinking reflective thinking, and unlike many of the other developers of theories of critical thinking, he did not suggest a series of steps to use in the process. Instead, he suggested that it was more of a disposition that included living with uncertainty and risk taking.

Halpern (1984) defined critical thinking as directed thinking and elaborated that critical thinking involved a purpose or a goal toward which it is directed. She differentiated critical thinking from other types of thinking that are routine and do not focus on a purpose. Problem solving, making an inference, or making a decision require critical thinking.

Perhaps the most directional definition in terms of how to teach critical thinking based on its attributes is the one offered by Kurfiss (1988): "Critical thinking is an investigation whose purpose is to explore a situation, phenomenon, question, or problem to arrive at a hypothesis or conclusion about it that integrates all available information and that can therefore be convincingly justified" (p. 2). It is a rational response to questions that cannot be answered definitively and for which all the relevant information may not be available. Further, in critical thinking, all assumptions are open to question, divergent views are aggressively sought, and the inquiry is not biased in favor of a particular outcome.

The array of definitions showcases the fact that critical thinking is considered important. But, the essential question is, does it actually improve learning for students in general and gifted students specifically? This author answers yes, unequivocally. Critical thinking is essential in all disciplines in order for gifted students to maximize their gifts. For gifted students who think critically both inside and outside the classroom and have since they arrived on the school steps on their first day, critical thinking fits their cognitive processes. Without it, classes are boring, activities are dumbed down, and school is generally not worth the effort.

Colangelo et al. (2004) write the following about the picture of American schools:

American high schools are becoming hiding places for a lot of untapped academic talent. Despite all those popular movies that show one lonely scholar in a huge gray suburban high school, researchers are finding surprisingly large numbers of students who can steamroll through high school in record time. . . . Clearly these students require our attention. Their performance, year after year, proves that we need to find challenges for them. . . . Typical teenagers are thinking about parties, friends, and love relationships. But studies show that academically gifted students are thinking about these issues and something else, too. They're thinking about thinking. They want to be challenged academically. They love learning and they love many subjects. And they require a different curriculum, a curriculum planned for the motivated and highly able student. (p. 1)

Whether through radical acceleration in content or through the opportunity to use critical thinking process skills in their courses, gifted students respond to challenges and require them (Colangelo et al., 2004).

Empirically Validated Studies on Critical Thinking

It is not easy to find reports of studies with empirical evidence for gains in critical thinking. Further research in this area concerning gifted adolescents' thinking is needed. The next portion of this review delineates those available.

The National Assessment of Educational Progress (NAEP; U.S. Department of Education, 2000) provides some empirical evidence that suggests that although basic skills have their place in pedagogy, critical thinking skills are essential. In mathematics and science at both the fourth- and eighth-grade levels, practices that emphasize critical thinking skills are associated with higher student achievement. Apparently, students learn even simple content more effectively if they understand the conceptual framework that lies behind that content. Based on these data, Wenglinsky (2004) suggests that teachers should introduce advanced skills in math and science early to motivate students to learn these subjects effectively. If this is the case for regular students in grade-level situations, the necessity for gifted students who need challenging material is evident.

Evidence from the Trends in International Mathematics and Science Study (TIMSS; Stigler & Hiebert, 1999) provides support for using critical thinking in classrooms. Stigler and Hiebert analyzed videotapes of classes in the United States, Germany, and Japan. They found that Japanese eighth-grade teachers were more likely to emphasize critical thinking by having students fashion their own solutions to problems and by introducing advanced material (e.g., algebra) at a relatively early stage. Overall, Japanese students outperformed their U.S. and German counterparts in mathematics.

Dixon (1996) found that gifted students trained in the Hegelian Dialectic as a heuristic for critical thinking performed significantly better in writing essays than gifted students in a control group. As they used the Hegelian Dialectic to analyze literature, they were able to suggest a thesis, counter with an antithesis, and arrive at a synthesis. Their writing was clear and critical thinking was evident in their work.

Dixon, Cassady, Cross, and Williams (2005) found gender specific gains in critical thinking in essays. Specifically, boys who used computers to write their essays received higher ratings on a structured rubric than those boys who wrote their essays without computers. Girls scored the same in both conditions and performed consistently at a level on par with the boys using computers.

At the collegiate level, early longitudinal studies of critical thinking in education indicated that education does influence reasoning about everyday questions, such as bias in the news and evaluation of food additives. However, only graduate students seem to recognize that different points of view can be compared and evaluated through contextual reasoning (King, Kitchener, & Wood, 1985). Perkins (1985) found that depth of argument on controversial issues is minimal and increases marginally as a result of college instruction. Seniors are more adept than freshmen at evaluating position papers, but their overall level of performance is low. Compared to freshmen, seniors in liberal arts and engineering are more aware of evidence in reasoning, but they still believe judgment is a matter of individual idiosyncrasies (Welfel, 1982). College students make judgments on the basis of unexamined personal preferences (Belenky, Clinchy, Goldberger, & Tarule, 1986; Welfel, 1982).

In general, most studies indicate that critical thinking can be improved with increased practice. The idea that it has to be taught to all is somewhat interesting. The behaviors involved in critical thinking seem to align themselves well with analytic, synthetic, and evaluative thinking. If gifted students perform these types of operations as characteristics or manifestations of their giftedness, then their behaviors on standardized assessments and in classroom discussions (whether pleasant or not) are consistent indicators of successful thought. Teaching them to think seems less important than teaching to their thinking. The remainder of the chapter concentrates on strategies and models across disciplines that focus on critical thinking and are appropriate for gifted students.

STRATEGIES

Kurfiss (1988) suggests several general principles for teachers to use as guides as they construct activities that teach to thinking:

1. Critical thinking is both a learnable skill and an improvable skill. The instructor and peers are resources in developing critical thinking skills.
2. Problems, questions, or issues are the point of entry into the subject and a source of motivation for sustained inquiry.
3. Successful courses balance challenges to think critically with support tailored to students' developmental needs.
4. Courses are assignment-centered rather than text- and lecture-centered. Goals, methods, and evaluation emphasize using content rather than simply acquiring it.

5. Students are required to formulate and justify their ideas in writing or other appropriate modes.
6. Students collaborate to learn and to stretch their thinking, for example, in pair problem solving and small group work.
7. Several courses, particularly those that teach problem-solving skills, nurture students' metacognitive abilities.
8. The developmental needs of students are acknowledged and used as information in the design of the course. Teachers in these courses make standards explicit, and help students learn how to achieve them. (pp. 88–89)

To fully appreciate these principles and how they align with gifted education, consider the following suggestions for systematic tailoring of the curriculum suitable for meeting the needs of gifted students. Curriculum should include:

- provisions for acceleration and compression of content;
- use of interrelated higher order thinking skills (e.g., analysis, synthesis, and evaluation);
- integration of content by key ideas, issues, and themes;
- advanced reading level of materials employed;
- opportunities for students to develop advanced products;
- opportunities for independent learning based on student capacity and interest; and
- consistently focused use of inquiry-based instructional techniques. (VanTassel-Baska & Little, 2003, pp. 14–15)

These two sets of guidelines should help the teacher modify curriculum to meet the needs of gifted students whether they are in self-contained gifted classes (in high school these are usually designated as honors or Advanced Placement classes) or classes designated as academic (usually for students who plan to further their education after high school). If curriculum is not appropriately modified for gifted students by the time they reach high school, they have already learned that they can do their homework on the bus on the way to school or that it doesn't make any sense to ask questions because they already know more than the teacher anyway. These are sad indictments on secondary education, but these issues are prevalent. Hence, teachers must modify curriculum. Even in a prepared curriculum, such as Advanced Placement or International Baccalaureate programs, teachers must use strategies like the ones suggested by Kurfiss (1988) and VanTassel-Baska and Little (2003) in order to engage students.

The following strategies can be used with gifted students in both middle and high schools. If the school has adopted block scheduling, the extra time with peers allows for a more in-depth pursuit of the issues being discussed. These strategies are especially relevant to gifted students in homogenous classes. Every discipline can use these particular strategies, but the specific examples in this chapter come from humanities classes. All strategies address the lists of guidelines (Kurfiss, 1988; VanTassel-Baska & Little, 2003) offered at the beginning of this section. These four strategies are constructivist in nature in that they allow students to construct knowledge (Biehler & Snowman, 1997). However, it is important to note that a good lecture can engage students in critical thinking, as well. But, lectures must be prepared carefully and used sparingly so that the wealth of knowledge present in the classroom can be shared. If one thinks of middle and high school classes for gifted students as thinking communities, then the result is learning for all.

Strategy 1: Problem-Based Learning

Problem-based learning (PBL; Stepien, Gallagher, & Workman, 1993) is an excellent strategy for use with both middle and high school students. Students work through their curricula (either in its entirety or in selected problems) in the form of ill-structured problems. They are presented an ill-structured problem in an engaging way that piques interest and motivates them to learn. The textbook becomes one of several research tools to examine the problem effectively. Students usually engage in the problem-solving process by moving through four distinct phases: engagement in the problem, inquiry and investigation, problem solution, and debriefing. All students receive the same problem, but depending on their existing knowledge, they may approach the phases leading to a solution in vastly different ways. The actual problem presented is very important to initiate this strategy.

An ill-defined problem has the following characteristics (Stepien et al., 1993):

1. The problem is presented as a messy situation rather than a perfectly presented problem statement.
2. The problem is complex and embedded with a variety of information, which is not necessarily presented sequentially. This necessitates a variety of potentially different searches on different aspects of the problem within the same class.
3. The problem may have many distracters in it, which means it is essential for students to define what the problem means.
4. There is more than one answer to the problem; the important idea is that the resolution to the problem must make sense and be well supported.
5. The problem becomes clearer as students work on it and investigate it thoroughly.

Teachers can build a problem into their curriculum to add interest, or they can completely restructure their whole curriculum around ill-structured problems. Knowing how much time they have to devote to a problem sets the parameters for the length of time students have to engage in each separate part. Indeed, deciding how to present the solution can be left to individual groups of students or can be stipulated by the teacher at the beginning of the problem. An example of an ill-defined problem, the Shetland Island Problem, is presented in Figure 1. For a complete description of the merits of this strategy, see Stepien et al. (1993).

Before leaving this strategy, it is essential to discuss the importance of the debriefing phase. If left out, teachers may lose an important glimpse into the individual

You are the mayor of the Shetland Islands. It is June 23, 1995, and you have just been approached by the CEO of Shell Oil and the Director of Greenpeace concerning the Brent Spar Oil Spill. You have a town meeting in two days prompted by an angry group of citizens who want the Brent Spar dismantled as far away as possible. Everyone is frustrated and angry; your family has received death threats; and CNN is camped outside the door.

Figure 1. Shetland Island Problem

student's analysis of his or her own thinking process. This chance to openly encourage metacognition in the classroom is essential for the critical thinking process and is very important for students as they evaluate how they processed the problem.

Finally, assessment is an authentic companion to this strategy. Any part or phase of the problem can be assessed with a written analysis turned in by the group or by the use of a rubric completed by either the teacher or the group members. In addition, students can web or graphically represent any part of this process. The inquiry and investigation phase can be assessed with these same measures or with e-mails turned in daily by the students. The teacher may assign the form of the final solution presentation, or students may choose a variety of ways to present, depending on the problem. Finally, a formal debriefing can be held with a written product as the result, or a group discussion with certain points addressed can transpire. The more input the students have into the form of evaluation, the better.

The only weakness of this strategy may be the class time required to do it. As with any constructivist strategy, students deliberate and construct responses to each phase. The time to complete a problem may take more class sessions than a teacher would like to devote. However, for gifted students, the time spent doing both group work and independent work is well worth the extra time.

Strategy 2: The Dixon-Hegelian Process

Thesis, antithesis, and synthesis are the hallmarks of this strategy (Dixon, 1996; Dixon et al, 2004). Students constantly use these words as they interact with the curricular tasks. This strategy directly meets the needs of gifted students in providing a framework for class discussion, writing, and future reading activities. Figure 2 graphically presents the Dixon-Hegelian Process.

To use this strategy, the curriculum must be viewed as open to discussion and examination. Students are divided into groups in order to discuss the issue of interest for the day's class. However, it is also possible to assign the determination of the thesis as individual work to be shared later. Students discuss the entire reading and determine the most logical thesis they find for the reading. For example, if they read an assignment from a novel, they determine the overarching idea represented in the day's reading. If they are studying an historical event, they determine a thesis that describes the action involved in the event or what was accomplished by one of the

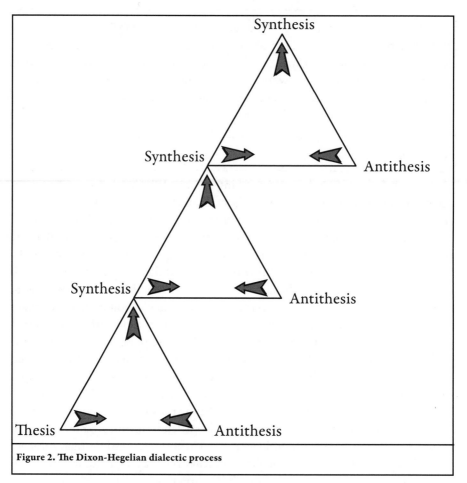

Figure 2. The Dixon-Hegelian dialectic process

interested parties. Groups must agree on a thesis before they present it to the whole forum for further analysis. Just as in writing, the thesis is the statement of the main idea. Since all groups report, groups have the right to question other groups' theses. The presenting group must then provide support from the text for their thesis. This dialogue between groups, as well as the initial dialogue within the group, is one of the positive aspects of this strategy. During this dialogue, the teacher is not the focal point of class; the students are dialoguing with each other.

Subsequently, students return to their groups to work on the antithesis that may be presented in the reading. The more widely read students are, the more interesting these discussions can be. Students who revel in discussing current events often find other perspectives presented either in the form of a thesis or its antithesis. Even if outside information is brought in, it is important that support come from the shared reading if possible. Again, students present their antitheses in the group forum for added discussion.

An alternate method to this strategy has half of the class work on a thesis and the other half work on an antithesis at the same time. To do this, the teacher must assign a character or group that represents a specific position. In science, when students are viewing alternate ways of understanding a situation or discovery, the various views can be examined by different students. This can be a productive way to have biased students confront their own biases, as they must present them rationally to the group for further examination.

Finally, students work through these two-sided issues to find a synthesis. If there is not one presented in the reading they have been assigned, they may suggest one of their own. When using this strategy with novels, synthesis may not be achieved until the entire book has been read. Sometimes students can individually predict a plausible synthesis given the ramifications of the reading. If they write their prediction in a journal, they can go back and check it when they have finished the book or chapter.

A logical extension for this process is writing. Since good writing is predicated on determining a thesis and supporting it to its conclusion, students who work with a thesis and antithesis regularly find their writing makes more sense. In addition, writing often reflects their critical thinking in a logical and systematic way. Hence, writing is a good assessment for this strategy. A second consistent assessment that matches the task is debate. Groups logically debate issues, finding support to advance their thesis. This can also be a means of assessment. As with problem-based learning, the more input the students have in determining the criteria used for assessment, the better.

If there is a weakness in this strategy, it would have to be overusing it so the students would cease to consider it important as a heuristic. Gifted students often become saturated with process strategies and need variety. This is a sound strategy, but must be used with other strategies for maximum effectiveness.

Strategy 3: The Treasure or Scavenger Hunt

Gifted students love to pursue clues. For that matter, most students enjoy mysteries. This strategy is based on the traditional treasure hunt format in which the teacher writes clues taken from the readings or assignments during a grading period or semester (Dixon, 1994). The following list of "rules" given out ahead of time help advance a productive treasure hunt:

1. You have been divided into groups to complete this treasure hunt. Each group must have one set of all the materials read for this grading period. Carry these with you in a backpack because you will need to refer to them to complete the hunt successfully.

2. You will be given a video camera to record your hunt. Everyone in the group must help solve the clues. In other words, one person cannot be the cameraperson the entire time because that would not allow him or her to participate in the activities suggested. Share the responsibility.

3. Each clue sends you to some reading you did during the semester. In addition, you will have a relevant activity to perform at each stop. Do both and record these.

4. At the end of the hunt, you must bring back all of the clues, create a map of the stops, and sequence them in the order that they were completed. Your map must be accurate and neat when you turn it in. You will also need to

name your group and create a slogan that you will chant as you are return-ing to the classroom. All materials must be returned in good order at the end of the hunt.

5. Accuracy and completeness are as important as time in this hunt. You are not competing with the other groups, so do not sabotage them by taking any clues other than your own.

6. Good luck and have fun.

From the author's perspective, this strategy tends to work well, and it has been used effectively in all disciplines. It has even been used in short-term courses of high interest. For example, it was used in a course that focused on the *Lord of the Rings*. The hunt took the form of a quest and all participants wore a "ring" (a plastic curtain ring wrapped with gold ribbon) for the duration of the hunt. At the end, the final action was to get rid of the ring at Mount Doom (in this case, a designated power plant at a Midwestern university). The motivation, interest, and attention to detail were evident in each group's map and videotape, which were the forms of assessment used.

The weakness in this strategy would be that it takes time to accomplish and time to write clues and distribute them. In addition, it may need to be completed outside of school so students can travel to the destinations to find the clues. Safety must be considered in all aspects. If teachers are willing to plan and implement the treasure hunt, it is an excellent example of synthesis in action.

Strategy 4: The Right Six Words

This is a very successful strategy to use with high-ability students in any disci-pline. The teacher must know what the important aspects of the lesson are and what he or she hopes the students will gain from the study of the lesson. That said, the strategy develops as follows:

1. Choose the catalytic six points you want to cover in the lesson (or any num-ber of words that covers the concept/reading for the day).

2. List these on the board at the beginning of class.

3. Begin by stating, "Where would you like to begin?"

4. Let the students choose where to begin the discussion. In order to do this, the teacher needs to know how to reorder the progress of the lesson. Gifted students will also know how to do this, but it helps if the teacher can foresee where the discussion is going.

5. Either proceed with a whole-class discussion, or divide the students into groups to discuss the words in the order the group finds most interesting. In other words, there are six ideas that must be covered; as long as they are covered, students may discuss them in any order. Convene at the end for a wrap-up to the lesson.

6. Often, students may become so wrapped up in the discussion that they do not finish all six terms. If that happens, and you do not want the lesson to

carry over to the next day, specify that they need to finish all six and then come back to their most interesting conversation if time permits.

7. Frequently the six terms can be integrated into the next day's lesson as a starting point.

This constructivist strategy can be used productively in humanities classes to cover major time periods or works (art history, history, or genres or quotations in literature). The author saw an adaptation used in an AP Physics class in which students were discussing electrical circuits. The term on the board was the formula that governed completing the circuit. Students discussed each term of the formula that was written on the board. This was an excellent example of analysis, synthesis, and evaluation, and the teacher guided the student discussion, never over-teaching. The teacher had a model on the lab station at the front of the class. When the students explained which term actually indicated the completion, the teacher had them come and complete the circuit by connecting the wires. The students were virtually responsible for the class content.

Assessment for this strategy could take the form of a collaborative rubric, constructed by the class as a whole at the beginning of the semester and modified as the semester progresses and the students become adept at using it in class. It is a classroom strategy, and the assessment should be formative to let the students know how they fare in both small and large group discussion. Assessment criteria should include participation and quality of issues raised concerning each of the points.

This strategy really depends on the environment of the individual class as to its effectiveness. In a 50-minute session with the right six words and high-ability students, the teacher may not finish all six. This requires that teachers are flexible enough to modify the strategy if they need to. If six are not enough, they need to add to the list. Teachers can use quotations, single words, characters, current events, formulas, definitions, or issues. Students should do the analysis and synthesis—the teacher should not do it for them. This is a great preparation for understanding text.

All four of these strategies are constructivist (Snowman & Biehler, 2000) and focus on critical thinking. Students synthesize material as they work through the curriculum. They assess themselves and learn the importance of evaluation. Further, they learn from each other as they work together. The result is a community of critical thinkers in secondary classrooms. It is important to note that at any time in the process, the teacher can step in and provide guidance through lecture, guided discussion, or other means of teaching targeted at deficiencies noticed. However, it is important for high-ability students to listen to each other and share strengths.

CONCLUSION

McKeachie, Pintrich, Lin, and Smith (1986) suggested that classrooms focus on regular discussions, problem-solving activities, and verbalization of metacognitive strategies to encourage critical thinking. According to Delisle (1997), gifted adolescents deserve to express their opinions and lifestyle choices. They want to succeed as surely as we want them to (albeit, in some different areas of focus), but are still teen-agers, concerned about zits, dates, cars, clothes, and college—despite their advanced intellects and stunning powers of mind. These characteristics held true for Seth, Jenna, Sadiyya, and Kate, the students presented at the beginning of this chapter, as they experienced school. The important aspect for teachers and other school personnel to consider is that challenging content, coupled with rigorous activities that demand critical thinking, are essential elements for talented teenagers in this post-Sept. 11 era.

REFERENCES

Aiken, H. D. (1962). *The age of ideology: The nineteenth-century philosophers.* Boston: Houghton Mifflin.

Belenky, M. F., Clinchy, B. M., Goldberger, N. R., & Tarule, J. M. (1986). *Women's ways of knowing: the development of self, voice, and mind.* New York: McKay.

Biehler, R., & Snowman, R.F. (1997). *Psychology applied to teaching* (8th ed.). Boston: Houghton Mifflin.

Carnegie Council on Adolescent Development. (1995). *Great transitions: Preparing adolescents for a new century.* New York: Carnegie Corporation of New York.

Colangelo, N., Assouline, S., & Gross, M. U. M. (2004). *A nation deceived: How schools hold back America's brightest students* (Vol. 2). Iowa City: The Connie Belin & Jacqueline Blank International Center for Gifted Education and Talent Development.

Cox, J., Daniel, N., & Boston, B. O. (1985). *Educating able learners: Programs and promising practices.* Austin: University of Texas Press.

Csikszentmihalyi, M., Rathunde, K., & Whalen, S. (1993). *Talented teenagers.* New York: Cambridge University Press.

Davidson, J., Davidson, B., & Vanderkam, L. (2004). *Genius denied.* New York: Simon & Schuster.

Delisle, J. R. (1997). Gifted adolescents: Five steps toward understanding and acceptance. In N. Colangelo and G. Davis (Eds.), *Handbook of Gifted Education* (pp. 475–482). Boston: Allyn & Bacon.

Dewey, J. (1933). *How we think.* (Rev. ed.). New York: Heath.

Dixon, F. A. (1994). Literature seminars for gifted and talented students. *Gifted Child Today, 16,* 12–16.

Dixon, F. A. (1996). *The use of the Hegelian Dialectic as a heuristic in literature classes to improve critical thinking skills.* Unpublished doctoral dissertation. Purdue University.

Dixon, F. A., Prater, K. A., Vine, H. M., Wark, M. J., Williams, T., Hanchon, T., et al. (2004). Teaching to their thinking: A strategy to meet the critical thinking needs of gifted students. *Journal for the Education of the Gifted, 28,* 56–76.

Dixon, F. A., Cassady, J. C., Cross, T. L., & Williams, D. (2005). Effects of technology on critical thinking and essay writing among gifted adolescents. Manuscript submitted for publication.

Ennis, R. H. (1985). Goals for a critical thinking curriculum. In A. Costa (Ed.), *Developing minds: A resource book for teaching thinking* (pp. 54–57). Alexandria, VA: Association for Supervision and Curriculum Development.

Halpern, D. (1984). *Thought and knowledge: An introduction to critical thinking.* Hillsdale, NJ: Erlbaum.

Inhelder, B., & Piaget, J. (1958). *The growth of logical thinking from childhood to adolescence.* New York: Basic Books.

Kanevsky, L. (1992). The learning game. In P. S. Klein & A. J. Tannenbaum (Eds.), *To be young and gifted* (pp. 204–241). Norwood, NJ: Ablex.

King, P. M., Kitchener, K. S., & Wood, P. K. (1985). The development of intellect and character: A longitudinal study of intellectual and moral development in young adults. *Moral Education Forum, 10*(1), 1–13.

Kurfiss, J. G. (1988). *Critical thinking: Theory, research, practice, and possibilities* (ASHE-ERIC Higher Education Report No. 2). Washington, DC: Association for the Study of Higher Education.

Labouvie-Vief, G. (1980). Beyond formal operations: Uses and limits of pure logic in life-span development. *Human Development, 23,* 141–161.

Maker, C. J. (1982). *Curriculum development for the gifted.* Rockville, MD: Aspen.

McKeachie, W., Pintrich, P., Lin, Y., & Smith, D. (1986). *Teaching and learning in the college classroom: A review of the research literature.* Ann Arbor, MI: National Center to Improve Postsecondary Teaching and Learning.

Nasar, S. (1998). *A beautiful mind: A biography of John Forbes Nash, Jr.* New York: Simon & Schuster.

Paul, R., & Elder, L. (2001). *Critical thinking: Tools for taking charge of your learning and your life.* Upper Saddle River, NJ: Prentice Hall.

Perkins, D. N. (1985). Postprimary education has little impact on informal reasoning. *Journal of Educational Psychology, 77,* 562–571.

Pascual-Leone, J. (1984). Attentional, dialectic, and mental effort. In L. M. Commons, F. A. Richards, & C. Armon (Eds.), *Beyond formal operations* (pp. 182–215). New York: Plenum.

Reis, S. M., & Burns, D. (1991). Developing a thinking skills component in the gifted education program. *Roeper Review, 14,* 72–79.

Riegel, K. F. (1973). Dialectical operations: The final period of cognitive development. *Human Development, 16,* 346–370.

Shore, B. M., & Kanevsky, L. (1993). Thinking processes: Being and becoming. In K. A. Heller, F. J. Mönks, and A. H. Passow (Eds.), *International handbook of research and development of giftedness and talent* (pp. 133–147). Oxford, England: Pergamon Press.

Snowman, J., & Biehler, R. (2000). *Psychology applied to teaching* (9th ed.). Boston: Houghton Mifflin.

Stepien, W. J., Gallagher, S. A., & Workman, D. (1993). Problem-based learning for traditional and interdisciplinary classrooms. *Journal for the Education of the Gifted, 16,* 5–17.

Sternberg, R. J., & Williams, W. M. (2002). *Educational psychology.* Boston: Allyn & Bacon.

Stigler, J. W., & Hiebert, J. (1999). *The teaching gap: Best ideas from the world's teachers for improving education in the classroom.* New York: Free Press.

U.S. Department of Education. (2000). *National assessment of educational progress 2000.* Washington, DC: Author.

VanTassel-Baska, J., & Little, C. A. (2003). *Content-based curriculum for high-ability learners.* Washington, DC: National Association for Gifted Children.

Welfel, E. R. (1982). How students make judgments: Do educational level and academic major make a difference? *Journal of College Student Personnel, 23,* 490–497.

Wenglinsky, H. (2004). Facts or critical thinking skills? What NAEP results say. *Educational Leadership, 62*(1), 32–35.

CREATIVE THINKING

CHAPTER 13

by Cheryll M. Adams
& Rebecca L. Pierce

ADOLESCENCE AND ADOLESCENTS' NEED FOR CREATIVE EXPRESSION

*T*he second decade of life is considered by Lerner and Steinberg (2004) to be the period of time associated with adolescence. Susman and Rogol (2004) identify several characteristics of adolescent development: emotional responses due to hormones, antisocial behavior, concern with body image, achievement related to maturation, heightened responses to peer network, and cognitive movement from inductive to deductive reasoning. Vygotsky suggests adolescents' overly critical attitudes lead them to abandon their creative efforts. He indicates creativity in adolescence reflects the transition from immature, childhood fantasies to mature creativity, showing an interaction between reasoning and imagination (Smolucha, 1992, p. 56).

Schools have a great impact on the development of adolescents (Eccles, 2004). At the classroom level Eccles states, "Teachers who trust, care about, and are respectful of students provide the social-emotional support that students need to approach, engage, and persist on academic learning tasks and to develop positive achievement-related self-perceptions and values" (p. 129). Furthermore, she suggests teachers use a variety of instructional practices to increase student motivation, such as designing activities that require a variety of cognitive operations, presenting a problem in multiple ways, and teaching students specific strategies. For many students, having a creative component as part of a learning activity promotes motivation and fosters achievement (Piirto, 1991). According to Sternberg and Lubart (1999), recent research shows that when students are given an opportunity to be creative, they may not choose to become disengaged from school instruction; instead, they may find their interest captured.

In a study of high school students, Damm (1970) found that students who received high scores on both intelligence and creativity measures were superior in self-actualization to those with high scores in only intelligence or only creativity or low scores in both. Based on his results, Damm argues that the curriculum should incorporate "both intellectual and creative abilities, rather than a concentration on one to the exclusion of the other (p. 569). As Feldman (1999) states, "the enduring belief that great creativity is developed alone, without assistance from teachers, mentors, peers and intimate groups is largely a myth" (p.176).

THEORETICAL RATIONALE FOR TEACHING CREATIVITY TO GIFTED ADOLESCENTS

What is creativity? That all depends to whom you have directed the question. Almost everyone who is prominent in the field of creativity defines it in a relatively different manner (Amabile, 1983; Csikszentmihalyi, 1996; Sternberg, 1999; Torrance, 1988). Creativity is hard to define, and we might go so far as to say that its definition depends on the context. It may be defined as a process, a product, as the content, or even as a personality condition. According to Piirto (2004), "Creativity is in the personality, the process, and the product within a domain in interaction with genetic influences and with optimal environmental influences of home, school, community and culture, gender, and chance. Creativity is a basic human need to make new" (p. 37). Creativity is the opposite of conformity. It is relatively safe to say that there is no succinct definition of creativity that will be agreeable to everyone. For our purposes, we prefer to use the definition Paul Torrance (1988) calls his "research definition." This process definition was chosen by Torrance because he could address person, product, and environment through process.

> I tried to describe creative thinking as the process of sensing difficulties, problems, gaps in information, missing elements, something askew; making guesses and formulating hypotheses about these deficiencies; evaluating and testing these guesses and hypotheses; possibly revising and retesting them; and finally communicating the results. (Torrance, 1988, p. 47)

Eminent creativity, or creativity with a "Big C," is synonymous with the concept of genius. The "Big C" creative person is eminent, well-known within a domain (e.g., mathematics) and a field (e.g., the gate keepers of the mathematics), while a "little c" creative person is not (Csikszentmihalyi, 1996; Simonton cited in Kersting, 2003; Sternberg & Lubart, 1996). Genius is not a subject that is taught, but an innate attribute of a person. Consequently, in this chapter we are discussing "little c" creativity, which is everyday creativity by ordinary people.

Why Teach Creativity to Adolescents?

Now that we have a definition, what place does creativity have in teaching gifted adolescents? It is a topic that should be introduced to children in elementary school and continue to be developed and explored by students in a variety of middle and high school courses. A number of authors believe that creativity can be developed and have created instructional materials for this purpose (see Baer, 1997; Eberle, 1987; Gordon, 1981; Parnes, 1981; Sternberg & Williams, 1996; Torrance & Safter, 1990; Treffinger, Isaksen, & Dorval, 2000; Williams, Markle, Brigockas, & Sternberg, 2002). As evidence that creativity training for elementary and secondary students has had some success in promoting creative production, Torrance (1987) offers these five indicators:

1. sense of well being in the participants;
2. improvements in attitude toward school subjects, such as mathematics;
3. decisions made by the students to follow creative pursuits or careers;
4. an increase in type and length of creative writing; and
5. improvement in self-concept. (p. 113)

Scholars generally recognize the unique characteristics of the gifted and often structure the curriculum around their needs based on these characteristics. Characteristics such as productivity, independent thought, persistence, concern for the future, imagination, and curiosity imply needs that may be addressed through the addition of creativity into the program. It should be noted that many creative adolescents exhibit personality traits that may be viewed as negative, such as being disorganized, uncooperative, or rebellious (Davis, 1986).

What teachers do in the classroom is vital to the development of students' creativity. Teachers play an important role as facilitators of their students' creativity (Cropley, 1994; Fishkin, Cramond, & Olszewski-Kubilius, 1999; Lynch & Harris, 2001; Runco, 1990; Sak, 2004; Sternberg, 1999). Cropley's model of teachers' behaviors that are necessary to foster students' creativity in the classroom includes three aspects: teacher as role model, a classroom atmosphere that fosters positive risk taking, and instructional activities that foster and reward creativity.

Why Teach Creativity in the Classroom?

Why are we interested in teaching creativity in a content area, such as science? Cross (1990) points out that there is a mismatch between how scientists actually do science and how we describe the process of science in our classrooms. We are spending too much time learning about the products of science and little time on the processes that allowed the products to happen (Cross; Pollack, 1988; Root-Bernstein, 1989; Yager, 1992). Pollack explains that "the statement of science is the testable prediction. The creative event of science is the demonstration that the prediction was correct" (p. 15). So creativity in science plays out in the process of actually doing science and thinking about solving problems, not simply reading about science. The same can be said about the learning of language arts, history/social studies, mathematics, and other content areas.

We're not advocating throwing away the texts and ignoring content in favor of process. We can't have one without the other. However, in many classrooms we are spending too much time on content to the near exclusion of process. Let us anticipate your protests at this point. "But, I teach science processes," you say. "Isn't that the 'scientific method' that is in all our texts?" Our answer is, "Yes and no." Yes, the scientific method is in nearly every science text and we require our students to memorize the steps. But, there are two flaws in this approach. First, there is no one process that could be called *the* scientific method, but many methods that scientists use to solve problems. Second, we usually teach the method in our texts as a set of steps—a linear process. In fact, the process of doing science is cyclical. The various stages feed back into each other many times before the problem is solved. A similar argument can be made for problem solving in any other content area.

Looking back at Torrance's definition of creativity, we see that he characterizes it in terms of creative thinking. Creative thinking, as he describes it, is similar to the processes practicing professionals work through as they solve problems. Assouline and Lupkowski-Shoplik (2003) and Brandwein (1988) suggest that creativity and process play major roles in identifying and nurturing those students who are gifted and talented. They advise that paper and pencil creativity tests and IQ tests will not necessarily help us find these students. Other factors such as personality traits, competency in a content area, and previous opportunities to practice the skills of a content area are not reflected in the scores on these tests. They state that actually working successfully through the process of a content area as a professional would is a sign of talent in the content area.

In the classroom we can't separate process from content, product, affect, and environment. The same holds true in a discussion of creativity. We look at the creative process within a context of personality, product, and environment. A few examples will show more closely what is meant by looking at personality, process, product, and environment:

> When asked to comment how one of her stories came into existence because of its literary worth, Dorothy Canfield commented, "The chance, remote as it might be of usefulness to students, would outweigh this personal consideration. What is more important is the danger that some students may take the explanation as a recipe or rule for the construction of other stories, and I totally disbelieve in such rules or recipes." (Ghiselin, 1981, p. 168)

> Henri Poincaré, after 15 days of trying to prove there couldn't be a particular set of functions, Fuchsian functions, drank black coffee and couldn't

sleep. He states, "Ideas rose in crowds; I felt them collide until pairs inter-locked, so to speak, making a stable combination. By the next morning, I had established the existence of a class of Fuchsian functions, those which come from the hypergeometric series; I had only to write out the results, which took but a few hours," (Ghiselin, 1981, p. 36).

Fleming himself told another biographer that "I was just playing" when he discovered penicillin. And, in 1945, shortly after receiving his Nobel Prize, Fleming said again, "I play with microbes. There are, of course, many rules to this play . . . but when you have acquired knowledge and experience it is very pleasant to break the rules and to be able to find something nobody had thought of," just as he often did in his games (Root-Bernstein, 1989, p. 147).

The Importance of Parents and Teachers

From studies of eminence (Bloom, 1985; Goertzel, Goertzel, Goertzel, & Hansen, 2004; Simonton, 1987, 1988), we have learned the importance of the role of parents on their children's creative potential. Families and special teachers provide the background and subject knowledge necessary to master a particular area while supporting a child's creative production. Bireley and Genshaft (1991) remind us that some gifted creative adolescents "will be lost to themselves and to society if they do not receive assistance dealing with problems emanating from family needs, self-imposed pressures, or the weight of the burden that society unwittingly places on those who seem to 'have it all'" (p. 14).

REVIEW OF THE CURRENT EMPIRICAL LITERATURE

As we stated previously, there is no agreed upon definition of creativity, and as Jackson and Messick (1965) indicate, the construct itself is hard to define: "It is well to remember that theories of creativity are themselves creative products. As such, they must abide by the same laws as those they are designed to unearth . . . The day on which we are certain about how to construct a theory of creativity will also be the day on which we are certain about how to construct a poem" (p. 328).

Sternberg and Lubart mention in their 1996 article that there is very little empirical research in the area of creativity. Guilford (1950) said that less than two-tenths of 1% of *Psychological Abstracts* up to 1950 focused on creativity. Sternberg and Lubart analyzed the number of references in *Psychological Abstracts* from 1975 to 1994 and found that approximately one half of 1% of the articles listed dealt with creativity. However, they feel the study of creativity is just as important as the study of intelligence because it is through creativity that people are able to find novel solutions to everyday problems. Most universities and teacher education programs lack formal courses on creativity. Creativity receives only a brief introduction in psychology texts.

A review of the literature revealed very little evidence of empirical research dealing with creativity and giftedness. Most studies addressed divergent thinking strategies and few included gifted adolescents. Creative problem solving appears to have the most empirical research indicating its effectiveness (Cramond, Martin, & Shaw, 1990; Feldhusen & Clinkenbeard, 1986; Parnes & Brunelle, 1967; Rose & Lin, 1984; Schack, 1993; Torrance, 1987). Researchers still do not agree about the extent of teachers' knowledge concerning the characteristics of creative students or about how teachers foster students' creativity in the classroom (Alencar, 1993; Cropley, 1994; Fleith, 2000; Fryer & Collings, 1991; Gentry, Rizza, & Owen, 2002; Mayfield, 1979; Rash & Miller, 2000; Starko, 1995; Tan, 2001). One small study asks students to compare their recognition by teachers at school for having creative ideas with the recognition by the instructors in the Torrance Creative Scholars Program. The proportion of students who felt that recognition given to creative ideas in their home schools was 33%, while 76% indicated that recognition was given to creative ideas in the Creative Scholars Program. For second year creative scholars, the proportions were 27% and 84% on the same variables (Parker, 1998). The program has as its primary purposes the identification and nurturance of creative potential. To qualify for the program students must have completed any grade 4–8 and score at or above the 87 percentile on either the Creative Average or the Creative Index of the Torrance Test of Creative Thinking.

CHALLENGING CURRICULUM

Plucker and Beghetto (2003) suggest that there is a lack of creativity in creativity education, including creativity curriculum. However, Plucker and Runco (1999) conclude that "In response to the question, 'Can creativity be enhanced?' the best answer is yes, because creative potentials can be fulfilled. Efforts to enhance creativity will not expand one's in-born potentials but can ensure that potentials are maximized" (p. 670). Most packaged creativity programs (e.g., Creative Problem Solving) and strategies to enhance creative thinking (e.g., SCAMPER) focus largely on developing divergent thinking. What once were novel approaches for enhancing creative thinking now lack originality. Plucker and Beghetto suggest three possible causes for this stagnation over the last few decades: the overemphasis and misunderstanding of "Big C" creativity; over-emphasis on psychometric approaches to the study of creativity, using divergent thinking as an outcome variable; and the isolation of research efforts in the areas of creativity and innovation in gifted education.

To solve the above problems and to keep creativity education creative, Plucker and Beghetto (2003) suggest the following:

- Distinguish between the kind of creativity that is being emphasized (i.e., Big C versus little c) and be certain not to overemphasize Big C conceptions in the training.
- Dispel the numerous myths, misconceptions, and stereotypes about creativity and creative individuals and organizations.

- Scrutinize the claims and the theoretical and empirical support of the growing number of "popular" creativity training programs.
- Do not neglect the importance of divergent thinking in training, but rather balance the training of divergent thinking with the training of convergent thinking and other noncognitive aspects of creativity.
- Consider the use of problem-based learning and other approaches that are based on systems theories of creativity.
- Search for and apply innovative approaches from various fields to help guide students' creative endeavors.

In applying the systems model of creativity to schools, Csikszentmihalyi and Wolfe (2000) define domain as the body of knowledge to be transmitted, teachers who control the knowledge as the field, and students as the individuals. At the individual level, they indicate six implications for educational practice:

- students' curiosity and interest are the main sources of potential creativity,
- potential creativity is enhanced by intrinsic motivation and suppressed by excessive reliance on extrinsic rewards,
- activities need to be designed with the conditions necessary for flow in mind,
- learning to formulate problems should be part of the curriculum,
- respecting creative personality traits, and
- promoting the internalization of learning.

At the level of the domain, they suggest several questions that teachers should consider:

- How attractive is the information presented to students?
- How accessible is the information?
- How integrated is the information?
- Are there opportunities for mentorships and apprenticeships?

In the educational application of the systems model, teachers are considered the field since they assess the ideas and products of students. Csikszentmihalyi and Wolfe (2000) suggest five questions teachers should answer to operate as a field:

- Does the school have the material resources to foster creativity?
- How open are teachers to new ideas?
- Do teachers stimulate students' curiosity and interest?
- Can teachers distinguish good new ideas from bad ones?
- Are there ways of implementing student creativity in the school?

Hence, for creativity to exist in schools these three elements, the individual, the domain, and the field, must work in concert with each other.

Plucker and Beghetto (2003) cite problem-based learning (PBL) as one promising approach to creativity education. PBL (for a complete discussion of PBL see Delisle, 1997; Lambros, 2004; Torp & Sage, 1998) is an approach that uses real-world problems as a springboard to the acquisition of new knowledge. These problems are fuzzy, messy, interdisciplinary, and allow for multiple solutions. The problems create new learning experiences and the reinforcement of existing knowledge. The real-world nature of the problem encourages students to take on a specific role in the scenario, and the ownership that students feel while working with the problem is particularly important to adolescents. A characteristic of gifted adolescents is that they need opportunities to determine their own learning needs and the student-centered nature of PBL allows them this chance. As students determine what they need to know to solve the problem, the teacher responds with mini lessons to address these needs. Plucker and Beghetto indicate several advantages of PBL for enhancing creativity education. First, the real-world problems model the systems theories of creativity. Second, PBL is "little c" creativity-focused. Third, the interdisciplinary nature encourages students to access other information sources. Fourth, the PBL approach is flexible.

While PBL appears to be an effective approach to developing student talent and creativity (Barron et al., 1998; Gallagher & Stepien, 1996; Krajcik et al., 1998; Reis & Renzulli, 1999; Renzulli & Reis, 1994), creativity was generally not considered as an outcome of the PBL activities. On the other hand, others found that students engaged in PBL activities gained more content knowledge, as well as creative skills, including a greater understanding of the creative process (Gorman, Plucker, & Callahan, 1998; Plucker & Gorman, 1995, 1999; Plucker & Nowak, 2000).

Another recent addition is the Creative Intelligence for School Program (CIFS; Williams et al., 2002), which is a tool, inspired by the theories of Sternberg and Gardner, specifically designed for middle and high school students. The authors deem it equally appropriate for both levels. CIFS consists of 21 lessons designed to teach students basic skills and methods to become more creative. Teachers may choose to use the entire set of lessons over one semester or a whole year, or they may choose to use only a few of the lessons. The authors see CIFS as different from other creativity programs because it emphasizes "specific skills, outlooks, and abilities that underlie creative performance. CIFS is an intensive course on how to open a student's mind and potential and release her or his creativity" (p. 2). There are lessons such as Why Be Creative?, Somebody Created That!, When *Not* to Be Creative, and Creativity in Everyday Occupations. The program focuses on four basic steps for developing creativity:

1. Remove barriers to creativity by *increasing* motivation and self-efficacy.
2. Remove barriers to creativity by *decreasing* school and peer evaluation anxiety.
3. Encourage growth in creativity through training, experience, and practice.
4. Develop personal control, evaluation, and refinement of the creative process. (p. 6)

The program is advantageous, in that it was designed specifically for middle and high school students. Along with PBL, it is the nearest we have found to an actual

Table 1
Programs to Enhance Creative Thinking

Program	Grades	Web Address
Future Problem Solving	K–12	http://www.fpsp.org
DestinationImagiNation®	K–12	http://www.destinationimagination.org
Invention Convention	1–6	http://www.eduplace.com/science/invention
Science Olympiad	K–12	http://www.soinc.org
Creative Problem Solving	K–12	http://www.creativelearning.com
deBono's CoRT & Six Thinking Hats	K–12	http://www.edwdebono.com

creativity curriculum, and the skills learned can be used to solve problems across the content areas, as well as those that are practical or social.

Other commercial and competitive programs designed to enhance creative thinking are featured in Table 1. However, like PBL and CIFS, these programs fall short of providing a comprehensive curriculum for creativity but are good venues to stimulate creative processes and products.

STRATEGIES USED TO IMPART CURRICULUM

According to Sternberg (1995/1996), there are 12 methods teachers can use to make students more creative:

1. Serve as a role model for creativity.
2. Encourage questioning of assumptions.
3. Allow mistakes.
4. Encourage sensible risk taking.
5. Design creative assignments and assessments.
6. Let students define problems themselves.
7. Reward creative ideas and products.
8. Allow time to think creatively.
9. Encourage tolerance of ambiguity.
10. Point out that creative thinkers invariably face obstacles.
11. Be willing to grow.
12. Recognize that creative thinkers need to find nurturing environments. (p. 81–84)

A number of instructional strategies have been developed and marketed for teachers to use to foster creative thinking in the classroom. We discuss several of these below. By using these methods teachers can address some or all of the items on Sternberg's list.

SCAMPER

The acronym SCAMPER represents the techniques of Substitute, Combine, Adapt, Modify/Magnify/Minify, Put to Other Uses, Eliminate, and Reverse/Rearrange. This instructional strategy had its start in the 1950s when Osborn (1953) provided checklists of questions to improve divergent thinking. Eberle (1987) arranged some of Osborn's questions into the acronym SCAMPER. SCAMPER can help students generate diverse ideas to solve problems, develop products, or stimulate creative imagination. An advantage of this strategy is that it can be used with all ages, including middle and high school students. For example, a physics teacher could encourage students to use the SCAMPER strategy to improve their science fair projects. Suppose a student wants to design a new invention. She may choose to adapt some existing materials, such as a garden hose, a Lazy Susan, a belt and a cup and brainstorm ways to put them to other uses.

Creative Problem Solving

Creative Problem Solving (CPS) has been developed over a period of more than 20 years by Osborn (1963), Parnes (1981), and Treffinger and Isaksen (1992). The Treffinger and Isaksen version contains six specific stages: Mess-finding, Data-finding, Problem-finding, Idea-finding, Solution-finding, and Acceptance-finding. Each stage begins with divergent thinking and concludes with convergent thinking. One feature of CPS during the problem-finding stage is to use the prompt "In what ways might we . . ." (IWWMW) to generate as many alternative problem statements as possible. During the convergent portion of this stage one statement must be selected. Firestien and Treffinger (1983) suggest the "Head and Shoulders" test as a method to focus on a problem statement. Simply put, "Does one of the problem statements stand head and shoulders above the others?" If the answer is yes, Firestien and Treffinger strongly consider this problem as the choice. For example, in a 10th-grade American Studies class, students work with CPS to determine "IWWMW improve America's image in today's world?"

Object Analogy

Object Analogy is another strategy to enhance creative thinking. Through analogy, everyday objects are used to help solve problems (Hanks & Parry, 1983). A student may define a problem such as, "How might I improve my study habits in order to become a better student?" The everyday object the student chooses is an AA battery. The student identifies each part of the battery and shows how it will help solve the problem. For example, Energizer™—put more energy into my school work; AA—work hard and get A+ grades; Eveready™—always be prepared for class; and so forth.

Attribute Listing

Attribute Listing (Crawford, 1954) fosters flexibility, originality, imagination, elaboration, and complexity, A problem or product is separated into its key attributes, each of which are addressed separately. By examining each key attribute, students then decide how each could be modified or combined to form a new product or to solve a problem. In a unit on inventions, students could develop new products from current ones. For example, the components (microchip, crystal, watch hands, etc.) of a quartz watch could be listed in one column, the characteristics in another, and the improvements in a third. A classic use of attribute listing is creative writing. With the current interest in space and science fiction, students could generate a list of situations, resources, physical characteristics of planets, and environmental factors, then choose items from each area to use in writing a science fiction short story for their ninth-grade English class.

Brainstorming

In classic brainstorming (Osborn, 1953), the object is to list as many ideas that come to mind regarding a question or problem without judging the quality of the ideas. This is Osborn's "principle of deferred judgment." There are seven rules of brainstorming: no criticisms; record all ideas; get ideas out—do not discuss them; quantity, not quality counts; expect wild ideas; be spontaneous; and build on the ideas of each other. A distinct advantage of brainstorming is that it may be used in any subject at any grade level anytime there is a need to produce quantities of ideas. Hence, brainstorming increases creativity by fostering fluency.

Synectics

Synectics was developed by W. J. J. Gordon (1981) and comes from the Greek word meaning the joining of different and apparently irrelevant elements or ideas. Synectics was designed to enhance creativity and problem solving abilities by using metaphoric activities. The three phases in this strategy are direct analogy, personal analogy, and compressed conflict (oxymorons). A direct analogy is a simple comparison of two things. For example, how is an emotion like a rose? A personal analogy requires empathic identification with a living or nonliving thing or an idea. For example, how does it feel to be a traffic light? Probably the most difficult analogy is that of compressed conflict. During this phase, students are asked to use words that are in opposition to each other and put them into a unique combination. This is often called an oxymoron, for example, restricted freedom or loud silence. Basically, the three phases give students the opportunity to "make the familiar strange" and allow students to see old problems in a new light. Students refer back to their original idea after gaining insights using these analogies. Synectics enhances creative thinking by encouraging flexibility of thought.

APPROPRIATE ASSESSMENT

Testing for creativity is controversial. Among noted professionals of the field, there are two schools of thought about the value of assessing creativity. One group encourages the testing for completeness of identifying all strengths of students, while the other group holds that creativity is a process explainable by observing and studying the thinking of creative people. Despite the controversy, Treffinger (1987) gave seven reasons why schools attempt to measure creativity:

1. Helping to recognize and affirm the strengths and talents of individuals.
2. Expanding and enhancing our understanding of the nature of human ability and giftedness.
3. Providing baseline data for assessing individuals or groups to guide teachers in planning and implementing instruction.
4. Obtaining data, such as pre- or posttest data, for group comparisons.
5. Helping instructors, counselors, or individuals on their own to discover unrecognized and untapped resources and talents.
6. Advancing research progress in understanding the nature, development, and nurture of creative behavior.
7. Helping to remove the concept of creativity from the realm of mystery and superstition. (p. 104)

"Creativity is the underpinning, the basement, the foundation that permits talent to be realized . . . but with all due respect to Mensa, having scored high on an intelligence test is not necessary" (Piirto, 2004, p. 38). However, creativity testing has never been as prolific as IQ testing (Treffinger, 1987). Current research indicates that creativity is both content and task specific (Baer, 1993, 1994; Csikszentmihalyi, 1988; Gardner, 1993; Runco, 1989; Sternberg & Lubart, 1995).

There are a number of tests and checklists that have been developed to assess creativity. Here, we describe several appropriate for adolescents. (For a complete discussion of these and many other instruments see Callahan, 1978; Cropley, 1997; Csikszentmihalyi & Wolfe, 2000; Plucker & Runco, 1998; Starko, 1995; Treffinger, 2004.)

Torrance Tests of Creative Thinking (TTCT; Torrance, 1966)

This popular and frequently used assessment instrument measures creative thinking ability. It is comprised of two parts: thinking creatively with pictures and thinking creatively with words. In both parts, students react to various prompts and their answers are scored for fluency, flexibility, originality, and elaboration (figural version only). Although widely available, one of the biggest drawbacks of the TTCT is that the tasks are open-ended and scoring is extremely time-consuming. Cost of the instrument is minimal if you score it yourself. The reliability and validity of this instrument have mixed results (Piirto, 2004; Rosenthal, DeMers, Stilwell, Graybeal, & Zins, 1983; Starko, 1995; Torrance, 1987).

Group Inventories for Finding Interests I & II (GIFFI; Davis & Rimm, 1982)

GIFFI is a self-report instrument designed for middle school and high school students, respectively. Students respond to statements formulated to assess imagination, independence, and interests. The test must be scored by the publisher and some of the items may have cultural bias since they have not been renormed recently. GIFFI has strong split-half reliabilities, but there is a need for additional validity data. Its internal consistency reliabilities are above .90.

Creativity Checklist (CCh; Johnson, 1979)

The CCh is another self-report instrument. It has eight items "developed specifically to identify overt creativity observed by at least one other person" (Johnson, 1979, p. 1). It generally takes less than 15 minutes and can be scored by hand. The instrument has an interrater reliability between .70 and .80, and product-moment correlation with the TTCT verbal total scores is .56.

Creativity Assessment Packet (CAP; Williams, 1980)

CAP consists of two group administered instruments: a Test of Divergent Thinking and a Test of Divergent Feeling. The tests are suitable for students ages 8–18. In addition, there is a rating scale, The Williams Scale, for parents and teachers to use to rate students on eight divergent factors: fluent thinking, flexible thinking, original thinking, elaborative thinking, risk taking, complexity, curiosity, and imagination. These are the same factors that are tested in the group administered parts. Validity for the two group administered tests is .71 and .76, respectively. Pairs of tests and the parent/teacher ratings correlate significantly at .74. Unfortunately, the CAP has been criticized for reliability and validity limitations (Damarin, 1985; Rosen, 1985).

Beyonders Checklist (Torrance & Safter, 1999)

This checklist was developed by Torrance and presented in the book by Torrance and Safter. It represents a recent addition to the self-report assessment of creativity. It has 35 questions and attempts to identify exceptional creativity. There is no evidence that the instrument has been used or validated with adolescents. However, one can easily determine his/her own score and compare it to the norming sample of beyonders and superior adults. This instrument could be used appropriately with juniors and seniors.

Based on knowledge present at the time, Treffinger (1980) made 13 recommendations for creativity assessment practice. We state the recommendations here since they are still applicable today.

1. Clarify goals and objectives for creativity learning.
2. Select and evaluate instruments carefully.
3. Avoid using "homemade" instruments.
4. Be alert for many sources of data.
5. Sample student work early and often.
6. Assess complex aspects of creativity.
7. Gather a portfolio of students' creative efforts.
8. Use group tests carefully.
9. Develop a written plan for creativity assessments.
10. Build a database.
11. Combine clinical and statistical analyses.
12. Don't settle for decisions you can't defend.
13. Retain flexibility about decisions. (p. 28–32)

There are no recent creativity assessments and most of those available have pros and cons. The most problematic is that the instruments available generally are time-consuming to score. We would greatly discourage the practice of taking one part (e.g., circle portion of the TTCT) and using it for high stakes decisions such as placement into gifted programs.

In conclusion, Jane Piirto (2004) provides an excellent summary of the issues of assessing creativity with the following nine statements:

1. Teachers are often not well trained in administering creativity tests and checklists.
2. School districts should understand the research base that went into a particular checklist or creativity test.
3. Sometimes the research is confusing since validity and reliability can be defined in different ways.
4. Predictive validity of creativity tests, creativity training, and creativity checklists are most difficult to establish because the tasks on the tests have little relationship to real life creativity.
5. Scoring is difficult on creativity tests because the scoring requires subjective judgment and scorers must be trained.
6. When reading about results of studies that claim that the treatment made the group "more creative," check whether that meant more fluent, flexible, etc. and judge the results accordingly.
7. There is no normal curve of creativity.
8. Behavioral checklists used to make decisions about students' lives are problematic.
9. Creativity test results used to make decisions about students' lives are problematic. (p. 406)

FINAL THOUGHTS

All indications are that creativity does not hold a place of importance in the secondary classroom. However, we assert that it can be used as a means of expanding and enriching any content area. Given its ability to empower gifted adolescents to tap into new realms of thinking, creativity needs to be given a front row seat in the classroom, rather than relegated to a dark spot in the back corner.

So, what else can be done in the classroom to encourage the use of the creative processes in any content area? First, teach the content as action. We learn new knowledge by doing rather than by passively listening. In the content areas, use real-world problems and have students work as a practicing professional would in that field. That's the real key to the issue. Content, process, product, affect, and learning environment must all interact. One can't be missing or be taught in isolation. Ditch the cookbook activities. Have students read essays, biographies, and autobiographies of prominent people in the field, paying close attention to the process by which they sought solutions, not just who they were and what they discovered. Invite professionals to come into your classroom and talk about the processes they use to solve real problems. Help students with high ability and interest in content areas to find mentors in their area of interest. In order to foster creativity students need contact with complexity, ambiguity, puzzling experiences, uncertainty, and imperfection (Runco & Albert, 1986). Creativity needs to be infused in all content areas and educational experiences. We offer the following 10 ideas to infuse creativity into the curriculum:

1. Look for places in the curriculum to encourage flexibility, fluency, originality, and elaboration.
2. Teach conceptually.
3. Use open-ended activities and assignments.
4. Help students be tolerant of ambiguity.
5. Allow and encourage out-of-the-box thinking.
6. Include a creation or design assignment in every subject.
7. Teach creative strategies such as SCAMPER and attribute listing.
8. Include the study of creative individuals in all content areas.
9. Value creativity as a teacher and encourage students to value it also.
10. Understand that creativity is a continuum and there are varying degrees of creativity.

Remember: Mistakes equal learning and each "no" brings you closer to a "yes." Creativity isn't a single light bulb; it is a lot of little flashes!

REFERENCES

Alencar, E. (1993). Thinking in the future: The need to promote creativity in the educational context. *Gifted Education International, 9,* 93–95.

Amabile, T. M. (1983). *The social psychology of creativity.* New York: Springer-Verlag.

Assouline, S., & Lupkowski-Shoplik, A. (2003). *Developing mathematical talent.* Waco, TX: Prufrock Press.

Baer, J. (1993). Why you shouldn't trust creativity tests. *Educational Leadership, 51*(4), 80–83.

Baer, J. (1994). Why you still shouldn't trust creativity tests. *Educational Leadership, 52*(2), 72 –73.

Baer, J. (1997). *Creative teachers, creative students.* Needham Heights, MA: Allyn & Bacon.

Barron, B. J. S., Schwartz, D. L., Vye, N. J., Moore, A., Petrosino, A., Zech, L., et al. (1998). Doing with understanding: Lessons from research on problem- and project-based learning. *The Journal of the Learning Sciences, 7*, 271–312.

Bireley, M., & Genshaft, J. (Eds.). (1991). *Understanding the gifted adolescent.* New York: Teachers College Press.

Bloom, B. (Ed.). (1985). D*eveloping talent in young people.* New York: Ballantine.

Brandwein, P. (1988). Science talent: In an ecology of achievement. In P. Brandwein & H. Passow (Eds.), *Gifted young in science: Potential through performance.* Washington, DC: National Science Teachers Association.

Callahan, C. M. (1978). *Developing creativity in the gifted and talented.* Reston, VA: Council for Exceptional Children.

Cramond, B., Martin, C. E., & Shaw, E. L. (1990). Generalizability of creative problem solving procedures to real-life problems. *Journal for the Education of the Gifted, 13*, 141–155.

Crawford, R. P. (1954). *The techniques of creative thinking.* New York: Hawthorne Books.

Cropley, A. (1994). *More ways than one: Fostering creativity.* Norwood, NJ: Ablex.

Cropley, A. J. (1997). Fostering creativity in the classroom: General principles. In M. A. Runco (Ed.), *The creativity research handbook* (pp. 83–114). Cresskill, New York: Hampton Press.

Cross, B. (1990). A passion within reason: The human side of process. *Science and Children, 27*(4), 16–21.

Csikszentmihalyi, M. (1988). Society, culture, and person: A systems view of creativity. In R. J. Sternberg (Ed.), *The nature of creativity: Contemporary psychology perspectives* (pp. 325–339). New York: Cambridge University Press.

Csikszentmihalyi, M. (1996). *Creativity: Flow and the psychology of discovery and invention.* New York: HarperCollins Publishers.

Csikszentmihalyi, M., & Wolfe, R. (2000). New conceptions and research approaches to creativity. In K. A. Heller, F. J. Mönks, R. J. Sternberg, & R. F. Subotnik (Eds.), *International handbook of giftedness and talent* (2nd ed., pp. 81–93). Kidlington, Oxford: Elsevier Science Ltd.

Damarin, F. (1985). [Review of Creativity Assessment Packet]. In J. Mitchell, Jr. (Ed.), *The ninth mental measurements yearbook.* (Vol. 1., pp. 410–411). Lincoln, NE: University of Nebraska Press.

Damm, V. J. (1970). Creativity and intelligence: Research implications for equal emphasis in high school. *Exceptional Children, 36*, 565–569.

Davis, G. A. (1986) *Creativity is forever* (2nd ed.). Dubuque: Kendall/Hunt.

Davis, G. A., & Rimm, S. (1982). Group Inventory for Finding Interests (GIFFI) I and II: Instruments for identifying creative potential in the junior and senior high school. *Journal of Creative Behavior, 16*, 50–57.

Delisle, R. (1997). *How to use problem-based learning in the classroom.* Alexandria, VA: Association for Supervision and Curriculum Development.

Eberle, R. F. (1987). *SCAMPER.* Buffalo, NY: D.O.K. Publishers.

Eccles, J. S. (2004). Schools, academic motivation, and stage-environment fit. In R. M. Lerner & L. Steinberg (Eds.), *Handbook of adolescent psychology* (2nd ed., pp. 125–153). Hoboken, NJ: John Wiley & Sons.

Feldhusen, J. F., & Clinkenbeard, P. R. (1986). Creativity instructional materials: A review of research. *Journal of Creative Behavior, 20*, 153–182.

Feldman, D. H. (1999). The development of creativity. In R. J. Sternberg (Ed.), *Handbook of creativity* (pp. 169–186). Cambridge: Cambridge University Press.

Firestien, R. L., & Treffinger, D. J. (1983). Ownership and converging: Essential ingredients of creative problem solving. *Journal of Creative Behavior, 17,* 32–38.

Fishkin, A. S., Cramond, B., & Olszewski-Kubilius, P. (1999). *Investigating creativity in youth.* Cresskill, NJ: Hampton Press.

Fleith, D. S. (2000). Teacher and student perceptions of creativity in the classroom environment. *Roeper Review, 22,* 148–153.

Fryer, M. & Collings, J. A. (1991). British teachers' views of creativity. *The Journal of Creative Behavior, 25,* 75–80.

Gallagher, S. A., & Stepien, W. J. (1996). Content acquisition in problem-based learning: Depth versus breadth in American studies. *Journal for the Education of the Gifted, 19,* 257–275.

Gardner, H. (1993). *Creating minds.* New York: Basic Books.

Gentry, M., Rizza, M. G., & Owen, S. V. (2002). Examining challenge and choice in classrooms: The relationships between teachers and their students and comparisons between gifted students and others. *Gifted Child Quarterly, 46,* 145–155.

Ghiselin, B. (1981). *The creative process.* New York: Mentor.

Goertzel, V., Goertzel, M., Goertzel, T., & Hansen, A. (2004). *Cradles of eminence* (2nd ed.). Scottsdale, AZ: Great Potential Press.

Gordon, W. J. J. (1981). *The new art of the possible: The basic course in synectics.* Cambridge, MA: Porpoise Books.

Gorman, M. E., Plucker, J. A., & Callahan, C. M. (1998). Turning students into inventors: Active learning modules for secondary students. *Phi Delta Kappan, 79,* 530–535.

Guilford, J. P. (1950). Creativity. *American Psychologist, 5,* 444–454.

Hanks, K., & Parry, J. (1983). *Wake up your creative genius.* Los Altos, CA: William Kaufmann.

Jackson, P. W., & Messick, S. (1965). The person, the product, and the response: Conceptual problems in the assessment of creativity. *Journal of Personality, 33,* 309–329.

Johnson, D. L. (1979). *Creativity checklist.* Chicago: Stoelting Co.

Kersting, K. (2003). What exactly is creativity? *Monitor On Psychology, 34*(10), 40–41.

Krajcik, J., Blumenfeld, C. P., Marx, R. W., Bass, K. M., Fredricks, J., & Soloway, E. (1998). Inquiry in project-based science classrooms: Initial attempts by middle school students. *The Journal of the Learning Sciences, 7,* 313–350.

Lambros, A. (2004) *Problem-based learning in middle and high school classrooms: A teacher's guide to implementation.* Thousand Oaks, CA: Corwin Press.

Lerner, R. M., & Steinberg, L. (2004). The scientific study of adolescent development: Past, present and future. In R. M. Lerner & L. Steinberg (Eds.), *Handbook of adolescent psychology* (2nd ed., pp. 1–12). Hoboken, NJ: John Wiley & Sons.

Lynch, M. D., & Harris, C. R. (2001). *Fostering creativity in children, K–8: Theory and practice.* Needham Heights, MA: Allyn & Bacon.

Mayfield, B. (1979). Teachers' perceptions of creativity, intelligence, and achievement. *Gifted Child Quarterly, 23,* 812–817.

Osborn, A. F. (1953). *Applied imagination.* New York: Scribner's Sons.

Osborn, A. F. (1963). *Applied imagination* (3rd ed.). New York: Scribner's Sons.

Parker, A. P. (1998). The Torrance creative scholars program. *Roeper Review, 21,* 32–38.

Parnes, S. J. (1981). *Magic of your mind.* Buffalo, NY: Bearly Ltd.

Parnes, S. J., & Brunelle, E. A. (1967). The literature of creativity (part 1). *Journal of Creative Behavior, 1,* 52–109.

Piirto, J. (1991). Encouraging creativity and talent in adolescents. In M. Bireley & J. Genshaft (Eds.), *Understanding the gifted adolescent* (pp. 104–121). New York: Teachers College Press.

Piirto, J. (2004). *Understanding creativity.* Scottsdale, AZ: Great Potential Press.

Plucker, J. A., & Beghetto, R. A. (2003). Why not be creative when we enhance creativity? In J. H. Borland (Ed.), *Rethinking gifted education* (pp. 215–226). New York: Teachers College Press.

Plucker, J. A., & Gorman, M. E. (1995). Group interaction during a summer course on invention and design for high-ability secondary students. *The Journal of Secondary Education, 6,* 258–272.

Plucker, J. A., & Gorman, M. E. (1999). Invention is in the mind of the adolescent: Evaluation of a summer course one year later. *Creativity Research Journal, 12,* 141–150.

Plucker, J. A., & Nowak, J. (2000). Creativity in science for K–8 practitioners: Problem-based approaches to discovery and invention. In M. D. Lynch & C. R. Harris (Eds.), *Fostering creativity in children, K–8* (pp. 145–158). Boston: Allyn & Bacon.

Plucker, J. A., & Runco, M. A. (1998). The death of creativity measurement has been greatly exaggerated: Current issues, recent advances, and future directions in creativity assessment. *Roeper Review, 21,* 15–24.

Plucker, J. A., & Runco, M. A. (1999). Enhancement of creativity. In M. A. Runco & S. Pritzker (Eds.), *Encyclopedia of creativity* (pp. 669–675). San Diego, CA: Academic Press.

Pollack, R. (1988). Science as a creative process. *Liberal Education, 74*(2), 11–15.

Rash, P. K., & Miller, A. D. (2000). A survey of practices of teachers of the gifted. *Roeper Review, 22,* 192–194.

Reis, S. M., & Renzulli, J. S. (1999). Research relating to the development of creative productivity using the enrichment triad model. In A. S. Fishkin, B. Cramond, & P. Olszewski-Kubilius (Eds.), *Investigating creativity in youth: Research and methods* (pp. 367–387). Cresskill, NJ: Hampton Press.

Renzulli, J. S., & Reis, S. M. (1994). Research related to the schoolwide enrichment triad model. *Gifted Child Quarterly 38,* 7–20.

Root-Bernstein, R. S. (1989). *Discovering: Inventing and solving problems at the frontiers of scientific knowledge.* Cambridge, MA: Harvard University Press.

Rose, L. H., & Lin, H. (1984). A meta-analysis of long-term creativity training programs. *Journal of Creative Behavior, 18,* 11–22.

Rosen, C. L. (1985). [Review of Creativity Assessment Packet]. In J. Mitchell, Jr. (Ed.), *The ninth mental measurements yearbook* (Vol. 1, pp. 411–412). Lincoln, NE: University of Nebraska Press.

Rosenthal, A., DeMers, S. T., Stilwell, W., Graybeal, S., & Zins, J. (1983). Comparison of interrater reliability on the Torrance Tests of Creative Thinking for gifted and nongifted children. *Psychology in the Schools, 20,* 35–40.

Runco, M. A. (1989). Parents' and teachers' ratings of the creativity of children. *Journal of Social Behavior and Personality, 4,* 73–83.

Runco, M. A. (1990). Divergent thinking of children: Implications of the research. *Gifted Child Today, 13*(4), 37–39.

Runco, M. A., & Albert, R. S. (1986). The threshold hypothesis regarding creativity and intelligence: An empirical test with gifted and nongifted children. *Creative Child and Adult Quarterly, 11,* 212–218.

Sak, U. (2004). About creativity, giftedness, and teaching the creatively gifted in the classroom. *Roeper Review, 25,* 216–222.

Schack G. D. (1993). Effects of a creative problem-solving curriculum on students of varying ability levels. *Gifted Child Quarterly, 37,* 32–38.

Simonton, D. K. (1987). Genius: The lessons of historiometry. In S. G. Isaksen (Ed.), *Frontiers of creativity research* (pp. 66–76). Buffalo, NY: Bearly Limited.

Simonton, D. K. (1988). *Scientific genius: A psychology of science.* New York: Cambridge University Press.

Smolucha, F. (1992). A reconstruction of Vygotsky's theory of creativity. *Creativity Research Journal, 5,* 49–67.

Starko, A. J. (1995). *Creativity in the classroom: Schools of curious delight.* White Plains, NY: Longman Publishers.

Sternberg, R. J. (1995/1996). Investing in creativity: Many happy returns. *Educational Leadership, 53*(4), 80–84.

Sternberg, R. J. (1999). *Handbook of creativity.* Cambridge: Cambridge University Press.

Sternberg, R. J., & Lubart, T. I. (1995). *Defying the crowd: Cultivating creativity in a culture of conformity.* New York: Free Press.

Sternberg, R. J., & Lubart, T. I. (1996). Investing in creativity. *American Psychologist, 51,* 677–688.

Sternberg, R. J., & Lubart, T. I. (1999). The concept of creativity: Prospects and paradigms. In R. J. Sternberg (Ed.), *Handbook of creativity* (pp. 3–15). Cambridge, MA: Cambridge University Press.

Sternberg, R. J., & Williams, W. M. (1996). *How to develop student creativity.* Alexandria, VA: Association for Supervision and Curriculum Development.

Susman, E. J., & Rogol, A. (2004). Puberty and psychological development. In R. M. Lerner & L. Steinberg (Eds.), *Handbook of adolescent psychology* (2nd ed., pp. 15–44). Hoboken, NJ: John Wiley & Sons.

Tan, A. G. (2001). Singaporean teachers' perception of activities useful for fostering creativity. *The Journal of Creative Behavior 35,* 131–146.

Torp, L., & Sage, S. (1998). *Problems as possibilities: Problem-based learning for K–12 educations.* Alexandria, VA: Association for Supervision and Curriculum Development.

Torrance, E. P. (1966). *Torrance Test of Creative Thinking: Norms and technical manual–research edition.* Princeton, NJ: Personnel Press.

Torrance, E. P. (1987). Recent trends in teaching children and adults to think creatively. In S. G. Isaksen (Ed.), *Frontiers of creativity research* (pp. 189–215). Buffalo, NY: Bearly Limited.

Torrance, E. P. (1988). The nature of creativity as manifest in its setting. In R. J. Sternberg (Ed.), *The nature of creativity: Contemporary psychological perspectives.* New York: Cambridge University Press.

Torrance, E. P., & Safter, H. T. (1990). *The incubation model of teaching: Getting beyond the aha!* Buffalo, NY: Bearly Limited.

Torrance, E. P., & Safter, H. T. (1999). *Making the creative leap beyond.* Buffalo, NY: Creative Education Foundation Press.

Treffinger, D. J. (1980). The progress and peril of identifying creative talent among gifted and talented students. *Journal of Creative Behavior, 14,* 20–34.

Treffinger, D. J. (1987). Research on creativity assessment. In S. G. Isaksen (Ed.), *Frontiers of creativity research* (pp. 103–109). Buffalo, NY: Bearly Limited.

Treffinger, D. J. (2004, Spring). Assessing creativity: Challenges and opportunities. *Quest, 15,* 11–14.

Treffinger, D. J., & Isaksen, S. G. (1992). *Creative problem solving: An introduction.* Sarasota, FL: Center for Creative Learning.

Treffinger, D. J., Isaksen, S. G., & Dorval, K. B. (2000). *Creative problem solving: An introduction* (3rd ed.). Waco, TX: Prufrock Press.

Williams, F. (1980). *Creativity assessment packet.* Buffalo, NY: D.O.K. Publishers.

Williams, W. M., Markle, F., Brigockas, M., & Sternberg, R. J. (2002). *Creative intelligence for school.* Boston: Allyn & Bacon.

Yager, R. E. (1992). Appropriate science for all. *Science Scope, 16*(3), 57–59.

SECONDARY ENGLISH FOR HIGH-ABILITY STUDENTS

CHAPTER 14

by Felicia A. Dixon

emember, you have been entrusted with a tremendous power, the power to decide. But, as you must know, the greater the power, the more frightening is the responsibility of wielding it! (Dostoevsky, *The Brothers Karamazov*, p. 894)

Gifted adolescents at the secondary level seek, choose, and decide what to do and how to do it. If they are given appropriate choices in a constructivist classroom atmosphere, they can achieve great things, possibly reaching their potential. In English classes these great accomplishments can occur in their writing, in their choice of reading material, and in their oral expressions—discussions, speeches, debates, and role-plays in class.

One of the early identifiers of giftedness in students is their advanced verbal ability. Often gifted children read early—well before they enter school—and they use advanced vocabulary to express themselves (Coleman & Cross, 2001; Piirto, 1999; VanTassel-Baska & Little, 2003). Further, they express themselves well, using language appropriately. As they grow into adolescence, their verbal ability grows as well. Verbally gifted students move into advanced reading material quite early, often finding challenge and enjoyment in adult materials rather than adolescent novels. They are able to use figurative language naturally, and they understand and use analogies and metaphorical thinking to express their ideas. If asked what they have read lately, these students can produce a list of books that puts most of their teachers' personal reading lists to shame in comparison. The issues of how to teach these students and how to foster their gifts and talents in middle school and high school must be resolved in order to encourage continual progress of their unique academic gifts. The goal of this chapter is to explore ways and means to foster these academic gifts through carefully designed curriculum that meets these unique needs. Consider the following vignette as a precursor to the theoretical rationale that follows.

Maya was at the end of her junior year in high school at a state-supported academy for gifted students. She had taken all of the advanced AP math and science classes and planned a career that focused on microbiology. But, Maya's real passion was her intrigue with Arthurian Literature. In fact, she petitioned to take an independent study, called a directed reading, in the Arthurian Legend during the first semester of her senior year. She was referred to a teacher who had previously taught at the academy and was now a college professor on an adjoining campus. Maya's initial e-mail to the professor read as follows:

Dear Professor:

I am sorry that I did not get back to you sooner about the independent study for next year, but I just got done with my AP tests.

I was looking through *La Morte D'Arthur* by Malory and I would like to split that up over a few weeks. I think that there are about 16 weeks in a semester. There are 21 books in Malory, so if I read four a week, we'd be done with that in 5 weeks or so.

I wanted to start off with Malory since his book is so often thought of as the primary "source" for the legends, but I really want to read Geoffrey of Monmouth's works since I think he's the one who really introduced Arthur and Merlin to literature.

Then I would like to read some of Cretien [*sic*] de Troyes's five romances (I definitely want to read Percival as well as Launcelot and Yvain) and spend maybe a week on his writings. I don't know if we can find any of the Vulgate Cycle, but that is something I have been wanting to look at for quite a while.

After that, I would like to cover some Tennyson. I tried reading *Idylls of the King* a while ago, but I really didn't retain much of it. I would primarily like to stay with the older literature written in the middle ages/Renaissance and the Victorian era, ending with the revival that Tennyson started.

Also, I am absolutely, totally in love with Merlin, and would like to devote the last few weeks to studying Merlin. I could try to get a copy of a translation of the *Vita Merlini* (I'm sure it exists somewhere), as well as de Boron's big long poem, some of the old Welsh/Scottish stories of Myrddain and Lailokin, and any other things we come across.

I'm not sure if you had anything in mind with assignments. I would definitely prefer writing smaller responses to the readings as opposed to papers, but I'd be willing to write papers if you feel that there's a need for that. I would want to meet with you at least once a week if not two or three to discuss the readings.

I hope that gives a good idea of what I hope to do for the directed study next fall, and I will try to get in touch with you again sometime before the beginning of the school year. I am so excited about studying Arthurian literature with you, and thank you so much for agreeing to instruct me!

Maya

THEORETICAL RATIONALE

It is difficult to tell who was teaching whom in the above e-mail. Certainly the zeal and pure excitement for Arthurian literature that Maya possessed came across in her e-mail. But, what came across equally was her knowledge of the material and her precise targeting of specific texts that she wanted to explore. Maya is not alone in her representation of the well-read adolescent. Her e-mail illustrates several of the obvious needs that verbally gifted students manifest. They have preferences in what they read, and, when given a chance, they will voice these preferences. In addition, they have preferences in designing a curriculum that satisfies their quest for knowledge. Finally, they know how they prefer to showcase what they know, and if given a chance to have input into type of assessment, they will offer suggestions for why their preferred mode should be acceptable.

Verbally gifted students at the secondary level must have rigorous content, challenging tasks that respond to the content with choices to satisfy their unique learning styles, and frequent discussions with peers of like minds in order to grow in their talent area. Coupling critical thinking tasks with the challenging content that demands such tasks makes for a meaningful educational experience for these students.

Indeed, verbally gifted secondary students are unique in their abilities and must be understood in order to teach them productively. Yet, they also are adolescents who are changing and experiencing new things both academically and socially. According to the Carnegie Council (1995),

Adolescence is one of the most fascinating and complex transitions in the life span; a time of accelerated growth and change second only to infancy; a time of expanding horizons, self-discovery, and emerging independence; a time of metamorphosis from childhood to adulthood . . . The events of this

365

crucially formative phase can shape an individual's life course, and thus the future of the whole society. (p. 7)

The right choice of literature in their English class can complement this period of changes, adding depth to adolescents' educational experience (Halsted, 1994).

Secondary students who have high verbal ability, that is, those whose cognitive performance exceeds the norm for their age group, must be challenged at their cognitive level for maximum educational value to be achieved.

While acceleration is usually suggested for students who manifest advanced abilities, classes that address the breadth and depth of the literary experience are often very worthwhile for verbally gifted secondary students. If the class is designed as an honors class that is directed toward gifted students, the collaborative effort of discussing ideas with those of like abilities provides a rich experience that challenges and enriches both the middle and high school levels.

A cautionary note is in order here: These students also need a firm grounding in language, including a good command of English grammar and regular writing assignments that focus on persuasive writing. These are basic needs in future schooling and careers that must not be ignored by assuming these students intuitively know grammar and writing because of their advanced vocabulary. Poor English usage quickly brands a person, and masking gifts with substandard language can close doors to opportunities for bright students. Hence, with the positive attributes that advanced vocabulary provides comes the serious charge that schools must not fail them by lacking to provide these basic language needs. While repetitive drill is not productive with these students, the study of language is a necessity.

REVIEW OF CURRENT EMPIRICAL LITERATURE

English classes for high-ability secondary students focus on language, literature, and vocabulary development. In addition, oral expression is a domain often relegated to the English class. Research in these areas reveals interesting ideas about what should be happening for talented teens. Thompson (1996), in arguing for the use of classic literature with gifted high school students because of the language used, states,

> This characteristic of the classics—the apt and creative use of words at a level that is brilliantly exciting—is really no surprise. Is it unexpected that humanity's most highly developed verbal talents would use many words and use them well? The best writers are the best users of words. If students are to have their vocabularies developed, they should read these writers. These are the writers who define and redefine the limits. These are the writers who show the path. (p. 65)

Thompson continues by stating that when verbally gifted students submerge themselves in reading the classics, they are exposed to an increasingly sophisticated use of vocabulary in the texts that models good writing, ultimately helping them become good writers as well.

In discussing the necessity to teach grammar, Thompson (2002) states,

> Grammar has been stereotyped as tedious, unteachable, and remedial, unfit for emphasis in language arts programs for gifted children . . . Grammar, however, is sometimes successfully taught, has symmetries and mysteries enough to fascinate the dullest mind, and is an introspective and metacognitive way of thinking about our own ideas—perfect for the higher level ruminations advocated for gifted children. (p. 64)

Gallagher (1975) urges language arts instructors to go beyond the "sterile presentation of grammar and syntax" (p. 198) in teaching English, but he also adds as one of the objectives for language arts classes, "To apply the conventions of general American-English usage, putting to use whatever function or variety of language is appropriate to the occasion" (p. 177). Similarly, VanTassel-Baska (1988) noted that,

> [in] a language arts class for the gifted, it is necessary to adopt a diagnostic-prescriptive approach to teaching grammar and usage since these students are capable of mastering the language system much more rapidly than other learners and in a shorter time period than currently is allotted in the regular school curriculum. (p. 167)

Advocating for a strong study element that allows students to understand English language from a variety of perspectives, VanTassel-Baska (1988, p. 167) suggests the following goals as appropriate for a gifted program focusing on English language study:

1. To understand the syntactic structure of English (grammar) and its concomitant uses (usage).
2. To promote vocabulary development.
3. To foster an understanding of word relationships (analogies) and origins (etymology).
4. To develop an appreciation for semantics, linguistics, and the history of language.

Adolescents must be able to express themselves in their writing and speaking, confident that they are not held back by inadequate expressions relative to their cognitive understandings. English classes must provide the opportunities for this crucial area of language practice.

Developing worldviews that are sensitive and considerate of many varying positions is certainly not the norm among untrained adolescents. Exposure to literature can help secondary students analyze their thoughts about the human condition in a thoughtful and considerate way, ultimately transforming their rough ideas into a productive worldview. Taylor (1996) writes:

We look to literature as a source of collective wisdom, for insights into our muddled human condition, to be reassured by the record of human heroism or restrained by the corrective drama of human folly. We look to literature for experience that enlarges understanding—understanding accessible only through experience. Indeed, understanding is supposed to be the goal of all learning . . . In spite of much earnest rhetoric to the contrary, guiding students to experience genuine understanding is not an educational priority. The vocabulary of education suggests instead a preoccupation with measurement—an urgency to demonstrate mastery of basic skills, performance of outcomes, the achievement of cultural literacy. (p. 75)

Taylor (1996) continues to describe the necessity for students to participate in the world the literature creates in order to truly understand that work. Literature "renders experience (remembered or imagined), and in an artificial act, holds the flux of experience in place for a moment of illumination. Magically, this moment, frozen but nonetheless vital, may be endlessly relived" (p. 77). The power of literature includes the following issues:

1. Literature tells us nothing new; it merely repeats, preparing a familiar situation within a novel script—a script the reader enters to rehearse the dialogue that allows us to define what is of human significance.
2. Literature models for us and invites us into the dialogic process—the process that allows us to narrate meaning and the life made coherent by story.
3. Literature imagines and articulates new possibilities.
4. Literature dramatizes active dialogue, and our instruction must invite students to participate in that dialogue.

Taylor (1996) concludes that the understanding of literature focuses on expression and its release into language. She writes, "We make it accessible to our students by showing them the processes of language, by allowing them to use those processes in the struggle for voice and expression" (p. 92). Both Taylor and Thompson (1996) suggest that educating high-ability students must include carefully chosen texts that challenge thought and action. Similarly, Kolloff (1996) states that the development of verbal talent among all students is the goal of the literate classroom. Little (2002) corroborates these thoughts, stating that the study of language also encourages the habits of mind of the critical reader and the practiced writer; the meaning created when reading or writing is constructed on a frame of words and their combinations into grammatical structures. These thoughts are consistent with characteristics of verbally gifted students who are voracious readers who find enjoyment in the way ideas are stated.

Piirto (1999) suggests that schools need to provide advanced work in literature and in the humanities to students with strong verbal ability. This work should include expository writing and criticism, analysis of literary form, study of foreign languages, and in-depth work in multicultural areas. She argues for a broad array of works to be read, avoiding the trap that many English classes fall prey to of focusing on D.W.M. (Dead White Male) writers. Indeed, her caution is one that has been voiced frequently: In this postmodern era of affirmative action, it serves students well to study a variety of literature and the plight of all people. Piirto continues by stating that the function of education in verbal areas is perhaps primarily to produce connoisseurs who enjoy and appreciate the written word and who can evaluate arguments, see logic, and appreciate aesthetics.

With regard to what should be taught in English classes, Singal (1991) stated,

> Changes in the teaching of literature matter greatly because reading is the primary vehicle by which students absorb the rhythms and patterns of language. The more a person encounters sophisticated prose, the more he or she will pick up varied sentence structure, vocabulary in context, and even spelling, as well as advanced descriptive techniques and narrative strategies. Feed a student the literary equivalent of junk food and you will get an impoverished command of English. (p. 66)

Stotsky (1995) reminds literature teachers that literature programs need to live up to the original promise of multiculturalism: to teach students to understand and appreciate one another's ethnic heritage, as well as their common heritage as Americans. E. D. Hirsch (as cited in Stotsky) argues that all American students deserve a "centrist curriculum" that encourages knowledge of and sympathy towards the diverse cultures of the world (p. 612).

Regarding what should occur in verbally oriented courses for gifted adolescents, Feldhusen (1998) suggested that there should be substantial reliance on large reading assignments. Ideally, the course syllabi should offer both required and optional reading lists. In addition, there should be an extensive reliance on the selection of books and articles that represent primary sources from leaders in the field of study, which is often college level material. The typical survey-type anthologies, so often used in middle and high school classes, are often far too low in reading level for verbally gifted youth. Similarly, Passow (1986) states that gifted students' talents will not be fully nurtured in secondary school; students should fully realize that they are not finished writers and need to continue to work in their talent area if they are to produce and create important products. Classes that encourage understanding and assessing one's talents are important to this growth.

What has been mentioned so far are ideas about what is necessary in classes for verbally gifted youth. These are all good ideas and certainly have merit and scholarly consideration behind them. However, empirical research that can substantiate the reason to use one method over another because it has been proven to be more effective with gifted students through experimental design is very difficult to find. Dixon (1996) conducted one such study in which a heuristic for critical thinking was used regularly with the experimental classes and not with the control classes; her work indicated gains in critical thinking expressed in written essays. In addition, VanTassel-Baska, Zuo, Avery, & Little (2002) used a quasi-experimental design in their research to investigate the effects of language arts units on gifted learners at primary, intermediate, and middle school levels. They found that the use of the

William and Mary language arts curriculum units produce significant and important gains for gifted learners in key aspects of language arts as assessed by demonstration of high level thinking on performance-based measures. Sadly, there is not much empirical evidence for what happens in English classes for high-ability verbal students. Most schools use the global term *best practice* to describe and defend what they do. Certainly there is a call for research focusing on effective methods to use in English classes for gifted adolescents.

Advanced Placement (AP)

As with other core classes at the high school level, much gifted education in English is left to the teachers of Advanced Placement classes. Feldhusen (1997) stated, "Talented youth should be allowed, encouraged, and counseled to take Advanced Placement (AP) courses whenever and wherever they are available" (p. 91). The AP exams also offer excellent tests of talent strengths, as well as college credit for those students who score well (i.e., usually a 3, 4, or 5 on an exam).

According to the College Board (2000), the description of the AP exams that apply to English are as follows:

> [English Exams consist of] two 3-hour examinations each covering a full year introductory college English course. Both include 60 minutes of multiple-choice questions and 120 minutes of free-response questions. The AP English Language and Composition Examination tests the student's skills in analyzing the reasoning and the expression of ideas in prose passages and asks students to demonstrate their skill in composition by writing essays in various rhetorical modes. The AP English Literature and Composition Examination tests the student's ability to read selected poems and prose passages analytically and to write critical or analytical essays based on poems, prose passages, and complete novels or plays. (p. 15)

The College Board does not qualify AP courses as being designed for gifted students. In fact, the selection criteria read as follows:

> Students should be selected to participate in AP courses on the basis of their preparation for such a course, their willingness and ability to meet its academic challenges, and the level of support they have from family and friends. When deciding whether a student is prepared to take the AP course, educators may wish to analyze the courses the student has already taken and to interview the student and family. The examinations are open to students in any grade. For particularly self-directed students, an AP program in the form of supervised independent study is a valid option; each year hundreds of students participate, and succeed, in this way. (p. 8)

Advanced Placement is considered an accelerative option for secondary students. Since these classes do offer challenging content that moves along at a fast pace, they are popular choices for gifted students. However, because students are not selected for these classes based on their special verbal gifts (other than teachers attesting for their ability to take the class), courses may not meet the unique needs of verbally gifted students in the breadth and depth of coverage that they should have. However, AP courses are popular with parents and with students, and many schools have adopted Advanced Placement as the gifted program at the secondary level.

Few can argue with the selections chosen for a given year. The classics from the past, as well as the current classic literature of Toni Morrison, Margaret Atwood, and Louise Erdrich (to name just a few of many listings) offer choices for writing essays and challenging texts for critical analysis in class. Hence, the argument is not with the choice of challenging literature covered in class. More problematic is the methodology employed regularly to cover the texts.

Burney (2002) stated,

> AP is not a pure example of gifted education. While it is a more rigorous curricular option than is frequently available to high school students, courses are not designed to promote many of the things that are present in good gifted education. True gifted education offers students of exceptional ability opportunities for both critical and creative thinking. True gifted education promotes interdisciplinary study, meta-cognition, exploration of areas of study outside traditional high school subjects, the use of mentors, seminars and independent study. True gifted education is much more than the greater depth-content or accelerated study of traditional subjects. Furthermore, success in AP is not limited to the gifted although most of those who achieve success on multiple AP exams would likely meet the criteria of local gifted programs. AP courses should be open to all students who are ready and willing to take on the challenge. (p. 138)

But being "ready and willing to take on the challenge" seems to speak more of high achievement than of specific giftedness in an area. So, perhaps the instructor of the AP class would need to differentiate instruction within the AP class in order to truly meet the cognitive needs of all the students. Tiering lessons based on the challenging content of either the AP Literature and Composition or the AP Language and Composition courses may meet the needs of gifted students more productively than standard courses open to everyone usually do.

International Baccalaureate (IB)

Similar to AP courses, the IB curriculum is rigorous; therefore, it offers a challenge to gifted students proficient in English areas. It is described as a rigorous, international, pre-university course of study leading to examinations that meets the needs of highly motivated and academically superior secondary school students. IB has a comprehensive classics curriculum (languages, sciences, mathematics, and humanities) that allows its graduates to fulfill education requirements of various nations. Only schools approved by the IB organization may offer the program.

FOCUS OF THIS CHAPTER

Gallagher (1995) writes that gifted education is a civil right of gifted students. It clearly follows that students who have high verbal abilities have the right to be in classes that foster these gifts. Such classes must offer challenging content; focus on higher level thinking processes every day in every activity; use discussion frequently, openly inviting debate on crucial issues presented in literature; and require persuasive writing regularly. Diagnosing problems that occur in individual students' performances and then prescribing appropriate work to help change the unproductive area is sound education for these students. Rather than stopping class for a group remediation activity that certainly does not apply to everyone, this diagnostic-prescriptive approach is much more productive. Further, constructivist classes that frequently invite and empower students to decide and choose how they want to showcase their responses to literature make use of the gifts these students possess. The next part of this chapter focuses on strategies and lessons appropriate for middle school and high school verbally gifted students.

APPROPRIATE STRATEGIES FOR SECONDARY VERBALLY GIFTED STUDENTS

Content, process, product, and learning environments are all essential elements of curricular differentiation for gifted students (Maker, 1982). In addition, Passow (1988) suggests that modification can occur in breadth and depth in the classroom, in tempo or pacing of the material, and in nature or in kind of class offered. Before moving to specific lessons focused on the gifted secondary student, it is necessary to discuss optimal formats conducive to teaching these students. One particularly appropriate theory for gifted students in English classes is constructivism. Constructivist classrooms do allow for student input on a regular basis and are excellent formats for encouraging discussion. Constructivist classes share the following common elements:

1. complex, challenging learning environments and authentic tasks;
2. social negotiation and shared responsibility as a part of learning;
3. multiple representations of content;
4. understanding that knowledge is constructed; and
5. student-centered instruction. (Snowman & Biehler, 2000)

The constructivist format allows for the characteristics of secondary gifted students to be considered in appropriate curriculum planning and implementation.

A second appropriate format for secondary English classes both at the middle school and the high school is the literature seminar format. Kolloff and Feldhusen (1986) state that the seminar format provides unique opportunities for gifted and talented youth to meet with precocious peers for discussions of higher-level concepts, to carry on independent study and research, and to be guided by a teacher in scholarly and/or artistic endeavors. Further, the seminar combines several crucial learning activities, notably the opportunity for in-depth research and the correlated activities of writing, discussion, and presentation (Feldhusen & Robinson, 1986). Many high-ability adolescents analyze, synthesize, and evaluate material routinely, and frequently they have read so avidly on their own that their background is rich with a variety of experiences to share. In most cases, students are anxious to discuss ideas with peers of like interests, and they encourage each other to pursue depth of understanding. In fact, the peer interaction becomes so important to seminar members that the teacher becomes part of the discussion group, sharing in the inquiry process instead of serving as information disseminator. Therefore, the seminar should be led by a teacher-mentor who can provide guidance in the investigative procedures (Dixon, 1994; Feldhusen & Robinson).

Seminars are appropriate for middle school or high school students dependent on the specific topic to be explored. Middle school students may love a seminar focused specifically on the works of J. R. R. Tolkien, or they might like a course that focuses on the works of several fantasy writers in order to compare and contrast the literary themes. In high school classes, topics such as the literature of war, Russian literature of the 19th century, Dickens and the Industrial Revolution, the literature of the Lost Generation, Shakespearean comedies or tragedies, or any other specifically grouped literature that arouses interest would be appropriate. Block scheduling would allow for more time to do research and presentations in the seminar along with the essential discussions about the literature.

Discussion focused, these seminars routinely focus on patterns that surface from one piece of literature to the next that force students to analyze, synthesize, and evaluate material on a personal level as well as to question each other's ideas. The teachers assume the role of participants in order to establish the shared responsibility of leadership necessary for the success of a true seminar (Dixon, 1994).

Before moving to specific strategies and lessons designed for gifted secondary adolescents, it is essential to mention the importance of focusing on critical thinking for all high-ability learners. This topic is covered in another chapter in this text (see Chapter 12), so it only will be touched on here. However, the way material is used in these lessons demands an understanding of critical thinking on the teacher's part. The design of the lessons presented focuses on the cognitive strengths of gifted students, and critical thinking activities constantly require them to use these strengths. Therefore, these lessons are not appropriate for regular classes because they are appropriately differentiated for gifted students.

The following strategies can be modified for use at the middle or high school depending on the content chosen by the teacher or the students. Further, they comply with the Standards for the English Language Arts as developed by the National Council of Teachers of English (1996), which state the following skills:

1. Students read a wide range of print and nonprint texts to build an understanding of texts, of themselves, and of the cultures of the United States

and the world; to acquire new information; to respond to the needs and demands of society and the workplace; and for personal fulfillment. Among these texts are fiction and nonfiction, classic and contemporary works.

2. Students read a wide range of literature from many periods in many genres to build an understanding of the many dimensions (e.g., philosophical, ethical, aesthetic) of human experience.

3. Students apply a wide range of strategies to comprehend, interpret, evaluate, and appreciate texts. They draw on their prior experience, their interactions with other readers and writers, their knowledge of work meaning and other texts, their word identification strategies, and their understanding of textual features (e.g., sound-letter correspondence, sentence structure, context, graphics).

4. Students adjust their use of spoken, written, and visual language (e.g., conventions, style, vocabulary) to communicate effectively with a variety of audiences and for different purposes.

5. Students employ a wide range of strategies as they write and use different writing process elements appropriately to communicate with different audiences for a variety of purposes.

6. Students apply knowledge of language structure, language conventions (e.g., spelling and punctuation), media techniques, figurative language, and genre to create, critique, and discuss print and nonprint texts.

7. Students conduct research on issues and interests by generating ideas and questions, and by posing problems. They gather, evaluate, and synthesize data from a variety of sources (e.g., print and nonprint, artifacts, people) to communicate their discoveries in ways that suit their purpose and audience.

8. Students use a variety of technological and informational resources (e.g., libraries, databases, computer networks, video) to gather and synthesize information and to create and communicate knowledge.

9. Students develop an understanding of and respect for diversity in language use, patterns, and dialects across cultures, ethnic groups, geographic regions, and social roles.

10. Students whose first language is not English make use of their first language to develop competency in the English language arts and to develop understanding of content across the curriculum.

11. Students participate as knowledgeable, reflective, creative, and critical members of a variety of literacy communities.

12. Students use spoken, written, and visual language to accomplish their own purposes (e.g., for learning, enjoyment, persuasion, and the exchange of information). (p. 3)

The first sequence of assignments are tests based on challenging texts. They focus on critical reading, critical thinking, and writing that focuses on text and on the issue presented. They are appropriate for gifted students because they require a thorough knowledge of the literature being tested, as well as an element of creativity in the type of question asked and the type of response elicited.

The Odyssey

This test (Ney, 2005) is appropriate for use in middle or high school classes.

1. Using passages from your text as a basis of comparison, create an odyssey for one of the following characters. Be sure that as your person journeys through life, he or she encounters parallel situations in contemporary life that Odysseus encountered in *The Odyssey* (50 pts.).
   1. a feminist
   2. a member of your family
   3. your best friend

2. Odysseus is the first alienated hero. He is truly alienated from society and foreshadows so many 20th-century heroes. Alienation allows one to see from a distance and usually creates difficulty, and thus knowledge, through crisis. The Greek word *krisis* carries within it the meaning of separation and judgment. In order to judge, one must separate, make distinctions, and make choices. Odysseus is a man of choices. Discuss, using passages from your text as support (50 pts.).

This test on *The Odyssey* has several qualities that make it very appropriate for gifted adolescents:

1. It focuses on classic literature and asks students to cite specific passages as a standard of comparison.
2. It asks for creative responses and offers choices for response (i.e., the persona of a feminist, a family member, or a best friend).
3. It focuses on a specific theme (i.e., the alienated hero) for a response.
4. Both writing activities are equally weighted and are open-ended in that they do not require one convergent response from all students.
5. This test is challenging and interesting for students.

The Lost Generation

The second test example is taken from a high school American Literature seminar entitled "The Lost Generation" (Ney, 2005), which focused on the literary expatriates who converged in Paris. This examination is based on the works of F. Scott Fitzgerald and is a take home examination.

1. Choose two of the following quotes and apply them to the material that you have read in the class thus far (25 points for each quotation):

A. "Paris," Gertrude Stein had said, "is where the twentieth century is."

B. "You can't have too much money. I believe in money and lots of it. I have to believe in it—because after all there's nothing else to believe in nowadays. Nothing!" (Zelda)

C. "Sometimes," Fitzgerald told a visitor late at night, "I don't know whether Zelda and I are real or whether we are characters in one of my stories."

2. Choose one of the following quotes and apply it to what you have read. Be sure to use textual evidence to support your statements (25 points):

A. In one of his "Notebook" entries, under the title "Description of Girls," Fitzgerald notes, "She was lovely and expensive, and about nineteen." His stories from the beginning bring many changes upon that formula. Gloria Gilbert of *The Beautiful and the Damned* is a preliminary sketch, and a good one, but Daisy Fay Buchanan of *The Great Gatsby* is a full and mature study of the "flapper" heroine's place in Fitzgerald's special world.

B. It is interesting to compare notes on Daisy's dependence upon wealth for the security and the "respectability" it grants, with Myrtle Wilson's lusty and even primitively arrogant assumptions of its momentary privileges in the apartment Tom Buchanan provides for her.

3. Apply the following quote to what you have read thus far. Include textual evidence (25 points):

The masculine ideal of the 1920s was what Fitzgerald called, "the old dream of being entire man in the Goethe-Byron-Shaw tradition, with an opulent American Touch . . ." The entire man would be one who "did everything," good and bad, who realized all the potentialities of his nature and thereby achieved wisdom. The entire man in the 1920s was the one who followed the rule "Do what you will." But, in the 1920s, young men had to will all sorts of actions and had to possess enough energy and courage to carry out even their momentary wishes. They lived in the moment with what they liked to call "an utter disregard of consequences."

This test is appropriate for gifted high school students because it is challenging and requires a high degree of critical thinking before responding to each item. In addition, students must use synthesis in order to respond to each item. Expressing ideas in writing is essential for success in life for these students, and this type of examination fosters that goal. The language used in the items on this examination is high level and cites outside sources in each item. Literary criticism is used to teach this course, and an examination that makes use of this literary criticism makes good sense. Finally, Taylor's (1996) notion that texts must be "read and reread, discussed, and then rethought in order to be understood. Repetition, delay, and participation are crucial elements in experiencing literature" (p. 93) is applied well in this examination. It is obvious that Fitzgerald's ideas and guiding theories must be thought out and understood in order to fare well on this type of examination. These are elements necessary for gifted students.

Jane Eyre

The next example (Ney, 2005) is another take home test that focuses again on a series of choices for responses. Based on the novel *Jane Eyre* by Charlotte Bronte it is more widely used with high school students, but highly talented middle school students would be challenged as well.

Directions: Select either A or B in each of the categories. Read the commentaries carefully, and determine the major points that should be addressed in each essay. Do not skip statements in the quotation that should be addressed. Use good style and support your comments with passages from the text (200 pts. total).

Part I: 50 points
A. "Almost all that we require in a novelist, Charlotte Bronte has: perception of character, and power of delineating it; picturesqueness; passion; and knowledge of life." —George Henry Lewes, 1847, "The Reality of Jane Eyre"
B. "There can be no question but that *Jane Eyre* is a very clever book. Indeed it is a book of decided power. The thoughts are true, sound, and original; and the style, though rude and uncultivated here and there, is resolute, straightforward, and to the purpose . . . There are, it is true, in this autobiography (which though relating to a woman, we do not believe to have been written by a woman), struggles, and misgivings, but in the end, the honesty, kindness of heart, and perseverance of the heroine, are seen triumphant over every obstacle . . ."—A. W. Fonblanque, 1847, *Examiner*

Part II: 50 Points
A. "Conventional romantic novels of love are essentially optimistic because they are expected to, and almost invariably do, conclude with the achievement of a much frustrated union of hero and heroine. But they achieve the sunlight only after a prolonged sojourn in the darkness of despair, anger, danger even. The final happy outcome is the greater because of the encircling gloom out of which it has leapt." —Barbara and Gareth Evans, 1982, *The Scribner Companion to the Brontes*
    Is this true of *Jane Eyre*?
B. "Some readers have regarded *Jane Eyre* as a religious novel because it is the record of the fidelity of a young woman to the inexorable laws of God as she sees them. Even more, in her adherence to duty, to order, and her fidelity to what is expected of her, it might be said that Jane demonstrates Christian principles in practice."—Barbara and Gareth Evans, 1982, *The Scribner Companion to the Brontes*

Part III: 25 Points

A. "It is true Jane does right, and exerts great moral strength, but it is the strength of a mere heathen mind which is a law unto itself. No Christian grace is perceptible upon her. She has inherited in the fullest measure the worst sin of our fallen nature—the sin of pride. Jane Eyre is proud, and therefore she is ungrateful too."—Elizabeth Rigby, 1848, "An Anti-Christian Composition"

B. "For the majority of readers, *Jane Eyre's* major 'romantic' appeal lay and still lies in its heroine, who is placed in a succession of situations which bare her vulnerability—physical, mental, spiritual, emotional, and moral." —Barbara and Gareth Evans, 1982, *The Scribner Companion to the Brontes*

Part IV: 25 Points

A. "If in Mr. Rochester we see only a Byronic hero and a Charlotte wish-fulfill-ment figure, we miss what is more significant, the exploration of a personality that opens up new areas of feeling in intersexual relationships."—Helman, 1958, "Charlotte Bronte's New Gothic"

B. "Bronte's men were all father figures. They all seem to have a paternal atti-tude toward the heroine. *Jane Eyre* depicts the experience of a girl/gov-erness whose desire for love is inextricably linked with a desire to have a protector—someone to be respected, looked up to, someone to whom she can indulge her yearning to be subservient without losing respect, love, or, what is most important, freedom of action." —Barbara and Gareth Evans, 1982, *The Scribner Companion to the Brontes*

Part V: 25 Points

A. "Charlotte Bronte was most concerned with the terrible vulnerability to exploitation of all kinds of young women, like herself and her sisters . . . the facts are that in early Victorian England, governesses were often treated with callous cruelty, were without any personal freedom, often had no one with whom to share their miseries, and were employed for longer hours and poorer wages than many millhands."—Barbara and Gareth Evans, 1982, *The Scribner Companion to the Brontes*
    Discuss in relation to *Jane Eyre*.

B. "The Bronte novels are concerned with the neuroses of women in a man's society. It is also obvious that *Jane Eyre* is a feminist tract, an argument for the social betterment of governesses and equal rights for women."—Richard Chase, 1971, "The Brontes, or Myth Domesticated"

Part VI: 25 Points

A. Discuss *Jane Eyre* as an autobiographical novel.

B. Discuss *Jane Eyre* as a Gothic novel.

The challenging way that this novel is treated in this examination takes the student to the text and to outside sources for a thorough understanding of how this novel fits into its time period and why it has remained so important in literature. The critical thinking aspects of the items are obvious. Students are well informed of how many points are awarded for each item, but within each item is a choice. This test is lengthy but fair and consistent. It suggests that the activities within class before the examination were focused on discussion of important elements of the novel and utilized outside sources as springboards to discussion, as well.

American Literature Exam

The final example of a test for high-ability verbal students was constructed for an American Literature class (Dixon, 2005). This is a final in-class exam, again in essay format.

Directions: Answer the questions that follow as completely as you can, giving specific examples from the texts. You must answer all six questions; the first five are worth 15 points each, and the final question is worth 25 points. Give examples from the readings (as you remember them) to support the points you make.

1. *Moby Dick* and *Walden*, published a few years apart, concern themselves (among other things) with the natural order ("nature") and humankind's place in it. In what ways do Melville and Thoreau see Nature the same in these books? In what ways do they differ?
2. Compare and contrast the uses of symbols and themes in one work by Poe and one work by Hawthorne. Choose either A or B:
   A. Use "Young Goodman Brown" and "The Cask of Amontillado."
   B. Use *The Scarlet Letter* and "Ligeia."
3. Franklin's *Autobiography* could, without too much damage to reason, be called a textbook on the "American Dream" (though Franklin might be a bit surprised at that grandiose term). What is clear is that Franklin intended his book to mark out a general way to success. Emerson's essays, especially "An American Scholar" also deal with man, dreams, and success. Compare and contrast ideas each man uses to arrive at the conclusion of what is most successful for humankind.
4. In a famous letter to Hawthorne, Melville said of *Moby Dick*, "I have written a wicked book, and feel spotless as the lamb." Discuss in what ways *Moby Dick* might be considered a "wicked book."
5. Melville and Hawthorne were known as the "Dark" Romantics of their period. What themes and motifs in *Moby Dick* and *The Scarlet Letter* would prove this statement true about these authors? Be careful to cite specific examples from the text to support your views.
6. This is a creative question that demands a creative and thoughtful response. You are in a situation in which time period is no factor. You are to invite the

following authors to a dinner: Hawthorne, Emerson, Thoreau, Franklin, and Melville. You must decide the following:

A. Where the dinner will take place (either a specific restaurant and place or the type of restaurant and reason for your choice).
B. The seating arrangement around the table at the restaurant (specifically, who will sit next to whom and why you placed them in the arrangement. In some cases, you may want to avoid putting people next to each other; explain this).
C. What each person will eat (you should have a rationale for the choice).
D. Where you will sit; what you will eat and why.
E. Finally, what topic of conversation will you, the host, choose to initiate during the dinner, and why will it be appropriate to your guests?

Again, this test demands creative production from students on some items and critical thinking throughout the items. Students are required to read the texts carefully and know and understand them in order to answer the questions. Literary criticism informs the content of the items, modeling synthesis for students as they write their own responses.

These examples were used to show the type of tests that work well for gifted students. Although none of the classes in which these tests were given were designated as AP, these items would well-prepare students for the AP examination. They ask for logical development, clear thinking that comes from understanding and analysis of a challenging text, and they demand support from the work(s) read. Further, material was handled at a high level. The essay format was obviously used in all of these. This is not to disparage the use of objective formats when needed in classes. However, the use of essays in which students must condense thoughts and think through a number of issues maximizes their critical thinking and more closely mirrors what goes on in class.

The Discussion Examination

Another type of examination used in literature classes for gifted students focuses on the discussion format, and is therefore called the discussion examination (Dixon, 2000). The rationale for this type of examination is that in classes that focus on discussion as the primary classroom activity, the assessment should match the instructional strategy. Discussion examinations make sense. Before the day of the examination, the students are informed of the rules that govern the process. They receive a handout that includes the following information:

1. Develop three themes that span the works read this semester. Examples of themes include the role of women, the growth of the hero/heroine, the use of nature, the use of metaphor, and the supernatural elements in the works.
2. Find examples of these themes in text and come to the examination with

all books, as well as carefully constructed lists of passages from the texts. Leafing through the books during the examination is inappropriate because it takes too much time. Rather, come with the examples written out and give page references so that others can locate the passages quickly.

3. For this examination, desks will be arranged in a circle. At the onset, I will ask the question, "What theme do you want to develop?" We will go around the circle and mention themes. You have developed three, but you will choose one to share with the group. The other two will ensure that you have one in case someone mentions your theme before you do. By preparing three themes, you will also be better prepared to discuss with the other members of the class the topics they introduce.

4. Each discussion examination will have a maximum of 12 students. We may have to have more than one examination session per class, but 12 is the absolute maximum number that I can assess in a single time period.

5. When everyone has mentioned a theme, I will state, "Who would like to begin?" The student who wants to get started will begin.

6. You are not competing with each other. You are showcasing knowledge and the ideas you wish to share. You may add to each other's ideas with text that you have researched whenever it applies. Interrupting each other is not appropriate.

7. I will assess you using the assessment grid based on the levels of Bloom's Taxonomy (see Figure 1). I will record a mark in the appropriate box when your statement reflects the thought level.

The discussion format works well if the teacher knows how to assess it appropriately according to the grid and the points listed on each area (i.e., fact, analysis, synthesis, and evaluation). Optimally, students are well acquainted with what each of these levels represents in practice. To prepare students, a teacher can simply tell the class when someone gives a good example of analysis, synthesis, or evaluation as opposed to fact in class discussion. If the teacher cannot tell the difference him- or herself, then this format does not work well. However, students comment that they study so hard for this type of examination, and usually the means justify the end. It certainly is authentic assessment in that it matches what is occurring in class.

Discussion Questions

Another area of concern for teachers of gifted students in a variety of classes focuses on determining appropriate discussion questions to use in small or large group discussions in class. Whether the class is designated as AP or Honors, students need high-level questions that stimulate active engagement. Consider the following examples as the type of questions (Ney, 2005) that ask students to engage in critical thinking.

Student	Theme	Fact(1)	Analysis(2)	Synthesis(3)	Evaluation(4)
Julie	Nature				
Terrence	Supernatural				
Bob	Hero				
Simon	Metaphor				
Suchi	Time				
Malea	Drama				
Micah	Education				
Jim	Archetypes				
Callie	Woman				
Tim	Art				
Josh	Awakening				
Katherine	Science				

Figure 1. Example of a grid for assessing discussion examination

Heart of Darkness

1. One critic said that there are at least 50 images of death, decay, and darkness in *Heart of Darkness*. Find passages that reveal these images. Are there an equal number of life, growth, and light images?

2. The reader is slowly introduced to Kurtz through reports from other people. Gather the details about him throughout the first two parts of the book. What is Marlowe's assessment of him?

3. Conrad is fond of using contrast in his works. He puts contrasting images back-to-back to make a point. Find some examples and try to determine the point he is trying to make.

4. Conrad is also fond of using different narrators and narrative techniques. How is this true and what effect does it have on the work?

5. Conrad is a very Jungian writer who loads up his works with archetypal imagery. What are the archetypes that you recognize? How is this novel a quest novel portraying the journey of the hero? Trace the pattern of the hero on his journey. What does the hero discover in the end? Provide textual evidence.

6. What are some possibilities of themes in this book? What is Conrad saying about what is at the heart of humanity? Consider other comments he might be making about imperialism? Good vs. evil? White savagery? Respect and responsibility? Ethics? Find text that supports your theories.

7. Consider the ending of the book: Part 3. What happens to Kurtz in the end, and what does it signify? What happens to Marlowe in the end, and what does it signify?

8. Give the significance of the minor characters:
   A. Marlowe's audience on the boat
   B. The two women Marlowe meets at the door

    C. The Swede
    D. The papier-mâché Mephistopheles
    E. The Russian
    F. The Helmsman
    G. Kurtz's native woman
    H. Kurtz's "Intended"
9. Analyze the following in terms of significance and meaning:
    A. The river
    B. Kurtz's pointing
    C. Kurtz's manuscript and "Exterminate the brutes!"
    D. The framework narrative
    E. Color symbolism
    F. Ivory
    G. Africa and the Congo, respectively
    H. The title of the novel
    I. Marlowe's lie in the end
    J. "The horror! The horror!"
10. How does this novel pertain to our life today?

These questions can be used in groups, individually to help students focus as they read, or in a large group forum. They all focus on analysis and synthesis of ideas in the text. They are open-ended and require careful reading in order to uncover the essence of the novel. The abstract style in which this novel is written, along with its historic relevance make it an excellent text to use with gifted students. The questions focus on helping students analyze the novel according to many different literary considerations, all of which could be essay topics, as well as discussion topics.

A Midsummer Night's Dream

A second example of discussion questions (Ney, 2005) focuses on Shakespearean Comedy, in this case the play *A Midsummer Night's Dream*. These questions are appropriate for both high school and middle school gifted students.

Consider these ideas:

1. *A Midsummer Night's Dream* does not take place in midsummer, as the title might suggest. The time of its action is around May Day, and the title merely alludes to the frivolous madness proverbially associated with the rites of Midsummer's Eve, or those of May Day. So, what is the significance of the title and how should the director/producer of this play convey this significance?

2. The masque was an elaborate show that emphasized spectacular elements, costumes, and scenic devices rather than dramatic plot and poetry. Music, dance, and pageantry were essential to the masque. Normally it had alle-

gorical figures—gods, goddesses, shepherds, shepherdesses, and other beau-
tifully costumed creatures of fancy who sang, danced, and paraded before
the guests. These creations had as foils a contrasting group known as the
antimasque, who might be anything from satyrs to earthy yokels comically
attired. *A Midsummer Night's Dream* is Shakespeare's nearest approach to
that form of spectacle. How would you direct this play to emphasize these
masque characteristics?

3. Although our main interest may be in the fairy world and the burlesque
   humor of the artisans, *A Midsummer Night's Dream* is not merely an
   entertaining spectacle like any number of masques from this time period.
   Shakespeare always provides a meaning and significance deeper than the
   surface ripples of mere entertainment. His plays are filled with commentary
   on life and love. Do you agree, or is *A Midsummer Night's Dream* what the
   17th-century diarist Samuel Pepys called, "the most insipid ridiculous play
   that ever I saw in my life"? Defend your answer with text.

4. In Greek New Comedy (342–291 BC) the hero and heroine are usually
   likeable but not very interesting people because their real lives are assumed
   to begin just after the play stops. The chief character interest thus falls on
   the blocking characters. Is this true of Shakespeare's *A Midsummer Night's
   Dream* lovers?

These questions could certainly follow a viewing of the play or a videotape of the
play. However, equally strong is the use of the questions for groups after the reading
of the play. By placing gifted students in the role of the director of the play, they must
analyze and synthesize the information of the play and decide what they want to
emphasize and de-emphasize for audiences to derive maximum understanding. Again,
the concept of choice is challenging for gifted students. According to Thompson
(1996), an interesting way to analyze classic literature such *as A Midsummer Night's
Dream* is to use the Wallas (1926) model that includes four stages: preparation,
incubation, illumination, and verification. With *A Midsummer Night's Dream*, the
first stage, preparation, focuses on study of the text. As Thompson states,

> Study and reread the text carefully collecting the data you will need.
> Incubation: Allow your study of the text to sink in, and allow interpreta-
> tions to bubble in the back of your mind. Illumination: When you have
> incubated long enough, your aha experience will come and you will sud-
> denly get a good idea for interpreting the text. Verification: Once you have
> an idea, patiently work it out, showing how it helps to explain the many
> separate details of the story. (p. 70)

Essays

The next example focuses on topics for writing essays. Again, as in the examination, the choices offered are interesting.

American Literature: Unit on Women's Studies (Ney, 2005)
Directions: Choose four of the 19th-century women characters we have studied and have each of them write a letter to the 20th-century woman as she is described in the poetry and the essay that follow. The letters should reveal whether or not the characters think things have changed for women between the 19th and 20th centuries. Be attentive to style and tone. Be specific and use textual evidence where appropriate.

Selections from which you may choose:

Kate Chopin
The Awakening
"Desiree's Baby"
"The Storm"
"The Story of an Hour"
"A Pair of Silk Stockings"
Charlotte Perkins Gilman
"The Yellow Wallpaper"
Willa Cather
My Antonia

This is an excellent example of choice, as students may choose which four characters from the above works they care to use for their letters. The format is prescribed, but the choice empowers the students on one level. In addition, they must know the literature and understand the format of a good letter in order to do well on this writing task. It is appropriate for secondary gifted students in the challenge of the content and the critical thinking that is required for a well-written response.

"Portrait of the Artist"
Taken from a course entitled "Portrait of the Artist in Contemporary British Literature" (Dixon, 2005), the following essay assignment comes at the completion of *A Portrait of the Artist as a Young Man* by James Joyce.

Directions: Write a five-paragraph essay on one of the following topics or choose one that you determine using the same guidelines. Be sure to use text to support your thesis.

1. Stephen Dedalus was influenced greatly by what he read. Some of the writers that he mentioned included Byron, Shelley, Dumas, Victor Hugo, Newman, Yeats, Aquinas. Discuss these literary "voices" and their influence on Stephen as a literary artist.

2. The name "Stephen Dedalus" is a combination of a biblical name (Stephen) and a mythical name, "Daedalus." Discuss Joyce's use of both biblical and mythical images in this text and the reason for his use of both.

3. Discuss Stephen's exile as a logical culmination of this text, or discuss this exile as a miserable failure in that Stephen is simply running from his problems.

4. The Irish backdrop for this novel serves as a metaphor for what Stephen is experiencing himself. Discuss this idea.
5. In this book, in which priests play such an integral part, Stephen describes himself as an artist, " . . . a priest of eternal imagination, transmuting the daily bread of experience into the radiant body of everliving life." Tie this quotation into the story of Stephen Dedalus.
6. Discuss Stephen's labyrinths or mazes in this novel.

This text is very challenging for all readers. It demands a high level of critical thinking continuously as the student navigates the text. Further, Borland (2000), in responding to papers at the American Educational Research Association's annual meeting, referred to the creative struggle of a verbally gifted individual as being well documented by James Joyce in *A Portrait of the Artist as a Young Man*. Through all of his struggles in life, his verbal gift remained steadfast. This reminder of the permanence of one's gift is a good lesson for gifted students as they ponder the issues presented in this book. These essay topics are short, focused, and open-ended enough for personal interpretation. However, they are precise enough to demand evidence through the text in the essay response. The key to this assignment is found in the challenging content read. Figure 2 provides an assessment rubric that is appropriate for essays of this type.

The Canterbury Tales

Finally, this third example comes from the very familiar *The Canterbury Tales* by Geoffrey Chaucer (Dixon, 2005).

Directions: Write an essay that answers one of the following questions or choose another topic of your own from *The Canterbury Tales* and examine it in a similarly complex way. Use textual evidence and think about elements of language and MLA format as you write this essay.

1. The Pilgrimage is over: The Pilgrims have returned to the Tabbard Inn and Harry Bailey (the host) is ready to seat the Pilgrims for the award dinner. Using the Pilgrims whose tales you have read as the group invited, determine how the host should seat them. Draw a diagram to include with this essay in which you provide a seating chart. Next, justify why Bailey should sit each person next to someone (instead of someone else) based on what you know about these characters. Finally, who does he choose as the winner, and why does he make this selection? Write this as a well-developed essay and include well-chosen quotations from the text.
2. Discuss how Chaucer treats the genre of writing known as the Courtly Romance in the "Knight's Tale," "The Wife of Bath's Tale," and "The Tale of Sir Topaz." In order to do this well, first establish the guidelines of a romance, then show how each of these does or does not fit.

Student_____ Total Points_____

Content: 50 Points Possible   _____ Points Received

Introduction (5 points)
_____Interesting or scholarly lead into the paper
_____Ends with thesis statement

Thesis (5)
_____Valid; provable
_____Stated concisely, but contains necessary information
_____Narrow enough for the length of the paper
_____Interesting; challenging (not an obvious fact or idea)

Body: 40 Points
_____Strong argumentative topic sentences for each point (5)
_____Sufficient exposition to explain the point (15)
_____Paper argues the points and does not "tell" the plot
_____Paper follows outline and does not digress
_____Sufficient number of examples to lend support to the point (10)
_____Concrete examples from the text are used
_____Paper is free of generalizations
_____Each point is strongly supported so that the paper is balanced
_____Direct quotes from text to lend authority to the point (10)
_____Appropriate number of direct quotes are used
_____Quotes are spaced so that there is no "stringing"

Form: 50 Points Possible   _____ Points Received
_____Organization (5)
_____Clarity and conciseness (5)
_____Grammar, sentence structure, punctuation, spelling, proofreading (5)
_____Diction (use of language) (5)

Use of MLA
_____Information block (1)
_____Headings, pagination (2)
_____Spacing, indentation (2)
_____Introducing quotes and weaving into text (5)
_____Citations (5)
_____Short Quotes (5)
_____Long Quotes (5)
_____Works Cited (5)

Figure 2. Rubric for assessing papers

3. Greed is one of the vices that the Pilgrims had to fight against. Discuss how Chaunticlear and Pertilote, the Pardoner, and the characters in "the Miller's Tale" all dealt with greed. Think of different ways greed is shown in these tales first, and finally try to conclude with what Chaucer is saying to his audience about greed.

This work is one that almost all students read in a British Literature class. These essay topics are challenging enough to provide a range of responses for gifted students. The creativity in the first question and the analysis and synthesis that are required for the responses for each of them provide for critical thinking and content rigor for gifted students.

Individual and Group Projects

Finally, in discussing high-ability students and strategies to use in the English classroom, it is important to examine both individual and group projects. The following assignments clearly incorporate the characteristics of gifted students with verbal strengths.

Portfolios
Portfolios can be used with any literature for middle school or high school. This example came from the Lost Generation seminar (Ney, 2005).
Contents of the portfolio should include:

1. Pictures of your author/artist during the 1920s. Accumulate as many as you can revealing him or her in different settings with different significant people.
2. Your author's work prior to the 1920s, his or her work during the 1920s, and works in progress or ideas for the future. Reviews of his or her works.
3. Your author's theories/opinions about the art of writing, as well as his or her opinions about the other writers and their opinions of your author and his or her writing.
4. Description of significant events that happened to the author/artist during the 1920s and the impact these events had on your artist's art.
5. Interesting stories about your artist and his or her friends, enemies, and rivals in the 1920s.
6. Present these at a tea in honor of these authors/artists.

This is an excellent way for gifted students to analyze major events of the time and how they affected the chosen author or artist. Creating a forum for sharing, such as a party or a tea makes the assignment an event.

The Character Party
The character party is appropriate for any literature for middle and high school students (Dixon, 2005) and can be as elaborate as the teacher desires. The example

below was created for a seminar on Russian Literature. The party was in the form of a meeting of the Russian Intelligentsia during the 19th century. Students had read the following works: short stories by Pushkin; *A Hero of Our Time* by Mikhail Lermontov; "The Nose" and "The Overcoat" by Gogol; *Fathers and Sons* by Ivan Turgenev; *Crime and Punishment,* by Fyodor Dostoevsky; and *the Kreutzer Sonata* by Leo Tolstoy.

1. Students choose a character, philosopher mentioned in the works, or the author of the works to portray at the party.
2. Students were required to dress as the character would dress or adapt the dress to a modern rendition of what the character would wear today.
3. At the party, students must stay in character, using language and mannerisms the person would use based on research completed prior to the party.
4. Students must have knowledge of political/social issues that would influence their character and join other characters at the party with similar views.
5. Students must visit with the teacher for assessment during the party.

This type of activity in which the student must assume a role is an excellent way for them to analyze the character and then synthesize the time period, other characters, and how these all influenced the literature of the time. It is very appropriate for gifted students, and they tend to enjoy these experiences.

Literary Quest/Treasure Hunt

The literary quest or treasure hunt example is based on Tolkien's *Lord of the Rings* series, but can be used with any group of literature read in middle or high school (Dixon, 2005). Students are divided into groups and instructed that one person in the group must have a complete set of the readings assigned for the quest. The quest will send them on a journey around the school, on a campus if you are near a college and can do this outside of school time, or in town if the school is in a rural area. The following rules must be followed and are presented to the students:

1. You will receive a video camera and a roll of paper and markers. You must video all stops, and all members of the group must appear an equal amount of time on the tape. You need to video what happens in response to each clue.
2. The paper is to be used to construct a map at the end of the quest. Your map must be a complete representation of where you have been. In addition, you must name your group and create a slogan that you will chant as you return at the end of the quest.
3. You will receive the first clue, which will send you on to the next clue. Figure out where you are to go and proceed to the next place. At each stop, you will need one of the texts you have read to find the passage and do what you are instructed to do on the clue (i.e., read a passage, do an activity). All activities will be recorded on tape.

4. Time is of the essence. Work efficiently, but have a good time. There are eight clues to complete.

This works very well as a strategy for gifted students. It can adapt well to many different literature classes and can be as complex as the teacher makes it. The assessment comes from the videotape turned in, as well as the map indicating where the students went during the quest.

CONCLUSION

Maya, the student at the beginning of this chapter who e-mailed the instructor about the independent study in Arthurian Literature, determined her own syllabus that directed the semester's readings. She continues to love this literature, having traveled to Glastonbury to visit the sites attributed to the Arthurian Legend. In addition, she taught a class on Arthurian Literature in college. Her zeal for this literature never quit. It is evident that this is what needs to happen for these students in English classes. The key is for teachers to understand the needs of high-ability students and then appropriately differentiate the classes to meet those needs. Even in AP classes, differentiation must occur if students are to work to their potential. Challenging content that sets the context for processes focused on vocabulary development, grammar study, writing assignments that provide rigor and yet precision, and literary discussions meet the needs of these students because they continually offer choices and challenge. Academic rigor is essential and with this type of curriculum, it can and must happen all the time.

REFERENCES

Borland, J. (2000, April). Discussant statements made at the Annual Meeting of the American Educational Research Association, New Orleans, LA.

Burney, V. (2002). Advanced placement in Indiana: Why you should support it. In The Indiana Association for the Gifted (Ed.), *A Gifted Education Resource Guide for Indiana Parents and Educators* (2nd ed., pp. 137–140). Indianapolis: Indiana Department of Education, Division of Exceptional Learners.

Carnegie Council. (1995). *Great transitions: Preparing adolescents for a new century.* New York: Carnegie Corporation.

College Board. (2000). *A guide to the Advanced Placement program.* Princeton, NJ: Author.

Coleman, L. J., & Cross, T. L. (2001). *Being gifted in school: An introduction to development, guidance, and teaching.* Waco, TX: Prufrock Press..

Dixon, F. A. (1994). Literature seminars for gifted and talented students. *Gifted Child Today, 18*(2), 12–16.

Dixon, F. A. (1996). *The use of the Hegelian Dialectic as a heuristic in literature classes to improve critical thinking skills.* Unpublished doctoral dissertation. Purdue University.

Dixon, F. A. (2000). The discussion examination: Making assessment match instructional strategy. *Roeper Review, 23,* 104–108.

Dixon, F. A. (2005). *Examples of curriculum units used in classes for high-ability students at the Indiana Academy for Science, Mathematics and Humanities.* Unpublished units.

Dixon, F. A. (in press). *Literature units for high-ability students.* Waco, TX: Prufrock Press.

Feldhusen, J. F. (1997). Secondary services, opportunities, and activities for talented youth. In N. Colangelo & G. Davis (Eds.), *Handbook of gifted education* (2nd ed., pp. 189–197). Boston: Allyn & Bacon.

Feldhusen, J. F. (1998). Strategies and methods for teaching the talented. In J. VanTassel-Baska (Ed.), *Excellence in educating gifted and talented learners* (3rd ed., pp. 363–379). Denver, CO: Love.

Feldhusen, J. F., & Robinson, A. (1986). The Purdue secondary model for gifted and talented youth. In J. S. Renzulli (Ed.), *Systems and models for developing programs for the gifted and talented* (pp. 153–179). Mansfield Center, CT: Creative Learning Press.

Gallagher, J. (1975). *Teaching the gifted child* (2nd ed.). Boston: Allyn & Bacon.

Gallagher, J. (1995). Education of gifted students: A civil rights issue? *Phi Delta Kappan, 76,* 408–410.

Halsted, J. W. (1994). *Some of my best friends are books.* Dayton: Ohio Psychology Press.

Kolloff, P. B. (1996). Gifted girls and the humanities. *Journal of Secondary Gifted Education, 7,* 486–492.

Kolloff, P. B., & Feldhusen, J. F. (1986). The seminar: An instructional approach for gifted students. *Gifted Child Today, 9*(5), 2–7.

Little, C. (2002). Reasoning as a key component of language arts curricula. *Journal of Secondary Gifted Education, 13,* 52–59.

Maker, C. J. (1982). *Curriculum development for the gifted.* Rockville, MD: Aspen.

National Council of Teachers of English. (1996). *Standards for the English language arts.* Urbana, IL: Author.

Ney, C. (2005). *Curriculum units used in courses at the Indiana Academy for Science, Mathematics and Humanities.* Unpublished units.

Passow, A. H. (1988). Educating gifted persons who are caring and concerned. *Roeper Review, 11,* 13–15.

Passow, A. H. (1986). Curriculum for the gifted and talented at the secondary level. *Gifted Child Quarterly, 30,* 186–191.

Piirto, J. (1999). *Talented children and adults* (2nd ed.). Upper Saddle River, NJ: Merrill, Prentice Hall.

Singal, D. J. (1991). The other crisis in American education. *The Atlantic Monthly, 71,* 59–74.

Snowman, J., & Biehler, R. (2000). *Psychology applied to teaching* (9th ed.). Boston: Houghton Mifflin.

Stotsky, S. (1995). Changes in America's secondary school literature programs: Good news and bad. *Phi Delta Kappan, 76,* 605–613.

Taylor, B. A. (1996). The study of literature: Insights into human understanding. In J. VanTassel-Baska, D. Johnson, & L. Boyce (Eds.), *Developing verbal talent* (pp. 75–94). Boston: Allyn & Bacon.

Thompson, M. C. (1996). Mentors on paper: How classics develop verbal ability. In J. VanTassel-Baska, D. Johnson, & L. Boyce (Eds.), *Developing verbal talent* (pp. 56–74). Boston: Allyn & Bacon.

Thompson, M. C. (2002). Vocabulary and grammar: Critical content for critical thinking. *Journal of Secondary Gifted Education, 13,* 60–66.

VanTassel-Baska, J. (1988). Verbal arts for the gifted. In J. VanTassel-Baska, J. Feldhusen, K. Seeley, G. Wheatley, L. Silverman, & W. Foster (Eds.), *Comprehensive curriculum for gifted learners* (pp. 153–189) Boston: Allyn & Bacon.

VanTassel-Baska, J., & Little, C. A. (2003). *Content based curriculum for high-ability learners.* Washington, DC: National Association for Gifted Children.

VanTassel-Baska, J., Zuo, L., Avery, L. D., & Little, C. A. (2002). A curriculum study of gifted student learning in the language arts. *Gifted Child Quarterly, 46,* 30–44.

Wallas, G. (1926). *The art of thought.* New York: Harcourt Brace.

"Pulling the Cat's Tail" in Social Studies and History Classrooms

CHAPTER

by William J. Stepien & William C. Stepien

"You can learn more about cats by pulling their tails than you can by reading about them in books," says Hal Holbrook in *Mark Twain Tonight*, Holbrook's critically acclaimed portrayal of the noted author and social commentator. The actor attributes the quote to Huckleberry Finn, who offers it as an explanation for why his school attendance record is so dismal. In the young rascal's view, school has little to do with learning about the real world.

If you asked today's middle and high school students about the value social studies and history education play in helping them understand the real world, would they respond differently? For too many students, social education fails to engage, challenge, or inspire, and it is not producing especially glowing results as measured by national assessment efforts either (Patrick, 2001).

How might this situation be improved? Even though Huck Finn's advice is not likely to appear in a scholarly journal, when taken as metaphor explaining why students disconnect from social studies and history, it does pack a potent message. Finn could be telling educators to engage students with real-world issues, topics, and problems—to give them the "tail of the cat" to investigate or "pull on"—and stop relying so heavily on textbooks and teacher talk as their *modus operandi*.

In this chapter, the authors argue that students, especially gifted and talented adolescents, can achieve significant subject matter outcomes and find motivation when social studies and history curricula reflect national standards, activate and nourish the talents of gifted students, and are delivered through constructivist methodologies, such as *problem-based learning* (PBL).

STUDENT ATTITUDES TOWARD SOCIAL EDUCATION

How closely does Huck Finn's view of formal education mirror the attitudes of adolescents toward social education? Research findings on attitudes toward selected subjects in elementary schools put social studies and history in the middle of the pack, but that soon begins to change. Fraser (1981) found that attitudes toward social studies and history deteriorate with each succeeding grade level, while Haladyna and Thomas (1979) discovered that diminishing status is not directly correlated to negative feelings toward school in general, nor is it explained by gender. Along with a general lack of interest in the fields, students also view the subjects as "unimportant" and "insignificant" in helping construct a better understanding of historic or contemporary issues (Schug, Todd, & Beery, 1984). And finally, even though a number of subjects have image problems in these grade levels (DiSibio & Savitz, 1983; Rakow, 1984; Reyes, 1984), social studies is the least stimulating and least liked subject students encounter in grades 6–12 (Shaughnessy & Haladyna, 1985).

Some insight into why this is true can be found in causal research probing the importance certain variables in learning environments play in attitude formation. These studies generally conclude that variables in the learning environment, taken together, are much more important than the content of the social studies curriculum in determining student attitudes toward the subject itself (Fancett & Hawke, 1982; Weible & Evans, 1984). In other words, social studies content does not explain why attitudes toward the subject are declining. Additionally, once variables such as respect for students, good management techniques, and teacher enthusiasm for the subject matter are held constant, *quality of instruction* seems to explain why students feel the way they do toward social studies (Haladyna & Shaughnessy, 1982). More recent findings suggest that attitudes of adolescents can improve when a mixture of diverse teaching strategies, active student participation in the lesson, and cooperative learning activities become regular components of the classroom environment (Fouts, 1989).

THE PRIMARY PURPOSE OF SOCIAL STUDIES AND HISTORY EDUCATION

Since antiquity, thinkers have extolled the importance of education as the foundation of a republic. At the beginning of our own republic, Thomas Jefferson, perhaps the most quoted of the founding fathers on the subject, pointed out that only when the people are well-informed can they be trusted with their own government.

In Jefferson's eyes, citizens of a democratic republic needed to prepare themselves for the role of citizen, a responsibility he viewed with an almost religious reverence. For Jefferson, education was the pathway to civic virtue.

But, what must young people know and be able to do in order to become virtuous citizens and understand how they and societies change over time? This should be the first question answered when designing meaningful curricula.

During America's early history, the major responsibility for preparing young people to be capable, responsible citizens rested in the study of history, civics, and geography. During the early 20th century, social studies, featuring a blend of subject matter from the social sciences and history, ascended in importance in elementary education and is now the place where children begin their journey toward becoming responsible, productive members of society. The need to feature patriotism in the social education curriculum also expanded during this time, fueled by increasing geo-political tensions and a need to help millions of immigrants find their places in the American salad bowl. With the dawn of the space race, the goals of social studies and history were expanded to include making students proficient in the process of rational inquiry, a first cousin to the scientific method.

Most recently, concerns over the scope and sequence of the curriculum and the need to specify standardized outcomes for each content area have brought renewed interest in the mission, methods, and materials of social studies, history, and the social sciences. But, one constant endures both the passage of time and the motives of reformers—the primary purpose of social studies and history is educating children for responsible, active citizenship.

Defining Social Studies

The National Council for the Social Studies' (NCSS) definition of social studies is especially useful to instructional planners because it establishes both the purpose and subject matter disciplines that are foundational for a meaningful social education curriculum. The NCSS (1994) defines *social studies* as:

> . . . the integrated study of the social sciences and humanities to promote civic competence. Within the school program, social studies provides coordinated, systematic study drawing upon such disciplines as anthropology, archaeology, economics, geography, history, law, philosophy, political science, psychology, religion, and sociology, as well as appropriate content from the humanities, mathematics, and natural sciences. The primary purpose of social studies is to help young people develop the ability to make informed and reasoned decisions for the public good as citizens of a culturally diverse, democratic society in an interdependent world. (pp. 2–3)

Two elements of the definition need to be carefully noted. First, the definition recognizes that civic competence requires understanding of concepts from disciplines and fields of study as varied as economics, history, political science, law, religion, humanities, and natural sciences. In other words, civic competence requires an

---

Table 1
The Process of Inquiry

Phases in the Process	Guiding Questions
1. Define a purpose for thinking	"What's the issue or the problem?"
2. Guess at a tentative answer or conclusion; form an hypothesis	"What could be the explanation?"
3. Test and investigate; gather relevant information from reliable sources	"What do I need to know?" "How can I find out?"
4. Draw valid conclusions	"What logical conclusions can I make?"
5. Apply the conclusions to new data and generalize	"What reasonable/defensible generalizations can I make?"

Note. The guiding questions were added by this chapter's authors.

---

interdisciplinary understanding of phenomena and movements in the real world. The artificial boundaries that separate academic disciplines must be made invisible when authentic understanding of concepts and issues are being sought. Today's citizen lives and makes decisions in a global village distinguished by its diversity, complexity, and web of interdependence. In this village, decisions about the public good in one place send shock waves of intended and unintended consequences around the planet, slowed little by political or geographical boundaries. Therefore, the NCSS posits, informed decisions regarding complex issues require understanding of concepts from any disciplines that shed light on human thought and behavior. The entirety of the recommended concepts needed to produce effective social studies curriculum are found at the NCSS Web site (http://www.ncss.org).

A second assertion to note in the definition is the importance assigned to "informed and reasoned decisions" as a basic competence of citizens in a democracy. Implied in this affirmation is the importance of coaching young people, as a part of social studies, toward proficiency in rational inquiry, with its foundation of critical thinking skills, and a disposition on the part of learners to use those skills when needed. Table 1 identifies the major phases of the inquiry process and the metacognitive questions critical thinkers use for focus as the process unfolds (Beyer, 1971).

THE PROCESS OF INQUIRY

This assertion is a daunting challenge because it requires more than *knowing* on the part of citizens. Rational inquiry requires the ability and proclivity to use high level thinking skills when faced with ambiguous, multifaceted problems that lend themselves to a variety of interpretations, are filled with conflicting value positions, and can usually be resolved in more than one way. Further, making "informed and reasoned decisions for the public good" requires the ability to view situations from multiple perspectives, to identify potential consequences of actions, and to recognize the importance of respecting minority rights and opinions. And, just hearing about issues, problems, and solutions in a classroom has little effect on the development of productive problem solvers or competent citizens. Competence in solving problems and making rational decisions requires that students have opportunities to investigate and work out solutions to real problems, contemporary and historical. Maybe Huck Finn was warning educators that education without a focus on real problems cannot produce genuine competencies.

A Special Place for History

Beside the fact that history has traditionally been a flagship discipline in social education, it is generally accepted that history plays a special role in the preparation of responsible citizens. The study of history offers students a chance to examine social change as both evolutionary and revolutionary processes, a perspective that reveals the importance of past and present interactions of people with places and issues, as well as the importance of being proactive regarding future interactions. As Neville Shute reminds the world in *On the Beach*: "Nothing is inevitable as long as people think."

Explicit, well-conceived standards for meaningful, high-quality history education can be found in two easy-to-find documents. The first, *U.S. History Framework for the 1994 and 2001 National Assessment of Educational Progress*, was produced by the U.S. Department of Education in collaboration with the American Historical Association, National Council for the Social Studies, Council of Chief School Officers, and National Council for History Education. The framework has two purposes: (1) to guide test makers as they prepare items for the National Assessment of Educational Progress (NAEP), the national "report card" on American schools, and (2) to provide educators with a vision and details for what adds up to quality in a history program. According to the framework (National Assessment Governing Board, 2002), students should:

> ... study all kinds of new (and sometimes conflicting) ideas, compelling stories of people and events, diverse traditions, economic booms and disasters, technological innovations, philosophical and political debates, religious convictions and influences, and the complex interactions among these various forces. Most of all, they study people—individually and in groups—in their complex settings and in their complex reactions to the world around them. (pp. 25–26)

The framework also lists the analytical skills, foundational to the study of history, that are necessary for citizens to use when making informed judgments and reasoned decisions in the public arena. As shown in Table 2, history's foundational skills begin with knowing significant subject matter and then evolve to more complex intellectual operations, those usually associated with rational inquiry and critical thinking.

Quality components of history education are expressed from a slightly different perspective in the Bradley Commission on History in Schools seminal report pub-

---

Table 2
History's Foundational Skills

Historical knowledge and perspective
- Knowing and understanding people, events, concepts, themes, movements, contexts, and historical sources
- Sequencing events
- Recognizing multiple perspectives
- Seeing an era or movement through the eyes of different groups
- Developing a general conceptualization of U.S. History

Historical analysis and interpretation
- Explaining issues
- Identifying historical patterns
- Establishing cause-and-effect relationships
- Finding value statements
- Establishing significance

Applying historical knowledge
- Weighing evidence to draw sound conclusions
- Making defensible generalizations
- Rendering insightful accounts of the past

---

lished in 1988. The recommendations from the 17 history teachers and professors, found in *History in Schools*, go beyond advocating the development of high level thinking skills. They assert that courses in history, geography, and government need to instill in students certain "habits of the mind" central to making thoughtful judgments. Habits of mind are the abilities required for making sound judgments, held so deeply by the decision-maker that they are put to use almost subconsciously. Table 3 outlines the habits of mind identified and thoroughly discussed in the Bradley Commission's report (Bradley Commission on History in Schools, 1988).

The outcomes from meaningful social studies and history education are a high bar to clear, but the payoffs for the learner and society are enormous. As John Dewey (1916) noted, "The assistance which may be given by history to a more intelligent, sympathetic understanding of the social situations of the present in which individuals share is a permanent and a constructive moral asset" (pp. 217–218).

But, putting the puzzle together that will result in meaningful, challenging social studies experiences for gifted learners requires more than just assembling pieces of subject matter and practicing sophisticated skills. It requires careful consideration of the unique characteristics gifted adolescents bring to the learning enterprise. These characteristics need to be honored, activated, and nurtured if gifted students are to construct the extraordinary insights and habits of mind they are capable of building along the way to becoming responsible citizens.

Table 3
Historical "Habits of Mind"

Exemplary curriculum and instruction in history will help students:

- understand the significance of the past to their own lives, both private and public, and to their society;
- perceive past events and issues as they were experienced by people at the time, to develop historical empathy as opposed to present-mindedness;
- understand how things happen and how things change, how human intentions matter, but also how their consequences are shaped by the means of carrying them out, in a tangle of purpose and process;
- prepare to live with uncertainties and exasperating, even perilous, unfinished business, realizing that not all problems have solutions; and
- appreciate the often tentative nature of judgments about the past, and thereby avoid the temptation to seize upon particular "lessons" of history as cures for social ills.

Note. Compiled from *Building a History Curriculum: Guidelines for Teaching History in Schools*, by Bradley Commission on History in Schools, 1998, Westlake, OH, National Council for History Education. Copyright ©1998 by National Council for History Education.

CHARACTERISTICS OF GIFTED LEARNERS

Schools are responsible for creating learning environments that stimulate and challenge students possessing a wide range of abilities and social/emotional needs, including adolescents who are capable of extraordinary intellectual, psychomotor, and creative performance. Because gifted students, like all other learners, are a diverse group, with representatives from all economic strata, cultural groups, and educational backgrounds, meeting their needs involves significant curricular and instructional modification at the level of individual learner. Satisfying the needs of gifted learners cannot be accomplished through "one size fits all" programming or simple administrative edict. Designing educational experiences for gifted middle and high school students requires strategies and methods that put the unique characteristics of these adolescents into play.

"Giftedness" is a general reference that takes into account both demonstrated performance and the potential for distinguished performance in any number of areas, not limiting itself to any single ability or talent. Giftedness can be viewed as a grouping of general abilities, such as leadership, academic capability, and creative thinking, and it can be looked at as specific talents that produce exceptionally high performance in specific disciplines, such as mathematics, social studies, or writing. In whatever context it is viewed, however, only about 3 to 5% of the general school population demonstrates exceptionalities strong enough to be classified as "gifted."

Although giftedness, by definition, is a general descriptor of learner performance, it does rest on observable learner characteristics that are extremely important

Table 4
Characteristics of Giftedness

In visual and performing arts, gifted learners:
- sense spatial relationships;
- express self feelings and moods through art, dance, drama, music;
- exhibit good motor coordination;
- express thoughts creatively;
- desire to produce their own products; and
- demonstrate refined powers of observation.

In general intellectual ability, gifted learners:
- formulate abstractions,
- process information in complex ways,
- demonstrate refined powers of observation,
- become excited about new ideas,
- enjoy hypothesizing,
- learn rapidly,
- use a large vocabulary,
- are inquisitive, and
- are self-starters.

In creative thinking, gifted learners:
- are independent thinkers,
- exhibit original thinking in oral and written expression,
- come up with several solutions to a given problem,
- demonstrate a sense of humor,
- create and invent,
- find challenge in creative tasks,
- improvise often, and
- do not mind being different from the crowd.

In leadership, gifted learners:
- assume responsibility;
- hold high expectations for self and others;
- use fluent, precise self-expression;
- foresee consequences and implications of decisions;
- show good judgment in decision making;
- like structure;
- are well liked by peers;
- are self-confident; and
- are organized.

In specific academic ability, gifted learners:
- demonstrate good memorization ability,
- are capable of advanced comprehension,
- show ability to acquire basic-skills and knowledge quickly,
- exhibit a wide background in special-interest areas from reading,
- attain high academic success in special-interest areas, and
- bring enthusiasm and vigor in the pursuit of their interests.

Note. Adapted from *Characteristics of Gifted Children,* by the National Association for Gifted Children, 1998, Retrieved May 1, 2005, from http://www.nagc.org. Copyright ©1998 by the National Association for Gifted Children. Copyrighted material from the National Association for Gifted Children (NAGC), 1707 L Street, NW, Suite 550, Washington, DC 20036. This material may not be reproduced without permission from NAGC. For more information on NAGC and gifted children contact NAGC at (202) 785-4268 or visit our Web site at www.nagc.org.

targets for the organization of subject matter and the design of learning activities. The National Association for Gifted Children's (NAGC; 1998) list of learner characteristics is one of the best guides for designing experiences that meet the needs of gifted adolescents while simultaneously honoring the criteria for meaningful instruction in social studies and history already mentioned in this chapter. Table 4 presents NAGC's list, organized into five categories often referred to as "areas" of giftedness. Note that some characteristics appear in more than one category.

These characteristics are vitally important for designing social education experiences because they identify both outcomes to be sought through instruction and learner attributes to be activated during instruction. As outcomes, the characteristics are clues for finding meaningful, stimulating subject matter and instructional methods, likely to nurture their very own development. As attributes of gifted adolescents, the characteristics identify what can be activated in the learner, by subject matter and learning activities, to make curriculum content engaging, meaningful, and challenging.

The standards for social studies and history education, taken along with the characteristics of gifted learners, provide two of the three elements for an equation that can produce meaningful, challenging experiences for this population. The element that still needs to be added is made up of instructional methods and strategies that activate and develop the unique characteristics of exceptional learners. What's still needed are the methodologies for "pulling the cat's tail."

"PULLING THE CAT'S TAIL"

Huck Finn prided himself on having become an "expert" in many things without ever needing much help from formal education. His classroom was the world and he learned through experience, like pulling a cat's tail to see how it would react. Huck prized the lessons he learned from his experiences because he saw their usefulness in his world.

What does it mean to "pull the cat's tail" in a social studies or history classroom? It means engaging students in issues and topics just as though they were experiencing them and working on them in the real world. What's required to get the cat's tail in the hands of adolescents are active learning strategies and materials that stimulate curiosity and activate the unique characteristics of every student—especially those of exceptional learners. Further, because the characteristics of gifted and talented adolescents are qualitatively different from their classmates, learners with exceptional abilities need experiences that are qualitatively different from what others are asked to do.

STANDARDS AFFECTING QUALITY

A range of instructional practices can have a positive affect on the quality of an adolescent's educational experience. Those that do often reflect standards and characteristics found in (1) authentic instruction and (2) principles of promising directions.

Authentic Instruction

The standards for authentic instruction emerged from classroom observation and lesson analysis by Fred M. Newmann and his colleagues at the University of Wisconsin as they searched for reasons why some innovations improve the quality of what students learn, while others do not, in schools attempting educational reform. The investigators examined instructional practices and classroom environments, looking for elements that produced higher-order thinkers with a deep understanding of how the real world works (Newmann & Wehlage, 1993). Concerned that even the most innovative strategies can be implemented in ways that undermine meaningful learning, Newmann looked for practices that produced *authentic achievement*—achievement that is significant and meaningful, not trivial and useless.

During their investigations, the researchers used three criteria to identify authentic achievement: (1) students construct meaning and produce knowledge, (2) students use disciplined inquiry to construct knowledge, and (3) students produce discourse, products, and performances that have value or meaning beyond success in school. These criteria, used to assess instructional practices and outcomes, frequently revealed two "maladies" that prevented high-quality instruction from taking place. Newmann and Wehlage (1993) explained,

> We were cautious not to assume that technical processes or specific sites for learning, however innovative, necessarily produce experiences of high intellectual quality. Even activities that place students in the role of a more active, cooperative learner and that seem to respect student voices can be implemented in ways that do not produce authentic achievement. The challenge is not simply to adopt innovative teaching techniques or to find new locations for learning, but deliberately to counteract two persistent maladies that make conventional schooling inauthentic:
> 1. Often the work students do does not allow them to use their minds well.
> 2. The work has no intrinsic meaning or value to students beyond achieving success in school. (p. 8)

From observations of teaching and lesson construction in classrooms where the maladies did not appear often, Newmann and his colleague formulated five standards, shown in Table 5, as the measure for high quality, authentic instruction (Newmann & Wehlage, 1993, pp. 9–12).

Principles of Promising Directions

A collaboration between gifted and middle school educators has recently produced agreement on "promising directions" that establish new, practice-based standards for middle school programs (Tomlinson, 1995a). Both groups of educators have come to agree that meaningful instruction for early adolescent, gifted learners should: (1) be theme based, (2) be interdisciplinary, (3) promote self-directed learn-

---

Table 5
Standards for Authentic Instruction

Standard	Standard Defined
Higher order thinking	Students manipulate information and ideas in ways that transform their meaning and implications. They synthesize, generalize, explain, or arrive at conclusions.
Depth of knowledge	Students understand complex, central ideas of topics or disciplines. They construct arguments, solve problems, or construct explanations.
Connectedness to the world	Students connect with the larger social context within which they live. They address real-world problems or use personal experiences as a context for applying knowledge.
Substantive conversation	Students engage in considerable, nonscripted interaction on ideas. They share higher order thinking, raise questions, or dialogue coherently on each other's ideas.
Social support	Students experience high expectations, respect, and inclusion. All students are asked to take intellectual risks, show respect, and receive assistance in reaching expectations.

Note. Adapted from "Five Standards of Authentic Instruction," by F. M. Newmann and G. G. Wehlage, 1993, *Educational Leadership, 50*(7), pp. 8–12. Copyright ©1993 by Association for Supervision and Curriculum Development. Adapted with permission. The Association for Supervision and Curriculum Development is a worldwide community of educators advocating sound policies and sharing best practices to achieve the success of each learner. To learn more, visit ASCD at http://www.ascd.org

---

ing, (4) incorporate basic skills, (5) be relevant to the learner and based on the study of significant problems, (6) promote student discovery, (7) value group interaction, (8) encourage critical and creative exploration of ideas, and (9) promote student self-evaluation (Currier, 1986; Kaplan, 1979; Maker & Nielson, 1995; Stevenson, 1992).

In Tomlinson's (1995a) account of the principles emerging from study of successful practices with gifted middle school students, consensus is reported on five recommendations to guide the reform of curricula and instructional practices in middle school programs for the gifted. The recommendations are to:

1. disavow theories that present middle school students as incapable of high level thought and complex learning;
2. abandon practices that couch middle school as a place for drill and skill;
3. establish complex, problem-based, student-centered curricula, differentiated for student readiness, interests, and learning style;
4. emphasize problem-based, cooperative strategies rather than skill-focus collaborative strategies; and
5. teach and balance cooperation, independence, and healthy competition. (pp. 3–4)

The recommendations offered by Tomlinson share a number of features with Newmann's standards for authentic instruction. First, both lists contain endorsements for challenging adolescents to attain deeper understanding of more sophisticated concepts, using more complex mental processes than what is currently being practiced in middle school classrooms. Second, both studies point out the need to make students more mentally active and engaged as learners, setting the objects of their inquiry more often in the real world. Using real-world issues and problems as the focus of investigation and inquiry leads students to make connections between concepts from numerous disciplines, because real-world issues and problems are interdisciplinary by their very nature. Last, both sets of recommendations rest on intellectual foundations that recognize the heterogeneous nature of any group of middle school students assembled for instruction. This heterogeneity, resulting from the uniqueness of each learner's readiness to learn, interests, and preferences for learning styles, makes practices that require all students to learn the same content, in the same way, and at the same pace unlikely to be productive.

DIFFERENTIATION IN SOCIAL STUDIES AND HISTORY

Whenever and wherever learners are grouped for instruction, a range of unique characteristics and needs is created that must be acknowledged and served. In addition, because most gifted students—especially in middle school—are taught in regular classrooms (Sousa, 2003), teachers need to find and use methods that lift performance restraints and promote exceptional, high quality achievement. To do this, grouping patterns, subject matter, instructional strategies, products, and assessments must be differentiated according to significant student characteristics so that gifted students, indeed all students, meet the highest levels of complexity and challenge they can manage.

Differentiation by Grouping

Differentiation can begin by grouping students in class around specific learner characteristics—an arrangement that can produce advantages for both gifted and regular populations of students (Gamoran, Nystrand, Berends, & LePore, 1995; Kulik & Kulik, 1992; Pallas, Entwisle, Alexander, & Stluka, 1994). Differentiated grouping practices can be used in limited time arrangements where students with similar abilities or interests work together on a specific teacher-designed task for a period of time as short as 15 minutes to an entire class period. Students in differentiated groups can also work together for longer periods of time, up to an entire semester, on self-directed, independent study projects, internships, and service learning projects. The following examples of high school and middle school strategies illustrate successful grouping patterns for differentiation.

Short Duration Grouping in High School—The Trial of Galileo
Students are given the role of judges representing the Inquisition for Galileo's heresy trial. Initially, the students are grouped homogeneously for a few class peri-

ods based upon the difficulty and complexity of the materials they are using to prepare questions for Galileo's interrogation. After the questioning phase of the trial, students are regrouped, heterogeneously this time, to determine the verdict and come up with an appropriate sentence (Stepien, Senn, & Stepien, 2000, pp. 137–152).

Short Duration Grouping in Middle School—Television News

Students are grouped around their ability to write with clarity and present ideas logically and are asked to prepare a one-minute long TV news story from a teacher-prepared list of world events. Some groups collaborate on stories that feature who, what, where, when, and why questions. Others prepare in-depth analyses or opinion pieces, using alternative viewpoints found on the Internet or in print sources. The stories are videotaped, played back, and new small groups evaluate the stories for clarity, accuracy, and logical development.

Long Duration Grouping in High School—Local Government or Service Learning

Students might confront a real community issue, such as where to build a second bridge over a river, as they did at St. Charles High School in St. Charles, IL. Differentiated groups constructed interview forms to sample community sentiment on the topic, arranged for guest speakers to appear in class, reviewed engineering and demographic studies, prepared policy alternatives, and delivered presentations at a city council meeting.

Differentiation by Ability Grouping

Full-time ability grouping, often referred to as "tracking," allows high performing students to meet more advanced content in special courses, seminars, independent study projects, early college enrollment programs, and internships. In schools with large student bodies, especially high schools, this can be achieved by creating a separate class section for gifted students. Implementing full-time ability grouping in smaller schools is more of a challenge.

More than 80% of recently surveyed high schools (Sytsma, 2001) indicate that they offer some combination of the options mentioned above. The most popular forms of full-time ability grouping are Advanced Placement (AP) and pre-AP programs offered by the College Board at Educational Testing Service and the International Baccalaureate (IB) sponsored by the International Baccalaureate Organization in New York.

Under the AP format, students capable of advanced work enroll in special courses, usually on their high school campus, that feature college-level subject matter. AP courses, such as American History, Economics, and Government, as well as the IB program, often appeal to students who learn rapidly, have a good ability to memorize, are capable of advanced comprehension, and can attain high academic success in special-interest areas because they often cover large amounts of material at a fast pace.

Recently, however, the conventional wisdom that Advanced Placement courses are the best way to group and instruct exceptional students has come into question (Gollub, Bertenthal, Labov, & Curtis, 2002). Their concern is based on the huge amount of content that must be covered in these courses, indicating a stronger preference for coverage than depth of understanding, and lack of attention to newer instructional strategies based upon emerging knowledge of how the brain works. Given the extensive and diverse abilities of gifted adolescents, some educators are concerned with what they see as an overemphasis on comprehension and memorization of subject matter, when equally important abilities such as problem solving, creative expression, and decision making are given little or no attention. Concentration on the coverage of introductory college level material means important characteristics of gifted learners can go untouched and undernourished.

An alternative for both middle and high schools would be to group students around a broader set of learner characteristics—characteristics having to do with complexity of thought, for example, and creating courses that use interdisciplinary content provided by teachers or discovered through investigations by students as they confront real-world issues and problems.

Grouping by Student Interest in High School—Science, Society, and the Future (SSF)

> At the Illinois Mathematics and Science Academy (IMSA), a public, residential high school for students with deep interest in mathematics and science, *SSF* was offered as an elective that engaged students in science problems with the potential to have great impact on society. The interdisciplinary teaching team coached their apprentice problem solvers through in-depth investigations that featured intensive practice with rational inquiry and often included analyzing the ethical implications of solutions. Student developed solutions were frequently presented before community groups. Topics for *SSF* included: developing policies for the control of infectious diseases, citing utilities to minimize health risks, conducting forensic anthropology in politically charged environments, responding to biological terrorism, and protecting endangered species. (Stepien & Gallagher, 1993, pp. 25–26)

Full time ability grouping using this type of course structure can help students with exceptional talent reach more advanced content while simultaneously honing inquiry skills, developing important habits of mind, making interdisciplinary connections, and utilizing oft overlooked characteristics of giftedness, such as inventiveness, artistic ability, and decision making.

Differentiating Content

Besides differentiating the way students are grouped, the needs of high performing students can be met by differentiating curriculum and instruction. Tailoring course content to ability level yields a consistently positive effect on the achievement of high-ability students (Kulik & Kulik, 1992).

Differentiating content requires giving gifted learners more advanced or complex subject matter in place of course content they may have already mastered and allowing these students to cover standard content at a more accelerated rate. Allowing high performing students to test out of subject matter, if they can demonstrate they already comprehend it, compacts subject matter content, freeing up time for more challenging material.

Curriculum compacting is a popular way of modifying content because it resolves the problem of what to do with learners who master standard course content faster than their classmates. Compacting reduces the amount of time students face content they are already familiar with by allowing them to demonstrate what they know through simple assessment devices, work on what they still need to master, and then move on to more advanced subject matter for enrichment and extension. Compacting can help reduce exposure to redundant content in a unit, semester, or entire course (Renzulli & Richards, 2000).

Sometimes this is as simple as reducing the amount of time spent on repetition or practice when skills are taught, or sometimes it can mean allowing students to skip reading assignments and discussions that feature recall and comprehension of basic information. The time freed through compacting is then filled with activities that probe the deeper meaning of concepts and themes that allow exploration of topics related to the unit and are intriguing to the students, or that provide practice with advanced application of important skills and thinking processes. All three reasons for compacting might result in a unit like the one described in the following example.

Curriculum Compacting in High School Civics—Candidates and Elections

Three versions of a unit on how political candidates are selected and elected, created around increasingly higher levels of Bloom's Taxonomy (Anderson & Kratwohl, 2001), are offered to students in the civics class. Students are placed in one version or another according to results from a simple teacher-prepared assessment. The assessment is constructed using test and quiz questions from the textbook's teacher supplement.

Students demonstrating a need to master basic information are placed in the version of the unit that features knowledge on how candidates are chosen and elections are conducted. The work for this group is organized around the *remember* and *understand* levels of Bloom's Taxonomy.

Another group of students, selected using pretest results again, is placed in a version that asks them to design a campaign strategy for a real or fictional political candidate. They have demonstrated a basic knowledge of how the election process works and are provided an opportunity to look into more advanced topics, such as the role of media, opinion polls, and patterns of voter turnout in planning political campaigns. Members of this group work primarily at *application* and *analysis* of election strategies, in the center of Bloom's Taxonomy.

The remaining students are challenged by activities at the most complex levels on the Taxonomy—*evaluate* and *create*. Their task is to evaluate a proposal for the innovative use of computer technology during elections and create appropriate applications of the innovation where possible. The innovation would allow citizens to vote directly for candidates by using personal computers or other communication devices and to even vote directly on pending legislation in Congress, allegedly making the legislative process more democratic.

Curriculum Compacting in Middle School World History—
Industrialization and Child Labor

In the following example of compacting that might take place in a middle school history course, only two versions of a unit are utilized. The first version features basic, introductory material on industrialization, while the second offers learners an opportunity to explore primary sources as they prepare material for the whole class to use during a simulation exercise that culminates the unit for both groups of students.

At the beginning of a unit on industrialization, students are assessed on their knowledge of people, places, and events in the unit. Using the outcomes from the assessment, students are placed in one of two groups. The first group works on acquiring basic knowledge of when industrialization began, who promoted its development, how it changed production, and how children were involved in the process.

The second group of students investigates the attitudes and involvement of factory owners, public health officers, reformers, and children working in mills or factories using relevant Web sites and print materials to determine how each would testify before a governmental body investigating child labor during the 19th century.

When both groups have completed their work, a simulated governmental hearing on child labor is conducted in class. The students who investigated conditions in the mills and factories present testimony before the students who worked on acquiring a basic understanding of industrialization—now playing the role of government officials. At the conclusion of testimony, the entire class produces legislation concerning working conditions for children and assesses the likelihood that their legislation could have passed during the reign of the "robber barons."

Compacting curriculum allows all students to cover content at a more individualized rate. For gifted students, this can also mean meeting and using more challenging processes, such as problem solving, creative thinking, and artistic expression during instruction and in the production of products from learning. For example, students working on tasks that require them to remember, understand, or apply knowledge might produce outlines, construct charts, draw maps, make models, create newspaper stories, or produce graphic organizers such as timelines. Students working on operations requiring them to analyze, evaluate, or create might produce cartoons, song lyrics, poetry, editorials, strategies, proposals, critiques, or graphic organizers such as flow charts and Venn diagrams.

The complexities of thought identified by Benjamin Bloom and his colleagues in their groundbreaking work done during the 1950s, and then revised in 2001, are

Table 6
Bloom's Taxonomy—Cognitive Domain

1. Remember—accurate recall or retrieval of terminology, specific facts, conventions, trends, classifications, criteria, methodology, principles, and one's past cognitive performance.
2. Understand—correct comprehension illustrated through translation, interpretation, summary, inference, and explanation.
3. Apply—selection and correct use or implementation of a procedure in a given situation.
4. Analyze—breakdown of wholes into constituent parts and seeing or differentiating the relationships between the pieces.
5. Evaluate—make judgments, based on criteria, regarding the value of ideas, methods, solutions and other cognitive products.
6. Create—plan and put elements together to form an original, coherent product.

Note. Adapted from *Bloom et al.'s Taxonomy of the Cognitive Domain,* by W. Huitt, 2004, Retrieved June 10, 2005, from http://chiron.valdosta.edu/whuitt/col/cogsys/bloom.html.

extremely helpful for the process of differentiating instruction and the products from instruction. Table 6 shows the increasingly more complex forms of thought identified by Bloom in the 2001 format.

Bloom's taxonomy came about from his work and the work of his colleagues on classifying the complexity of thought required to answer questions on standardized tests. The taxonomy portrays thinking as becoming more complex as it moves from the *remember* through *create* stages. The nature of thinking also changes from convergent thinking, fixed on finding facts, accepted understandings, and appropriate application, to divergent thinking, fixed on discovery, invention, and problem solving, as it becomes more complex.

It is also helpful for a discussion on differentiating tasks around learner characteristics to distinguish between *complexity* and *difficulty,* because increasing complexity for the learner is far different from increasing difficulty. Complexity increases as the brain engages in higher levels of thought, such as analysis, evaluation, and creating (Sousa, 2003, pp. 73–74). So, complexity increases when students are first asked to define dictatorship and are then asked to determine if a specific leader is a dictator or decide how a particular dictatorship might be ethically transformed into a more democratic form of government.

On the other hand, difficulty increases when the brain must increase its effort to complete a mental task as compared with completing a previous task—both tasks occupying the same level of thought. Difficulty increases when students are first asked to recall one dictator's name and are then asked to recall all the dictators they studied during a unit. Thinking remains at the recall level for both tasks, but the amount of information to recall is greater in the second task. When thinking about stimulating learners, especially gifted learners, *challenge* should be thought of as increased *complexity*.

Considering the earlier examples of compacting in civics and history, a fair question to ask before leaving the idea of differentiation would be: "In what group(s) will the gifted students find themselves?" The answer depends on how they fare during the assessment at the opening of each unit. It is possible that gifted learners could find their way into all of the groups. Students who do not demonstrate mastery of required content will need to join their classmates in the group in which the material they have not yet mastered is being considered. Even there however, modifications to instruction, such as acceleration, can be used because gifted learners are likely to need less time and practice to master the material than their age mates. It is also likely that some students not identified as "gifted" will find their way into each of the groups, supporting the idea that strategies appropriate for gifted learners can broaden the instructional choices in the classroom for a wide range of students.

CONSTRUCTIVIST METHODOLOGY

Grouping students around various learner characteristics and then maximizing the intellectual challenge for each group by differentiating materials, methods, and products improves the fit of the curriculum to diverse student populations. The fit is also improved by bringing methodology to instruction that promotes active construction of new knowledge and insights by each learner. Known as *constructivism*, this approach engages learners with subject matter in real-world settings as problem solvers and decision-makers.

Constructivism, as a learning theory, recognizes that every person, as an actively cognizing agent, constructs knowledge through interaction with the outside world. They progress through life processing new information and experiences, incorporating them into what they already know about the world. In this way, the purpose of their cognitive activity is to create viable meaning out of the world around them, not seek out some sort of objective "truth" constructed by others. In fact, meaning is so intimately connected to personal experience that it can hardly be imagined as objective at all (Jonassen, 1991).

Under constructivist theory, the learner adds to, revises, or replaces existing knowledge if new information and experiences make sense in light of what he or she already knows. But, these connections can only be built by the learner. In short, the learner must actively reconstruct existing mental frameworks for meaningful learning to occur; teachers can not just pass along knowledge, meaning, or truth to their students (Savery & Duffy, 1995; Tam, 2000). This way of looking at learning has serious implications for civic competence and for designing learning environments for high performing adolescents.

As mentioned earlier, the office of citizen requires understanding the world in its complexity and thinking and acting in ways that promote the public good. Learners need to understand the messy nature of social issues and the multitude of valid perspectives and opinions held by stakeholders in various situations. Merely remembering information about issues from reading, discussion, or lectures is not good enough.

When looking to history for help in the preparation of responsible citizens, teachers need to help students understand historical events and ideas as situated in specific times and places that shaped the lessons that evolve from them. To form the knowledge base required to competently hold the office of citizen, learners need to comprehend not only the significance of events, but also how they and other people come to understand those events and form their unique perspectives.

For all students, education must help illustrate that social dynamics, even formal interactions like those found in diplomacy, legal proceedings, and economic exchange, are not cut and dried. Interactions are painted in shades of gray and often leave the participants wondering, "How can that person believe what he does?" or "Why can't the other side understand how I'm thinking?" Knowledge of how people construct their ideas and viewpoints is essential to an understanding of what they believe.

Constructivists hold that social education needs to prepare students for the lifelong tasks of constructing knowledge, replacing old knowledge when appropriate, and accepting the idea that others learn by the same process, explaining why there can be varied points of view on an issue. By accepting and teaching a social studies curriculum that treats knowledge as static and completely objective, educators remove the connection to the realities that people experience every day. Dewey (1916) lamented that teaching history and geography as a body of factual information to be memorized separates it from its purpose—to illuminate the present and allow people to visualize the future.

Social studies and history classrooms should be full of opportunities for students to uncover information, think critically about that information, and build knowledge bases they can use to better comprehend the past, present, and near future. Merely accepting knowledge constructed by others without building it for oneself or examining how others came to hold those ideas results in knowledge that is inert, without much utility.

Constructivists also hold that presenting crucial social information in an always positivistic way serves to alienate and oppress elements of society (Apple, 1993; Freire, 1973; Giroux, 1997). By presenting positions, opinions, and beliefs as objective and static, the prevailing worldviews of the dominant groups in society are internalized by those outside the dominant groups who then struggle to imagine situations where they are not oppressed. In order for school curriculum to be transformative at all, it must help students build understanding of multicultural perspectives, and this can only take place when students learn to view knowledge as socially constructed (Banks, 1994). In this type of curriculum, students are required to confront multiple perspectives on issues and formulate their own positions, justifying their own construction of knowledge (Banks). The following two examples demonstrate how constructivist methodology might be applied to high school and middle school history courses.

Constructivist Methodology in High School—
Separate but Equal Doctrine

Students would be asked if the following principle would be good social policy for our country: "If the two races are to meet on terms of social equality, it must be the result of natural affinities, a mutual appreciation for each other's merits, and a voluntary consent of individuals . . ." (*Plessy v. Ferguson*, 1896). Next, they would be asked to put the Equal Protection and Due Process clauses from the Fourteenth Amendment into their own words, and students would determine when the two principles might clash. After a conceptual framework is built, the students could be put into teams to examine how black codes, Jim Crow laws, and more subtle forms of discrimination challenged ideas of racial equality. After the groups share the fruits of their investigations, they might be given historic civil rights challenges and asked what to do with each, keeping in mind the historical perspectives they developed during the opening of the unit. Finally, students would be asked to decide how their thinking might apply in a more modern case of alleged reverse discrimination.

Constructivist Methodology in Middle School—
Terror During the French Revolution

After investigating the use of terror during the French Revolution, students could be given case studies highlighting the behavior of more modern political regimes accused of using terrorism to accomplish political goals. Using what they have learned, students could draw up an indictment or present the opening argument in front of an international tribunal charged with determining if a contemporary political figure or other individual is a "terrorist."

PROBLEM-BASED LEARNING

The constructivist strategy that provides one of the best opportunities to "pull the cat's tail" is *problem-based learning* (PBL). PBL has evolved from the work of Canadian medical educators during the 1970s who were concerned that traditional methods of instruction could not keep up with the demands on medical education. Specifically, they were concerned that new information was emerging so rapidly and old information was being replaced so often that lecture-based teaching methods could not keep up with the pace of change. These educators also recognized that avalanching new information on students did not effectively increase their knowledge bases; it more often increased forgetting. But, most importantly, the Canadian innovators became determined to find educational practices that promoted construction of knowledge in ways that were useful for solving problems, the problems brought to physicians by their patients (Gallagher, 1997).

The adaptation of problem-based learning to high school classrooms began in 1989 at the Illinois Mathematics and Science Academy (IMSA). The faculty and staff at IMSA recognized many similarities between the pressures faced by medical schools and high schools, especially those schools wishing to deliver meaningful, challenging educational experiences to gifted students. IMSA's faculty was concerned that high school textbooks were so thick and courses so packed with information that they were beginning to resemble the science courses in medical school. Besides, the weight of content to be covered in most courses left little time for in-depth exploration of topics or for significant practice in using the content for real-world problem solving. As experimentation and research in PBL evolved at IMSA, it become clear that high school students required more than just hearing about problem solving, getting older, or stockpiling information if they were to become more *expert* as problem solvers (Gallagher, Stepien, & Rosenthal, 1994; Stepien & Gallagher, 1993; Stepien, Gallagher, & Workman, 1993).

The work at IMSA led to a new paradigm for what it takes for adolescents to become better problem solvers and acquire standard course content simultaneously (Gallagher, Sher, Stepien, & Workman, 1995; Stepien & Pyke, 1997). The task requires learners to build a pair of special "scissors" in their minds. The blades of the scissors represent the two primary attributes of expert problem solvers. One blade stands for the role of *knowledge* during problem solving. Expert problem solvers need significant knowledge bases in order to make progress in any problem they might be working on. Without reliable, relevant knowledge, and the ability to continually upgrade and supplement that knowledge, the problem solver is powerless, maybe even dangerous.

But, knowledge accounts for only one blade of the scissors. Another blade must be present to make the tool work. That blade is *experience*. Without experience with reasoning, the ability to productively solve problems is severely stunted. Experience comes from practice in solving problems and using the process of rational inquiry. Building this experience takes time, however, and the time needed, in both high schools and middle schools, to provide students experience in real-world problem solving, in a curriculum overflowing with material to cover and recall on end-of-course examinations, is hard to find.

Problem-based learning helps resolve the dilemma of how to build experience through practice while also helping learners master prescribed subject matter in two ways. First, PBL units can be constructed around topics, issues, and skills found in any school or state's standard course of study, so using PBL does not require adding more content to a course. In fact, in history, carefully constructed PBL units produce the same or better content retention than more traditionally designed and delivered units (Gallagher & Stepien, 1996). Second, experience in problem solving is added to the curriculum by simply remodeling portions of existing instructional units around applications of content to the solution of real problems. In their remodeled PBL formats, with the resolution of real-world problems at the center, the new units provide experience in solving problems as the students construct new knowledge about a unit's topics or issues. Additionally, it is not necessary to convert an entire course to PBL; in fact, it is not even desirable. A small number of strategically placed PBL units will produce significant results (Gallagher et al., 1994).

At the Core of Problem-Based Learning

Problem-based learning puts students into carefully constructed situations, created around authentic, *ill-structured* problems that require real problem solving on the part of the students. In the context of PBL, *problem* means any situation that requires action, decision, or solution on the part of someone. In this sense, problems include opportunities, as well as predicaments. So a photographer needs to solve an ill-structured problem when he or she decides to photograph an incredibly beautiful sunset. The problem turns out to be a wonderful opportunity: How can the beauty of the sunset be captured on film given the location of the photographer, the capabilities of the camera, and the type of film and lenses in the case?

Ill-structured or messy problems are at the core of PBL because they have characteristics that help create a potent learning environment. Ill-structured problems:

1. are complex, with hidden issues, and are unable to be completely understood when first encountered;
2. cannot be resolved by simple, formulaic thinking as they often change as more is learned about them;
3. can often be resolved in more than one way; and
4. sometimes require resolution before all issues in the problem are completely understood.

These characteristics make ill-structured problems challenging, engaging, and even more than a little frustrating at times. But, these elements also make them highly motivating to most students, especially gifted learners. Their special appeal rests on the way they need to be approached. They demand problem solving the way it is practiced by experts: issues must be identified, hunches and hypotheses investigated, and solutions justified by the way they fit relevant conditions in the situation. During their investigation of ill-structured problems, students structure searches for needed information, determine if discovered information is relevant and reliable, and often make interdisciplinary connections because real-world problems are, by their nature, interdisciplinary. The students move forward, hit dead ends, revisit ideas, revise their thinking and forge on. During the experience, they construct substantial knowledge bases and enter into real collaborations with classmates (Barrows, 1994). It's little wonder why this type of investigation stimulates gifted learners when one recalls NAGC's characteristics of gifted learners and notice how many of them have been activated by the process.

The Distinctive Flow of PBL

PBL is characterized by the distinctive phases or flow shown in Figure 1. The components of that flow, and their sequence, distinguish PBL from other constructivist strategies such as simulation, case study, and project-based learning.

The flow emphasizes four groups of intellectual activities often used by expert problem solvers as they apply the inquiry process, detailed in Figure 2 (Barrows,

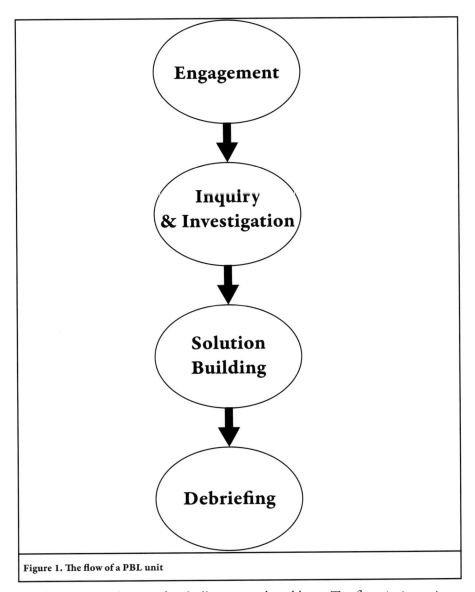

Figure 1. The flow of a PBL unit

1994), to the resolution of real, ill-structured problems. The flow, in its entirety, will be described further in this chapter as it might be found in a problem from an American History course following the explanation of the diagrams.

Each PBL unit begins with an *initiation* phase, a time when students meet their problem and become stakeholders—participants in the problem responsible for resolving at least a significant piece of it. As stakeholders, students are given as much responsibility for solving the problem as they can handle.

Initiation is followed in PBL's flow by an *investigation* phase. Here the students deepen their inquiry by identifying (1) what they know—the facts, (2) what might be going on in the problem—their hunches and hypotheses, (3) what they need to know—their search questions, and (4) how they might conduct their investiga-

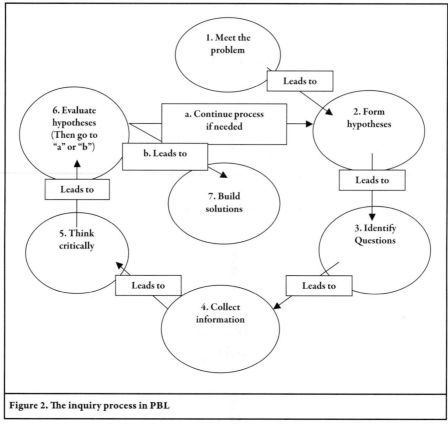

Figure 2. The inquiry process in PBL

tion—their action plan. As the investigation escalates, teachers become mentors and coaches, leaving the problem solving to the learners as much as possible.

When expert problem solvers become satisfied that they have a good understanding of the key elements in a problem, *investigation* gives way to *solution building*. During this phase, students create new hunches and hypotheses about potential solutions or actions to determine if they lead toward a viable, ethical resolution of the problem. Then they craft or select solutions that fit the problem as they have described it and prepare rationales for why their solutions are the best resolution for the problem.

A fourth phase, *debriefing*, brings the flow of the PBL unit to a close. A period of debriefing gives the coach and student problem solvers an opportunity to formally review the outcomes of the unit, focusing on subject matter that might need to be revisited or practiced more for mastery or on concepts from the problem that can be extended into additional historical situations. Debriefing is also used to help students gain insight into their metacognitive performance, their proficiency with the inquiry process.

Figure 2 shows the steps students use during their formal investigation of the problem. During its early stages, the process resembles the scientific method. But, an emphasis is added about halfway through the investigation that distinguishes it clearly as a problem-solving strategy—students use the information and insights they have acquired to find a reasonable solution to the problem they met at the beginning of the unit. The search for solutions distinguishes PBL from many classroom applications of the inquiry process that conclude with the construction of new knowledge and insights.

An interesting aspect of the inquiry or reasoning process at the center of PBL is how the human brain takes to it so willingly, in the beginning, that is. When a human being is confronted with a novel situation or becomes puzzled about something, the brain is likely to begin speculating about it, forming hunches that are largely intuitive and usually unexamined. But, then comes a choice of paths that separates novice from expert problem solvers. Novice problem solvers often stay on the road of uncritical, undisciplined thought; they propose and embrace solutions that spring from continued reliance on their intuition, not from rigorous inquiry. Expert problem solvers veer off onto a harder road, a path of reflective inquiry.

As depicted in Figure 2, the inquiry process appears to be made up of distinctive, isolated operations. In reality, the operations are more like periods of specialized focus during a broad flow of cognitive and affective activity. Hunches about the nature of the problem, springing from the investigator's imagination, lead him or her to asking the metacognitive question: "What do I need to know?" The specific questions that result from the metacognitive question guide the investigator's search for needed information. Gathered information is integrated with prior knowledge, rejected if it lacks relevance or reliability, and used to build new concepts. Armed with new knowledge and insights, problem solvers examine their original hunches and hypotheses, now able to see which should be pursued and which should be modified or abandoned. Iterations of this circular flow can be continued until the problem solver is satisfied that enough is known to begin considering possible solutions.

Notice again the place of the ill-structured problem in the inquiry process used for problem-based learning—at the top or beginning of the reasoning process. The process of inquiry begins with an unresolved question, intriguing situation, or challenging dilemma that needs to be investigated before it will reveal its true nature. Without an ill-structured problem at the top of the inquiry process, there is little reason ... to reason!

Problem-Based Learning in American History— The Fugitive Slaves

The following example, used both in middle or high school history courses, shows how a PBL unit unfolds through the four phases just discussed. During consideration of each phase of PBL's flow, attention is given to how the phase emphasizes a portion of the inquiry process and how teaching behavior can be transformed into coaching behavior.

The *Fugitive Slaves* problem (Stepien, 2001) is initiated when students are handed a short scenario on the first day of the unit. The class has been investigating sectionalism, slavery in America just before the Civil War, and the abolitionist movement. They are told that for the next several class periods they must each imagine themselves as the farmer in the story they are about to read. The scenario reads:

You are a farmer living with your family near the town of Alton, IL. The year is 1858. As you enter your barn one morning to prepare for a day of work in the fields, you hear noises behind equipment in the back of the building.

"Who's there?" you shout.

Slowly, two people emerge from the shadows. Both are Negroes, one a child and the other a woman. Their clothes are ragged, and they look tired and scared.

"Who are you? What are you doing in my barn?" you ask.

First one and then the other tells you a little something about themselves. As you listen to their stories, you begin to think to yourself: What am I going to do with these fugitive slaves?

The Fugitive Slave Stories

Tice (Woman)

I been runnin' and hidin' from the catchers since I cross the river by St. Louis. Now I'm followin' the drinkin' gourd. Gonna get all the way free. Met this little one a few days ago. Names Thomas. He been on the railroad longer than me. His Mamma's a house slave way down the river. His Daddy probably a field slave down there somewhere. Ain't no way I'm gonna let him go back and get the cowhide or collar put on him.

Thomas (Child)

Ma Mamma sez I'm 10 years old. They all sez we got it good working in the big house. But Mamma sez I'm goin' to the fields next year to pick cotton. She sez there's a better life in the North. Sez she'll find me if I tell the conductors who I am. Are you a conductor? Even if you ain't, you ain't gonna call the sheriff are you?

The Initiation Phase

To initiate the unit and the inquiry process, the teacher asks the students to imagine themselves as the farmer in the story. Discussion focuses on the reactions to finding the fugitives in the barn. Students are asked to imagine what they might be concerned or puzzled about as they face the runaways. The objectives for the teacher, now a coach of the inquiry process for the students, are to (1) engage or hook students using the situation's setting, unresolved issues, and upcoming decisions; (2) help students take ownership of the problem by imagining themselves in the situation; and (3) begin the inquiry process by identifying facts, imagining possibilities, and organizing questions to be investigated.

As the initiating discussion draws to a close, the teacher/coach draws a chart with three columns, called a frame, on the chalkboard. Students create a similar chart on their own paper or a copy of the frame can be provided. The columns are labeled "Facts," "Hunches," and "What do we need to know?" The just completed discussion is quickly reviewed by asking students to recall items that can be listed in the first two columns. As the items are put on the board and recorded on the student's individual charts, discussion focuses on why something is considered a "fact" as opposed to a "hunch" or conclusion. Then attention is turned to the "What do we need to know?" column. Students are asked to list questions that need to be answered in order for the farmer to determine if the hunches recorded on the board are accurate, true, and worthy of considering when it is time to determine what to do about the fugitives. The frame on the board will be used to organize and monitor the upcoming investigation of the problem.

During the initiation phase of a PBL unit, the teacher's role in the inquiry process is to help students, through probing questions and a demonstration of sound reasoning, (1) establish the context for the problem, (2) engage with the opening scenario, (3) collect facts and hunches about the problem from the scenario and the students' prior historical knowledge, and (4) identify important questions to guide the upcoming inquiry. The ability to recognize and use effective questions is a cornerstone of problem-based learning for both the teacher and the student problem solvers.

Coaching students to ask questions that, when answered, will supply the information they need to better understand the presented problem is an especially important responsibility of the teacher. As coach, the teacher not only elicits questions, but should also probe the relevance of questions to help students see how well-conceived questions fuel the inquiry process and produce needed information. For example, a question about the nature of the people living in Alton, IL might trigger the teacher to ask: "Why is that important to know?" The students must then make the case for relevance, citing the attitudes of Alton residents toward slavery as important for getting cooperation and determining any risk of trouble for the farmer and his or her family if the community learns about the fugitives.

Questions that are too abstract or too broad are also challenged. In response to a question such as, "What is a slave's life like on a plantation?," the coach might ask, "What specifically do you want to know about slave life?" The purpose of the probe is to explore the usefulness of the question for finding information relevant to the situation in which the students find themselves.

Finally, the initiating discussion for the unit focuses on the topic of how to best conduct the inquiry that will produce answers to the students' questions. Students should settle on sources of information to investigate, how they will organize themselves to gather the information, and how information will be shared.

The Investigation Phase

The *investigation phase* of the PBL unit requires teachers to (1) coach their students through collecting relevant information from reliable sources and forming reasonable conclusions based upon the collected data, (2) demonstrate sound critical thinking for the students to emulate, and (3) challenge sloppy thinking through the use of metacognitive questions when necessary. This phase begins with data collection as students answer the most significant "What do we need to know?" questions.

An effective way of organizing for this step is to break the class into differentiated small groups, each group being responsible for finding information that helps answer one question they pick or are assigned from the frame created during the previous day's activity. The questions that produce the most concrete information should be reserved for groups capable of doing that task well. More abstract, open-ended, or complex questions, or questions that demand more rigorous searches, can be assigned to students capable of successfully conducting them (Tomlinson, 1995b).

During investigation, the teacher's role in the inquiry process is to coach students as they (1) collect relevant, reliable information, (2) analyze and synthesize data to uncover and clarify issues in the problem, (3) modify or extend searches if necessary, and (4) present direct instruction or practice around inquiry skills if learners demonstrate a need for them.

During information gathering, differentiation should be considered again. Materials should be matched to student capabilities. Information sources assembled in the classroom or located in the school library or media center can be identified according to level of difficulty and presentation format. A short list of available resources tagged for difficulty and format, sometimes referred to as a *pathfinder*, can then be given to students to help them initiate their research into the question they are responsible for answering.

The Internet is an especially useful source of information to be tapped during the investigation phase of PBL (Stepien et al., 2000). Web sites can be discovered by students as an outcome of their own structured searches, or they can visit sites preselected by the teacher. The usual caveat must be shared here. It is always important for the teacher to visit preselected sites to be sure they are available on the day the searches are initiated. Additionally, the teacher must remember to double check search terms likely to be used by students planning their own Web searches so that inappropriate sites do not pop up.

During the *investigation phase* of PBL, teachers usually begin the process of student assessment. Quizzes and tests yield very limited useful information regarding student performance during PBL. What really works well is a portfolio approach to assessment. Portfolios can be easily constructed around the activities students are asked to do during the inquiry process. For example, in the fugitive slave problem, the students in each small group gathering information can be asked to collaboratively present what they find in an appropriate format such as a poster, briefing sheet, or outline that can be readily shared with the rest of the class during a follow-up discussion. Because their work has been done as a collaborative effort, each group member shares the same performance assessment or grade for the activity. But, to also assess individual performance during the search activity, each student should be

Standard: Criteria:	Exceeds standard for the unit (10–9)	Reaches standard for the unit (8–7)	Approaches unit standard (6)	Does not yet reach standard (5)
Depth				
Accuracy				
Relevance				

Group's Performance at Gathering Relevant, Reliable Information

Individual answers to the question being investigated

Clarity				
Logic				

Figure 3. A Rubric for Information Gathering
Note. Individual cells on the rubric can be filled in with check marks, point totals, or performance comments.

asked to write an answer to the question the group investigated, using the information the group collected as the basis for the answer. For this part of the assessment, students are required to work individually, and their answers are assessed according to a rubric like the one presented in Figure 3.

Extremely useful criteria for building rubrics is available at Richard Paul's Web site on critical thinking at Sonoma State University (http://www.criticalthinking.org). The criteria Paul uses to describe the attributes of critical thinkers serve as excellent assessment criteria, as well. Descriptors the authors find most helpful for the assessment of work done during PBL are shown in Table 7.

When preparing a rubric to use in the assessment of students' work, the teacher picks two or three of the most relevant descriptors from Table 7 and describes to the students how the descriptors will be used as performance criteria. For example, the criteria for the collaborative portion of the information collection activity discussed above might include "depth," "accuracy," and "relevance." The work of the group is then assessed in light of the depth of information students found. Was it previously unknown to the students and did it deepen their understanding of the problem? The second criterion, relevance, is used in the same way. Information gathered by the groups is assessed for its bearing on the question each group was answering. Lastly, the degree of accuracy reached by the group in paraphrasing or quoting the information it found would be assessed. By using just a few criteria, assessments are more tightly focused and results can be shared with students more quickly, giving

Table 7
Assessment Criteria

Depth—going beyond simple or superficial understanding
Breadth—involving more than one point of view or source
Accuracy—being correct, true, and factual
Precision—being specific and exact
Clarity—expressing oneself clearly and intelligibility
Relevance—staying connected to the topic in meaningful ways
Reliability—using information from trustworthy sources
Logic—building ideas from available evidence

Note. Adapted from *Universal Intellectual Standards*, by L. Elder and R. Paul, 2005, Retrieved January 22, 2005, from http://www.criticalthinking.org.

them time to use what they learn from the assessment during the continuation of the unit.

The *investigation phase* continues during subsequent class periods as students share what they uncovered during their searches, discuss the significance of what they found for the problem, and decide what needs to be done next. This phase can also include teacher led, direct instruction, but it should be used sparingly since it tends to take the investigation away from the students. Direct instruction can take the form of teacher explanation of complex ideas or concepts, practice of important skills by students, and short presentations on issues or events that emerge during the investigation. The *investigation phase* gives way to the *solution phase* as the issues in the problem are discovered and students come to understand them.

The Solution Phase

Solution building is the culmination of the inquiry process in problem-based learning. During the *solution phase* of PBL, the teacher is responsible for helping learners (1) define the problem, using insights gained from the investigation, (2) choose criteria for the selection of a solution that fits the problem as defined, (3) brainstorm solution options that fit the criteria, and (4) construct a rationale that explains why a chosen solution is reasonable.

The solution phase begins with students suggesting definitions for the problem they face as the farmers in the opening scenario. Along with formulating problem definitions, the students are asked to select criteria they will use to evaluate potential solutions for reasonableness and fit to the problem's definition. An example of a problem definition, constructed by a gifted student in one of the author's eighth grade classes, read like this: "What should I do about the slaves that takes into consideration the safety of my family, the Fugitive Slave Act, and the life the fugitives will face if they are returned to their owners?" Notice that the first seven words define the problem while the remainder of the statement establishes three criteria for the selection of a fitting solution. Students are often faced with important ethical considerations when they establish the criteria for an acceptable solution. After each member of the class builds a definition, students brainstorm actions they, as the farmer, might take to resolve the problem. The discussion focuses on ethical issues, state and federal laws of the time, the activities of abolitionists and slavery supporters in border states, the operation of the Underground Railroad, and other issues that have surfaced during the investigation. Then, each student is asked to construct a solution and a rationale for his or her choice. The solutions, with their rationales, become the final assessment product in each student's portfolio.

As with the initiation and investigation phases of the PBL unit, teachers have important coaching responsibilities during solution building. They must (1) expect and support critical thinking as students build definitions of the problem, generate criteria for fitting solutions, and select their solutions for the problem; (2) demonstrate solid critical thinking for their students; and (3) help learners develop the metacognitive insights needed to monitor their own performance as problem solvers.

The Debriefing Phase

The final phase of the PBL process, *debriefing*, is used to revisit complex issues in the problem, to reteach content students still don't understand, and to give students feedback or other insights into their metacognitve performance. Serious, thoughtful reflection on how they managed the inquiry process helps adolescents develop mental templates that can be used during future problem solving situations.

During debriefing, the teacher helps students (1) reflect upon and evaluate their performance as problem solvers, (2) review concepts and objectives of the unit, and (3) transfer or try out newly acquired concepts in additional settings.

Constructivist methodology, like problem-based learning, should not be the only instructional environment gifted students encounter in social studies and history classrooms. It should, however, become one of the more frequently selected resources in the teacher's toolkit because it offers enormous potential for activating the unique characteristics of gifted adolescents and producing authentic learning.

CONCLUSION

Challenging, meaningful experiences in social studies and history for gifted adolescents require regular opportunities for the students to "pull the cat's tail" in the classroom—sample issues and problems from the real world with as much complexity and student directed investigation as possible. Designing such opportunities begins by aligning the goals and purposes of instructional units with standards from national organizations and commissions so that choices regarding subject matter and methodology are intentional and based upon sound scholarship. Then, the characteristics of gifted adolescents must be factored into choices regarding content and methodology so their talents and abilities are activated, practiced, and polished during instruction. Finally, constructivist methodology, such as problem-based learning, must become a regular feature in the social studies classroom, along with other strategies that differentiate student grouping patterns and the complexity of content they meet, so that gifted adolescents can craft the uniquely complex understandings of themselves and the world they are capable of creating.

REFERENCES

Anderson, L. W., & Kratwohl, D. R. (Eds.). (2001). *A taxonomy for learning, teaching, and assessing.* Chicago: Longman.

Apple, M. (1993). *Official knowledge.* New York: Routledge.

Banks, J. (1994). *An introduction to multicultural education.* Boston: Allyn & Bacon.

Barrows, H. S. (1994). *Practiced-based learning: Problem-based learning applied to medical education.* Springfield, IL: Southern Illinois University.

Beyer, B. K. (1971). *Inquiry in the social studies classroom: A strategy for teaching.* Columbus, OH: Charles E. Merrill.

Bradley Commission on History in Schools. (1998). *Building a history curriculum: Guidelines for teaching history in schools.* Westlake, OH: National Council for History Education.

Currier, L. (1986). A declaration of independence. A creed for middle school educators. *Middle School Journal, 17*(2), 4–6.

Dewey, J. (1916). *Democracy and education.* New York: Macmillan.

DiSibio, R. A., & Savitz, S. R. (1983). *But, teacher, I don't like to read: Or how to make reading alluring.* (ERIC Document No. 237971)

Elder, L., & Paul, R. (2005). *Universal intellectual standards.* Retrieved January 22, 2005, from http://www.criticalthinking.org

Fancett, V. S., & Hawke, S. D. (1982). Instructional practices in social studies. In Project SPAN Staff (Eds.), *The current state of social studies* (pp. 207–262). Boulder, CO: Social Science Education Consortium.

Fouts, J. T. (1989). Classroom environments and student views of social studies: The middle grades. *Theory and Research in Social Education, 17,* 136–147.

Fraser, B. J. (1981). Deterioration in high school students' attitudes toward social studies. *Social Studies. 72*(2), 65–68.

Freire, P. (1973). *Pedagogy of the oppressed.* New York: Continuum.

Gallagher, S. A. (1997). Problem-based learning: Where did it come from, what does it do, and where is it going? *Journal for the Education of the Gifted, 20,* 332–362.

Gallagher, S. A., Sher, B. T., Stepien, W. J., & Workman, D. (1995). Implementing problem-based learning in the science classroom. *School Science and Mathematics, 95,* 136–146.

Gallagher, S. A., & Stepien, W. J. (1996). Depth versus breadth in problem-based learning: Content acquisition in American studies. *Journal for the Education of the Gifted, 19,* 257–275.

Gallagher, S. A., Stepien, W. J., & Rosenthal, H. (1994). The effects of problem-based learning on problem solving. *Gifted Child Quarterly, 36,* 195–200.

Gamoran, A., Nystrand, M., Berends, M., & LePore, P. C. (1995). An organizational analysis of the effects of ability grouping. *American Educational Research Journal, 32,* 687–715.

Giroux, H. A. (1997). *Pedagogy and the politics of hope: Theory, culture, and schooling.* Boulder: Westview Press.

Gollub, J. P., Bertenthal, M. W., Labov, J. B., & Curtis, P. C. (Eds.). (2002). *Learning and understanding: Improving advanced study of mathematics and science in U.S. high schools.* Washington, DC: National Academy Press.

Haladyna, T., & Shaughnessy, J. (1982). Correlates of attitudes toward social studies. *Journal of Social Studies Research, 10,* 1–26.

Haladyna, T. M., & Thomas, G. P. (1979). The attitudes of elementary school kids toward school and subject matters. *Journal of Experimental Education, 48*, 18–23.

Huitt, W. (2004). Bloom et al.'s taxonomy of the cognitive domain. *Educational Psychology Interactive*. Valdosta, GA: Valdosta State University. Retrieved June 10, 2005, from http://chiron.valdosta.edu/whuitt/col/cogsys/bloom.html

Jonassen, D. H. (1991). Objectivism versus constructivism: Do we need a new philosophical paradigm? *Educational Technology Research and Development, 39*(3), 5–14.

Kaplan, S. (1979). *Inservice training manual: Activities for developing curriculum for the gifted and talented*. Ventura, CA: National/State Leadership Training Institute.

Kulik, J., & Kulik, C. (1992). *An analysis of the research on ability grouping: Historical and contemporary perspectives*. Storrs, CT: The National Research Center on the Gifted and Talented.

Maker, J., & Nielson, A. (1995). *Training models in education of the gifted*. Austin, TX: Pro-Ed.

National Assessment Governing Board. (2002). U.S. history framework for the 1994 and 2001 national assessment of educational progress. Washington, DC: Author.

National Association for Gifted Children. (1998). *Characteristics of gifted children*. Retrieved May 1, 2005, from http:///www.nagc.org

National Council for the Social Studies. (1994). *Expectations of excellence*. Alexandria, VA: Author.

Newmann, F. M., & Wehlage, G. G. (1993). Five standards of authentic instruction. *Educational Leadership, 50*(7), 8–12.

Pallas, A. M., Entwisle, D. R., Alexander, K. L., & Stluka, M. F. (1994). Ability-group effects: Instructional, social, or institutional? *Sociology of Education, 67*, 27–46.

Patrick, J. (2001). *The 2001 NAEP in U.S. History*. Retrieved May 4, 2005, from http://www.indiana.edu/~ssdc/naephis2dig.htm

Plessy v. Ferguson, 163 U.S. 537 (1896).

Rakow, S. J. (1984). What's happening in elementary science: A national assessment. *Science and Children, 22*(2), 39–40.

Renzulli, J. S., & Richards, S. (2000). Gifted and in the middle: Addressing the needs of gifted middle school students. *Principal, 79*(4), 62–63.

Reyes, L. H. (1984). Affective variables and mathematics education. *Elementary School Journal. 84*, 558–581.

Savery, J. R., & Duffy, T. M. (1995). Problem based learning: An instructional model and its constructivist framework. *Educational Technology, 35*(5), 31–38.

Schug, M. C., Todd, R. J., & Beery, R. (1984). Why kids don't like social studies. *Research in Social Studies Education, 48*, 382–387

Shaughnessy, J., & Haladyna, T. M. (1985). Research on student attitude toward social studies. *Social Education, 49*, 692–695.

Sousa, D. A. (2003). *How the gifted brain works*. Thousand Oaks, CA: Corwin Press.

Stepien, W. J. (2001). *Problem-based learning across the curriculum*. Presentation at Centennial Campus Middle School, Raleigh, NC.

Stepien, W. J., & Gallagher, S. A. (1993). Problem-based learning: As authentic as it gets. *Educational Leadership, 50*(7), 25–29.

Stepien, W. J., Gallagher, S. A., & Workman, D. (1993). Problem-based learning for traditional and interdisciplinary classrooms. *Journal for the Education of the Gifted, 16*, 338–357.

Stepien, W. J., & Pyke, S. (1997). Designing problem-based learning units. *Journal for the Education of the Gifted, 20*, 380–400.

Stepien, W. J., Senn, P. R., & Stepien, W. C. (2000). *The Internet and problem-based learning*. Tucson, AZ: Zephyr Press

Stevenson, C. (1992). *Teaching ten to fourteen year olds*. New York: Longman.

Sytsma, R. E. (2001, November). *Gifted education in America's high schools: National survey results.* Paper presented at the meeting of the National Association for Gifted Children, Cincinnati, OH.

Tam, M. (2000). Constructivism, instructional design, and technology: Implications for transforming distance learning. *Educational Technology & Society, 3*(2), 50–60.

Tomlinson, C. A. (1995a). *Gifted learners and the middle school: Problem or promise?* Reston, VA: ERIC Clearinghouse on Disabilities and Gifted Education. (ERIC Document Reproduction Service No. ED386832)

Tomlinson, C. (1995b). *How to differentiate instruction in mixed-ability classrooms.* Alexandria, VA: Association for Supervision and Curriculum Development.

Weible, T., & Evans, C. S. (1984). Elementary students' perceptions of the social studies. *The Social Studies, 75,* 244–247.

GUIDING GIFTED STUDENTS TOWARD SCIENCE EXPERTISE

CHAPTER 16

by Shelagh Gallagher

O *nce a scientist experiences the exhilaration of discovery and once he has felt the deeper and more expansive feeling . . . that is the reward for any real advancement of the understanding—then he is hooked and no other life will do.* (Medawar, 1979, p. 7)

A healthy society requires experts whose inventive visions push culture forward, as well as a public capable of determining whether any given vision pushes the society in a desirable direction. When experts are well educated, a continuous flow of new ideas is ensured. When the public is well educated, undesirable, unnecessary, or unsafe ideas fail to thrive. This interplay is particularly important with respect to science, which has become more influential than ever in our cultural fabric. Concern over the public's ability to fill its part of the bargain has led to a nearly exclusive focus on education for scientific literacy; while necessary, this only attends to half the equation. Left this way, the social structure is all out of balance. New experts must also be prepared to maintain a healthy, independent society. The purpose of this chapter is to put the discussion of literacy aside for a while in order to focus on how to prepare students capable of future scientific expertise.

Understanding the endpoint is essential to understanding the path future experts should follow. Teasing out the details of three aspects of the modern scientist's life will help define what it takes to be considered an expert scientist in today's society. Each of the three components contributes a unique set of attributes: (1) the actual practice of modern science will provide information about skills and tools, (2) the source of new ideas in science will help establish behavior qualities of the expert, and (3) the framework of beliefs that guide scientific activity will reveal an important philosophical underpinning. Together the three perspectives allow for a theoretical rationale for an approach to science education for gifted students. It is hoped that this approach will ensure that gifted students are not only prepared to work, but are also able to experience "the exhilaration of discovery."

THEORETICAL RATIONALE

Practicing Modern Science

Ask the parents of any gifted young scientist what he or she will need and they will reply, "He (or she) will have to get a job!" Perhaps the answer sounds flippant, but the truth is that getting a job in a science-related field will require a set of skills quite different from those of previous generations, largely because of the huge expansion of scientific information. Modern technologies allow scientists to observe smaller and larger phenomena, store larger databases, and analyze at lightening speed. As a result, information accumulated so quickly that 29,000 new scientific journals were introduced between 1970 and 1993 (Hurd, 1993). The annual accumulation of new knowledge reported in these journals creates a virtual mountain of new data that never erodes.

The ever-increasing mountain of new information doesn't erode, but it does move. Sometimes there's a shift in the mountain of information, a shift caused by a single fact that transforms how phenomena are interpreted. Examples of these theoretical shifts are easy to find, such as the revolution in biology that accompanied the mapping of the human genome, or the transformation in astronomy provided by the Hubble Telescope. In fact, shifts in thought can come so quickly and so frequently that noted physician Lewis Thomas (1995) claimed:

> In the fields I know best, among life sciences, it is required that the most expert and sophisticated minds be capable of changing those minds, often with a great lurch, every few years.... The next week's issue of any scientific journal can turn a whole field upside down ... It is almost an everyday event in physics, in chemistry, in materials research, in neurobiology, in genetics, in immunology. (p. 207)

As scientists endeavor to organize new, shifting bodies of information, they sometimes find they need to create a whole new field to connect ideas that didn't seem related until a new fact or idea came along. An array of new hybrid science disciplines has emerged in the past 20 years. It is hard to remember that nuclear science is a hybrid of physics, chemistry, biology, and health, or that biology and chemistry weren't always joined through biochemistry; perhaps someday fields like bioastronautics and nanoelectronics will be similarly familiar. Right now, they provide both opportunity and confusion. Klein (1993) points out that the new hybrid science fields make it difficult to sort professionals into traditional disciplinary classifications. "Is it proper . . ." she ponders, "to classify the scientist investigating certain molecular structures of DNA as a molecular biologist, a geneticist, a biochemist or a quantum mechanic?" (Klein, p. 189). With the number of hybrid science fields on the rise, modern scientists actively acquire their own expertise, and also actively integrate their ideas with perspectives from other areas of science.

Working in a hybrid field requires collaboration (Curloss, 2004). One clear sign of this collaboration takes the form of scholarly articles, which have an average of 6.6 authors (Hurd, 1993). Collaboration reaches a massive scale in large research ventures such as the Fermi National Accelerator or the International Space Station. Scientists working on these large research ventures all want salaries and equipment: Big research requires big money. Acquiring big money requires communication early on to funding sources and later to the public at large. Ethical dilemmas emerge at both ends of this interplay between science and society:

> Urgent ethical and social questions are being raised in the behavioral sciences and in areas of biomedicine such as experimentation with human subjects, genetic engineering and behavior control, human reproduction, and the termination of life. Technology has generated extraordinary demands on space, energy, and natural resources. The resulting questions about pollution and about constraints on growth are essentially ethical . . . (Commission on the Humanities, 1980, p. 16)

With all these changes in the practice of science, it stands to reason that job requirements would change, too. Employers in scientific fields now seek scientists who are rapid learners and conceptual thinkers, at ease with ambiguity and shifts in ideas. Adaptability and sound procedural knowledge are more important than absolute certainty about a given content dogma (Duggan & Gott, 2002).

The stereotypical image of the isolated scientist spending lonely hours in his laboratory researching in chemistry, biology, or physics is fading. Modern scientific practice now entails flexible, interdisciplinary thought, skill in collaboration and communication, and conscious consideration of ethical implications. Preparing the next generation of scientists requires training in conceptual, flexible, and interdisciplinary thinking; information analysis; collaboration; communication; and ethics. This is a sizable agenda, to be sure, yet it's still incomplete, for all the tools in the world will do an expert no good without an idea to pursue.

Producing and Pursuing Scientific Ideas

Scientific ideas are tested in the lab, or in the field, or in space, they are discussed at conferences or in the news, but where do they come from in the first place?

They come from within. Science has always been dependent upon the imagination of scientists. Interviews with eminent scientists reveal a respect for the process of discovery in science and a commitment to scientific thinking as a way of life (Koro-Ljungbert, 2001). For creative scientists, the desire to question, solve problems and create new ideas seems to be integrated into their very personalities. Feist (1993) reviewed research studies that compared more creative scientists and less creative scientists; creative scientists were consistently found to be more autonomous, independent, dominant, self-sufficient, and intrinsically motivated. Subsequently, Feist and Gorman (1998) found that while all scientists tend to report qualities such as dominance, drive, independence, achievement orientation, and introversion, only eminent scientists also reported preferences for ambition, independence, autonomy, self-confidence, openness, flexibility, and hostility (attributed to professional defensiveness).

Personality traits cannot entirely account for a science experts' affinity for the field; for them, science is often a matter of the heart. Thagard (2005) noted that when scientists describe the qualities of a scientist, they are likely to list affective rather than cognitive traits. While classifying traits of scientists reported across several studies, Thagard labeled one set "Be Excited," but "excited" seems tame placed next to the words of a Nobel laureate: "Passion is indispensable for creation, no less in the sciences than in the arts. . . . This is the rage to know" (Judson, 1987, p. 5). Scientists' collective passion, intensity, and curiosity are the true catalysts of discovery.

Affinity for uncertainty and a love of exploration lead scientists into a world of wide ranging questions about the unknown. Questions born of passion require pursuit, and while on the hunt for answers, the expert scientist develops a set of cognitive attributes that aid in problem solving: a wealth of information, organized conceptually; skill in posing apt questions; flexible representation of ideas using models, theories, and concepts (Kozma, 2003; Larkin, McDermott, Simon, & Simon, 1980); flexible representation of material; abstract thinking; and forward problem solving (Chi, Feltovich, & Glaser, 1981).

The potential expert needs more than the pragmatics of day-to-day operational procedure; she needs a penchant for creativity, intrinsic motivation, and ease with open exploration of unanswered questions. Bolstering these more affective characteristics are a comprehensive knowledge base and mental tools for complex problem solving. The description seems complete, and yet it's still missing an essential element.

Beliefs Underlying Scientific Endeavors

The notion that science is dependent upon the imagination and experiences of individual scientists may seem contrary to students who believe that scientific knowledge emerges from detailed observation of the natural world. The difference between these two beliefs, that science emerges from theories formed by scientific imagination and the belief that science is derived from objective observation, is substantial, significant, and rarely directly addressed in schools.

Scientists share a way of thinking about the knowledge they pursue. Judson (1987) refers to it when he says, ". . . to know something—really to know it, not merely know *of* it—is to think in a particular way and, necessarily, not to think in certain other ways" (p. xii). Scientists have a particular way of looking at information, an *epistemology* that describes their assumptions about the origin and nature of scientific knowledge. Kuhn (1962) presented a groundbreaking description of this particular way of thinking in *The Structure of Scientific Revolutions*. Kuhn refuted the notion that scientific discoveries are "found" like pennies on a sidewalk. Instead, he described science as a human endeavor directed primarily through theories developed by scientists; a creative act. A penny is discovered because a scientist was looking for something like a penny instead of something like a ball. Other tenets of the epistemology of science include:

1. Observations made by scientists are not objective, they are colored by the scientists' ideas and past experiences; indeed, past experience inevitably affects all arenas of scientific understanding.
2. Scientists create paradigms or structures of thought. These human made theoretical structures affect the information they seek and the methods they use while seeking.
3. Compelling new evidence can require that a paradigm be abandoned or rearranged to account for the new information or insight—the paradigm shift.
4. Theoretical stance affects observation and interpretation.
5. Paradigm shifts change theory, and rearrange what facts are considered important when explaining a particular phenomenon. So while facts do not change, their relative importance does (Abimbola, 1983; Carey & Smith, 1993; Nelson, 1989; Ryan & Aikenhead, 1992).

Empirical research gives evidence that experts do tend to ascribe to this epistemology (Ferry & Ross-Gordon, 1998; Kuhn & Weinstock, 2002; Thorlindsson, 1994). In many ways this epistemology—Judson's particular way of thinking—connects directly to the scientific personality discussed in the previous section. Scientists are drawn to the lure of the unknown; they form theories about what they might find. These theories, in turn, guide the quest to see if their ideas hold true. They are not *discoverers* as much as they are the *architects* of future scientific understanding.

Scientists believe this epistemology is so important they have embedded it in science education reform. A notable example is *Science for All Americans: Project 2061,* where Rutherford and Alghren (1990) frame the chapter on the Nature of Science with headings that reflect this philosophy: Scientific Ideas Are Subject To Change; Science Knowledge Is Durable; Science Cannot Provide the Answers to All Questions; Science Is a Blend of Logic and Imagination; and Science Is a Complex Social Enterprise. Others have also suggested that epistemology is a kind of "gatekeeper" to understanding science: In order to see science as creative and exploratory, they must first believe that open-endedness is legitimate (Nelson, 1989). Bell (2004) insists that this particular way of thinking about science is equally important as content knowledge: "A student's ability to understand scientific advancement and any associated controversy hinges both on knowledge of the particulars at hand and about the epistemic practices of the discipline" (pp. 237–238). Becoming an expert requires a multifaceted approach. Training in content and skills alone won't work; these must be augmented with the attitudes, dispositions, and beliefs that are also characteristic of expertise.

EMPIRICAL RESEARCH

Gifted Students, Poised for Expertise

Gifted students have cognitive characteristics that are potential precursors for science expertise. Certainly, their minds show the capacity to work like a scientist's: Earlier than their age mates, gifted students use conceptual representation of information (Passow & Fraiser, 1996), forward problem-solving (Chi, Glaser, & Farr, 1988; Shore & Kanevsky, 1993), expert-like problem representation and capacity for problem definition (Rogers, 2001), and the use of executive (metacognitive) strategies to monitor their learning (Cheng, 1993).

In many ways, gifted adolescents are kindred spirits to expert scientists. The qualities common in the experts—passion, curiosity, intensity—are also common among gifted students. Gifted students and scientists are united together and distinguished from others in their intensity, curiosity, and desire to know the unknown (Rogers, 2001; Sak, 2004). Gifted students who have these characteristics and also an early love of science, are called "science prone." Science curriculum, if properly designed, could validate the science prone students' natural interests, revealing the reason why people who think the way they do find the field alluring.

Many gifted students who aren't science prone have the inclination for creating new ideas, asking questions, and desiring to learn. This suggests that among the pool of gifted students are those who could become devoted to science if they saw the inherent opportunity to explore. Tobias (1990) describes students suited to, but uninterested in, science as the "second tier." She argues that presenting these students with authentic science activity could ignite interest and persuade them to pursue science careers. Brandwein (1995) makes a similar point, noting that many students have not yet experienced a learning environment where they could discover their "proneness" to science. Cultivating science interest in the second tier of students, those with the predisposing skills and dispositions, will be essential to maintain a thriving science community (Tobias).

Science Achievement and the Gifted: Not Expert Yet

In theory, gifted students should feel a natural appeal for science: They share the same cognitive strengths, the same inclination for exploration, and the same desire to create original ideas. Unfortunately, evidence from Lupart, Cannon, and Telfer

(2004) suggests that by middle school gifted students' feelings about science are lackluster: In their survey of 600 middle school students, science received an average rank of third out of six career choices for boys, and last for girls. Achievement data are also dismaying. Analysis of the 2000 NAEP science results revealed only 4% of 8th graders and 2% of 12th graders scored in the Advanced category (U.S. Department of Education [USDOE], 2001). In a more targeted analysis, students taking advanced science classes received an average scaled score of 174 out of 300, just barely above the average of 150 (O'Sullivan & Grigg, 2001). Similar findings emerged from the Third International Mathematics and Science Study (TIMSS), where AP Physics students received the lowest average scores among advanced students in 16 countries (USDOE, 1998). By any of these measures, the science achievement of advanced US students is inadequate. Is the problem the lack of content in science classes? Actually, the problem may be that there's too much content:

> . . . Japanese eighth graders do not do better because of better prepared teachers, smaller classes, a longer school year, less TV, and more homework. The differences trace right to the classroom, where the learning goals are clear, the topics per year are few but treated in depth, and where students learn to understand and apply through real-world problem solving and verbalization for meaning. In U.S. schools, by contrast, learning goals are defuse, coverage is King (30–35 topics a year vs. 6–10 in Japan), textbooks get fatter by the year, and everything has to be taught and retaught again . . . (Marchese, 1998, p. 3)

The vocabulary alone is daunting: Somewhere between 2,000–5,000 new terms are introduced in a typical middle or high school level science class (Hurd, 1993).

Advanced curriculum in the U.S. is also packed with content. Comparing U.S. and international science curriculum, Callahan and colleagues (2000) note, "The math and science Advanced Placement exams . . . are based on rapid, surface-level coverage of a plethora of concepts. In contrast, curricula in those countries whose advanced students tend to score higher than their U.S. counterparts tend to focus on fewer concepts and give students the opportunity to study those concepts in greater depth" (Callahan, Tomlinson, Reis, & Kaplan, p. 789). Ironically, this fast paced, surface level approach may actually backfire with gifted students, as evidence suggests that routine, repetitive, rote curriculum contributes to underachievement, not expertise (Kanevsky & Keighley, 2003; Peterson & Colangelo, 1996).

Quality is as problematic as quantity. Content analyses of middle school science texts reveal the majority to be woefully deficient in providing relevance, creating and using scientific ideas, and encouraging students' thinking about ideas and phenomena (Kesidou & Roseman, 2002; Roseman, Kesidou, Stern, & Caldwell, 1999). Stern and Roseman (2004) compared middle school biology textbooks on their treatment of a single topic, energy transfer, and found the texts lacking in both the explanation and support to help student learn. Biology is not alone in the textbook problem. After a comprehensive review of middle school physics texts, Hubisz (2003) concluded, ". . . according to the criteria we set forth, none of the 12 most popular middle-school physical science texts was acceptable." Hubisz (2002) elaborated in his online report:

> Not one of the books we reviewed reached a level that we could call "scientifically accurate". . . . The sheer number of errors precludes such a designation. . . . no text emphasized and reminded the reader that the scientific approach was something to be learned and applied, . . . for the most part these [tests] were trivial from a physical science perspective. (pp. 92–93)

Hubisz did find some quality texts, most of which were rarely used. Many of the quality curricula were relics of the post-Sputnik curriculum era. Finally, content accuracy is not only a problem in middle school; only 1 out of 10 high school biology texts analyzed met a satisfactory standard (Roseman, Kulm, & Shuttleworth, 2001).

Study after study reports that science achievement among gifted students is lagging, and their overstuffed texts are inaccurate. Is it any wonder that science isn't their favorite subject? Fortunately, the literature also provides evidence of educational practices that will help ensure that potential experts take science, learn science, understand the goals of science, and ultimately, love science.

Encouraging Persistence

Studies identify prior achievement and positive attitudes towards science as variables with the greatest influence on continued enrollment in science (Gallagher, 1994; Gooding, Swift, Schell, Swift, & McCroskery, 1990). Prior achievement and positive attitude may be related because achievements bring about feelings of competence, and feeling competent often leads to a positive attitude (Rennie & Punch, 1991). Attitudes toward science also improve when students have access to role models (Evans & Whigham, 1995), and when the curriculum is inquiry-based (Linn & Hsi, 2000), personally relevant (Siegel & Ranney, 2003), and presented in a real-world context (Kauffman & Mann, 1997), suggesting that the closer students get to "authentic" science, the more pleased they are with their science class. Positive attitude toward science is an important predictor regardless of whether the science course has a laboratory component (Butler, 1999). However, no one seems particularly interested in science in early adolescence. College students, regardless of major, report having a relatively low interest in science in grades seven and eight; however, college science majors remember liking science in ninth grade significantly more than non-science majors (Eichinger, 1997).

Ensuring Content Acquisition

Policy makers in science education speak in a clear voice on this matter: Comprehensive reports from well-respected science organizations call for students to engage in science in an inquiry-based environment (National Research Council,

1996; Rutherford & Alghren, 1990) Well-designed, content-rich inquiry is superior for cultivating higher order thinking skills at no expense to content acquisition. The body of research supporting inquiry stretches back to the 1960s, when both initial and subsequent analysis of the Sputnik era science curricula demonstrated superior learning gains (Hardy, 1971; Shymansky, Hedges, & Woodworth, 1990). Modern studies support these findings. While researching inquiry-based high school physics, Tretter and Jones (2003) found that students in inquiry-based classes both participated more and had better grades than their traditionally instructed peers. Standardized achievement scores for the two groups were not dramatically different, but the inquiry group's scores were more uniform (Tretter & Jones). In a separate study of experiment-based physics, Reynolds (1991) found no significant differences in content acquisition, but significant improvement in the process skills of the experiment-based group. As a part of analysis of NAEP test scores, Schneider and colleagues looked at students in problems-oriented classrooms separately from others and found their performance to be superior on 44% of test items (Schneider, Krajcik, Marx, & Soloway, 2002). A larger study including a nationwide sample of more than 64 physics classrooms found students learned physics concepts more readily in inquiry-based classes than they did in didactic instruction (Hake, 1998). Classroom analyses conducted by the NAEP and the TIMSS both reveal students who scored higher on those tests tended to have had inquiry-based instruction (Tretter & Jones). At the very least, inquiry does no harm to content acquisition, and the additional gains that include higher order thinking (Reynolds, 1991), increases success in subsequent courses (Linn & Hsi, 2000).

Encouraging Mature Epistemologies

The failure of schools to address the epistemology of science may be the biggest stumbling block to the early cultivation of expertise. Without the capacity to see that science is about unanswered questions that evolve from theories and answered through research and discourse, how could students begin to understand what they were supposed to do? Those involved in educating young potential experts actually have two jobs related to epistemology: (1) encouraging mature personal epistemology, and (2) understanding the epistemology of science.

Encouraging Personal Epistemologies

Epistemology matures in a developmental, sequential, stage-based sequence. Like the more familiar Piagetian stages of cognitive development, movement from one stage to the next requires a transformation of point of view. Children start forming their beliefs in elementary school (Kuhn & Weinstock, 2002); development continues through adulthood. Movement from one stage to the next is dependent on cognitive development and experience; not all people acquire the highest levels.

Perry (1970) was among the first to present a framework describing stages of epistemological development. While many others have made important contributions that have expanded Perry's work (Belenky, Clinchy, Goldberger, & Tarule, 1986; King

> ## Table 1
> ## Examples of Students at Different Stages
> ## of Epistemological Development
>
> Polly and Portia are at their desks busily completing an assignment to compare and contrast two scientific theories, justifying why one is currently considered more valid. Polly is confused; she doesn't understand what "more valid" means—that sounds more like something she'd see in her World Studies class! Polly believes that because this is science class there's going to be a right answer. Why ask for her reasons when one is clearly right and the other clearly wrong? Duh. Polly's response focuses on why the first theory is right and fails to address possible strengths of the secondary theory. She gets a B-. One desk over, Portia is hard at work looking for strengths and weaknesses in each theory. She successfully identifies strengths of the "lesser theory," but her response is a bit awkward and she fails to draw strong comparisons. She gets a B. The students' grades are close, but their reasoning is not. Portia approached the assignment with the belief that both theories likely had some merit, and it was her job to figure out which had more merit. With practice, she'll get an A. Polly, on the other hand, was incapable of understanding the assignment, and she could not grasp that there could be competing theories in science. Polly will have to transform her view of science in order to obtain a higher grade on assignments like these.

& Kitchener, 1984; Schommer, 1994), his four-stage framework still provides a good, accessible grounding for the ideas they all present. Perry described four stages:

1. *Dualism*. Marked by a black-and-white perspective, students at this stage believe all legitimate questions have certain answers. So-called questions without answers are just nonsense questions, pointless.
2. *Multiplicity*. Students acknowledge that there are a few unanswered questions, but believe that in the absence of an answer all opinions on the matter are equally valid.
3. *Contextual Relativism*. Unanswered questions are investigated using the tools provided by each discipline; each discipline approaches questions in a different way. Certain answers are unlikely, but a "best answer" can be achieved using the proper tools.
4. *Dialectic*. Theories are used to set directions for important questions, most of which have no "right" or "wrong" answers. Gaining understanding requires building upon the possibilities presented by data as interpreted by a consciously selected point of view, but with willingness to changing perspective if the need arises.

Polly and Portia, presented in Table 1, might provide a more vivid example of how epistemology gives two similar students different outlooks.

Polly and Portia differ in their beliefs about science; one part of their personal epistemologies. Polly believes that science is black and white, right or wrong—in fact, Polly believes this about just about all subjects right now. Portia believes that science does have some unanswered questions worth exploring; she's just not quite sure how to address them.

Lower levels of epistemological development are generally referred to as "naïve" and higher levels "mature." Polly is representative of the naïve point of view; Portia's viewpoint isn't mature, but she's further along than Polly. Several sources are available for those who want more information about general implications of epistemological development and education (King & Kitchener, 1984; Kitchener, 1983; Perry, 1970; Schommer, 1994); here, the focus remains on the implications directly related for scientific practice and science education.

The highest levels of epistemological reasoning parallel the epistemology of science, incorporating an enthusiasm for unanswered questions, with the notion that understanding is gained from sorting through complexity, and individuals construct that understanding using a paradigm—Judson's particular way of thinking. It stands to reason that achieving a mature epistemology, or something close to it, is necessary for scientific expertise. Certainly a student whose views on knowledge are naïve is impeded by philosophical filters; he or she cannot see what is ambiguous, or that science understanding is constructed. Eventually, this will affect performance in classes where science is presented in an appropriate form:

> Students who have difficulties often view physics knowledge as a collection of facts, formulas, and problem solving methods, mostly disconnected from everyday thinking, and they view learning as primarily a matter of memorization. By contrast, successful learners tend to see physics as a coherent system of ideas, the formalism as a means for expressing and working with those ideas, and learning as a matter of reconstructing and refining one's current understanding. (Hammer & Elby, 2003, p. 54)

While the effect of epistemology on a student's perspective is complex (Roth & Roychoudhury, 2003), it is broadly influential, affecting the student's ability to create logical arguments (Weinstock, Neuman, & Tabak, 2004), to describe scientists' work, to note the purpose of scientific investigation (Mason & Boscolo, 2004), and to respond to open-ended learning (King & Kitchener, 1984).

Windschitl and Andre (1998) found while some students performed better in so-called "verification" labs, students with more mature epistemologies performed better in settings where inquiry was more open-ended and exploratory. Some evidence suggests that this limited view of science may have profound effects on young potential experts, for level of epistemological reasoning, not science attitudes, predict commitment to science as a college major (Enman & Lupart, 2000).

Understanding the Epistemology of Science

Having a more mature epistemology is a necessary, but insufficient condition to understand the true nature of science. All students form opinions about the nature of knowledge in a subject, eventually deciding that they are based on understanding "known facts," "constructed ideas," or something in between (Hofer, 2000). Judgments about the nature of knowledge in different subjects are independent of one another (Bell & Linn, 2001), and may not even resemble the actual structure of the subject in question. After all, even students whose own philosophies are more mature will believe that science is based on known knowledge if that is all they ever experience. So, while Portia is somewhat more mature in her viewpoint than Polly, and even though she understands that science is more than known facts, she might still consider history a simple collection of straightforward events from the past. The interaction between the students' level of reasoning (naïve to mature) and their beliefs about a subject (known to evolving) can ultimately determine their attitudes toward the subject, as presented in Table 2. Returning once again to Polly and Portia, Polly's attitude toward science would be consistent with the third line of Table 2, and Portia's attitude either the second or fourth, depending on the structure of her science classes.

Research consistently reveals that students believe science to be a field based on certain, unchangeable facts (Bell, 2004; Cavallo, Rozman, Blickenstaff, & Walker, 2003; Cavallo, Rozman, & Potter, 2004; Ryan & Aikenhead, 1992), largely because in the fact bound science curriculum " . . . students learn scientific content quite removed from learning about the nature of scientific inquiry. Not surprisingly, they develop a view that scientific knowledge is immutable" (Linn, Davis, & Eylon, 2004, p. 116).

By this point, the conundrum should be plain: To become expert, students must develop more mature epistemology *and* view science as aligned to this view, yet by all accounts the majority of science curriculum and instruction is more likely to reinforce false, limited views of science. In short, school science is anathema to the cultivation of potential expertise.

Gifted Students and Epistemology

A student who has more advanced views will be better able to draw meaning from open-ended science experiences and come closer to emulating true expertise. The few available studies comparing gifted students with their age mates suggest that the gifted are also somewhat advanced in epistemological reasoning (Goldberger, 1981; Schommer & Dunnell, 1997; Wilkinson & Maxwell, 1991; Wilkinson & Schwartz, 1987). Some evidence exists that measurable differences begin to emerge in high school (Schommer & Dunnell, 1994). Table 2 depicts what happens when students with advanced epistemologies think a subject is based on "known fact"; they reject the subject as unimportant. As a case in point, Neber and Schommer-Aikins (2002) found traditional high school physics caused work avoidance among gifted students, while nontraditional discovery-based physics motivated students to initiate learning and metacognitive reflection.

Encouraging Appropriate Epistemologies

Already established is the importance of inquiry for content acquisition and higher order skills. Added progress toward mature epistemology as a goal narrows

Table 2
Effect of Epistemological Development
on Attitudes Towards Science

Individual level of epistemological development	Perception of science	Attitude towards the discipline
Naïve beliefs: Understanding is the result of accumulating known facts	+ Science is a field based on "known facts"	= Acceptance based on false premises: Science is *accepted* as a field based on established certainty
Mature beliefs: Understanding is constructed from human ideas and facts	+ Science is a field based on "known facts"	= Rejection based on false premises: Science is *rejected* as limited and simplistic because it is based on established certainty
Naïve beliefs: Understanding is the result of accumulating known facts	+ Science is evolving, much is unknown, and facts are affected by human interpretation	= Rejection based on accurate premises: Science is *rejected* as a vague field with no known facts and where nobody is certain of anything
Mature beliefs: Understanding is constructed from human ideas and facts	+ Science is evolving, much is unknown, and facts are affected by human interpretation	= Acceptance based on accurate premises: Science is accepted as a field where theory, speculation, and analysis combine to interpret and reinterpret facts

more specifically to specific forms of inquiry, represented by specific characteristics. First, it is inquiry characterized by open-endedness and complexity; King and Kitchener (1984) found that curriculum involving ill-structured problems was most likely to result in movement toward sophisticated reasoning. Properly approached, open-ended inquiry involving ill-structured problems forms a framework where students can achieve many important goals:

. . . inquiry approaches successfully engage students in forms of scientific inquiry as they simultaneously develop scientific knowledge that is grounded in relevant to scientific and personal life institutions. . . . A powerful outcome of this kind of integrated approach is that students develop rich conceptual knowledge while also learning about the epistemic associated with the nature of science. (Bell, 2004, p. 116)

Second, the curriculum must incorporate *explicit* instruction about the nature of science (Khishfe & Abd-El-Khalick, 2002; Sandoval, 2003). Hammer and Elby (2003) describe how to make epistemological issues explicit in all areas of instruction, including labs, homework, in-class problems, and test questions. After testing curricula with these embedded components, they observed significant increases in epistemological reasoning.

Third, developing expertise requires practice in designing theories, as well as designing experiments. An effective curriculum will provide students this practice so they can experience how theoretical stance can affect research decisions (Bell, 2004). This orientation fits perfectly with the learning preferences of gifted adolescents, who tend to respond to curriculum that is both challenging and engaging (Csikszentmihalyi, Rathunde, & Whalen, 1994).

Fourth, role models and mentors play an important role in the cultivation of scientific "habits of mind," as they transmit tacit knowledge, including values and beliefs (Subotnik & Olszewski-Kubilius, 1997). This may be one reason why Eichinger (1997) found that gifted students who are interested in science value teachers who are competent, creative, and committed, while gifted students not interested in science like science teachers who established good rapport and had patience. Both groups reported a preference for active, student centered learning, but unfortunately both groups also reported that didactic instruction dominated their science instruction.

Creating an Optimal Program

Some of the perspectives used in the above sections may seem a bit foreign: Most educators are more familiar with tenets of education than they are with the lives of practicing scientists, personality theory, or epistemology. Serendipitously, when they are rearranged and placed into educational categories, they also bear a striking resemblance to differentiation principles long familiar among educators of gifted students. The final list of educational components to encourage science expertise is summarized in Table 3.

Science education that allows students to experience (or closely emulate) real science is more motivating and more instructive than traditional approaches. Above all, this seems clear: "Best practice" in science education for gifted students requires *comprehensive modeling of authentic science*. What remains is to find frameworks that will guide curriculum selection or development.

Table 3 Educational Components That Encourage Science Expertise	
Curriculum components	Advanced disciplinary or interdisciplinary content
	Depth versus breadth of content coverage
	Emphasis on open-ended discovery, complexity, and mystery
	Incorporation of significant concepts
	Focus on ill-structured problems
	Participation of role models/mentorships
Cognitive components	Conceptual reasoning
	Theoretical reasoning (including student derived theories)
	Interdisciplinary thinking
	Flexible thinking
	Explicit epistemological thinking
	Disciplinary thinking (cognitive apprenticeship; habits of mind)
Behavioral components	Collaboration
	Independence
	Self-initiation
	Communication (oral and written; technical and lay)
	Authentic practice
Assessment components	Performance-based
	Authentic audience
	Discipline-based peer critiques

CURRICULUM EXAMPLES: MIDDLE SCHOOL

Middle school science for gifted students is suffering from a lack of resources. Textbook analyses presented earlier reveal that standard texts do not meet the challenge of reform for general education, and certainly fall short of the level of rigor, complexity, and abstractness required for gifted learners. Research and development models of middle school science for gifted students is all but nonexistent. Any promising direction must be gleaned from the few models that have evolved for general education that also provide natural opportunities

Table 4
Components of the KIE Curriculum Framework

KIE Category	Description	Components
Making science accessible	Accessible in this context means cognitively accessible, built upon student ideas, on issues relevant to students, and supported by diverse inquiry tasks	Model scientific thinking Scaffold students to make their thinking visible Provide multiple representations of information
Listen and help students learn from others	Classroom encourages discussion, engaged listening, and incorporates multiple cultural values and a variety of social activities structures.	Encourage listening to others: Students learn from each other, as well as from the instructor Design discussions Highlight cultural norm Employ multiple social activity structures; vary groups and types of activity
Promote autonomy and life-long learning	Encourage reflection on issues and on thinking (metacognition): provide complex projects; revisit and generalize inquiry processes for diverse science projects; engage in critiques of science information; critique ideas regardless of source	Encourage monitoring: Engage students in metacognitive reflection Provide complex projects: Projects based in varied, sustained science Revisit and generalize inquiry processes Scaffold critique: Require students to critique science information

Note. Information synthesized from "The Scaffolded Knowledge Integration Framework for Instruction," by M.C. Linn, E. A. Davis, & B. S. Eylon, 2004, in M.C. Linn, E. A. Davis, & P. Bell (Eds.), *Internet Environments for Science Education* (pp. 47–72), Mahweh, NJ: Lawrence Erlbaum Associations.

to add depth and complexity for the gifted; they also focus on school-based instruction.

In *Internet Environments for Science Education*, Linn, Davis and Eylon (2004) present a curriculum framework and tested applications of the framework. The Knowledge Integrated Environments (KIE) team combined effective types of inquiry and authentic science activity to derive principles for effective inquiry in science. The framework is comprised of three components: making science accessible, listening and helping students learn from others, and promoting autonomy and life-long learning. Each category is described and aligned to its major components in Table 4.

Knowledge Integrated Environments

The KIE framework has been used as the basis for a number of curriculum projects demonstrating the many variations that fit under its umbrella. Consistent with the goals of the project, the KIE curricula also integrate use of the Internet or other technology. Each of these is briefly described in Table 5. The diversity of the projects developed under KIE, and these are only a few, provide comfort to those who fear that a framework will inherently limit a teacher's creativity. Instead, the KIE model seems to suggest that a framework like this provides necessary structure for creative efforts to evolve in productive directions.

Table 5
Curriculum Projects Developed Using the KIE Framework

Project WISE	Web-Based Inquiry Science Environment (WISE) is an Internet-based platform for middle and high school science where students collaborate and find information on the Web. The format of the activities varies, but includes designing solutions to problems, critiquing interpretations of science information found on the Internet, and debates on scientific controversies.
Project SCOPE	Science Controversies: Online Partnerships for Education (SCOPE) engages students in the investigation of scientific controversies, including the reasons why frogs are deformed, the treatment and control of malaria, and genetically modified food.
CSILE	Computer Supported Intentional Learning Environments (CSILE). An Internet-based curriculum that requires students to critique arguments built on scientific data, and to build alternate arguments when necessary.
CLP: House Design	Computer as Learning Partner (CLP) is actually an umbrella title for a number of KIE projects; the House Design curriculum demonstrates how effective collaboration can occur both online and off as students tackle the problem of designing a human dwelling in the desert.

Note. Synthesized from *Internet Environments for Science Education,* by M.C. Linn, E. A. Davis, & P. Bell, 2004, Mahweh, NJ: Lawrence Erlbaum Associatons.

Learning by Design

The KIE team recognized that curriculum grounded in cognitive science would also look like authentic science. Kolodner et al. (2003) worked from the same premise in a model called Learning by Design. Using a carefully constructed set of authentic science activities, teachers and students engage in a series of design-and-build activities, punctuated by moments of reflection about important scientific concepts and the nature of authentic science practice—an aspect of scientific epistemology. Program developers note that curriculum alone is not sufficient to have a successful program; it also requires fostering a collaborative classroom culture in which students want to be engaged in deep learning and where the teacher sees herself as both a learner and a facilitator of learning, trusts that with her help the students can learn, and enthusiastically assumes the roles she needs to take on. (Kolodner et al., p. 495)

Ill-Structured Science: S/T/S and PBL

Authentic science, ill-structured science, and problem-based instruction are all included in our list of components for expertise. Two tested approaches that take this approach are Science/Technology/Science (S/T/S; Yager, 1993) and problem-based learning (Barrows & Tamblyn, 1980). More generally familiar, many would turn to S/T/S as the perfect model to engage gifted students in science. However, others have questioned whether S/T/S is useful for gifted students:

Some teachers see the STS approach as great for the average to below average student, but less rigorous than desirable for the college bound student, particularly those oriented toward science and engineering. Some science teachers, trained under National Science Foundation (NSF) stipends to teach science curriculum, such as BSCS, IPS, PSII, ESCP, CHEM Study, still believe that those programs represented the zenith of U.S. science curriculum development. (Clarke & Agne, 1997, p. 251)

S/T/S could well be a valuable starting place for teachers with gifted students as long as they adapt the level of challenge and complexity.

Problem-based learning (PBL), described in another chapter in this section, is a valuable and effective curriculum structure for virtually any field of study, and science is no exception. Examples of PBL science curriculum are available in both middle school and high school (Dods, 1997; Gallagher, 1997; Lambros, 2003). Recent examples of science-oriented interdisciplinary and discipline specific PBL units emerged from Project Insights, as a part of a larger effort to create a model middle school program for gifted disadvantaged students (Gallagher & Gallagher, 2005). Taking advantage of the PBL model's ability to embrace a variety of instructional goals, unit developers incorporated a central concept (risk), higher order thinking, metacognition, open-ended investigation, and a rich, authentic content base. Middle school units developed under this model included *Mosquito Coast*, investigating West Nile Virus; *A Sizable Dilemma*, centered around the human-elephant conflict in Zimbabwe; *That Sinking Feeling*, which investigates global warming; and *SPUD!*, a unit about genetically modified foods. Research testing the efficacy of the units demonstrated that 1) students learned important science concepts during the PBL units and 2) the PBL environment allowed for identification of students who were not considered gifted using traditional measures to emerge (Gallagher & Gallagher). Once again, however, a cautionary note is warranted: PBL is not inherently appropriate for gifted students; just like S/T/S, rigor, complexity, and abstractness must be embedded (Gallagher, 2001, 2005).

CURRICULUM EXAMPLES: HIGH SCHOOL

As students enter the high school years, the programming challenges increase. Some gifted students require differentiated curricula that help them dig into a number of different science arenas. The science prone gifted student may need to narrow rather than to focus. As they mature, both groups of students are ready for increasingly authentic levels of intense science experience.

Restructured Science

Since its inception, The Illinois Mathematics and Science Academy tested "sacred cow" assumptions of the standard science curriculum. Even in its first years, IMSA challenged the status quo, placing physics at the beginning of the high school science sequence. Today, IMSA continues to innovate in some areas of its science curriculum, offering an integrated, double credit, full year course. By integrating the three fields, chemistry, biology, and physics, students learn to approach science as a field where individual fields of study are united by common assumptions, providing new students with a strong epistemological foundation. Without concern for disciplinary boundaries, this is also the perfect environment for students to discover the hybrid science fields so common to modern practice. Later in their schooling at IMSA, students will learn science through authentic methods such as PBL, and will also have the opportunity to participate in a program similar to Authentic Science Research, described below.

Rutgers University Program

Authentic training in science takes on a third form at Rutgers University. In the Rutgers program, gifted high school students have a chance to work with professors to learn about modern science and conduct their own original research. Using the model of a cognitive apprenticeship (Collins, Brown, & Holum, 1991) students become immersed in the world of science, studying and emulating the behaviors of experts in the field. Quantitative and qualitative data gathered on student performance indicated that the students were able to discriminate between models and data, could design and conduct authentic research, and had the tools to analyze and interpret experimental research results. They also report that students' scores on the AP test items were comparable to those of students who had participated in an AP Physics course (Etkina, Matilsky & Lawrence, 2003).

Internet Options

Rapidly expanding and diversifying, Internet courses provide many opportunities to administrators who wish to broaden the scope of their science offerings. For example, the Concord Consortium offers a virtual high school that offers many different AP science courses, as well as courses on Bioethics, DNA Technology, Meteorology, and Veterinary Medicine (see http://www.govhs.org/Pages/Academics-Catalog). Many schools of the National Consortium of Specialized Secondary Schools of Mathematics, Science, and Technology (NCSSSMST) partially fulfill their outreach mandates by providing distance education courses. Useful in themselves, these courses can also support early specialization.

Models for Science Prone High School Students

Subotnik (2003) turned to the world of music conservatory to describe the optimal learning environment for the science prone gifted student. She notes that musically talented adolescents receive specialized and highly individualized training. Drawing from the wisdom of the long established and highly successful Julliard program, she recommends the following components for training young potential scientists:

- employ some form of audition as a part of admissions;
- view each student as a unique challenge, with an individual profile of abilities, traits, and interests;
- provide regular opportunities to publicly demonstrate both skills and new creative products; and
- make public the skill and creativity of the faculty—this can then be used to motivate students who might hope to work with a specific faculty member.

Gifted musicians do not study all instruments; they specialize early. Opportunities for early specialization are also possible for science prone high school students. One program that allows students to develop a singular research agenda is Authentic Science Research (Robinson, 2004). The principle goal of Authentic Science Research is to help students become independent science researchers. Students who elect to participate in Authentic Science Research are first connected with a mentor who will monitor their work. With that mentor, students select the single research topic they will follow for 3 years. The curriculum is carefully structured to help students analyze and critique science writing, develop their own research topics, investigate, and provide oral and written reports of their results. Throughout, they keep a portfolio that includes records of laboratory work, intensive analysis, and practice in scientific communication. In the 12th-grade program participants are required to enter the Intel Science Search. In one year of the program, seven out of nine seniors in the contest were selected as semifinalists and three went on to be finalists (Robinson). While the original program was open to anyone interested, it is clearly the kind of learning experience that would draw science prone gifted students. This innovative program also aligns closely with Subotnik's (2003) recommendations: the program is small, uses interview and student interest as criteria for participation, depends on a strong relationship between student and mentor, is structured around the student's interests and abilities, and provides several opportunities for increasingly authentic performance.

Evanston Township High School in Evanston, IL, provides a slightly different form of intense science experiences for science prone students. School administrators recognized that science prone students needed qualitatively different alternatives beyond their existing advanced science program. They devised three options for science prone students: (1) enrollment in a course at a local university; (2) study of a particular area of interest with a school faculty member; or (3) independent, original research conducted at the school. Founders of the three-pronged approach were particularly emphatic about the importance of student-designed research: "In [the university] setting, high school students often join a research project already in progress. They usually end up missing much of the research process that takes place prior to actual research activity, particularly the development of a research question and the experimental design process" (Ngoi & Vondracek, 2004, p. 145).

The Really Big Picture

The previously noted tendency for scientists to think conceptually allows them to make interdisciplinary connections that reach far beyond the realm of science. At this largest level scientists come to see the profound universality in the world, as when Thomas Levenson describes the connections between science and art:

> Science is something that human beings have always done to help them make sense of the world. Art, in its own way, aims at the same end. . . . Art and science don't just track the same quarry; they form between them a common endeavor, each presenting one face of the same impulse. (Levenson, 1995, p. 17)

Revealing this unity to gifted students takes them a step forward on the journey to expertise. The Israel Arts and Science Academy, a public residential school in Israel, has taken the bold step of organizing its academic programs around demonstrating the underlying parallels between science and art, each sharing elements of rigor, creativity, discovery, justification, aesthetics, and ethics. At the heart of the program is an understanding that depth of study is essential to creative productivity, "We choose to encourage creative excellence. This means that we cannot expect students to be profoundly and sincerely interested in too many domains" (Erez, 2001, p. 8). Erez also notes that the focus on depth allows the opportunity for discussions of ethics and the impact of science on human endeavors.

On a somewhat smaller scale, the connections between science and art are demonstrated in a distance learning course offered by the North Carolina School of Science and Mathematics. In the course called Honors Art of Science and Math, students explore the scientific principles that emerge when art is considered in detail. Students create artwork that integrates scientific principles as part of the course assignments; some of these are available for viewing online (see http://www.dlt.ncssm.edu/distance_learning/Teachers/Jliles.htm). Other forms of interdisciplinary connection reveal a different kind of unity. In the long-standing Science, Society, and the Future course, students at the Illinois Mathematics and Science Academy learn about the reciprocal impact of science on society and of society on science as they investigate real-life science dilemmas using problem-based learning (Gallagher, Stepien, & Rosenthal, 1992).

Extracurricular Opportunities

While formalized curricula for students gifted in science are scarce, academic competitions in science are plentiful. Often sponsored by science and technology related industries, the majority of these contests are designed to provide students with authentic science experiences. Sorting through the plethora of opportunities can be challenging, however, the Institute for Educational Advancement (IEA) runs a comprehensive academic competition search engine that allows users to include parameters such as grade level and target subject area (see http://www.education-aladvancement.org/resources/search/contest.php).

The number of summer science programs is also on the rise. Summer programs provide many opportunities that often seem impossible during the school year, such as travel to a specific research site or extended time with a mentor. The IEA search engine can also help identify summer programs by age, subject area, and/or location. Talent search programs such as Johns Hopkins University's Center for Talented Youth and Duke University's Talent Identification Program are also valuable resources. Camps run by science organizations are also popular, such as NASA Science Space Camps.

Academic contests and summer programs are invaluable for the experience, motivation and collegiality they provide to students. At the same time, they do not substitute for systematic, long-term curricula during the school year. Providing balance to a potential experts' experience requires both the unique excitement provided through competitions and summer experiences and an engaging, rigorous, authentic school year experience.

PICKING AMONG THE PROJECTS

Finding or creating good inquiry-based science curriculum is clearly imperative, yet plagued with challenges. Simply finding decent curricula is one challenge, judging it's worthiness is another, and judging one unit in comparison to another is a third. A recent development from the Inquiry Synthesis Project (Minner, Levy, & Century, 2004) helps illuminate why two inquiry based curricula can look so different, and why it is important to make knowledgeable selections of inquiry based materials.

Researchers at the Inquiry Synthesis Project developed a classification tool to help them code hundreds of research studies on inquiry-based science. While designed to aid in their mammoth undertaking, the tool can also help guide teachers and administrators who want to make purposeful choices about inquiry learning for their students. The evaluation tool is divided into three sections. The first two sections are fairly straightforward, listing (1) the science discipline(s) addressed in the unit, and (2) the types of student engagement or the kinds of activities students complete during the unit. The third section creates a cross section of Components of Instruction (question, design data, conclusion, communication) with Element of Inquiry (student responsibility for learning, students active thinking, student motivation). As a result, reviewers could determine first which Component of Instruction is emphasized and then what kind of student activity is required while students are engaged in that component. Curricula with more components and stronger emphases on the elements of inquiry are considered "saturated" in inquiry opportunities. When used systematically, teachers and administrators could describe not only the qualities of inquiry present in a given curriculum, but also the level of saturation. Balance in inquiry experience could be achieved by using the tool to ensure that students are exposed to different forms of inquiry throughout the school year (Minner, Levy & Century, 2004).

INSTRUCTION IN MIDDLE AND HIGH SCHOOL

Curriculum and instruction have a natural synergy; sometimes their individual effects are hard to determine because they seem so intertwined. Even so, they are distinct, each bringing a unique element to the classroom. Curriculum establishes a content framework, a mode of engagement, and an opportunity to learn; instruction sets the academic tone and, to a large extent, determines whether students' thinking about the curriculum will be shallow or deep. Students need to have deliberate practice in thinking like experts in order to acquire expertise, regardless of the field of study (Ericsson, Krampe, & Tesch-Romer, 1993). Other instructional models derived from cognitive research support the premise that becoming an expert requires immersion in the thinking patterns, or habits of mind, of practitioners; these include anchored instruction (Bransford, Vye, Kinzer & Risko, 1990), cognitive apprenticeship (Brown, Collins & Duguid, 1989), and cognitive flexibility theory (Spiro, Coulson, Feltovich, & Anderson, 1988).

The scientific community also advocates for inquiry instruction as a realistic model of scientific thinking. Its commitment to inquiry instruction is so strong the National Research Council (NRC) has published a book on the topic (Olson & Loucks-Horsley, 2000). Through inquiry instruction teachers model and encourage modes of scientific thought and attitudes. Inquiry instruction also encourages scientific epistemologies:

> Inquiry teaching requires that students combine processes and scientific knowledge as they use scientific reasoning and critical thinking to develop their understanding of science. Engaging students in activities of and discussions about scientific inquiry should help them to develop an understanding of scientific concepts; an appreciation of "how we know" what we know in science; understanding of the nature of science; skills necessary to become independent inquirers about the natural world; and the dispositions to use the skills, abilities, and attitudes associated with science. (NRC, 1996, p. 6)

Judging the quality of inquiry instruction can be as difficult as judging the quality of curriculum. The NRC Standards set a baseline by defining five essential characteristics of inquiry-based instruction:

1. learners are engaged by scientifically oriented questions;
2. learners give priority to evidence, which allows them to develop and evaluate explanations that address scientifically oriented questions;
3. learners formulate explanations from evidence to address scientifically oriented questions;
4. learners evaluate their explanations in light of alternate explanations, particularly those reflecting scientific understanding; and
5. learners communicate and justify their proposed explanations (NRC, 1996, p. 14).

Beerer and Bodzin (2003) take the NRC characteristics a step further by using them as the basis for an observation tool called the Science Teacher Inquiry Rubric (STIRS). Each of the NRC essential characteristics is transformed into a continuum ranging from learner-centered behaviors to teacher-centered behaviors. Descriptive indicators allow observers to accurately place observed instruction on the continuum. Beerer and Bodzin (2003) found high levels of interrater reliability using this scale, suggesting that it holds promise as a guide for teachers and administrators interested in promoting skills in science inquiry instruction. Originally designed as a guide for use in elementary school, STIRS holds several possible uses for middle school and high school, as well. First, the indicators are sufficiently broad to apply to observations of middle or high school instruction. Second, the indicators for each characteristic could provide a set of guideposts for teachers who seek a systematic, supportive means of moving their students from dependent to independent classroom activity. Third, the indicators could be used as a differentiation tool, since the progression from teacher-centered to learner-centered activity also involves systematically more complex tasks for students.

ASSESSMENT

Nothing undermines open, authentic curriculum more than closed, artificial assessment, because assessments are, among other things, the means students use to determine what teachers really want them to *learn*. If an open unit is followed by a closed test, students may well believe that the open experience was a waste of time, or worse, deceptive. Wiggins (1992) was among the first to provide a thorough description of the qualities of an authentic assessment, including that they are:

1. essential—not needlessly intrusive, arbitrary, or contrived to "shake out" a grade;
2. enabling—constructed to point the student toward more sophisticated use of the skills or knowledge;
3. contextualized, complex intellectual challenges, not "atomized" tasks;
4. [based on] the student's own research or use of knowledge, for which "content" is a means;
5. [measures of] student habits and repertoires, not mere recall or plug-in skills;
6. *representative* challenges—designed to emphasize *depth* more than breadth;
7. engaging and educational; and
8. involve somewhat ambiguous (ill-structured) tasks or problems. (Wiggins)

What is rarely mentioned is that a single authentic assessment is seldom sufficient. An open-ended environment requires a set of authentic assessments, each taking a different form depending on the nature of the assessed activity. At one point, a drawing may be appropriate, while at another, a written reflection may be necessary.

Fortunately, resources are becoming more plentiful. A comprehensive overview of authentic science assessments is provided on the Web site for the Center for Science Education (http://cse.edc.org). Examples are provided for elementary, middle school, and high school grades with complete descriptions. At each grade grouping, descriptions and concrete examples are provided for five kinds of assessment: observations, interviews, and discussions; written assessments; performance assessments; graphics; and self-assessments. Sample assessments provided as examples are drawn from existing published curricula, ensuring proper alignment. What these assessments lack are attention to conceptual or abstract ideas; teachers of gifted students would have to add this more complex layer. A second Web site, Performance Assessment Links in Science (PALS; http://pals.sri.com) is a similar repository that provides links to quality authentic science assessments that assess more advanced cognitive skills. Like the CSE Web site, PALS provides assessment examples from K–12, sorted by subject matter.

ADVANCED PLACEMENT, INTERNATIONAL BACCALAUREATE, AND THE NATIONAL RESEARCH COUNCIL

Designed from well-intended philosophies, both the Advanced Placement (AP) and International Baccalaureate (IB) programs have provided millions of students a chance for early exposure to rigorous and challenging content. Provided in individual course packages from the College Board or in full programmatic structure from the International Baccalaureate Organization (IBO), each provides established curricula and relatively accessible training programs; an appealing feature to many teachers and administrators. However, despite their popularity—or perhaps partly because of their popularity—each program has come under scrutiny by those concerned that (1) pressure to increase course enrollments results in a slower, less rigorous pace, and (2) the highly structured formats of the programs prevents them from keeping pace with rapidly changing scientific content.

Notable among the concerned are the scientists and educators of the NRC. In 2002, several panels were commissioned to investigate the quality of advanced training in science and mathematics. The panels produced one general report and several discipline-specific reports (Gollub, Bertenthal, Labov, & Curtis, 2002; Spital, 2002; Stanitski, 2002; Wood, 2002). The general report makes specific mention of the need for a rich and diverse set of contemporary, rigorous and advanced curricular offerings to challenge gifted students that include, but are not limited to, AP and IB. Alternatives advanced in the report include using alternate curriculum models; internships and mentorships; specialized schools; dual or concurrent enrollment in college; education through electronic media (computer-based curricula, televised courses, Web-based courses, and virtual high schools); summer enrichment opportunities; and academic competitions. This very important report provides both examples of sample programs and Web sites with helpful resources.

Each of the discipline-specific panels was ostensibly assembled to conduct an analysis of advanced high school course offerings in their area; however, analysis of the AP and IB coursework dominate the discussion. Thoughtful analyses of the advantages and disadvantages of each program are considered; in some cases specific analyses are presented comparing the two programs as well. Like the more general report, each of the discipline-specific reports concludes with detailed, often courageous, recommendations. Naturally, the recommendations from biology, chemistry, and physics are not identical; while teachers of each discipline may be tempted to read only recommendations for their field, each of the reports is worthy of attention for any advanced science high school teacher.

Challenges to Change

The need for scientific expertise is increasing; models for curriculum and instruction, though few in number, do exist; the scientific community is united behind the philosophy reform, and yet didactic, fact-driven classrooms still dominate the landscape. Why? The forces that militate against reform are potent, and in the interest of time and space each is mentioned only briefly.

Standardized Tests

Among the biggest blockades to reform is the domineering presence of state and national standardized accountability tests:

> [high stakes] tests tempt textbook authors and teachers to provide information at the same grain size and level of connection as found on the test. Administrators and parents may reinforce these decisions, worrying that college admissions or advanced placement tests require extensive factual knowledge of numerous topics and rarely assess inquiry. These forces oppose research-based innovations and push the complex educational system back toward the status quo. (Linn, Davis, & Bell, 2004, p. 7)

As already noted in this chapter, this is a counter-productive position, since inquiry based instruction, when used with rigorous content, results in learning gains that are equal to or greater than didactic instruction.

Calcified Scope and Sequence Structures

Schools and colleges have historically divided science into an ascending trilogy: first, biology, then chemistry, and finally physics. Even the most motivated high school teacher is influenced by this pervasive structure. Rarely discussed is the fact that this division is not in and of itself a force of nature; rather, it is fairly arbitrary and was initially designed for the convenience of college instruction (Aikenhead, 2003). Science texts follow these traditional disciplinary boundaries, and core texts are selected for the very reason that they match a traditional scope and sequence. True to the adage, "if you always do what you always did, you'll always get what you always got," true innovation will be difficult unless this structure can be successfully challenged by alternate scope and sequences.

Isolated Innovation

Similarly, reform efforts are usually course-based and dependent on an individual motivated teacher. These courses are received by students as a welcome relief or as decidedly odd, but not as "normal" school. Frequently these courses disappear if the motivated teacher takes another position. Powerful, enduring change takes more than one innovative course, especially when the course is surrounded by traditional curriculum and static pedagogy. While these individual efforts are valuable and worthy of support, enduring reform will likely only occur with a comprehensive revision of an entire scope and sequence.

Inaccessible Innovations

Valuable classroom innovations are not only isolated, they are often unseen by the public at large. As expert practitioners, teachers of advanced science are often more skilled in instruction than they are in formal curriculum writing. The result is that many valuable ideas often remain shut behind classroom doors. A model program combining innovative teachers with curriculum writers could well provide a much richer field of curriculum materials for the field at large.

Qualified Teachers

Schools across the country face a crisis of teacher shortages, especially in high school (USDOE, 2004). Science is one of the most challenged fields, and while the No Child Left Behind Act may minimize the practice of assigning teachers out-of-field, it will not address rapid turnover, nor will it ensure that they will be the kind of role models gifted students need.

Science Literacy Versus Science Training

Schools have limited resources and unlimited needs, making it difficult for many to manage the training in scientific literacy that most students need. Adding a second strand focusing on developing scientific expertise is simply beyond the reach of some schools. Half-day magnet schools, regional or state-based full-day magnet schools, Internet courses, mentorships and summer enrichment programs are invaluable options for smaller schools.

College Is Calcified, Too

Teachers and parents alike are more likely to look to the near future than the distant future when judging the success of a high school program. Colleges and universities are still largely entrenched in traditional curriculum and instruction models. Greater attention to innovative college programs may loosen the belief many hold that preparation for colleges requires unyielding dedication to ineffective practices.

FACING THE FUTURE

Times of enormous challenge are also ripe with opportunity. Never have there been so many challenges, or so many opportunities, for science teachers with gifted students in their care. The agenda can seem overwhelming and the obstacles insurmountable. Entropy is powerful and often appealing, yet it is ultimately counterproductive. Yet, the world that young gifted scientists face is full of excitement and wonder; the act of providing gifted students the tools to enter that world is a teacher's astonishing gift. Teachers who go through the effort to make their classrooms more authentic routinely say that it is both more work and more rewarding, for they also get to experience the wonder of discovery. So, perhaps the best place to close is back at the beginning, back to the qualities of the scientist that draw them toward the quest to know. The advice of Lewis Thomas (1983) can serve as a guide:

> Let it be known, early on, that there are deep mysteries, and profound paradoxes. . . . Teach at the outset, before any of the fundamentals, the still imponderable puzzles . . . that there are some things going on in the universe that lie beyond comprehension, and make it plain how little is known. . . .Teach that. (pp. 151–152)

REFERENCES

Abimbola, I. A. (1983). The relevance of the "new" philosophy of science for the science curriculum. *School Science and Mathematics, 83*, 181–193.

Aikenhead, G. S. (2003). Chemistry and physics instruction: Integration, ideologies, and choices. *Chemistry Education: Research and Practice, 4*, 115–130.

Barrows, H. S., & Tamblyn, R. M. (1980). *Problem-based learning: An approach to medical education.* New York: Springer Publishing Company.

Beerer, K., & Bodzin, A. (2003). Promoting inquiry-based science instruction: The validation of the Science Teacher Inquiry Rubric (STIR). *Journal of Elementary Science Education, 15*(2), 39–49.

Belenky, M. F., Clinchy, B. M., Goldberger, N. R., & Tarule, J. M. (1986). *Women's ways of knowing.* New York: Basic Books.

Bell, P. (2004). Promoting students' argument construction and collaborative debate in the science classroom. In M. C. Linn, E. A. Davis, and P. Bell (Eds.), *Internet environments for science education* (pp. 115–143). Mahwah, NJ: Lawrence Erlbaum Associates.

Bell, P. & Linn, M. C. (2001). Beliefs about science: How does science instruction contribute? In B. Hofer & P. Pintrich (Eds.), *Personal epistemology: The psychology of beliefs about knowledge and knowing.* (pp. 321-346). Mahwah, NJ: Lawrence Erlbaum Associates.

Butler, M. P. (1999). Factors associated with students' intentions to engage in science learning activities. *Journal of Research in Science Teaching, 36*, 455–473.

Brandwein, P. (1995). *Science talent in the young expressed within ecologies of achievement.* Storrs, CT: National Research Center on the Gifted and Talented.

Bransford, J. D., Vye, N., Kinzer, C., & Risko, V. (1990). Teaching thinking and content knowledge: Toward an integrated approach. In B. F. Jones & L. Idol (Eds.), *Dimensions of thinking and cognitive instruction* (pp. 381–413). Hillsdale, NJ: Lawrence Erlbaum Associates.

Brown, J. S., Collins, A., & Duguid, S. (1989). Situated cognition and the culture of learning. *Educational Researcher, 18*(1), 32–42.

Callahan, C. M., Tomlinson, C., Reis, S. N., & Kaplan, S. N. (2000). TIMMS and high-ability students: Message of doom or opportunity for reflection? *Phi Delta Kappan, 81,* 787–790.

Carey, S., & Smith, C. (1993). On understanding the nature of scientific knowledge. *Educational Psychologist, 28,* 235–251.

Cavallo, A. M. L., Rozman, M., Blickenstaff, J., & Walker, N. (2003). Students' learning approaches, reasoning abilities, motivational goals, and epistemological beliefs in differing college science courses. *Journal of College Science Teaching, 33,* 18–23.

Cavallo, A. M. L., Rozman, M., & Potter, W. H. (2004). Gender differences in learning constructs, shifts in learning constructs, and their relationship to course achievement in a structured inquiry, yearlong college physics course for life science majors. *School Science and Mathematics, 104,* 288–301.

Cheng, P. W. (1993). Metacognition and giftedness: The state of the relationship. *Gifted Child Quarterly, 37,* 105–112.

Chi, M., Feltovich, P., & Glaser, R. (1981). Categorization and representation of physics problems by experts and novices. *Cognitive Science, 5,* 121–152.

Chi, M. T. H., Glaser, R., & Farr, M. J. (1988). *The nature of expertise.* Hillsdale, NJ: Lawrence Erlbaum.

Clarke, J. H., & Agne, R. M. (1997). *Interdisciplinary high school teaching: Strategies for integrated learning.* Needham Heights, MA: Allyn & Bacon.

Collins, A., Brown, J. S., & Holum, A. (1991). Cognitive apprenticeship: Making thinking visible. *American Educator, 6*(11), 38–46.

Commission on the Humanities. (1980). *The humanities in American life: Report of the Commission on the Humanities.* Berkeley: University of California Press.

Csikszentmihalyi, M., Rathunde, K., & Whalen, S. (1994). *Talented teenagers: The roots of success and failure.* Boston: Cambridge University Press.

Curloss, R. R. (2004). Individual and contextual variables among creative scientists: The new work paradigm. *Roeper Review, 26,* 126–127.

Dods, R. (1997). An action research study of the effectiveness of problem-based learning in promoting the acquisition and retention of knowledge. *Journal for the Education of the Gifted, 20,* 423–437.

Duggan, S., & Gott, R. (2002). What sort of science education do we really need? *International Journal of Science Education, 24,* 661–679.

Eichinger, J. (1997). Successful students' perceptions of secondary school science. *School Science and Mathematics, 97,* 122–131.

Enman, M., & Lupart, J. (2000). Talented female students' resistance to science: An exploratory study of post-secondary achievement motivation, persistence, and epistemological characteristics. *High Ability Studies, 11,* 162–178.

Erez, R. (2001). The interrelationships among science, art, and values: Significance for advancing holistic excellence. *Journal of Secondary Gifted Education, 8,* 6–10.

Ericsson, K. A., Krampe, R., & Tesch-Romer, C. (1993). The role of deliberate practice in the acquisition of expert performance. *Psychological Review, 199,* 363–406.

Etkina, E., Matilsky, T., & Lawrence, M. (2003). Pushing to the edge: Rutgers astrophysics institute motivates talented high school students. *Journal for Research in Science Teaching, 40,* 958–985.

Evans, M. A., & Whigham, M. (1995). The effect of a role model project upon the attitudes of ninth-grade science students. *Journal of Research in Science Teaching, 32,* 195–204.

Feist, G. J. (1993). A structural model of scientific eminence. *Psychological Science, 4,* 366–371.

Feist, G., & Gorman, M. (1998). The psychology of science: Review and integration of a nascent discipline. *Review of General Psychology, 2,* 3–47.

Ferry, N. M., & Ross-Gordon, J. M. (1998). An inquiry into Schon's epistemology of practice: Exploring links between experience and reflective practice. *Adult Education Quarterly, 48,* 98–112.

Gallagher, S. A. (1994). Middle school predictors of science achievement. *Journal for Research in Science Teaching, 31,* 721–734.

Gallagher, S. A. (1997). Problem-based learning: What is it, what does it do, and where is it going? *Journal for the Education of the Gifted, 20,* 332–362.

Gallagher, S. A. (2001). But does it work? Testing the efficacy of problem-based learning: A review of the literature and research agenda for educators of the gifted. In S. G. Assouline, & N. Colangelo (Eds.), *Talent development IV: Proceedings from the 1998 Henry B. and Jocelyn Wallace National Research Symposium on Talent Development.* (pp. 179–204). Scottsdale, AZ: Great Potential Press.

Gallagher, S. A. (2005). Adapting problem-based learning for gifted students. In F. A. Karnes & S. M. Bean (Eds.), *Methods and materials for teaching the gifted.* (pp. 285–312). Waco, TX: Prufrock Press.

Gallagher, S. A., & Gallagher, J. J. (2005). Using problem-based learning units to discover potentially gifted students. Manuscript submitted for publication.

Gallagher, S. A., Stepien, W. J., & Rosenthal, H. (1992). The effect of problem-based learning on problem solving. *Gifted Child Quarterly, 36,* 195–201.

Goldberger, N. R. (1981). Developmental assumptions underlying models of general education. *Liberal Education, 67,* 233–243.

Gollub, J. P., Bertenthal, M. W., Labov, J. B., & Curtis, P. C. (Eds.). (2002). *Learning and understanding: Improving advanced study of mathematics and science in U.S. high schools.* Washington, DC: National Academies Press.

Gooding, C. T., Swift, J. N., Schell, R. E., Swift, P. R., & McCroskery, J. H. (1990). A causal analysis relating previous achievement, attitudes, discourse, and intervention to achievement in biology and chemistry. *Journal of Research in Science Teaching, 27,* 789–801.

Hake, R. R. (1998). Interactive-engagement vs. traditional methods: A six-thousand survey of mechanics test data for introductory physics courses. *American Journal of Physics, 66,* 64–75.

Hammer, D., & Elby, A. (2003). Tapping epistemological resources for teaching physics. *Journal of the Learning Sciences, 12,* 53–91.

Hardy, C. A. (1971). Achievement and level of critical thinking in CHDM study and traditional chemistry. *Journal of Educational Research, 65,* 159–162.

Hofer, B. K. (2000). Dimensionality and disciplinary differences in personal epistemology. *Contemporary Educational Psychology, 25,* 378–405.

Hubisz, J. L. (2002). *Review of middle school physical science texts: Final report to the David and Lucile Packard Foundation.* Retrieved February 12, 2005, from http://www.science-house.org/middle-school/reviews/hubisz.rtf

Hubisz., J. L. (2003). Middle-school texts don't make the grade. *Physics Today, 56*(5), 50–55.

Hurd, P. (1993). *Postmodern science and the responsible citizen in a democracy.* Presentation at the International Conference on the Public Understanding of Science and Technology, Chicago, IL.

Judson, H. F. (1987). *The search for solutions.* Baltimore: The Johns Hopkins University Press.

Kanevsky, L., & Keighley, T. (2003). To produce or not to produce: Understanding boredom and the honor in underachievement. *Roeper Review, 26,* 20–29.

Kauffman, D. M., & Mann, K. V. (1997). Basic sciences in problem-based learning and conventional curricula project: Students' attitudes. *Medical Education, 31,* 177–180.

Kesidou, S., & Roseman, J. E. (2002). How well do middle school science programs measure up?

Findings from Project 2061's curriculum review. *Journal of Research in Science Teaching, 39,* 522–549.

Khishfe, R. & Abd-El-Khalick, F. (2002). Influence of explicit and reflective versus implicit inquiry-oriented instruction on sixth graders' views of nature of science. *Journal of Research in Science Teaching, 39,* 551–578.

King, P. M., & Kitchener, K. S. (1984). *Developing reflective judgment: Understanding and promoting intellectual growth and critical thinking in adolescents and adults.* San Francisco: Jossey-Bass.

Kitchener, K. S. (1983). Cognition, metacognition, and epistemic cognition: A three-level model of cognitive process. *Human Development, 4,* 222–232.

Klein, J. T. (1993). Blurring, cracking, and crossing: Permeation and the fracturing of discipline. In E. Messer-Davidow, D. R. Shumway, & D. J. Sylvan (Eds.), *Knowledge: Historical and critical studies in disciplinarity* (pp. 185–211). Charlottesville: University of Virginia Press.

Kolodner, J, Camp, P. J., Crismond, D., Fasse, B., Gray, J., Holbrook, J., et al. (2003). Problem-based learning meets case-based reasoning in the middle-school science classroom: Putting learning by design into practice. *Journal of the Learning Sciences, 12,* 495–548.

Koro-Ljungbert, M. (2001). Creative game in science. *Journal for the Education of the Gifted, 25,* 32–51.

Kozma, R. (2003). The material features of multiple representations and their cognitive and social affordances for science understanding. *Learning and Instruction, 13,* 205–226.

Kuhn, D., & Weinstock, M. (2002). What is epistemological thinking and why does it matter? In B. K. Hofer & P. R. Pintrich (Eds.), *Personal epistemology: The psychology of beliefs about knowledge and knowing* (pp. 121–144). Mahwah, NJ: Lawrence Erlbaum.

Kuhn, T. S. (1962). *The structure of scientific revolutions.* Chicago: University of Chicago Press.

Lambros, A. (2003). *Problem-based learning in middle schools and high schools: A teacher's guide to implementation.* Thousand Oaks, CA: Corwin Press.

Larkin, J., McDermott, J., Simon, D. P., & Simon, H. A. (1980). Expert and novice performance in solving physics problems. *Science, 208,* 1335–1342.

Levenson, T. (1995). *Measure for measure: A musical history of science.* New York: Touchstone Books.

Linn, M. C., Davis, E. A., & Bell, P. (Eds.). (2004). *Internet environments for science education.* Mahwah, NJ: Lawrence Erlbaum Associates.

Linn, M. C., Davis, E. A., & Eylon, B.S. (2004). The scaffolded knowledge integration framework for instruction. In M. C. Linn, E. A. Davis, & P. Bell (Eds.), *Internet environments for science education,* (pp. 47–72). Mahwah, NJ: Lawrence Erlbaum Associates.

Linn, M. C., & Hsi, S. (2000). *Computers, teachers, peers: Science learning partners.* Mahwah, NJ: Lawrence Erlbaum Associates.

Lupart, J. L., Cannon, E., & Telfer, J. (2004). Gender differences in adolescent academic achievement, interests, values and life-role expectations. *High Ability Studies, 15,* 25–42.

Marchese, T. J. (1998). The new conversations about learning: Insights from neuroscience and anthropology, cognitive science and work-place studies. Retrieved November 29, 2004, from http://www.aahe.org/members_only/TM-essay.htm

Mason, L., & Boscolo, P. (2004). Role of epistemological understanding and interest in interpreting a controversy and in topic-specific change belief. *Contemporary Educational Psychology, 29,* 103–128.

Medawar, P. D. (1979). *Advice to a young scientist.* New York: Harper and Row.

Minner, D. D., Levy, A. J., & Century, J. R. (2004). Describing inquiry science instruction in existing research: A challenge for synthesis. Paper presented at the National Association for Research in Science Teaching Annual Conference, Vancouver, British Columbia. Retrieved February 12, 2005, from http://cse.edc.org/work/research/inquirysynth/default.asp

National Research Council. (1996). *National science education standards.* Washington, DC: National Academy Press.

Neber, H., & Schommer-Aikins, M. (2002). Self-regulated science learning with highly gifted students: The role of cognitive, motivational, epistemological, and environmental variables. *High Ability Studies, 13*, 59–74.

Nelson, C. E. (1989). Skewered on the unicorn's horn: The illusion of the tragic tradeoff between content and critical thinking in the teaching of science. In L. W. Crow (Ed.), *Enhancing critical thinking in the sciences* (pp. 17–27). Washington, DC: National Science Teachers Association.

Ngoi, M., & Vondracek, M. (2004). Working with gifted science students in a public high school environment: One school's approach. *Journal of Secondary Gifted Education, 15*, 141–147.

Olson, S., & Loucks-Horsley, S. (2000). *Inquiry and the national science education standards: A guide for teaching learning.* Washington, DC: National Academy of Sciences.

O'Sullivan, C. Y., & Grigg, W. S. (2001). *Assessing the best: NAEP's 1996 assessment of twelfth-graders taking advanced science courses, NCES 2001-451.* Washington, DC: U.S. Department of Education.

Passow, A. H., & Fraiser, M. M. (1996). Toward improving identification of talent potential among minority and disadvantaged students. *Roeper Review, 18*, 198–202.

Perry, W. G., Jr. (1970). *Forms of intellectual and ethical development in the college years: A scheme.* New York: Holt, Rinehart, and Winston.

Peterson, J., & Colangelo, N. (1996). Gifted achievers and underachievers: A comparison of patterns found in school files. *Journal of Counseling and Development, 74*, 399–408.

Rennie, L. J., & Punch, K. F. (1991). The relationship between affect and achievement in science. *Journal of Research in Science Teaching, 28*, 193–209.

Reynolds, A. J. (1991). Effects of an experiment-based physical science program on cognitive outcomes. *Journal of Educational Research, 84*, 296–302.

Robinson, G. (2004). Replicating a successful authentic science research program: An interview with Dr. Robert Pavlica. *Journal of Secondary Gifted Education, 15*, 148–155.

Rogers, K. B. (2001). Effects of acceleration on gifted learners. In M. Neihart, S. M. Reis, N. M. Robinson, & S. M. Moon (Eds.), *The social and emotional development of gifted children: What do we know?* Waco, TX: Prufrock Press.

Roseman, J. E., Kesidou, S., Stern, L., & Caldwell, A. (1999). Heavy books light on learning: AAAS Project 2061 evaluates middle grades science textbooks. *Science Books & Films, 35*, 243–247.

Roseman, J. E., Kulm, G., & Shuttleworth, S. (2001). Putting textbooks to the test. *ENC Focus, 8*(3), 56–59.

Roth, M., & Roychoudhury, A. (2003). Physics students' epistemologies and views about knowing and learning. *Journal of Research in Science Teaching, 40* (Suppl.), 114–139.

Rutherford, F. J., & Alghren, A. (1990). *Science for all Americans: Project 2061.* New York: Oxford University Press.

Ryan, A. G., & Aikenhead, G. S. (1992). Students' preconceptions about the epistemology of science. *Science Education, 76*, 559–580.

Sak, U. (2004). A synthesis of research on psychological types of gifted adolescents. *Journal of Secondary Gifted Education, 15*, 70–79.

Sandoval, W. A. (2003). Conceptual and epistemic aspects of students' scientific explanations. *Journal of the Learning Sciences, 12*, 5–51.

Schneider R. M., Krajcik, J., Marx, R. W., & Soloway, E. (2002). Performance of students in project-based science classrooms on a national measure of science achievement. *Journal of Research in Science Teaching, 39*, 410–422.

Schommer, M. (1994). An emerging conceptualization of epistemological beliefs and their role on learning. In R. Garner & P. A. Alexander (Eds.), *Beliefs about texts and instruction with text* (pp. 25–40). Hillsdale, NJ: Lawrence Erlbaum.

Schommer, M., & Dunnell, P. A. (1994). A comparison of epistemological beliefs between gifted and non-gifted high school students. *Roeper Review, 16*, 207–210.

Schommer, M., & Dunnell, P. A. (1997). Epistemological beliefs of gifted high school students. *Roeper Review, 19,* 153–156.

Shore, B. M., & Kanevsky, L. S. (1993). Thinking processes: Being and becoming gifted. In K. A. Heller, F. J. Mönks, & H. A. Passow (Eds.), *International handbook of research and development of giftedness and talent* (pp. 133–147) Oxford, UK: Pergamon Press.

Siegel, M. A., & Ranney, M. A. (2003). Developing the changes in attitude about the relevance of science (CARS) questionnaire and assessing two high school science classes. *Journal for Research in Science Teaching 40, 151–175.*

Shymansky, J. A., Hedges, L. V., & Woodworth, G. (1990). A reassessment of the effects of inquiry-based science curricula of the 60's on student performance. *Journal of Research in Science Teaching, 27,* 127–144.

Spiro, R. J., Coulson, R. L., Feltovich, P. J., & Anderson, D. K. (1988). Cognitive flexibility theory: Advanced knowledge acquisition in ill-structured domains. In V. Patel (Ed.), *Proceedings of the 10th annual conference of the Cognitive Science Society* (pp. 375–383). Hillsdale, NJ: Lawrence Erlbaum Associates.

Spital, R. (Ed.). (2002). *Learning and understanding: Improving advanced study of mathematics and science in U.S. high school: Report of the content panel for physics.* Washington, DC: National Academies Press.

Stanitski, C. (Ed.). (2002). *Learning and understanding: Improving advanced study of mathematics and science in U.S. high school: Report of the content panel for chemistry.* Washington, DC: National Academies Press.

Stern, L. Y., & Roseman, J. E. (2004). Can middle school science textbooks help students learn important ideas? Findings from Project 2061's curriculum evaluation study: Life science. *Journal for Research in Science Teaching, 41,* 538–568.

Subotnik, R. F. (2003). Adolescent pathways to eminence in science: Lessons from the music conservatory. In P. Csermely & L. Lederman (Eds.), *Science education: Talent recruitment and public understanding* (pp. 295–302) Burke, VA: I0S Press.

Subotnik, R. F., & Olszewski-Kubilius, P. (1997). Restructuring special programs to reflect the distinctions between children's and adults' experiences with giftedness. *Peabody Journal of Education, 72,* 101–116.

Thagard, P. (2005). How to be a successful scientist. In M. E. Gorman, R. D. Tweney, D. C. Gooding, & A. P. Kincannon (Eds.), *Scientific and technological thinking* (pp. 159–171). Mahwah, NJ: Lawrence Erlbaum Associates.

Thomas, L. (1995). *Late night thoughts on listening to Mahler's Ninth Symphony.* East Rutherford, NJ: Penguin Books.

Thorlindsson, T. (1994). Skipper science: A note on the epistemology of practice and the nature of expertise. *Sociological Quarterly, 35*(2), 329–345.

Tobias, S. (1990). *They're not dumb, they're different: Stalking the second tier.* Tucson, AZ: Research Corporation.

Tretter, T., & Jones, M. G. (2003). Relationships between inquiry-based teaching and physical science standardized test scores. *School Science and Mathematics, 103,* 345–350.

U.S. Department of Education. (1998). *Pursuing excellence: A study of U.S. twelfth-grade mathematics and science achievement in international context* (No. NCES 98-049). Washington, DC: U.S. Government Printing Office.

U.S. Department of Education. (2001). *The nation's report card: Science highlights 2000* (No. NCES 2002-452). Washington, DC: National Center for Education Statistics.

U.S. Department of Education. (2004). *Qualifications of the public school teacher workforce: Prevalence of out-of-field teaching, 1987–88 to 1999–2000.* Washington, DC: National Center for Education Statistics.

Weinstock, M., Neuman, Y., & Tabak, I. (2004). Missing the point or missing the norms: Epistemological norms as predictors of students' ability to identify fallacious arguments. *Contemporary Educational Psychology, 29,* 77–94.

Wiggins, G. (1992). Creating tests worth taking. *Educational Leadership, 49*(8), 26–33.

Wilkinson, W. K., & Maxwell, S. (1991). The influence of college students' epistemological style on selected problem-solving processes. *Research in Higher Education, 32,* 333–350.

Wilkinson, W. K., & Schwartz, H. H. (1987). The epistemological orientation of gifted adolescents: An empirical test of Perry's model. *Psychological Reports, 61,* 976–978.

Windschitl, M., & Andre, T. (1998). Using computer simulations to enhance conceptual change: The roles of constructivist instruction and student epistemological beliefs. *Journal of Research in Science Teaching, 35,* 145–160.

Wood, W. B. (Ed.). (2002). *Learning and understanding: Improving advanced study of mathematics and science in U.S. high schools: Report of the content panel for biology.* Washington, DC: National Academies Press.

Yager, R. E. (Ed.). (1993). *The science, technology, society movement: What research says to the science teacher.* Washington, DC: National Science Teachers Association.

SECONDARY MATHEMATICS FOR HIGH-ABILITY STUDENTS

by Scott A. Chamberlin

CHAPTER 17

RATIONALE FOR CHALLENGING HIGH LEVEL MATHEMATICIANS

For years, teachers have questioned the need for additional instruction for the mathematically gifted. Principally two reasons exist for neglecting instruction of the mathematically gifted. First, some teachers believe that if they don't instruct the mathematically gifted, these students will still know as much as their peers. This reasoning is based on the premise that these students are so far ahead that they can miss significant parts of the curriculum and still be average or above average students. Second, instructors often are simply nervous about instructing the gifted, as it can be an ominous task. This reasoning often comes from teachers who don't want to reveal their mathematical inadequacies. Both responses are poor excuses. All students, the gifted notwithstanding, have a right to be instructed. Not (adequately) challenging the mathematically gifted precipitates negative ramifications. For instance, boredom is likely the by-product of low challenging mathematical experiences (Gallagher, Harradine, & Coleman, 1997). Also, data exist to suggest that poorly challenged math students choose unchallenging math classes in the future and highly challenged math students seek highly challenging math classes in the future (Hammer, 2002; Ryan, 2000). The mathematically gifted may be challenged using two approaches: acceleration and enrichment.

DEFINITION OF MATHEMATICAL GIFTEDNESS

Numerous definitions have been presented to define mathematical giftedness in the secondary grades. Stanley, Keating, and Fox (1974) have suggested that a set score on a norm-referenced test (i.e., more than 700 on the Scholastic Aptitude Test-Math (SAT-M) prior to age 13), constitutes mathematical giftedness, as only about one in 10,000 students can accomplish this task. High school teachers might suggest that any student passing an Advanced Placement (AP) examination for a mathematics course should be considered gifted. The National Council of Teachers of Mathematics (NCTM) task force on mathematically promising students defines mathematical giftedness as a function of ability, motivation, belief, and experience or opportunity (Wertheimer, 1999). The most comprehensive list of traits associated with mathematical giftedness comes from the former Soviet Union (Krutetskii, 1976); a short list of these traits includes: willingness and eagerness to engage in math problems, ability to concentrate for long periods of time on math, ability to transfer knowledge from one problem to another, ability to reason spatially, ability to identify faulty reasoning, and ability to be creative. Others have suggested that some component of creativity be considered when identifying the mathematically gifted (Glas, 2002). Sheffield (1999) defines mathematical giftedness from a statistical point of view. She states that a certain percentage of the population, for example, 1–5%, should be defined as gifted. For this chapter the Sheffield and Stanley definitions of mathematical giftedness have been merged. Specifically, any mathematics student scoring in the top 2.5% on a national standardized test is considered gifted, because 2.5% of the population encompasses standard deviations of two and above (see Figure 1). Any student more than three standard deviations from the mean is well beyond the average student and represents a very minute percentage of the population. With the definition in place, an argument for why to teach mathematics to the gifted is presented.

THEORETICAL RATIONALE FOR TEACHING MATHEMATICS TO GIFTED ADOLESCENTS

The theoretical rationale for teaching high-ability adolescents mathematics is based on two tenets. First, mathematically gifted adolescents require services in addition to those provided for the typical student. Second, adolescents advanced in mathematical ability and knowledge cannot be neglected or they may perish academically.

Adolescents advanced in mathematical ability and knowledge require instruction that varies from instruction provided for the typical student (Johnson, 2000). If mathematically gifted adolescents fail to receive adequate services, this omission

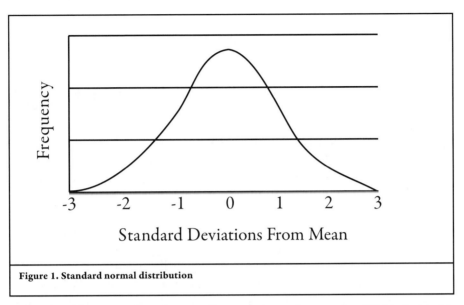

Figure 1. Standard normal distribution

will negatively impact their decision for an undergraduate major (Webb, Lubinski, & Benbow, 2002). Examples of services deemed adequate for gifted learners include compacting curriculum (Stanley et al., 1974), differentiating curriculum (Reed, 2004; Tomlinson, 1995), using enrichment and acceleration (George, Cohn, & Stanley, 1979; Southern, Komes, & Stanley, 1993), and using higher order thinking tasks (Sheffield, 1999). Generally it is accepted that if a student can exhibit proficiency when asked to complete a task, he or she has learned the material. Whether the student has learned the material from a previous class or from another source is not important, but redundancy should be limited in the gifted mathematics curriculum.

Compacting curriculum refers to the elimination of material students have previously learned (Stanley et al., 1974). As a result of eliminating redundancy, compacting curriculum may help students avoid boredom. Differentiation of material refers to altering or adapting activities to appropriately challenge students. As with compacting, differentiation holds promise for adequately challenging students, and this strategy can be accomplished practically by enriching or accelerating the curriculum. In some situations, activities provided for the mainstream population of a class are suitable for advanced students in mathematics if adapted appropriately; in these cases enrichment may occur. Enrichment refers to the investigation of (mathematical) concepts in such a manner as to provide deeper coverage of the subject than is generally provided (Slavin, 2003). Acceleration refers to speeding through or skipping large parts of the curriculum to get a student on track with his or her appropriate mental age (Colangelo, Assouline, & Gross, 2004). The decision of when to accelerate and when to enrich is best left to the qualified teacher of the gifted, but a combination of the two is most logical for mathematics. Some form of adaptation must take place to instruct the student who is greatly advanced from his or her peers. Higher order thinking tasks are requisite for all gifted students (Friedman, 1984), but they are particularly necessary for the mathematically gifted. Simply engaging the mathematically gifted in routine calculations and algorithmic thinking will not enable them to view mathematics conceptually (National Council of Teachers of Mathematics [NCTM], 2000).

The second tenet is that mathematically gifted adolescents cannot be neglected or they may perish academically. Webb et al. (2002) argue that experiences in the adolescent years significantly impact college major choices later in life. Johnson (2000) suggests that for years the fallacy has been promulgated that if gifted students are left alone, they will succeed. The gifted mathematician is the most neglected regarding the realization of full potential (NCTM, 1980). If mathematically gifted adolescents are neglected, the potential learning ramifications can be quite negative. Boredom may be the greatest enemy of students gifted in mathematics. Gifted adolescents require instruction well beyond that provided in the mainstream classroom (House, 1999).

To provide a comparison with the neglect of the gifted student, his or her counterpart, the student in the bottom 2.5% nationally (Sheffield, 1999), should be examined. Rather than asking if the gifted student should be neglected, perhaps one should ask whether any student should be neglected. Letting gifted students *explore* mathematics independently on a daily basis while the teacher works with less able students is poor pedagogical practice and no longer acceptable. Students with learning disabilities requiring special services are not asked to *explore* subjects autonomously, and gifted students should not be asked to engage in subject (e.g., mathematics) *exploration* either.

By providing challenging curricula to mathematically gifted adolescents, their interests can best be met (Bleske-Rechek, Lubinski, & Benbow, 2004). Adolescents report feeling most challenged and socially at ease when they work with peers of similar ability in mathematics. Additionally, gifted adolescents have the opportunity to work at a pace commensurate with their abilities in advanced classes (Lubinski & Benbow, 2000). The demands of working with mathematically gifted adolescents are much greater than they are when working with traditional students.

In summary, students advanced in mathematics require services in addition to those provided to the typical student, and they cannot be neglected academically. Mathematically gifted adolescents require genuine academic challenges, which are often provided by a venue outside of the normal math classroom, such as Advanced Placement coursework.

REVIEW OF CURRENT EMPIRICAL LITERATURE

A review of current empirical literature from 1993 to the present for mathematically gifted students in the secondary grades shows parallels with mathematics education. Three themes emerge: Gender differences are being reduced, problem solving is of paramount importance to learning mathematics, and a genetic basis for mathematical talent exists.

Niederer, Irwin, Irwin, and Reilly (2003) suggest that most of the empirical mathematics research is based on high school students. Extensive hand and computer searches revealed contrary findings in gifted education. Most of the empirical research in gifted mathematics students appears to be in the elementary grades. In any event, empirical research in secondary grades is sparse.

Gender Differences

Girls who hold high math self-concepts fare better in higher level mathematics courses and are more likely to pursue mathematics in college than their peers (Gavin, 1996). A contributing factor to a high mathematics self-concept for gifted adolescents is the influence of parent(s) and home environments. Positive comments such as, "You were so strong in math and I still believe that you are; you can't lose your self-confidence" (Gavin, p. 480), coupled with support from the home environment are integral components for girls' success in secondary mathematics classes. Conversely, negative comments and little or no home support for mathematics discourage girls from pursuing higher level mathematics in college.

A similar study investigated five factors and the impact each factor had on gifted girls taking calculus courses (Reynolds & Conaway, 2003). Factors studied included socioeconomic status (SES), number of siblings, mother's education, father's education, and educational aspirations. Reynolds and Conaway studied 1,244 eighth grade females using National Educational Longitudinal Data (National Center for Educational Statistics [NCES], 1989). Their study revealed that SES, mother's education, and aspirations for graduate school had a significant effect on whether or not women took calculus in high school. Girls in households making more than $75,000 per year were significantly more likely to take calculus than peers in households making less than $35,000 per year. Also, girls with mothers who attended a 4-year or junior college were 1.5 times more likely to take calculus than girls with mothers who did not attend college. If girls had mothers who had attended graduate school, their likelihood to take calculus was increased to 1.6 times. The desire to attend graduate school had the largest effect on whether girls took calculus. Girls with graduate school aspirations were three times more likely to take calculus than those whose goals were less than a college degree. Number of siblings and father's education did not have a significant effect on girls taking calculus.

Gender differences among gifted mathematicians continue to be a topic of interest. Initially, men were considered to reason spatially better than women (Voyer, Voyer, & Bryden, 1995). Today disagreement exists regarding spatial reasoning by gender. When giftedness is considered as a factor, the difference in spatial reasoning between genders is eliminated (Voyer, 1998). Voyer further suggested that laboratory measures, such as the SAT-M, may be faulty measures of mathematical ability because they underestimate achievement potential for women. For the teacher of the mathematically gifted, men and women can be considered more similar than once thought.

Gender difference also impacts problem solving. When 14 high school boys and 14 high school girls took the SAT-M and the GRE-Quantitative sections, boys outperformed girls on the spatial reasoning items (Gallagher et al., 2000). The difference in performance appears to be attributed to strategy flexibility. This study further showed that the use of intuitive strategies by men and women for unconventional problems was evident only among high-ability students. Recent studies have suggested that equity is being approximated between genders.

Problem Solving

Problem solving is of paramount importance in developing gifted mathematicians. For instance, Sriraman's (2003) study on problem solving revealed that gifted students in freshmen algebra classes reason differently from the way nongifted students reason. According to Sriraman's study, three components differentiate the mathematically gifted from the typical mathematician at the high school level. Qualitative data indicate that the mathematically gifted "isolate similarities in the structures of problems" better than typical students do. Specifically, they compare unequal quantities more effectively than their nongifted peers do. Also, they are likely to exhibit more perseverance and curiosity than typical peers do. In general, gifted mathematicians maintained a more positive attitude than their peers. The implication for teaching is that high school mathematics teachers need to identify appropriate problem-solving tasks that enable all, and particularly gifted students, to reason abstractly.

Livne and Milgram (2000) studied the use of problem-solving strategies and the impact they had on math development and the identification of the gifted. Creativity in mathematics is often overlooked with gifted students (Livne & Milgram). The researchers developed a 12-item instrument to assess creativity in problem solving among 11th- and 12th-grade Israeli students during out of school activities. By using the instrument, the researchers found that four distinct levels of creative ability exist. They further found that the mathematically gifted were seldom challenged and needed to seek extracurricular mathematical tasks more difficult than those available in school. If appropriate activities are not located, boredom may surface resulting in disengagement in mathematical learning.

Genetic Basis for Mathematical Talent

While speculation regarding a genetic basis for advanced mathematical ability has existed for some time, until recently empirical evidence did not exist to support the notion. Scientists now believe that advanced mathematical abilities, in part, may be inherited (Carol, 1993; Fisher et al., 1999; Weiss, 1994; Wijsman et al., 2004). The Wijsman study analyzed three generations, $n = 34$ females and $n = 32$ males, to investigate whether or not mathematical ability is inherited. Participants were sorted by their parents' mathematical attainment. In addition, a semiquantitative scale of mathematical talent was used to measure mathematical performance and interest. In both cases, participants from high mathematical attainment families outperformed participants from families of low mathematical attainment. Results suggest that some genetic basis may exist for mathematical talent. Two limitations of the study were that environmental factors, such as education and family/parental values, may have clouded the picture, and that the sample size was small.

MIDDLE SCHOOL AND HIGH SCHOOL TEACHING STRATEGIES

A perpetual dilemma when selecting curricula is whether one should engage in acceleration or enrichment. Each approach should be encouraged and the situation should not be viewed as dichotomous; rather, the two approaches should be viewed as working in harmony (Stanley, 1986). A principal component of giftedness is developing expertise (Sternberg, 2000), and developing expertise in mathematics is precipitated by the interplay between enrichment and acceleration. Strategies for implementing challenging curricula are discussed in the following section followed by a discussion of exemplary curricula for middle school and high school students.

To discuss the implementation of challenging curricula, the term must first be defined. Challenging curricula within the context of secondary gifted education is interpreted to mean complex curricula. To be complex in mathematics, several activities are requisite such as "organizing materials, recognizing patterns or rules, changing the representation of the problem and recognizing patterns and rules in this new area, comprehending and working with highly complex structures, reversing and inverting processes, and finding and constructing related problems" (Wieczerkowski, Cropley, & Prado, p. 415). A central focus in accomplishing these activities is problem solving. Not surprisingly, problem solving appears as a key element in all curricula for gifted secondary mathematicians.

Problem Solving

Engaging students in problem solving has multiple advantages for gifted mathematicians. Problem solving may enhance the likelihood that students develop the four characteristics Krutetskii (1976) defines as necessary for mathematical giftedness (flexibility, curtailment, logical thought, and formalization). In addition, problem solving fosters the recognition of interrelatedness of concepts which breeds higher level thinking (NCTM, 2000).

Quality problem-solving tasks often seriously engage students in mathematical discussions (Wood, Merkel, & Uerkwitz, 1996) and they can help students invent their own meaning for mathematics (Hiebert et al., 1997). Students can begin to approximate the tasks required of expert mathematicians rather than merely engaging in "mathematics bulimia." Mathematics bulimia refers to the phenomenon when students merely shove facts into their minds and regurgitate them meaninglessly at a later time. The mathematically gifted in the secondary grades should progress through the curriculum quicker than peers (Johnson, 2000), but this acceleration should not come at the expense of enrichment. Students must be expected to reason mathematically on a high level if the needs of the mathematically gifted are to be served adequately (Usiskin, 1999).

The most significant task for teachers of the mathematically gifted is to spend quality time identifying what constitutes complex problem-solving tasks and what content generally interests and challenges students. Students have the potential to make mathematical learning meaningful when they invent their own algorithms (Hiebert et al., 1997; Kamii & Dominick, 1998). Showing students standard algorithms is no longer an acceptable method of mathematics instruction (Kamii & Dominick). Furthermore, showing students algorithms has potentially more harmful effects for the gifted learner than it does for any other learner. The emphasis on problem solving should enable the instructor of the mathematically gifted to downplay the significance of algorithms in the classroom. Ideally one by-product of problem solving is that students create their own algorithms or formulae to solve problems. The mathematically gifted should not be encouraged to adopt one line of reasoning (Hiebert et al.; Tretter, 2003), as it stifles creative thinking.

Creative Thinking

Creative thinking is generally considered to be the generation or production of novel ways of thinking. In the past 15 years, creative thinking has emerged as an area of investigation in the field of mathematics education as a result of its strong connection to constructivism. Teachers of the gifted can promote creative thinking by asking students to develop their own problems (Runco, 1993). When students design their own problems, they use personal knowledge from their daily lives. After designing the problems, students are then asked to solve them using whatever approach they want. Engaging in this process requires students to solve problems with more than one solution, which also fosters creativity (Sheffield, 1999; Wheatley, 1999). A curricular suggestion for implementing creative thinking is Creative Problem Solving (CPS). CPS is one way to foster problem solving while also including creative thinking (Schack, 1993).

Critical Thinking

Critical thinking refers to the assessment, evaluation, or comparison of ideas (Walsh & Paul, 1988). A focus of critical thinking is reducing the amount of time students engage in algorithmic thinking and memorization of facts. When non-algorithmic thinking is promoted, students are asked to reason like actual mathematicians (Sheffield, 1999). Critical thinking often entails both enrichment and acceleration.

One way to promote critical thinking in mathematics is to use problems that have more than one solution. These problems are sometimes referred to as open-ended questions or complex tasks. Some experts feel that using problems with more than one process to solve the problem is one way to identify actual problem solving tasks (Wieczerkowski et al., 2000). One familiar problem is presented below:

One of my favorite activities is attending parties. Some time ago I was at a boring party and I got to thinking about how many handshakes will take place at this party. Assuming there are 10 people at the party, and none of them know each other, if each person introduces him- or herself to everyone else, how many handshakes will take place? As a follow-up task create a formula that will enable you to figure out the answer for parties in the future with estimated numbers of 7, 23, and 36.

Students should be asked to find as many ways as possible to solve the problem (Sheffield, 1999), and teachers should not suggest how many solutions actually exist because this practice stifles critical, as well as creative thinking. A second way to promote critical thinking is to have students develop their own problem-solving questions (Runco, 1993). By forcing students to evaluate what constitutes a problem, they more readily develop problems that are proximal to their interest. Additionally, increased persistence may occur as a result of ownership being created (Cuccio-Schirripa, 1999; Driscoll, 2000).

Independent Study

Fostering independent study may seem counterintuitive to contemporary curricular suggestions because collaboration currently is stressed in mathematics work in the United States. Students need to spend time together mediating solutions to problems for greater achievement in mathematics (Sowell, 1993). Wheatley (1999) and Wood et al. (1996) write that students should spend time debriefing on their solutions to create a context for discussing mathematics.

Many mathematics curricula today emphasize working with peers. However, well-balanced instructional approaches contain a blend of group work and independent study. Independent study is included in this section as instrumental to comprehensive curricula because in real life, professional mathematicians often work both with colleagues and alone. Teachers should ensure that students have ample time to work on projects individually, and simultaneously they should be able to call on peers for assistance. Additionally, enabling students to work independently lets them pursue their own interests, which may lead to positive educational outcomes (Chamberlin, 2002).

Gifted students, like professionals, need time to work with peers of similar ability and time to work alone. One way to accomplish individual and group work is by encouraging students to work on individual projects and have peers provide feedback on how the projects could be improved. A second iteration of the project can then be completed. This process mimics real-life mathematics. In the professional world, it would be common for a mathematician to work on a project, introduce it to colleagues, and subsequently make revisions to the initial body of work.

Students with an intense interest in statistics and probability, for example, may pursue statistics and probability, those with an intense interest in calculus, may pursue calculus, and so forth. Pursuing topics of individual interest can lead students to appreciate the beauty or aesthetics of mathematics (Sheffield, 1999). One strategy significant to fostering independent study is to have students work on individual math projects much like in a science fair. Both statistics and probability lend themselves nicely to independent projects as students are able at a young age to collect, analyze, and draw inferences from data. Once data are compiled, students can assemble projects and share their findings with peers.

CHALLENGING CURRICULA FOR MIDDLE SCHOOL AND HIGH SCHOOL

As stated previously, two approaches—acceleration and enrichment—may be used when educating the mathematically gifted adolescent. Most experts agree that some combination of the two is the best approach. This section focuses on curricula that have an emphasis on acceleration and enrichment. Curricula have been placed with the descriptor that is most emblematic of their approach.

Acceleration

The most notable approach when accelerating high school, and some middle school or junior high, students is Advanced Placement (AP) classes. The International Baccalaureate (IB) program also demands recognition, but it is not discussed separately as advanced mathematics classes in the IB program either mimic closely or are substituted with AP mathematics classes (International Baccalaureate Organization, 2004). The principal difference in AP and IB is that the IB program was created to instruct students who might reside in various countries during their high school years. Initially, AP classes were offered only in the United States, but they have expanded to more than 100 countries (DiYanni, 2003). Consequently, many IB programs have adopted AP coursework.

AP classes have the potential to meet the needs of mathematically gifted high school students by accelerating the mathematics introduced. For example, a mathematically gifted 10th grader might take AP calculus (AB) in the 10th grade, AP calculus (BC) in 11th grade, and a college math course in 12th grade. AP courses are the most widespread approach to advancing mathematical knowledge for high school students. The benefits of AP courses are dramatic (VanTassel-Baska, 2001); the main advantage for gifted students is the potential for challenge and the potential to eliminate one or more required college math courses while still in high school.

AP math-oriented courses offered include calculus AB, calculus BC, and statistics. Calculus AB is the introductory course, and calculus BC is intended to be an extension rather than an enhancement of AB. Statistics is designed to provide students with a comprehensive overview of statistics as a whole. The emphasis is consistent with an introductory college statistics course as it covers descriptive statistics, limited inferential statistics, and material related to probability.

Courses that entail mathematics, but are not specifically AP mathematics courses, are physics B, physics C, computer science A, computer science AB, macroeconomics, and microeconomics (College Board, 2004). Thus, AP courses offer a significant number of math related courses in addition to the three math specific courses. The purpose of each course is to offer coursework consistent with that offered in college.

These courses count as college credit, so advanced mathematicians may start course-work in college at a higher level than peers not taking AP courses.

One example of curricula that emphasizes advanced placement is Stanford's Educational Program for Gifted Youth (EPGY). EPGY is a comprehensive distance learning program that appears to show great promise for instructing the secondary gifted mathematician. EPGY provides online courses with supplemental texts and CD-ROMs in mathematics, physics, and writing (Educational Program for Gifted Youth, 2004). It has great potential for schools with scant time and monetary resources to accelerate middle school and high school students. EPGY may be particularly appropriate for rural schools with advanced students.

EPGY has been used successfully within the framework of a regular classroom, and it individualizes instruction for students so they can progress at an adequate pace. Much like Johns Hopkins University's Center for Talented Youth's (Stanley, 1986) emphasis on acceleration, EPGY moves rapidly through the curriculum. Feedback is provided on homework sets by Stanford instructors. High school students can attain college credit through Stanford's Continuing Studies Program (CSP; 2004). This program appears to be the most systemic of all programs discussed in this chapter. EPGY appears to stress acceleration at the expense of enrichment; however, students are genuinely challenged mathematically.

An exemplar online program in the Midwest is the Indiana Academy for Science, Mathematics, and Humanities at Ball State University. The Academy offers online math courses in calculus, statistics, and physics. These courses help schools with minimal financial or human resources. Like EPGY, the online courses at the Academy provide AP course credit, and their principal emphasis is rapid acceleration through the curricula. One difference in the Academy and many other university courses is that students may actually watch the instructor on a compressed video in real time or request a tape version of the session if absent.

Enrichment

Much like acceleration, enrichment is a viable option for instructing the mathematically gifted adolescent. Each approach has its place in mathematics. The enrichment discussion pertains to middle school or junior high students and the acceleration discussion pertains to high school students. An ideal program would have some enrichment and acceleration at all levels.

The difference in enrichment and acceleration is that enrichment of mathematics enables students to pursue topics on a deeper level than acceleration does. Acceleration enables students to progress through content very quickly, while enrichment enables a student to learn about a specified topic in depth. For instance, if an adolescent desires to explore the concept of scaling in greater detail than the classroom teacher provides, enrichment (not acceleration) is necessary. Engaging students in enrichment may produce mathematicians who appreciate the aesthetics of the discipline more than those who accelerate through areas of mathematics (Sheffield, 1999). While enrichment may take longer than acceleration, it may create more comprehensive mathematicians. Furthermore, enrichment may provide students the opportunity to pursue individual interests.

A positive enrichment approach for mathematics instruction in the secondary grades is Model Eliciting Activities (MEAs). This approach is comprised of mathematical activities, designed by professors and graduate students, to elicit the production of models by middle school and junior high students. The curriculum is intended to be used throughout the summer or school year. MEAs were initially designed to investigate student cognition. Few MEAs have been designed for high school and college students although the activities are designed to engage students in pre-college mathematical reasoning (Lesh, Hoover, Hole, Kelly, & Post, 2000).

The process of modeling is considered a substantive component of math curriculum for students of all ages, but in the middle grades modeling can promote an understanding of advanced mathematics. Given the need for advanced mathematics, MEAs act to fill a void in the gifted educators' curriculum by engaging the mathematically gifted in problem solving, higher order thinking, and the creation of models to solve problems (Chamberlin, 2002).

Designing models can be thought of as similar to designing formulae. Students create models to solve problems immediately in front of them and later seek to identify instances in which previous learning and creation of models can be generalized to mathematical situations. As a result of creating models, students notice the interconnectedness of mathematics (Lesh et al., 2000). MEAs are not intended to replace curricula, but they may serve to fill a void in curricula that overemphasize acceleration. To learn more about MEAs, visit http://crlt.indiana.edu/research/csk.html.

Consistent with enrichment, MEAs meet the needs of mathematically gifted adolescents by providing a comprehensive curriculum. An interrelationship of mathematical concepts is a focus of implementing the MEA approach. Often students jump from one topic to another in mathematics class without noticing connections. MEAs are designed to help students notice connections in mathematics (Lesh & Lamon, 1992).

Reasoning skills are developed when using MEAs. In particular, gifted students are rarely forced to reason with what are considered traditional textbook problems. Rather, they learn an algorithm and then they are expected to replicate it. A problem-solving approach fosters self-directed learning and the development of skills such as scrutinizing information (Norman & Schmidt, 1992).

SAMPLE PLAN OF STUDY FOR GIFTED MATH STUDENTS

While a single set of courses that gifted students must take to progress through the field of mathematics does not exist, the suggestion presented is quite typical for a student advanced by at least 2 to 3 years. Naturally, the extent to which one is advanced in mathematics determines how closely this plan may be followed.

A sample plan of study is outlined below.

Grade 6   Algebra and geometry
Grade 7   Algebra II
Grade 8   Precalculus and/or trigonometry
Grade 9   Calculus AB (Vector calculus enrichment activities)
Grade 10   Calculus BC (Vector calculus enrichment activities)
Grade 11   Multivariable calculus (online or at a local university) and/or AP
            statistics
Grade 12   Linear algebra (online or at a local university)

Precalculus is optional in the ninth grade, but given the emphasis on calculus throughout high school and college, precalculus holds great value in setting the foundation for deep understanding of calculus principles. In the event precalculus is omitted, it may be replaced with trigonometry in 10th grade, assuming calculus AB is taken the 9th-grade year and calculus BC is taken the 10th-grade year. Calculus AB and BC will not require 2 entire years of coursework for the mathematically gifted, so the teacher must be prepared to enhance curricula with genuine mathematical problem solving activities. Activities in vector calculus prepare students for higher level mathematics courses from a local university. Multivariable calculus, along with AP statistics, could be taken during the junior year, and the most logical option during the senior year would be a college course such as linear algebra. Following this plan of study, a student advanced in mathematics may enter college with as many as 12 credits in mathematics. In certain circumstances, an independent study or program may be the best course of action for a gifted high school mathematician. This option is best when a highly capable mentor exists and the university option is inadequate for geographical, developmental, or financial reasons.

NCTM Standards

The NCTM principles and standards document (NCTM, 2000) has had a major influence on what and how math is taught. The principles (equity, curriculum, teaching, learning, assessment, and technology); the content (data analysis and probability, geometry, number sense, algebra, and measurement); and the principles (problem solving, reasoning and proof, communication, connections, and representations) are reasonable guides for expectations in the classroom. However, instructors of mathematically gifted students should heed one caveat as they interpret the NCTM principles and standards. Following the discussion of the principles, content, and standards, the NCTM document outlines expectations for each grade band (K–2, 3–5, 6–8, and 9–12). The expectations for each grade band are often well below those that should be used with mathematically gifted students. Due to the extensiveness of the NCTM document, all expectations cannot be discussed in this chapter. Consequently, a sample has been provided.

In the content area of geometry, for example, students are expected to:

- analyze properties and determine attributes of two- and three-dimensional objects;
- explore relationships (including congruence and similarity) among classes of two- and three-dimensional geometric objects, make and test conjectures about them, and solve problems involving them; and
- use Cartesian coordinates and other coordinate systems, such as navigational, polar, or spherical systems, to analyze geometric systems.

While more demanding expectations are listed, the expectations presented here are typical and not challenging for the mathematically gifted. These expectations are in line with level two of Van Hiele's model, but advanced mathematicians should be working on Van Hiele's highest level—four (Bassarear, 2001). One suggestion regarding how to instruct the mathematically gifted is to apply Bloom's top three levels—analysis, synthesis, and evaluation—regularly to the mathematics classroom.

A qualified expert in the field of secondary mathematics for the gifted is most prepared to explain what expectations provide a good fit for the mathematically gifted. As a default, the content in AP classes works well to gauge how well a mathematically gifted student is doing. This is a safe assumption because AP classes are designed to qualify as college credit. Hence, if a student can pass the AP exam in calculus or statistics, for example, the student has met expectations on par with a college student (VanTassel-Baska, 2001).

Assessment

Assessment is a crucial component of all curricula. Without assessment, direction cannot be provided to regulate what material to teach in the future. Two types of assessment, norm- or criterion-referenced and authentic assessment, are discussed in this section and their value is discussed relative to gifted secondary mathematics.

Criterion- and norm-referenced tests are often used to gauge one's mathematical learning. Criterion-referenced tests have been so named because test results provide data about how the respondent compares relative to the objectives or preestablished criterion specified for the test (Ward & Murray-Ward, 1999). A chapter test or a final examination is an example of a criterion-referenced test because the respondent's score is provided relative to the material covered. Norm-referenced tests have been so named because test results provide data about how the respondent compares to peers in a larger group (Ward & Murray-Ward). For example, a respondent attaining a certain score on a test might rate in the 87th percentile nationally. State tests of progress are typically examples of norm-referenced tests; Indiana Statewide Testing for Educational Progress (ISTEP+), Wyoming Comprehensive Assessment System (WyCAS), and Colorado Student Assessment Program (CSAP) are examples of tests that assess mathematical understanding for secondary students.

Since Julian Stanley's Study of Mathematically Precocious Youth in the early

1970s (Stanley et al., 1974), tests such as the SAT-M and ACT-M have been used to assess mathematical understanding for gifted students. These tests are valid if used for the appropriate intent, which is to predict success in mathematics in college. The tests are designed to assess high school seniors, and as such, they can be used to assess where a student is relative to other high school seniors in the country. Stanley suggested that any student 13 years of age or younger scoring a 700 or above, with 800 being the maximum attainable score, on the SAT-M should be considered gifted mathematically (Stanley et al., 1974). He further stated that approximately one out of every 10,000 students could score more than 700, which defines the student as gifted. The ACT has similar qualities to the SAT, although the SAT was likely used during the start of SMPY because of its popularity and familiarity on the east coast.

Using high school tests such as the ACT or SAT in middle school or junior high is referred to as off-grade-level testing. Using a state standardized test such as ISTEP+, WyCAS, or CSAP is problematic because the gifted student is generally only permitted to take the on-grade-level test. State tests are therefore poor assessors of advanced mathematical talent because the ceilings are too low. Practically speaking, a low ceiling means that there are not sufficient items on the test to discriminate between mildly, moderately, and profoundly gifted mathematicians. Typical test results might indicate that a profoundly gifted student missed zero items, while a mildly or moderately gifted student might have missed one or no items. Ostensibly, no dichotomy exists in the talent levels.

While tests have a place in mathematics, assessment is flawed if it is based entirely on norm- and criterion-referenced tests such as aptitude, achievement, state proficiency, or college entrance exams. Assessment of student mathematical learning cannot be reduced to multiple-choice or fill-in-the-blank tests (Sheffield, 1999). When these sorts of tests are used, the emphasis on student thinking is reduced or eliminated altogether. Alternative forms of assessment, such as authentic assessment, must be encouraged to attain a true picture of students' mathematical progress. In this chapter authentic assessment means the assessment of real-life mathematical tasks (Lesh & Lamon, 1992).

A crucial component to success in authentic math assessments is the selection of authentic activities. Suggestions to identify authentic activities in mathematics are:

- problem solutions may take nearly an hour to finish,
- the contexts for problems might be seen in students' everyday lives,
- the problem meshes with students interests and experiences,
- personal knowledge can be brought into the solution,
- higher order thinking tasks are noticeable in the problem,
- realistic tools (Hiebert et al., 1997) can be used to solve the tasks, and
- more than one solution may be designed to solve the problem (Lesh & Lamon, 1992).

In the mathematical world, authentic assessment may take the form of collected work samples (Baron & Boschee, 1995; Ginsburg, et al., 1992) such as portfolios, interviews, oral or written reports, and activities. An example of such an activity is a math fair. These fairs are similar to a science fair, and they are positive venues in which students may engage in serious discourse on mathematical projects. Expectations at a math fair are similar to those at a professional academic conference. Typically, the order for a conference presentation is formal paper and oral presentation, concluded by a question and answer session.

Teachers must seek alternate ways to assess students. In so doing, teachers may attain local information on individual students in addition to state and national information. In turn, teachers will be able to guide instruction carefully. For curriculum and assessment, students must complete real-life mathematical tasks that are germane to successful completion of their coursework or degree in a gifted program. Inherent in the identification of authentic assessment tasks is the notion of an actual problem-solving task such as that described by Wieczerkowski et al. (2000). Real-life problems lend themselves to real-life assessment.

CONCLUSION

A damaging attitude exhibited by many educators is that we need not pay special attention to the mathematically gifted because those students will survive without special instruction. An appropriate response to this claim is that the mathematically gifted may survive, but they won't likely realize their full potential. All students are entitled to a challenging curriculum, and for the mathematically gifted, a challenging curriculum may be more necessary than for other students because much of the ordinary curriculum may seem mundane. A challenging curriculum includes both enrichment and acceleration. The mathematically gifted can move through the curriculum more quickly than peers, but still appreciate the beauty and aesthetics of mathematics.

The mathematically gifted are done a disservice if only assessed with criterion or norm-referenced tests. Authentic assessment can provide significantly more information regarding the development of the individual mathematics student than criterion- or norm-referenced tests can on their own. Authentic assessment should be used in tandem with criterion- and norm-referenced tests to provide the instructor of the gifted with a complete picture of academic progress.

* A special thanks is offered to Dr. Barbara Chatton, University of Wyoming, and Dr. Felicia Dixon, Ball State University, for providing feedback on this chapter.

REFERENCES

Baron, M. A., & Boschee, F. (1995). *Authentic assessment: The key to unlocking student success.* Lancaster, PA: Technomic Publishing Company.

Bassarear, T. (2001). *Mathematics for elementary school teachers* (2nd ed.). Boston: Houghton Mifflin.

Bleske-Rechek, A., Lubinski, D., & Benbow, C. (2004). Meeting the needs of special populations: Advanced Placement's role in developing exceptional talent. *Psychological Science, 15,* 217–224.

Carol, J. (1993). *Human cognitive abilities: A survey of factor-analytic studies.* Cambridge, United Kingdom: Cambridge University Press.

Chamberlin, S. A. (2002). *Analysis of interest during and after model-eliciting activities: A comparison of gifted and general population students.* Unpublished doctoral dissertation, Purdue University.

Colangelo, N., Assouline, S. G., & Gross, M. U. M. (2004). *A nation deceived: How schools hold back America's brightest students: Vol. II.* Iowa City, IA: The Connie Belin & Jacqueline N. Blank International Center for Gifted Education and Talent Development.

College Board (2004). *About AP.* Retrieved October 7, 2004, from http://www.collegeboard.com/student/testing/ap/about.html

Continuing Studies Program (2004). *Welcome to Stanford's continuing studies.* Retrieved November 12, 2004, from http://continuingstudies.stanford.edu

Cuccio-Schirripa, S. (1999). Science question level and its relationship to seventh graders' interest and achievement in science. *Journal of Elementary Science Education, 11,* 1–13.

DiYanni, R. (2003). The internationalization of the Advanced Placement program. *International Schools Journal, 22,* 25–33.

Driscoll, M. P. (2000). *Psychology of learning for instruction* (2nd ed.). Boston: Allyn & Bacon.

Educational Program for Gifted Youth. (2004). *EPGY instructional support for schools.* Retrieved June 9, 2004, from http://www-epgy.stanford.edu/schools

Fisher, P. J., Turic, D., Williams, N. M., McGuffin, P., Asheron, P., Ball, D., et al. (1999). DNA pooling identifies QTLs on chromosome 4 for general cognitive ability in children. *Human Molecular Genetics,* 8, 915–922.

Friedman, M. (1984). *Teaching higher order thinking skills to gifted students: A systematic approach.* Springfield, IL: C. C. Thomas.

Gallagher, J., Harradine, C. C., & Coleman, M. R. (1997). Challenge or boredom? Gifted students views on their schooling. *Roeper Review, 19,* 132–136.

Gallagher, S., De Lisi, R., Holst, P. C., McGillicuddy-De Lisi, A. V., Morely, M., & Cahalan, C. (2000). Gender differences in advanced mathematical problem solving. *Journal of Experimental Child Psychology, 75,* 165–190.

Gavin, M. K. (1996). The development of math talent: Influences on students at a women's college. *Journal of Secondary Gifted Education, 7,* 476–486.

George, W. C., Cohn, S. J., & Stanley, J. (1979). *Educating the gifted, acceleration or enrichment.* Baltimore, MD: Johns Hopkins University Press.

Ginsburg, H. P., Lopez, L. S., Mukhopadhyay, S., Yamamoto, T., Willis, M., & Kelly, M. S. (1992). Assessing understandings of arithmetic. In R. Lesh & S. Lamon (Eds.), *Assessment of authentic performance in school mathematics* (pp. 265–289). Washington, DC: American Association for the Advancement of Science.

Glas, E. F. (2002). Klein's model of mathematical creativity. *Science and Education, 11,* 95–104.

Hammer, E. J. (2002). Changes in math attitudes of mathematically gifted students taught in regular classroom settings from fourth to seventh grade (Doctoral dissertation, Michigan State University, 2002). *Dissertation Abstracts International, 63,* 1708.

Hiebert, J., Carpenter, T., Fennema, E., Fuson, K., Wearne, D., Murray, H., et al. (1997). *Making sense: Teaching and learning mathematics with understanding.* Portsmouth, NH: Heinemann Publishers.

House, P. (1999). Promises, promises, promises. In L. Sheffield (Ed.), *Developing mathematically talented students* (pp. 1–7). Reston, VA: NCTM.

International Baccalaureate Organization (2004). *Education for life.* Retrieved October 7, 2004, from http://www.ibo.org

Johnson, D. T. (2000). *Teaching mathematics to gifted students in a mixed-ability classroom.* Retrieved March 31, 2004, from http://ericec.org/digests/e594.html

Kamii, C., & Dominick, A. (1998). The harmful effects of algorithms in grades 1–4. In L. J. Morrow & M. J. Kenney (Eds.), *Teaching and learning of algorithms in school mathematics* (pp. 130–140). Reston, VA: NCTM.

Krutetskii, V. A. (1976). *The psychology of mathematical abilities in schoolchildren.* Chicago, IL: The University of Chicago Press.

Lesh, R., Hoover, M., Hole, B., Kelly, A., & Post, T. (2000). Principles for developing thought-revealing activities for students and teachers. In A. Kelly & R. Lesh (Eds.), *The handbook of research design in mathematics and science education* (pp. 591–646). Hillsdale, NJ: Lawrence Erlbaum and Associates.

Lesh, R., & Lamon, S. (1992). Assessing authentic mathematical performance. In R. Lesh & S. J. Lamon (Eds.), *Assessment of authentic performance in school mathematics* (pp. 17–62). Washington, DC: American Association for the Advancement of Science.

Livne, N. L., & Milgram, R. M. (2000). Assessing four levels of creative mathematical ability in Israeli adolescents utilizing out-of-school activities: A circular three-stage technique. *Roeper Review, 22,* 111–116.

Lubinski, D., & Benbow, C. P. (2000). States of excellence. *American Psychologist, 55,* 137–150.

National Center for Educational Statistics (1989). *User's manual, national longitudinal study of 1988, base year student component* (No. NCES-90-464). Washington, DC: US Government Printing Office.

National Council of Teachers of Mathematics (1980). *An agenda for action.* Reston, VA: Author.

National Council of Teachers of Mathematics (2000). *Principles and standards for school mathematics.* Reston, VA: Author.

Niederer, K., Irwin, J. R., Irwin, K. C., & Reilly, I. L. (2003). Identification of mathematically gifted children in New Zealand. *High Ability Studies, 14,* 71–84.

Norman, G. R., & Schmidt, H. G. (1992). The psychological basis of problem-based learning: A review of the evidence. *Academic Medicine, 67,* 557–565.

Reed, C. (2004). Mathematically gifted in the heterogeneously grouped mathematics classroom: What is a teacher to do? *Journal of Secondary Gifted Education, 15,* 89–95.

Reynolds, N. G., & Conaway, B. J. (2003). Factors affecting mathematically talented females' enrollment in high school calculus. *Journal of Secondary Gifted Education, 14,* 218–228.

Runco, M. A. (1993). Divergent thinking, creativity, and giftedness. *Gifted Child Quarterly, 37,* 16–22.

Ryan, R. H. (2000). High school students' math course enrollment decisions. (Doctoral dissertation, UCLA, 2000). *Dissertation Abstracts International, 60,* 2375.

Schack, G. D. (1993). Effects of a creative problem solving curriculum on students of varying ability levels. *Gifted Child Quarterly, 37,* 32–38.

Sheffield, L. (1999). Serving the needs of the mathematically promising. In L. Sheffield (Ed.), *Developing mathematically talented students* (pp. 43–55). Reston, VA: National Council of Teachers of Mathematics.

Slavin, R. E. (2003). *Educational psychology: Theory and practice* (7th ed.). Boston: Allyn & Bacon.

Southern, W. T., Komes, E. D., & Stanley, J. C. (1993). Acceleration and enrichment: The context and development of program options. In K. A. Heller, F. J. Mönks, & A. H. Passow (Eds.), *International handbook of research and development of giftedness and talent* (pp. 387–409). New York: Pergamon Press.

Sowell, E. J. (1993). Programs for mathematically gifted students: A review of empirical research. *Gifted Child Quarterly, 37,* 124–132.

Sriraman, B. (2003). Mathematical giftedness, problem solving, and the ability to formulate generalizations: The problem-solving experiences of four gifted students. *Journal of Secondary Gifted
Education, 14,* 151–165

Stanley, J. C. (1986). Fostering use of mathematical talent in the USA: SMPY rationale. In A. J.
Cropley, K. K. Urban, H. Wagner, & W. Wieczerkowski (Eds.), *Giftedness: A continuing worldwide challenge* (pp. 227–243). New York: Trillium.

Stanley, J. C., Keating, D. P., & Fox, L. H. (1974). *Mathematical talent: discovery, description, and
development.* Baltimore, MD: Johns Hopkins University Press.

Sternberg, R. J. (2000). Giftedness as developing expertise. In K. Heller, F. Mönks, R. J. Sternberg, &
R. F. Subotnik (Eds.), *International handbook of giftedness and talent* (pp. 55–66). New York:
Pergamon Publishers.

Tomlinson, C. A. (1995). Deciding to differentiate in middle school: One school's journey. *Gifted
Child Quarterly, 39,* 77–87.

Tretter, T. R. (2003). Gifted students speak: Mathematics problem-solving insights. *Gifted Child
Today, 26,* 22–36.

Usiskin, Z. A. (1999). The mathematically promising and the mathematically gifted. In L. Sheffield
(Ed.), *Developing mathematically promising students* (pp. 57–70). Reston, VA: NCTM.

VanTassel-Baska, J. (2001). The role of advanced placement in talent development. *Journal of Secondary
Gifted Education, 12,* 126–132.

Voyer, D. (1998). Mathematics, gender, spatial performance, and cerebral organization: A suppression
effect in talented students. *Roeper Review, 20,* 251–266.

Voyer, D., Voyer, S., & Bryden, M. P. (1995). Magnitude of sex differences in spatial abilities: A meta-
analysis and consideration of critical variables. *Psychological Bulletin, 117,* 250–270.

Walsh, D., & Paul, R. (1988). *The goal of critical thinking: From educational ideal to educational reality.*
Washington, DC: American Federation of Teachers.

Ward, A. W., & Murray-Ward, M. (1999). *Assessment in the classroom.* Belmont, CA: Wadsworth
Publishing.

Webb, R. M., Lubinski, D., & Benbow, C. P. (2002). Mathematically facile adolescents with math-science aspirations: New perspectives on their educational and vocational development. *Journal of
Educational Psychology, 94,* 785–794.

Weiss, V. (1994). Mathematical giftedness and family relationship. *European Journal of High Ability,
5,* 58–67.

Wertheimer, R. (1999). Definition and identification of mathematical promise. In L. Sheffield (Ed.),
Developing mathematically promising students, (pp. 9–26). Reston, VA: NCTM.

Wheatley, G. (1999). Effective learning environments for promising elementary and middle school
students. In L. Sheffield (Ed.). *Developing mathematically promising students* (pp. 71–80). Reston,
VA: NCTM.

Wieczerkowski, W., Cropley, A. J., & Prado, T. M. (2000). Nurturing talents/gifts in mathematics.
In K. A. Heller, F. J. Mönks, R. J. Sternberg, & R. J. Subotnik (Eds.), *International handbook of
giftedness and talent* (2nd ed., pp. 413–426). New York: Pergamon Press.

Wijsman, E. M., Robinson, N. M., Ainsworth, K. H., Rosenthal, E. A., Holzman, T., & Raskind, W. H.
(2004). Familial aggregation patterns in mathematical ability. *Behavior Genetics, 34,* 51–62.

Wood, T., Merkel, G., & Uerkwitz, J. (1996). Creating a context for talking about mathematical thinking. *Educacao e matematica, 4,* 39–43.

Secondary Affective Curriculum and Instruction for Gifted Learners

by Joyce VanTassel-Baska

The world of secondary gifted learners, unless they are in selective schools, can be brutal, to say the least. They are often ostracized by age peers and thus desperate for social relationships that are meaningful, concerned about their futures and the future of the world in general, and unsure about their abilities and aptitudes as they are now being tested in new environments. As gifted students move from elementary settings to secondary ones, there are many organizational reasons for this heightened anxiety. One of the reasons for it is that the organizational structure of secondary schools is much more complex, requiring these students to navigate multiple teachers and classrooms across limited time frames. This split in how time is organized and how physical space is allocated can cause new challenges for these learners who like to concentrate for longer periods on areas of interest. A second issue has to do with having multiple teachers. These students, if they have been in elementary programs, have expectations for teacher acceptance of their abilities and interests, not a likely situation in secondary programs, as many secondary teachers encountered will have no background in gifted education and not be attuned to their needs. Finally, the curriculum in secondary school also becomes more challenging in

481

respect to content expectations, requiring more effort on the part of gifted learners. If learning skills rather than just performance skills have not been internalized by these students, then problems at this level of learning are likely to arise.

All of these issues related to the development of the individual and the context of secondary schooling conspire to cause affective needs of these learners to become more pronounced at this transition point in the schooling process (Pfeiffer & Stocking, 2000). Thus, a prevention program of special seminars, group and individual counseling sessions, and individual exploration appear to be an important adjunct to the secondary experiences created for these learners. These opportunities need to be carefully crafted by the coordinator of gifted programs in concert with selected school counseling staff and teachers of advanced courses in order to ensure both acceptance and coherence in the plan to assist these learners in the affective domain. Not incidental to forming such an allied group are the insights gained informally by participants about gifted and talented adolescents.

REVIEW OF RELEVANT THEORY AND RESEARCH

The basis for considering the importance of affective development of the gifted as the cornerstone of gifted programming comes from several recent sources in emerging theory in the field. Moon (2003) has proposed a theory of personal talent that suggests a strong overriding role of metacognitive control in the capacity to convert aptitudes to developed skills to useful talents. Like Sternberg's (2003) idea of executive processes, the individual's capacity to direct the talent development process in a proactive way is essential to optimal realization of positive outcomes. Ambrose (2002, 2003) has suggested that aspirations can either impede or promote talent development in gifted individuals, suggesting that for low income and minority students, necessary aspirations are too often thwarted at early stages of development in such a way that they impede future talent development prospects. Like Gottfredson's (1996) career development model that suggests individuals can inadvertently circumscribe their own future development by making choices that limit and constrict future options, Ambrose sees a critical role for gifted educators in helping students engage in more open goal-setting behaviors. The developmental theory of Feldman and Goldsmith (1991) is also instructive in our understanding that gifted learners may move through typical stages of cognitive development more rapidly, thus creating a dyssynchrony in their capacity to function in all spheres or dimensions of their lives. Csikszentmihalyi's (1991) concept of flow further suggests that cognitive and affective features of the individual must be aligned in order for creative productivity to emerge. All of these understandings about the factors that must work together to bring about talent development implicate the role of the affective dimension as a necessary part of effective cognitive functioning.

Lovecky (1993) identifies five traits of gifted children that can cause internal and external conflict: divergent thinking ability, excitability, sensitivity, perceptiveness, and entelechy (a determination to achieve self-actualization). Although divergent thinking can lead to success in many fields in adulthood, it can cause problems for a gifted adolescent. It often leads to difficulty in organizing thoughts, feelings, and materials. In addition, its inherent nonconformity often elicits negative responses from both teachers and peers who don't understand the divergent thinker's mind; this can lead to feelings of isolation and a negative self-image in the gifted adolescent (Strop, 2002).

The reigning social emotional theory is Dabrowski's (1938) Theory of Overexcitabilities (OEs). Dabrowski defines five OEs—psychomotor, emotional, intellectual, imaginative, and sensual. Although these are not entirely unique to gifted people, they are more common in the gifted than in those of average intelligence. Ackerman (1997) found that in her sample, which included both students who had been identified as gifted by their school district and those who had not been, 70.9% of the students could be correctly classified as identified or unidentified according to their scores on an overexcitability questionnaire for psychomotor, intellectual, and emotional OEs. She also found higher questionnaire scores for all five OEs in gifted children than in the unidentified. Each OE, while giving a gifted child certain advantages, also poses its own problems (Silverman, 1993). Children with psychomotor OE may be misidentified as ADD; those with emotional OE are easily hurt and often seen as "too sensitive." Without understanding and properly trained teachers, intellectual and imaginational OEs can both lead to problems in school when gifted children do not approach problems and assignments in the same ways as their peers. Sensual OE, though it is more common in gifted adults than children, often manifests itself as intense reactions to noise or discomfort.

In her analysis of the Gulbenkian study, Freeman (1994) found that children with higher IQs were more sensitive to the differences between them and their peers. In addition, they were more likely to have a pessimistic view of the world's future (in particular, more likely to predict nuclear holocaust), a sign of sensitivity toward world events and problems. Gifted individuals are also more sensitive when it comes to moral issues such as fairness and honesty (Silverman, 1994). Because of gifted adolescents' asynchronous development, heightened sensitivity to these issues often comes before they can deal with the issue emotionally, which can lead them to worry excessively and even become depressed (Robinson, 1996).

Highly perceptive students are adept at taking others' points of view and understanding different layers of an issue (Lovecky, 1993). Although this contributes greatly to their intellectual development and understanding of concepts and theories, the absence of this trait in others can be very frustrating. Left unchecked, this frustration can lead to disillusionment, cynicism, arrogance, and distrust. Strong-willed behavior, perfectionism, and a tendency to put others' needs before one's own can all be the results of entelechy (Lovecky). At the same time, students with high entelechy are highly motivated to create their own destiny, and this can help them to surmount the obstacles presented to them (Piechowski, 1998).

In addition to theoretical literature supporting the importance of affective development in the lives of gifted learners, some empirical research supports key approaches to interventions, as well. Bibliotherapy can be useful in helping students explore issues of decision making (Friedman & Cataldo, 2002), identity development (Frank & McBee, 2003), emotional intelligence (Sullivan & Strang, 2002), empathy (Ingram, 2003), social problems (Hébert & Kent, 1999), and multicultural-ism (Ford, Tyson, Howard, & Harris, 2000), among others. Although the facilitator should choose books based on the goals of the bibliotherapy, if possible, the students involved can be given some choice to increase their interest and thus motivation (Abdullah, 2002; Schlichter & Burke, 1994). It may be useful to have a selection of suitable books on hand for students to choose from at any given time (Hébert & Kent), including books that employ themes related to giftedness (Halsted, 2002). To increase the effectiveness of the intervention, bibliotherapy can be combined with project work that explores the student's relationship to the book (Frank & McBee; Hébert & Kent; Sullivan & Strang).

The process for videotherapy is much like that for bibliotherapy, but uses mov-ies or television shows rather than books as the vehicle for self-discovery (Milne & Reis, 2000). This can be accomplished in many ways; a single movie can be shown in one sitting or in segments over time with questioning after each segment, or a series of scenes from different movies and shows revolving around a similar theme can be used (Hébert & Speirs Neumeister, 2002). The movies can be shared with a large group of gifted adolescents, a smaller group needing help with a particular issue, or even gifted students and their parents together. Extroverted students may respond better to the group viewing atmosphere of a movie than to the individual experience of reading a book, and teachers may find it easier to ensure all students are familiar with the material in this setting (Frank & McBee, 2003). Discussion of films portraying gifted adolescents (whether realistically or in stereotypes) can also be a useful tool in training teachers who are unfamiliar with the characteristics of the gifted (Nugent & Shaunessy, 2003).

Counseling strategies of various types have also been recommended for gifted adolescents, ranging from psycho-social counseling (Neihart, Reis, Robinson, & Moon, 2002), family therapy (Moon & Volker, 2003), and career and academic counseling (Colangelo, 2002; Greene, 2003). Peterson (2003) stresses the role of teachers and counselors working together to cofacilitate discussion groups. Nugent (2000) focuses on the role of teachers in addressing these needs through establish-ing classrooms that value listening and self-assessment activities. Use of the arts has also been advocated as a way to help students be open to experience (VanTassel-Baska, Evans, & Baska, in press). Other writers have addressed specific strategies for addressing key affective characteristics such as perfectionism (Nugent) and height-ened sensitivity (Mendaglio, 2003). Regardless of the strategies suggested, a key aspect of enhancing the affective development of gifted adolescents is through the provision of appropriate curriculum and instruction. An exploration of what such curriculum and instruction might look like follows.

THE INTEGRATED CURRICULUM MODEL AS A FRAMEWORK FOR AFFECTIVE CURRICULUM

The effectiveness and use of the Integrated Curriculum Model (ICM) for cogni-tive development in several academic areas has been well-documented in other work

(VanTassel-Baska, Ries, Bass, Poland, & Avery, 1998; VanTassel-Baska, Zuo, Avery, & Little, 2002). However, it is also an important framework to consider in building an affective curriculum for secondary learners. It posits that three interrelated dimensions of curriculum are equally important in constructing curriculum for this population. One critical dimension is advanced content. Even in the affective realm, the content level must be sufficiently high to challenge gifted learners. The example of using emotional intelligence as a content in the following section illustrates that well. Using adult level concepts with adolescent gifted learners, especially as it relates to their understanding of self and others is a critical part of an appropriate curriculum response.

A second critical dimension of ICM is higher order thinking and problem-solving skills leading to generative products. In an affective curriculum for the gifted, this aspect is critical to enhancing growth. In the four sample lesson plans on emotional intelligence that follow there is a major emphasis on critical thinking, metacognition, and creation in both the activities and questions.

A third dimension of the ICM model calls for a focus on abstract concepts, issues, problems, and themes that allow gifted students to grapple with the complexities of the real world. The use of issue-based and problem-based scenarios as deliberate ways to motivate and challenge the gifted is exploited in the various applications provided in the strategies section. The adaptability of the ICM for affective curriculum purposes broadens its potential for use in important ways.

EMOTIONAL INTELLIGENCE

While much rhetoric about emotional intelligence has not progressed to the level of sustained research (see Goleman, 1993), the work of Salovey and Mayer (1990; Mayer & Salovey, 1997) and Mayer, Caruso, and Salovey (2000) has. Their continued work to develop a theoretical framework for understanding emotional intelligence and a test to assess it provide an important avenue for developers of gifted curriculum to forge curriculum emphases at each relevant stage of development for K–12 learners in school. Salovey, Bedell, Detweiler, and Mayer (2000) define emotional intelligence as "the ability to perceive and express emotions, to understand and use them, and to manage emotions so as to foster personal growth" (p. 506). This type of emphasis on emotional intelligence feeds into our concerns about gifted learners' development in this area and uses a metacognitive orientation to enhance student growth. Because it is defined well within a framework, approaches to assessment can be readily developed, and the overall structure supports existing gifted programs well, dispelling some of the more common criticisms leveled against including such an emphasis in a gifted program.

The following section of this chapter outlines each aspect of the emotional intelligence framework and includes a prototypical lesson that may be used as a model for translating framework ideas into discrete classroom use. It is presented for use in secondary classrooms at the high school level. It may be considered one manifestation of a "prevention" curriculum for gifted learners in social-emotional areas to be implemented by both counselors and teachers.

The framework begins with being able to perceive, appraise, and express emotion in a variety of contexts, then moves to using emotions to facilitate thinking and on to applying emotional knowledge. The last component of the framework emphasizes the regulation of emotion. The lesson plans exploit the opportunities to learn in each element of the framework and provide active learning situations for gifted students that employ psychology and the arts as media for understanding.

The Emotional Intelligence Framework: Perception, Appraisal, and Expression of Emotion

Objectives: In a classroom setting, gifted students will be able to:

- Identify emotion in one's physical and psychological states. *Recognition of their emotions such as anger.*
- Identify emotions in other people and objects. *How other people respond to us— what emotions we evoke (fear, dislike).*
- Express emotions accurately, and express needs related to those feelings. *Owning one's emotions to the extent of being able to depict them: "I am angry because . . ." "I feel stupid when I don't know an answer and need to be affirmed."*
- Discriminate between accurate and inaccurate, or honest and dishonest, expressions of feelings. *How to read social cues; such as paying a compliment to someone authentically or recognizing sycophants (false flatterers).*

Sample Lesson Design #1

Study of emotion

Goal: To study emotion in self and others.

Outcome: Students will be able to analyze, evaluate, and express emotions in various forms.

Activities:

1. Analyze feelings based on your response to selected art, music, and poetry.
2. Express an emotion that frequently affects you in an artistic form of choice.
3. Evaluate a scene from a Shakespearean play for its emotional content or watch a film or create a role play. What emotions are displayed? How authentic are they?
4. Use a real world scenario to analyze emotions—yours and others'.
5. Analyze your emotional response to given stimuli such as various video clips depicting interactions.

Assessment:

Prepare a written response that documents emotional understanding of a predetermined scenario. Provide your *emotional* response, as well as your understanding of others' emotions based on the perspectives represented in the scenario.

This lesson plan provides students direct access to emotional content through literature, film, and other art forms, as well as real life experiences. It provides the cognitive avenue of analysis to allow students to recognize and understand emotion in themselves and others.

The Emotional Intelligence Framework: Emotional Facilitation of Thinking

Objectives: In a classroom setting, gifted students will be able to:

- Redirect and prioritize one's thinking based on the feelings associated with events and other people.

  In life, people come to like other people who share their values. These feelings produce a desire to spend more time together, leading to shared projects done in the company of these people. Students need to understand how positive and negative associations with others, as well as events, affect their thinking about structuring friendship patterns and activities.

- Generate or emulate vivid emotions to facilitate judgments and memories concerning feelings.

- Gifted students need to call up emotions in order to cognitively reflect on them, much the way that an actor does in order to learn a part. Through this process students may come to clarify their emotional reactions.

- Capitalize on mood swings to take multiple points of view.

  Students need to develop the ability to integrate mood-induced perspectives, and use emotional understanding of different selves to reflect on the impact of specific emotional states on human behavior.

- Use emotional states to facilitate problem solving and creativity.

  Students, for example, can learn that feeling sad might lead one to write poetry or that feeling happy might cause one to work on a hard problem. Gifted students, given their sensitivity and intensity, can learn to use these characteristics in the service of their own creative production.

Sample Lesson Design #2

Channeling emotion to promote thinking

Goal: To apply emotional understanding to cognitive tasks.

Outcome: Students will be able to use emotional understanding to advance cognition.

Activities:
1. Use your understanding of emotional issues surrounding selected current events to craft an explanation of how emotions affect the perception of the problem. Select from the following list or add your own example:
    *   emotional reactions to terrorism
    *   emotional reactions to political candidates (e.g., the 2004 election)
    *   emotional reactions to gay marriage
    *   your own choice
2. Analyze the emotional content of the Gettysburg Address and its potential impact on soldiers, families, and people in the local area.
3. Use a given emotional state or memory of it in your life to create a product of interest.

Assessment:

Prepare a journal entry reflecting on how you were able to employ "emotion" to enhance your problem solving in a given situation.

This lesson plan provides students the opportunity to apply their understanding of emotional states to real-world situations and grapple with the implications. They may come to appreciate that feelings color human actions everywhere in the world.

The Emotional Intelligence Framework: Understanding and Analyzing Emotional Information and Employing Emotional Knowledge

Objectives: In a classroom setting, gifted students will be able to:
*   Understand how different emotions are related.
    For example, students can come to know how shame leads to anger and how extended sadness can lead to depression and despair. Joy, on the other hand, can enhance positive feelings towards others.
*   Perceive the causes and consequences of feelings.
    Gifted students often have unpleasant experiences with peers including bullying. These encounters may lead to sadness which in turn may lead to lowered achievement patterns in school. Gifted students then can see the need to talk about their emotions before these emotions begin to work against them.
*   Interpret complex feelings, such as emotional blends and contradictory feeling states.
    Gifted students often experience deep feelings of abandonment when a friend moves away. They can analyze the mixed feelings of regret and happiness for the friend.
*   Understand and predict likely transitions between emotions.
    Students can come to understand the power of joy in anticipating a given event that, when it occurs, produces positive feelings. They also can come to appreciate that the aftermath may bring about feelings of letdown and sadness.

Sample Lesson Design #3

Developing and applying emotional knowledge

Goal: To develop and apply emotional knowledge.

Outcome: Students will be able to analyze and evaluate emotional content.

Activities:
1. Read selected books with a gifted protagonist who experiences emotional problems. Describe in a paragraph the emotional state of the key characters.
2. Analyze more fully the emotions displayed, their antecedents and consequences, and the ambiguity of individual emotional states.
3. Create a dialogue between two of the characters who could be angry with one another over a misunderstanding. Show how their emotions change as they discuss their perspective.

Assessment:
Assess the dialogue created in Activity #3, using a rubric that focuses on demonstrated effectiveness in
- interpreting feelings,
- knowing feeling transitions, and
- showing contradictions in feelings.

This lesson plan design provides students opportunities to "try out" their understanding of emotions through a careful analysis of literary characters. The safe distance promoted by this technique heightens their capacity to analyze emotional properties of human states and interactions.

The Emotional Intelligence Framework: Regulation of Emotion

Objectives: In a classroom setting, gifted students will be able to:
- Be open to both pleasant and unpleasant feelings.
  Gifted students need to be open to experience because of the importance of the quality for creativity. This includes being open to their own natures so that feelings can be explored and studied.
- Monitor and reflect on emotions.
  Gifted students, once emotions have surfaced, need to use the information from the emotional experience to think about the way that their emotional state impacted on their mood, others in the environment, and future events.
- Engage, prolong, or detach from an emotional state, depending upon its judged informativeness or utility.
  Students may learn to use emotions to perform important tasks or subdue them to prevent their interfering with other tasks.

- Manage emotions in oneself or others.
  Students can learn to control their emotions, given the situation. This may include checking anger or moderating sadness, or subduing elation in the face of a given social situation.

Sample Lesson Design #4

Regulation of emotions

Goal: To regulate emotion in self and others.

Outcome: Students will be able to apply judgment to the use of emotional knowledge.

Activities:
1. Use selected moral dilemmas as a basis for judging emotional reactions. How does emotion work in the situation and how can it be controlled? Should it be controlled in all cases?
2. Discuss the dilemmas, noting different emotional perspectives that prevail in the scenario and in yourselves.
3. Write an essay on the positive and negative role of emotion in dealing with real-life problems and dilemmas.

Assessment:
Have students engage in three-person role plays where two people are in conflict and the third is a mediator. After 10 minutes, rotate roles. Engage in peer, teacher, and self-assessment of the efficacy shown in emotional regulation.

Example: Role play a situation where Party A has just had her brand new car hit by a new teenage driver, Party B. Both Party A and Party B are upset. Party A is very irritated, as she has waited 6 months to get this car. Party B is worried that her insurance rates will go up or she will lose her license that has taken her 2 years to acquire. Party C observed the incident.

In this lesson plan design, students work through the emotional content of moral dilemmas, working through issues of appropriate outrage at situations, yet finding ways to mediate behavior to bring about a more satisfactory outcome. Hopefully they will learn that successful conflict resolution is partially about regulating emotions.

SUMMARY OF LESSONS

These lessons highlight the importance of understanding emotions at levels that promote application of that understanding to improve human functioning in both cognitive and affective areas. They also illustrate the importance of gifted students' use of emotions to enhance thinking and spur creative responses to stimuli.

Moreover, they offer strategies that teachers and counselors may employ to engage gifted secondary students in understanding self and others.

WRITING ABOUT EMOTIONS

Newer research suggests that writing and talking about emotional trauma can minimize its detrimental effects. Pennebaker (1997) has shown that disclosing emotional traumas in writing has numerous beneficial effects. These can be achieved by writing just once to a few times over several weeks, and writing can be anonymous. Benefits include fewer health center visits and improved grades among college students; enhanced immune system functioning; and in some cases, fewer self-reports of physical symptoms, distress, and depression. These have been replicated many times in diverse populations. Outward linguistic expression appears to facilitate the coping process, whereas internally ruminating over a negative event makes things worse (Salovey et al., 2000). Thus the lesson designs are structured to encourage written and oral communication about emotional issues.

STRATEGIES FOR WORKING WITH GIFTED SECONDARY LEARNERS ON AFFECTIVE ISSUES

In addition to differentiating curriculum for gifted learners by content, process, and conceptual dimensions, there are also selected strategies teachers, counselors, and other educators may employ to work successfully with these students at the secondary level. Most of the strategies involve an emphasis on oral and written communication, two modes that research suggests are effective in promoting "safe openness" (Pennebaker, 1997; Salovey et al., 2000). The use of such techniques, however, requires a careful understanding of student needs (Coleman & Cross, 2001) coupled with skilled facilitation of group discussion skills (Peterson, 2003). The following approaches have been used by both counselors and teachers to help gifted learners develop and mature in affective development.

Socratic Seminars

The use of Socratic seminars is especially useful in the context of exploring affective issues and concerns. It is based on a model of inquiry dating back to Socrates (thus the name) where the group leader assumes the role of question-asker and question-prober, but never provides an answer for any of the questions. Rather, she leads students to explore the issue among themselves and arrive at answers as a result of careful and guided exploration. Popularized by Mortimer Adler in the 1980s through his Paediea Proposal (1982), the technique is used by teachers of the gifted predominantly in secondary English and social studies classrooms. Several authors have described the process and found it effective with adolescent learners (Moeller & Moeller, 2002; Strong, 1996). Steps in implementing the process include: (1) begin by raising a mega-question about the topic; (2) have students complete a reading and an activity related to it; (3) divide the class into two sections and reseat them in an inner or outer ring. (The inner ring students respond directly to the discussion questions posed by the teacher, while the outer ring students take notes on the discussion for additional comment later to a different set of questions); (4) hold the discussion with inner ring students, using questions and follow-up probes; (5) assign an application activity as homework; (6) hold the discussion with outer ring students, using appropriate questions and probes; (7) use a global question to conclude the discussion with both groups, culminating in the sharing of samples of student work on the application activity; and (8) assess the individual homework samples and provide appropriate feedback.

A Model Lesson: The Socratic Seminar Approach

Purpose: To explore personal decision-making processes (three class periods required)

Mega-question: How important is decision making in today's world? Illustrations? How equipped do you feel to make prudent decisions in your life?

Activity:
   All students read a set of scenarios where a decision is called for. (One might be on making decisions about college, another about course taking, a third about peer pressure to participate in a questionable activity). Students then work in small groups to reach decisions on each scenario, rotating to a new scenario every 15 minutes. A full discussion of the scenarios would be carried out the next two class periods.

Discussion questions to be asked:
- What processes did you employ to address the scenarios? Probes: Were they the same or different across the group of situations? Why do you think that was the case?
- What would happen if your decisions were implemented for each scenario? Probes: Are the outcomes appropriate in your view? Why or why not?
- How did the decisions you made affect other people in each scenario? Probes: Were the decisions moral and ethical in nature? In what ways?
- What criteria are important to consider in making real world decisions? Probe: Why?
- Follow-up assignment: Describe in a two- to three-page statement an important decision you have to make and how you will use the criteria we generated to make it. (Due the next class period.)

Follow-up discussion with "observer" students:
- What key ideas did you hear in the discussion about the scenarios that you thought were important to emphasize further? (Facilitator probes each response.)

- What three criterion you heard discussed are the most critical in decision making in your opinion? Probes: Why these three? How did you apply them in your statement of personal decision making?
- What did you learn from observing the discussion yesterday as opposed to participating in it? Probe: Why did such learning occur for you as a passive observer?

Whole class question: What do you now know to apply to personal decision-making that you did not know before? Will these processes work for you in all situations? Why or why not?

Homework follow-up:
Let's hear a few of the application statements you worked on last night. (Have three read. Comments on each one may be solicited.)

Assessment:
All statements are collected and read by the teacher. Feedback is posted electronically to each student. The statement is placed in a portfolio on affective development to be student-developed.

Shared Inquiry Using The Literature/Arts Web

This approach is more simplistic in execution than the Socratic seminar in that it relies primarily on a core set of questions constructed by the teacher ahead of time to guide discussion of a specific reading or core stimulus related to a relevant affective topic. Art objects, as well as literature may be used to provoke discussion. Shared inquiry may or may not feature probes or follow-up assignments. The major emphasis is placed on a careful search for meaning in the text-based reading and student reactions to the text. Based loosely on the shared inquiry process of Junior Great Books, the technique involves five steps, moving from simple to complex interpretation of the stimulus provided:

1. students come up with words that describe their initial reactions to the stimulus,
2. students now declare their overall feelings about the stimulus,
3. students articulate the main ideas they think the author/artist is trying to convey by the art object,
4. students discuss images and symbols that the artist is working with in the piece, and
5. students comment on the structure of the artwork as it reinforces the intended meaning.

In conducting the discussion, the facilitator should present the stimulus on an overhead or computer and provide students with a web that requires their response to each of the five areas delineated. At stage one of the implementation of the activity, students should traverse all five aspects of the web individually.

493

At stage two of the process, students should work in dyads to discuss each web and compare findings. At stage three, the facilitator should hold a whole group discussion to determine the multiple insights gleaned through the process.

Model Lesson: Literature/Arts Web

Purpose: To engage learners in using the arts to understand self, others, and life issues.

Activities:
1. Ask students to view Millet's "Mariana."
2. Ask students to read Tennyson's poem by the same name.
3. Ask students to explore each art piece separately, using the following literature/arts web as a guide (see Figure 1).
4. Discuss the insights gained through the web exploration in small groups and then as a whole group.
5. Ask students to write a comparison of the two works, based on their web responses.
6. Ask students to reflect on the following questions:
    *   How does the theme of longing pervade both works?
    *   What changes occur in understanding as one moves from one art form to another?
7. Use the following questions to think through ideas about the concept of change. Create a poem and visual that reflects a state of change you are experiencing in your life.
    *   How does the *concept* of change apply to your life now?
    *   What *evidence* do you have that it is occurring?
    *   What is your *perspective* on whether the change is good or bad?

Assessment:
Facilitators may wish to collect three webs from students throughout the course of seminars, demonstrating their internalization of the process. Students should also be encouraged to include webs in their portfolios. After using this approach a few times, instructors may wish to ask students to comment on how the web encourages them to express feelings about what they encounter and how it helps them process those feelings within a cognitive framework.

Problem-Based Learning

The use of problem-based learning techniques to spur discussion and learning in respect to affective development is a powerful tool that gifted educators can benefit from employing at the secondary level, especially where the development of abstract reasoning renders such problems fraught with complexity that these students can rec-

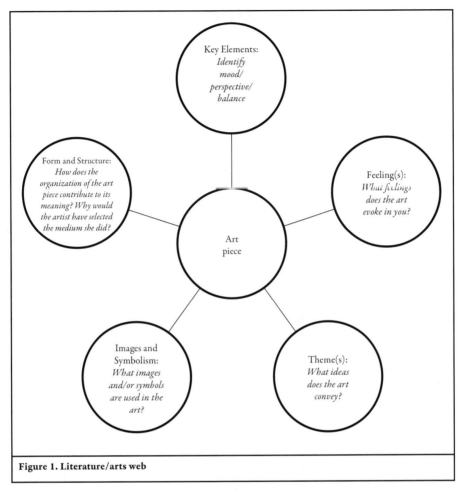

Figure 1. Literature/arts web

ognize and key into in a myriad of ways. The process of problem-based learning has been employed in secondary classrooms at selective high schools (Gallagher & Stepien, 1996) and in middle school settings (VanTassel-Baska et al., 1998). Problem-based learning has been used predominantly as a tool to promote cognitive-based learning in specific subject areas, notably science and social studies. However, it is a tool that can easily be employed in the pursuit of more affective goals, as well. The steps in the process of implementation include: (1) the teacher provides students with a real world problem related to human relations, (2) students work in small investigatory groups of two to four on the problem, (3) students receive additional data from the teacher about the problem and independently locate resources that inform them about the problem, (4) students are given a deadline to resolve the problem and are asked to publicly present that resolution to a real world audience, and (5) students in the class "role play" the audience and ask each team relevant questions about their resolution. The teacher then asks students to assess each other's approaches to resolution and handling questions. An overall discussion of learning accrued through this process should conclude the instructional module.

Model Lesson: Problem-Based Learning (PBL)

Purpose: To develop self-understanding in the context of developing social relationships (2 weeks should be allowed for this lesson module).

Activities:
Students are given the following problem:

You are the manager of personnel for a small company and have been alerted to a problem in one of the departments. A conflict has been reported to you over the work habits of a given employee, known to be very intelligent, but somewhat lazy. This employee appears to have failed to complete his part of a team project in a timely manner. Moreover, he has "verbally abused" his colleagues when confronted about the issue, according to one source. This person's input is vital to the success of the project. He has reported to work regularly, but appears to be sullen in his attitude toward the group. The project is due to your boss by the end of the month. What do you do?

Ask students to work through a "need to know" board to begin understanding the problem—What do they know? What do they need to know? How are they going to find out?

Students then begin to explore identified resources that may help them with the problem. The teacher should stress the use of people, as well as written material in the process.

New information should be provided to each group: *The employee in question has filed a complaint against the company, charging discrimination in the workplace.*

A few days later the following should be provided to all teams—
New information: *One of the team members has resigned unexpectedly, without giving proper notice or cause.*

The teacher-facilitator may wish to circulate as groups are working on the problem and raise the following questions:

- What do you think is the real problem here?
- How has your view of the problem changed in light of new information?
- Have you considered all the types of resources available to you in addressing this problem? (i.e., Have you talked firsthand to people who supervise employees in a similar context? Have you checked personnel rights and responsibilities handbooks? Do you know laws that govern such practices?)
- What questions do you have about the problem that stump you? What can you do about that situation?

Students present their resolutions, with five class members acting as a board of inquiry into the situation for each group's presentation. (Class members will rotate for this purpose.)

Assessment:

Students will assess each other's resolutions, using a rubric, citing additional commentary for each criterion (see Figure 2).

The inclusion of affective curriculum for gifted learners at the secondary level is not innate to most secondary educators, nor is the topic of gifted education incorporated in most education courses at the undergraduate level. Therefore, targeted professional development within the secondary schools should be included as part of the district plan. Secondary educators who work primarily with gifted students may consider certification in gifted education. The school district may also provide workshops and seminars on the social-emotional and cognitive characteristics and needs of gifted adolescents including specific instructional strategies, such as those suggested in this chapter, as ways to meet the needs of the gifted population. Furthermore, district leaders must ensure that the appropriate mechanisms and resources are available when the professional development occurs to encourage implementation. Unfortunately, there are sometimes logistical and philosophical barriers related to meeting the needs of gifted learners at the secondary level that must be addressed.

The ubiquitous problems associated with scheduling any special options for learners at the secondary level must be worked out first in respect to the proposed program. Too many good ideas are mercilessly blocked from fruition by rigid, one-size-fits-all scheduling practices, and an antipathy on the part of many administrators regarding gifted students' needs. The opportunities that need to be put on a schedule are bimonthly sessions that constitute seminar time, scheduled during existing homeroom time or brought about by scheduling a schoolwide "quest" period within which such options as delineated in this chapter might be offered. Coupled with a specific academic option, these sessions can be embedded with other content. An example comes to mind of a high school gifted coordinator offering a critical thinking option on the schedule for gifted students and then using that period to insert at regular junctures issues related to social and emotional development. Such a compromise may seem limited in some respects, but at least it guarantees a presence on the school schedule and assures students and parents that these issues will be addressed.

ORGANIZING SECONDARY CURRICULUM OPTIONS

Curriculum within the classroom can also be organized and integrated within the regular content areas. Secondary educators need to consider several issues in developing an affective component for gifted learners. First of all, it must be deliberate and planned, not put in place in response to problems, but rather proactively forged to prevent their occurrence. Secondly, it must be developed with an eye

Criteria	Exemplary	Satisfactory	Needs Improvement
Clarity of thought in explicating the problem	Thoughts were very clearly expressed and insightful in explicating the problem.	Thoughts were reasonably clear and adequately expressed in assessing the problem.	Thoughts were not clearly expressed in attempting to explicate the problem.
Comments:	*Comments:*	*Comments:*	*Comments:*
Evidence of the use of relevant resources	Resources were exemplary in respect to choice and use.	Resources were satisfactory in respect to choice and use.	Resources were limited in respect to choice and use.
Comments:	*Comments:*	*Comments:*	*Comments:*
Probable effectiveness of the resolution in the context	Resolution effectiveness was highly probable.	Resolution effectiveness was possible.	Resolution effectiveness was rather unlikely.
Comments:	*Comments:*	*Comments:*	*Comments:*
Appropriate concern shown for individual and group needs related to the problem	Needs of stakeholders were carefully considered.	Needs of stakeholders appeared to be considered.	Needs of stakeholders appeared not to be considered.
Comments:	*Comments:*	*Comments:*	*Comments:*
Credible presentation, based on the nuances of the problem	The presentation was highly credible and recognized the nuances of the problem.	The presentation was reasonably credible, given the problem.	The presentation was not credible because it lacked insight into the problem.
Comments:	*Comments:*	*Comments:*	*Comments:*

Figure 2. Example rubric

to developmental changes within adolescence, acknowledging that student needs will change as students mature. Finally, curriculum development in the affective realm should provide connections to cognitive development and the content being studied to serve as an appropriate catalyst for enhancing student productivity through the types of strategies employed (VanTassel-Baska & Stambaugh, 2006). Curriculum can then be ordered by integrating the curriculum with gifted students' universal concerns, by helping gifted students understand themselves and their future, by discussing and organizing the curriculum around major concepts and philosophical questions, and by helping students with metacognition and goal setting.

Researchers, teachers, and counselors have observed a rather consistent set of issues that plague gifted students. Strop (2002) found that a group of seventh- and eighth-grade talent search students worried most about universal concerns, performance, and getting along with others. When these students were asked to rank order specific issues, the following 10 emerged in order of priority:

1. establishing and maintaining positive relationships with peers,
2. dealing with oversensitivity to what others say and do,
3. making appropriate career choices,
4. developing the ability to relax and relieve tension,
5. maintaining the motivation and desire to achieve,
6. developing positive leadership skills,
7. getting along with siblings,
8. developing tolerance,
9. dealing with the need or desire for perfectionism, and
10. avoiding prolonged periods of boredom.

Such a list could be used as a basis for organizing special sessions or mini-units for discussion and writing with gifted students throughout the secondary levels of schooling. The social studies, the humanities, and literature seem to be the most logical places for these discussions to be embedded, but science, mathematics, and the arts are not excluded. Students may study eminent figures that contributed to the field or area of study and relate personal life issues with the eminent figures and their contributions to a domain. Casual class discussions regarding an assignment can be embedded within the curriculum to discuss motivation or perfectionism, for example. Service learning opportunities related to specific content domains or issues of world concern for students can also be implemented as a class or individual project. Product options with opportunities for creative expression and choice will help gifted students with their psycho-social needs and contribute to the affective curriculum organization.

Another key to organizing an affective curriculum is to understand how one fits in respect to predisposition, temperament, and ability. Helping gifted students understand their abilities in light of their personalities, aptitudes, and interests is a critical component of any social-emotional emphasis in a gifted curriculum. Consequently, giving a battery of relevant tests and interpreting test results in achievement, ability, aptitude, and vocational interests would seem prudent. Not all gifted people can become anything they want to be, based on predispositions, values, and personality (Achter, Lubinksi, Benbow, & Eftekhari-Sanjani, 1999). Thus, helping them understand optimal matches during their early high school years is a special need.

Similarly, organizing the curriculum to contemplate difficult life questions can contribute to further development within the affective domain. Helping students discern their true values and beliefs can ward off problems during adolescence with excessive experimentation. Students need to start addressing the large questions of: How do I define "meaning" for myself? What do I believe in and value? What are my life themes? Such questions then can lead to creating reflective journals where ideals are readily shared in a number of written and graphic forms. Opportunities for students to study great thinkers provide a vocabulary and a set of thinking processes to promote such philosophical study. Gaarder's book *Sophie's World* offers students a protagonist who is also studying the great philosophers. The book is written at an accessible level for high school students with the history of philosophy meted out in enjoyable pieces. The Philosophy for Children program, especially *Harry Stottlemeier*, also provides younger secondary students a basis for discussion of the great archetypal questions of identity and purpose in life.

Curriculum may also be organized around major concepts, such as suggested through the Integrated Curriculum Model. Halsted (2002) has organized affective themes and assigned them to grade level considerations and particular texts that she has arranged for easy use by readers. Sample themes might include achievement, aloneness, arrogance, creativity, uniqueness, drive to understand, identity, intensity, introversion, moral concerns, perfectionism, relationship with others, sensitivity, and using ability. Issue-based current fiction that has gifted youth as protagonists can be effective as a tool for discussions and allow gifted students to see themselves in the fiction, and for viewing affective issues of development at a safe distance.

Finally, students can be taught goal setting and metacognition. Students need to develop their goals at each year of development, monitor progress across a year, and assess outcomes at the end of a year. Keeping a journal might be a part of recording worthwhile crystallizing experiences that occur during the year and link them to a goal of the plan. Students could be afforded the opportunity to sign up for an independent study based on a topic of importance for affective development or pursuits of individual interests. Independent study opportunities can embed self-monitoring and goal setting, allow for in-depth discovery of a given topic, and encourage self-reflection about issues, careers, or oneself.

Many schools for the gifted require student portfolios to demonstrate cognitive growth; these plans could exemplify affective growth across the same span of time as well. Goals could be affective, cognitive, and/or aesthetic with clear implementation strategies and resources to be outlined for dealing with homework, planning a large scale research paper, or dealing with perfectionism or social relationships.

Conclusion

Both curriculum and instructional approaches matter in addressing the affective needs of secondary gifted students. The ideas presented in this chapter use the Integrated Curriculum Model as a framework to tap into an understanding of emotional intelligence at the level of curriculum interventions and the key strategies that support them. The interventions suggested are shaped into lesson modules for easy implementation by facilitators who may be teachers or counselors. They have also been organized for use as embedded experiences within an academic subject for groups of gifted learners; in addition, they could be used in special seminars or small group sessions. The inclusion of affective curriculum can be organized within the content domains with a focus on major concepts and philosophical questions, as well as the promotion of self-understanding, metacognition, and goal setting. Moreover, the need for professional development regarding the needs of gifted learners at the secondary level cannot be ignored. Addressing affective issues should be a major way to reach gifted adolescents, help them create meaning in their lives, relieve their anxieties about being gifted, and contribute to the development of strong peer networks for them. What could be more important in a secondary program plan?

REFERENCES

Abdullah, M. H. (2002). *Bibliotherapy.* Bloomington, IN: ERIC Clearinghouse on Reading English, and Communications. (ERIC Document Reproduction Service No. EDOCS0208)

Achter, J. A., Lubinski, D., Benbow, C. P., & Eftekhari-Sanjani, H. (1999). Assessing vocational preferences among gifted adolescents adds incremental validity to abilities: A discriminant analysis of educational outcomes over a 10-year interval. *Journal of Educational Psychology, 91,* 777–786

Ackerman, C. M. (1997). Identifying gifted adolescents using personality characteristics: Dabrowski's overexcitabilities. *Roeper Review, 19,* 229–236.

Adler, M. J. (1982). *The paediea proposal: An educational manifesto.* New York: Macmillan.

Ambrose, D. (2002). Socioeconomic stratification and its influences on talent development: Some interdisciplinary perspectives. *Gifted Child Quarterly, 46,* 170–180.

Ambrose, D. (2003). Barriers to aspiration development and self-fulfillment: Interdisciplinary insights for talent discovery, *Gifted Child Quarterly, 47,* 282–294.

Colangelo, N. (2002). *Counseling gifted and talented students.* Storrs, CT: National Research Center on the Gifted and Talented.

Coleman, L. J., & Cross, T. L. (2001). *Being gifted in school: An introduction to development, guidance, and teaching.* Waco, TX: Prufrock Press.

Csikszentmihalyi, M. (1991). *Flow: The psychology of optimal experience.* New York: HarperCollins Publishers.

Dabrowski, K. (1938). Typy wzmozonej pobudliwosci: Psychicnej (Types of increased psychic excitability). *Biul. Inst. Hig. Psychicznej, 1*(3–4), 3–26.

Feldman, D. H., & Goldsmith, L. T. (1991). *Nature's gambit: Child prodigies and the development of human potential.* New York: Teachers College Press.

Ford, D. Y., Tyson, C. A., Howard, T. C., & Harris III, J. J. (2000). Multicultural literature and gifted Black students: Promoting self-understanding, awareness, and pride. *Roeper Review, 22,* 235–240.

Frank, A. J., & McBee, M. T. (2003). The use of Harry Potter and the Sorcerer's Stone to discuss identity development with gifted adolescents. *Journal of Secondary Gifted Education, 15,* 33–41.

Freeman, J. (1994). Some emotional aspects of being gifted. *Journal for the Education of the Gifted, 17,* 180–197.

Friedman, A. A., & Cataldo, C. A. (2002). Characters at crossroads: Reflective decision makers in contemporary Newbury books: Characters in fine literature serve to model decision-making skills. *The Reading Teacher, 56*(2), 102–113.

Gallagher, S. A., & Stepien, W. J. (1996). Content acquisition in problem-based learning: Depth versus breadth in American studies. *Journal for the Education of the Gifted, 19,* 257–275.

Goleman, D. (1993). *Emotional intelligence: Why it can matter more than IQ.* New York: Bantam Books.

Gottfredson, L. S. (1996). Gottfredson's theory of circumscription and compromise. In D. Brown and L. Brooks (Eds.), *Career choice and development* (3rd ed., pp. 179–232), New York: Guilford Press.

Greene, M. J. (2003). Gifted adrift? Career counseling of the gifted and talented. *Roeper Review, 25,* 66–72.

Halsted, J. (2002). *Some of my best friends are books: Guiding gifted readers from pre-school to high school.* (2nd ed.). Scottsdale, AZ: Great Potential Press.

Hébert, T. P., & Kent, R. (1999). Nurturing social and emotional development in gifted teenagers through young adult literature. *Roeper Review, 22,* 167–171.

Hébert, T. P., & Speirs Neumeister, K. L. (2002). Fostering the social and emotional development of gifted children through the guided viewing of film. *Roeper Review, 25,* 17–21.

Ingram, M. A. (2003). The use of sociocultural poetry to assist gifted students in developing empathy for the lived experiences of others. *Journal of Secondary Gifted Education, 14,* 83–92.

Lovecky, D. V. (1993). The quest for meaning: Counseling issues with gifted children and adolescents. In Silverman, L. K. (Ed.), *Counseling the gifted and talented* (pp. 29–50). Denver, CO: Love.

Mayer, J. D., Caruso, D., & Salovey, P. (2000) Emotional intelligence meets traditional standards for an intelligence. *Intelligence, 27,* 267–298.

Mayer, J. D., & Salovey, P. (1997). What is emotional intelligence? In P. Salovey & D. Sluyter (Eds.), *Emotional development and emotional intelligence: Implications for educators* (pp. 3–31). New York: Basic Books.

Mendaglio, S. (2003). Heightened multifaceted sensitivity of gifted students: Implications for counseling. *Journal of Secondary Gifted Education, 14,* 72–82.

Milne, H. J., & Reis, S. M. (2000). Using video therapy to address the social and emotional needs of gifted children. *Gifted Child Today, 23*(1), 24–29.

Moeller, V., & Moeller, M. V. (2002). *Socratic seminars and literature circles for middle and high school English.* Larchmont, NY: Eye on Education.

Moon, S. M. (2003). Personal talent. *High Ability Studies,* 14, 5–21.

Moon, S. M., & Volker, T. (2003). Family therapy with gifted and talented adolescents. *Journal of Secondary Gifted Education, 14,* 107–113.

Neihart, M., Reis, S. M., Robinson, N. M., & Moon, S. M. (Eds.). (2002). *The social and emotional development of gifted children: What do we know?* Waco, TX: Prufrock.

Nugent, S. A. (2000). Perfectionism: Its manifestations and classroom-based interventions. *Journal of Secondary Gifted Education, 11,* 215–221.

Nugent, S. A., & Shaunessy, E. (2003). Using film in teacher training: Viewing the gifted through different lenses. *Roeper Review, 25,* 128–135.

Pennebaker, J. W. (1997). Writing about emotional experiences as a therapeutic process. *Psychological Science, 8,* 162–166.

Peterson, J. S. (2003). An argument for proactive attention to affective concerns of gifted adolescents. *Journal of Secondary Gifted Education, 14,* 62–71.

Pfeiffer, S. I., & Stocking, V. B. (2000). Vulnerabilities of academically gifted students. *Special Services in the Schools, 16,* 83–93.

Piechowski, M. M. (1998). The self victorious: Personal strengths, chance, and co-incidence. *Roeper Review, 20,* 191–198.

Robinson, N. M. (1996). Counseling agendas for gifted young people: A commentary. *Journal for the Education of the Gifted, 20,* 128–137.

Salovey, P., Bedell, B. T., Detweiler, J. B., & Mayer, J. D. (2000). Current directions in emotional intelligence research. In M. Lewis & J. M. Haviland-Jones (Eds.), *Handbook of Emotions* (2nd ed., pp. 504–520). New York: Guilford Press.

Salovey, P., & Mayer, J. D. (1990). Emotional intelligence. *Imagination, Cognition, and Personality, 9,* 185–211.

Schlichter, C. L., & Burke, M. (1994). Using books to nurture the social and emotional development of gifted students. *Roeper Review, 16,* 280–283.

Silverman, L. K. (1993). The gifted individual. In L. K. Silverman (Ed.), *Counseling the gifted and talented*. Denver, CO: Love.

Silverman, L. K. (1994). The moral sensitivity of gifted children and the evolution of society. *Roeper Review, 17,* 110–116.

Sternberg, R. J. (2003). Giftedness according to the theory of successful intelligence. In N. Colangelo & G. A. Davis (Eds.), *Handbook of gifted education* (3rd ed., pp. 88–99). Boston: Allyn & Bacon.

Strong, M. (1996). *The habit of thought: From Socratic seminars to Socratic practice.* Chapel Hill, NC: New View Publications.

Strop, J. (2002). Meeting the social emotional needs of gifted adolescents: A personal and contextual journey. *Understanding Our Gifted, 14*(3), 7–11.

Sullivan, A. K., & Strang, H. R. (2002). Bibliotherapy in the classroom: Using literature to promote the development of emotional intelligence. *Childhood Education, 79*(2), 74–81.

VanTassel-Baska, J., Evans, B., & Baska, A. (in press). The role of the arts in the socio-emotional development of the gifted. In R. Olenchak (Ed.), *Affective Development*, Washington, DC: NAGC.

VanTassel-Baska, J. & Stambaugh, T. (2006). *Comprehensive curriculum for gifted learners* (3rd ed.). Boston: Allyn & Bacon.

VanTassel-Baska, J., Ries, R., Bass, G., Poland, D., & Avery, L. (1998). A national pilot study of science curriculum effectiveness for high-ability students. *Gifted Child Quarterly, 42,* 200–211.

VanTassel-Baska, J., Zuo, L., Avery, L. D., & Little, C. A. (2002). A curriculum study of gifted student learning in the language arts. *Gifted Child Quarterly, 46,* 30–44.

SECONDARY PROGRAM MODELS AND THE EVALUATION OF SECONDARY PROGRAMS

CHAPTER

by Carolyn M. Callahan

As with all decisions about programming or selecting curriculum for gifted students, the choices made at the secondary level should be internally consistent and consonant with beliefs about giftedness and the most appropriate goals for gifted students. Therefore, before consideration of the models of programming for gifted students, it is important to note that the models presented here represent a wide range of assumptions about the appropriate definition of giftedness and the identification of the students to be served and also about the functions and purpose of the education of gifted students. For example, the model of Advanced Placement is based on a conception of ability that is cognitive only (high ability in one or more discipline areas characterized by an ability to learn rapidly and understand advanced, complex knowledge, concepts and principles of the discipline). Accordingly, the curriculum of this model reflects the importance of covering an advanced college level curriculum with dual purposes: (1) to give students the opportunity to earn college credit and placement in more advanced courses once enrolled in college, and (2) to prepare students for the rigors of college study. In contrast, the conception of giftedness offered by Reis and Renzulli (1985, 1986) in the Secondary Triad

Model (STM) includes both cognitive traits (above-average ability and creativity) and affective traits (task commitment). Further, while one goal of the STM is clearly advanced knowledge and understanding of the discipline, this model focuses more on outcomes reflecting the behavior of those recognized as gifted adults, including creativity. Thus, the ultimate goals in this model become the development of the skills, ability, and willingness to engage in self-selected investigations of real-life problems to produce solutions or research products that have audiences for the products of the study or investigation. These goals reflect Renzulli's belief that creative productivity is a more important outcome of gifted education than knowledge acquisition alone. In the Autonomous Learner Model, Betts (1986, 2004) takes an even stronger position on the importance of meeting the affective needs (social and emotional), as well as cognitive needs of gifted students and stresses outcomes specifically aimed at becoming life-long, autonomous learners.

The definition of giftedness (or lack of a definition) influences the range of learners that the model is designed to serve. The population served is also influenced by the development of the model either as one specifically intended for gifted students (e.g., Enrichment Triad/Schoolwide Enrichment Model, Autonomous Learner Model, or Purdue Three Stage Model and Purdue Secondary Model) or as one that has evolved de facto as a model for gifted learners (e.g., Advanced Placement). Some offerings are targeted specifically at students with highly developed talents in one discipline such as the DT-PI (Diagnostic Testing followed by Prescriptive Instruction), which evolved from the Study of Mathematically Precocious Youth (SMPY; Benbow, 1986) and the *Introduction to College Mathematics* curriculum (North Carolina School of Science and Mathematics, 1988). Others are designed to address talents in any area in which they are manifest, with any discipline area being a potential area of talent (e.g., Schoolwide Enrichment Model).

The wide variations in conceptions of giftedness underlying each model, as well as the differing goals and objectives of the models, suggest that decisions about the appropriateness of given program options for secondary level gifted students must be based on the context of the school and the accepted beliefs about giftedness and the values and goals of gifted education. Furthermore, the models are also distinct across many other dimensions, including intended audience and their place in the secondary school structure. Some are conceived as specific courses to be introduced into the secondary level curriculum (e.g., Advanced Placement courses) with little specification of requirements for enrollment. Others include extensive student commitment to fulfilling specific course and program requirements and usually are highly selective with expectations that students will have the background knowledge and aptitude to engage in high-level academic challenge across multiple disciplines (e.g., International Baccalaureate). Yet, others are programs that have both academic classroom components and supplemental components to address social and/or emotional development (e.g., the Autonomous Learner Model).

CATEGORIES AND DESCRIPTIONS OF MODELS

While all of the program models offered at the secondary level are unique, they are all based on a belief that gifted students are unique in their learning characteristics and that the traditional or standard school curriculum as delivered in a lock-step fashion in the heterogeneous classroom is insufficient to meet the needs that arise from the distinguishing characteristics that these learners present. The ways in which the differences are defined and the suggested responses differ across models, although the models share some common attributes or assumptions that allow general categorization as either enrichment or acceleration models.

Models of Acceleration

Acceleration models are those that are based on an assumption that the gifted learner is a rapid learner, has already mastered advanced level curriculum, and is ready to learn curriculum offered at a more advanced grade or school level. The models of acceleration do not demand change in the school curriculum; the learner is served by placement in a more advanced level of the existing curriculum within a school or by attendance at another school or in college. The models that fall in this category include radical acceleration, dual enrollment, Advanced Placement courses, and the International Baccalaureate Program.

Radical Acceleration

Programs of radical acceleration allow students to skip one or more grade levels. Examples of radical acceleration at the middle school level include entering sixth grade at the age of 9 or 10 or even younger, skipping a grade while in middle school, or moving to high school at the end of seventh grade. At the high school level, radical acceleration might include options similar to those described for the middle school or early entrance into college. Two less dramatic forms of acceleration are telescoping and course-by-course acceleration. Telescoping provides for condensing two or more grade levels of content into one year. Students may also only accelerate their learning in one subject area (e.g., going to the high school in seventh grade to take geometry). The theoretical rationale of the acceleration options is that the more advanced course(s) will provide a sufficient level of challenge. The model does not provide for a modification in the curriculum or the instructional strategies for the student, and the goals of the curriculum remain the same.

Diagnostic Testing Followed by Prescriptive Instruction (DT/PI)

A specific model for implementing acceleration models, the DT/PI model, was developed at Johns Hopkins as part of the Study of Mathematically Precocious Youth (Benbow, 1986; Stanley, 1978, 1979). This individualized instructional approach is recommended for use in either individual or group settings and begins with analysis of results of standardized testing (using out-of-level tests to ensure adequate measurement range) to assess students' current level of knowledge and areas of weakness.

Based on the item analysis, an instructional program is developed that targets the area of weakness. The student is then assessed on a second form of the test to assure mastery of the newly acquired knowledge and skill, and if successful, proceeds to the next higher level of learning. The model is intended for use in highly sequential disciplines such as "arithmetic or basic mathematics, precalculus, calculus, the sciences and other subjects such as the mechanics of standard written English" (Benbow, 1986, p. 12).

The developers of the model recommend that the process begin with an estimate of the point at which a student would score at the 85th percentile based on "stringent national norms" (an indicator that the student has mastered that level of mathematics). On an Algebra test, for example, the student would be compared to other students who have completed Algebra. If the student scores at the 85th percentile or above, Algebra II would be the appropriate starting point. Another guide provided is that the assessment should begin at a level where the student scores at least halfway between a pure chance score and a perfect score. For the fast-paced mathematics courses offered as part of Northwestern University's Center for Talent Development, a score of at least 500 on the SAT-M is used to signify that testing of Algebra I is warranted.

Following the scoring of the first administration of the test, students are then instructed to retry missed items. Examination of missed items by a mentor then leads to identification of areas of difficulty. "By considering the points underlying the twice-missed items, by querying the examinee . . . , the mentor should be able to 'read the examinee's mind' and devise an instructional program to perfect the examinee's knowledge of that level of mathematics" (Benbow, 1986, p. 15). The mentor sets the instructional content and the pace of the instruction. According to Benbow, this process can be implemented by teachers, teachers' aids, mentors, and qualified volunteers from the community so long as these individuals are "intellectually able, fast-minded, and well-versed in the subject area" (p. 15).

Dual Enrollment

A variation of radical acceleration is the practice of offering middle school or high school students the opportunity to enroll in college courses and simultaneously earn high school and college credit. These programs are usually dependent on the physical proximity of a community college or 4-year college and students usually enroll for only one or two courses. Several states have provided specific funding to support such opportunities and have further encouraged the development of these programs by supporting the widespread acceptance of the credits by state universities in those states (Oregon University System, Oregon State Department of Education and Office of Community College Services, 1999).

Advanced Placement and International Baccalaureate

The evolution of Advanced Placement courses and International Baccalaureate Programs as the dominant means of serving gifted students in high schools is a relatively recent phenomenon even though both options have been available for sev-

508

eral decades. The Advanced Placement courses were developed in the early 1950s to provide students with an opportunity to earn college credit while in high school without having to actually attend college. In response to concerns about a Ford Foundation program that encouraged high school students to attend college early, the Educational Testing Service first developed a set of exams using college level syllabi as the basis for setting standards for successful mastery of introductory college courses. These exams were, and still are, scored independently by raters hired and trained by the College Entrance Examination Board. The CEEB does not award credit for the courses, but advises that a score of 3 or greater (out of a possible high score of 5) is acceptable to most colleges and universities for granting credit or advanced standings (Morgan & Ramist, 1998). However, individual colleges and universities determine the level of performance required for credit, and some colleges and universities do not grant Advanced Placement credit based on these exams. Lichten (2000) reports that even though two-thirds of test takers earn scores of 3 or higher, only 49% receive college credit and that there is an increased tendency for many highly selective institutions of higher education to require higher scores in some areas than in others.

The Educational Testing Service has also prepared course syllabi to accompany each area in which an exam is offered, including topical outlines and recommended texts and readings, specifications that outline the relative topical emphasis on the exam, recommended laboratory time and exercises, and sample exam questions. These materials, including the exam, are prepared by a review of courses offered at the introductory level across a broad range of colleges and universities and vetted with a panel of college and high school instructors experienced in teaching the course. Hence, course syllabi do not conform to a particular introductory course at a particular college; rather, they represent an amalgam of those courses. As trends in curricular development have occurred at the college level and demand for more courses has increased, the CEEB has responded with the addition of art and music, computer science, and additional languages. In addition, pre-AP courses of study are now offered as is schoolwide articulation of coursework leading to the AP courses. Teacher training is also provided to prepare teachers to provide instruction that conforms to the syllabi. The CEEB has never claimed that Advanced Placement courses were designed specifically for gifted students.

These courses, designed to prepare the students for the Advanced Placement exam, are offered as part of the regular high school schedule. Students may elect any number of the AP courses available in their school and may or may not choose the exam, although in some schools participation in the exam is required. The AP courses and exams were initially developed for the top 5% of high school seniors, but they are now elected by as many as 10–20% of students and are taken by high school juniors and even younger students.[1] Advanced Placement courses are offered across all disciplines from art to the sciences, computer science, economics, calculus, lan-

---

1   The Stanford Education Program for Gifted Youth reports calculus and physics AP courses have been offered via computer to students in grades 8–10.

guages, history, government, music, geography, psychology, statistics, and English literature and composition. Within some subjects more advanced levels of course and exam are offered (e.g., calculus). The College Entrance Examination Board now offers AP scholar program award certificates ranging from AP Scholar (a grade of 3 or higher on 3 or more AP exams in full year courses) to National AP Scholar (an average grade of at least 4 on all AP exams taken and grades of 4 or higher on 8 or more of these exams; College Board, n.d.).

The number of Advanced Placement schools offering AP courses has grown from 104 in 1955–1956 to 13,680 in 2001. The number of exams taken in 1956 was 2,199; the number had grown to 1,139,516 taken in the U.S. in 2001.

While Advanced Placement courses were not developed specifically for gifted students, the initial claims of the developers of the International Baccalaureate program (IB) were that it was "a rigorous pre-university course of study, leading to examinations, that meets the needs of highly motivated and academically gifted students" (International Baccalaureate, 1987, p. 1). That claim has been dropped from later literature which now describes the target students as "highly motivated secondary students" (International Baccalaureate Organisation [IBO], 2000). The IB program is significantly different from the AP course options in that it requires students to successfully complete one subject from each of six categories (a first language, a second language, individuals and societies, experimental sciences, mathematics, and arts and electives). To earn the IB diploma, students must also successfully complete at least three subjects at the "higher level" (two years of in-depth study before sitting for examinations). Successful completion of the program also requires satisfactory performance on an extended essay on an independent study topic (chosen from approximately 60 topics) and a "creative, aesthetic, or social service activity." The goals of the IB program also go beyond the achievement of particular content related goals to include providing students "with values and opportunities that will enable them to develop sound judgment, make wise choices, and respect others in the global community" (IBO, 2000, p. 1.). Grading of IB examinations and projects is done by independent IB examiners; however, teacher examinations and project grading count for 20% of the final grade. To participate in the IB program, a school must submit a formal application and receive the approval of a review board certifying that the teachers and the program meet standards set by the IB organization. Participation in the program requires an application fee; annual participation fees; participation in training, which include release time; travel and training fees; costs of authorized IB consultants; and funding of the position of IB coordinator.

The course offerings are in some ways similar to AP courses, but not unexpectedly, are wider ranging in scope (e.g., philosophy, social anthropology) and are much more global in nature. Going beyond what one might expect in traditional Western curricula, the course offerings include options such as history of the Islamic world, world literature studies, and information in a global society. More than 80 languages have been offered for examination.

The growth of IB programs has been slower, but significant, with more than 36,000 students enrolled in more than 350 schools in the United States (Gehring, 2001).

The growth of Advanced Placement and International Baccalaureate Programs has been attributed to:

- readily available curriculum and training,
- lack of rigor and challenge in other secondary options,
- government support for students and schools offering these programs,
- the trend toward increased time to complete a baccalaureate degree,
- beliefs about advantages in the college admissions process,
- the use of AP and IB as indicators of school quality,
- the relative quality of the curriculum,
- level of challenge and learning environment in the classes, and
- recommendations in the literature about the fit for gifted and talented learners (Callahan, 2003).

Models of Enrichment

Enrichment, as the term is used here, characterizes those models in which the assumption is made that the development of the full potential of gifted students requires substantial modification to the curriculum and to the instructional practices that characterize the traditional curriculum. Each of the models specifies ways in which the curriculum and instructional modification addresses a specific set of needs of gifted students. Included in this category are the Autonomous Learner Program (ALP; Betts, 1986), the Secondary Triad Model (STM; Reis & Renzulli, 1986), and the Purdue Three Stage Model (PTSM; Feldhusen & Kolloff, 1986). The Purdue Secondary Model (Feldhusen & Reilly, 1983; Feldhusen & Robinson, 1986) includes an array of acceleration and enrichment options.

The Secondary Triad Model (STM)

First proposed in the mid 1980s, the STM was posited as a response to (1) middle and high school gifted students who were offered a "homogenized" school curriculum at a low level of cognitive challenge, (2) the relatively small number of students who had the option of enrolling in Advanced Placement courses, and (3) the demands of students and parents who had experienced the Enrichment Triad Model/Revolving Door Identification Model (ETM/RDIM) at the elementary school level (Reis & Renzulli, 1985; 1986). Like those models, the STM relies on a definition of giftedness based on a confluence of above average ability, creativity, and task commitment. Hence, the program implementation begins with the identification of a Talent Pool of students consisting of the top 15–20% of the general population in either general ability or one or more specific areas of ability (e.g., mathematics, language arts). Talent Pool students are provided the opportunity to test out of already learned facts and low level understandings or are given the opportunity to master the material with less instructional practice (compacting).

Students in the Talent Pool are also offered the opportunity to enroll in Talent Pool classes according to specific areas of talent. The Talent Pool classes are offered in addition to the traditional honors or accelerated classes. The students are introduced to Type I enrichment opportunities designed to provide the learner perspectives on new topics or areas of study related to the discipline of the Talent Pool class, but not ordinarily covered as part of the traditional curriculum. This type of enrichment is predicated on the assumption that gifted students benefit from a broadened range of knowledge and that development of interests and task commitment will lead to the development of gifted producers in school and in adulthood. The presentation of Type I enrichment is designed for students to see how knowledge of the discipline leads to real-life problem solving and production and gives the student the opportunity to determine whether he or she is interested in further study or research in that area. To extend enrichment opportunities within the Talent Pool classes, Type II enrichment is designed to develop specific thinking skills and affective processes that move the students to higher levels of cognitive processing of information using the tools of that discipline. Advancement to Type III enrichment occurs when the student demonstrates exceptional interest in or excitement about a particular topic or area of study. Type III enrichment consists of self-selected and self-directed investigations of a topic using advanced methodology and knowledge of the discipline to produce a creative product or pursue an original research study. Students in Talent Pool classes are also offered the compacting option. The model, as presented by Reis and Renzulli, is accompanied by specific forms and suggestions for developing student interest and learning style and for identifying emerging commitment to study and research.

Reis and Renzulli claim several unique features of the Talent Pool classes. First, because a Talent Pool class can be substituted for a traditional class, there need not be a disruption of schedules. Because the students may enroll in one or several classes based on interest and aptitude, the model does not have the drawbacks of tracking where students are usually required to enroll in advanced classes in all subject areas. The unique opportunity to pursue their own research within the structure of the classes differentiates this option from Advanced Placement, which follows a more structured and predetermined acquisition of knowledge model.

The Purdue Three Stage Model (PTSM)

The PTSM, a model similar to the STM, has been advocated as an enrichment model for both elementary and secondary school programs (Feldhusen & Kolloff, 1986; Moon, 1994; Moon, Feldhusen, Powley, Nidiffer, & Whitman, 1993). The model provides for students identified in specific talent areas to experience increasingly sophisticated and independent learning activities. Nidiffer and Moon (1994) note that the model is not the most appropriate choice for gifted students who have been identified as highly gifted in a single discipline area or for students who are considered academically gifted, rather than intellectually gifted. They also caution against using the model with underachieving gifted students.

Stage I and Stage II of the PTSM emphasize mastery of the core content, but Stage I also includes the goal of enhancing divergent and convergent thinking skills, and Stage II goals include development of complex problem-solving abilities. These goals and activities are parallel to those of Type II activities. At Stage III, students are expected to apply knowledge to real problems, function as a professional in the talent area, and develop real products to share with real audiences (akin to Type III enrichment activities). When used in homogeneous classrooms, the most advanced students would be expected to master Stage I content outside of class with class time spent on Stage II and Stage III activities.

The Purdue Secondary Model (PSM)

While the Purdue Three Stage Model is offered as a model for elementary or secondary students, the PSM was offered as a model for secondary learners only (Feldhusen & Reilly, 1983; Feldhusen & Robinson, 1986). Based on the assumption that "gifted learners share the common characteristics of capacity to absorb great amounts of information and to transform that information in complex and creative ways" (Feldhusen & Robinson, p. 156) and the premise that a comprehensive program consisting of acceleration and enrichment is most effective, the PSM offers "functional components" (i.e., counseling, vocational programs, cultural experiences) and components that are considered "service delivery" modes (i.e., out-of-school instruction and seminars). Hence, Feldhusen and Robinson describe the model as an "eclectic" approach (p. 154). The counseling component is decreed to be of primary importance because of the role of the counselor in identifying specific talents of gifted students, in providing assistance to gifted students experiencing adjustment problems, and in providing specialized career and counseling services. As in earlier models, in-depth research is considered a critical component of the model and is incorporated into the seminar component along with writing, discussion, and presentation activities. Seminars may either be related to career exploration or academic topics incorporating library or empirical research, but should focus on the study of broad topics.

The "Advanced and Enriched Curriculum Opportunities" include Advanced Placement courses (described later in this chapter), honors classes (focusing on the methods of a discipline) in areas other than mathematics and the physical sciences, math-science acceleration, and foreign languages beyond the typical 4-year study in high school. The "Arts and Cultural Experience" component is designed to address the needs of gifted learners to stimulate imagery, imagination, and spatial ability. The authors of the model suggest that this component may be addressed within the seminar component, as part of outside of school activities, the honors courses, or special music and arts courses. The "Career and Vocational Education" component is aimed at career education needs of gifted students and at developing talents of students in vocational areas traditionally overlooked. The "Extra-School" component (summer and Saturday programs) may be used to deliver nearly all of the other components of the model. A variety of curriculum models and principles are offered to guide the development of instruction within each component (Feldhusen & Robinson, 1986). Case studies illustrate how particular students are directed to particular components of the model, depending on identified talent area, and level of relative strength *and* weakness.

The Autonomous Learner Model (ALM)

While authors of each of the models discussed above make mention of the positive social and emotional consequences of being involved in the curricular and programmatic adaptations proposed in the models, the ALM more directly and specifically includes components aimed at social, emotional, and physical outcomes, with special emphasis on the affective domain (Betts, 2004). The categories of giftedness that the model is designed for include students who are (1) intellectually gifted (high achieving and highly intelligent), (2) creatively gifted (creative and divergent thinkers), and (3) talented (students who excel in one specific area such as mathematics or music). Betts also notes that learners identified according to the dimensions as defined by Renzulli (described above) may also benefit from this model. Furthermore, his model suggests that attainment of the goal of being an autonomous, self-directed learner is dependent on discovering the areas of study about which we can be passionate. This dimension is similar to the task commitment that is described by Renzulli.

Based on the premise that programs for these gifted learners should be focused on helping these students maximize their career potential and experience a sense of personal fulfillment or self-actualization, the model includes five components designed to lead to those goals: orientation, individual development, enrichment, seminars, and in-depth study (Betts, 1986; Betts & Kercher, 2000). Activities in the first component are aimed at students, educators, and parents with the goal of helping all learn more about the concepts associated with giftedness and the program. During the individual development component, students are expected to learn skills (cognitive, social, physical, and affective) associated with lifelong, autonomous learning. This component also includes career and college involvement. The enrichment dimension is structured to provide exploration in content not traditionally included in the school curriculum with two stages of exploration: an introduction to a broad range of topics across disciplines and the way in which they will be studied in the second phase of the enrichment dimension. Explorations, investigations, cultural activities, service, and adventure trips are included within this dimension of the program. Seminars are designed as an opportunity for groups of three to five students to study a topic (at an advanced level) and present it to the rest of the class and other interested observers. Finally, as with the STM and the PTSM, students pursue long-term small group or individual in-depth study. This last phase also includes mentorships as part of the in-depth study

Within secondary schools, ALM is structured as a separate course with an expectation that it would be offered and selected for more than one year. A 3-year timeline is offered for full implementation of the model (Betts, 1986). The assumption is made that special courses are necessary for total development of the gifted individual (Betts & Kercher, 2000); however, if that is not possible, Betts (1985) recommends using the model as a component of a regular classroom in the language arts or social sciences.

The following standards are provided as fundamental to the program and are offered as student/learner goals (Betts, 1985; Betts & Kercher):

1. Develop more positive self-concepts.
2. Comprehend own abilities in relationship to self and society.
3. Develop skills to interact effectively with peers, parents, and other adults.
4. Increase knowledge in a variety of areas.
5. Develop critical and creative thinking skills.
6. Develop decision-making and problem-solving skills.
7. Integrate activities which facilitate the cognitive, emotional, social, and physical development of the individual.
8. Develop individual passion area(s) [of] learning.
9. Demonstrate responsibility for own learning in and out of the school setting.
10. Ultimately become responsible, creative, independent, lifelong learners. (Betts & Kercher, p. 360)

Integrated Curriculum Model (ICM)

The Integrated Curriculum Model (ICM) is based on addressing three major characteristics of gifted learners in grades K–9: (1) precocity, or advanced knowledge and development in a school-related curriculum area—usually verbal or mathematical subject domains; (2) intensity, or capacity to focus or concentrate for extended time periods; and (3) complexity, or the ability to use higher level and abstract thinking, as well as their proclivity to enjoy hard work and challenge. This tripartite, integrated model is also a hybrid of acceleration and enrichment with acceleration serving as a base for emphasis on advanced content knowledge (VanTassel-Baska, 1995). The accelerative component mirrors the diagnostic prescriptive approaches of the DT-PI model, but with emphasis on using end-of-year or end-of-chapter assessments. The second component of the model focuses on student use of generic thinking models to manipulate information and knowledge at complex levels to create new ideas or products. The final component is learning experiences based on major themes, issues, or ideas that lead to a "deep understanding of ideas" (VanTassel-Baska, p. 99). A language arts curriculum for grades 6–10 based on the model includes these goals:

1. To develop analytic and interpretive skills in literature.
2. To develop persuasive writing skills.
3. To develop linguistic competency.
4. To develop listening/oral communication skills.
5. To develop reasoning skills in the language arts.
6. To understand the concepts of change in the language arts. (Center for Gifted Education, 1998, pp. 3–4)

Recommendations for implementation are based on context variables that are considered critical for success. The first is flexibility in student placement and progress because "ungraded multi-age contexts where high-ability learners access appropriate work groups and curriculum work stations is critical" (VanTassel-Baska, 1995, p. 103). The second is grouping gifted students together for delivery of the curriculum. This grouping may be in special homogeneous classes of gifted students, pull-out classes, or clusters within the regular classroom. Finally, trained teachers and a climate of excellence are deemed to be vital factors in the successful execution of the curriculum.

Specialized Courses

While Advanced Placement and International Baccalaureate courses have dominated the course offerings at advanced levels in the high school—particularly for juniors and seniors, several other promising curricula have emerged that should be given consideration. For example, the Carnegie Corporation funded the development of the Introduction to College Mathematics based on principles of calculus, discrete mathematics, statistics, and mathematical modeling applied to the disciplines of engineering, the physical sciences, the life sciences, business, finance, and computer science (North Carolina School of Science and Mathematics, 1988). Three units were developed (matrices, data analyses, and geometric probability) to be offered to students who have completed the equivalent of Algebra II. Designed to prepare students for the range of mathematics courses they will encounter in college, the units cover such topics as using matrices to model real-world phenomenon, solving problems that are not feasibly solved without matrix algebra, determining probabilities of events for which the number of possible outcomes is infinite, using mathematical modeling, and exploring data presentations and finding the best curve to use in fitting the data. Computer software with examples, exercises, and simulations, accompanies each unit.

RESEARCH AND EVALUATIONS OF EFFECTIVENESS

While most of the accelerative and enrichment models have been implemented for 20 or more years, there is only limited research and meager evaluation data on student outcomes or the impacts of the models. Little of the research or evaluation data reported is based on strong experimental design that allows for clear attribution of effects.

Radical and Moderate Acceleration

The acceleration and course-specific models are based on goals for groups of students that are very content specific; hence, success can be more easily tied to successful course completion, high performance on examinations (AP and IB), or quality products (IB).

Studies of radical acceleration programs have focused on two populations: the early college entrants and the students who were part of the Johns Hopkins program where the DT/PI model has been implemented. Studies of moderate acceleration conclude that acceleration yields clear advantages in academic achievement (Kulik & Kulik, 1992) Follow-up surveys report high mathematics achievement and participation in high level mathematics courses by students who had been identified as part of the SMPY Talent Search and had experienced acceleration in mathematics (Kolitch & Brody, 1992). The students (62% of those surveyed) reported high achievement in calculus (as measured by scores on Advanced Placement exams) and those who took postcalculus courses only found those courses moderately challenging. Their results affirmed earlier studies of the benefits of acceleration in follow-up survey studies of accelerated students (see Southern & Jones, 1991).

Because of many concerns that are raised about potentially negative social or emotional outcomes of acceleration, many researchers have examined the affective outcomes of such programs, as well. Much of this research is based on post hoc survey reports from the students about their perceptions of the experience, its influence on their goals and their perceptions of the programs. Studies of middle school students who take high school courses early and early college entrants at the University of Washington, for example, reported being equally as happy, satisfied with their lives, and psychologically healthy as a group of equally able adults who had chosen to enter college early (Noble, Robinson, & Gunderson, 1993)

Noble and Smyth (1995) and Cornell, Callahan and Loyd (1991) focused particularly on gifted females in studying radical (early entrance to college) acceleration. Cornell et al. found that in contrast to females who had not been accelerated, the young women who had been accelerated were more independent, resourceful, and self-sufficient, more self-assured, more self-disciplined, and more strongly oriented toward completing tasks. They did note that some of the young women in the accelerated program experienced serious adjustment problems. The young women in the Noble and Smyth study reported that their perceptions of ability were greatly affected by the early entrance program in which they participated.

Cornell, Callahan, Bassin, and Ramsay (1991) concluded that while studies of radical acceleration have concluded that there are adverse effects of the model, most of these studies have research flaws that temper those conclusions. In particular, there is (1) an over-reliance on self-report measures rather than standardized and validated measures of social and emotional adjustment; (2) a failure in cross-sectional studies to control for preexisting conditions that might distinguish accelerants from comparison groups, (3) a failure to recognize selective factors, which results in overgeneralization of findings; (4) an absence of group differences that may be attributable to methodological factors such as lack of statistical power, influence of confounding variables, or excessive measurement error; (5) drop-out bias; and (6) a problem with the choice of comparison groups.

Southern and Jones (1991) have summed up the literature on acceleration succinctly by noting that while group results appear very positive, concentrating on whether or not groups were helped or harmed masks the effects on individuals. Callahan and Hunsaker (1991; Hunsaker & Callahan, 1991) have provided guidelines for monitoring the effectiveness of acceleration programs and student placement in those programs. See Table 1 for a summary of those guidelines.

Table 1
Guidelines for Monitoring the Effectiveness of Acceleration Programs and Student Placement in Acceleration Programs

Assessment of Potential Accelerants
- Are thorough evaluations of the students' intellectual functioning, academic skill levels, social adjustment, and emotional status conducted by a psychologist and considered in the decision making?
- Are the options for acceleration matched to the assessment of intellectual functioning and academic skill level, as well as social and emotional status? (For example, a student who is very advanced in only one discipline should only be placed above grade level for instruction in that area.)
- Is appropriate consideration given to variables such as motivation and persistence in challenging academic situations?
- Are student self-evaluations of readiness and student wishes taken into consideration?
- Are clear options for "reversing" the acceleration in place that are free of pressure and stigmas of failure? That is, are acceleration options presented clearly as trials with clear options for returning to the earlier placement? Have those been discussed with the student and the parent?
- Have teachers been screened for positive attitudes toward acceleration and the accelerated student? Do they understand and accept developmental differences that are unrelated to cognitive functioning (e.g., motor skills, ability to sit for extended periods of time)?

Thoroughness and Rigor
- Have provisions been made to ensure that the students have mastered the content of the discipline in which they are accelerated?
- Has an assessment been done to ensure that "skipped" standards have been addressed?
- If content is compacted, is there a provision for ensuring deep understanding, rather than surface level achievement?
- Are teachers prepared to provide scaffolding as necessary or to further challenge a student who may still be beyond grade level peers after acceleration?
- Do the teachers have the content knowledge to address student needs (especially in secondary level Advanced Placement or International Baccalaureate programs)?
- Are there provisions to evaluate the appropriateness of the placement in terms of academic challenge?
- From a program evaluation perspective, is data collected to document that achievements are attributable to the acceleration program and not to maturation?

Social and Emotional Issues
- Are the student and the student's parents comfortable with the student's ability to relate to peers and form friendships?
- Does the student feel comfortable with the social opportunities provided?
- Is the student comfortable with level of expectation set in the new setting?
- Have provisions been made, as appropriate, for ensuring desired opportunities to continue or form age peer relationships?
- Are there provisions to monitor the social and emotional development of the students?
- Are the students in the classroom in which an accelerated student is placed given adequate information and instruction to make the transition a positive one?
- Are counselors prepared to guide the accelerant in college choice and career development activities that are an appropriate response to cognitive, personality, and developmental variations that are different from the norm?
- Are teachers and counselors trained to detect signs of maladjustment?

Advanced Placement and International Baccalaureate

Most research on AP courses has been limited to student satisfaction surveys and studies of the success of students in college. The survey study (Casserly, 1968) reported overall high satisfaction ratings; however, there was a very large range and standard deviation in responses, indicating that considerable numbers of students at that time gave ratings at the middle and below the middle of the range. Other researchers (Morgan & Crone, 1993; Morgan & Ramist, 1998) report that AP students perform as well or (often) better in related college courses as their peers who were not in AP courses. However, a review of these studies by a panel appointed by the National Academy of Sciences (NAS, 2000) concluded that

> [T]he methodology used in conducting the studies makes it difficult to determine how often and under what circumstances there is a positive advantage for AP students relative to non-AP students in second level courses. . . . [The methodological flaws also] make it difficult to determine whether any apparent advantage held by AP students over non-AP students is a function of the colleges they enter, their own academic backgrounds and abilities, or the quality of the AP courses they took in high school. (p. 193)

As with the AP courses, independent research on the impact of the International Baccalaureate program is limited. Further, like the AP research, the lack of control for aptitude and motivational variables inhibits interpretation of the results. Feldhusen and Poelzer (1996) found that students in the high level IB courses outperformed students in equivalent AP courses on AP exams. However, the teachers noted that the students in the more highly selective IB program "demonstrated greater task commitment, questioning, independence, intelligence, ability to see connections among concepts, desire to understand, management skills, and taking responsibility for their own learning" (p. 33). Grexa (1988) found that the grade point averages of IB students during college exceed those of AP students, but weakly concluded, "IB students perform at least as well as their counter-parts from the same or other schools that do not offer IB" (p. 5).

The NAS panel (2000) challenged the assumption that the AP mathematics and science courses "reflect the content coverage and conceptual understanding that is developed in good college courses" (p. 192). The panel also raised pedagogical concerns about the course structures based on learning research, and the Commission on Life Sciences (1990) raised concerns about the biology course structure.

Recent data collected in a qualitative study of Advanced Placement and International Baccalaureate classrooms documented that teachers, whether teaching in affluent or impoverished schools, tended to view their students as a homogeneous group and, as such, designed curriculum and instruction in accordance with their expectations of the class as a whole, rather than in accordance with expectations of individual students (Callahan, Hertberg, Kyburg, Brighton, Hench, & You, 2005). The resulting "one-size-fits-all" curriculum and instruction did not always fit all students in the class. Teachers and students alike tended to view the mismatch between the offered curriculum and instruction and an individual learner's needs as a failing on the part of the student.

Further, AP and IB teachers felt immense pressure to prepare students for end-of-year tests, believing that rapid-paced lectures and drill-and-practice approaches were the most effective methods of doing so. In a few AP classrooms, the teachers' beliefs that students could not pass the AP tests led the teachers essentially to abandon the AP curriculum in favor of less challenging content. Additionally, most teachers in AP and IB courses defined the main difference in curriculum between these courses and non-AP and -IB courses as "level of challenge." Nearly all teachers' instruction reflected a definition of "greater challenge" as meaning "more work." The majority of students taking AP and IB classes were satisfied with the nature of the curriculum and instruction within these courses, perceiving the courses as challenging and as representing the "best" classes offered at their schools. Students seemed to believe that AP and IB courses were the "best" because they were taught by the most experienced teachers, required students to take on the heaviest workload, and were populated by the most advanced students. Most students did not question the importance of what they were learning, whether or not they found the content interesting, or the teachers' instructional methods, even when asked to do so in interviews. Student satisfaction with the nature of these courses also rested on assumptions that the courses were preparing them for the types of challenging experiences they would encounter in college and in the workplace.

Students who had dropped out of AP and IB programs told a different story, however. These students made their decisions to leave the programs precisely because they believed that the curriculum, instruction, and environment of the classes were inappropriate for their individual needs. All of these students indicated that they originally took the courses because they desired greater challenge than that offered in non-AP or -IB classes, but that the way AP and IB courses were taught did not allow them to succeed, feel welcome, or learn in the ways that they liked to learn. Clearly, for these students, AP and IB courses did not provide a good fit.

Enrichment Models

The enrichment models are often predicated on cognitive outcomes not so easily measured (e.g., creativity or creative productivity, critical thinking); are directed toward affective outcomes such as the expansion and development of interests, the development of independence, and self-directed learning; and/or are characterized by outcomes that vary individually by child (e.g., independent study, mentorships, or production of individualized products such as those called for in the Secondary Triad Model or the Autonomous Learner Model).

Secondary Triad Model

A two-part qualitative longitudinal study of the Secondary Triad Model gathered retrospective data from students in grades 9–12 enrolled in programs using the model (but also enrolled in Advanced Placement, honors classes, and special seminars) who had "produced at least three performances or products . . . with four or more years of participation in a [gifted] program" (Delcourt, 1994, p. 408).[2] In the first part of the study, 18 students who were surveyed and interviewed reported that work on their projects increased characteristics such as their interest, task commitment, their ability to generate ideas, the quality of later projects, and the ability to accept criticism. They reported skill acquisition in research, writing, communication, and technical abilities and improvement in personality dimensions such as self-satisfaction, patience, self-assurance, responsibility, and independence. Success was tied to the opportunity to share products with appropriate audiences. The eight students responding to a follow-up survey 3 years later engaged in creating products in areas of interest relating to college courses (no information was provided relative to course requirements). Taylor (as cited in Renzulli & Reis 1994) found that participation in Type III activities significantly increased the mean number of years that students in a vocational/technical school planned to attend postsecondary schools.

The Autonomous Learner Model

One evaluation of a modified version of the ALM program over a 3-year time frame documented student reports of broadened interests, greater inquisitiveness, and more positive attitudes toward school. Students' grade point averages were not improved in other courses as expected (Burgess, 1990). Experimental studies of the effectiveness of the model have not been reported.

Purdue Three Stage Model

An evaluation study (Nielsen, 1985) using a quasi- experimental design found that students in the program in grades 7 and 8 did not earn significantly higher scores on measures of critical thinking and general self-concept than the control students (students initially identified as potential program candidates, but who did not participate in the gifted program). The program students demonstrated significantly improved self-concepts related to giftedness, but general self-concept scores of the females in the program decreased through grade 6. Participation in the enrichment program significantly improved critical thinking skills and self-concepts related to giftedness in this age group. However, critical thinking skills and self-concepts of high school students were not improved by participation in the course based on the model. While high school and elementary school students were positively supportive of the program, junior high school students expressed dissatisfaction with the pullout program format.

Integrated Curriculum Model

Evaluations of units developed using this model are reported as group results across elementary and middle school grades. A study of a language arts unit for grades 4–6 produced data (VanTassel-Baska, Johnson, Hughes, & Boyce, 1996)

---

2   Eighteen students were studied in Phase 1; one student did not agree to further contact.

documenting significant change for the experimental group on measures developed by the model originators (reading, persuasive writing, and grammatical understanding), while control group students did not exhibit significant gains. Control groups were not necessarily comparable groups of students. The study also raised cautions about use of the unit in regular classroom settings because teachers reported that the advanced level of the readings and the abstractness and complexity of the concepts made the units too difficult for average learners. A second, similarly designed study (VanTassel-Baska, Zuo, Avery, & Little, 2002) on several language arts units in grades 2–8 yielded overall significantly greater results for an experimental group on literary analysis and interpretation skills and persuasive writing skills. Data on a third unit (science), also implemented in grades 4–6, revealed small, but significant differences between experimental and control groups on a performance assessment of science inquiry, but control and experimental groups were not randomly assigned (VanTassel-Baska, Bass, Ries, Poland & Avery, 1998). Data were not reported by grade level in any of these studies so it is impossible to gauge the effects for middle school students.

In summary, the evidence of effectiveness of the enrichment models at the secondary level is extremely weak. One could try to generalize from the limited research on the application of parallel models implemented at the elementary level to outcomes at the secondary level, but such generalizations are tenuous at best and even these data are limited by the nonexperimental design of most studies (most often retrospective), emphasis on student perception data rather than student outcome data, and lack of replication. Further, the distinct nature of elementary schools compared to secondary schools, and more importantly, the developmental stage of the preadolescent and adolescent makes generalization debatable.

SELECTING OPTIONS FOR GIFTED PROGRAMS

It is clear from the discussion of the variety of program models that have been developed and implemented at the secondary level that there is no one program that fits all types of gifted students. In planning for gifted students at this level, educators must first determine the types of giftedness accepted and valued by the community. Are the constituents of the schools vested in providing programs for those who are academically advanced achievers in particular disciplines? Are they interested in those who are creative and intellectually facile? Are they interested in serving those who are underachievers, as well as those who have evidenced extraordinary achievement? These decisions do not need to be either/or decisions. A school community may determine that there are several categories of giftedness that warrant services.

A second question that must be asked is: "What are the goals we have for providing educational programs to gifted students?" If those goals are rapid advancement through the regular curriculum for students identified as extraordinary achievers in a particular discipline, then acceleration options are the best considerations. However, if the goals extend to high creative productivity, then enrichment options may be most appropriate. Hence, the second step in good program development is to match the needs of the students who are deemed gifted with school goals and the model or models that seem best suited in terms of the type of gifted student to be served. It is critically important that the schools not limit their options to "a gifted program," but rather, that they consider a continuum of services that will best serve all types of giftedness recognized within that community and seek to match educational services with student learning needs.

To that end, a school may determine that it needs to have Advanced Placement courses available in all high schools that are options for traditional gifted learners who excel, exhibit giftedness in one or more particular discipline area, and whose goals include the rapid learning of the broad general ideas from one or more disciplines. If these courses are to be offered at the high school level and issues of equity are to be addressed, the schools must prepare to offer sufficiently challenging options at the middle school to prepare gifted learners from all populations for these courses and must prepare teachers in scaffolding techniques to provide the support for a range of learners in those classes (Hertberg et al., 2005). In addition, a school might offer International Baccalaureate programs at a select number of schools that would provide an option for learners who seek advanced learning across disciplines, are capable of meeting the standards for high level performance across many disciplines, and are focused on the depth of knowledge and understanding, as well as the broader projects and goals that characterize the IB program. In addition, the data from the Hertberg et al. study suggest that options within advanced classes or seminars that focus on creative productivity as goals (based on models such as the Schoolwide Enrichment Model) are necessary to meet the needs of students whose talents lie in areas of creative productivity combined with advanced cognitive abilities and motivation to go beyond the known discipline knowledge and make contributions of their own to the area of study.

The most critical concern of all schools should be to evaluate the outcomes of the options that are offered. Current research does not clearly support any one of the available options as the best or most appropriate for the achievement of the goals we have outlined for successful education for gifted students. Clearly, differences in definitions of giftedness and beliefs about giftedness, as well as the expectations and meaning of success in any community will drive the goal-setting and evaluation processes. A clear evaluation plan that has been approved by the stakeholders in the education of gifted students will be the best test of whether or not a given set of options is successful in addressing the needs of these students.

REFERENCES

Benbow, C. P. (1986). SMPY's model for teaching mathematically precocious students. In J. S. Renzulli (Ed.), *Systems and models for developing programs for the gifted and talented* (pp. 1–26). Mansfield Center, CT: Creative Learning Press.

Betts, G. T. (1985). The autonomous learner model. Greeley, CO: Autonomous Learning Publications and Specialists.

Betts, G. T. (1986). The autonomous learner model for the gifted and talented. In J. S. Renzulli (Ed.), *Systems and models for developing programs for the gifted and talented* (pp. 27–56). Mansfield Center, CT: Creative Learning Press.

Betts, G. T. (2004). Fostering autonomous learners through levels of differentiation. *Roeper Review, 26,* 190–191.

Betts, G. T., & Kercher, J. K. (2000). Appendix B: The autonomous learner model. In Kay, K. (Ed.), *Uniquely gifted: Identifying and meeting the needs of the twice-exceptional student* (pp. 356–360). Gilsum, NH: Avocus.

Burgess, R. (1990, September). *Creative and talented studies: An application of Betts' model of the autonomous learner.* Paper presented at the SAGE (Society for the Advancement of Gifted Education) Conference, Calgary, Alberta, Canada. (ERIC Document Number ED337967)

Callahan, C. M. (2003). *Advanced Placement and International Baccalaureate programs for talented students in American high schools: A focus on science and mathematics* (RM03176). Storrs, CT: University of Connecticut, National Research Center on the Gifted and Talented.

Callahan, C. M., & Hunsaker, S. (1991). Evaluation of acceleration programs. In W. T. Southern & E. D. Jones (Eds.), *The academic acceleration of gifted children* (pp. 181–206). New York: Teachers College.

Callahan, C. M., Hertberg, H. L., Kyburg, R. M., Brighton, C. M., Hench, E. P., You, H. (2005). *AP and IB programs: A fit for gifted students?* Manuscript submitted for publication.

Casserly, P. L. (1968). *Advanced Placement revisited.* New York: College Entrance Examination Board.

Center for Gifted Education (1998). *The 1940s: A decade of change. A language arts unit for high-ability learners.* Dubuque, IA: Kendall-Hunt.

College Board. (n.d.). *AP scholar awards.* Retrieved May 25, 2005, from http://apcentral.collegeboard.com/article/0,3045,150-157-0-2057,00.html#name1

Commission on Life Sciences (1990). *Fulfilling the promise: Biology education in the nation's schools.* Washington, DC: National Academy Press.

Cornell, D. G., Callahan, C. M., Bassin, L. E., & Ramsay, S. G. (1991). Affective development in accelerated students. In W. T. Southern & E. D. Jones (Eds.), *The academic acceleration of gifted children* (pp. 74–101). New York: Teachers College.

Cornell, D. G., Callahan, C. M., & Loyd, B H. (1991). Personality growth of female early college entrants: A controlled prospective study. *Gifted Child Quarterly, 35,* 135–143.

Delcourt, M. (1994). Characteristics of high-level creative productivity: A longitudinal study of students identified by Renzulli's three-ring conception of giftedness. In R. F. Subotnik & K. D. Arnold (Eds.), *Beyond Terman: Contemporary longitudinal studies of giftedness and talent* (pp. 401–436). Norwood, NJ: Ablex.

Feldhusen, J. F., & Kolloff, P. B. (1986). The Purdue three-stage enrichment model for gifted education at the elementary level. In J. S. Renzulli (Ed.), *Systems and models for developing programs for the gifted and talented* (pp. 126–152). Mansfield Center, CT: Creative Learning Press.

Feldhusen. J. F., & Poelzer, G. H. (1996). An empirical study of the achievement of International Baccalaureate students in biology, chemistry, and physics in Alberta. *Journal of Secondary Gifted Education, 8,* 28–40.

Feldhusen, J. F., & Reilly, P. (1983). The Purdue secondary model for gifted education: A multi-service program. *Journal for the Education of the Gifted, 4,* 230–244.

Feldhusen, J. F., & Robinson, A. (1986). Purdue secondary model for gifted and talented youth. In J. S. Renzulli (Ed.), *Systems and models for developing programs for the gifted and talented* (pp. 155–179). Mansfield Center, CT: Creative Learning Press.

Gehring, J. (2001, April 25). The International Baccalaureate: "Cadillac" of college prep programs. *Education Week, 20,* 19.

Grexa, T. (1988, Fall). A case for the International Baccalaureate. *The Journal of College Admissions,* 2–6.

Hertberg, H. L., Callahan, C. M., Kyburg, R. M., Brighton, C. M., Hench, E. H., & You, H. (2005). *AP and IB programs: A "fit" for gifted students?* Manuscript submitted for publication.

Hunsaker, S. L., & Callahan, C. M. (1991). Student assessment and evaluation. In W. T. Southern & E. D. Jones (Eds.), *The academic acceleration of gifted children* (pp. 207–222). New York: Teachers College.

International Baccalaureate North America. (1987). *International Baccalaureate.* New York: Author. (ERIC Document Reproduction Service No. ED285450)

International Baccalaureate Organisations (2000). *Diploma Program* [Brochure]. Geneva, Switzerland: Author.

Kolitch, E. R., & Brody, L. E. (1992). Mathematics acceleration of highly talented students: An evaluation. *Gifted Child Quarterly, 36,* 78–86.

Kulik, J. A., & Kulik, C. C. (1992). Meta-analytic findings on grouping programs. *Gifted Child Quarterly, 36,* 73–77.

Lichten, W. (2000). Whither Advanced Placement? *Educational Policy Analysis, 8*(29). Retrieved May 25, 2005, from http://epaa.asu.edu/eppa/v8n29.html

Moon, S. M. (1994). Using the Purdue three-stage model: Developing talent at the secondary level. *Journal of Secondary Gifted Education, 5,* 31–35.

Moon, S. M., Feldhusen, J. F., Powley, S., Nidiffer, L., & Whitman, M. W. (1993). Secondary applications of the Purdue three-stage model. *Gifted Child Today, 16*(3), 2–9.

Morgan, R., & Crone, C. (1993). *Advanced Placement examinees at the University of California: An examination of the freshman year courses and grads of examinees in biology, calculus, and chemistry* (Statistical Report 93-210). Princeton, NJ: Educational Testing Service.

Morgan, R., & Ramist, L. (1998). Advanced Placement students in college: An investigation of course grades at 21 colleges. Princeton, NJ: Educational Testing Service.

National Academy of Sciences (2000). *Learning and understanding: Improving advanced study of mathematics and science in US high schools.* Washington, DC: National Academy of Sciences.

Nidiffer, L., & Moon, S. M. (1994). Middle school seminars: The Purdue three-stage model provides exciting opportunities for pull-out programs. *Gifted Child Today, 17*(2), 24–27, 39, 40

Nielsen, M. E. (1985). Evaluation of a rural gifted program: Assessment of attitudes, self-concepts, and critical thinking skills of students in grades 3–12. (Doctoral dissertation, Purdue University, 1984). *Dissertation Abstracts International, 45, 3114 A.*

Noble, K. D., Robinson, N. M., & Gunderson, S. (1993). All rivers lead to the sea: A follow-up study of gifted young adults. *Roeper Review, 15,* 124–131.

Nobel, K. D., & Smyth, R. K. (1995). Keeping their talents alive: Young women's assessment of radical post-secondary acceleration. *Roeper Review, 18,* 49–55.

North Carolina School of Science and Mathematics, Department of Mathematics and Computer Science. (1988). *Matrices.* Reston, VA: National Council of Teachers of Mathematics.

Oregon University System, Oregon State Department of Education, & Office of Community College Services. (1999). *Oregon early options study.* Eugene, OR: Authors. (ERIC Document Reproduction Service No. ED 430 470)

Reis, S. M., & Renzulli, J. S. (1985). *The secondary triad model: A practical plan for implementing gifted programs at the junior and senior high level.* Mansfield Center, CT: Creative Learning Press.

Reis, S. M., & Renzulli, J. S. (1986). The secondary triad model. In J. S. Renzulli (Ed.), *Systems and models for developing programs for the gifted and talented* (pp. 216–266). Mansfield Center, CT: Creative Learning Press.

Renzulli, J. S., & Reis, S. M. (1994). Research related to the schoolwide enrichment model. *Gifted Child Quarterly, 38,* 7–20.

Southern, T. W., & Jones, E. D. (1991). Conclusions about acceleration: Echoes of debate. In T. W. Southern & E. D. Jones (Eds.), *The academic acceleration of gifted children* (pp. 223–228). New York: Teachers College.

Stanley, J. C. (1978). SMPY's DT-PI model. Diagnostic testing followed by prescriptive instruction. *ITYB, 4*(10), 7–8.

Stanley, J. C. (1979). How to use a fast-pacing math mentor. *ITBY, 5*(6), 1–2.

VanTassel-Baska, J. (1995). The development of talent through curriculum. *Roeper Review 18,* 98–102.

VanTassel-Baska, J., Bass, G., Ries, R., Poland, D., & Avery, L. D. (1998). A national study of science curriculum effectiveness with high-ability students. *Gifted Child Quarterly, 42,* 200–211.

VanTassel-Baska, J., Johnson, D. T., Hughes, C., & Boyce, L. N. (1996). A study of language arts curriculum effectiveness with gifted learners. *Journal for the Education of the Gifted, 19,* 461–480.

VanTassel-Baska, J., Zuo, L., Avery, L. D., & Little, C. A. (2002). A curriculum study of gifted-student learning in the language arts. *Gifted Child Quarterly, 46,* 30–44.

Extracurricular Activities

by Eric Calvert
& Eric Cleveland

Extracurricular activities are organized student activities not generally considered part of the regular school curriculum. Sports and arts programs are the most well-known extracurricular activities. Small towns and suburbs in Texas are famous (and sometimes notorious) for their devotion to their high school football teams, where crowds and facilities match or surpass those of many universities elsewhere in the country. In Indiana, high school basketball is followed with such intensity that many television stations extend their late news broadcasts on Friday nights to allow time to cover high school scores and highlights. Similarly, school music and theatre programs have long been a part of the cultural lives of their communities. Perhaps sports and arts activities come first to mind among extracurricular activities because they are often spectator-friendly; attract local news coverage; and provide opportunities for parents, alumni, and community members to maintain connections to the school.

However, the typical middle or high school also supports dozens of other activities, such as clubs organized around areas of academic interest (e.g., math clubs), service organizations (e.g., Key Club), honor societies, advocacy organizations (e.g., environmental issue clubs), religious groups, and hobby clubs. For example, the high school alma mater of one author of this chapter includes a directory of 16 interscholastic sports teams and 19 different clubs. Activities range from National Honor Society to "Goth Club," which lists its club goal as, "To conform to nonconformity," and then states that "Membership is open to all students who wear black. See Mr. Hughes or a Goth Club member" (Belton High School, n.d.). Clearly schools are devoting significant staff time and resources to providing such a range of extracurricular options. But, does all this activity contribute to academic achievement or provide other benefits to students?

GENERAL EFFECTS

Many researchers have explored the academic, social and emotional, and talent development effects of extracurricular programs on students. However, because extracurricular offerings are so varied, there are few broadly generalizable studies. Further, few studies have examined extracurricular activities through the lens of gifted education. Nonetheless, the body of research on student participation in extracurricular activities is generally positive, and studies exploring the effects of extracurricular participation on gifted students specifically have also been encouraging.

In studies of heterogeneous secondary school populations, positive correlations have been found between extracurricular participation during the secondary grades and a variety of positive short- and long-term outcomes. For example, Zaff, Moore, Papillo and Williams (2003) reported that participation in extracurricular activities was associated with academic achievement, likelihood of attending college, likelihood of voting, and likelihood of volunteering.

Some critics of extracurricular activities have questioned whether after-school activities draw students' energy and focus away from academics. However, there is little empirical evidence to suggest that extracurricular participation is academically harmful to students. Rather, Gerber (1996) found that participation in extracurricular activities was associated with academic achievement among eighth grade students, and concluded that participation in extracurricular activities was not academically harmful. Positive effects of extracurricular participation have also been found in the gifted population. For example, Renzulli and Park (2000) evaluated the National Education Longitudinal Study (NELS) of 1998 data and found that gifted dropouts participated less in extracurricular activities than gifted students who were not dropouts.

Others have noted that extracurricular activities provide training opportunities in specific talent areas in an environment where achievement is generally valued. Further, extracurricular activities may provide opportunities for some students to develop skills that can be applied to the pursuit of goals in a variety of areas. Csikszentmihalyi, Rathunde, and Whalen (1993) assert there is a set of "metaskills" that enables talent to develop. Essential metaskills include the development of attention management, emotional self-regulation, and intrinsic enjoyment of work and activities related to the student's talent. Extracurricular activities that develop these metaskills may facilitate talent development in participating students of potential.

If the value of extracurricular activities is to be enhanced for gifted students, it is worth exploring how extracurricular activities influence student development. Because most extracurricular activities involve individual goals, group or team goals, and a social aspect, it is logical to suspect that participation in extracurricular activities influences students in a variety of ways. These influences may be both direct and indirect.

For example, Horvat, Weininger, and Lareau (2003) suggest that some of the benefits of extracurricular participation for students may relate to the effect their participation has on their parents. These researchers hypothesize that in the course of facilitating students' participation in extracurricular activities, parents enhance their social networks and learn about additional educational opportunities and resources for their children by word of mouth, often from other parents. The opportunity to observe their children outside the home may provide parents with additional insights about their children. Additionally, witnessing their children succeed may reinforce the parents' efforts in supporting the development of the child's talents.

Others have suggested that "activity" is the key concept in the benefits of extracurricular activity participation. Milgram (2003) classified extracurricular activities as "active," in comparison to passive activities such as watching television. Passive activities are, by nature, unchallenging and are rarely goal-directed. Therefore, they are comparatively less stimulating and do not provide students with opportunities for challenge and growth. Milgram's study suggests that participating in challenging and creative activities in a talent area can lead to real accomplishments in adulthood in the domain of the activity. Regardless of one's views on the innateness of talent potential, there is near universal accord in the talent development literature that achieving at the highest levels in a talent area invariably involves training, practice, and challenging experiences.

Unfortunately, for many gifted teens, school is seldom optimally challenging. Extracurricular activities may provide opportunities for challenge that may be lacking in the regular school curriculum. Competitive activities, when similarly talented competitors are available, are inherently challenging, requiring students to continuously train and improve in order to match and best their competitors who are also working to improve their performance. Talented teenagers in Csikszentmihalyi et al.'s (1993) study often reported that extracurricular activities were the most engaging part of school life. The authors suggest extracurricular activities provide opportunities for accomplishment with interesting and appropriate challenges. These challenges may reinforce a talented student's motivation to participate and encourage further growth and the desire to take on still greater challenges as the student attains goals and experiences success.

Others have suggested that the social aspects of extracurricular participation influence positive outcomes, perhaps by helping students feel more connected to the school and to peers. For example, team membership emphasizes the similarities between students and involves shared commitment that contributes to a sense of belonging (Janos & Robinson, 1985). Shared goals and common competitors can help form social bonds between members of teams, clubs, and organizations. In

American high schools, this concept of membership is echoed by the fact that students' social identities among their peers are often largely defined by the activities in which they participate. While cliques vary from school to school, groups designated "jocks," "drama geeks," and "band kids" (or some variation of the preceding) are common. Beyond simply identifying where a given student is likely to be found after the last bell of the day, these terms have socially important connotative meanings. Uniforms, slogans, initiation rites, team rituals, and shared successes and defeats all serve to reinforce this sense of membership. Teams and clubs also provide students with almost instant social networks, so it should not be surprising that friendships often develop from, and revolve around, extracurricular activities.

Many effective coaches and activity sponsors take good advantage of the bonds and sense of commitment that can be formed by shared experiences in activities to help students succeed. For example, in a qualitative study of high-ability male students in an urban high school, Hébert's (2000) academically successful subjects seemed to gain a sense of accomplishment from participation in extracurricular activities and benefited from opportunities to develop their talents. The students named coaches and club sponsors as important role models within and beyond the context of the sport or activity. For gifted students in economically distressed communities plagued by crime and violence, positive adult role models may be essential in successfully navigating youth and young adulthood. For students who lack positive role models in the home, a caring coach or activity sponsor who provides support and encouragement may help protect students from a variety of possible negative outcomes. Additionally, competition might provide needed challenges for gifted students from populations too often viewed with lowered expectations.

TYPES OF EXTRACURRICULAR ACTIVITIES

The extracurricular activities offered in public schools across the United States are extremely varied. Due to this variety it is reasonable to expect that different activities will attract students with different interests, abilities, and goals, resulting in different participation outcomes. To facilitate a discussion of these diverse outcomes, we will divide the universe of extracurricular activities into four categories: academic clubs and competitions, leadership and service activities, visual and performing arts activities, and athletic activities.

Academic Clubs and Competitions

Academic clubs and competitions are enrichment and talent development opportunities related to academic domains. Math leagues, science fairs and Olympiads, Model United Nations programs, mock trials, computer clubs, debate teams, video production clubs, and student newspapers are examples of academic clubs and competitions. A survey of gifted students in grades 4–11 found that math clubs and competitions were the most popular academic extracurricular activity among gifted students (Olszewski-Kubilius & Lee, 2004).

McNeal (1998) found that students who participated in extracurricular activities outperformed their peers on quantitative measures of academic success. Higher academic achievement and higher educational expectations are less consistently associated with involvement in extracurricular athletics than non-sports-related extracurricular activities. Academic achievement, ambition, and participation in nonathletic extracurricular activities are positively associated (Guest & Schneider, 2003). However, there are conflicting findings in the research on the benefits of academic extracurricular activities. For example, minority female students in the general population involved in science competitions, academic clubs, speech and drama, and leadership organizations reported higher grades than minority female students who did not participate in such activities (Lisella & Serwatka, 1996). However, Lisella and Serwatka did not find evidence of academic benefits to participation in most extracurricular activities for minority male students. Rifner and Feldhusen (1997) found in a small study of junior high chess club participants that involvement in the club improved students' skill at chess and had a modest but positive effect on participants' scores on an unrelated problem-solving task.

This variability in research findings is not unexpected considering the variety and variability of extracurricular programs. In most public schools, curriculum and instruction are heavily influenced by official curriculum standards and the content of standardized state assessments. However, even with these influences that should make schools more similar, there is still tremendous variability in the progress of students in some schools compared to others. It should be expected that the quality and impact of extracurricular activities would vary even more widely since comparatively few standards guide extracurricular programs and there is far less effort expended in evaluation. Additionally, where teacher licensure requirements ensure a minimal level of training for regular classroom teachers, extracurricular programs typically have no such requirements, so the level of training and expertise of coaches and activity sponsors can also be expected to vary widely.

It is likely that some high quality extracurricular activities promote academic achievement and talent development while low quality extracurricular activities do not. In addition to investigating whether extracurricular activities are beneficial to students, future research should focus on identifying the characteristics of high quality extracurricular activities. It may also be useful to survey the needs and interests of gifted teens so that extracurricular activities can be molded to more deliberately complement and supplement the curriculum.

In addition to influencing academic achievement, participation in extracurricular activities may have social and emotional effects on students. Gross (1998) noted that gifted children, like all children, have a desire for companionship that may sometimes conflict with their strong achievement motivation. Gifted students may sometimes hide or deny their gifts to win peer acceptance (Swiatek, 1995). Therefore, challenging activities that value the abilities of the gifted student, while providing opportunities for companionship and collaboration, can be ideal for gifted students. Goldstein and Wagner (1993) note that academic competitions give students opportunities to meet and interact with "equally able" students.

Additionally, extracurricular activities provide an easier and safer point of entry to the social life of the school for particularly introverted students or for gifted students who feel different from their peers due to their advanced abilities. Cross and Dixon (1998) note that involvement in extracurricular activities by gifted students in rural schools helps gifted students be seen and treated as individuals rather than just the embodiments of their academic gifts. However, earlier studies (West, 1996) also noted that gifted students in rural settings sometimes feel intellectually isolated and may cope by reading voraciously. While reading provides intellectual benefits, it is also a socially isolating activity. After-school interest-based book clubs that encourage socialization around reading may thus be more beneficial for gifted students. Considering the recent rise in popularity of book clubs, particularly among women, schools should consider assessing student interest in extracurricular activities related to reading and creative writing.

Because of their advanced interests and abilities, gifted students often prefer the companionship of older students to the company of same age peers (Janos & Robinson, 1985). For middle school and early high school students, extracurricular activities often provide opportunities for interaction and friendship with older students that may be unavailable in the classroom environment, particularly in schools that offer few opportunities for accelerated course placement.

For example, interscholastic debate is an intellectually demanding activity that requires strategic thinking, the ability to analyze, synthesize, and critique information, as well as verbal fluency and interpersonal skill. Collaborating with teammates in preparation and during competition provides opportunities for social companionship in an environment where peers value, rather than belittle, the abilities of gifted students. Additionally, Silverman (1993) notes that gifted students often develop concerns about local and global issues before their age peers, which can cause social difficulties. Therefore, activities like debate and Model United Nations programs may provide venues for gifted students to study and discuss complex issues that concern them.

Gifted students are often very competitive in regards to grades. While this concern for academic success is generally positive, when taken to the extreme, concern for grades may limit students' willingness to take a challenging course in a topic that is new to them or is outside their perceived area of strength. Obviously, this limits opportunities for growth. Silverman (1993) has noted that gifted students sometimes suffer from a "fear of failure." Extracurricular activities may provide opportunities for students to explore novel fields without having to worry that their grade point average will suffer if they do not excel.

Academic extracurricular activities that provide opportunities for career exploration may be particularly valuable. Greene (2003) argues that career counseling focuses almost exclusively on getting into college and that more needs to be done to provide opportunities for career exploration, including consideration of the broader lifestyles associated with prospective careers. A few organizations, such as the Future Educators of America, explicitly focus on students' exploration of a particular career path. Additional school-based career focused activities include mentorships and internships. Feldhusen (1995) criticized the lack of availability of high quality vocational talent development opportunities for gifted students oriented towards areas like agriculture and industrial technology, saying that vocational programs are often a "'dumping ground' for weak students" (p. 62). Competitions in these areas may give gifted vocational students opportunities to find a more appropriate level of challenge and opportunities to share ideas with other talented peers.

Leadership and Service Activities

Service learning and leadership development programs have been growing in popularity in recent years. These programs typically have a broader focus than other academic activities focusing on specific academic domains. The prevalence of volunteerism and participation in public service among members of the "Millennium Generation" has been widely noted in the popular media. This has often been attributed to a desire to make a contribution to society by a generation that is assumed to be mistrustful of the motives and ability of elected officials and established institutions to create positive change. Indeed, one survey of entering college freshman found that 83% had participated in some form of volunteer work during high school (Higher Education Research Institute, 2003). School-based service programs may be helping to fuel this trend.

Service projects have long been a component of student honors organizations such as the National Honor Society. More recently, service-focused clubs have emerged with specific focus areas. For example, in some school computer clubs, talented students donate their time to develop and maintain Web sites for nonprofit agencies or refurbish damaged equipment to be donated to charitable organizations or disadvantaged individuals. Because gifted teens are often highly idealistic, empathetic, and concerned with global problems, leadership and service organizations may be highly attractive to them. Further, because of their talents and intellect, many gifted teens are capable of making real and significant contributions to their communities at an early age. Additionally, competition plays a diminished role in service and leadership organizations in comparison to sports and academic competitions. While competition is not significantly harmful for most students, service organizations may provide opportunities for the involvement of students who prefer noncompetitive activities. Finally, for gifted students who are bored with, and disconnected from, the regular curriculum, service activities may provide opportunities for learning that seems relevant, in contrast to the regular curriculum that may seem unchallenging and irrelevant.

Few studies have been conducted specifically focusing on gifted students' involvement in leadership and service activities. However, because of the powerful mutual benefits possible to both gifted students and their communities, ways to integrate service and leadership opportunities with principles of gifted education should be explored. For example, Terry's (2003) qualitative study of a service learning program for gifted students in Georgia found that participation in the program contributed to positive attitudes such as a sense of accomplishment, pride, and respect for the community. Notably, the Georgia program integrated instruction on the Creative Problem Solving (CPS) model, long popular in gifted enrichment curricula, and attempted to have students work through the steps of the CPS model to address a real community problem.

While the research in this area is promising, more is needed to determine all possible effects on gifted students of this kind of extracurricular involvement and to identify ways to maximize the benefits of participation. Exploring the application of strategies for differentiating instruction in the general curriculum to extracurricular service programs might be a useful starting point for this line of research. Service activities might also be effective settings for developing leadership talent.

Visual and Performing Arts Activities

Extracurricular activities in the visual and performing arts can provide valuable talent development opportunities for creatively and artistically gifted students. Many schools, faced with tight budgets and a renewed national focus on achievement in so-called "core" academic content areas, have eliminated or scaled back formal arts programs and opportunities for creative expression during the regular school day. Therefore, for students in these schools, participating in extracurricular arts activities may be the only school-based option for exploring their interests and cultivating their talent. This is particularly true for students from families who cannot afford to support the development of students' talents outside of school by enrolling the student in dance studio classes, music lessons, drama workshops, or arts-focused summer camps.

The downsizing of arts programs is unfortunate as numerous studies have documented the positive effects of artistic activities on academic achievement and social and emotional development among students from populations with limited outside opportunities. For example, Lisella and Serwatka (1996) found that minority girls who participated in music, art, speech, or drama reported higher grade point averages than minority female students who did not participate in these activities. McLaughlin (1993) reported that urban teenagers who participated in extracurricular activities that produced a product or performance enhanced students' sense of self.

In addition to general academic and psychological benefits, participation in quality extracurricular arts activities can develop students' abilities in the area of artistic activity. For example, some creative students find competitions and formal recognition of their work motivating (Piirto, 1998), encouraging them to devote increased time and effort in developing their talents. However, arts activities may also be attractive to students who do not enjoy competition. For example, apart from the casting process, participation in a school play is largely noncompetitive, at least in the sense that no students are deemed winners or losers at the final curtain. Nonetheless, as in competitive activities, participation in theatre still provides the experience of collaborating with peers and working together toward a shared goal.

Athletic Activities

It is often asserted that school sports programs help prevent students from "dropping out." However, Melnick, Sabo, and Vanfossen (1992) found conflicting data in regards to this belief. They reported positive relationships between athletic participation and graduation for some groups in rural and suburban schools, but found no differences in dropout rates between athletes and non-athletes in urban schools. Athletic activities appear to have more modest effects on academic achievement than nonathletic activities. McNeal (1998) found that participation in extracurricular athletics was not associated with high academic achievement.

Nonetheless, there is little data to suggest that participation in athletic activities negatively impacts academic performance. That extracurricular activities seem to correspond with academic achievement, whereas athletic extracurricular activities show little effect may be due to the fact that students who are already academically successful are most likely to be recruited to participate in math competitions, science Olympiads, and debate. Ellis, Riley, and Gordon's (2003) study of athletically talented females found that the athletes valued their athletic ability and participation in sports, but generally felt that academic performance should be a higher priority than athletic achievement.

However, there may be excellent reasons for intellectually and creatively gifted students to participate in sports. The physical fitness of school-aged children has become a topic of great interest in the media and among public health researchers. A lack of physical activity among youth has been cited as a leading cause of the alarming increase in health problems like obesity and diabetes among children and young adults. Additionally, regular exercise provides benefits related to managing stress, regulating sleep, and managing depression. High quality athletic programs can provide opportunities and motivation for increasing physical activity, which can yield physical and psychological benefits.

Aside from the well-documented health benefits of regular exercise, sports may provide opportunities for positive social interaction. In a study of talented female athletes (Ellis et al., 2003), participants listed opportunities to meet new peers, team affiliation, social opportunities at games and tournaments, and being connected with a peer group with similar interests and abilities as benefits of participation. However, 70% of the research participants reported feeling uncomfortable displaying their talents in front of peers, and 39% disagreed or strongly disagreed that athletic talent has positive effects on friendships.

Additionally, participation in sports may provide opportunities for gifted students to gain attention for something other than academic success. In some school environments, athletic achievements may enhance the standing of a student in the school social hierarchy. Guest and Schneider (2003) suggested that the social benefits of participation in sports may vary depending on the circumstances of the student or the culture of the school. For example, students in lower income communities valued sports as a way to experience success, and more often saw sports as a possible path to upward mobility than students in wealthier communities. Participants in

"Nerds" versus "Jocks"

The statistics on gifted adolescents' participation in extracurricular activities do not support the popular stereotypes of weak, bookish nerds or meathead jocks. Participation in sports was the most frequently reported extracurricular activity in a survey of gifted students (Olsezeski-Kubilius & Lee, 2004). Nonetheless, the stereotype of gifted students as "nerds" persists in school culture and influences the self-concepts and behavior of some gifted students. Many adolescent girls admit to sometimes hiding their abilities so they can "fit in," (Kerr, 1985), and Brown and Steinberg (1990) have argued that some gifted students participate in athletics partly to draw attention away from their academic accomplishments and win peer acceptance.

Hébert's (2000) study of intelligent urban male students often identified coaches as important mentors and role models.

Sports seem to provide natural opportunities to teach strategic thinking, build leadership skills, and develop persistence, resilience, and work ethic. It would be interesting to explore employing a "differentiated" training program for bright athletes that emphasized the strategies of their sports, organizational leadership, performance psychology, and physiological principles of physical training that would allow them to develop their intellectual gifts while participating in athletic programs. This may also help athletic programs overcome the perception of some that athletic activities are anti-intellectual (Ellis et al., 2003) and encourage a school atmosphere that values knowledge and intellectual talent.

COMPETITION

While caring parents and educators worry about students' stress levels and self-esteem, there is little evidence to support the idea that the competition typical in competitive extracurricular activities and sports is significantly harmful to most students. Many gifted students enjoy and are motivated by competition and benefit from competitive activities when the desire to win is kept in perspective.

Gifted students may participate in competitive extracurricular activities in part as a way to measure their own abilities and monitor their own progress (Udvari & Schneider, 2000). In a single subject qualitative study, Lee (2002) found that the friends of a gifted adolescent male were seen as competitors, as well as role models and supporters. Friendly competition seemed to motivate the boys to work and practice and did not have obvious negative effects. Academic competition may have similar effects (Rizza & Reis, 2001). Students benefit from opportunities to compare their abilities against talented peers, which may motivate them to study, practice, or train harder in order to improve.

In addition to increasing motivation, participation in a competitive activity can have social benefits for many students. Competition with an "other" (such as rival high school across town) can help build a sense of community and friendship among team members. Gifted students are disproportionately introverts who spend a greater proportion of their time in solitude (Csikszentmihalyi et al., 1993), and often have unusual interests and hobbies. Because of these characteristics, some gifted youth have difficulty meeting new peers and forging new friendships. Extracurricular activities may provide opportunities for such students to find peers who share their interests, and working with their peers toward shared goals can help the students form enjoyable social bonds.

However, excessive competitiveness may be unhealthy. Competition may be extremely stressful for children for whom competitive achievement defines self-esteem, and for students who exhibit a dysfunctional degree of perfectionism. There is a significant difference between training to achieve challenging goals and training out of fear of finishing second. Rimm (1986) suggested that competition contributes to underachievement in students who do not handle competition well, possibly to hide their abilities and lower the expectations of others for their performance.

While some students may be troubled by the risk of failing to achieve their own goals in competitive events, some gifted students may be worried about the costs of success. First, gifted adolescents sometimes deliberately hide their intellectual ability to better fit in with their peers. Therefore, some may be embarrassed by the attention that earning awards in activities not socially valued in the peer group might bring.

Second, many gifted teens are highly empathetic and may be concerned about hurting the feelings of their opponents. For example, in a qualitative study of gifted girls in an academically rigorous parochial school, Rizza & Reis (2001) found that students perceived head-to-head competition with their peers as negative, with some being "conflicted" about participating in competitive activities. The authors concluded that competition can increase student motivation, but may also cause problems in relationships between students. They also noted that the girls involved in their study sometimes used informal friendly competition as a way to encourage and support their peers.

Rimm (1986) suggests that competition can be a positive experience if parents and teachers emphasize individual achievement and improvement rather than winning and losing. Research has suggested that individuals who attribute achievement to a combination of ability and effort are the most successful (Powers & Wagner, 1984). Therefore, schools can help ensure that competition is healthy by helping students set challenging but attainable goals, celebrating excellence and progress, emphasizing mutual support and sportsmanship, and helping students attribute successes and failures in psychologically adaptive ways.

EXTRACURRICULAR ACTIVITIES IN THE COLLEGE PORTFOLIO

It should be noted that, in addition to enjoying participating in activities and benefiting from the opportunities for learning, many students who hope to attend highly competitive colleges and universities after graduation join clubs and teams in part to build an impressive college application. Guest and Schneider (2003) note that, in schools where most students are expected to go on to college after they graduate, non-sports activities are likely to be viewed in part as opportunities for "portfolio building," whereas extracurricular sports are less valued as experiences that help lay a foundation for future success.

Schneider and Stevenson (1999) suggested that ambitious adolescents can feel pressured by the perceived need to engage in "portfolio building" through participation in a significant number of extracurricular activities. For example, the lead author of this chapter saw this phenomenon vividly displayed on the day yearbooks were distributed to students in a predominately middle class high school. At the back of yearbook was an index of students' names organized alphabetically. Next to each name was a listing of the pages on which a picture that included the student appeared. Most students simply used the index to find their pictures and pictures of their friends. However, the most competitive students used the number of pages upon which a student's picture appeared as a rough measure of accomplishment, and would count the number of page references for themselves and their peers as though the index was a scorecard. The more clubs, sports teams, and activities a student participated in, the higher his or her page count "score," a rough quantitative measure of achievement.

This is not to say that students who sample a variety of activities are necessarily trying to pad their college applications. Students who are extremely concerned with maintaining a high grade point average may avoid signing up for courses in new topics of interest out of fear of earning low grades when they are novices in the subject. Extracurricular activities may provide a "safe" way for academically competitive gifted students to explore new fields of study without jeopardizing their academic class rankings. For example, a student could decide to attend a few meetings of a foreign language club before signing up for an actual course in the language to sample the material and determine whether the class would be a good fit.

Nonetheless, because many gifted students are concerned with being admitted to selective colleges, it may be useful to investigate what influence extracurricular participation is likely to have on admissions officials at colleges and universities of interest. While different colleges have different priorities, generally speaking, participation in extracurricular activities can give students an edge in the competition for admission to highly selective colleges and universities.

However, in recent years, college admissions officers have shifted from seeking students with extremely broad extracurricular experiences to valuing students whose experiences show commitment, persistence, and depth in narrower areas of interest (College Board, n.d.). The College Board's Web site now advises that

> admission officials are more likely to consider an applicant who is very committed to one or two activities, rather than a student who has taken on too many activities and has not shown serious commitment to any single one. Colleges want students who can bring unique skills and interests to the student body. The emphasis should be on quality, not quantity, and depth, not breadth. (¶ 5)

Similarly, the online Princeton Review (n.d.) advises students to sample a wide variety of activities in the ninth grade, and then narrow down extracurricular participation to the activities the student finds most enjoyable and challenging. Admissions officials now prefer students who show a record of achievement or hold leadership positions in a small number of activities in comparison to students who are superficially involved in a large number of activities.

Further, students who are applying to a specific college program of study, or for a scholarship awarded for potential or achievement in a specific domain, may benefit from participating in extracurricular activities related to that domain. For example, a student interested in applying for an engineering program or scholarship might benefit from participating in activities like science Olympiads, math clubs and competitions, technical theatre, or even involvement with Habitat for Humanity, a volunteer organization that builds and remodels affordable homes for low income families.

Finally, while extracurricular participation is certainly considered in college admissions and scholarship applications, consideration of extracurricular activity is usually secondary to consideration of test scores and transcripts. Therefore, students should select extracurricular activities based primarily on personal interest and enjoyment, rather than the impact their participation might have on an admissions counselor in the future. Gifted students should focus first on succeeding in challenging course work. Taking on a hectic schedule of extracurricular activities may be counterproductive if a student has to take low level, unchallenging classes to keep grades up and homework load down to cope with a large number of nonacademic commitments. A high school transcript showing good grades, Advanced Placement coursework, and four years of challenging math, science, and language arts courses, but only a handful of extracurricular activities, will usually be more attractive to competitive colleges than a transcript showing dozens of extracurricular activities but less rigorous course work.

FINDING BALANCE

Wes Anderson's 1998 film *Rushmore* is a coming of age film about Max Fischer, a creative and ambitious gifted young man who is the only son of a widower who operates a barbershop. Max attends an elite prep school on a scholarship he earned by writing a play and becomes heavily involved in extracurricular activities. An expository montage early in the film shows glimpses of Max's extracurricular involvement, which includes serving as president of the French club, the ambassador from Russia for the Model United Nations, stamp and coin club president, lacrosse team manager, calligraphy club president, astronomy society founder, fencing team captain, junior varsity decathlon competitor, 2nd chorale choir master, the founder of the "Bombardment Society" (an intramural dodge ball league), Kung Fu Club yellow belt, Trap and Skeet Club Founder, Rushmore Beekeeper's president, Yankee Racers (go-kart club) founder, Max Fischer Players director, Piper Cub (aviation) club member, and wrestling team alternate. Max is portrayed as a daydreamer in classes, but thrives in extracurricular activities—until he finds himself on "sudden death academic probation" due to chronically low grades.

While Max's extracurricular involvement is obviously a fictitious exaggeration, many gifted students do become involved in dozens of extracurricular activities. While the effects of participation in extracurricular activities are generally considered to be positive, it is possible to have "too much of a good thing." In helping students choose extracurricular activities, parents and educators should have realistic expectations for the mental and physical endurance of talented youth. For example, teens typically need more sleep than adults to function optimally. The National Sleep Foundation (2000) recommends that adolescents sleep between 8.5 and 9.25 hours per night for optimal performance, but reports that, on average, American teens sleep just over 7 hours per night on weeknights. Sleep deficits can have serious consequences for teens. A lack of quality sleep can lead to decreased short-term memory, can negatively affect mood, and can make it more difficult to focus and concentrate. Considering these effects, it is not surprising that students with low grade point averages are disproportionately likely to have irregular sleep patterns.

In addition to an increased need for sleep of teenagers in general, gifted students often need more "alone time" than non-gifted students. In their study of talented teenagers, Csikszentmihalyi et al. (1993) found that teens do spend approximately 20% more time in solitude than average peers. As students enter middle and high schools where more extracurricular activities are available to them, it may be prudent to start with participation in just a few activities and then monitor the student's ability to manage the time and responsibilities that go along with the activities. If the student is able to manage participation in the activities without significant compromises related to academic work, sleep, physical and psychological health, and other priorities, then it seems reasonable to allow the student to add additional activities to his or her schedule.

Feldhusen and Wood (1997) argue for the inclusion of extracurricular activities in "growth plans" for gifted students, suggest students choose clubs and activities related to their talents, and specifically recommend math, debate, and drama clubs, as well as the Future Problem Solving program. Further, Moon (2003) has argued that developing time management skills and learning how to set appropriate goals and monitor progress are important parts of developing one's talents and converting potential to achievement. Participation in a variety of extracurricular activities may facilitate learning these skills. The experience of having to manage time and set priorities while parental supervision and support are available may better prepare students for the college environment, where students have greater responsibilities for managing their own schedules and ensuring work gets done without parents there to exhort and encourage them.

Parents and teachers have an important role to play in helping students learn to set priorities and manage commitments. Because gifted students are often strong in a variety of areas and have diverse interests, they are frequently recruited by coaches and teachers to participate in a variety of activities. Due to the departmentalized nature of many secondary schools, coaches and teachers may unintentionally contribute to overloading a gifted student by adding time demands and responsibilities because they are unaware of an individual student's other commitments. Schools may help gifted students by developing systems to monitor students' participation in activities so coaches and activity sponsors can be sensitive to the demands on students' time. Parents of gifted students can help by encouraging involvement in extracurricular activities while helping their children develop strategies for time management, discussing priorities, and by monitoring the mental and physical well-being of active gifted students.

EXTRACURRICULAR ACTIVITIES AND GIFTED STUDENTS: RECOMMENDATIONS FOR EDUCATORS

To summarize, in order to best serve gifted students in extracurricular activities, the research literature suggests the following:

1. *Provide a variety of extracurricular options, including a variety of academically and artistically oriented extracurricular activities.* Extracurricular activities that provide opportunities for intellectual challenge and creative expression can be particularly attractive and beneficial to gifted students, although many gifted students also enjoy and benefit from participating in athletic activities. Math and science related activities are particularly popular with gifted students, as are speech and debate programs and visual and performing arts programs. However, schools should not use the provision of a variety of extracurricular opportunities as a substitute for providing appropriate challenges for gifted students in the regular curriculum.

2. *Encourage gifted students to participate in extracurricular activities.* Participation in appropriate extracurricular activities can benefit gifted students by providing talent development opportunities, increasing connectedness to the school community, and improving the student's profile for college admissions and scholarship applications. Educators may need to actively recruit and encourage some gifted teens to participate, particularly those students who are more introverted or who are reluctant to display their abilities due to negative experiences in the past. Schools should also value accomplishment and celebrate student achievements. Creating an environment in which students' abilities and achievements are acknowledged and valued is crucial for developing talents through extracurricular activities (Ellis et al., 2003).

3. *Facilitate the involvement of at-risk gifted students.* While most gifted students are socially and academically successful, a significant number feel alienated from their peers and schools. Gifted students exist in every population, income level, and type of neighborhood, and are not immune to the effects of family problems, crime, poverty, pregnancy, or other factors that increase the risk of dropping out. Renzulli and Park (2000) advocate maintaining and expanding extracurricular options and offering specific encouragement to gifted students at risk of dropping out. Gifted boys, particularly minority gifted boys, are at a much greater risk of dropping out than gifted girls. Finding new ways to engage gifted boys, particularly in academic extracurricular activities, may help address this issue.

Removing economic barriers to participation may also be necessary. Affluent students are more likely to participate in extracurricular activities than less affluent students. This may be because students from lower income families, particularly boys, are often called on to work wage earning jobs to help the family provide basic necessities. Other gifted teens may be responsible for providing after school childcare to younger siblings. Additional barriers may include a lack of reliable transportation or a lack of money to cover the direct costs of participating in an activity, such as purchasing or renting clothing and equipment. These barriers may be growing more significant as an increasing number of schools are instituting "pay to play" policies that require students to pay a fee for participation in extracurricular activities to help school systems defray the costs of transportation, supplies, and coaching stipends. Because many at-risk gifted students are from economically disadvantaged families, schools may need to find ways to subsidize and facilitate the involvement of lower income gifted students in extracurricular activities. Educators may also need to identify local barriers to participation and find creative solutions to address them.

4. *Monitor and advise students.* School districts should periodically evaluate extracurricular offerings. Part of the evaluation should examine which students are participating and which students may be opting out of, or being excluded from, extracurricular involvement. First, barriers to participation should be identified and addressed. These barriers may be financial, cultural, perceptual, or issues of scheduling. Second, schools should determine whether the menu of extracurricular offerings should be modified or expanded to match the current needs and interests of students. Finally, schools should endeavor to measure the academic, social, and talent development effects of extracurricular programs to ensure that students have positive and healthy experiences in these activities. (See Table 1 for additional recommendations.)

Students should be encouraged to document their participation in extracurricular activities. Artifacts of a student's extracurricular involvement, such as awards, certificates, statistics, news clippings, training logs, photographs, and video recordings can be excellent portfolio items. Talent development portfolios allow students to see evidence of their own growth, measure progress toward long-term goals, reflect on their interests and abilities, and help them prepare for college entrance and scholarship applications.

Future Directions

More research is needed on the effects of participation in extracurricular activities on gifted youth. Because research findings have found varying effects in studies of extracurricular participation, it is also clear that research is needed to identify the essential characteristics of *high quality* extracurricular activities. At the local level, schools should develop and implement ongoing evaluation processes to monitor and improve the quality of extracurricular activities and to regularly update the "menu" of extracurricular offerings to match the changing needs and interests of students. The field of gifted education should expand its focus to assist coaches and club spon-

Table 1
Recommendations for Coaches and Club Sponsors for Meeting the Needs of Gifted Youth

Type of Activity	Recommendations
Academic activities	• Encourage broad participation, and avoid overlooking potential participants in populations traditionally underrepresented in gifted programs. • Provide opportunities for participation in events and competitions that allow students to apply subject-specific knowledge to solving authentic, open-ended problems. • Recognize and celebrate the progress and accomplishments of students. • Help students develop specific goals and plans for improvement. • Monitor the stress level and well being of students.
Athletic activities	• Help students develop specific goals and plans for improvement. • Engage bright students by involving them in developing strategy, managing the team, analyzing statistics, or evaluating potential competitors. • Manage perceptions of competition. Set high standards for ethical sportsmanship. • Emphasize the importance of improvement over winning. • Document student progress and celebrate individual improvement and team accomplishment. • Monitor and emphasize dedication to academics, address anti-intellectual stereotypes of athletes, and emphasize the importance of the mental aspects of the sport to overall success.
Leadership and service activities	• Provide opportunities for students to develop and exhibit leadership skills. • Take advantage of opportunities to teach problem solving, management skills, and communication skills through service projects. • Recognize that gifted students are often highly empathetic and idealistic and may "carry the weight of the world" at an early age. Provide these students with authentic opportunities to make a difference while helping them develop realistic expectations. • Provide opportunities for students to reflect on their activities and evaluate their efforts. • Help students set realistic goals and develop plans. • Recognize and celebrate individual and group accomplishments.
Artistic activities	• Provide opportunities for student exposure to a variety of visual and performing arts experiences. • Participate in regional competitions and exhibitions to provide students with opportunities to interact with peers who have similar interests and abilities. • Expose students to the history, theory, criticism, and social relevance of their art form. • Look for talent in students from populations traditionally underrepresented in gifted programs. • Provide opportunities for mentorship and career counseling for students highly talented in the arts. • Recognize and celebrate accomplishments in the arts. Work to develop a school culture in which artistic achievements are valued.

sors in applying principles of talent development in extracurricular activities. Finally, as the American high school becomes a focus of educational reform efforts, the place of extracurricular activities in the school experience should be carefully considered in the conversation of change.

ORGANIZATIONS AND RESOURCES ON THE WEB

Academic

4-H	http://www.4-h.org
American Computer Science League	http://www.acsl.org
Destination Imagination	http://www.destinationimagination.org
Future Educators of America	http://www.pdkintl.org/fea
Future Problem Solving Program	http://www.fpsp.org
MathCounts	http://www.mathcounts.org
Model United Nations	http://www.nhsmun.org
National Forensic League	http://www.nflonline.org
National History Day	Nationalhistoryday.org
Science Olympiad	http://www.soinc.org
Thinkquest	http://www.thinkquest.org
U.S. Academic Decathlon	http://www.usad.org

Service and Leadership

Amnesty International	http://www.amnesty.org
Corporation for National Service	http://www.nationalservice.org
Do Something	http://www.dosomething.org
Interact	http://www.rotary.org/programs/interact
Key Club International	http://www.keyclub.org
National Honor Society	http://www.nhs.us
National Service-Learning Clearinghouse	http://www.servicelearning.org
National Youth Leadership Council	http://www.nylc.org
Sierra Student Coalition	http://www.ssc.org

Visual and Performing Arts

Educational Theatre Association	http://www.edta.org
National Art Education Association	http://www.naea-reston.org
American High School Theatre Festival	http://www.ahstf.com
Music Teachers National Association	http://www.mtna.org
National Dance Education Organization	http://www.ndeo.org

REFERENCES

Belton High School. (n.d.). *Goth club*. Retrieved November 28, 2004, from http://www.beltonschools. org/bhs/index.htm

Brown, B. B., & Steinberg, L. (1990). Skirting the "brain-nerd" connection: Academic achievement and social acceptance. *The Education Digest, 55*, 57–60.

College Board (n.d.) *The extracurricular edge: Quality over quantity*. Retrieved November 13, 2004, from http://www.collegeboard.com/parents/article/0,3708,703-704-0-21282,00.html

Cross, T. L., & Dixon, F. A. (1998). On gifted students in rural schools. *NASSP Bulletin, 82*, 119–124.

Csikszentmihalyi, M., Rathunde, K., & Whalen, S. (1993). *Talented teenagers: The roots of success and failure*. New York: Cambridge University Press.

Ellis, C. J., Riley, T. L., & Gordon, B. (2003). Talented female athletes: Are they going for the gold? *Journal of Secondary Gifted Education, 14*, 229–242.

Feldhusen, J. F. (1995). Talent development during the high school years. *Gifted Education International, 10*, 60–64.

Feldhusen, J. F. & Wood, B.K. (1997). Developing growth plans for gifted students. *Gifted Child Today, 20*(6), 24–26, 48.

Gerber, S. B. (1996). Extracurricular activities and academic achievement. *Journal of Research and Development in Education, 30*, 42–50.

Goldstein, D., & Wagner, H. (1993). After school programs, competitions, school olympics, and summer programs. In K. A. Heller, F. J. Mönks, & A. H. Passow (Eds.), *International handbook of research and development of giftedness and talent* (pp. 593–604). New York: Pergamon Press.

Greene, M. J. (2003). Gifted adrift? Career counseling of the gifted and talented. *Roeper Review, 25*, 66–72.

Gross, M. U. M. (1998). The "me" behind the mask: Intellectually gifted students and the search for identity. *Roeper Review, 20*, 167–174.

Guest, A., & Schneider, B. (2003). Adolescents' extracurricular participation in context: The mediation effects of schools, communities, and identity. *Sociology of Education, 76*, 89–109.

Hébert, T. P. (2000). Defining belief in self: Intelligent young men in an urban high school. *Gifted Child Quarterly, 44*, 91–114.

Higher Education Research Institute. (2003). *The American freshman: National norms for fall 2003*. Retrieved November 28, 2004, from: http://www.gseis.ucla.edu/heri/findings.html

Horvat, E. M., Weininger, E. B., & Lareau, A. (2003). From social ties to social capital: Class differences in the relations between schools and parent networks. *American Education Research Journal, 40*, 319–351.

Janos, P. M., & Robinson, N. M. (1985). Psychosocial development in intellectually gifted children. In F. D. Horowitz & M. O'Brien (Eds.), *The gifted and talented: Developmental perspectives*. (pp. 149–195). Washington, DC: American Psychological Association.

Kerr, B. A. (1985). *Smart girls, gifted women*. Dayton, OH: Ohio Psychology Press.

Lee, S. Y. (2002). The effects of peers on the academic and creative talent development of a gifted adolescent male. *Journal of Secondary Gifted Education, 14*, 19–29.

Lisella, L. C., & Serwatka, T. S. (1996). Extracurricular participation and academic achievement in minority students in urban schools. *The Urban Review, 28*, 63–81.

McLaughlin, M. W. (1993) Embedded identities: Enabling balance in urban contexts. In S. B. Heath & M. W. McLaughlin (Eds.), *Identity and inner-city youth: Beyond ethnicity and gender* (pp. 36–68.) New York: Teachers College Press.

McNeal, R. B. (1998). High school extracurricular activities: Closed structures and stratifying patterns of participation. *Journal of Educational Research*, 91, 183–191.

Melnick, M., Sabo, D., and Vanfossen, J. (1992). Educational effects of interscholastic athletic participation of African-American and Hispanic youth. *Adolescence, 27*, 295–307.

Milgram, R. M. (2003). Challenging out-of-school activities as a predictor of creative accomplishments in art, drama, dance, and social leadership. *Scandinavian Journal of Educational Research, 47*, 305–315.

Moon, S. M. (2003). Personal talent. *High Ability Studies, 14*, 5–21.

National Sleep Foundation. (2000). *Adolescent sleep needs and patterns: Research report and resource guide.* Washington, DC: National Sleep Foundation.

Olszewski-Kubilius, P., & Lee, S. Y. (2004). The role of participation in in-school and outside-of-school activities in the talent development of gifted students. *Journal of Secondary Gifted Education, 15*, 107–123.

Piirto, J. (1998). *Understanding those who create.* Scottsdale, AZ: Gifted Psychology Press.

Powers, S., & Wagner, M. (1984). Attributions for school achievement of middle school students. *Journal of Early Adolescence, 4*, 215–222.

Princeton Review. (n.d.). *Sophomore year: Time to narrow down your extracurricular activities.* Retrieved November 13, 2004, from http://www.princetonreview.com/college/research/articles/prepare/extracurriculars.asp

Renzulli, J. S., & Park, S. (2000). Gifted dropouts: The who and the why. *Gifted Child Quarterly, 44*, 261–271.

Rifner, P. J., & Feldhusen, J. F. (1997). Checkmate. *Gifted Child Today, 20*(1), 36–40.

Rimm, S. B. (1986). *Underachievement syndrome: Causes and cures.* Watertown, WI: Apple Publishing.

Rizza, M. G., & Reis, S. M. (2001). Comparing and contrasting: Stories of competition. *Gifted Child Quarterly, 45*, 54–62.

Schneider, B., & Stevenson, D.L. (1999). *The ambitious generation.* New Haven, CT: Yale University Press.

Silverman, L. K. (1993). Social development, leadership, and gender issues. In L. K. Silverman (Ed.), *Counseling the gifted and talented* (pp. 291–327). Denver: Love.

Swiatek, M. A. (1995). An empirical investigation of the social coping strategies used by gifted adolescents. *Gifted Child Quarterly, 39*, 154–161.

Terry, A. W. (2003). Effects of service learning on young, gifted adolescents in their community. *Gifted Child Quarterly, 47*, 295–308.

Udvari, S. J., & Schneider, B. H. (2000). Competition and the adjustment of gifted children: A matter of motivation. *Roeper Review, 22*, 212–216.

West, J. (1996). In God's country: Rural gifted women. In K. Arnold, K. Noble, and R. Subotnik (Eds.), *Remarkable women: Perspectives on female talent development* (pp. 69–80). Cresskill, NH: Hampton Press.

Zaff, J. F., Moore, K. A., Papillo, A. R., & Williams, S. (2003). Implications of extracurricular activity participation during adolescence on positive outcomes. *Journal of Adolescent Research, 18*, 599–630.

SPECIAL SCHOOLS FOR THE GIFTED AND TALENTED

by Michael F. Sayler

Gifted adolescents have special educational needs. The term "gifted adolescent" is a good description of these individuals if we take each part of the phrase seriously. They are adolescents with many of the same developmental and personal issues as all young people. They are also gifted, which means they have aptitudes exceeding many of their age peers, and sometimes exceeding many adults. Although gifted adolescents go through the same developmental stages as their age peers, they may do so more quickly and deal with the changes and transitions differently (Dixon, 1998). What are the appropriate educational placements for the gifted adolescent? The group is not homogeneous in terms of abilities or aptitudes, interests and desires, current performance and life goals, social and emotional development, or the match between their current school placement and their educational needs. Many gifted adolescents function well in the options and opportunities provided by their local public or private schools. Others, although appreciative of the options available, are hungry for more.

Middle schools and high schools have a variety of options for addressing the needs of the gifted and talented. Gifted programs often serve about 5–15% of students in the school or district, although the percentage of students

547

identified as gifted varies from state to state. For example, four states identify more than 10% of their students as gifted and talented, while in 21 states fewer than 5% are identified as such (U.S. Department of Education, 1993). Typically, middle school programs for the gifted involve part-time pullout classes, after school academic competitions, and weekend or summer opportunities (Swiatek & Lupkowski-Shoplik, 2003). High school options often include Advanced Placement (AP) courses, International Baccalaureate (IB), honors classes, acceleration, and extra-school learning experiences (Feldhusen, 1998). Even with these many options, there are some gifted students whose unique needs go beyond what a school can easily provide.

School personnel might think about individual instruction or mentoring for these students, but individualized programs of instruction may not be possible due to a lack of qualified teachers to provide this accelerated level of instruction or just the time and effort needed to provide so much individualized help for a single person. Psychologically, the best instructional arrangement is one in which the adolescent's special academic, performance, or vocational needs are addressed. This is made easier when the gifted and talented are allowed to work and study with their intellectual or talent peers. The best arrangements of all are those where the highly gifted and talented adolescents can receive advanced training and education among intellectual or talent peers, some of whom are of a similar age (Sayler, 1993). Important and viable alternatives to a totally individualized and accelerated program for these students are the many kinds of special schools.

SPECIAL SCHOOLS FOR THE GIFTED

Some special schools for the gifted and talented address accelerated academic content across all domains. These schools are operated by school districts, private entities, or universities. Other special schools provide advanced curriculum in a specific area with a strong, but less advanced, curriculum in the other academic areas. These schools might focus on mathematics, science, engineering, medicine, business, agriculture, or the humanities. In some cases, such as the early college entrance academies, students receive a curriculum that matches their high performance by taking courses normally taught to students one or more years older. Other special schools focus on students with high levels of performance in music, drama, or dance. A few special schools focus on populations not immediately obvious as gifted, such as schools for the vocationally talented or schools for bright students with learning disabilities. Some of the special schools demand that all students live at the school, others are commuter schools with no housing facilities, and some are attended by both residential and nonresidential students.

Students may even attend a school electronically through programs such as the A. Linwood Holton Governor's School for the Gifted, which has no classrooms or buildings. Students in 13 counties in southwestern Virginia have access to this school, which focuses on offering advanced science and math courses not readily available in their rural and small-town home high schools. Students remain in their home high school physically, but take courses via the Internet. A number of virtual schools for the gifted are now available, some full-time and many part-time or as summer opportunities (ERIC, 2005).

Once the students are identified and begin attending classes, many teachers recognize that these exceptional children or youth are not homogeneous in makeup (Strop, 2003). Lovecky (1992) noted that gifted children differ as much from each other as they differ from average children. Studies of the makeup of gifted classes show that they are at least as variable, and in some cases more variable, as the range of abilities and interests found in regular classrooms (Reis & McCoach, 2000; Ruf, 2003). Why would this be so? Whenever individuals are selected on one set of markers, and selected for having a lot of the characteristics measured, the group will vary widely in other issues (Winner, 2000). For example, if we were picking a basketball team and searched for any high-school student above 6'5", we would find a wide range of students: some who were just 6'5" tall, but others who were taller; some who were passionate about basketball, but others who could care less; some who like classical music, others who hate it.

Middle schools may pose special problems for those gifted students whose needs are most unique. The middle school philosophy, with its emphasis on homogeneous grouping and socialization while minimizing rigorous academics, is at odds with the needs of these unique students. Typical middle school approaches are not well matched to the advanced developmental levels, formal operational thinking, or psychological development of the highly gifted and talented. Even the best middle schools seldom make modifications in their curriculum for the gifted (VanTassel-Baska, Bailey, & Hammett-Hall, 1995), and consequently may not see the need for placement of a student in a special school for the gifted.

A common concern when considering special schools for the gifted and talented is whether or not the special school is accredited. Accreditation, whether private or state, impacts the viability of any credit earned, the legitimacy of a diploma, and the student's ability to matriculate into a good university. Some special schools are part of the public school systems and are accredited by the state. Others are private institutions and have obtained accreditation through regional or national accreditation bodies. Some are not high schools in the normal sense at all, but are part of colleges or universities. University programs deal with the issue of high school diplomas differently (Brody, Muratori, & Stanley, 2004). State legislatures authorize some schools to issue a high school diploma (e.g., the Texas Academy of Mathematics and Science at the University of North Texas). Others rely on the high school from where the students came to issue the diploma (e.g., The Advanced Academy of Georgia at the University of West Georgia), and others ignore the problem as being irrelevant when students are on an accelerated bachelor's track (e.g., the Early Entrance Program at the University of Washington).

University-Based Special Schools

Many opportunities exist for very talented adolescents to enter college early (Colangelo, Assouline, & Gross, 2004). The proliferation of university-based special programs grows out of the observation that certain gifted adolescents have academic needs that are very high and, consequently, are difficult to meet in many schools. Capable students, some in middle schools and more in high schools, are ready for college-level coursework and the myriad opportunities a college or university offers. Early college entrance programs provide an ideal blend of opportunities for these students: college courses, increased intellectual- and age-peer interaction, and economical use of these students' time (Brody et al., 2004).

Students who are attracted to the early college entrance programs often come from good schools or schools with gifted programs. These students often liked their home schools and being with their friends, but they found the pace of their middle- or high-school classes was too slow, the amount of practice work was wearying as it was typically paced for those with on- or below-level academic needs, the assignments did not challenge them to work hard or to think deeply, and their teacher's style and approaches focused more on helping students struggling with school (Cross, Stewart, Coleman, 2003; Muratori, Colangelo, & Assouline, 2003).

The college-level courses and experiences in schools such as the National Academy of Arts, Sciences, and Engineering (NAASE) at the University of Iowa are challenging, but exciting to the students attending (Muratori et al., 2003). Often participants initially feel enthusiastic, but also a little strange at being surrounded by age peers who are as bright as or brighter than they are—a unique experience for many who never experience this in their home schools. Some of these students have or quickly develop good organization, study habits, a strong sense of efficacy in doing college work, and academic competence (Dixon, Lapsley, & Hanchon, 2004). Others struggle in an environment where things are not easy. Issues of underachievement, perfectionism, and weak time management may surface as these students, for the first time, have to be organized in order to understand the content of their courses.

School personnel, parents, and students are also rightly concerned about the social and emotional development the early college entrants will experience and the possibilities for developing good friendships while avoiding bad experiences in a college setting (Arnold, 1994). The empirical research on the social and emotional healthiness of early entrance to college is limited, but what has been done is generally positive (Sayler, 1990). It is especially positive when students attend a special school rather than enter college early on their own at a university without a special program. Early entrance high schools are designed to facilitate the successful academic, social, and psychological success of gifted students by providing structure, support, guidance, and equally talented age peers. This minimizes the concerns of leaving adolescents on their own in a college setting with older students. Students who attend these special schools find good friends and fit in well with the other early entrants and with the students at the university or college (Muratori et al., 2003).

In the residential high schools for gifted students, the curriculum often incorporates a strong math and science focus (Britton Kolloff, 2003). Students attending these special schools on college campuses either take university courses, advance rapidly though the high school curriculum and take Advanced Placement (AP) courses, or participate in special classes that build on broad themes or philosophical foundations of the content areas.

Students attending the 2-year Texas Academy of Mathematics and Science (TAMS) at the University of North Texas take the university courses normally taken by freshman and sophomores who are majoring in high-level science, mathematics, engineering, or medical tracks. TAMS is special high school created and accredited by the state of Texas. Students typically have completed their sophomore year in high school and enter the Academy the fall of their 11th-grade year. Students take a sequence of college courses, but no additional high school classes. At the end of the 2 years, they graduate with both a Texas high school diploma and at least 60 university semester credit hours in math, science, and general studies. About 200 students enter the program each year.

TAMS students must live on campus in a special residence hall. For the students' safety and efficiency of operations, this hall is used exclusively for students in the TAMS program and has its own specially trained residential, student life, and counseling staffs. Separate wings of the hall are used for men and for women. There are commons rooms, a computer lab, recreation areas, and TAMS staff offices in the hall.

Several thousand students have completed TAMS since its first class entered in the fall of 1988. Most of the students have done very well academically, in their careers, and in their personal lives. All participants are similar in their academic preparation and performance at entry into TAMS, but not all come from similar home backgrounds or have similar psychological profiles. Students most likely to be successful academically and psychologically at TAMS were those students who came from families that were cohesive and expressive and low in conflict (Caplan, Henderson, Henderson, & Fleming, 2002). The same study found that success at TAMS facilitated having a positive self-concept.

Taking college courses while at TAMS gives students an early and a deep knowledge of the basic content they will use in their professional careers. This early amassing of real-world professional content in mathematics and science allows many of the participants to be involved in real research efforts. High ability is not sufficient for access to real scientific or technical problem solving and research. The deep knowledge of the fundamentals of biology, chemistry, physics, and mathematics received in their college courses, combined with high natural ability and enthusiasm for mathematics, science, medicine, engineering, and so forth prepare TAMS students for participation in real scientific investigations.

TAMS students are key contributors on many research teams while they are still 15–18 years old. Recent research activities of TAMS students include exploring functions in neuronic cilia as they relate to neurological diseases such as Alzheimer's and ALS; research on the enzyme ATCACE; creating carbon nanotubes in epoxy with no defects; studying fumagillin, an antibiotic derived from fungi that has proven to shrink tumors by inhibiting the blood flow that keeps them alive; manipulating the polymer polyanilan on silicon surfaces that would provide an inexpensive way to manufacture low-current circuit boards; or developing a mathematical model of human muscle contractions. These projects are done with faculty at the university, at regional medical centers, at private research centers, and other places where real scientists work. TAMS students have done research at the University of North Texas, aboard a research vessel sailing near Antarctica, at Houston's NASA Johnson Space Center, at M. D. Anderson Cancer Center, at University of Texas-Houston Health Science Center, at Southwest Medical Center, and at Moscow State University in Russia.

The university classes, living with other highly gifted and motivated adolescents, and the research opportunities prepare TAMS graduates to enter prestigious programs in their content fields at universities around the country at least 2 years earlier than their age peers. This then allows them to finish their education and enter their professions early, a positive advantage that facilitates their future contributions to society. Alternately, the time saved by attending TAMS allows them the freedom to explore academic or personal interests that they might not have had time to explore had they stayed in their home high school and graduated with their age peers before starting college.

A different approach to early-college entrance is that of the Clarkston School Bridging Year Program at Clarkston University. This special school provides a one-year early-entrance transition from high school to college. Participants are not limited to individuals with interest in mathematical and scientific fields.

Students attend Clarkston during what would be their senior year in high school. While in the Bridging Program they take classes with other university students and earn 15 to 18 credits in each of two semesters of enrollment. Students cross-register at nearby colleges and universities for specific courses in art, music, and languages. The program does not issue a high school diploma, but students have several options for earning one: They may take the 2-day New York State General Equivalency Exam (GED), after which they may apply for a diploma from the New York State Education Department upon successful completion of twenty-four credit hours in six different disciplines, or they can make arrangements to receive a high-school diploma from their home high school after completing the Clarkston program.

Some early entrance schools, such as the Program for the Exceptionally Gifted (PEG) at Mary Baldwin College in Staunton, VA, target specific populations. The PEG program is the only early entrance school in the country exclusively for young women. PEG was a natural extension of the mission of Mary Baldwin College, which has a 150-year tradition of higher education for women. Talented young women enter PEG after eighth or ninth grade; they live in a special hall and receive more intensive supervision and support. After 10th grade, students have more freedom and can choose other living arrangements. PEG students take core courses in their first 2 years before pursuing specific academic programs. Students earn a bachelor's degree, but not a high school diploma.

A consideration for school personnel as they talk to parents and gifted students about the possibilities of a special school on a college campus or in any place away from the home campus of the student is the location of the school and whether the student can commute from home to attend it. Many of the special schools are day schools; some have residential facilities, and others require living on campus. As a specific school is being considered, it is important to look over these aspects carefully to determine if the school is a good match for the needs of the particular student and if the student can attend given the distance or residential requirements.

Students, mostly seventh and eighth graders, attending the Transition School of the Early Entrance Program (EEP) at the University of Washington in Seattle usually live with their families somewhere in the area. Long commutes by bus, ferry, or carpool are not uncommon. Some students come to live with relatives or other families in the Seattle area. The Transition School students eventually become Early Entrance Program students and by their sophomore or junior year are living in a residence hall or group living situation near campus (Robinson & Noble, 1992).

The EEP program has undergone a rigorous and comprehensive analysis of its students, their intellectual and psychological makeup and experiences, and success of the program (e.g., Janos & Robinson, 1985; Janos, et al., 1988; Janos, Robinson, & Lunneborg, 1989; Janos, Sanfillippo, & Robinson, 1986; Noble, Arndt, Nicholson, Sletten, & Zamora, 1999; Noble & Drummond, 1992; Noble, Robinson, & Gunderson, 1993; Noble & Smyth, 1995). The studies found the students generally did very well academically, were able to make good friends both within EEP and in the general university population, were satisfied with the early entrance experience, and had healthy psychological adjustment.

In other schools located on college campuses, but not primarily offering college courses, students take a specially designed high-school curriculum or a mix of these special high-school classes and college classes. Students receive a high-school diploma and may concurrently earn some college credit. Students at the Indiana Academy of Science, Mathematics, and Humanities at Ball State University, for example, earn an Indiana academic honors diploma and take a variety of Advanced Placement (AP) courses, some of which earn college credit. The Academy is accredited by the state of Indiana and the regional accreditation agencies.

Early college entrance or attending a school on a college campus is not for every highly gifted middle- or high-school student. Just being very smart and successful in high school, having a high IQ, or being bored in their home schools is not enough to decide to go to college early. Brody et al. (2004) warn:

> Content knowledge, motivation, and emotional maturity seem to be important factors in contributing to high achievement and good social adjustment among young college students. Students who go to college just to avoid problems in their home and school environments often find that they take their problems with them to college. (p. 105)

The structure and support provided to highly gifted young people in the special schools at universities maximize their chances for academic success and a healthy transition from K–12 education, through college, and into the careers of their choice.

Non-University-Based Special Schools

Special schools that serve the needs of gifted and talented individuals are not always housed on university campuses. These non-university-based special schools may be readily identifiable or their names may make finding them a challenge. Many of the special schools for middle and high school students do not use the words gifted or talented in their school names or in their promotional information. Special schools for the gifted go by many names: academies; conservatories; charters; centers for a specific content or domain; honors schools; governor's schools; magnet schools; or schools of fine arts, mathematics, science, or other specific content area.

It is obvious that a special school is addressing the needs of selected gifted students when they identify themselves by using the terms gifted or talented in their title. These special middle and high schools are often magnet academies. For example, the award-winning Dunbar Magnet Middle School for Gifted and Talented in Little Rock, AR, is a public middle school that began in the 1920s as an inner-city school, but which added magnet programs in international studies and for gifted students in 1990. All students participate in the international studies program by taking at least one of the foreign language interdisciplinary electives each year. Gifted and talented students take an accelerated curriculum in math, science, social studies, and English.

Another example is the Enloe Gifted & Talented/International Baccalaureate High of the Wake County Public School System in Raleigh, NC. Enloe offers programs in the humanities, science and mathematics, the visual and performing arts, and an International Baccalaureate program. Students from this magnet school have earned national and regional awards for their art, music, writing, forensics, horticulture, science, mathematics, technology, and engineering. Students in multiple years earned Emmys for their video productions. The school was awarded the International Education Award of Excellence. The curriculum focuses on critical thinking and problem-solving skills. Students have access to professional and technological equipment and instruction such as engineering labs and faculty. The research science courses include lab work supervised by scientists at North Carolina State University and from the Research Triangle.

A third example of a special school identifying itself as serving the gifted is the School for the Talented and Gifted in Dallas, TX. The school prides itself as being the only school in the district with a student body that is evenly ethnically diverse—one-third Anglo, one-third Black, and one-third Hispanic. This gifted magnet school is part of a cluster of six magnet programs at the Townview Magnet Center. This cluster of magnet schools allows students to match their abilities and interests to different academic foci and approaches. In addition to the School for the Gifted and Talented, Townview Center houses a nationally ranked School of Science and Engineering, the School of Health Professions, the School of Business & Management, the School of Government and Law, and the School of Educational and Social Services. All of the magnet schools have access to a high-speed network allowing students to access hundreds of multimedia CD-ROMs, scores of software application tools, educational videotapes, and cable and satellite television broadcasts. The center has more than 1,000 computers with Internet connections, 11 file servers, 14 CD-ROM servers, and 300 laser printers (Watson, 1996). Online textbooks are replacing traditional books.

Students attending Townview have opportunities for research in regional and state medical and research facilities. Students from the different schools at Townview have, for example, participated in summer research projects with teams at the Southwestern Medical Center. Townview students conducted behavior tests to determine the efficacy of an antidepressant on mice, sought to understand addictions by looking at pathways of CDK5 in neurotransmission, studied natural killer (NK) cell receptors in chimeric mice, and studied methods of crystallizing different proteins.

Some special schools-within-schools, ones that serve specific kinds of gifts and talents, have names that do not suggest their special purposes. The name of the school is like any typical middle or high school. An illustration of this kind of school-within-a-school is the dance program in Jefferson High School in Portland, OR. The Dance Academy at Jefferson offers classes in ballet and pointe, jazz, modern, tap, and African dance; these classes are taught by professional dancers who have national and international experience. Talented dance students who train at Jefferson compete in regional and national dance opportunities; numerous graduates have gone on to professional careers in dance.

The Thomas Jefferson High School for Science and Technology in Fairfax, VA, grew out of a partnership between local businesses and schools seeking to improve education in science, mathematics, and technology. The school is also the Governor's School for Science and Technology in Northern Virginia and consequently is supported by the Virginia Department of Education. This regional feature provides access to the high-level interventions at the school to qualified students in multiple school districts. Students follow an intensive 4-year program that includes the ninth-grade Integrated Biology, English, and Technology Program (IBET); computer science; humanities; foreign languages; fine arts; and physical education. All seniors are required to complete a technology laboratory project either in one of the specialized research laboratories at the school or in the TJ Mentorship Program with firms and laboratories throughout the metropolitan Washington, DC, area.

Looking quickly at a list of local schools might not suggest any special schools for the gifted and talented; however, a closer look is often required to determine any special opportunities that are available. Garland High School in Garland, TX, sounds like any high school in any city, but a closer examination reveals that it offers special tracks for qualified students in the International Baccalaureate program and in the GHS Performing Arts Endorsement program. Garland High School students entering the Performing Arts Endorsement Program are provided a coherent sequence of courses designed for artistically gifted and talented students. From their freshman or sophomore years forward, these students take a specified sequence of academic and performing arts professional study.

International Baccalaureate (IB) programs are available in many larger school districts. There are elementary, middle, and high school diploma IB programs offered in 1,485 schools in 119 countries worldwide (International Baccalaureate Organization, 2005). The standardized IB curriculum at the high school level is a comprehensive and integrated 2-year diploma-oriented curriculum that prepares students for higher education programs both internationally and in the United States.

Gifts and talents in the vocational or technical areas may not always be recognized as being a part of the conception of gifted education, nor assessed as a need of gifted and talented students (Feldhusen, Hoover, Sayler, 1990; Sayler, 1998). There are a few special schools that serve talented students with vocational and technical talent although neither the schools nor the students may consider themselves "gifted and talented."

Students with high levels of ability and performance in vocational and technical areas can find appropriate services in the special magnet program in the A. J. Ferrell Middle School in Tampa, FL. This award-winning school offers technology-oriented opportunities that are rather unique among middle schools: telecommunications technology, pre-engineering, media publishing, aerospace, art technology, business, communications, explorations, music technology, and video production.

Similarly, Duncan Polytechnical High School in Fresno, CA, is located in the San Joaquin Valley, one of the nation's prime agricultural regions. This special vocational agricultural school, winner of substantial federal research grants in conjunction with California State University at Fresno, provides gifted agricultural education for students heading towards high-level careers in agriculture. The school also involves regional middle school students in its agricultural research opportunities.

The Denver School of the Arts is both a special middle school and a special high school for those talented in the areas of creative writing, dance, theatre, instrumental music, stagecraft/design, video/cinema arts, visual arts, and vocal music. This magnet school admits students in grades 6–12 with more than 600 students in attendance and is the only arts school in the Rocky Mountain region. The school organizes its years around broad themes that teachers of the gifted would recognize (e.g., change, process, elements, relationships, and journeys).

Some special schools are privately owned and operate outside of the school district or university structures. These schools are accredited not by states, but by nationally recognized accreditation bodies such as one of the regional accreditation associations for colleges and schools. The Walnut Hill School in Natick, MA, affiliated with the New England Conservatory of Music, is a private high school for the arts. Along with training in ballet, music, theater, visual art, and writing, students get a rigorous college-preparatory academic curriculum.

CONCLUSIONS

Just labeling students as gifted is not addressing their needs (Feldhusen, 1998); the real measure of success is found in the appropriateness of the curriculum received by the identified gifted individual. High schools and middle schools offer many different services for gifted and talented students. Schools create their gifted programs and program options to address the greatest unmet needs of their students. Yet, inevitably, some of these students have academic, performance, or vocational needs that go well beyond the needs of the other gifted students in the school. These needs often exceed the capability of the local school to address them easily or efficiently.

The measure of effectiveness of the curriculum offered to a gifted student is whether it actually works, that is whether or not it actually addresses effectively the important but unmet needs of a particular student. VanTassel-Baska and Brown (2001) outline fundamental questions for schools to ask when assessing the question of whether or not a curriculum actually works for the gifted students to whom it is delivered. Most schools are unable to offer the diversity of courses and depth of learning necessary for those students whose needs exceed even the gifted program options. Special schools for the gifted grow out of the advanced needs of some students; some because their potential or current performance exceeds that of other gifted students, others because their advanced needs are in areas that the local school does not or cannot address easily.

References

Arnold, K. D. (1994). The Illinois valedictorian project: Early adult careers of academically talented male high school students. In R. F. Subotnik & K. D. Arnold (Eds.), *Beyond Terman: Contemporary longitudinal studies of giftedness and talent* (pp. 24–51). Norwood, NJ: Ablex.

Britton Kolloff, P. (2003). State-supported residential high schools. In N. Colangelo and G. A. Davis (Eds.), *Handbook of gifted education* (pp. 238–246). Boston: Allyn & Bacon.

Brody, L. E., Muratori, M. C., & Stanley, J. C. (2004). Early entrance to college: Academic, social, and emotional considerations. In N. Colangelo, S. Assouline, and M. U. M. Gross (2004). *A nation deceived: How schools hold back America's brightest students* (Vol. 2). Iowa City, IA: The Connie Belin & Jacqueline N. Blank International Center for Gifted Education and Talent Development.

Caplan, S. M., Henderson, C. E., Henderson, J., & Fleming, D. L. (2002). Socioemotional factors contributing to adjustment among early-entrance college students. *Gifted Child Quarterly, 46,* 124–134.

Colangelo, N., Assouline, S. G., & Gross, M. U. M. (2004). *A nation deceived: How schools hold back America's brightest students* (Vol. 1). Iowa City, IA: The Connie Belin & Jacqueline N. Blank International Center for Gifted Education and Talent Development.

Cross, T. L., Stewart, R. A., & Coleman, L. J. (2003). Phenomenology and its implications for gifted studies research: Investigating the lebenswelt of academically gifted students attending an elementary magnet school. *Journal for the Education of the Gifted, 27,* 201–220.

Dixon, F. A. (1998). Social and academic self-concepts of gifted adolescents. *Journal for the Education of the Gifted, 22,* 80–94.

Dixon, F. A., Lapsley, D. K., & Hanchon, T. A. (2004). An empirical typology of perfectionism in gifted adolescents. *Gifted Child Quarterly, 48,* 95–106.

ERIC Clearinghouse on Disabilities and Gifted Education. (2005). *Virtual schools for the gifted.* Retrieved April 1, 2005, from http://ericec.org/fact/virtualsch.html

Feldhusen, J. F. (1998). Programs and services at the secondary level. In J. VanTassel-Baska (Ed.), *Excellence in educating gifted and talented learners* (pp. 225–240). Denver, CO: Love Publishing.

Feldhusen, J. F., Hoover, S. M., & Sayler, M. F. (1990). *Identification and education of the gifted and talented at the secondary level.* New York: Trillium Press.

International Baccalaureate Organization. (2005). *FAQ.* Retrieved April 1, 2005, from http://www.ibo.org/ibo/index.cfm?page=/ibo/faq&language=EN

Janos, P. M., & Robinson, N. M. (1985). The performance of students in a program of radical acceleration at the university level. *Gifted Child Quarterly, 29,* 175–180.

Janos, P. M., Robinson, N. M., Carter, C., Chapel, A., Cufley, R., Curland, M., et al. (1988). Social relations of students who enter college early. *Gifted Child Quarterly, 32,* 210–215.

Janos, P. M., Robinson, N. M., & Lunneborg, C. E. (1989). Markedly early entrance to college. *Journal of Higher Education, 60,* 495–518.

Janos, P. M., Sanfillippo, S. M., & Robinson, N. M. (1986). "Underachievement" among markedly accelerated college students. *Journal of Youth and Adolescence, 15,* 303–311.

Lovecky, D. V. (1992). Exploring the social and emotional aspects of giftedness in children. *Roeper Review, 15,* 18–25.

Noble, K. D., Arndt, T., Nicholson, T., Sletten, T., & Zamora, A. (1999). Different strokes: Perceptions of social and emotional development among early college entrants. *Journal of Secondary Gifted Education, 10,* 77–84.

Noble, K. D., & Drummond, J. E. (1992). But what about the prom? Students' perceptions of early college entrance. *Gifted Child Quarterly, 36,* 106–111.

Noble, K. D., Robinson, N. M., & Gunderson, S. A. (1993). All rivers lead to the sea: A follow-up study of gifted young adults. *Roeper Review, 15,* 124–130.

Noble, K. D., & Smyth, R. K. (1995). Keeping their talents alive: Young women's assessment of radical, post-secondary acceleration. *Roeper Review, 18,* 49–55.

Muratori, M., Colangelo, N., and Assouline, S., (2003). Early-entrance students: Impressions of their first semester of college. *Gifted Child Quarterly, 47,* 219–237.

Reis, S. M., & McCoach, D. B. (2000). The underachievement of gifted students: What do we know and where do we go? *Gifted Child Quarterly, 44,* 152–170.

Robinson, N. M., & Noble, K. D. (1992). Acceleration: Valuable high school to college option. *Gifted Child Today, 15*(2), 20–23.

Ruf, D. L. (2003). *Use of the SB5 in the assessment of high abilities* (Stanford-Binet Intelligence Scales, Fifth Edition Assessment Service Bulletin No. 3). Itasca, IL: Riverside Publishing.

Sayler, M. F. (1990). *Early college entrants at Purdue University: A study of their academic and social characteristics.* Unpublished doctoral dissertation, Purdue University, West Lafayette, IN.

Sayler, M. F. (1993). Helping students and their parents understand early college entrance. *Educating Able Learners, 18*(1), 3–5.

Sayler, M. F. (1998). *Gifted education: School-to-work information.* Sherman, TX: Texoma School-to-Work Partnership.

Strop, J. (2003). The affective side of gifted identification and the call to advocacy. *Understanding our Gifted, 15*(3), 24–26.

Swiatek, M. A., & Lupkowski-Shoplik, A. (2003). Elementary and middle school student participation in gifted programs: Are gifted students underserved? *Gifted Child Quarterly, 47,* 118–129.

U.S. Department of Education, Office of Educational Research and Improvement (1993). *National excellence: A case for developing America's talent.* Washington, DC: U.S. Government Printing Office

VanTassel-Baska, J., Bailey, J., & Hammett-Hall, K. (1995). Case studies of promising change schools. *Research in Middle Level Education Quarterly, 19,* 89–116.

VanTassel-Baska, J., & Brown, E. F. (2001). An analysis of gifted education curriculum models. In F. A. Karnes & S. M. Bean (Eds.), *Methods and materials for teaching the gifted* (pp. 93–132). Waco, TX: Prufrock Press.

Watson, O. (1996) A networked learning environment: Toward new teaching strategies in secondary education. *Educational Technology, 36*(5), 40–43.

Winner, E. (2000). Giftedness: Current theory and research. *Current Directions in Psychological Science, 9*, 153–156.

WHAT TEACHER EDUCATION CAN DO

Professional Development: An Overview

by Felicia A. Dixon

*T*he final portion of *The Handbook of Secondary Gifted Education* focuses on teachers, counselors, and administrators and their important roles in the education of gifted adolescents. Three of the four chapters in this section focus on teachers, offering characteristics of effective teachers of secondary adolescents and describing preservice, in-service, and licensure programs for teachers, as well as standards and degree programs that are important to teacher training for working with high-ability adolescents. A chapter on professional development that offers ongoing training in the current research-based strategies in gifted education continues the focus on teacher preparation, but suggests that the entire school staff is responsible to work together collaboratively for the education of gifted adolescents at the secondary level. The final chapter in this book challenges counselors, principals, and superintendents to understand gifted students and charges this administrative team to consider why specific programming both in coursework and in other school dimensions is essential for effectively educating secondary gifted students and those who teach them. Cognitive, personal, and social dimensions of gifted students at the secondary level (see Chapter 1) are again important dimensions in all of the chapters in Part IV.

"Teachers who love to learn inspire students who love to learn" (Davidson, Davidson, & Vanderkam, 2004, p. 139).

Continuing education for teachers in the form of professional development and courses leading to a license in gifted education are as important to secondary teachers as they are to elementary teachers. Although it is difficult to work through the content disciplines to "get to" the teachers concerning the giftedness of their students, it is possible, and training certainly helps it happen. Gallagher (2000) stated that it was unthinkable for teachers of the gifted to have a haphazard hodge-podge of courses (i.e., a summer workshop, an in-service activity during one semester of the school year, and a 3-day conference the other semester) and call themselves specialists in gifted education. Similarly, Feldhusen (1997) stated that too often teachers of the gifted were left to find additional courses on their own to prepare them to teach gifted students. If secondary teachers are offered the choice of which courses to take from a smorgasbord of professional development choices, most of them go directly to their content domain. Although it is paramount that secondary teachers are very well grounded in their content, it is also important that they know the unique characteristics of their students, as well as the instructional strategies to appropriately instruct them. They must know how to differentiate instruction in order to reach out to the extreme variability that exists even in homogeneously grouped classes at the secondary level.

Often, secondary teachers are "difficult pupils" when it comes to professional development. They have no interest in sitting and listening to presenters outside their content (See Chapter 24). This makes professional development for them a very difficult and challenging enterprise for those consultants hired for special in-services on topics relevant to teaching gifted adolescents. In regard to this general disinterest outside of their subject area, attending to Reis' (1983) advice makes sense. She states, "If the classroom teachers are encouraged to participate actively in the gifted program, they may eventually come to regard efforts to meet the special needs of advanced students as shared responsibility" (p. 21). But, they must be invited first, and they must see the advantage of gifted education.

In a study focusing on perceptions of college students concerning the impact of their participation in gifted programs, Hertzog (2003) found that elementary experiences in gifted programs were not vividly remembered. Rather, she stated,

> . . . from the students' perspective, the greatest impact came later through participation in secondary programs that included honors, AP courses, and extracurricular competitions. Of course this may be a function of time and the fact that they may have better remembered their more recent experiences. However, their articulation of the importance of their secondary experiences to their future must be acknowledged. Educators should pay particular attention to making those secondary experiences challenging and available to as many students as possible. (p. 141)

Teachers and administrators are those responsible for making the system of educational experiences successful for these students, and they must not take the responsibility lightly. These chapters help with this endeavor.

Indeed, teachers are important to the education of gifted adolescents. They make it work both in the classroom and in the extracurricular activities that they coach, direct, and mentor. Their presence is paramount to success, but without supportive principals and superintendents, individual classes may thrive, but whole schools can flounder in the collective array of services offered. Leaving the programming to Advanced Placement (AP) classes or International Baccalaureate (IB) just doesn't meet everyone's needs in secondary schools for gifted adolescents. Successful programming requires a team effort. As Landrum (2001) suggests, "Gifted education programming must begin to move away from a separate and segregated role to become integrated with the total school program." (p. 139).

The four chapters in Part IV focus on helping secondary school personnel understand these foundational roles necessary in collaborating on the whole program. In Chapter 22, "Teachers of the Secondary Gifted Students: What Makes Them Effective," Roberts focuses specifically on the characteristics of successful middle and high school teachers. She argues that they must be in the business of talent development, offering opportunities that allow young people to have their talents and abilities recognized, nurtured, and celebrated. Roberts further suggests that the goal for teachers at the secondary level is to prepare students to be successful in postsecondary opportunities that lead to careers in science, mathematics, technology, the humanities, social sciences, and the arts. Roberts outlines several strategies that successful teachers employ as they support students in the development of their talents, abilities, and interests.

In Chapter 23, Robinson and Kolloff continue the focus on teachers with their chapter, "Preparing Teachers to Work With High Ability Youth at the Secondary Level: Issues and Implications for Licensure." From their wealth of experience in advocacy for gifted students and programs (Robinson & Moon, 2003), and their knowledge of curriculum for gifted students (Feldhusen & Robinson, 1986; Kolloff, 1996; Kolloff & Feldhusen, 1986), they present essential issues for teachers to consider and follow in becoming more proficient in working with gifted adolescents. They review selected literature on teacher preparation in gifted education with a focus on secondary issues and implications; summarize the shift from certification to licensure in teacher preparation; explore the teacher outcomes jointly proposed by the Council for Exceptional Children (CEC) and the National Association for Gifted Children (NAGC); and recommend the integration of specific secondary topics, readings, and resources into teacher preparation courses in gifted education. The chapter is laced with interesting anecdotes that continually illustrate and highlight the points Robinson and Kolloff present.

The difficulty of conducting professional development activities with a secondary audience has already been mentioned in this introduction. In Chapter 24, Dettmer, Landrum, and Miller bring their expertise in planning and implementing professional development to focus on secondary audiences. "Professional Development for the Education of Secondary Gifted Students," outlines the issues surrounding this very important form of teacher education, the pitfalls that may result if careful planning does not occur, and the benefits of successful implementation. Stating that perhaps a professional development session is the first or only chance general education teachers have to learn about the dimensions of gifted students, Dettmer,

Landrum, and Miller reiterate the need for schools to plan these activities and to plan them well. Recent changes in how sessions are conducted, goals of sessions, and practical "how-to" guides to use when conducting a professional development session at the middle and high school levels are presented factually, comprehensively, and supportively. The authors end with several outlines for professional development programs that teachers, gifted coordinators, administrators, and counselors can implement immediately. The ongoing education of educators is a worthy goal for all schools to pursue, and this important chapter lays the groundwork essential for practice.

The final chapter in *The Handbook of Secondary Gifted Education* is entitled "Superintendents, Principals, and Counselors: Facilitating Secondary Gifted Education." In Chapter 25, Peterson focuses on the leadership team of a secondary school: superintendents, principals, and school counselors. Peterson's understanding of the distinct role of each administrator augments her focus on the necessary collaboration that must exist among these roles to run a gifted-supportive secondary school, attuned to both culture and climate. All of these administrators deal holistically with students, and they are concerned about student attitudes, family environment, student safety and wellness, and collective school morale. They spend considerable time working with parents and building bridges to the community in order to ensure school success. Supported by knowledge of gifted students' affective and academic concerns, both administrators and counselors can be advocates for appropriate programming, including opportunities to attend to developmental concerns beyond academics. Peterson's suggestions for how to help administrators know more about gifted students and their academic and affective needs are practical and tested for effectiveness. Her own extensive work with discussion groups (Peterson, 1990) in schools is clearly outlined in this chapter and is useful for exploring issues associated with gifted adolescents. Peterson clearly advocates for administrators and counselors, as members of the school leadership team, to help to ensure that critical needs of gifted adolescents are met.

In summary, Part IV completes the picture presented in this book of the many dimensions that must be considered in the education of gifted secondary students. Schools and the people who are employed by schools are integral to the positive experiences gifted adolescents encounter daily. However, they may also be connected to the negative experiences that many gifted students endure in the time before graduation. The authors of the final four chapters offer practical suggestions and sage advice in considering what to do for teachers, counselors, and administrators who are all focused on educating adolescents. Part IV complements the other three parts, which are more focused on the dimensions of the student. This portion seeks to educate the educators, always keeping the reason for their education centered on the gifted adolescents they teach. Themes from Part IV that teachers need to keep in mind when working with talented teenagers are (a) the importance of understanding the dimensions of giftedness in adolescence when planning instructional strategies, (b) the necessity of coursework and professional development to involve the teacher in continuing education on the strategies and issues relevant to gifted adolescents, and (c) the necessity of collaboration among the school leadership team in order to ensure a school culture that encourages the education of gifted adolescents.

Part IV is the culmination of the book. The themes and issues presented in this volume are all devoted to secondary gifted adolescents. Those who have worked with adolescents know that there is always more to learn, more to understand, and more to do. Talented teens never stop being talented, and therefore will always provide a challenge. Our goal has been to provide a way to sort out the issues in order to understand the dimensions of adolescence and schooling that impact the gifted secondary student. If, as Pipher (1994) asserts, adolescence is a journey, then helping to plan and implement the journey are our tasks.

REFERENCES

Davidson, J., Davidson, B., & Vanderkam, L. (2004). *Genius denied: How to stop wasting our brightest young minds.* New York: Simon and Schuster.

Feldhusen, J. F. (1997). Educating teachers for work with talented youth. In N. Colangelo and G. Davis (Eds.), *Handbook of gifted education* (2nd ed., pp. 547–552). Boston: Allyn & Bacon.

Feldhusen, J. F., & Robinson, A. (1986). The Purdue Secondary Model for gifted and talented education. In J. S. Renzulli (Ed.), *Systems and models for developing programs for the gifted and talented* (pp. 153–179). Mansfield Center, CT: Creative Learning Press.

Gallagher, J. (2000). Unthinkable thoughts: Education of gifted students. *Gifted Child Quarterly, 44,* 5–12.

Hertzog, N. B. (2003). Impact of gifted programs from the students' perspectives. *Gifted Child Quarterly, 47,* 131–143.

Kolloff, P. B. (1996). Gifted girls and the humanities. *Journal of Secondary Gifted Education, 7,* 486–492.

Kolloff, P. B., & Feldhusen, J. F. (1986). The seminar: An instructional approach for gifted students. *Gifted Child Today, 9*(5), 2–7.

Landrum, M. S. (2001). An evaluation of the catalyst program: Consultation and collaboration in gifted education. *Gifted Child Quarterly, 45,* 139–151.

Peterson, J. S. (1990). Noon-hour discussion groups: Dealing with the burdens of capability. *Gifted Child Today, 13*(4), 17–22.

Pipher, M. (1994). *Reviving Ophelia: Saving the selves of adolescent girls.* New York: Ballantine Books.

Reis, S. M. (1983). Creating ownership in gifted and talented programs. *Roeper Review, 5*(4), 20–23.

Robinson, M., & Moon, S. M. (2003). A national study of local and state advocacy in gifted education. *Gifted Child Quarterly, 47,* 8–37.

TEACHERS OF SECONDARY GIFTED STUDENTS

CHAPTER 22

What Makes Them Effective

by Julia Link Roberts

ourtney Lee was named 2004's Mr. Basketball in Indiana. A headline in the *Courier-Journal* in Louisville, KY, read "Gifted freshman playing significant role for Hilltoppers" (Grant, 2005). Undoubtedly, Courtney's abilities were recognized, nurtured, and celebrated during his years in high school. Most of us would agree that the top basketball player is indeed gifted athletically. This point raises a few questions:

- Do students in high school resent the teachers and coaches who recognized Courtney's talent and developed his skills to the highest level possible?
- Could Courtney's skills have reached the same high level without the specialized teaching the coaches provided?
- Would Courtney's possibilities for success in postsecondary athletic endeavors have been the same if he had not had not played varsity basketball, gone to summer basketball camps, and had opportunities to play against very talented basketball players?

Think about your answers to those questions. If you answered "no" to each of the questions, how would you answer if the questions asked were directed to developing talent and abilities in academic areas of mathematics, science, social science, and language arts? How would you answer if the questions were focused on developing talent in creativity, leadership, and the visual and performing arts? Did your answers change? Lee's gifts and talents had been nurtured and developed and most of us celebrate that; consider, though, those young people who are very talented in the core academic areas, as well as in creativity, leadership, and the visual and performing arts. What happens if their talents are not recognized and developed during their secondary school experience?

Teachers in middle and high schools must be in the business of talent development. Educators must offer opportunities that allow young people to have their talents and abilities recognized, nurtured, and celebrated. The goal for secondary teachers is to prepare students to be successful in postsecondary opportunities as they anticipate careers in science, mathematics, technology, the humanities, social sciences, and the arts. This chapter will focus on the characteristics of effective secondary teachers and strategies they employ as they support gifted students in the development of their talents and abilities, nurture their interests, and prepare them to be successful in whatever they pursue following high school.

Some people think that teaching gifted students is easy. Others believe that fairness is evident when everyone has the same learning experiences so all students are taught at the same level. Still others voice the myth that gifted children will make it on their own, so there is no need to make accommodations for them. None of these responses to teaching gifted students recognizes that gifted young people have needs that require instruction that motivates and challenges if they are to reach their potential. Of course, gifted young people do not look needy. Their needs are usually created by strengths rather than deficiencies, yet the needs of gifted students are intense and must be addressed in order to prepare them to be successful in postsecondary educational opportunities and later in their careers. Their needs cannot be met through isolated classes such as Advanced Placement (AP) or honors classes—they need challenge and continuing growth in all classes.

CHARACTERISTICS AND PRACTICES OF EFFECTIVE TEACHERS

What characteristics do great teachers have? Babbage (2002) reported survey results that found participants emphasizing four important points about effective teachers:

1. They challenged students, and they challenged themselves.
2. They used a variety of teaching methods with emphasis on active involvement of students.
3. They were enthusiastic and encouraging.
4. They connected learning with students' lives now, in their real worlds. (p. xi)

The authors of *Making the Most of Middle School: A Field Guide for Parents and Others* (2004) say that teachers "who convey excitement for their subjects, demonstrate relevant applications of their lessons, and provide a framework for understanding new ideas help students learn more than instructors who just regurgitate information" (Jackson, Andrews, Holland, & Pardini, p. 21). They emphasize the importance of teachers setting high expectations and caution that "Educators who recognize adolescents' vast capacity for learning and who spice their instruction with clarity and enthusiasm will be astounded by the response" (p. 21). They describe effective teachers as those with enthusiasm who organize the content to present it in interesting and relevant ways.

Similar characteristics are effective for high school teachers. Relevance, challenge, affection, and respect are the four qualities that Tomlinson and Doubet (2005, p. 9) describe as key for effective teachers to have. The title of the article conveys the essential message—"Reach Them to Teach Them." The authors tell how four teachers engage their high school students in learning in spite of the pressures of time, testing, and number of students.

During the 2004 summer program at Western Kentucky University, 165 gifted 7th–10th graders responded to a questionnaire focused on teachers (Roberts, 2004). The first question asked the students to list the three characteristics they valued most in their teachers. The five characteristics most frequently given were: knowledgeable, having a sense of humor, creative, understanding, and enthusiasm for teaching.

As a follow-up to the open-ended question about characteristics of teachers, the students were asked to respond to what teachers do to encourage students to learn at high levels. Sample responses were:

- "They personally 'zoom in' on you and your work and help you learn at a different level."
- "If the teacher is excited about a subject, that encourages me to learn at high levels."
- "They assign problem solving and have class discussion."
- "They expect a high level performance from you."
- "They want you to succeed and make you work for your grades."
- "They don't put me down or allow the class to put me down when I express my opinions. They listen and encourage us to think outside the box."
- "They offer new material for me to learn."
- "They give me stimulating questions to answer and something new to learn."
- "If the teacher is excited and passionate about his/her subject, it makes it much easier for me to put a lot of effort into whatever I'm doing. Recommending extracurricular learning opportunities also encourages me."

The next question for the summer students concerned what teachers do that discourages students from learning at high levels. Sample responses were:

- "Busy work (excessive amounts of work that requires little thought but takes a lot of time)."
- "Regular questions in assignments that we already know about. They should give us work that makes us think a lot."

- "Worksheets. They don't help at all; they just keep us busy."
- "Redundant assignments."
- "Review on lessons learned in previous grades or earlier in the year."

All middle and high school students deserve high quality teaching from teachers who believe that each student should make continuous progress. Each student is entitled to make at least one year's achievement in each subject he or she studies. Each student needs the opportunity to work hard on challenging tasks, and what content is challenging will differ a great deal among middle or high school students who are the same age. This wide range of abilities, interests, and levels of readiness also is present among our young athletes, and teachers and coaches nurture and develop their athletic talents to reach their potential. The same emphasis on nurturing and developing potential must be applied to academic talents and abilities.

Teachers have a big impact on their students, and the impact is especially great among young people who are gifted and talented in all areas—intellectually, as well as in specific academic areas, creativity, leadership, and the visual and performing arts.

> Gifted students appear to be more profoundly impacted by their teachers' attitudes and actions than are other students. Although their teachers must possess the same characteristics and competencies of all good teachers, the most successful teachers of the gifted develop areas of specific expertise not required in general education. (Croft, 2003, p. 558)

RESEARCH ON TEACHER EFFECTIVENESS

Student achievement is the most direct measure of teacher effectiveness. The teacher makes more difference on student achievement than any other variable. Sanders (1998) stated, "the single largest factor affecting academic growth of populations of students is differences in effectiveness of individual classroom teachers" (p. 27). He makes many observations from the Tennessee Value Added Assessment System (TVAAS) data, and describes students at the highest levels of achievement as having "somewhat less academic growth from year to year than their lower-achieving peers" (pp. 26–27). High-potential and high-ability young people are most likely to make less academic growth than other students are, and the hallmark of teacher effectiveness is producing achievement gains among all students in the class.

Wenglinsky (2000) has studied indicators of teacher quality related to students' performance. In *How Teaching Matters: Bringing the Classroom Back Into Discussion of Teacher Quality*, the report of the Milken Foundation, Wenglinsky found that "certain types of professional development prepare teachers to use specific techniques in their classrooms that result in higher student achievement" (pp. 5–6). The findings link classroom practices and professional development designed to impact classroom practices to student achievement.

The following findings describe such linkages:

- In mathematics, students whose teachers participated in professional development in working with diverse or different populations outperformed their peers by more than a full grade level.
- Students in math whose teachers participated in professional development that emphasized higher-order thinking skills outperformed their peers by 40% of a grade level.
- Students whose teachers participated in professional development that focused on hands-on learning activities outperformed their peers by more than 70% of a grade level in math and 40% of a grade level in science.
- Students in science whose teachers participated in professional development on laboratory skills outperformed their peers by 40% of a grade level. (p. 9)

A switch has been made in the assessment of teacher effectiveness from examining inputs or aspects of preparation to teach or characteristics of teachers to outputs or student achievement. The only teacher input that Wenglinsky found to make a difference in student achievement was the teacher's major or minor in a relevant subject. Students whose teachers had majors or minors in the subject they were teaching outperformed their peers by 40% of a grade level in both mathematics and science (p. 9). Achievement goes up when teachers have preparation in relevant content areas.

Because there is a strong connection between student achievement and professional development on classroom practices focusing on higher-level thinking, hands-on learning, and strategies for working with diverse learners, it is discouraging that only a very small percentage of school districts provide professional development on topics related to gifted education (Westberg et al., 1998). The results of the national survey of professional development practices in gifted education indicated that districts spend 4% of their professional development budget on gifted education, including classroom practices (Westberg et al., p. 5).

The National Middle School Association (NMSA) and the National Association for Gifted Children (NAGC) issued a joint position statement called *Meeting the Needs of High-Ability and High-Potential Learners in the Middle Grades* (NMSA/NAGC, 2004). In the discussion of preservice and in-service staff development in this position statement, it reads that "teachers with training in gifted education are more likely to foster high-level thinking, allow for greater student expression, consider individual variance in their teaching, and understand how to provide high-end challenge" (p. 5). Undoubtedly, the initial teacher preparation and the professional development of teachers needs to focus on strategies for dealing with diverse learners to allow for continuous progress, as well as strategies to develop creative and critical thinkers—ones who can ask good questions and engage in high level thinking.

The National Council for Accreditation of Teacher Education (NCATE) has six standards that must be met by institutions of higher education as they pursue accreditation for their educator preparation programs (2002). Faculty must plan and gather evidence that their graduates have the knowledge, skills, and dispositions to be effective teachers. The focus of the evidence must be on student learning. One of the standards addresses diversity. Specifically, "the unit designs, implements, and evaluates curriculum and experiences for candidates to acquire and apply the knowledge, skills, and dispositions necessary to help all students learn" (NCATE, p. 25). Of course, "all students" includes young people who are gifted and talented. The NCATE standards apply to all individuals who will be applying for certification as educators.

What do secondary teachers need to know and be able to do in order to be effective in teaching students who are gifted and talented? In 2004 the National Association for Gifted Children (NAGC) and The Association for the Gifted (TAG), an affiliate of the Council for Exceptional Children (CEC), launched an initiative to develop joint standards for the preparation of teachers to work with gifted students. Currently the CEC/NAGC standards are in draft form, but are moving through the approval process in both organizations. These standards will be used in the initial preparation of teachers in gifted education, and the advanced standards will be used by institutions as they prepare teachers who have already demonstrated that they have met the initial standards. Once the CEC/NAGC standards are approved by both organizations, they will be submitted to NCATE, and institutions will follow the joint standards as they seek accreditation in gifted education from NCATE. Both NAGC and CEC are members of NCATE. NCATE standards focus on knowledge about the cognitive and social-emotional needs of children who are gifted and talented and strategies to address them. The standards spell out the knowledge, skills, and dispositions needed to be effective educators with students who are gifted and talented.

What effective teachers know and are able to do has a tremendous impact on the learning opportunities available to young people. Teachers who have the knowledge and repertoire of skills to teach their content at high levels challenge all students to work hard learning what they don't already know. They nurture and develop the talents of young people in their classes.

NATIONAL CONCERN ABOUT SECONDARY TEACHING

Secondary education is the subject of conversation and concern among educators, politicians, and the public. In February 2005, the National Governors Association meeting focused on the need for high schools to change dramatically. Educators (Gallagher, 2005; Renzulli, 2005) as well as commissions and other groups (National Governors Association, 2005b; National Science Board, 2004; The Technology Network, 2005; U.S. Commission on National Security/21st Century, 2001) describe "a quiet crisis" in which the numbers in the pipeline for scientists, mathematicians, and engineers in the United States are inadequate to fill the positions in the future; the crisis is the result of not developing our intellectual and creative potential. The Technology Network emphasizes the "critical link between innovation and economic growth and identifying the key public policies that will determine whether and how our nation reaches its innovation potential" (p. 1). Furthermore, the network states, "American prominence in this new era is not assured. In fact, on every front, U.S. global competitiveness is being challenged" (p. 1). Various organizations have produced reports detailing the need to redesign the American high school, and all of the reports address the issue of increased rigor to prepare students to be successful in postsecondary opportunities (Achieve, Inc. & National Governors Association, 2005; Harvey & Housman, 2004; National Commission on the High School Senior Year, 2001; National Governors Association, 2005b). The Gates Foundation has provided millions in grants to support changes in high schools. An Educational Testing Service (ETS, 2005) poll found that only 9% of the U.S. public said they believe that students are challenged by their high school coursework. International comparisons show that high school students in the United States do not perform near the top; in fact, the PISA study indicated that 15-year-olds' scores in mathematics dropped from 18th three years ago to 24th out of 29 Organisation for Economic Co-operation and Development (OECD) countries in 2004 (OECD, 2003; Port & Carey, 2005).

Governor Mark Warner (2005), Chairperson of the National Governors Association, has said that redesigning the American high school is his highest priority. He stated, "It is time for a new approach to high school, one that challenges students and gives them new opportunities to transition to colleges and careers." The National Governors Association (2005a) has a plan called "Ready? Set? Go!: Redesigning the American High School," outlining 10 steps governors can take to accomplish the task. Three of the steps in the plan include defining a rigorous college and work preparatory curriculum for high school students; providing financial incentives for disadvantaged students to take rigorous AP exams and college-preparatory and college-level courses; and expanding college-level learning opportunities in high school for minorities, English language learners, low-income students, and youth with disabilities. The focus is on raising the level of rigor and increasing opportunities for high school graduates to be successful as they proceed in postsecondary opportunities.

High schools are the focus of discussion and planning across the country. In *Raising Our Sights: No High School Senior Left Behind* (2001), the National Commission on the High School Senior Year "unequivocally responds that the primary goal of high school should be graduating students who are ready (and eager) to learn more, capable of thinking critically, and comfortable with the ambiguities of the problem-solving process" (pp. 9, 11). "The Commission calls for more (and more rigorous) alternatives to traditional senior years that merely prolong 'seat-time' by encouraging the development of capstone projects, the development of meaningful internships, and opportunities to take college courses" (p. 5). Of course, the implication of this statement is that secondary teachers must be prepared to focus on high-level content at the same time that they embed high-level processes into their teaching.

Reports have been issued that show that many, if not most, high school students are not well prepared to be successful in postsecondary opportunities. Far too many students are being required to take remedial work in college because they are not prepared adequately. Gifted students who have earned easy A's are among the students who are ill-prepared to pursue a rigorous course of study. A word that is repeated throughout the reports is *rigor*. All of the reports call for increased rigor to ensure that students are ready and able to be successful in their pursuits after high school.

What Effective Teachers of Gifted Students Need to Know, Understand, and Be Able to Do

Middle and high school teachers, counselors, and administrators need to know about the characteristics of young people who are gifted and talented. They need to recognize the needs of gifted individuals, both cognitive and social-emotional needs, and know the research related to the needs of gifted students (Neihart, Reis, Robinson, & Moon, 2002). Educators at all levels must recognize that the needs of gifted young people are often created by a strength or strengths; consequently, the young people may not evoke sympathy. Numerous checklists have been developed, and one for educators to use in assessing high-potential students is presented in Figure 1 in the Teacher Referral Checklist. The checklist includes a place to indicate factors that may inhibit behaviors indicating high potential.

Effective teachers in secondary schools prepare students, including those who are gifted and talented, to be successful in postsecondary education and careers. These students need to experience challenges that will allow them to accept educational opportunities with confidence. These students need a vision of potential career options that will match their interests and maximize their strengths. Effective secondary teachers provide the challenge and vision to enable students to be successful in challenging educational opportunities that lead to careers of their choice.

What do secondary students wish for their teachers to be? A teen interviewed for the Louisville, KY, *Courier Journal* (2005) was asked what he appreciated most in a teacher. The response was "their ability to stimulate my mind." Challenge is an important goal for all students, yet learning experiences that will challenge one student or a cluster of students will be too much of a challenge or present too little challenge for others. Secondary teachers who differentiate learning experiences can address a range of students' interests, needs, abilities, and levels of readiness. Three key components of differentiation and an accompanying question guide the planning and implementation of differentiated learning experiences (Roberts and Inman, in press):

- Planning—What do I want the students to know, understand, and/or be able to do?
- Preassessment—Who already knows, understands, and/or can use the content or demonstrate the skills?
- Differentiation—What will I do for him, her, or them so they can make continuous progress and extend their learning?

Differentiation must be planned; it must be intentional. Responding to differences among students is important; however, responding will not take the place of

The following criteria are useful in assessing high potential of students. Please use one form per student to assign a value of 3 (to a considerable degree), 2 (to some degree), or 1 (to little if any degree) for each characteristic.

1. Learns rapidly and easily   _____
2. Uses much common sense and practical knowledge   _____
3. Retains easily what has been presented   _____
4. Knows about many things of which other students are unaware   _____
5. Uses a large number of words easily and accurately and appreciates word power   _____
6. Recognizes relationships, comprehends meanings, and seems to "get more out of things"   _____
7. Is alert with keen powers of observation and responds quickly   _____
8. Likes difficult subjects and challenging tasks for the fun of learning   _____
9. Asks penetrating questions and seeks out causes and reasons   _____
10. Is a good guesser with an intuitive sense   _____
11. Reads voraciously well beyond age level, and sets aside time for reading   _____
12. Questions the accepted ways of doing things   _____
13. Prefers to work independently with minimal direction   _____
14. Has a longer attention span than age peers   _____
15. Has little patience for routine drill and practice   _____
16. Tends to be critical of self and others, with high standards and seeking perfection   _____
17. Seldom needs more than one demonstration or instruction in order to carry out an activity   _____
18. Perseveres on projects and ideas   _____
19. Is withdrawn yet very capable when pressed   _____
20. Demonstrates remarkable talent in one or more areas   _____
21. Uses materials in innovative an unusual ways   _____
22. Creates unusual stories, pictures, examples, models, or products   _____
23. Has many interests and follows them with zeal   _____
24. Makes extensive collections, with sustained focus   _____
25. Invents contrivances, gadgets, and new ways of doing things   _____
26. Prefers to be around older students or adults, communicating effectively with them   _____
27. Has an advanced sense of humor and "gets it" when others may not   _____
28. Influences other students to do things   _____
29. Is serious-minded and intolerant of prolonged foolishness   _____
30. Shows much sensitivity toward people, social issues, and right and wrong   _____

Please check any of the following factors which apply. If present along with a number of the attributes above, they may provide additional validation of high ability.

   A. A disability that affects learning and/or behavior   _____
   B. Living in a home where English is the second (or third) language   _____
   C. Transience (three or more moves)   _____
   D. Social or educational isolation from resources and stimulation   _____
   E. Home responsibilities or employment that interferes with school   _____
   F. Irregular school attendance   _____
   G. Little or no interaction between school personnel and family   _____

Additional comments:

Figure 1. Teacher Referral Checklist
Note. From *Consultation, Collaboration, and Teamwork for Students With Special Needs* (p. 5e), by P. Dettmer, L. P. Thurston, & N. J. Dyck, 2005, Boston: Allyn & Bacon, Copyright ©2005 by Pearson Education. Reprinted with permission.

planning because students will differ in their levels of readiness to study a particular content area. Strickland (2005) emphasized the need to be intentional when planning for differentiating learning experiences.

Each student deserves the opportunity to make continuous progress—to make academic growth—in school. In sports, the top athletes are allowed to advance with special learning opportunities to help them develop their abilities and talents.

> A precocious Vinny would not have the high-jump bar (note the adjective high) frozen at a designated low level until everyone else grows into his skill; he would be given time, equipment, space, instruction, and encouragement to develop his special talents. A tall, precocious freshman basketball player would not be relegated to the bench for the next one or two years if she could contribute to school victory and pride now. It is unfortunate when schools and the public forego age-/grade-level constraints for performance areas that don't really matter all that much in the overall aim of education (skills needed primarily for competitive sports, not fitness skills needed for quality of life), but then "throttle down" bright minds that could contribute so much to quality of life for all. (Dettmer, Thurston, & Dyck, 2005, p. 251)

The pace and the complexity of the curriculum will differ for young people with varying levels of readiness for learning about specific content. *A Nation Deceived: How Schools Hold Back America's Brightest Students* (Colangelo, Assouline, & Gross, 2004) outlines 18 types of acceleration. The report states, "Acceleration levels the playing field of opportunity because any cost to the family or school is minimal" (p. 7). Acceleration options provide teachers with a means to address the need of gifted students to learn at an accelerated pace. Preassessment is an essential step in determining the level at which students are ready to learn. Stanley (2000) described the goal accurately in the title of an article: "Helping Students Learn What They Don't Already Know." Teachers who challenge all young people understand and have strategies to alter the pace and complexity of content to match students' interests, abilities, and levels of readiness.

Preadolescent and adolescent students who are gifted and talented need teachers who understand and respect differences in the social-emotional development of young people. One of their needs is to have peers who share their interests and have similar abilities. After her daughter participated in a summer program for gifted young people, novelist Barbara Kingsolver (2002) wrote, "Her experience at SCATS helped her understand the potential rewards of belonging to a peer group that's more interested in Jane Austen and Shakespeare than Calvin Klein and Tommy Hilfiger" (p. 9). Another young person reported that he often worried that the teachers thought he knew too much. Gifted young people need teachers who understand and support their needs to be with intellectual peers and teachers who understand and support their social-emotional, as well as their cognitive development. They need to be celebrated and nurtured—just like Mr. Basketball.

Teachers who are talent finders and developers understand that children who are gifted and talented come from all ethnic and racial groups, as well as from all socioeconomic levels. Teachers must recognize and develop talent among children who are diverse, including young people with disabilities and gifts. They have strategies for incorporating curriculum that reflects multicultural understanding. In Table 1, Ford and Trotman (2001) describe what teachers must know and be able to do to work effectively as they develop the talents and skills of diverse populations of young people who are gifted and talented. Undoubtedly, gifted and talented young people come from diverse backgrounds.

RECOMMENDATIONS

All secondary students deserve teachers who are enthusiastic about teaching, well-versed in the content they teach, respectful of individuals, and able to relate to young people. In addition, middle and high school teachers who develop the abilities and talents of young people who are gifted and talented will:

1. be familiar with and use state and national curriculum standards, recognizing that they are minimum standards and that some young people have already exceeded the levels established by standards and that every student deserves to make continuous progress;
2. implement differentiation strategies that intentionally match what is learned and how it is learned based on data gleaned from pre- and on-going assessment;
3. know the research related to acceleration and implement acceleration options as appropriate; and
4. understand and respond appropriately to the social-emotional, as well as the cognitive, needs of secondary young people who are gifted and talented to develop their abilities and talents, foster positive self-esteem, and ensure study skills needed for success in postsecondary opportunities.

The goal for teachers is to develop talents and abilities of all students to optimum levels. Reaching minimum standards will hold back many young people from reaching their potential. Without hard work and challenge, many young people will not be ready for opportunities that could have been in their futures. When talents and abilities are nurtured and developed, all young people, including those who are gifted and talented, will be successful in postsecondary opportunities and later on in their careers.

> You don't prepare a young man or woman to become a world class athlete by keeping him or her in regular gym classes and by not allowing him or her to compete against other youngsters who can provide appropriate levels of challenge. . . . . You don't develop world leaders such as Martin Luther King, Golda Meir, and Mahatma Gandhi by having them practice basic skills over and over again or by reiterating mundane concepts that they can undoubt-

Table 1
Characteristics of Effective Teachers of Gifted Diverse Students

Characteristics of Gifted Education Teachers	Characteristics of Multicultural Education Teachers	Characteristics of Gifted Multicultural Education Teachers
Knowledge of the nature and needs of gifted students.	Knowledge of the nature and needs of diverse students.	Knowledge of the nature and needs of students who are gifted and diverse.
Ability to develop methods and materials for use with gifted students.	Ability to develop methods and materials for use with diverse students.	Ability to develop methods and materials for use with students who are gifted and diverse.
Skills in individual teaching.	Skills in addressing cultural differences in students' learning styles, cognitive styles, and behavioral styles.	Skills in addressing individual and cultural differences.
Skills in teaching higher level thinking skills and questioning techniques.	Skills in teaching higher level thinking skills and questioning techniques using multicultural resources and materials.	Skills in teaching higher level thinking skills and questioning techniques using multicultural resources and materials.
Ability to identify gifted students.	Ability to recognize the strengths of diverse students.	Ability to recognize the strengths of students who are gifted and diverse.
Seeks to develop students' self-concept.	Seeks to develop students' concept as a person of color (i.e., racial identity).	Seeks to develop students' sense of self as a gifted individual and diverse individual.
Skills in counseling gifted students.	Skills in counseling diverse students (multicultural counseling skills).	Skills in counseling students who are gifted and diverse.
Skills in creating an environment in which gifted students feel challenged and safe to explore and express their uniqueness.	Skills in creating an environment in which diverse students feel challenged and safe to explore and express their uniqueness.	Skills in creating an environment in which diverse gifted students feel challenged and safe to explore and express their uniqueness.

Note. From "Teachers of Gifted Students: Suggested Multicultural Characteristics and Competencies," by D. Y. Ford and M. F. Trotman, 2001, *Roeper Review*, 23, p. 236. Copyright ©2001 by Roeper Review, P.O. Box 329, Bloomfield Hills, MI 48303. Reprinted with permission.

edly learn faster than all their schoolmates and, in some cases, even many of their teachers. Talent development is the "business" of our field, and we must never lose sight of this goal (Renzulli & Reis, 2004, p. 17).

REFERENCES

Achieve, Inc., & National Governors Association. (2005). *An action agenda for improving America's high schools*. Washington, DC: Achieve.

Babbage, K. (2002). *Extreme teaching*. Lanham, MD: The Scarecrow Press.

Colangelo, N., Assouline, S. G., & Gross, M. U. M. (2004). *A nation deceived: How schools hold back America's brightest students* (Vol. 1). Iowa City: Connie Belin & Jacqueline N. Blank International Center for Gifted Education and Talented Development.

Croft, L. J. (2003). Teachers of the gifted: Gifted teachers. In N. Colangelo & G. A. Davis (Eds.), *Handbook of gifted education* (5th ed., pp. 558–571). Boston: Allyn & Bacon.

Dettmer, P., Thurston, L. P., & Dyck, N. J. (2005). *Consultation, collaboration, and teamwork for students with special needs* (5th ed.). Boston: Pearson Education.

Educational Testing Service (2005). *New ETS Poll*. Retrieved June 25, 2005, from https://www.ets.org

Ford, D. Y., & Trotman, M. F. (2001). Teachers of gifted students: Suggested multicultural characteristics and competencies, *Roeper Review, 23*, 235–239.

Gallagher, J. J. (2005). National security and educational excellence. *Education Week, 24*(38), 32–33, 40.

Grant, M. (2005, January 24). Gifted freshman playing significant role for Hilltoppers. *Courier-Journal*, p. C1.

Harvey, J., & Housman, N. (2004). *Crisis or possibility? Conversations about the American high school*. Washington, DC: National High School Alliance.

Jackson, A. W., & Andrews, P. G. (with Holland, H., & Pardini, P.). (2004). *Making the most of middle school: A field guide for parents and others*. New York: Teachers College Press.

Kingsolver, B. (2002, Winter). Letter. *The Challenge*, p. 9.

Martin is center stage (2005, March 25). *Courier-Journal*. p. E3.

National Commission on the High School Senior Year. (2001). *Raising our sights: No high school senior left behind*. Washington, DC: U.S. Government.

National Council for Accreditation of Teacher Education. (2002). *Professional standards for the accreditation of school, colleges, and departments of education*. Washington, DC: Author.

National Governors Association. (2005a). *Ready? Set? Go?: Redesigning the American high school*. Retrieved May 5, 2005, from http://www.nga.org

National Governors Association. (2005b). *America's high school: The front line in the battle for our economic future*. Retrieved on May 2, 2005, at http://www.nga.org

National Middle School Association, & National Association for Gifted Children. (2004). *Meeting the needs of high-ability and high-potential learners in the middle grades: A joint position statement of the National Middle School Association and the National Association for Gifted Children*. Washington, DC: Authors.

National Science Board. (2004). *A companion to science and engineering indicators 2004*. Retrieved March 1, 2004, from http://www.nsf.gov/nsb/documents

Neihart, M., Reis, S. M., Robinson, N. M., & Moon, S. M. (2002). *The social and emotional development of gifted children: What do we know?* Waco, TX: Prufrock Press.

Organisation for Economic Co-operation and Development. (2003). *Learning for tomorrow's world: First results from PISA 2003*. Paris: Author.

Port, O., & Carey, J. (2005, March 28). The Intel award winners: Meet the best and brightest. *Business Week Online*. Retrieved August 15, 2005, from http://www.businessweek.com/magazine/content/05_13/b3926401.htm

Renzulli, J. J. (2005), A quiet crisis is clouding the future of R&D. *Education Week*, *24*(38), 32–33, 40.

Renzulli, J. J., & Reis, S. M. (2004). The reform movement and the quiet crisis in gifted education. In J. J. Renzulli & S. M. Reis (Eds.), *Public policy in gifted education* (pp. 1–19). Thousand Oaks, CA: Corwin Press.

Roberts, J. L. (2004). *Middle and high school gifted students' perceptions of teachers*. Unpublished manuscript.

Roberts, J. L., & Inman, T. F. (in press). *Differentiation for beginners*. Waco, TX: Prufrock Press.

Sanders, W. L. (1998, December). Value-added assessment. *School Administrator*, 55, 24–27,

Stanley, J. C. (2000). Helping students learn what they don't already know. *Psychology, Public Policy, and Law*, *47*, 216–222.

Strickland, C. A. (2005, April). Differentiation or differentiation? *National Middle School Association Middle E-Connections*. Retrieved May 25, 2005, from http://www.nmsa.org

The Technology Network. (2005, March). *The TechNet innovation initiative and 2005 innovation policy agenda*. Retrieved April 15, 2005, from http://www.technet.org

Tomlinson, C. A., & Doubet, K. (2005). Reach them to teach them. *Education Leadership*, *62*, 8–13.

U.S. Commission on National Security/21st Century. (2001). *Road map for national security: Imperative for change*. Retrieved January 15, 2005, from http://www.nssg.gov

Warner, M. (2005, February). *Wilbur J. Cohen lecture*. Keynote speech presented at the annual meeting of the American Association for Colleges of Teacher Education, Washington, DC.

Wenglinsky, H. (2000). *How teaching matters: Bringing the classroom back into discussions of teacher quality* (A Policy Information Center Report). Princeton, NJ: Educational Testing Service. (ERIC Document Reproduction Service No. ED447128).

Westberg, K. L., Burns, D. E., Gubbins, E. J., Reis, S. M., Park, S., & Maxfield, L. R. (1998, Spring). Professional development practices in gifted education: Results of a national survey. *The National Research Center on the Gifted and Talented Newsletter*, 3–4.

PREPARING TEACHERS TO WORK WITH HIGH-ABILITY YOUTH AT THE SECONDARY LEVEL

CHAPTER 23

Issues and Implications for Licensure

by Ann Robinson
& Penny Britton Kolloff

GLENN'S HIGH SCHOOL STORY

Glenn is thinking about his next assignment for 10th-grade English. He's got a plan to write an essay integrating the themes from *The Tale of Two Cities*, *Les Misérables*, and *Don Quixote*. His teacher, Mrs. Naylor, asked students to select one of these works for the writing assignment; each novel is 300–400 pages long. However, Glenn has already read all three; he is a fast and voracious reader. He's determined to modify the assignment, and Mrs. Naylor genially comments that he's "thematically astute and attentive to literary style." She observes that he's "voluble, but not smart alecky." Mrs. Naylor appreciates Glenn, tolerates his eccentricities, and understands that attention to detail takes a back seat to his big picture analysis. She comments, "Here's a kid who is grateful to his teachers and who takes advantage of absolutely everything the school has to offer."

Glenn sounds like a secondary teacher's dream, but there is more to the story. Glenn is a significant challenge. His blended dysfunctional family didn't want him to take advanced classes nor want to help him with the modest fees for Advanced Placement (AP) exams. In an apparent contradiction, he is punished by his stepmother if he does not make straight A's (which he does not).

In the remaining years of high school, Glenn takes as many AP courses as he possibly can—12 in all. In some cases, he signs up for exams for which there is no corresponding course in his high school—Psychology, Comparative Government, and French Language and Literature. During his senior year, Mrs. Naylor guides Glenn in his choices; she persuades him to take eight, rather than 11 AP exams and helps him to get fee reductions on the ones he is desperate to complete. Glenn is determined to go to college even though he will receive no financial support from either of his professional parents.

Despite the lack of familial understanding, support, or dollars, Glenn went to college with advanced standing, secured a small tuition remission to an excellent university, and went deeply into debt in order to stay in school. He is now in a war zone as an interpreter trying to make enough money to pay off his college loans and expenses. Glenn literally put himself in harm's way in order to stay in school and learn. Mrs. Naylor's heart still aches.

Glenn's teacher is skilled. She holds a master's degree in gifted education and is also prepared to teach Advanced Placement Language and Composition. Her knowledge about the development of talent, particularly in specific content domains helps her "understand a kid like Glenn," she says. "I learned about the family and classroom dynamics surrounding a bright, creative and highly nonconforming adolescent. I learned to modify assignments to challenge (or rather to keep up with) him. It wasn't easy knowing when to step in with a guiding hand, or how to leverage help for him when he needed it most, but I did the best I could." Glenn and the other gifted adolescents in Mrs. Naylor's class are fortunate. She cared enough about her bright students to seek out additional training, and she was able to put her preparation to work.

MIDDLE SCHOOL CONVERSATIONS AT JEFFERSON

Dr. Brooks, principal of Jefferson Middle School, enters the seventh grade team planning area. Coffee cup in hand, she greets the four teachers seated around the small table and pulls up a chair.

"We are enrolling two new students, twins, next week," she begins. "They are moving here from North Carolina, and their parents have called me to talk about their placements. Each has been in a program for gifted students since entering school early. Keily is a math whiz, and David excels in reading and writing. Their parents want to be sure that their needs will be met here at Jefferson."

"But, we don't have a gifted program," says Debbie, math teacher on the team. "We agreed in our planning process 2 years ago that we wouldn't group kids or give them labels."

"It goes against our philosophy," adds Bill, the science teacher.

Dr. Brooks nods. "I conveyed that to the parents. But, they described the things the kids were doing in their program, and they asked we continue to meet the needs of these students when they arrive at Jefferson."

"Look," Amelia chimes in, "most of our students' scores on the state tests are above average for the state and the district. We must be doing something right. Our kids feel good about themselves, and they have lots of opportunities to explore different areas." Amelia is proud that her students score exceptionally well in language arts year after year.

"Hey, none of us has any training in what to do with gifted kids, and the district isn't likely to offer any since our emphasis is keeping everyone up to the standards on the state assessments." Debbie's voice takes on a note of frustration. "How can we be expected to offer special programs for a couple of new students with pushy parents?"

Dr. Brooks listens patiently as the teachers express themselves. Jonathan, a social studies teacher, can usually be counted on to smooth out the conversation, and he scratches his beard thoughtfully. "What kinds of things have the students been doing in their current school?"

Dr. Brooks looks at her notes from the conversation with the parents. "Keily has been in an accelerated math program for the past 2 years. She's working with a group of six 7th graders who are taking algebra this year under the direction of the high school math department chair."

"Whoa," Debbie says, "We don't have anything like that, and I can't imagine the mess we'd be in if our parents got wind that acceleration was a possibility."

Dr. Brooks continues, "David has been grouped with other verbally talented students and has been reading advanced materials. His group has also been in a writing workshop taught by one of the middle school language arts teachers. From what I gather, the school from which the twins are coming has a wide variety of programs and services that can accommodate talented students. What I would like to do at this point is ask you to review the records that are coming from the North Carolina school and see if we can come up with ways to continue their educational programs within our school. I believe that we have resources here at Jefferson to address the specific needs of these students."

Dr. Brooks and her staff have encountered key issues in serving gifted learners—grouping, acceleration, and the distinct differences in the profiles and interests of students who are all too often assumed to be the same. In order to meet the needs of Keily and David, the faculty at Jefferson Middle School need to know how to recognize giftedness, what to expect from such learners, how to adapt instruction for them, and how to plan across grade levels to ensure their progress through school.

As the two preceding scenarios illustrate, the challenges facing teachers of high-ability adolescents and emerging adolescents are significant. What knowledge, skills, and dispositions are necessary for highly qualified teachers of high-ability learners at the secondary level?

PURPOSE

The purpose of this chapter is to review selected literature on teacher preparation in gifted education with a focus on secondary issues and implications, to summarize the shift from certification to licensure in teacher preparation, to explore the teacher outcomes jointly proposed by the Council for Exceptional Children (CEC) and the National Association for Gifted Children (NAGC), and to recommend the integration of specific secondary topics, readings, and resources into teacher preparation courses in gifted education.

LITERATURE ON TEACHER PREPARATION IN GIFTED EDUCATION

The literature on teacher preparation in gifted education is part of a broader knowledge base on teacher characteristics, proposed skills and competencies, and classroom practices with respect to high-ability learners. These strands of inquiry converge to set the context for the small, but consistent research literature investigating the effects of training in gifted education on teacher knowledge and skill. A selective review of representative studies in the field traces the shift from characteristics for the selection of teachers to delineating knowledge, skills, and dispositions as outcomes of professional preparation programs at the preservice and in-service levels.

Teacher Characteristics

The interest in teacher characteristics with respect to high-ability learners has engaged the field over several decades. One of the influential early studies by Bishop (1968) was carried out with secondary teachers. By surveying 186 high school seniors from 65 different districts in a southern state, Bishop identified 109 teachers who were nominated by one or more gifted students as "most successful." For comparison purposes, Bishop also randomly selected 97 teachers from a pool of 500 educators who taught the adolescents, but were not identified as their most successful teachers. Both groups were surveyed; a subset of the 30 most successful teachers was also interviewed and given a measure of verbal intelligence. Bishop focused on the differences between the two groups evidenced through their survey responses. In terms of interests and activities, identified teachers tended toward intellectualism with reported literary hobbies, cultural involvement, and a strong need for achievement. Student descriptions of successful teachers noted their subject matter expertise and the desire to learn more themselves, as well as motivating and inspiring their students. The data sources of the survey, interview, and student descriptions also converged on the importance of teacher attitude toward bright learners. Teachers identified as most successful were praised by their high-ability students for their positive attitude, reported that they preferred to teach high-ability learners, and saw their teaching role as student centered.

In addition to the early study of secondary teachers by Bishop (1968), other researchers have investigated the characteristics of successful teachers of the gifted through student nomination. For example, a recent study focused on secondary teachers and their students to examine teacher background and personal characteristics. Using a survey and the Myers-Briggs Type Inventory, Mills (2003) reported successful teachers held advanced degrees in a content area, infrequently reported training or preparation in gifted education, and were more likely to prefer intuition and thinking as measured by the Myers-Briggs personality inventory. In terms of personality characteristics, Mills concluded that exemplary teachers resembled their high-ability adolescent students. It is worth noting that Mills' sample was drawn from individuals teaching in a university talent search rather than in a school setting. Whether the results concerning teacher background, training, and personality variables would be robust across a more general teacher sample is not clear.

As Feldhusen (1997) noted, not all studies of teacher characteristics rely on surveys and questionnaires. To investigate the ideal teacher of the gifted, Whitlock and DuCette (1989) identified 10 excellent and 10 average teachers of the gifted for an in-depth interview study. Their results focused on several variables that appear to be characteristics rather than teacher competencies: teacher enthusiasm, self-confidence, and achievement motivation. While these characteristics in teachers of high-ability youth are certainly desirable, they do not appear to be unique. In a review of the literature on teachers and teacher preparation in gifted education, Feldhusen concluded

> ... studies of the ideal teacher of the gifted seem to list virtues that should characterize all teachers or all leaders. They also indicate stable, long-range traits that may be useful in selecting teachers but little value as guides in developing teacher education programs. (p. 548)

Classroom Practices

If personal characteristics are not sufficient to guide preparation programs, examining classroom practices of preservice and in-service teachers with respect to high-ability learners serves to identify gaps and to locate promising practices that can inform the development of appropriate experiences for educators. The research on classroom practices can be divided along two axes describing the teachers sampled: preservice versus in-service and trained versus untrained teachers.

In-Service Teachers

Unfortunately, large scale studies indicate that little is done by in-service teachers to adapt instruction for high-ability learners (Archambault et al., 1993; Gentry, Rizza, & Owen, 2002; Starko & Schack, 1989; Westberg, Archambault, Dobyns, & Salvin, 1993). In both a national survey (Archambault et al.) and a follow-up to an observational study of 46 classrooms (Westberg et al.), little differentiation was reported or observed for high-ability learners. The national survey and the classroom observational study focused on elementary classrooms and should be cautiously generalized to middle school or high school classrooms.

Another large scale study, however, specifically included middle schools and investigated the relationship between teachers' and students' perceptions of choice and challenge in the classroom (Gentry et al.). Using comparisons between student responses on the My Class Activities measure (Gentry & Gable, 2001) and the Classroom Practices-Teacher Survey (Archambault et al., 1993), the researchers found no agreement between students and teachers in the perceived level of opportunities for choice or challenge. The study included 64 middle school teachers who reported a range of professional development experiences in gifted education: 84% reported attending at least one in-service in gifted education and 56% had taken graduate coursework. In other words, approximately half of the middle school teacher sample had taken some graduate course work related to high-ability learners. Neither the scope nor the intensity of the training is known, nor were the data analyzed by the training variable. What can be concluded from the study by Gentry and her colleagues is that teachers more often believe they are offering choices and challenges in their classrooms than students perceive them to be. The findings hold constant across both elementary and middle level settings.

Finally, a study by Starko and Shack (1989) also investigated the perceptions of teachers related to high-ability learners and included the comparison among specialist teachers of the gifted, classroom teachers, and preservice teachers. Unlike the previous studies that did not focus on differences in preparation among teachers, Starko and Shack analyzed teacher perceptions by group. Of the three groups, teachers of gifted students were more likely to perceive that high-ability learners needed specific strategies and practices, had higher self-efficacy in terms of providing those opportunities in the classroom, and reported a higher incidence in providing them. Among the strategies Starko and Shack selected were acceleration, independent study based on student interest, higher level thinking, eliminating previously mastered material, grouping for instruction, creativity, use of alternate texts, simulations, and learning centers. While the focus of the study was not to evaluate the effects of training, Starko and Shack found that teachers of the gifted reported more experience with and more formal training in gifted education. They also found that across all three groups, the recognition of a strategy as one which met the needs of high-ability learners was not sufficient to prompt the reported use of that strategy.

Overall, the studies by Archambault and colleagues (1993), Westberg and colleagues (1993), and Starko and Shack (1989) present a picture of limited adaptation in classroom practice to meet the needs of high-ability learners. If we adopt these reports as our baseline for in-service educators, then postgraduate preparation programs have considerable ground to cover.

Preservice Teachers

To trace teacher dispositions, knowledge, and skills backwards, studies of preservice teachers are necessary. In addition to the research on in-service educators, there are a small number of studies that focus on the perceptions, knowledge, and skills of preservice teachers with respect to high-ability learners. To investigate perceptions of the concept, "gifted student," Ribich, Barone and Agostino (1998) presented preservice teachers with taped interviews of gifted secondary students who were either achieving or underachieving. The sample included 85 preservice teachers, 21 of whom were secondary majors. The preservice teachers responded to a semantic differential measure prior to and following the presentation of the taped interviews of achieving and underachieving high-ability learners. For the most part, preservice teachers viewed gifted learners positively; their attitudes did not change after viewing taped interviews of achieving gifted secondary students. However, when the secondary student was an underachiever, preservice teachers were far less positive about the concept, "gifted student."

Other studies of preservice teachers report complementary findings. In an observational and interview study of 10 preservice teachers, Tomlinson et al. (1994) investigated preservice teachers during their student teaching experiences. The purpose of the study was to examine "factors in the student teaching experience of 10 preservice teachers which relate to their instruction of academically diverse learners, among whom are gifted learners." (p. 108). Across the 10 cases, the researchers extracted five common themes. First, preservice teachers believe there are student differences with respect to need. Second, preservice teachers are ambiguous in their operational definitions of learners who are academically able or who are academic strugglers. They tended to equate compliant or happily engaged behavior with giftedness and frustration with learning difficulties. Third, preservice teachers have narrow conceptualizations of differentiated instruction. Fourth, preservice teachers have few strategies for responding to the academic diversity in their classrooms. The predominant strategy noted by Tomlinson and colleagues was to have the more able students tutor lower achieving learners. Finally, there are factors that actively discourage preservice teachers from addressing academic diversity. Preservice teachers focus on classroom management and content and skill coverage, are uncertain how to assess prior knowledge or readiness, and are actively discouraged from adapting instruction for high-ability learners by cooperating teachers and university supervisors.

The pattern, then, from the research on teachers is that few adaptations are made among in-service general educators and that recognition of the needs of high-ability learners does not necessarily result in adaptations to meet their needs. For preservice teachers, the message is similar. Needs are generally recognized, but the skill for meeting them in initial teaching placements is limited or nonexistent.

Clinkenbeard and Kolloff (2001), acknowledging the paucity of training for those who are preparing to teach, formulated a set of approaches for including gifted education in preservice education. These strategies suggest various ways to equip new teachers with introductory knowledge of characteristics and needs of gifted learners. Croft's (2003) recent review also highlights promising practices.

Effects of and Responses to Training

Given the baseline of minimal modification by teachers, even those with exposure to professional development in gifted education, what bright spots in the training literature can guide professional preparation in preservice and in-service programs? Early work by Feldhusen and colleagues suggested topics and practicum activities with high-ability learners for in-service teachers (Feldhusen, 1973), described a program for selecting and training teachers through Saturday experiences (Feldhusen & Hansen, 1987), and evaluated the same training model (Feldhusen &

Koopmans-Dayton, 1987). In later studies, a practicum was evaluated by the participating teachers (Feldhusen & Huffman, 1988) and finally a rigorous comparison study of trained and untrained teachers documented that both trained observers in the classroom and students themselves observed differences due to training (Hansen & Feldhusen, 1994).

Three studies that investigated formal preparation are instructive. Although secondary teachers were not a primary focus in the analyses, inferences about the preparation of secondary teachers may be teased out of them. First, Hanninen (1988) reported a scenario study in which 15 teachers were asked to respond to ambiguous cases of high-ability learners. Five of the teachers were classified as experts with at least one formal course in gifted education and additional professional development workshops. Another five teachers were experienced, but had no formal training in gifted education; the third group was comprised of preservice teachers. Hanninen found that expert teachers with training in gifted education took longer to respond to the scenarios, perceived the ambiguous scenarios as problems to be solved, and produced more elaborated responses to them than did the experienced, untrained teachers and the preservice teachers.

Second, Copenhaver and McIntyre (1992) surveyed 85 in-service teachers to determine the effects of formal training on teachers' perceptions of the characteristics of gifted children. Of the 85 teachers, 27 taught grades 7–12. In terms of training, Copenhaver and McIntyre report differences in response to their open-ended instrument, but these did not form a clear pattern. They did note that trained teachers were more likely to report creative characteristics, extensive vocabulary, and motivational level than were untrained educators. When analyzing responses by grade level, secondary teachers were less likely than elementary teachers to mention negative characteristics of gifted learners. Unfortunately, it is not clear whether there were differences between trained and untrained secondary teachers; the differences appear to be main effects between elementary and secondary teachers in general.

Finally, a rigorously designed field study compared trained and untrained teachers and found differences in classroom practice (Hansen & Feldhusen, 1994). In a sample of 82 teachers, trained and untrained teachers were observed in their own classrooms by observers blind to their level of training. Using a structured classroom observation instrument, the Purdue Observation Form, observers detected differences in classroom practice on 11 of 12 dimensions. Elementary teachers scored higher than did secondary teachers. Trained teachers with more coursework were rated higher than those with less or no coursework. The differences noted by the trained observers (who were skilled in gifted education) were mirrored by student perceptions. Students reported their trained teachers lectured less, emphasized higher level thinking more, conducted more discussions, and placed less emphasis on grades.

Overall, the literature on training does not focus on secondary teachers. The focus of the field on elementary concerns is mirrored in the training literature. However, secondary teachers were included in the samples of at least two of the three training studies reviewed here. What is clear from the small cluster of training studies is that training does matter. Trained teachers are more likely to focus on the concerns of high-ability learners, report a richer array of their characteristics, and engage in classroom practices adapted to their needs than untrained educators.

From Input Systems to Output Systems in Teacher Preparation: A Short History

The preparation of teachers to work with high-ability learners is situated in the general trends in the preparation of teachers. According to Roth and Pipho (1990), early efforts to license teachers employed examinations to indicate mastery, but this trend began to shift in the 1920s to the program approval approach in which teacher certification was largely the result of candidates completing an approved university program. These programs generally specified required courses, but did not rest heavily on entrance examinations, nor exit performance of the candidates. During the 1980s, school reform efforts affected teacher preparation, as well as other areas of education. Key reforms involve the increased participation of professional associations in developing and gaining consensus on the knowledge, skills, and dispositions required for capable teachers and an increased emphasis placed on documentation of candidates' performance through an array of assessments.

In terms of gifted education, the shift can be traced from prescriptive lists of courses, recommended experiences, and needed resources (inputs) to measures of what teachers know and are able to do (outcomes). Although the work on teacher competencies in gifted education is minimally empirical, attention has been steadily devoted to identifying a set of skills and a knowledge base necessary for teachers to work with high-ability youth effectively. Early work by Seeley (1979), Hultgren (1981), and Hultgren and Seeley (1982) surveyed university personnel and practitioners to identify teacher competencies.

In the 1980s, the National Association of Gifted Children (NAGC) Professional Training Institutes, initiated by then-President John Feldhusen of Purdue University, brought together university personnel and practitioners to discuss professional development issues and produce a set of documents to guide the training efforts in the field. Teams of educators developed recommendations for in-service training, certification programs, and graduate programs in gifted education. These early documents identify topics and course titles for various levels of training, including in-service, certification, master's and doctoral programs (National Association for Gifted Children, 1982).

In the latter 1990s, building on the work of the Professional Training Institutes, Jeanette Parker of the University of Southern Louisiana convened 50 educators to develop program standards in response to the National Council for Accreditation of Teacher Education (NCATE) requirements for teacher preparation programs (Parker, 1996). The document is organized by the four categories required by NCATE at that time: Conceptual Framework, Candidates for Graduate Programs in Gifted Education, Professional Education Faculty, and Resources. In the NAGC position paper on Standards for Graduate Programs in Gifted Education (1995), the subsection on Professional Studies under the category of Conceptual Framework best captures the teacher outcomes. Divided into knowledge and skills, the 1995 NAGC Standards for Graduate Programs in Gifted Education identify 13 topics and 17 distinct skills for prospective specialists in gifted education. They range across the familiar territory of foundations of gifted education, characteristics of gifted learners, theoretical models, special populations, current issues, development of learning experiences, identification, assessment, and the integration of general and gifted education.

During the 1990s, the Council for Exceptional Children (CEC) also engaged in the development of teacher competencies for special educators and identified a special education core of knowledge and skills for all beginning special educators. In addition to this shared core, the divisions of CEC developed knowledge and skill outcomes related to particular exceptionalities. As a member of the Executive Board of the CEC Division, The Association for the Gifted (TAG), and a member of the CEC Board of Governors, Karen Rogers, from the University of St. Thomas, crafted a set of competencies for the field of gifted education. Through a national validation survey of professionals in the field, these competencies became the specialized knowledge base for gifted education in relationship to NCATE professional societies.

As teacher preparation continued to evolve into an accountability and outcome-based effort, the two professional organizations, CEC-TAG and NAGC, forged links to examine the outcomes and chart a course of action. In 2002, two joint committees with some overlapping membership were appointed by the two organizations; the result led to the development of joint teacher outcomes for initial and advanced teacher candidates in gifted education.

In the spring of 2004, a series of work sessions and meetings of the leadership of CEC-TAG and NAGC resulted in a set of joint outcomes for initial teacher licensure in gifted education. Approved by the board of NAGC and the board of TAG, they currently await final CEC approval. These outcomes now form the core of knowledge and skills that the field adopted to guide the preparation of beginning teachers of high-ability learners. These teacher outcomes and how they relate to the preparation of secondary teachers to work with high-ability adolescents are presented in the next section.

OUTCOMES AND ASSESSMENTS FOR TEACHER PREPARATION: IMPLICATIONS FOR SECONDARY TEACHERS

Reflecting the demands for increased accountability in K–12 education, teacher preparation programs have moved to the assessment of teacher candidate performance through their quality control mechanism of NCATE. The alignment of the curricular and field experiences, explicit outcomes, and relevant assessments provide guidance to the providers of teacher preparation programs in gifted education and to prospective and in-service teachers of high-ability learners. There are three key issues affecting secondary teachers: the scope of the standards, the relevance of the outcomes to secondary teachers, and the alignment of the professional preparation experiences with the assessments to document teacher knowledge and skill.

Currently, the joint CEC-TAG and NAGC teacher preparation document has 10 standards and 72 discrete outcomes for initial licensure. Of the discrete outcomes, 32 are knowledge outcomes and 40 are skill outcomes. An examination of the standards and outcomes is instructive because it reflects the consensus emphasis of the field for the preparation of teachers.

Scope of the Standards

The titles of the standards summarized in Table 1 range across a broad conceptual landscape. The 10 standards begin with foundational knowledge and include learner development and characteristics, individual learning differences, instructional strategies, learning environments and social interactions, language and communication, instructional planning, assessment, professional and ethical practice, and collaboration.

Relevance of the Outcomes to Secondary Teachers

Of the 72 outcomes across the 10 standards, several are explicitly attentive to the preparation of secondary teachers. Nine of the 72 outcomes or 12.5% are particularly relevant to the preparation of secondary teachers. Two of the outcomes specifically mention adolescence or secondary education; an additional four have a content focus that is often associated with the preparation of secondary teachers. Another references lifelong learning. The eighth outcome focuses on academic and career guidance issues associated with emerging adolescents and secondary education. The final outcome with a secondary perspective focuses on the role higher education plays in the development of talents. The nine outcomes explicitly related to adolescence, secondary issues, or secondary teachers are summarized in Table 2, Selected Teacher Outcomes (see p. 594). Certainly, many of the other outcomes are relevant to the preparation of secondary teachers to work with high-ability adolescents. The learning experiences supporting many of them can be shaped to be relevant to the preparation of secondary teachers, but this attention to secondary issues is primarily found in syllabi, assignments, products, and their accompanying assessments rather than in the language of the outcomes themselves. Thus, to address the preparation of teachers to work with high-ability adolescents, content and resources must be infused into the courses. The following section identifies key content and resources for each of the 10 NCATE standards.

RECOMMENDED SECONDARY CONTENT AND RESOURCES FOR TEACHER PREPARATION PROGRAMS

Preparation of educators who will work with gifted middle and high school students must include exposure to key areas that relate to gifted education and gifted

Table 1	
Joint Initial Teacher Standards	
Standard	Description
Foundations	Local, state/provincial, federal laws Definition and identification Historical foundations Philosophies, theories, models Societal, cultural, economic factors Issues and trends
Development and characteristics of learners	Cognitive, affective characteristics Effects of culture and environment Role of families and communities Developmental milestones Learner similarities and differences
Individual learning differences	Influences of diversity on talents Individuals with talents and disabilities Differences in learning patterns Variations in beliefs, traditions, values Perspectives of diverse groups
Instructional strategies	Identify resources Describe strategies Apply content pedagogical knowledge Interest-based research Preassess learning/adjust instruction Pacing Multicultural curricula Information and assistive technologies
Learning environments and social interactions	Analyze stereotypes Social and emotional development Affective learning experiences Develop lifelong learning Individual and group learning Appreciate linguistic/cultural differences Social interaction and coping skills
Language and communication	Communication Effects of diversity on communication Exceptional communication needs Communicate with families Advanced communication tools Promote multilingualism

Table 1 continued	
Instructional planning	Theories/research models of curriculum Distinguish general from differentiated curricula Articulate cognitive, affective, aesthetic, social curricula Align curricular standards Design learning plans Develop scope and sequence Select resources, strategies, products Advanced curricular content Integrate academic and career guidance
Assessment	Critique identification processes Uses, limitations, interpretation of assessments Equitable approaches for identification Technically adequate assessment Develop differentiated curriculum-based assessments Use alternative assessments
Professional and ethical practice	Reflection Identify organizations/publications Comply with laws, ethics, standards Improve practice
Collaboration	Culturally responsive collaboration Respond to concerns of families Collaborate to deliver services Advocacy Communicate with families, communities, school personnel

students at the secondary level, as asserted in a recent position statement issued jointly by the National Association for Gifted Children and the National Middle School Association (2004). Earlier, Gallagher (2001) called for attention to the needs of secondary students and for training of secondary teachers and gifted education specialists who work within secondary education. He proposed specific knowledge and skills that effective gifted specialists at the secondary level must have. These are reflected in proposed CEC/NAGC Joint Initial Teacher Standards. The broad areas of the professional standards include the following knowledge and skills.

- a foundation that includes the history, sociology, and philosophy of gifted education;
- knowledge of cognitive and affective characteristics and the development of learners with gifts and talents;

Table 2 Selected Outcomes for Secondary Teachers		
Standard	Knowledge or Skill	Outcome
Development and characteristics of learners	Knowledge	Describe the advanced developmental milestones, from early childhood through adolescence, among individuals with gifts and talents
Instructional strategies	Knowledge	Identify school and community resources, including content specialists that support differentiation
Instructional strategies	Skill	Apply relevant pedagogical content knowledge to instructing learners with gifts and talents
Instructional strategies	Skill	Apply higher level thinking and metacognitive models to relevant content areas to meet the needs of learners with gifts and talents
Learning environments and social interactions	Skill	Create learning environments for individuals with gifts and talents that support lifelong learning
Instructional planning	Skill	Select and adapt a variety of differentiated curricula that incorporate advanced, conceptually challenging, in-depth, distinctive, and complex content
Instructional planning	Skill	Integrate academic and career guidance experiences into the learning plan for learners with gifts and talents, including those from diverse backgrounds
Collaboration	Skill	Collaborate with higher education, research agencies, service providers, networks, and other organizations to serve learners with gifts and talents and their families
Collaboration	Skill	Collaborate with learners with gifts and talents, their families, general and special educators, and other school staff to articulate a comprehensive preschool through secondary educational program

- knowledge of individual learning differences that affect gifted learners, with particular attention to culture, ethnicity, socioeconomic status, language, gender, sexual orientation, and ability/disability;
- knowledge and skills to develop and adapt curriculum content and instructional strategies in order to meet the academic needs of learners with gifts and talents;
- knowledge of learning environments, especially those which foster the social and emotional well-being of individuals with gifts and talents;
- knowledge of the influence of language and communication on the cognitive and affective development of learners with gifts and talents;
- knowledge of appropriate curriculum and instructional planning for learners with gifts and talents;
- knowledge of and skill to use assessments for identifying learners with gifts and talents and to monitor their instructional progress;
- knowledge of professional and ethical practices; and
- knowledge of behaviors that characterize effective collaboration with others in and outside of school in order to promote the learning and well being of learners with gifts and talents (Council for Exceptional Children/The Association for the Gifted and the National Association for Gifted Children, 2004).

Gifted education courses are unlikely to target the specific needs of secondary teachers, while undergraduate and graduate courses in special or general education do not focus to any great extent on gifted learners as a subgroup of the secondary population. Therefore, there is a need to identify areas that secondary educators can explore in greater depth. The key standards-based areas above form appropriate guidelines for the preparation of preservice and graduate teachers, whether incorporated into general education courses or courses specifically for those who will work with gifted learners. The standards provide a framework so that instructors can tailor readings and assignments specifically for secondary teachers within course sequences. The following portion of this chapter suggests specific topical content and supporting resources to address secondary teacher preparation. Each of these areas and selected readings may be incorporated into coursework or professional development for secondary educators who work with gifted learners.

Foundations

A broad understanding of the historical underpinnings of gifted education is important for those who teach gifted learners. To understand the evolution of gifted education, it is critical to know how the field has developed, and what theories, philosophies, and sociological factors have shaped current practice. Some of the information is important for all educators, but there are certain elements that are particularly relevant to an understanding of older gifted learners. Theories of giftedness that describe characteristic stages of adolescent development and identify influences on that development may be instructive. Three such theoretical models are those of Tannenbaum (2003), Gagné (2003), and

Feldman (1986); Tannenbaum and Gagné define giftedness in terms of lifespan, and each takes into account multiple areas of ability. These two theorists describe both inherent and external factors that shape giftedness. Gagné explicitly identifies talent as mastery of skills in specific school-related domains, offering secondary teachers an understanding of young people who are at peak levels of a particular subject or discipline. Feldman studied prodigious talent in a select group of extremely precocious young children. Goldsmith (2000) published a follow-up description of the lives of some of Feldman's subjects through young adulthood.

Within the context of foundations, secondary educators should also be aware of factors that hinder the development of giftedness, particularly among diverse populations. Ford (2003) identifies issues that affect the appropriate identification and placement of gifted young people of color. This work helps educators understand cultural differences and styles that may be at odds with characteristics and expected behaviors of students who are typically identified as gifted. These differences may also work against retention of culturally diverse students in gifted programs; thus, it is essential that educators become familiar with techniques and curricular approaches that are supportive of all students.

The following are suggested readings concerning the foundations of gifted education:

- Ford, D. Y. (2003). Equity and excellence. In N. Colangelo & G. A. Davis (Eds.), *Handbook of gifted education* (3rd ed., pp. 506–520). Boston: Allyn & Bacon.
- Gagné, F. (2003). Transforming gifts into talents: The DMGT as a developmental theory. In N. Colangelo & G. A. Davis (Eds.), *Handbook of gifted education* (3rd ed., pp. 60–74). Boston: Allyn & Bacon.
- Goldsmith, L. T. (2000). Tracking trajectories of talent: Child prodigies growing up. In R. C. Friedman & B. M. Shore (Eds.), *Talents unfolding: Cognition and development* (pp. 89–117). Washington, DC: American Psychological Association.
- Tannenbaum, A. (2003). Nature and nurture of giftedness. In N. Colangelo & G. A. Davis (Eds.), *Handbook of gifted education* (3rd ed., pp. 45–59). Boston: Allyn & Bacon.

Development and Characteristics

As gifted individuals grow and develop, characteristics that were present in their earlier development may become more evident and distinctive. The verbally talented child may become an adolescent with extraordinary writing ability. The young child who is artistic may become an inspired sculptor in high school. Additionally, adolescents are likely to become more sensitive and intense, a developmental pattern that may lead to positive or negative outcomes (Schultz & Delisle, 2003). Gifted adolescents often face pressures from within themselves, as well as outside. Their wide-ranging capabilities and desire to explore numerous directions can lead to overextension and frustration. Academic pressures begin or intensify in adolescence with the demands of rigorous courses and the need to plan ahead toward college and career.

Peterson (2003) explores particular challenges in the affective domain, citing various social-emotional concerns that emerge in middle or high school. These issues are often present in the general population; however, gifted individuals may respond differently because of their heightened sensitivity. Family problems, inter- and intra-personal conflicts, difficulties with peer relationships, and potentially more serious concerns such as eating disorders or suicide can shape the lives of young gifted learners. As with typical adolescents, these young people need to make social connections and find the companionship of others like themselves. Teachers who are knowledgeable about adolescent development can respond appropriately and supportively, or they can make referrals to counselors.

Some suggested readings about the development and characteristics of gifted students include:

- Peterson, J. S. (2003). An argument for proactive attention to affective concerns of gifted adolescents. *Journal of Secondary Gifted Education, 14,* 62–71.
- Schultz, R. A., & Delisle, J. R. (2003). Gifted adolescents. In N. Colangelo & G. A. Davis (Eds.), *Handbook of gifted education* (3rd ed., pp. 483–492). Boston: Allyn & Bacon.

Individual Learning Differences

Middle and high school gifted students differ from others in a variety of academic and affective characteristics. Culture and gender play significant roles in the way gifted adolescents perform in school, and educators are often the key individuals who observe and respond to specific issues. Observant teachers notice, for example, when female students lower their performance and their goals in individual courses and in their overall pattern of course-taking (Kerr, 2003; Siegle & Reis, 1998). Informed and observant counselors can help these students look beyond high school to the goal of maintaining their long-term options by acquiring a broad and advanced preparation. These same teachers and counselors may observe perfectionistic behaviors in talented students that may be healthy or maladaptive (Adderholdt-Elliott, 1991; LoCicero & Ashby, 2000; Schuler, 2000).

Members of diverse cultural and racial groups are often underrepresented in programs for gifted students, and those who do participate during elementary school frequently do not continue in middle and high school. Moore, Ford, and Milner (2005) identify obstacles and call for recognition and response to factors related to the persistence of talented African American students that are critical to their continued engagement in programs and opportunities.

Suggested readings for individual learning differences include:

- Kerr, B. A. (2003). Gender and giftedness. In N. Colangelo & G. A. Davis (Eds.), *Handbook of gifted education* (3rd ed., pp. 493–505). Boston: Allyn & Bacon.

- Moore, J. L., Ford, D. Y., & Milner, H. R. (2005). Recruitment is not enough: Retaining African American students in gifted education. *Gifted Child Quarterly, 49*, 51–67.
- Schuler, P. A. (2000). Perfectionism and gifted adolescents. *Journal of Secondary Gifted Education, 11*, 183–196.

Instructional Strategies

Among the programs and services that comprise appropriate education for gifted middle and high school students are formal programs such as the AP program, talent searches, and the International Baccalaureate (IB) program. Each offers a coordinated, systematic approach that challenges and advances the gifted learner. Both talent searches and AP can fit seamlessly into existing secondary schools. Teachers of middle and high school students should be knowledgeable about these opportunities in order to inform and encourage talented students.

Talent searches are offered in all 50 states for the purpose of identifying young people at middle school age or younger who reason extremely well mathematically and/or verbally. Students who have scored well (usually 95th–99th percentile) on grade level standardized tests are eligible to become a part of one of the talent searches and take more challenging standardized tests designed for older students (usually the SAT I or the ACT). Academic planning assistance, as well as summer and school year programs are offered to students who score well on these tests. (Lupkowski-Shoplik, Benbow, Assouline, & Brody, 2003)

The AP program, a division of College Board, currently offers more than 30 advanced courses to high school students, which can be taken as a part of the school curriculum or as independent studies in the case of homeschooled students or those whose schools do not have a formal AP program. Rigorous, college-level coursework prepares students for AP exams. One advantage of AP is that many colleges and universities accept students' scores on these exams for credit or placement in advanced courses, allowing students to enter with advanced standing and thus save time and money in college. Secondary teachers of the AP classes participate in specialized professional development to prepare to teach these courses. Research on AP students who are in college reveals a variety of strengths attributed to their high school participation (Curry, MacDonald, & Morgan, 1999).

IB programs are part of a worldwide program for students in their final 2 years of high school (called the Diploma program). There is also a Middle Years program for ages 11–16. While not created exclusively for gifted students, many schools and districts that adopt IB have done so with their high-ability students in mind (Tookey, 1999/2000). The IB consists of an international common curriculum, based on intercultural understanding and critical thinking, which prepares students for entrance into higher education, as well as other IB schools. The curriculum framework includes the intensive study of their own language plus another, experimental sciences, social sciences, mathematics and computer science, and the arts; it is understandable that this model appeals to schools that seek ways to provide appropriate levels of challenge for their gifted students (Tookey).

A number of instructional options exist for talented middle school and secondary students. Each has specific benefits and characteristics schools should consider in determining direction and opportunity for gifted students. Olszewski-Kubilius and Limberg-Weber (1999) efficiently chart program options and their matches with appropriate experiences for gifted learners, including such elements as opportunity for adult work, access to adult professionals, opportunity to earn college credit, and opportunity for access to advanced coursework, to name several.

Among the appropriate learning accommodations for gifted secondary students are those that allow them the opportunity to accelerate their progress through middle and high school. The Templeton Report on Acceleration (Colangelo, Assouline & Gross, 2004) delineates advantages of acceleration in terms of time and cost saving, and suitable rigor and challenge to secondary students.

In concert with programs that originate from formal organizations outside local schools, there are approaches that are incorporated into the instruction of high-ability students. For example, one instructional strategy that has been widely implemented at the secondary level is problem-based learning (Gallagher, 1997). Borrowing from an established medical education model, problem-based learning (PBL) is well-suited to gifted learners at the secondary level whose interests are broad and deep, and who thrive on the challenge of open-ended problems. In PBL, students engage in solving ill-structured, multidisciplinary, multifaceted, real-world problems under the guidance of their teachers.

School counseling centers possess their own potential for strategies that encompass a number of opportunities to provide support for students. Among these are the establishment of mentorship and shadowing relationships between gifted students and adults in domains of common interest. Counselors also provide gifted individuals and their families with information about summer programs, academic competitions and talent searches, scholarships, internships, and study programs. Knowledgeable and committed counselors are critical to the futures of gifted students in the college selection and application process. Beyond these typical counseling responsibilities, there are often opportunities for counselors to assist students as they investigate possible career directions. Savvy counselors can help students match their interests with institutions of higher education that have strong programs in these areas of appeal (Peterson, 2003).

The following are suggested readings for instructional strategies:

- Colangelo, N., Assouline, S. G., & Gross, M. U. M. (2004). *A nation deceived: How schools hold back America's brightest students* (Vol. 1). Iowa City: Connie Belin & Jacqueline N. Blank International Center for Gifted Education and Talent Development.
- Curry, W., MacDonald W., & Morgan, R. (1999). The Advanced Placement program: Access to excellence. *Journal of Secondary Gifted Education, 9,* 17–23.
- Gallagher, S. A. (1997). Problem-based learning: Where did it come from, what does it do, and where is it going? *Journal for the Education of the Gifted, 20,* 332–362.
- Lupkowski-Shoplik, A., Benbow, C. P., Assouline, S. G., & Brody, L. E. (2003). Talent searches: Meeting the needs of academically talented youth. In N.

Colangelo & G. A. Davis (Eds.), *Handbook of gifted education* (3rd ed., pp. 204–218). Boston: Allyn & Bacon.

• Olszewski-Kubilius, P., & Limberg-Weber, L. (1999). Options for middle school and secondary level gifted students. *Journal for Secondary Gifted Education, 11,* 4–10.

• Tookey, M. E. (1999/2000). The International Baccalaureate: A program conducive to the continued growth of gifted adolescents. *Journal of Secondary Gifted Education, 11,* 52–66.

Learning Environments and Social Interactions

The most appropriate learning environments for gifted learners at the secondary level are those that provide both academic and social support. As is true of programs and services for younger gifted children, one of the critical elements is interaction among gifted students in a safe, supportive environment. Also essential are relationships with compassionate and encouraging adults—teachers, counselors, and other educational personnel. Certainly the classroom should be the heart of the environment as it offers students opportunities for challenge, choice, and intellectual and social sustenance. Positive interactions with intellectual peers and understanding teachers who are knowledgeable about gifted learners should characterize the school experiences of the gifted.

Appropriate learning environments may also be beyond the walls of the school. Recognizing that gifted students' needs, interests, and levels of readiness may best be addressed in the larger community, schools often establish mentorships that allow individuals to work with an expert in a specific field or career. Casey and Shore (2000) suggest that mentorship experiences benefit students not only in their chosen vocational area, but also in their affective and social development. They cite, particularly, benefits to gifted females. Schatz (1999/2000) suggests a model characterized by collaboration between a local school district and a local college or university, providing detailed procedures and guidelines, interspersed with commentary by students and mentors and several specific examples of program application.

Beyond the school week and year, specialized programs exist for the benefit of gifted young people. Frequently associated with colleges and universities, Saturday and summer programs offer a change of place and a focus on the gifted learner in a group of peers under the guidance of specially trained teachers and other staff (Olszewski-Kubilius, 2003). Summer residential programs allow young people to explore not only advanced academic content, but also the expanse of opportunities and resources available on a campus. In an environment where all students are academically talented, peer connections flourish, self-awareness and self-esteem develop or are reinforced, and aspirations are likely to be raised (Olszewski-Kubilius).

A number of states have acknowledged the need to provide for gifted students at the secondary level by establishing state-supported residential schools

(Kolloff, 2003). These schools, beginning in 1980 with the North Carolina School for Science and Mathematics, bring together talented students from their states for the final 2–3 years of high school. Within a residential setting, students engage in advanced, demanding coursework in classes with others like themselves. Approximately 15 states currently have such schools. Beyond serving students, these schools also provide outreach to educators and school districts through professional development, internships, summer workshops, and distance learning.

Some suggested readings for learning environment and social interactions include:

- Olszewski-Kubilius, P. (2003). Special summer and Saturday programs for gifted students. In N. Colangelo & G. A. Davis (Eds.), *Handbook of gifted education* (3rd ed., pp. 219–228). Boston: Allyn & Bacon.
- Schatz, E. (1999/2000). Mentors: Matchmaking for young people. *Journal of Secondary Gifted Education, 11,* 67–87.

Language and Communication

The skills of oral and written language are essential to the education of gifted learners. Depending on the foundation established in the elementary grades, gifted students will be either well- or ill-prepared to apply their language knowledge and skills to their writing and speaking. It is hoped that a solid foundation results from early, extensive reading of rich literature, continuing through middle and high school levels. Beyond reading, however, the well-prepared secondary student will also study, in a more formalized way, the structure of the language through vocabulary and grammar (Thompson, 2002). Gifted students must have extensive opportunities for advanced writing and speaking, as well as reading. Their products must be assessed against criteria that are appropriate to the level of gifted learners, often using nontraditional tools, including rubrics, performance-based assessments, and portfolios (VanTassel-Baska, 2002).

Another issue relating to language and communication at the secondary level is the fact that students whose first language is not English are often overlooked during the screening and placement for gifted programs and services. Matthews and Matthews (2004) suggest that such students can benefit from courses taught in their first or "heritage" language so that they can focus on further development of their abilities, as well as their motivation and association with cultural/linguistic role models.

The following are suggested readings for language and communication:

- Thompson, M. C. (2002). Vocabulary and grammar: Critical content for critical thinking. *Journal of Secondary Gifted Education, 13,* 60–66.
- VanTassel-Baska, J. (2002). Assessment of gifted student learning in the language arts. *Journal of Secondary Gifted Education, 13,* 67–72.

Instructional Planning

Curriculum is at the center of the secondary experience. For gifted learners, curriculum defines what it is that distinguishes their educational needs from those of other students. In middle school and high school, content, strategies and outcomes in the various subject areas are the essence of differentiation. Verbally gifted learners are ready for advanced content combined with activities designed to produce critical thinking, specifically synthesis and evaluation (Dixon, 2002). Describing high-level content selections and rigorous activities that promote analysis, synthesis, and evaluation, Dixon demonstrates ways in which a literature curriculum may be appropriately differentiated for gifted students. Verbally talented learners also may deepen their understanding of language and thought by pursuing Latin (VanTassel-Baska, 2004). VanTassel-Baska presents a framework of elements for the study of Latin, as well as a timeline for acceleration of Latin along with another foreign language.

Usiskin (2000) explores what it takes to develop mathematical talent, delineating levels ranging from level 0 (no mathematical talent) to level 7 (all-time mathematical greats). He also describes how students develop into each of the levels—what it takes for a student to reach, for example, level 3, or the top 1–2% of mathematical talent. Secondary educators should understand these levels and the ways in which students may advance from one to the next. Usiskin also provides a view of the educational environment in which students may, or may not, reach their potential.

In the area of science, schools are often faced with a small group of exceptionally talented students who need more challenge than even an advanced science curriculum can offer. One such school, described by Ngoi and Vondracek (2004), identifies those students and designs a variety of educational options for them, including independent study, university courses, independent research, and academic competitions.

Implementing broad curricular change in a traditional school presents a considerable challenge to educators. Tomlinson (1995) reports a qualitative study of a middle school that made a commitment to differentiation for its gifted learners, an undertaking that required significant changes in philosophy and practice on the part of individual educators, as well as the entire school. The process took considerable time as new learning and beliefs replaced long-held practices. Tomlinson's account highlights the elements of change at all levels of the school, with examples of how the process was carried out.

Robinson and Kolloff (1994) encouraged secondary educators to create interdisciplinary units centered on broad themes. Such units provide students with opportunities for open-ended exploration of content, as well as experiences that promote the development of frameworks for understanding how concepts fit together across subject areas.

Another umbrella encompassing individual subjects is the meaningful integration of multicultural education into the preparation of gifted learners. Ford and Harris (2000), building on the work of James Banks and Benjamin Bloom, created a framework for looking at multicultural curriculum. Rich with examples, the matrix suggests ways to examine and enhance traditional curriculum so that the perspectives and issues of diverse cultures are explored.

Finally, in the area of curriculum, secondary educators should be knowledgeable about the criteria that distinguish curricula suitable for all learners from that appropriate for the gifted. Passow (1986) articulated the scope of differentiated curriculum at the secondary level. The curriculum division of NAGC created a rubric that describes such criteria (Purcell, Burns, Tomlinson, Imbeau, and Martin, 2002), and Robinson (2002) identified indicators for differentiated classrooms and schools.

Suggested readings for instructional planning include:

- Dixon, F. A. (2002). The memorable link: Designing critical thinking activities that stimulate synthesis and evaluation among verbally gifted adolescents. *Journal of Secondary Gifted Education, 13,* 73–84.
- Ford, D. Y., & Harris, J. J. (2000). A framework for infusing multicultural curriculum into gifted education. *Roeper Review, 23,* 4–10.
- Ngoi, M., & Vondracek, M. (2004). Working with gifted science students in a public high school environment. *Journal of Secondary Education, 15,* 141–147.
- Passow, A. H. (1986). Curriculum for the gifted and talented at the secondary level. *Gifted Child Quarterly, 30,* 186–191.
- Purcell, J. H., Burns, D. E., Tomlinson, C. A., Imbeau, M. B., & Martin, J. L. (2002). Bridging the gap: A tool and technique to analyze and evaluate gifted education curricular units. *Gifted Child Quarterly, 46,* 306–321.
- Robinson, A., & Kolloff, P. B. (1994). Developing secondary thematic units. In J. B. Hansen & S. M. Hoover (Eds.), *Talent development: Theories and practice* (pp. 153–183). Dubuque, IA: Kendall/Hunt.
- Tomlinson, C. A. (1995). Deciding to differentiate instruction in middle school: One school's journey. *Gifted Child Quarterly, 39,* 77–87.
- Usiskin, Z. (2000). The development into the mathematically talented. *Journal of Secondary Gifted Education, 11,* 152–162.

Assessment

Educators of gifted learners recognize the importance of determining appropriate assessments in order to document and evaluate student learning. Traditional tests and products such as research papers do not adequately measure the outcomes of appropriately differentiated curriculum for gifted learners. Graffam (2003) puts forth an assessment model, Teaching for Understanding (TfU), which is in place at an IB school. The assessment is authentic and on-going, and it can be applied to a variety of studies at the secondary level.

Dixon (2000) describes a model for conducting an exam using a discussion format. The model was applied in a literature course for gifted high school students and includes the guidelines for conducting this kind of assessment and a method for scoring students' level of participation.

Nowak and Plucker (1999) present an assessment that is aligned with problem-based learning. After pointing out the frequent mismatch between authentic experiences in problem-based learning and subsequent assessments, they provide examples of appropriate assessment activities for PBL activities.

The following are suggested readings for assessment:

- Dixon, F. A. (2000). The discussion examination: Making assessment match instructional strategy. *Roeper Review, 23,* 104–108.
- Graffam, B. (2003). Constructivism and understanding: Implementing the teaching for understanding framework. *Journal of Secondary Gifted Education, 15,* 13–22.

Professional and Ethical Practice

Secondary educators are generally well-informed about resources in their specific content areas. Those who work with gifted students also must be able to identify specific organizations and publications in the field of gifted education in order to access information for their own preparation and to carry out their roles as educators and resources to gifted students and their families. Among the organizations they should know are NAGC and CEC/TAG. Important journals include *Gifted Child Quarterly, Journal of Secondary Gifted Education, Journal for the Education of the Gifted,* and *Roeper Review*. Additional resources include gifted organizations in a majority of states.

Suggested resources for professional and ethical practice include:

- Council for Exceptional Children: http://www.cec.sped.org
- ERIC Information Center on Disabilities and Gifted Education: http://www.ericec.org/gifted/gt-menu.html
- *Gifted Child Quarterly*: http://www.nagc.org/Publications/GiftedChild
- *Journal of Secondary Gifted Education*: http://www.prufrock.com
- *Journal for the Education of the Gifted*: http://www.prufrock.com
- National Association for Gifted Children: http://www.nagc.org
- *Roeper Review*: http://www.roeperreview.org

Collaboration

At the middle and high school levels, collaboration becomes an important factor in the education of gifted learners. As students' educational programs become more diverse and more individualized, it is beneficial to students, parents, and educators that ongoing conversation and interaction take place. Ward and Landrum (1994) propose a model that engages the regular classroom teacher and the gifted specialist, with the additional involvement of a team when necessary. Although this model was studied in an elementary school setting (Landrum, 2001), the concept of a collaborative approach to addressing the needs of gifted learners is widely applicable.

A suggested reading on the topic of collaboration is:

- Landrum, M. S. (2001). An evaluation of the catalyst program: Consultation and collaboration in gifted education. *Gifted Child Quarterly, 45,* 139–151.

The above portion of the chapter describes specific areas of knowledge and skills important for the secondary educator. Each section relates to one of the 10 Joint Initial Teacher Standards. Suggested readings align with each standard to provide further elaboration or examples of essential ideas in the education of gifted adolescents. In the next section of the chapter, the linkage between the content, the expected teacher outcomes, and the assessment are described.

ALIGNMENT OF THE OUTCOMES AND THE ASSESSMENTS

From a discussion of resources or inputs, we return to the topic of outcomes expected of teachers. In an output model, accountability for teacher preparation programs is integrated into the system. In addition to the teacher outcomes identified by CEC and NAGC, NCATE requires that each approved university teacher preparation program collect performance data on its teacher candidates through six to eight assessments. In terms of gifted education, six of the assessments are tied to specific standards. Additional assessments may be identified at the discretion of the particular teacher preparation program.

One of the key assessment tools is a specific gifted education examination under revision by the Educational Testing Service (ETS) for the Praxis II series of teacher assessments. While the test was originally developed for use in a specific state, West Virginia, items are currently being retired, undergoing revision, or being written to align with the new standards and outcomes. It is instructive to compare the standards of the professional societies, the headings of the test specifications for the Praxis, and the relative weight assigned to each in order to accomplish a rough kind of alignment that might be used to plan teacher preparation programs. Table 3, Alignment of Praxis Table of Specifications and Teacher Preparation Standards, summarizes these comparisons.

By examining Table 3, the relative emphasis in the Praxis examination can be compared with the emphasis in the newly emerging Joint Standards. The alignment is reasonable, but does have gaps that can and should be addressed through the use of other assessments. For example, in the licensure program at the University of Arkansas at Little Rock, a case study of a gifted student with a rubric developed at the Center for Gifted Education, the Curriculum Unit rubric developed by members of the Curriculum Studies Division of NAGC, and the Purdue Teacher Observation Form are used to assess teacher outcomes (Robinson, 2004; Wood, Hunter, Robinson and Wood, 2005). The assessments are general enough to apply to both elementary and secondary teachers. However, the content of the case study can be structured to include a middle or high school example and thereby focus on the needs of high-ability adolescents.

Conclusion

The stories of Glenn and the middle school twins, Keily and David, are based on real events. Teachers need information about high-ability youth like them and

Table 3
Alignment of Praxis Table of Specifications and Joint Professional Standards

Praxis content	Percentage of total test items joint standards	Outcomes	Percentage of total
Definitions, development, and characteristics of giftedness	15	Foundations Characteristics Individual differences	9.7 6.9 6.9
Identification, assessment, and eligibility of gifted students	15	Assessment	9.7
Curricular and instructional modifications for gifted students	35	Instructional strategies Instructional planning	12.5 12.5
Program placements for gifted students	15	No comparable standard	
Professional knowledge	20	Foundations Collaboration	9.7 9.7

are unlikely to acquire the content and skills to work effectively with and advocate for such learners unless topics, resources, outcomes, and assessments are included in formal teacher preparation programs.

The implications for teacher licensure are manifold. First, the collaboration on Joint Teacher Standards will have far-reaching effects on preparation programs. These outcomes articulate what the field of gifted education thinks is important for teachers to know and be able to do. Second, whether specific outcomes are structured into specialized courses or infused into general education ones, the existence of a licensure system with explicit outcomes and accompanying assessments will provide avenues for holding teachers, including secondary teachers, accountable for educating high-ability learners.

REFERENCES

Adderholdt-Elliott, M. (1991). Perfectionism and the gifted adolescent. In M. Birely & J. Genshaft (Eds.), *Understanding the gifted adolescent: Educational, developmental, and multicultural issues* (pp. 65–75). New York: Teachers College Press.

Archambault, F. X., Westberg, K. L., Brown, S. W., Hallmark, B. W., Zhang, W., & Emmons, C. L. (1993). Classroom practices used with gifted third and fourth grade students. *Journal for the Education of the Gifted, 16,* 103–119.

Bishop, W. E. (1968). Successful teachers of the gifted. *Exceptional Children, 34,* 317–325.

Casey, K. M., & Shore, B. M. (2000). Mentors' contributions to gifted adolescents' affective, social, and vocational development. *Roeper Review, 22,* 227–230.

Clinkenbeard, P. R., & Kolloff, P. B. (2001) Ten suggestions for including gifted education in preservice teacher education. *The Teacher Educator, 36,* 214–218.

Colangelo, N., Assouline, S. G., & Gross, M. U. M. (2004). *A nation deceived: How schools hold back America's brightest students* (Vol. 1). Iowa City: Connie Belin & Jacqueline N. Blank International Center for Gifted Education and Talent Development.

Copenhaver, R. W., & McIntyre, D. J. (1992). Teachers' perceptions of gifted students. *Roeper Review, 14,* 151–154.

Council for Exceptional Children, The Association for the Gifted, & National Association for Gifted Children. (2004). *Draft joint standards for initial teacher preparation in gifted education.* Washington, DC: Author.

Croft, L. J. (2003). Teachers of the gifted: Gifted teachers. In N. Colangelo & G. A. Davis (Eds.), *Handbook of gifted education* (3rd ed., pp. 558–571). Boston: Allyn & Bacon.

Curry, W., MacDonald W., & Morgan, R. (1999). The Advanced Placement program: Access to excellence. *Journal of Secondary Gifted Education, 9,* 17–23.

Dixon, F. A. (2000). The discussion examination: Making assessment match instructional strategy. *Roeper Review, 23,* 104–108.

Dixon, F. A. (2002). The memorable link: Designing critical thinking activities that stimulate synthesis and evaluation among verbally gifted adolescents. *Journal of Secondary Gifted Education, 13,* 73–84.

Feldhusen, J. F. (1973). Practicum activities for students and children in a university course. *Gifted Child Quarterly, 17,* 124–129.

Feldhusen, J. F. (1997). Educating teachers for work with talented youth. In N. Colangelo & G. A. Davis (Eds.), *Handbook of gifted education* (2nd ed., pp. 547–552). Boston: Allyn & Bacon.

Feldhusen, J. F., & Hansen, J. (1987). Selecting and training teachers to work with the gifted in a Saturday program. *Gifted Education International, 4,* 82–94.

Feldhusen, J. F., & Huffman, L. E. (1988). Practicum experiences in an educational program for teachers of the gifted. *Journal for the Education of the Gifted, 12,* 34–45.

Feldhusen, J., & Koopmans-Dayton, J. (1987). Meeting special needs of the gifted through Saturday programs: An evaluation study. *Gifted Education International, 4*(2), 89–101.

Feldman, D. H. (1986). *Nature's gambit: Child prodigies and the development of human potential.* New York: Basic Books.

Ford, D. Y. (2003). Equity and excellence. In N. Colangelo & G. A. Davis (Eds.), *Handbook of gifted education* (3rd ed., pp. 506–520). Boston: Allyn & Bacon.

Ford, D. Y., & Harris, J. J. (2000). A framework for infusing multicultural curriculum into gifted education. *Roeper Review, 23,* 4–10.

Gagné, F. (2003). Transforming gifts into talents: The DMGT as a developmental theory. In N. Colangelo & G. A. Davis (Eds.), *Handbook of gifted education* (3rd ed., pp. 60–74). Boston: Allyn & Bacon.

Gallagher, J. J. (2001). Personnel preparation and secondary education programs for gifted students. *Journal of Secondary Gifted Education, 12,* 133–138.

Gallagher, S. A. (1997). Problem-based learning: Where did it come from, what does it do, and where is it going? *Journal for the Education of the Gifted, 20,* 332–362.

Gentry, M. L., & Gable, R. K. (2001). From the students' perspective—My class activities: An instrument for use in research and evaluation. *Journal for the Education of the Gifted, 24,* 322–343.

Gentry, M., Rizza, M. G., & Owen, S. V. (2002). Examining perceptions of challenge and choice in classrooms: The relationship between teachers and their students and comparisons between gifted students and other students. *Gifted Child Quarterly, 46,* 145–155.

Goldsmith, L. T. (2000). Tracking trajectories of talent: Child prodigies growing up. In R. C. Friedman & B. M. Shore (Eds.), *Talents unfolding: Cognition and development* (pp. 89–117). Washington, DC: American Psychological Association.

Graffam, B. (2003). Constructivism and understanding: Implementing the teaching for understanding framework. *Journal of Secondary Gifted Education, 15,* 13–22.

Hanninen, G. E. (1988). A study of teacher training in gifted education. *Roeper Review, 10,* 139–144.

Hansen, J. B., & Feldhusen, J. F. (1994). Comparison of trained and untrained teachers of gifted students. *Gifted Child Quarterly, 38,* 115–121.

Hultgren, H. (1981). Competencies for teachers of the gifted. *Dissertation Abstracts International, 2,* 2082A. (University Microfilms No. 812/433).

Hultgren, H., & Seeley, K. (1982). *Training teachers of the gifted: A research monograph on teacher competencies.* Denver, CO: University of Denver, School of Education.

Kerr, B. A. (2003). Gender and giftedness. In N. Colangelo & G. A. Davis (Eds.), *Handbook of gifted education* (3rd ed., pp. 493–505). Boston: Allyn & Bacon.

Kolloff, P. B. (2003). State-supported residential high schools. In N. Colangelo & G. A. Davis (Eds.), *Handbook of gifted education* (3rd ed., pp. 238–246). Boston: Allyn &Bacon.

Landrum, M. S. (2001). An evaluation of the catalyst program: Consultation and collaboration in gifted education. *Gifted Child Quarterly, 45,* 139–151.

LoCicero, K. A., & Ashby, J. S. (2000). Multidimensional perfectionism in middle school age gifted students: A comparison to peers from the general cohort. *Roeper Review, 22,* 182–185.

Lupkowski-Shoplik, A., Benbow, C. P., Assouline, S. G., & Brody, L. E. (2003). Talent searches: Meeting the needs of academically talented youth. In N. Colangelo & G. A. Davis (Eds.), *Handbook of gifted education* (3rd ed., pp. 204–218). Boston: Allyn & Bacon.

Matthews, P. H., & Matthews, M. S. (2004). Heritage language instruction and giftedness in language minority students: Pathways to success. *Journal of Secondary Gifted Education, 15,* 50–55.

Mills, C. J. (2003). Characteristics of effective teachers of gifted students: Teacher background and personality styles of students. *Gifted Child Quarterly, 47,* 272–281.

Moore, J. L., Ford, D. Y., & Milner, H. R. (2005). Recruitment is not enough: Retaining African American students in gifted education. *Gifted Child Quarterly, 49,* 51–67.

National Association for Gifted Children. (1982). *Professional training committee reports, 1982.* St. Paul, MN: Author.

National Association for Gifted Children. (1995). *Position paper on standards for graduate programs in gifted education.* Washington, DC: Author.

National Middle School Association, & National Association for Gifted Children. (2004). *Meeting the needs of high-ability and high-potential learners in the middle grades: A joint position statement of the National Middle School Association and the National Association for Gifted Children.* Washington, DC: Authors.

Ngoi, M., & Vondracek, M. (2004). Working with gifted science students in a public high school environment. *Journal of Secondary Education, 15,* 141–147.

Nowak, J. A., & Plucker, J. A. (1999). *Do as I say, not as I do? Student assessment in problem-based learning.* Retrieved February 27, 2005, from http://www.indiana.edu/~legobots/q515/pbl.html

Olszewski-Kubilius, P. (2003). Special summer and Saturday programs for gifted students. In N. Colangelo & G. A. Davis (Eds.), *Handbook of gifted education* (3rd ed., pp. 219–228). Boston: Allyn & Bacon.

Olszewski-Kubilius, P., & Limberg-Weber, L. (1999). Options for middle school and secondary level gifted students. *Journal of Secondary Gifted Education, 11,* 4–10.

Parker, J. P. (1996). NAGC standards for personnel preparation in gifted education: A brief history. *Gifted Child Quarterly, 40,* 158–164.

Passow, A. H. (1986). Curriculum for the gifted and talented at the secondary level. *Gifted Child Quarterly, 30,* 186–191.

Peterson, J. S. (2003). An argument for proactive attention to affective concerns of gifted adolescents. *Journal of Secondary Gifted Education, 14,* 62–71.

Purcell, J. H., Burns, D. E., Tomlinson, C. A., Imbeau, M. B., & Martin, J. L. (2002). Bridging the gap: A tool and technique to analyze and evaluate gifted education curricular units. *Gifted Child Quarterly, 46,* 306–321.

Ribich, F., Barone, W., & Agostino, R. (1998). Semantically different: Preservice teachers' reactions to the gifted student concept. *Journal of Educational Research, 91,* 308–312.

Robinson, A. (2002). Differentiation for talented learners—what are some indicators? *Understanding Our Gifted,* 3–5.

Robinson, A. (2004, May). *Preparing (selecting, developing and organizing) NCATE assessment.* Presentation to Defining the Field of Gifted Education: University Preparation at Advanced Levels, Crystal City, VA.

Robinson, A., & Kolloff, P. B. (1994). Developing secondary thematic units. In J. B. Hansen & S. M. Hoover (Eds.), *Talent development: Theories and practice* (pp. 153–183). Dubuque, IA: Kendall/Hunt.

Roth, R. A., & Pipho, C. (1990). Teacher education standards. In W. R. Houston (Ed.), *Handbook of research on teacher education* (pp. 119–135). New York: Macmillan.

Schatz, E. (1999/2000). Mentors: Matchmaking for young people. *Journal of Secondary Gifted Education, 11,* 67–87.

Schuler, P. A. (2000). Perfectionism and gifted adolescents. *Journal of Secondary Gifted Education, 11,* 183–196.

Schultz, R. A., & Delisle, J. R. (2003). Gifted adolescents. In N. Colangelo & G. A. Davis (Eds.), *Handbook of gifted education* (3rd ed., pp. 483–492). Boston: Allyn & Bacon.

Seeley, K. (1979). Competencies for teachers of gifted and talented children. *Journal for the Education of the Gifted, 3,* 7–13.

Siegle, D., & Reis, S. (1998). Gender differences in teacher and student perceptions of gifted students' ability and effort. *Gifted Child Quarterly, 42,* 39–47.

Starko, A. J., & Shack, G. D. (1989). Perceived need, teacher efficacy, and teaching strategies for the gifted and talented. *Gifted Child Quarterly, 33,* 118–122.

Tannenbaum, A. (2003). Nature and nurture of giftedness. In N. Colangelo & G. A. Davis (Eds.), *Handbook of gifted education* (3rd ed., pp. 45–59). Boston: Allyn & Bacon.

Thompson, M. C. (2002). Vocabulary and grammar: Critical content for critical thinking. *Journal of Secondary Gifted Education, 13,* 60–66.

Tomlinson, C. A. (1995). Deciding to differentiate instruction in middle school: One school's journey. *Gifted Child Quarterly, 39,* 77–87.

Tomlinson, C. A., Tomchin, E. M., Callahan, C. M., Adams, C. M., Pizzat-Tinnan, P., Cunningham, C. M., et al. (1994). Practices of preservice teachers related to gifted and other academically diverse learners. *Gifted Child Quarterly, 38,* 106–114.

Tookey, M. E. (1999/2000). The International Baccalaureate: A program conducive to the continued growth of gifted adolescents. *Journal of Secondary Gifted Education, 11,* 52–66.

Usiskin, Z. (2000). The development into the mathematically talented. *Journal of Secondary Gifted Education, 11,* 152–162.

VanTassel-Baska, J. (2002). Assessment of gifted student learning in the language arts. *Journal of Secondary Gifted Education, 13,* 67–72.

VanTassel-Baska, J. (2004). Quo vadis? Laboring in the classical vineyards: An optimal challenge for gifted secondary students. *Journal of Secondary Gifted Education, 15,* 56–60.

Ward, S. B., & Landrum, M. S. (1994). Resource consultation: An alternative service delivery model for gifted education. *Roeper Review, 16,* 276–279.

Westberg, K. L., Archambault, F. X., Dobyns, S. M., & Salvin, T. J. (1993). The classroom practices observation study. *Journal for the Education of the Gifted, 16,* 120–146.

Whitlock, M. S., & DuCette, J. P. (1989). Outstanding and average teachers of the gifted: A comparative study. *Gifted Child Quarterly, 33,* 15–21.

Wood, B. K., Hunter, K., Robinson, A., & Wood, S. C. (2005). Evaluating a practicum for gifted education graduate students. *Gifted Child Today, 28*(2), 38–43.

Professional Development for the Education of Secondary Gifted Students

CHAPTER 24

by Peggy A. Dettmer, Mary S. Landrum, & Teresa N. Miller

Scenario

*I*n a typical high school conference room, an Advanced Placement teacher, the high school gifted education resource teacher, the principal, and parents of a 12th grade gifted student meet after school to discuss the student's performance in calculus. The teacher tells the parents that their son will receive a failing grade in the course for the current grading period. Although he has an average score of 103 out of 100 possible points (because of earning extra credit) on six graded assignments and tests, he received a grade of zero for either failing to complete homework assignments or for completing homework correctly, but not showing his work. The parents are concerned because they believe this grade is not a fair representation of their son's mathematical ability. The principal is concerned because the math department does not want to set a precedent for students who fail to complete assignments as directed.

The classroom teacher in this scenario demonstrates a lack of understanding about the unique characteristics of learning for gifted students, as well as an inability to provide appropriately challenging learning experiences for him. It is clear that with such a commanding mastery of the material this student does not need more practice via homework. Furthermore, the teacher is not open to having the student complete the work using mental math versus working out the problems by a more conventional method. The teacher is neither vindictive toward the student nor uncaring about the student's performance, but is simply ill-prepared to accept his advanced ability and adjust instruction and grading practices accordingly. These kinds of school situations can be avoided with professional development for secondary personnel that targets gifted students' learning characteristics and educational needs.

Professional development is an integral component of being prepared as a teacher for instruction of gifted students. General education teachers, school counselors, school psychologists, and related services personnel have important roles in providing for gifted student needs. In addition, support personnel and classified staff need to be aware of provisions that are being made. Administrators are a key factor in ensuring that awareness, understanding, and competencies for gifted programs are present among all personnel in their attendance centers. School board members and central administration staff also are a part of the picture. They may be unclear about the purposes of professional development activities and a little skeptical about their value, therefore hesitant to fund professional development institutes, travel expenses for conferences, or release time to prepare differentiated learning experiences. They may feel less than knowledgeable about this sector of the school program, undecided about the overall importance, and apprehensive about the cost effectiveness in achieving school goals.

DEFINING PROFESSIONAL DEVELOPMENT

The term *professional development* has come to be favored over other terminology such as personnel preparation, staff development, in-service, and training as being more descriptive of experiences and activities that nurture the professional growth of educators. In-service tends to be a short-term or single-session activity included in more broad staff development plans that typically extend for a semester or a year. Personnel preparation typically refers to the sequence of coursework that leads to an initial degree or new licensure or certification. The term *training* is more suitable for emphasizing recall and memorization of procedures, and will not be used here except when needed in citing other references.

In recent years there have been major shifts in the nature of professional development (Sparks & Hirsch, 1997). Those most relevant to the material discussed here are:

1. *From fragmented, piecemeal improvement efforts to clear strategic plans for district, schools, and departments.* In high schools in particular, it is important that academic departments have professional development plans that address the issues, demands, and unique nature of the specific discipline. For example, English departments will be concerned about the gifted adolescent who has brilliant ideas and creative approaches to writing, but does not follow guidelines and dismisses the discipline imposed by high school writing assignments.

2. *From focus on adult satisfaction to focus on student learning outcomes.* Too often secondary teachers come to the profession with a focus on content rather than individual student needs, and for elementary teachers the reverse tends to be the case. Without professional development and preparation, secondary teachers are more likely to teach in a manner that fits their preferences for emphasizing subject matter over specific learning needs of individual students.

3. *From orientation toward presentation of knowledge and skills by experts to the study of the teaching and learning processes.* Secondary educators approach the study of their discipline uniquely. The methodologies, practices, and products that represent each discipline of study are varied. Therefore, the teacher expects teaching and learning to be unique to each discipline. It follows then that professional development that models how teaching and learning occur within a particular discipline will be most appealing to participants. The challenge for a staff development planner is to construct and implement professional development initiatives that equally represent models and outcomes for all disciplines of study, from mathematics and science, to psychology and technology.

4. *From staff developers as disseminators to staff developers who provide consultation, planning, and assistance.* Secondary educators in particular will expect staff developers to practice what they preach. Professional development participants expect to have a consultant, a role model, and a coach—in other words, a facilitator. In order to lead the secondary educator, the staff developer must be able to facilitate the development of foundational understanding and instructional competencies for education of gifted adolescents in any discipline or area of study.

5. *From staff development directed primarily toward teachers to improvement in performance by all who are involved with students' learning.* Pooling expertise and sharing responsibility for the education of gifted adolescents is an efficient way of providing for their needs. For example, English teachers can depend on teachers of technology to support advanced research and media specialists for accelerated reference sources. Similarly, any teacher working with a twice-exceptional gifted adolescent should be able to depend on the expertise of a special educator who is aware of the nuances and implications that accompany giftedness with learning disability.

6. *From staff development as a frill to professional development as an indispensable process.* When secondary educators see professional development as a process—in essence, a journey—then it is manageable. It is easy to avoid temporary expectations for change. But, when knowledge and competencies for educating gifted students are required of all educators, the process will be perceived as permanent and ongoing.

GUIDELINES FOR EXPECTED COMPETENCIES

Professional development is not without cost to schools and their personnel. It requires expenditures of precious time, energy, and focus. It can confound complicated schedules, particularly at the secondary level. If ill-planned and poorly administered, it can even be a turn-off rather than a turn-on to the featured topic. Generic sessions may be dismissed by some as not applicable to their teaching area, or they may have outcomes so short-lived that no changes or improvements result (Wineburg & Grossman, 1998). But, professional development is too often the first and perhaps only opportunity that educators who are teaching will have to focus directly on the nature and needs of gifted students in the school learning environment. A course in individual exceptionalities may have been included in preservice preparation programs of teachers, principals, counselors, or school psychologists, but not always. If included at all, it typically consisted of just one chapter in a general textbook discussed during one class session as directed by an instructor having little or no experience with gifted students and gifted education programs.

Several primary sources exist for guidelines to obtain licensure or a graduate degree for working with gifted students. Although none of these sources provides guidelines specifically for professional development, the important content they contain is a requisite part of professional development in education of secondary gifted students. Gifted programs require some of the content presented in these sources. Most of the documents overlap in that they refer to the study of education for gifted students with implications for the professional development of secondary educators.

One source is the *Standards for Graduate Programs in Gifted Education*, which was developed by the National Association for Gifted Children (NAGC; 1995). These standards represent core knowledge and competencies for high-quality graduate programs in gifted education. The document includes a conceptual framework, professional studies indicators, and indices of related field experiences. The competencies and foundational understandings are delineated as observable, measurable, and accountable indices of behavior. These very indices should be the expected outcomes of ongoing professional development initiatives. For example, all high school teachers must recognize the importance and understand the practice of modifying core curricula so that gifted students are provided opportunities to develop their advanced interests. Furthermore, this document outlines indicators for qualifications and composition of high school faculties for teaching gifted adolescents. Diversity, for example, is important so that all gifted students, including those from culturally and linguistically diverse populations, can see themselves culturally represented among their academic facilitators and leaders in classrooms.

A complementary document developed by the same organization, *NAGC Pre-K–12 Gifted Education Program Standards* (Landrum & Shaklee, 1998), contains a section on standards for professional development in gifted education. This document clearly delineates the minimal and exemplary benchmarks for measuring the adequacy of Pre-K–12 professional development programming in gifted education.

For example, one minimal competency indicates that all high school personnel must be aware of the nature and needs of gifted adolescents and the implications for teaching and learning. A related exemplary standard calls for ongoing staff development effort for secondary gifted students whereby the study of their nature and needs gives way to teaching methodologies, policies for student evaluation and grading, and more.

The Council for Exceptional Children (CEC) published a similar set of standards, *Standards for Programs Involving the Gifted and Talented* (CEC, 2001). Not unlike the NAGC documents, the contents of this document include specific competencies, practices, and attitudes deemed necessary for educators of gifted learners. As in the NAGC documents, measurable benchmarks for educator competence are outlined. However, unique competencies referring to the provision of gifted education services within the umbrella of exceptional children are unique to this document. For example, the inclusion of competencies referring to due process and related considerations is provided.

The European Council for High Ability (ECHA) also publishes a source of professional competencies and core understandings for teaching gifted students. This organization outlines the theoretical and practical components of a professional degree program for the specialist in gifted education. Specifically, ECHA emphasizes: (1) conceptions of giftedness; (2) identification of the gifted and talented; (3) instructional models and practices; (4) special issues such as family, socio-emotional needs, and special populations; and (5) methodological topics (Mönks & Mason, 2000). The implications of this document for professional development design and implementation are evident as the five sections provide the basis of a content outline for ongoing professional studies in gifted education at all levels, including secondary education. The study of socio-emotional development, for example, has unique elements for adolescence as compared with early childhood. Although young gifted children have early emergence of interests, gifted adolescents often have intense and well-developed interests, if not passions, by their secondary school days.

PROFESSIONAL DEVELOPMENT COMPONENTS

Plans for professional development must be crafted with utmost care if they are to help school personnel design educational programs and provide classroom experiences to maximize the potential of highly able students. Professional development has a history and a research base from which much has been learned about its successes and failures (see Dillon-Peterson, 1991; Guskey, 1985; Joyce & Showers, 1988). Professional growth activities need not be irrelevant, impractical, time wasting, frustrating, and dull. When constructed upon a solid base of school district and building goals, designed with careful planning that emanates from expressed needs of all constituents, conducted by experts with skill and enthusiasm, and evaluated meticulously with follow-through and follow-up to apply the professional development content, they can be rewarding experiences from which educators gain and, consequently, their students gain more. Key components to include in this careful planning are:

1. a realistic rationale,
2. appropriate purposes and goals,
3. participant involvement in the planning process,
4. suitable models and methods,
5. relevant topics,
6. excellent delivery,
7. a useful evaluation component, and
8. follow-up and follow-through activities.

Even as these general conditions are being assured, others specific to education of gifted and talented must be addressed. One important consideration is whether the goals, participants, and themes are to be directed toward elementary or secondary level personnel. In a study of teacher attitudes about staff development (McBride, Reed, & Dollar, 1994), secondary teachers found staff development activities less relevant and not as well planned, and felt less involved than did their elementary counterparts. The elementary teachers reported being able to use and apply the activities in their classrooms to a greater extent than did the secondary teachers.

Secondary school personnel tend to be a difficult constituency for planners and facilitators of professional development. First, the numbers of participants typically are large, which makes offering whole-group sessions seem more expedient and efficient than offering an array of choices for smaller groups. Also, secondary participants may ask hard, no-nonsense questions about what the focus of the professional development activity will be and how much it can be expected to subtract from their time and energy. They tend to be somewhat skeptical about short-term, easy-fix proposals tossed out by visiting experts and dismiss them as too-simplistic solutions for the monumental challenges they face each day. As a large, diverse group they bring a wide range of past experiences and a broad array of interests and talents. Even in nondepartmentalized settings, there are department-type considerations that influence their interactions with colleagues and administrators. One worrisome factor is an unyielding schedule that structures the school day into short periods and includes many extracurricular events, leaving little time for professional growth, collaboration, and reflection.

As content-specific educators, secondary teachers want relevant professional development consisting of valid presenters from content areas similar to theirs, or who demonstrate specific applications in various content areas. Furthermore, most secondary teachers want activities to emphasize content with instructional techniques that focus on student learning outcomes rather than on pedagogy.

RATIONALE FOR PROFESSIONAL DEVELOPMENT

School personnel must be engaged in continuous growth and development in order to teach, counsel, model for, and lead young generations wisely in this complex world. So, how are schools to find enough time, flexibility, energy, and resources for all, including professional development that focuses on education for gifted students? A sensible, defensible rationale must be presented for gifted education professional development.

Although general teacher education programs typically offer little instruction on gifted students and gifted programs, most teachers will have gifted students in their classrooms. Secondary teacher education programs tend to focus on content preparation exclusively. Yet, new middle school and high school teachers are caught up in dealing with the wide ranges of individual differences within their classes and faced very soon with the realization that when good teaching occurs for all students, the range of differences will widen each year. They must deal with restrictive schedules that inhibit creative production and in-depth learning, and with legislative and administrative pressures to increase test scores, often at the expense of providing enriched and accelerated content. Furthermore, attitudes toward brilliance in the gifted secondary student, particularly the studious, non-athletic type, generally have not been favorable on the part of students or their teachers (Cramond & Martin, 1987).

The most practical rationale for promoting specialized professional development in gifted education is that highly able students will find themselves in general classrooms for most of their school day whether their teachers are ready for them or not. Unfortunately, the "one-size-fits-all" method of teaching still exists, even in many honors and other advanced courses, due to teachers' false sense of student homogeneity. Furthermore, unfounded fears surrounding popular myths about acceleration too often limit educational options that might be offered to secondary students. Therefore, administrators, counselors, school psychologists, and teachers must work together to modify and supplement existing school policies to ensure appropriate academic and psychosocial development of gifted adolescents. They must help students deal with psychosocial vulnerabilities such as perfectionism and underachievement, and with issues related to multipotentiality and asynchronous development. The need to create an appropriate and nurturing academic environment in which the gifted student can thrive is the most obvious rationale for professional development for all teachers who have advanced students in their classrooms.

Excellent professional growth activities can help high schools avoid inertia caused by inflexibility and overreliance on outdated teaching strategies and materials. Understanding the importance of academic rigor, advanced content, and high expectations for student outcomes will lead teachers to accept diverse teaching methodologies and instructional approaches such as independent study, Socratic discussion, and the use of supplemental off-grade-level texts. It is imperative that all school personnel become adequately prepared to work with advanced students in their capacities as teachers, administrators, counselors, psychologists, and support personnel.

Purposes and Goals of Professional Development

School-based education is driven by numerous agenda items, school improvement goals, and decision-making instances. Important examples are the No Child

Left Behind Act (NCLB; 2001) that focuses on adequate yearly progress (AYP), equitable school funding, special needs of students with disabilities, emphasis on improved performances by students who underachieve, a clarion call for collaboration and teamwork among school personnel, changing structures of families and communities, and the exodus of many students from public schools to private schools and home schooling. Attention to high-ability students' needs is influenced by all of these issues and must be included as one of the issues in its own right. Strong professional development experiences that produce positive outcomes are vital for keeping the needs of very able, very talented, and highly creative learners up front in the total plan for student-appropriate classroom instruction and special services.

Professional development must be an integral part of a deliberately developed, continuous improvement effort (Zmuda, Kuklis, & Kline, 2004). Goals must be set that empower staff to lead wherever they are within the school structure, to designate parameters, and to allow creativity to emerge. All must "buy into" the concept of professional growth through professional development. Zmuda et al. point out that some teachers feel they can emerge from such experiences unchanged or unscathed. These feelings of disengagement contribute to the decades-old practice of rejecting innovations before they have been implemented (Hall & Hord, 1987).

When formulating goals for professional development, school personnel need to envision a system. A flow chart is a useful tool for showing how the goals fit with building and district goals—for example, School Improvement Goals, goals for enhancing student performance on state assessments, or for adhering to the NCLB mandate. School personnel will want to see a direct correlation of the staff development activities to student performance. The system should be adjusted to support multiple options for school personnel, and school staff should be urged to be flexible, even when the system is not.

A major challenge in professional development activity is ensuring that what is learned by participants makes its way into the daily instruction of students (Caldwell, 1989). This must be the singular aim of any professional development activity for teachers. "Integrating a new practice into the structure, system, and routines of a school or district enhances the probability that the practice will remain" (Caldwell, p. 120). Therefore, professional development in gifted education must be integrated into the school infrastructure, rather than regarded as an add-on. For example, grading policies and practices that address the advanced nature of some school options such as college level coursework should be integrated into the overall policy and practice of assigning grades to students. Then this must result in teacher adjustments of expectations for student outcomes in order to appropriately challenge gifted students, as well. When a goal of professional development is achieved and implemented successfully, and teachers and students feel good about the results, the practices are likely to carry on to other students in the future, creating an ever-widening circle of positive ripple effects.

DETERMINING THE PROFESSIONAL NEEDS OF POTENTIAL PROFESSIONAL DEVELOPMENT PARTICIPANTS

Busy secondary teachers, already overworked and heavily scheduled and straining to meet federal, state, and local demands of NCLB (2001) and the Individuals with Disabilities Education Act (IDEA; 1990), quality performance accreditation, school improvement goals, and more, may inwardly regard special attention to students who already "get it on their own" as unnecessary and wasteful. Planners of professional development opportunities must ferret out these attitudes and concerns before they can put together meaningful goals. Needs sensing and needs assessment processes will help identify issues and concerns that relate to education of gifted students.

Needs Sensing

Before formal planning for professional development takes place, the wants and needs of anticipated participants should be ascertained. This process typically is referred to as needs assessment. However, respondents to a needs assessment may not always know what they need to know, or they may be reluctant to voice their needs. This is the time for *needs sensing* that will help planners construct more useful needs assessment tools. As a precursor to needs assessment, needs sensing efforts probe for sensitivity and readiness toward staff development themes.

Useful techniques for needs sensing include informal interviews, dialogue with individuals or small groups, observations in classes and during school events, visits to other schools and programs for purposes of comparison, analysis of requests for materials and other resources, perusal of relevant comments by school personnel, and study of reactions to any mentioning of gifted students and gifted programs. Frequent internal scans of the learning environment are useful for picking up strong concerns that can be addressed in gifted program staff development. Sources of information must be treated with confidentiality and handled in a nonjudgmental manner. Analysis of existing school data, performance trends, and common requests or complaints by parents may lead to patterns of issues, concerns, or problems that could be addressed by professional development initiatives.

Needs Assessment

Needs assessment uses the informal information gleaned from needs sensing to construct more formal, measurable instruments for determining staff wants and needs. If needs assessment is conducted effectively, teachers feel that they have some ownership in professional development activities. When needs assessment data are analyzed and used in appropriate, visible ways to form goals, teachers will know that they have ownership in the process and the activities.

Useful techniques for needs assessment include the following: formal interviews, surveys, checklists, questionnaires, and brainstorm sessions. Time and space should be left for recording volunteered information and open-ended comments.

Gifted education facilitators or department chairs might visit classrooms and observe common needs or areas that should be improved. A focus group interview at staff meetings or departments can provide a laundry list of needs. Checklists or questionnaires with forced choices or open-ended questions can generate more individualized input.

PARTICIPANT INVOLVEMENT IN PLANNING PROFESSIONAL DEVELOPMENT

Teachers do not want to have in-service or staff development "done to them"; rather, it should be developed and implemented by them for the ultimate benefit of students. Therefore, representatives of the intended participants must be integral members of the professional development planning team. This team should be charged with writing the professional development plan so that it addresses different role groups, including general education teachers, special education teachers, related services and support staff, school administrators, school counselors and school psychologists, classified staff, and school board members. It is helpful also to communicate with the school community about the goals and activities of professional development.

Professional development is not just for teachers; it is for a wide range of roles, including school administrators, related services and support personnel, classified staff, and school board members (Sparks & Vaughn, 1994). Parents and students also have important roles in planning and participating in the professional growth of school personnel.

School Administrators

Building administrators have the primary responsibility of setting and clarifying goals of staff development in their school(s). Developing these goals with the staff should be their aim. In schools where a climate of collegiality has overcome teacher isolation and the extreme kind of self-reliance that shuns help, and where teachers are concerned about academic progress of all students, not just those at risk of failure, a healthy environment for professional development activity is already in place.

Another responsibility of building leaders is integrating staff development into the school schedule. Staff can and should help solve the problem of addressing this difficult aspect. As noted earlier, time allocation for professional development activity is a major concern. Teachers overwhelmingly favor scheduling staff development during the school day with time released from regular duties to participate.

General Educators in Middle Schools

The student population of a typical middle school includes a wide range of physical, social, emotional, and intellectual maturity; therefore, no one strategy, plan, or practice will be adequate for dealing with middle school students (Tomlinson, 1992). Professional development directed expressly to middle school needs is essential for positive outcomes. Content should relate to specific characteristics and needs of middle-grade students and the requirements for teaching them (Epstein, Lockard, & Dauber, 1991). Sometimes teachers are transplanted from higher or lower grades with little or no preparation for middle school issues.

One issue, for example, is how to help students make successful transitions from lower grades to middle school and then from middle school to higher grades. When differentiated curriculum for very able learners is added to a transition agenda that includes readying low-achieving students for mandated testing, the planning and decision-making aspects become quite complex.

Another issue stems from heterogeneous grouping and other structures for differentiating learning experiences of middle school gifted students. Studies by Gallagher, Coleman, and Nelson (1995) showed that little collaboration was taking place among gifted education personnel and general education personnel. Furthermore, both groups disagreed substantially on gifted students' needs. But, survey respondents did agree that there is serious need for more professional development and support to assist teachers with gifted students in their classrooms.

Middle-school staff development that features strategies for enhancing performance of gifted learners and all other learners could have an additional payoff of raising the school's test scores. Professional development planners should select first those teachers who are most interested in differentiating for their very able students and show promise of being most successful with the strategies. Then, other teachers can be expected to catch their enthusiasm and follow their lead.

General Educators in High Schools

Teachers and classroom environments at the high school level present numerous challenges to effective education of gifted learners. Again, the best hope for overcoming obstacles is effective professional development that empowers teachers to make appropriate modifications in curriculum and instruction and also to structure appropriately advanced studies for gifted students. Likewise, administrators gain from professional development emphasizing policy and instructional leadership that promotes educational interventions needed for advanced study in high school and beyond.

High schools traditionally rely on adoption of specialized programs of study for advanced learning such as Advanced Placement (AP) and/or International Baccalaureate (IB). The primary purpose for expanding advanced studies programs is the provision of high-level, challenging curricula specifically designed for high school students. Gifted learners are likely to be in AP or IB courses, either by default or because of concentrated efforts to place them there. Many students already enroll in such courses, and the numbers are growing larger. Thus, the diversity of students in AP or IB classes could come to resemble a heterogeneous classroom.

A recent study of trends in these high school programs examined the viability of such programs for gifted students (Callahan, 2003). Results of the study show that the truly advanced nature of the courses is largely undocumented. Although the alignment of AP and IB coursework with introductory college courses has been noted as a recruitment device for student enrollment, evidence of such congruency does not exist. Further, instruction in these courses can be relatively undifferentiated for student needs. Similar reports cite a breadth-over-depth approach to the content in these courses (National Research Council, 2002). Other shortcomings include shortage of highly qualified teachers to provide appropriately challenging instruction to gifted students, as well as lack of significant recruitment and retention efforts for gifted learners.

School Counselors and School Psychologists

School counselors must be alert to the natures and needs of very able students. They share responsibility with administrators for helping identify needs and arranging learning alternatives to serve those needs. They might reasonably be considered part of the professional development team to plan and deliver gifted program staff development. However, research from the 1960s indicates the presence of surprisingly negative attitudes toward gifted education programs by a significant number of school counselors and psychologists (Deiulio, 1983). This is another area in need of new research, and if further findings hold to this course, intensive efforts must be made to provide graduate-level coursework and ongoing staff development for these role groups. One example could be using research studies that focus on social and academic self-concepts of gifted adolescents (Dixon, 1998; Cross, Coleman, & Terhaar-Yonkers, 1991) as professional growth materials for counselors.

School psychologists have many opportunities and responsibilities in gifted education programs. They are integral to identification, placement, and individual goal-setting for gifted students. They often represent building administrators during IEP conferences, and they can be powerful advocates for differentiated services to address gifted students' needs. Some of their most important contributions can occur when working to identify and serve twice-exceptional students such as those with giftedness and learning disabilities or giftedness and Attention Deficit/Hyperactivity Disorder.

Special Education Teachers, English as Second-Language Teachers, and Support Personnel

Special education teachers, English as second-language teachers, related services and support personnel, along with gifted education personnel must collaborate in order to address the needs of twice-exceptional gifted students. Each group should be aware of curriculum and instructional methodology used by educators in the other groups. For example, the special education staff needs to know what general classroom teachers teach, and general classroom teachers need to be aware of special education strategies and materials the special education teachers use.

Some gifted education facilitators receive assistance from paraeducators. The paraeducator is a partner in providing special services for special needs. The prefix "para" means to come alongside and help. Paraeducators often reside in communities where they are employed and thus may reflect the cultural and linguistic backgrounds of students. They can be supportive links to the community, assisting as translators of cultural needs and collaborators with family members (Dettmer, Thurston, & Dyck, 2005). Although paraeducators are not to plan instruction, make decisions about student needs, or evaluate student performance, they may help conduct routine business of the classroom, prepare instructional materials, conduct small group activities, and monitor student progress.

Appropriate educational decision making is characterized by diversity and the presence of broad perspectives where others are valued and respected. Members of all groups of educators should be participants in professional development experiences for middle school and secondary gifted programs in order to gain competence in working with the specialized groups of gifted adolescents so woefully unrrrepresented in many regular education and advanced courses.

School Board Members

School board members have a complex, multifarious agenda to address and tend not to be focused on education for gifted students or experienced in gifted student needs. This lack of focus is particularly apparent in the demographics of districts that have too few students identified for gifted programs. However, the instructional policies, budgetary matters, and staffing practices typically guided by school board actions have great impact on provision of appropriate services for gifted learners. An example of such influence is the level of monies invested in appropriate professional development for secondary level gifted education and recognition of the need for highly qualified teachers in advanced courses.

Examples of negativity toward needs of gifted students include reluctance to permit dual enrollment of students in college courses to make challenging coursework available, and reluctance to allow early graduation that makes early entrance into post-secondary education possible. Furthermore, school board actions in matters such as course offerings and staff assignments can result in unintended obstacles to differentiated instruction for secondary gifted students in both advanced courses and general classrooms.

If school boards can have impact on the education of gifted students so dramatically, it follows that positive influences are possible, as well. Conscientious school board members do want the best for each student, but they might not have a grasp on how difficult that aim is to achieve and how often the needs of some students are overlooked. Gifted program staff can explain gifted student needs and advocate for appropriate learning arrangements. Students also can be very effective in presenting a case for curriculum differentiation and the teacher preparation needed to provide it.

School board members want to know about policies and processes that can bring about school excellence and parent satisfaction. Advocacy for gifted education is not uncommon on a school board; however, it typically emanates from one individual rather then a majority of the board. The presence of gifted program facilitators at school board meetings, and not just when gifted education issues are on the agenda, helps convey a commitment to school improvement goals. Professional development activities provided to school boards can inform them about gifted education issues in secondary schools and build advocacy for addressing those issues constructively.

Families of Gifted Students

Families also must be aware of issues relevant to their adolescents. Professional development may include families as participants or may be designed specifically for families. Research has shown that parents of gifted individuals have special needs just as their children do (Kaufmann & Sexton, 1983). Workshops for helping parents understand the nature and needs of gifted children have achieved positive outcomes (Wolf, 1987). For example, some parent participants have affiliated with state organizations for gifted education; others have stepped forward to serve on committees in groups such as the local Parent Teacher Organization to represent education of gifted students.

Gifted Students

In the all too rare instances where students have been asked to voice their opinions about schools, teachers, textbooks, classroom routines, teaching techniques, grading policies and the like, they have delivered powerful critique and sensible suggestions. When asked how they would change the curriculum, gifted students state their desire for more open discussion on current and controversial topics. They feel that more emphasis should be placed on quality of material rather than quantity. They definitely want the pace of instruction geared to their ability to learn and produce.

A professional development team might meet informally with students in small groups or individually and ask questions to elicit their input. Care should be taken to abide by a ground rule that no name or location of school personnel will be mentioned in the interview. The following list contains examples of relevant questions for hearing students' collective voice:

- What do you like best about your school?
- Why do you like to come to school?
- What motivates you to do well in a class?
- What kinds of learning present a challenge for you in the learning process?
- What qualities in teachers are most effective for you?
- What do you see as the purpose of textbooks and other class materials?
- What services now offered by the school help you most?

- If you are or have been in a gifted program, how is that program different from the regular classroom program?
- What educational services would you like for the school to offer?
- What kinds of educational experiences help you to do your best and feel good about learning?
- Are there other thoughts and feelings you would like to convey about your schooling?

This list of questions could be altered and others added to reflect local situations, ages of students, and purposes of the interview. The list is positive in tone. Questions could be used such as "What don't you like about school?" and "What teaching methods and materials do not work for you?" But, these types of questions necessitate caution; the responses they draw out may accentuate the need for firm enforcement of the "no names of people or schools" rule.

TOPICS FOR PROFESSIONAL DEVELOPMENT

The overarching goal of professional development in gifted education is to prepare school personnel for making appropriate decisions about the education of gifted students. Professional developers will want to see that educators are aware of curriculum differentiation and the program options gifted students need. They should emphasize the reality that conventional acceleration and enrichment structures such as AP classes and tests, IB curriculum, and honors classes in a few select subjects will not fill the bill of educational differentiation for highly able students.

Many options at the middle school and secondary levels necessarily take place outside school confines, such as correspondence courses, early college entrance, university courses, and mentorships. Others are provided in the school, but with involvement of fewer teachers—for example, dual enrollment, testing out of courses, independent study and research, before- or after-school accelerated classes, and the AP and honors classes mentioned previously. School counselors serve a vital role in setting up these arrangements and guiding students to them; however, there is also a need to approve the option by administrators and a need to know about it by teachers and classified staff. For coordination and support, addressing these needs to know and approve cannot be stressed too strongly.

Professional development specialists for gifted education straddle a fine line of differentiation that marks a two-handed dilemma. On one hand is the idea that, "These strategies and materials can benefit all students, including the identified gifted students in your classes." On the other hand is the concern that, "If all students can do it, then it isn't challenging and intellectually satisfying enough for the gifted students." With this paradox in mind, planners and presenters of professional development should proceed with caution. One negative-minded teacher or a single confrontational question not attended to appropriately could wreck an afternoon of progress, as many unfortunate presenters have found out the uncomfortable way.

General themes to be considered for professional development sessions, provided they reflect the concerns and interests that surface in the needs assessment data, include but are not limited to these:

1. Learning how to compact curriculum to remove previously mastered material, thus buying time for curricular alternatives;
2. Facilitating multilevel enrollment, perhaps in preparation for early graduation;
3. Setting up mentorships, on or off campus;
4. Assisting students with designing independent studies and research projects that interest them and stretch their abilities, such as how to select a topic, analyze data, describe conclusions, and disseminate results;
5. Facilitating powerful discussions in class with high-road transfer of learning activated by processes of application, analysis, synthesis, and evaluation;
6. Going beyond basal textbooks with alternative resources selected and collected in collaboration with the gifted program facilitator;
7. Challenging gifted students who underachieve to be successful learners;
8. Differentiating assignments and tests in ways that encourage students to maximize their potential;
9. Developing assessments that tap into high abilities and stretch intellectual powers;
10. Providing Saturday institutes with learning experiences that challenge;
11. Incorporating flexible scheduling plans that accommodate options such as dual enrollment and other modifications needed to individualize learning experiences on and off campus;
12. Offering special-subject seminars, perhaps county-wide or district-wide;
13. Procuring mobile enrichment units that can be brought to a school site as a reasonable option for remote areas;
14. Studying tactics of high achievers such as champion spellers and history and geography contestants that can be replicated in the classroom with more students and in different subjects;
15. Discussing incidences of suicide among gifted teenagers, the prevention of, and coping strategies if there is such an unfortunate occurrence;
16. Using electronic portfolios and other technological devices for projects, data collection, record-keeping, data analysis, and other accelerative, enriching functions;
17. Giving demonstrations and practice in providing instructive feedback and critique to gifted students rather than perfunctory comments and unsupported high grades;
18. Presenting advance organizers for introducing new topics in ways that intrigue and stimulate learners to go beyond the expected; and
19. Constructing differentiated homework assignments, if homework is to be assigned, that engage gifted learners and catalyze their learning.

Most topics suggested above could be beneficial at both the middle school and high school levels. Others that are more suitable for high school personnel include:

1. Analyzing early-graduation policies, with input from a panel of former students who did leave early, and adjustments schools need to make because of the policy. Counselors would be particularly helpful as active participants, and inclusion of parents would be warranted.
2. Managing details required to facilitate enrollment in university classes, correspondence courses, online accelerated courses, career shadowing, and internships.
3. Exploring opportunities for cultural trips and exchanges abroad or within the country, such as a rural/urban exchange. Facilitators from schools that already have such programs in place could be invited as presenters and consulted as coaches.
4. Developing community service projects for groups or for individuals; for short-term, semester, or a year; during or outside school time; and for credit or no credit.
5. Studying social issues and stigmas experienced by highly gifted or very creative students, and the residual effects on their self esteem.

DIVERSITY ISSUES IN PROFESSIONAL DEVELOPMENT

Professional development goals must be sensitive to and responsive to diversity issues. Americans who are White comprise 85% of the teaching force (Ford & Harris, 1999), and many school personnel do not understand issues that minority students and students of poverty face. The reality of this, together with the growing ethnic and linguistic diversity of the student population, calls for development of multicultural competencies in all teachers.

Diversity issues are twofold. One concern is a lack of diversity within the ranks of school personnel. The other is imbalance of diversity among students placed in programs for gifted students. To address the first of these issues, more diversity must be encouraged in teacher education programs, with particular emphasis given to preparing gifted program facilitators from minority populations. For the second issue, more students from special populations must be placed in gifted programs. Significant progress is even more likely when these issues are addressed simultaneously in both preservice and in-service professional development.

Areas that the professional development should target for attention are: developing knowledge of the nature and needs of culturally, linguistically, and ethnically diverse students; developing an understanding of the impact of poverty on the nurturing and actualizing of giftedness; recognizing viable teaching techniques consistent with the unique characteristics and needs of diverse gifted learners; and recognizing the importance of setting high standards and expectations to help students from diverse and special populations succeed.

Effective teachers are both socially responsive to, and responsible for, development of characteristics and competencies needed to teach diverse groups of gifted learners effectively (Ford & Trotman, 2001). Any teacher can become culturally responsive without becoming an expert in every culture; however, a foundation of knowledge about cultural diversity and its impact on student learning and self-actualization is fundamental (Ford & Trotman). Culturally sensitive and respectful teaching strategies assist teachers in developing culturally responsive classrooms. Applying the appropriate modifications, adaptations, or accommodations in instruction will contribute to a culturally relevant classroom built on congruency of instructional practices and student identities. Relevant teaching techniques, along with strong commitment to teaching diverse students, will produce teachers who are cultural advocates (Ford & Trotman).

Professional development provides opportunities for willing educators to develop the competencies and general understandings about the nature, needs, and education of culturally, linguistically, and ethnically diverse students. Resources such as *We Can't Teach What We Don't Know* (Howard, 1999) and *Multicultural Gifted Education* (Ford & Harris, 1999) can help; teacher exchanges with other schools that have different demographics also can be useful. Materials and workshops are available as resources (Payne, 1998; Payne & Krabill, 2002).

MODELS AND METHODS OF PROFESSIONAL DEVELOPMENT

Five models for professional development, described by Sparks and Loucks-Horsley (1989), are not indigenous to gifted education, but can serve as solid foundations on which to build more specifically targeted professional development.

General Models

Individually-Guided

The individually-guided staff development model is a process in which teachers judge their own learning needs, and then plan for and pursue activities they think will promote their learning. This might be attendance at a workshop or conference or designing and carrying out special projects driven by incentive grants.

Observation and Assessment

Observation and assessment involve reflection on one's own practices enhanced by observation and feedback from other professionals. In order to be effective, this technique must be separated from evaluation processes.

Development/Improvement Process

A development/improvement process is based on the assumption that adult learners learn most effectively when there is a need to know or a problem to solve. By being involved in developing or adapting curriculum, designing programs, or engaging in school improvement processes, educators become more knowledgeable and skillful.

Awareness or Knowledge

Awareness or knowledge development depends upon the staff developer's ability to select activities such as demonstration, role-playing, or microteaching for helping participants achieve outcomes that address school improvement goals. Improvement of the educator's thinking is an important goal, and staff development techniques focusing on this goal would be useful for replication in the classroom.

Inquiry

Inquiry can be a solitary activity, a small-group activity, or one conducted by an entire school faculty. It can be formal or informal, but it is predicated on a belief in teachers' abilities to form valid questions about their own practices and pursue objective answers to those questions. The assumption is that the best professional development experience is a teachers' cooperative study of problems and issues that emanate from their attempts to make their instruction consistent with their educational values.

Guskey's Approach to Professional Development

One of the most practical approaches to planning professional development is a simple but elegant concept put forth by Guskey (1985) and underscored by Reis and Westberg (1994). Guskey asserts that significant changes in teacher beliefs and attitudes will occur only after positive learning outcomes for students occur. Activities that are successful with students and improve learning outcomes tend to be repeated by teachers, and those that are not successful tend to be avoided. Teachers like to "look good," and they very much want their students, for the students' sakes, to succeed.

Therefore, the first step for initiating change is to adopt an innovative instructional approach that includes curriculum differentiation, teaching modification, and challenging material. For example, the instruction could provide for curriculum compacting or independent study or mentorship. But, it must be a "sure-thing" strategy that will work for teachers in their setting. Upon seeing students succeed and grow with the innovation, teacher beliefs and attitudes will change in positive ways.

The Schoolwide Enrichment Model

Professional development is an integral part of the Schoolwide Enrichment Model (SEM) (Renzulli & Reis, 1985). Building on Guskey's (1985) philosophy of altering teacher attitudes through use of strategies that improve student performance, the model depends heavily on staff development to meet the needs of gifted and talented students in general classroom settings. Reis and Westberg (1994) maintain that traditional, single-shot in-service sessions will not change practices in classrooms. But, peer coaching, videotape presentations, observation of curriculum compacting, and practice under guidance with extending and enriching activities that address gifted students' needs can change teacher practices, thereby improving their beliefs and attitudes.

The Resource Consultation Model

In the resource consultation model, the gifted program consultant role is that of collaborator, not expert. Teachers and resource consultants share decision making and focus on common goals. The collaborative teaching approach enables a consultant and teacher(s) to work together in developing teacher confidence and skills (Kirschenbaum, Armstrong, & Landrum, 1999).

Some teachers acknowledge the importance of specific instructional strategies for gifted students, but cannot implement them successfully. Then the resource consultant must decide when and how much in-service should be provided. Within a collaborative climate, the resource consultant can go beyond the relatively ineffective practice of simply informing teachers what they should be doing, and show them how to modify curriculum by working with them to implement the strategies.

The gifted education specialist shares responsibility for curriculum differentiation of gifted learners with school personnel who are engaged in collaborative efforts (Landrum, 2001). But, when needed, the consultant also can provide direct service to students; thus, a combination of indirect and direct services is readily available for all learning situations. Research shows that with the resource consultation model in place, academic performances of gifted students and students not identified as gifted are enhanced, and teacher competencies in differentiating instructional practices are improved (Landrum).

Other Methods

Ways of providing professional development experiences that focus on gifted students and their educational programs are as varied as the school personnel and their schools. The possibilities include these:

- *Professional conferences and conventions* can be powerful vehicles for networking, professional growth, and inspiration. Educators who attend regional or national conventions will find it helpful to prepare thoughtfully for the experience (Dettmer & Landrum, 1998). An adult version of the student IEP form can be used advantageously as an adult's Personal Development Plan (PDP) to assess the following: What strengths and needs will I be taking to the convention? What are my purposes (goals) for attending this convention? In what measurable ways (objectives) can I attain those goals? What resources will I need, and how and when will I evaluate the outcomes? The PDP can be part of a staff development activity later for sharing conference experiences and products with colleagues.
- *Administrators must have keen awareness of gifted students and their needs* in order to make good decisions in their schools. Feldhusen, Haeger, and Pellegrino

(1989) describe a three-credit graduate course for school administrators that includes visiting gifted and talented program sites in the state and reporting about those visits. The course also includes creating an administrative design for developing, implementing, or expanding gifted education in the participant's own school district. When this approach was evaluated, two of the most highly rated outcomes by participating administrators were "The areas of gifted and talented education I needed to know about were well covered," and "The course caused me to reconsider some of my prior attitudes."

- *University coursework and continuing education* are two of the more obvious and conventional forms of professional development. Coursework that extends teachers' knowledge in their subject areas can be particularly beneficial for teachers of bright secondary students in the general classroom. One study choice might be a class in characteristics and needs of gifted students; long-standing research demonstrates that teachers' attitudes toward gifted education and exceptionally able students can be altered positively after just one such course (Cohn, 1977; Hord, 1982; Solano, 1977). Other course choices could be nurturance of creativity, research methods, assessment, learning theory, or curriculum development.

- *Brown bag seminars* conducted by teachers provide a means by which teachers can become more aware of gifted student needs and curricular modifications for those needs. This approach, typically a noontime activity, works well in geographically isolated areas where the gifted education consultant is scheduled for some time in each school and can serve as convener and discussion leader.

- *Lesson plan analysis* is useful as a program evaluation tool (Ferrell, 1992). This method also can be a vehicle for staff development to align plans for differentiated instruction with program goals. Lesson plans that show responsiveness to learner needs, continuity of content, flexibility of pace, diversity of material, increasing levels of abstraction and difficulty, and evidence of higher taxonomy functions both cognitive and affective, can be discussed by teachers as ways of differentiating and flexibly pacing the learning experiences.

- *Textbook and curricular unit analysis* is another useful tool for including curriculum differentiation and flexible pacing strategies gifted students need. It is well known among educators of gifted students that many textbooks fail to challenge very able learners and a significant number of other learners, as well. Examining textbooks, including the basal series in science, math, social studies, literature, health, and English, can be a catalyst for reflecting on levels of information needed to stimulate higher order thinking and production for all students.

- *Professional portfolios* are effective as a framework for professional development activities. Participants set their own goals, determine how they want to learn, and decide how to integrate the learning into their teaching (Dietz, 1995). They evaluate the outcomes of their learning by assessing how it enhanced their students' learning.

- *Professional reading and discussion* with colleagues can provide learning opportunities while helping to overcome feelings of isolation and strengthen communication links among school personnel. Such discussions have been held during regular school hours where university faculty teach the teachers' classes one month and sit in on a discussion session another month (Sullivan, 1987). Discussions can center around book chapters, research articles in journals, application articles in periodicals, papers from classes and meetings, news articles on timely topics, or media presentations on educational issues.

- *Guided book review* is a variant of professional reading. A small group of teachers read a book pertaining to a subject—for example, self-esteem of gifted adolescents, think about what they have read, and meet to discuss their reactions. The process promotes synthesis of theory and practice, and helps establish a common language and shared meaning about the subject (Schmale, 1994).

- In the *cyclical professional development* approach, teachers use data to set specific targets for student learning and prepare for the activity. They collaborate to write curriculum and assessments, examine students' work, serve on committees, observe in colleagues' classrooms, participate in study groups, and coach and mentor new teachers. They participate in individualized professional growth experiences such as a conference or a course. They conduct action research and discuss what they learned, and they engage in external experiences such as summer externships and visits to other schools. The culmination is self-reflection and sharing of experiences with colleagues (Kelleher, 2003).

- *Teachers Helping Teachers (THT)* is a peer coaching method where teachers instruct colleagues in a particular area of expertise during informal sessions at their school (Dettmer et al., 2005). They might then be invited to instruct other groups in schools throughout the district or in cooperative arrangements with other nearby districts. The presenting teachers become participants in additional THT sessions where colleagues teach in areas of their expertise.

- *Mentoring* provides opportunities for an experienced teacher to take a direct interest in the professional development of a younger or less experienced teacher (Krupp, 1987). A mentoring relationship might be spontaneous or it might emanate from a school improvement plan. It need not always be directed at novice teachers; it can be equally effective for experienced teachers who have changed their grade level or curricular area.

- *Coaching* is attached to development programs as coached personnel learn to implement new knowledge and skills (Joyce & Showers, 1988). Coaching relationships are to be separate from supervision and evaluation. Principals must assume the responsibility of establishing a climate that makes participants feel good about being coached in experiences that involve collaboration, observation by others, and constructive feedback. Two typical types of coaching relationships are peer-coach and expert-coach. The peer relationship includes two participants with similar levels of experience who work together to achieve new knowledge, skill support, and encouragement. They are "in the same boat," so to speak. The expert or consultant coaching relationship for gifted education pairs two individuals with different levels of expertise to work in a consulting situation where one relies on the expertise of the other for feedback, modeling, and support.

- *Video clubs* provide opportunities for teachers to watch and discuss videotapes of their own teaching and develop understanding of what is taking place during lessons. This can lead to new ways of looking at what is happening in the classroom (Sherin, 2000). Videotapes that target gifted education interests can supply professional development material on knowledge about characteristics of giftedness, modified instructional strategies, differentiated curriculum, student diversity, motivational techniques, and advanced talent development (Karnes & Lewis, 1996). Videos must be selected very carefully; the right ones can be used advantageously in a variety of settings—university courses, parent group meetings, seminars for administrators, business and industry symposia where mentorships are arranged, and many more venues.

- *Classified staff sessions* are important for secretaries, transportation personnel, security personnel, custodians, school health care professionals, library and media personnel, food service personnel, and others who are involved with students in providing academic assistance, nurturing their health and well-being, and helping them come and go within a flexible schedule. An afternoon workshop is a doable format for such staff development (Welch, 1990). It allows for introductions and icebreaker activities, a well-organized delivery of key information, a question-and-response period, and a snappy, inspirational wrap-up. Beginning the half-day session with a lunch (perhaps served by students or parents) can be a much-appreciated icebreaker.

RURAL AREA PROFESSIONAL DEVELOPMENT

Rural schools in remote areas tend to be characterized by geographic distance and isolation, lack of diversity, too few students for expediting some grouping arrangements, limited resources, too few personnel covering too many curricular areas, and all too frequent resistance of students toward being singled out within their tight-knit communities (Dettmer et al., 2005). Rural educators often are left somewhat to themselves to acquire new knowledge and skills and solve school-related problems. These realities have ramifications for professional development planning.

Rural teachers differ from urban and suburban counterparts in a number of ways, including how they perceive their teaching situations and the kinds of incentives that keep them in those roles (Killian & Byrd, 1988). Although pupil-teacher ratios may be low, teachers might have five or six preparations daily, often outside their areas of expertise. They may be isolated from current development in their areas of specialization. Those at the secondary level tend to have many extracurricular duties.

A priority of rural teachers is survival; therefore, they are less likely to welcome staff development that promotes much change or carries much risk (King, 1988). However, they tend to have a long-term commitment to their positions and may have personal ties within the community that can do much to facilitate interactions between families and school personnel.

Small rural districts typically do not have personnel assigned solely to professional development. Furthermore, collaboration with peers in other districts is difficult due to schedules (particularly the busing schedules) and travel distances. Therefore, professional development design is often built around telecommunication using computer technology. Effective methods of professional development for rural areas include those described earlier, but also can employ techniques such as the following:

- *Telecommunications* can involve such means as videotapes of presentations by experts, demonstrations by practicing teachers of gifted students, printed readings, and a study guide. Telephone networks and computerized bulletin boards can make a wide variety of information readily accessible (Clasen & Clasen, 1989).
- *Online help sites and chat rooms* provide collegial interaction and help lessen feelings of isolation when they are used to convey useful strategies posted by colleagues for managing curriculum, schedules, and public relations for gifted education programs in rural areas.
- An instructional, interactive *satellite television system* for transmission is another way to provide professional and support staff development. In-services that would be prohibitively expensive can be provided at minimum cost with this system.
- A cooperative staff development model to tap rural strengths (Killian & Byrd, 1988) provides a *renewal institute for practicing educators* that has three strands: math, science, and language arts. After spring and summer workshops, instructors go to participants' classrooms in the fall for follow-up observation and feedback about implementation of workshop content. University tuition waivers provide incentive for participation in the workshops.
- *Collaboration among education service agencies and school district staff* can be initiated to establish benchmarks based on federal and state standards, with subsequent development of a procedure for laying groundwork, checking up in mid-year, and having a big wrap-up time to digest and reflect (Allen, 2004).

FORMATS AND TECHNIQUES
FOR PROFESSIONAL DEVELOPMENT

The overall process of conceptualizing, planning, conducting, and assessing a professional development activity is complex. It requires time, energy, and concentration by a number of school personnel to tailor each component. The plan must be comprehensive yet specific, appealing but cost effective, with long-range expectations of benefits, but the need for early assessment of effects. A generic template for keeping on track to ensure inclusion of necessities and refrain from veering off course can be very helpful. Figure 1 outlines basic parts of an activity in a professional development plan.

Delivery of In-Service and Staff Development

A group of adult learners presents a broad range of personal goals and a wide variety of learning styles and preferences (Dettmer, 1986). Adults learn best in

- Alignment of gifted program philosophy with school improvement goals
- Needs sensing and needs assessment in all schools involved
- Topic(s) for the professional development activities
- Participants who will be involved
- Dates and times
- Goals formulated, as based on needs sensing and needs assessment data
- Title(s) of the activities or sessions
- Presenter(s)
- Incentive(s) for participation
- Promotion and publicity
- Format for the sessions
- Facilities to be arranged
- Materials to be prepared
- Preparation and rehearsal
- Assessment and evaluation of outcomes
- Follow-up and follow-through functions

Figure 1. Template for Designing a Professional Development Activity

physical and psychological comfort (Nowak, 1994). Food and drink, pleasant surroundings, and comfortable (but not too comfortable) seats, preferably with tables, set the stage for receptivity and good will. Door prizes, tokens for special privileges such as a choice parking spot for a week, or coupons donated by local businesses, can add fun and anticipation to the event. These enticements are very important when calling for busy people to put down their immediate involvements of planning lessons, preparing materials, grading, and conferring with students and parents, in order to tackle new ideas and challenges as learners themselves.

Detailed discussion of specific presentation techniques for in-service and staff development is beyond the scope and length of this chapter. Numerous professional and commercial sources are available for guidelines on how to deliver material in interesting ways that will appeal to the novice and the most seasoned veteran educator. One example is *How to Make Presentations That Teach and Transform* (Garmston & Wellman, 1992) a resource that offers ways to "crack the ice," elicit participation, and handle criticism. The *Journal for Staff Development* provides columns on "how-to" ideas for making effective presentations. As just one example, Garmston (1993) offers an article on suggestions for podium humor. The NAGC service publication, *Staff Development: The Key to Effective Gifted Education Programs* (Dettmer & Landrum, 1998), includes a "dos" and "don'ts" list along with presentation techniques.

Recommendations when planning professional development experiences include the following: basing session material on determined needs and letting participants know that this has been done; rehearsing the presentation (especially if it is to be in front of "home folks," which often is the most anxiety-inducing audience); having a survival box of emergency supplies; making sure the room is comfortable; having food and drinks available; personalizing the material as much as possible; beginning on time; adhering to principles of adult learning; delaying distribution of the well-prepared, uncluttered, readable handouts until the moment they are needed; interspersing a delivery of information with brief activities and occasional breaks; involving participants actively as much as possible; having a succinct evaluation instrument ready with time built into the session for its completion; explaining planned follow-up and follow-through activities; and ending on time.

Those who conduct professional development activities must find a balance between arranging small, content-specific group sessions and whole-group general sessions. Most participants will want to stay in their specific work group. However, all need to be brought together at some point in order to understand the broad scope of the event's significance for their building and for the entire district. Within and beyond the sessions, participants should acquire and develop a common language about teaching and learning. This effort blends into performance evaluation, thus helping schools become more consistent in working toward the all-school goals.

Scheduling Professional Development Activities

Optimal scheduling of release time for professional development activities occurs at regular intervals during a school year to allow participants to try out their new learning and then return for additional staff development to problem-solve and continue learning (Caldwell, 1989). Such an approach utilizes concepts featured in Guskey's (1985) model for staff development:

1. First, change teacher practice(s).
2. Next, look for changed teaching that creates positive student outcomes.
3. Then, expect these outcomes to change teachers' beliefs and attitudes.

Administrators and staff in various settings have come up with creative and workable ways of buying time for professional development. These include the following: a cadre of substitutes to provide enrichment activities for students of teacher participants; arrangements in which one teacher manages two classes so the other teacher is free to participate in staff development; a visiting expert to instruct students on a topic of keen interest to them while their teachers are attending staff development; administrators, guidance counselors, and other qualified personnel who substitute for participating teachers; team planning and staff development time structured within the school day; a permanent substitute who can replace any staff member during staff development; and creative formats that modify block schedules and teacher planning time to free up time for staff development (Tanner, Canady, & Rettig, 1995).

EVALUATION, FOLLOW-UP, AND FOLLOW-THROUGH
OF PROFESSIONAL DEVELOPMENT

Evaluation

Evaluation methods for professional development experiences must be developed at the same time as the goals are developed. A goal is not useful if it cannot or will not be evaluated.

Multiple and varied assessment methods are needed. The ideal evaluation tool is a longitudinal assessment to measure student achievement resulting from participants' experiences. However, this ideal is not often realized. Evaluation results also should be used to improve future professional development activities. At the very least, evaluators should assess the following four areas (Dettmer & Landrum, 1998):

- *Participant critique of the activity.* A questionnaire at the conclusion of the event is a workable tool. A checklist would be efficient, but would deliver less-detailed data. (See Figure 2 for an example.)
- *Participant self-report of learning.* This might be assessed in paper-pencil formats, simulations, or interviews.
- *Participant on-the-job use of techniques presented.* An observation, videotape, or interview could serve this purpose. An open-ended questionnaire would be next best.
- *Participant assessment of differences the experience(s) made in classrooms and schools.* Survey forms and Likert scale-type instruments are effective.

Follow-Up Checks

After the professional development event(s) and the evaluation process are completed, a follow-up visit, phone call, or e-mail to participants is important in order to inquire about outcomes from the experience. All staff should be informed about anonymous, aggregated evaluation results from their building(s), and those from the entire district if applicable. Areas of growth should be highlighted first and then areas of further need pointed out, with a tentative plan and timeline provided for continuing the professional development process. Figure 3 is an example of a questionnaire with an open-ended format for collecting follow-up information.

Follow-Through Assistance

A final component of the professional development process is the follow-through. If a participant indicates wanting more information about a topic, or wanting to initiate a collaborative relationship, there must be an early response from the staff developer or gifted program facilitator. If evaluation data indicate little progress

---

Staff Development Activity Evaluation

Your name (optional): _____

Your teaching area(s): _____

Your teaching level(s): _____

Staff development site(s) and date(s): _____

Staff development topic(s): _____

RATING SCALE:

4 = to a great extent

3 = considerably

2 = somewhat

1 = very little

0 = none at all

____ 1. The staff development reflected needs that our needs assessment and planning identified.

____ 2. The staff development increased my understanding of nature and needs of gifted students.

____ 3. The staff development directed my attention to learning opportunities for gifted students.

____ 4. The session(s) provided me with ideas and techniques to use in my own teaching.

____ 5. The material was presented effectively and efficiently.

____ 6. The facilities were satisfactory.

____ 7. Resources for the staff development were well chosen or prepared, and useful.

____ 8. Because of this experience I am interested in collaborating with gifted program personnel.

____ 9. I have at least one thing in mind I will try because of this staff development experience.

10. Strengths of this staff development activity were:

11. The staff development could have been improved by:

12. I would like to have more information from gifted program personnel about:

provided for me (name)_____ at

(address)_____.

Figure 2. Example of a staff development questionnaire

Professional Development Activity Follow-Up

Please take a few minutes to respond to the following items concerning our recent professional development activity about _____ on the date _____.

1. Have you implemented any idea or strategy that was presented during the professional development activity? If so, please describe it briefly and rate the success level you have had with it by checking the appropriate category of your response.

_____

____ 1 = not effective ____ 2 = somewhat effective ____ 3 = very effective

---

2. Would you like to learn more about this topic beyond what was presented? If so, what?

_____

---

3. If you did not use the techniques and materials presented, please explain why you did not.

_____

---

4. Have you observed any use of the ideas by others so that it created a positive ripple effect beyond the immediate area? If so, please describe, and then rate the extent to which this happened.

_____

____ 1 = a little ____ 2 = somewhat ____ 3 = considerably ____ 4 = to a great extent

---

Figure 3. Example of professional development activity follow-up

toward goals of the professional development concepts and school improvement plans, coaching or mentoring may be appropriate.

Cashion and Sullenger (2000) remind educators that introducing new ideas will require gaining approval, and then, seeing the results will take time. Their findings from a summer institute on gifted education, gathered after 2 years' time, show change as a continuous process that includes recognizing a problem, learning about it, experimenting with potential solutions, integrating those ideas that do work into the system, reflecting on what is lacking, and trying again. Sometimes an experience is powerful because it occurs at a "teachable moment" or as an inspiration from addressing a student's needs.

SAMPLE PROFESSIONAL DEVELOPMENT PLANS

In order to see the integration of various components of effective professional development, three samples of professional development plans are presented here. Four other examples are available in the previously cited NAGC service publication on staff development (Dettmer & Landrum, 1998), including one for an information session directed to parents of gifted teenagers.

Example One

Title
Understanding Underachievement in High School Students

Rationale
One of the predictable vulnerabilities of being gifted is the potential for underachievement. This problem often surfaces with intensity during adolescence. Secondary teachers need to be aware of the potential problem and how to intervene.

Purpose and Goals
1. Introduce the concept of underachievement among gifted students.
2. Recognize the characteristics of underachievement.
3. Identify the preventable factors related to underachievement.
4. Consider potential interventions for secondary students who are underachieving.

Participants Involved
Teachers of advanced courses (e.g., AP, IB, honors, etc.), guidance counselors, administrators, special education teachers (most suitable for educators in rural or large, urban school districts)

Topics
A. Underachievement among gifted adolescents
B. Characteristics of underachieving gifted adolescents
C. Factors related to underachievement
D. Potential interventions for situational and chronic underachievement

Models and Methods
This staff development initiative will take the form of professional reading and discussion.

Format
Selected readings will be distributed to participants via electronic means (e.g., attachments to e-mail or posting on a Web site). Small-group discussions of the read-

ing materials will be conducted through electronic forums such as discussion boards or chat rooms.

Scheduling

The activities will be outlined over 5–6 weeks. Participants will be given a calendar indicating which discussion questions are addressed on a weekly basis. Students can post their discussion at any time during the start and finish dates indicated by the calendar.

Evaluation

Participants will respond to a 10-item questionnaire distributed electronically regarding the usefulness and efficiency of the staff development activities. Follow-up activities will be developed in response to evaluation data.

Example Two

Title

Recognizing the Characteristics of Giftedness in Adolescents

Rationale

The nature and needs of gifted adolescents are best understood as observable characteristics and behaviors. These characteristics are identifiable and must be addressed when they signal needs for modifying, adapting, or supplementing standard and advanced courses of study.

Purpose and Goals

1. Recognize the characteristics and behaviors of gifted adolescents.
2. Recognize the unique characteristics and behaviors of culturally and linguistically diverse, as well as impoverished gifted adolescents.
3. Recognize concomitant problems associated with giftedness.

Participants Involved

Teachers of advanced courses (e.g., AP, IB, honors, etc), guidance counselors, administrators, special education teachers, support personnel

Topics

1. Characteristics of gifted adolescents
2. Characteristics of underserved populations of gifted adolescents
3. Needs and concomitant problems of giftedness

Models and Methods

Participants will meet to watch and analyze videos that contain characters portraying giftedness in adolescents. Teachers will watch *October Sky* and *Stand and Deliver*. Using checklists for concomitant behavior and characteristics of giftedness in all, and in special populations of gifted learners, participants will analyze the presence of giftedness in the fictional characters for the films viewed.

Format
Participants will attend a full-day workshop. The two films are shown and followed by small-group discussion.

Scheduling
This will be a full-day workshop.

Evaluation
Approximately 3 months after the workshop, participants will receive an evaluation form that focuses on the benefits of attending the workshop and the impact it had on their teaching. Results will be used to develop follow-up activities and to improve future professional development programs.

Example Three

Title
Enhancing Learning and Teaching in the Classroom

Rationale
Teachers have the responsibilities to meet individual needs as specified in Individual Education Plans (IEPs), and to improve performances of all students.

Purpose and Goals
1. Increase awareness of student strengths and needs, and their educational concerns.
2. Increase awareness of multiple teaching strategies to enhance performance of all students and staff.
3. Increase awareness of the links to improved performance by all students through differentiated instruction and to success with adequate yearly progress (AYP).
4. Embed accommodations and modifications training into the building's staff development plan.

Participants Involved
General classroom teachers, school counselors and school psychologists, special education facilitators, administrators

Topics
A. Overview of the situation: A reality check
  1. Legal requirements of IEPs and 504s
  2. Adequate yearly progress requirements/the down side of closing the gap

       3.   AYP building status for current year/disaggregated groups
       4.   Consequences of not addressing the needs
   B. Teaching strategies that work
       1.   Differentiated instruction
       2.   Classroom strategies that work
       3.   Curriculum compacting and acceleration
       4.   Problem solving and higher order thinking skills
       5.   Curriculum modifications and accommodations

Models and Methods

A video of a student panel reacting to the question "How are your learning needs being met in the classroom?"

Format

Departmental discussions in small groups with special education facilitators discussing:

1. What are our current strengths in serving special education students?
2. What areas need to be improved and/or strengthened?
3. How can we organize this year to address needs and maintain strengths?
4. What resources do we need to accomplish the goal of improved student performance?

Scheduling

A full-day in-service, with the student panel video in the morning followed by an early lunch, and discussion groups in the afternoon followed by a concluding synthesis session.

Evaluation and Follow-up

In approximately 4 weeks, participants respond to an open-ended questionnaire:

1. What strategies are working for all student populations?
2. What strategies are working for staff problem solving and decision-making?
3. What strategies seem to be supported by employers and teacher educators?

Follow-up activities include monthly book study clubs, opportunities for summer training seminars, and Web site and print resources that provide information on a regular basis.

All are voluntary, with encouragement and perhaps fun kinds of incentives provided by administrators.

CONCLUSION

In a national study of 1,027 science and math teachers to compare effects of different characteristics of professional development on teachers' learning, results point to three core features having significant, positive effects on teachers' self-reported gains and changes in classroom practices (Garet, Porter, Desimone, Birman, & Yoon, 2001):

- a focus on content knowledge,
- opportunities for active learning, and
- coherence with other learning activities.

The researchers found that sustained and intensive professional development has more impact than shorter professional development. That which features academic subject matter to give opportunities for active learning and integration into daily school life (coherence) is more likely to produce enhanced knowledge and skills. Therefore, it is more important to focus on duration, collective participation, and core elements of content, active learning, and coherence than on type. Collective participation of groups of teachers from the same school, subject, or grade level is related to coherence and active learning, which in turn relates to changes in classroom practices. The research also reiterates the profound importance of subject-matter focus in designing high-quality professional development.

Many constituencies will want to know what gains have resulted from the schools' professional growth and development activities. These include school board members, parents, and students, many of whom are concerned about time lost from learning, disruption of routine, cost, and change of morale that can be results of staff development. When exemplary materials and methods that work in the classroom are presented and teachers find that students gain with these innovations, then beliefs and attitudes will change. Teacher morale improves as well when teachers move from passive experiences to application of the material and expectations of positive outcomes. Just about every member of a school staff comes into contact at one time or another with a gifted student. However, few have been prepared for facilitating the development of these individuals so that their remarkable potential is tapped and they do not become students who are held behind. Novice teachers in teacher preparation programs have learned the rhetoric for accommodating all learners, but may not have developed the understanding and skills to convert rhetoric to practice (Robinson, 1994). Teachers who have had preparation for gifted students are more likely to emphasize higher order thinking and to use concept-based approaches, in-depth study techniques, and flexible pacing than those who have not had such preparation. These strategies have been recognized as essential by external observers visiting the classroom, and by the students themselves (Hansen & Feldhusen, 1994).

All in all, professional development for secondary teachers with gifted students should help professional educators to:

- fulfill required goals and objectives of the district and the school;
- use what they have at hand as much as possible, including their own personal and collective strengths;
- know whom to call on for assistance and with whom to collaborate for achieving success;

- adopt positive attitudes toward students who can learn easily and produce remarkably; and
- put the school's best foot forward with excellent teaching skills that *hold no student behind in maximizing her or his potential.*

To fulfill goals of NCLB (2001) and also goals of No Child *Held* Behind (NCHB; Dettmer et al., 2005), school personnel must adopt the concepts of curriculum differentiation and alternative learning options, and cultivate a climate of curricular innovation and flexibility as preferred professional practice in their schools. It is a tall order, but it can be filled by school personnel who:

- formulate a defensible rationale for professional development;
- designate goals for it that dovetail with school improvement plans;
- inspire all role groups to be willing, involved participants;
- select models and methods for specific groups' preferences and needs;
- focus on topics of keen interest and immediate concern to middle school and secondary level educators;
- conduct professional development activities effectively; and
- assess the outcomes with follow-up and follow-through experiences to ensure ongoing professional growth and development and improved professional development practices.

In today's complex world, there is great need for continuous, ongoing education of educators. School personnel must participate in focused professional development that helps teach, counsel, model for, and lead wisely the brightest and most potentially productive students for the welfare of all.

REFERENCES

Allen, R. (2004). Sustaining professional development: Collaboration and technology reshape training. *March ASCD Curriculum Update, 44*(2), 1, 6–8.

Caldwell, S. D. (Ed.). (1989). *Staff development: A handbook of effective practices.* Oxford, OH: National Staff Development Council.

Callahan, C. M. (2003). *Advanced Placement and International Baccalaureate programs for talented students in American high schools: A focus on science and mathematics.* Storrs, CT: NRC/GT, University of Connecticut.

Cashion, M., & Sullenger, K. (2000). "Contact us next year": Tracing teachers' use of gifted practices. *Roeper Review, 23,* 18–21.

Clasen, D. R., & Clasen, R. E. (1989). Using telecommunications to meet the staff development and networking needs of educators of the gifted in small or rural school districts. *Roeper Review, 11,* 202–205.

Cohn, S. J. (1977). Changing teachers' attitudes and behaviors toward the gifted student. *Talents and Gifts, 19,* 23–26.

Council for Exceptional Children (2001). *CEC knowledge and skill base for all beginning special education teachers of students with gifts and talents.* Reston, VA: Author.

Cramond, B., & Martin, C. E. (1987). Inservice and preservice teachers' attitudes toward the academically brilliant. *Gifted Child Quarterly, 31*, 15–19.

Cross, T. L., Coleman, L. J., & Terhaar-Yonkers, M. (1991). The social cognition of gifted adolescents in schools: Managing the stigma of giftedness. *Journal for the Education of the Gifted, 15*, 44–55.

Deiulio, J. M. (1983). Attitudes of school counselors and psychologists toward gifted children. *Journal for the Education of the Gifted, 7*, 164–169.

Dettmer, P. (1986). Characteristics and needs of adult learners in gifted program inservice and staff development. *Gifted Child Quarterly, 30*, 131–134.

Dettmer, P., & Landrum, M. (Eds.). (1998). *Staff development: The key to effective gifted education programs*. Waco, TX: Prufrock.

Dettmer, P., Thurston, L. P., & Dyck, N. J. (2005*) Consultation, collaboration, and teamwork for students with special needs* (5th ed.). Boston: Allyn & Bacon.

Dietz, M. E. (1995). Using portfolios as a framework for professional development. *Journal of Staff Development, 16*(2), 40–43.

Dillon-Peterson, B. (1991). Reflection on the past, present, and future of staff development. *Journal of Staff Development, 12*(1), 48–51.

Dixon, F. A. (1998). Social and academic self-concepts of gifted adolescents. *Journal for the Education of the Gifted, 22*, 80–94.

Epstein, J. L., Lockard, B. L., & Dauber, S. L. (1991). Staff development for middle-school education. *Journal of Staff Development, 12*(1), 36–41.

Feldhusen, J. F., Haeger, W. W., & Pellegrino, A. S. (1989). A model training program in gifted education for administrators. *Roeper Review, 11*, 209–214.

Ferrell, B. G. (1992). Lesson plan analysis as a program evaluation tool. *Gifted Child Quarterly, 36*, 23–26.

Ford, D. Y., & Harris, J. J., III. (1999). *Multicultural gifted education*. New York: Teachers College Press.

Ford, D. Y., & Trotman, M. F. (2001). Teachers of gifted students: Suggested multicultural characteristics and competencies. *Roeper Review, 23*, 235–239.

Gallagher, J. J., Coleman, M. R., & Nelson, S. (1995). Perceptions of educational reform by educators representing middle schools, cooperative learning, and gifted education. *Gifted Child Quarterly, 39*, 66–76.

Garet, M. S., Porter, A. C., Desimone, L., Birman, B. F., & Yoon, K. S. (2001). What makes professional development effective? Results from a national sample of teachers. *American Educational Research Journal, 38*, 915–945.

Garmston, R. J. (1993). The persuasive art of presenting: Podium humor. *Journal of Staff Development, 14*(4), 68–69.

Garmston, R., & Wellman, B. M. (1992). *How to make presentations that teach and transform*. Alexandria, VA: Association for Supervision and Curriculum Development.

Guskey, T. (1985), Staff development and teacher change. *Educational Leadership, 42*(7), 57–60.

Hall, G. E., & Hord, S. M. (1987). *Change in schools: Facilitating the process*. Albany, NY: SUNY Press.

Hansen, J. B., & Feldhusen, J. F. (1994). Comparison of trained and untrained teachers of gifted students. *Gifted Child Quarterly, 38*, 115–121.

Hord, S. M. (1982). The concerns of teachers of gifted youth: Using concerns to improve staff support. *Roeper Review, 5*, 32–34.

Howard, G. R. (1999). *We can't teach what we don't know: White teachers, multiracial schools*. Columbia, NY: Teachers College Press.

Individuals With Disabilities Education Act, 20 U.S.C. §1401 et seq. (1990).

Joyce, B. R., & Showers, B. (1988*). Student achievement through staff development.* New York: Longman.

Karnes, F. A., & Lewis, J. D. (1996). Staff development through videotapes in gifted education. *Roeper Review, 19,* 106–110.

Kaufmann, F. A., & Sexton, D. (1983). Some implications for home-school linkages. *Roeper Review, 6,* 49–51.

Kelleher, J. (2003). A model for assessment-driven professional development. *Phi Delta Kappan, 84,* 751–756.

Killian, J. E., & Byrd, D. M. (1988). A cooperative staff development model that taps the strengths of rural schools. *Journal of Staff Development, 9*(4), 34–39.

King, C. E. (1988). Some basic understandings about rural education and staff development. *Journal of Staff Development, 9*(4), 8–11.

Kirschenbaum, R. J., Armstrong, D. C., & Landrum, M. S. (1999). Resource consultation model in gifted education to support talent development in today's inclusive schools. *Gifted Child Quarterly, 43,* 39–47.

Krupp, J. (1987). Mentoring: A means by which teachers become staff developers. *Journal of Staff Development, 8*(1), 12–15.

Landrum, M. S. (2001). An evaluation of the catalyst program: Consultation and collaboration in gifted education. *Gifted Child Quarterly, 45,* 139–151.

Landrum, M., & Shaklee, B. (Eds.). (1998). *Pre-K–grade 12 gifted program standards.* Washington, DC: National Association for Gifted Children.

McBride, R. E., Reed, J. L., & Dollar, J. E. (1994). Teacher attitudes toward staff development: A symbolic relationship at best. *Journal of Staff Development, 15*(2), 36–41.

Mönks, F. J., & Mason, E. J. (2000). Developmental psychology and giftedness: Theories and research. In K. A. Heller, F. J. Mönks, R. J. Sternberg, & R. F. Subotnik (Eds.), *International handbook of giftedness and talent* (2nd ed., pp. 141–155). Oxford: Pergamon.

National Association for Gifted Children. (1995). *Standards for graduate programs in gifted education.* Washington, DC: Author.

National Research Council. (2002). *Learning and understanding: Improving advanced study of mathematics and science in U.S. high schools.* Washington, DC: National Academy Press.

No Child Left Behind Act, 20 U.S.C. §6301 (2001).

Nowak, S. J. (1994). New roles and challenges for staff development. *Journal of Staff Development, 15*(3), 10–13.

Payne, R. K. (1998). *A framework for understanding poverty.* Highlands, TX: RFT Publications.

Payne, R. K., & Krabill, D. L. (2002). *Hidden rules of class at work.* Highlands, TX: Aha! Process.

Reis, S. M., & Westberg, K. L. (1994). The impact of staff development on teachers' ability to modify curriculum for gifted and talented students. *Gifted Child Quarterly, 38,* 127–135.

Renzulli, J. S., & Reis, S. M. (1985). *The Schoolwide Enrichment Model: A comprehensive plan for educational excellence.* Mansfield Center, CT: Creative Learning Press.

Robinson, A. (1994). Teachers, talent development, and talented students. *Gifted Child Quarterly, 38,* 99–102.

Schmale, R. L. (1994). Promoting teacher reflection through guided book reviews. *Journal of Staff Development, 15*(1), 30–32.

Sherin, M. G. (2000). Viewing teaching on videotape. *Educational Leadership, 57*(8), 36–38.

Solano, C. H. (1977). Teacher and pupil stereotypes of gifted boys and girls. *Talents and Gifts, 19,* 4–8.

Sparks, D., & Hirsch, S. (1997*). A new vision for staff development.* Alexandria, VA: Association for Supervision and Curriculum Development.

Sparks, D., & Loucks-Horsley, S. (1989). *Five models of staff development for teachers.* Oxford, OH: National Staff Development Council.

Sparks, D., & Vaughn, S. (1994). What every school board member should know about staff development. *Journal of Staff Development, 15*(2), 20–22.

Sullivan, M. A. (1987). Staff development through professional reading and discussion. *Journal of Staff Development, 8*(1), 39–41.

Tanner, B., Canady, R. L., & Rettig, M. D. (1995). Scheduling time to maximize staff development opportunities, *Journal of Staff Development, 16*(4), 14–19.

Tomlinson, C. A. (1992). Gifted education and the middle school movement: Two voices on teaching the academically talented. *Journal for the Education of the Gifted, 15,* 206–238.

Welch, K. D. (1990). The job-alike workshop: Staff development for classified personnel. *Educational Leadership, 47*(8), 79–80.

Wineburg, S., & Grossman, P. (1998). Creating a community of learners among high school teachers. *Phi Delta Kappan, 79,* 350–353.

Wolf, J. S. (1987). Workshops for parents of the gifted. *Roeper Review, 9,* 243–246.

Zmuda, A., Kuklis, R., & Kline, E. (2004*). Transforming schools: Creating a culture of continuous improvement*. Alexandria, VA: Association for Supervision and Curriculum Development.

SUPERINTENDENTS, PRINCIPALS, AND COUNSELORS

CHAPTER 25

Facilitating Secondary Gifted Education

by Jean Sunde Peterson

T he leadership team of a secondary-level school usually includes principals and school counselors. These individuals are generalists, concerned with more than just one or a few grade levels or academic domains. Their training differs considerably, given their contrasting roles, but both are concerned with more than academic matters, and both pay attention to school culture and climate. Principals and counselors typically also deal holistically with students, concerned about student attitudes, family environment, student safety and wellness, and collective school morale. Both spend considerable time working with parents and building bridges to the surrounding community in the interest of ensuring school success and support for students. Superintendents monitor all of these aspects of school leadership, paying attention to the health and performance of the entire district or corporation program. All have their eyes open and "their ear to the ground," listening to the system as it functions. However, each listens at different frequencies and uses a different lens when monitoring the context.

As generalists, responsible for establishing district and school policies and concerned with how programs and policies affect students and families, administrators and counselors potentially have great impact on the school experience of gifted adolescents. Therefore, preparatory programs in educational administration and school counseling should discuss the concept of giftedness and include general perspectives about appropriate curriculum for gifted students; their cognitive, social, and emotional needs; and strategies for meeting these needs. Graduate students in both areas should also be made aware of state and federal laws related to gifted education, including the important notion that pertinent legislative policy differs from state to state (Assouline, 1997). Indeed, policies regarding gifted education program mandates for schools and requirements for certification, endorsement, or licensure for teachers vary widely. Later, as administrators and counselors in practice, they can pursue continuing-education opportunities to add knowledge about giftedness and about appropriate services for gifted students.

Gifted adolescents do indeed have "special needs" and can be conceptualized as requiring accommodations in order to have an "appropriate education" in the "least restrictive environment," phrases usually associated with special education mandates in the United States (e.g., Individuals with Disabilities Education Act, 1990). As one criterion of qualifying for special programs for gifted students, many school districts require scores on a standardized test that are two standard deviations above the mean (Jackson & Klein, 1997). It is important that administrators- and counselors-in-training recognize that students in the top 2–3% of the school population are as different from those with average ability as are students who qualify for special education programs on the basis of limited mental ability. Both potentially have difficulty relating to, and communicating with, most age peers across a continuum of ability and are poorly served by an undifferentiated classroom curriculum. Furthermore, just as at the opposite end of a normal population distribution, the top tail of the bell curve can extend for a great distance. Profound giftedness (Gross, 2002) means extreme differentness—more than is inherent in being "just" two standard deviations from the mean, where identification for programs often begins. Such an extreme means extreme needs.

One can argue that gifted students are handicapped in the school environment. Earlier chapters have indicated that they may also be uniquely at risk. However, because administrators and counselors may not recognize these possibilities in the exceptional students at the upper end of the scale, professional preparation programs need to include formal attention to giftedness. Superintendents, though usually not operating in specific schools, need this awareness, as well.

SUPERINTENDENTS

Superintendents establish direction for education locally, and, in that important role, they have the power to "make or break" programs that focus on meeting the needs of gifted students. They and the school board have the power to effect change, certainly through managing financial allocations and exerting influence on which programs are supported and nurtured and stay viable when budget cuts are necessary. Their vision and priorities can drive an entire school system—toward an emphasis on science and math, on the arts, on athletics, or on service learning, for example. In the current era of school accountability and school transformation, they are certainly interested in students' academic success. They recognize that a good academic reputation has a ripple effect related to community support, potential demographic shifts, "good marks" in public listings of school quality, and competitive status among peer schools, not to mention compliance with the federal No Child Left Behind legislation (NCLB; 2001).

Preparatory programs for administrators can help future superintendents recognize that providing an environment where *all* gifted adolescents can thrive, not just those who have supportive, educated, economically secure parents, enriches the lives of those students and the total school environment, as well. In terms of school-performance measures, superintendents are likely to realize higher standardized test scores if they encourage support for both mainstream and nonmainstream gifted students. The latter, for a variety of complex reasons, may not be able to achieve school success otherwise, given their particular circumstances at that time in their lives.

Up to half of all students with high abilities may not be identified for gifted programs (Birely & Genschaft, 1991). Because of that possibility, superintendents should encourage, and potentially be involved in, discussion about program philosophy and procedures—so that multiple criteria for selection are more than just cosmetic, and so that the district definition of *giftedness* is appropriately inclusive. Superintendents who agree with the definition and ensure that programs fit the definition (e.g., programs with inclusive definitions embracing gifted students who face extreme challenges in their home contexts) are a great asset to schools, special programs, and gifted students.

Some, but not all, of the highly able individuals who are missed may be in groups already targeted for scrutiny through NCLB. Wise superintendents, therefore, encourage principals and counselors to target gifted underachievers for special assistance. Attention to this group may not only offer crucial individual assistance, but also positively affect scores on measures of school performance. These well-informed superintendents work with gifted-program personnel to encourage identification procedures that find students who do not fit common stereotypes of "gifted" individuals and, to accommodate those students, support more than just one-size-fits-all special programs.

By insisting on creative, stimulating, differentiated instruction in the classroom and/or interesting pull-out programming, and by perhaps bringing in experts to give guidance toward those ends, superintendents can ensure that all bright students thrive. Gifted students need that kind of support, and schools benefit when programs develop talent and inspire excellence. Communities and the nation also benefit when the abilities of gifted students are developed and channeled into positive directions. Superintendents might follow the lead of peers who have mandated that new hires take classes in gifted education so that they have some understanding of complex needs of gifted students and of interventions that can potentially meet those needs. Actually, many superintendents believe that courses required for gifted endorsement or licensure are beneficial for all teachers because they encourage new perspectives and strategies.

Gifted education programs are often understaffed, and that is the reality of many programs at the secondary level. Many high schools offer only honors and college-level Advanced Placement (AP) courses as the gifted program, incorrectly assuming that such courses meet the educational needs of all highly able students. A designated teacher may simply organize the AP exams and serve as the AP liaison for the school. In general, job descriptions of gifted education teachers may not allow adequate attention to programming and other responsive services for gifted students, such as extracurricular activities, counseling, and extra-school opportunities (Feldhusen, Hoover, & Sayler, 1990). They may be asked to serve large numbers of gifted adolescents, with highly idiosyncratic academic and personal needs, while additionally teaching in the regular classroom.

Superintendents-in-training should be made aware that gifted adolescents, even those who are stellar performers, may in fact have pressing social and emotional concerns, including high-stress lives that put them at risk for poor educational and personal outcomes. Standardized, one-dimensional, more-and-faster programs may appeal to many with high ability, certainly those for whom school is a good fit. However, those who support the idea of varying kinds of intelligences (Gardner, 1983) and learning styles (Gregorc, 1985; Shearer, 1999) argue for differentiation within programs, as well as in the classroom. By making funding available to employ an adequate number of gifted education staff, superintendents ensure that those faculty have time to collaborate with classroom teachers in the interest of differentiating instruction, to offer creative and appropriately individualized gifted education programming outside of the classroom, and to attend to students' social and emotional development, as well.

In their future positions, superintendents-in-training will have the power to provide budget support for in-service programs that raise awareness of the needs of gifted adolescents—and attend these programs themselves. The more they learn about this special population, the more they are likely to see that, even when programming is not mandated, gifted students need an education appropriate to their ability. In addition to providing support for in-service programs focused on giftedness, offering financial support for pertinent conference attendance and curriculum development is crucial to maintaining program viability, particularly since education for the gifted cannot rely on available textbooks for guidance in meeting complex academic needs. In addition, educators need to stay abreast of pertinent developments in fields such as neurological, clinical, social, and educational psychology, representatives of which often present sessions and workshops at conventions. Gifted education coordinators and teachers need professional development specific to their positions, of course, but classroom teachers can also benefit from attending conferences focused on gifted education, such as the annual meetings of the National Association for Gifted Children (NAGC), state affiliates, and the Council for Exceptional Children's (CEC) division focusing on gifted students, The Association for the Gifted (TAG).

PRINCIPALS

Ultimately, a secondary-level head principal is responsible for keeping the school on a secure foundation and on course. As members of the leadership team, assistant principals might assume leadership for specific areas of the school, such as curricula, student behavior, or attendance, but also exert general leadership in tandem with the head principal. In the following discussion, *principal* refers to the person at the helm, regardless of the number of principals who share leadership.

Coursework in preparatory programs for school administrators includes considerable attention to school leadership. Whether responding to school crises or charting a course for curricular or policy changes, principals are expected to lead. Administrative leadership means paying attention to the health and safety of students, including those with special needs; implementing programs to foster learning; establishing measures to determine outcomes; ensuring up-to-date and effective curricula; supporting and nurturing teachers and other school personnel; providing opportunities for professional development; establishing and maintaining special programs; and monitoring the health and use of the physical structure of the school. A principal's wisdom and actions related especially to health and safety, accountability, curricula, personnel, special programs, and physical structures have potential impact on the school experiences of gifted students.

Understanding a Special Population With Special Needs

Preparatory programs and continuing education for principals can help to ensure that needs of gifted students are met by providing pertinent information about giftedness and by offering guidelines for administrative support for programs for gifted students. Fundamentally, administrators-in-training should learn that gifted adolescents may have invisible risk factors, fueling the extremes of underachievement, hyperachievement, or desperation. Gifted students "are generally quite socially adept, popular with their peers, and emotionally stable," (Gallagher, 1997, p. 16), but vary widely in regard to any personal characteristic. In fact, although high ability has been associated with resilience in the literature (Higgins, 1994), various characteristics related to giftedness may also contribute to difficulties, no less for adolescents than for younger children.

Just as with superintendents, when principals agree with, and are invested in, a district definition of *giftedness* and general program philosophy, they serve as crucial support for students and program alike. They can initiate staff-development programs and help faculty build a knowledge base about giftedness and concerns of gifted students. Principals potentially also raise their own awareness through these programs, which may address a wide range of topics, including not only issues related to academic curricula, but also areas related to social and emotional development. In that regard, much of the following discussion in this section may appear to be related more to school counselors than to principals. However, it is important that principals be aware of counseling-related issues, since many of these are related to student safety and well-being, school climate, and school mission.

Related to affective issues, for instance, exceptional cognitive ability, global or domain-specific (Tannenbaum, 1997), may contribute to a gifted adolescent's feelings of discomfort and psychological pain (cf. Piechowski, 1997) in school, and even classrooms may feel unsafe to them. Sensitivity and overexcitability, the latter an intense response to experiences (Piechowski), may exacerbate problems with normal and expected developmental transitions, such as movement into puberty, choosing a college, or leaving home. These characteristics may also be problematic in response to life events, such as the death of someone close, parental separation and divorce, blending families, relocation, parental unemployment, and terminal illness in the family. Intensity and drive (Lovecky, 1992) may affect relationships. Divergent (in contrast to convergent) thinking (Guilford, 1987) may not fit with teacher personality or approach. Asynchrony, with differing levels of social, emotional, cognitive, and physical development (Silverman, 2002), may contribute to a poor social fit with peers. Gifted adolescents may overly control or deny emotions, be preoccupied with avoiding error, feel stress from high expectations of self and others (Peterson, 1998), and feel no permission to differentiate from parents (Peterson, 1999b). Their idealism, strong sense of justice, advanced moral development, and sensitivity to peers may contribute to distress in the competitive school environment (Piechowski). Particularly during middle school, some may reject achievement in favor of social acceptance, particularly females (Swiatek & Dorr, 1998).

Raising *all* school administrators' awareness of cognitive and affective concerns may result in crucial support for gifted adolescents. When well-prepared administrators communicate important information to school personnel and support pertinent professional development related to giftedness in the context of adolescent development, they potentially affect the well being of gifted students. Appropriately differentiated curricula for intellectually precocious students is essential; however, monitoring the out-of-classroom behaviors of gifted and other students is likewise important. Administrators who understand the vulnerabilities of gifted individuals may be more vigilant regarding student behaviors and quicker to respond to reports of harassment, for instance.

Paying Attention to Health and Safety

School administrators are responsible for creating and maintaining a school climate conducive to learning. That climate reflects each school's unique culture, including attitudes of all school personnel. A healthy school climate includes both physical and psychological safety. Bullying, broadly defined, potentially impinges on both (Bosworth, Espelage, & Simon, 1999). Harassment in general, but certainly when it is related to sexual orientation, can be devastating to those who are targeted (Huegel, 2003). Administrators-in-training need to be aware of the prevalence and effects of bullying for gifted students and assume responsibility for critical and appropriate systemic school climate change. The following discussion about bullying, harassment, and attitudes of administrators as related to gifted students relates to the work of all secondary-level principals, regardless of school level, given the trends that are presented. The findings pertinent to middle-school students make the discussion of bullying particularly important for administrators at that level, but the discussion of harassment related to sexual orientation relates to all secondary-level administrators.

Bullying

A retrospective national study of gifted eighth graders ($n = 432$) looked at bullying among gifted children in grades K–8 (Peterson & Ray, in press-b) and provides important information for school administrators and school counselors at both middle and high school levels. The study found that 67% of gifted eighth graders (73% of males) had been bullied in one of 13 listed ways sometime during their K–8 school years. In grade 6, the peak year, 46% of gifted eighth graders (54% of males) had been bullied, and 11% (14% of males) had been bullied repeatedly. In grade 8, 42% were still being bullied. Name-calling was the most frequent kind of bullying reported by victims (35% in grade 6), and physical assaults were not uncommon (13% pushed and shoved and 12% beaten up in grade 6). However, the kind of bullying with the most significant relationship with psychological effect was teasing about appearance. Noteworthy is the fact that most students did not tell adults about being bullied.

In the qualitative part of that study (Peterson & Ray, in press-a), 57 gifted victims of bullying articulately explained their inner world. An important and unsettling theme that emerged in interviews was that victims tended to assume responsibility for stopping the bullying—externalizing the cause (e.g., attention-seeking bullies; not enough supervision of hallways or recess; a substitute teacher with poor classroom management), but internalizing the responsibility to the extent that they did not tell teachers (e.g., "It's *my* problem"). In fact, "no one" ranked fourth among those told about the bullying, and even school counselors ranked fifth. Additional major themes were that a single incident of verbal abuse could have intense and prolonged effects, that victims became preoccupied with avoiding "mistakes" in order to avoid being bullied, and that being known helped to prevent bullying.

A finding about perpetrators was that 28% of gifted eighth graders had been a bully sometime during their school years, and 16% bullied others in grade 8, the peak year. The percentage had steadily increased since kindergarten. Most of these bullied verbally. The study went no farther than grade 8, and therefore the researchers could not assess the extent to which bullying continues during high school. However, the steady escalation suggests that it does continue, perhaps in somewhat altered forms; in addition, gifted bullies used more kinds of bullying as they aged. The study also could not determine whether the gifted bullies had been bullied, although that was true of a few interviewees. In a study of the general population, Haynie et al. (2001) found that more than half of bullies reported being victims, as well, and, therefore, it might be assumed that this phenomenon is also true for gifted students.

With school shootings in mind, the researchers asked participants if they had violent thoughts and found increasing percentages, to 29% (37% of males) in grade 8 who stated they had had violent thoughts. Several interviewees mentioned that teachers and administrators did nothing about bullying, even when it was reported. Bullying can be normalized and excused, of course, in schools and community (Will & Neufeld, 2002), and administrators may not understand the potential impact of bullying on students in general and on those who are gifted in particular—with residue affecting relationships and performance of some victims later in high school. Regarding effects, 13% were bothered "a lot" by bullying in grade 5, the peak year for that measure, after which the percentage declined slowly through grade 8.

Administrators-in-training should consider implementing anti-bullying programs (e.g., Newman-Carlson & Horne, 2004; Olweus, 2003) in their schools, particularly at the middle-school level, but also in high schools, establishing clear policies against it, ensuring more adult presence in nonclassroom areas, and recognizing that females may bully in ways that are subtle, but devastating. Principals can also meet with parents of bullies and work to change a culture that excuses and normalizes bullying and blames the victim. Principals should also be aware of particular vulnerabilities in gifted children, including the idea that sensitivity and intensity may contribute to extreme responses to bullying. Several interviewees in Peterson and Ray's (in press-a) study noted that being victimized contributed to depression, poor school attendance, and long, painfully uncomfortable school years.

Many of the interviewed students in the study believed they were bullied because they were different, not because they were gifted. Height, weight, and interests may make a gifted adolescent different, of course, but some may also be targeted because they pursue interests and behave in ways that do not fit cultural stereotypes of male and female (Hébert, 2002). It is also possible that victims who were not accustomed to social banter (cf. Will & Neufeld, 2002) and aggressivity were perceived as different and therefore targeted. The bullying literature suggests that other aspects also contribute to vulnerability, some of it reflecting the literature related to sensitivity in gifted children (e.g., Piechowski, 1997). Olweus (1973) distinguished between passive and provocative victims, with the former being lonely, not aggressive, not teasing others, and physically weaker than same-age peers. Parent interviews suggested that male victims were sensitive at a young age and generally had close contact and positive relations with their parents. Teachers identified them as overprotected by parents. Hoover (2003) noted that a sad, anxious response to the school milieu contributes to victimization.

Peterson and Ray's (in press-a, in press-b) study was not comparative, and it is difficult to know if similar percentages would be found in the general population. Research on bullying in the United States is a relatively recent phenomenon (e.g., Berthold & Hoover, 2000; Hunter & Boyle, 2002; Juvonen, Graham, & Schuster, 2003), and many surveys ask only if respondents have been bullied, without defining bullying, thereby probably underestimating prevalence. In this study, even after completing a survey listing various types of bullying, students who volunteered to be interviewed initially denied that they had been bullied or hesitated to identify nonphysical harassment as bullying (e.g., "Last year the eighth graders picked on seventh graders I knew, throwing in trash cans, calling names, pushing—[but] nothing like hitting"). Principals who want to improve school climate and student safety need to counter assumptions that verbal and other harassment is not a serious concern. Given the finding that gifted victims typically did not ask for help, principals also need to be aware that bullying may be occurring under the radar, and that bullied gifted adolescents may be highly distressed.

Harassment Related to Homosexuality

Teasing about sexual orientation was not listed in the survey in the study just discussed, but that kind of name-calling increased dramatically during grades seven and eight, according to responses to an open-ended question. "Gay" is a common negative epithet in school hallways (Fontaine & Hammond, 1996; Huegel, 2003), and any student may be called "gay." However, gay, lesbian, bisexual, transgendered, or questioning (GLBTQ) adolescents are particularly vulnerable, and gifted adolescents with nonstereotypical gender behaviors and interests may also be targeted. Tolan (1997) noted that they may even foreclose prematurely regarding sexual identity because of their complex understanding of sexuality. Cohn (2002) noted that adolescents who are both gifted and gay may feel particularly marginalized, since they are not likely to feel safe seeking others like themselves, and it is also unlikely that they will find each other.

A retrospective qualitative study of 18 gifted male and female homosexual college-age individuals (Peterson & Rischar, 2000) found that 50% had wondered seriously about their sexual orientation before leaving elementary school and had been suicidal at some time during their school years. Many had felt in danger at school, and some responded to their awareness with becoming "ultra-hetero," depressed, anti-gay, or extremely involved in extracurricular activities and extreme academic achievement. Most (94%) were convinced of their sexual orientation by grade 10, but 72% did not reveal their sexual orientation to anyone until after leaving high school (one came out during junior high and four during high school), with great distress and vulnerability in the intervening years, during which 83% experienced depression. Only 33% of those who experienced depression told their parents about their distress and none told teachers.

Study participants gave several suggestions to educators, most of them particularly relevant in high schools. Teachers can let GLBTQ students know they are OK and not alone; can mention the sexual orientation of gay literary figures; can realize that there are probably gay students in every class they teach; can be alert to the possibility that sexual orientation might be connected to dropping out, being involved with substance abuse, or adolescent suicide; can treat GLBTQ students with compassion; can maintain safe, respectful classrooms; can stop harassment related to sexual orientation in classrooms and hallways; and can recognize that being gay and gifted includes two dimensions of differentness. Teachers might even be concerned—or at least inquire—about intense extracurricular involvement. A theme in the study was that hyper-involvement in structured activities served as both compensation and self-protection. One gay student wished retrospectively that someone had been concerned about his frenetic pace, but noted that his successes probably precluded that. Harbeck (1994) noted that academic or athletic overachievement, perfectionism, or overinvolvement might be socially acceptable adaptations to uncertainty about sexual orientation.

Secondary-level principals can keep these concerns and suggestions in mind as they help teachers make school a safer place for GLBTQ adolescents. These administrators are in a position to offer other support as well with risk of criticism, of course. They can specifically communicate that counselors' offices are safe for GLBTQ youth and establish schoolwide zero tolerance for harassment, specifically delineating words related to sexual orientation. They can encourage the school counselor to make psychoeducational literature available (e.g., Huegel, 2003) and visible to students and provide funding to make that possible. They might even support bringing in a credible speaker to talk objectively and rationally about homosexuality in discussion groups for gifted students or for the school as a whole.

Administrator Attitudes

All educators, including principals, should examine their attitudes about giftedness and gifted students. Based on her experience in K–12 schools, the author proposes the following questions for consideration:

1. What are administrators' feelings and perspectives related to high achievement, underachievement, school "success" and "failure," "at-risk gifted," arrogance, shyness, and perfectionism?
2. Do secondary-level principals feel a need to compete with gifted adolescents' impressive intellect or talent?
3. Do they use humor in a competitive, "one-up," or even sarcastic mode?
4. Do they view beautiful, handsome, successful students as not needing support for social, emotional, cognitive, or career development?
5. Do they believe that highly able students need *less* support than others?
6. Do they see honors courses and gifted programs as inappropriate for highly able nonmainstream adolescents, such as those from nondominant cultures, low-socioeconomic status, or difficult family environments?
7. Do they interact uncomfortably with musical, artistic, and theater-oriented males and athletic, dominant, mechanically oriented females?

Attitudes of school personnel can have great impact on gifted adolescents' comfort level, sense of personal support, upward social mobility, and ability to thrive academically, socially, and emotionally at school.

Most gifted adolescents do quite well in school and elsewhere (Gallagher, 1997). The research literature suggests that gifted individuals have no more and no less incidence of mental health disorders than the rest of the population (Neihart, 2002). However, administrators-in-training should consider that gifted adolescents are not exempt from unsettling life events and trauma. In addition, if 80% of school-age individuals with mental illness are not identified and receiving treatment (National

Institute of Mental Health Policy Research Institute, 2004), serious mental-health issues of gifted adolescents may also be undetected. They may struggle with depression and suicidal ideation, eating disorders, or an obsessive-compulsive personality or disorder, not to mention existential angst, emotional upheaval related to earlier trauma, abusive relationships, or severe anxiety about the present and future. In fact, some clinical disorders, such as anorexia nervosa and obsessive-compulsive disorder, often appear first in high school (American Psychiatric Association, 1994).

The competitive school environment may overwhelm some gifted students. A particular danger lies in the fact that because of others' preoccupation with their abilities, troubled gifted teens may not reveal their concerns, worried that they may lose their identity and disappoint adults who are invested in them. A façade of composure may remain firmly intact, regardless of home or school circumstances, and may mask life-threatening despair. In addition, perfectionism can be an issue (Dixon, Lapsley, & Hanchon, 2004; Greenspon, 2000; Schuler, 2001). In the extreme, it may rob gifted adolescents of the ability to begin, end, or *enjoy* school projects. Especially in the dominant culture (Peterson, 1999a), highly able students may feel valued only for performance and achievement—for doing, not for being. They may be extremely self-critical or critical of others and may be preoccupied with avoiding mistakes. They may be averse to social and academic risk-taking because they cannot be certain of their performance (Dweck, 1992).

Principals who are aware of these possibilities can be sensitive to gifted students and support programming that attends to both affective and academic concerns. Intense, heavy curricula may not be appropriate for all gifted adolescents. Developmental or family distress, low English proficiency, heavy responsibilities at home, or after-school employment that provides crucial family support may preclude being able to devote time and energy to advanced courses. Principals can advocate for a complex, multifaceted program that fits their particular school context and community, even in high schools. Effective programs are not necessarily costly, since differentiated instruction usually happens in existing classrooms, and community volunteers may be available to teach various program components. However, it is important to have adequate staffing in order to ensure that consultation with teachers is possible and that there is adequate time to manage the logistical challenges of a multifaceted secondary-level program. Complex programs, directed with energy, especially those which open some components to the entire student body, can help to create a school culture characterized by learning, challenge, and respect for intellect (cf. Peterson, 2003).

One Strategy: Discussion Groups

With student health and safety in mind, principals can advocate for program components related to social and emotional support, which ultimately affects mental health and motivation for learning. One such offering, high school discussion groups focused on affective, not academic, development, has been described in the literature (Peterson, 1990, 1995, 2003). Those groups involve mutual, reciprocal learning, in contrast to teacher-directed classrooms, and are appropriate for all students. In fact, many middle schools use them in teacher-adviser programs (Gonzales & Myrick, 2000), as well. Gifted adolescents appreciate being grouped homogeneously by ability and trust that gifted peers can understand them (Peterson, 1990). Gifted students who are shy can gain a great deal by having social access to their peers and support for social and emotional development—as much at the high school level as earlier in the school years.

In addition, groups humanize members for themselves and other members. However, the presence of the groups may also humanize the participants to the rest of the student body and to teachers, especially if the groups are perceived as meeting critical needs. Because school personnel may not think of gifted adolescents as having special needs, it is important for administrators to consider and communicate to staff that *all* gifted children, including those who are from high-functioning families and who are excelling in school (or from not-so-well functioning families who are excelling in school), have social and emotional concerns related to life circumstances and "normal development." Because of their impressive talents, teachers, coaches, and parents may all forget that gifted adolescents need attention to social and emotional development—until one of them is diagnosed with a psychiatric disorder, does not finish the first year of college, or commits suicide.

Restricting the size of groups to five or six in grade six and to eight or nine in late high school, with all members from the same grade level, helps meet individual needs. Groups are also most effective and defensible to skeptics when there is a curriculum and when meetings are structured. Curriculum may be in the form of developmentally appropriate discussion topics (Peterson, 1993; 1995). The structure may include a paper-and-pencil activity for 5 minutes at the outset and then open-ended questions to elicit discussion. Training facilitators in basic listening and responding skills helps them to maintain structure, ensure that all students are heard at a level comfortable for them, and avoid problematic group behaviors.

Developmental topics that are appropriate across all adolescent years can include, for example, coping with stress, establishing an identity, finding career direction, dealing with peer relationships, assessing learning styles, articulating mood range, dealing effectively with authority, and assessing family roles (cf. Peterson, 1993, 1995). Because gifted adolescents face the same developmental challenges as the rest of the adolescent population, these topics are as appropriate for them as for anyone else.

Support for Personnel and Programs

Special programs help meet the special needs of gifted students, not just affectively, but cognitively as well. Administrators hold the key to whether such programs are possible. Future principals can ensure a viable, inspiring program by offering oral support for it at faculty meetings, affirming and quietly noting creative efforts of gifted education teachers and coordinators, and even making sure that gifted education has physical space. Good programs require materials, adequate storage, a telephone, ready access to technology, and administrative time, including time to pursue external funding.

A program for gifted high school students (Peterson, 1993) illustrates the importance of administrative support in establishing and maintaining a largely nonclassroom secondary-level curriculum for gifted students. One program option focused on social and emotional development, certainly associated with school counseling, but discussed in this section because that component was facilitated by the gifted education teacher, with crucial support from the principal. The structure reflects Feldhusen's (2003) views that high-school-level programs for gifted students may not resemble programs at other levels and can include special opportunities in and outside of school. The author once coordinated this complex program with several options available concurrently. Perhaps unusual was a weekly after-school lecture series, involving local college professors, artists, physicians, therapists, community scientists, creative business leaders, and community activists. Classroom teachers gave extra credit to their students for attending lectures on topics pertinent to their courses and sometimes attended themselves. The lectures were open to all students and helped to counter perceptions of program elitism. Some lectures and panels were taped by the school's television studio and shown on the local education channel. The topics were of interest to adults, as well. The presenters donated their time.

In addition, a college professor annually taught a noon-hour philosophy class at the school for 9 weeks. Community volunteers directed mime and dance troupes and taught music appreciation, Chinese, and Arabic. A group of underachievers met for breakfast before school to write and share poetry. One-day career-shadowing was available, and students learned about the broad, hard-to-explain field of engineering by taking field trips to see civil, mechanical, chemical, electrical, and architectural engineers at work. Several Future Problem Solving (FPS) teams met throughout the year to prepare for tournaments. Underachievers found successful community mentors who were once underachievers themselves. Some students took courses at the local college. Small groups in heterogeneous math and science classrooms worked quietly and independently a few days a week outside of the classroom in library conference rooms. An art teacher worked collaboratively with the program to support gifted artists. Several AP courses were available. Panels of graduates, home from college at Thanksgiving, described social, emotional, and academic adjustments. Discussion groups, like those mentioned earlier, involved the most students—115 per week (of approximately 140 identified students). The program earnestly pursued underachievers by examining school files and asking teachers to refer students for further assessment. Discussion groups were comprised of approximately 30% underachievers, and they and the achievers found commonalities in discussion focusing on development. In fact, underachievers were often more able than achievers to articulate the experience of development.

Administrators supported the program by making a formal conference room available over the double lunch hours every day for the discussion groups, funding travel related to academic competitions, providing a glassed bulletin board in the halls to display student poetry, being responsive to program needs related to logistics, and supporting the purchase of a few materials. In general, the program was inexpensive beyond the teacher's salary. In terms of labor, the program was intense and fragmented during each school day, continuing for one hour or more after school 4 days per week. In addition, FPS competitions required time and energy outside of school. However, the intensity was balanced by little homework, per se.

After 5 years, feedback from parents, teachers, several administrators, current students, and graduates suggested that the program had affected the school climate positively. Teachers were aware of, and could affirm, the students who were involved, including extreme underachievers, because a program newsletter listed students involved in each program component. Clever fliers for the open lectures were expected weekly on hallway walls, and the well-attended lectures became known as substantive and thought-provoking. The mime and dance troupes gave performances, and the breakfast group's poetry and the gifted artists' work were displayed. Many of the students who were involved defied the stereotypes of "gifted kids." According to informal teacher comments, beginning in the second year, the presence of the discussion groups helped them to see that gifted students could have concerns related to development—as much as anyone else did. In addition, because the groups "leveled the field" with their attention to social and emotional concerns, arrogance disappeared. Since the focus of the groups was on affective concerns, no one bragged about grade point average or college-entrance test scores. Arrogance was usually discussed once, per group, and was concluded to be ineffective for building social networks and to reflect a lack of interpersonal intelligence (cf. Gardner, 1983). Preoccupation with performance was left at the door when the students gathered in the noncompetitive, nonevaluative atmosphere of the groups.

It should be noted that the head principal was careful not to call attention to this program publicly, and the program, in fact, was relatively low-key. The newsletter came out only quarterly. Sensitivity to perceptions is important for the viability of any program, especially those involving highly able students. In fact, principals can offer crucial guidance to gifted education teachers regarding public relations for such programs.

In summary, principals who are aware of needs and vulnerabilities of gifted adolescents realize that paying attention to their safety and well being is important. Proactive and responsive support helps ensure that these individuals can learn comfortably and be challenged appropriately. Enlightened principals are not only alert to potential for bullying and harassment, but also monitor their own attitudes about giftedness. They encourage and support programming that gives attention to social and emotional development, as well as to academic concerns.

SCHOOL COUNSELORS

Like those who work with administrators, university educators who prepare school counselors ultimately have an indirect impact on the school life of gifted adolescents. Much of the information just presented about administrators can help to raise the awareness of school counselors, as well. School counselors are expected to attend to student concerns, behaviors, and attitudes that interfere with learning. Gifted adolescents deserve such attention also, of course. In addition to assisting

with planning for the future, counselors can play an important role by simply helping gifted students feel comfortable in the present—without having to be preoccupied with the future. Burdened by heavy expectations, some students might even
need to be encouraged to play (cf. Elkind, 1981)—and relax.

Counselor Attitudes

Like principals, counselors need to self-assess their attitudes and issues related
to giftedness and their comfort level when interacting with a wide range of gifted
students. No less than when they work with other students, nonjudgment is appropriate when working with gifted adolescents, as is openness to learning about their
complex world. Similarly, counselors should resist rushing in to fix a problematic
situation instead of guiding students to solve their own problems. As with any issue,
counselors' feelings about their own school experiences and their own gifts may
tempt them not to behave according to their training.

They should certainly be aware of the ubiquitousness of bullying, as mentioned
earlier, and how it is manifested among gifted students. They also need to be alert
to issues related to sexual orientation—not just harassment, but also truancy, hyperachievement, depression, and suicidal ideation or attempts, which may reflect the
distress of sexual orientation or being teased for appearing to be gay. In general, being
knowledgeable about characteristics, vulnerabilities, and academic needs related to
giftedness might help counselors contribute to school climate change, given their
potential to be part of school transformation (cf. Littrell & Peterson, 2005).

Their training should help them to be open to the idea that giftedness is a construct, one which is not defined similarly across cultures, and one which does not
resonate at all with some cultures. Such awareness can help counselors to advocate
for services for high-ability students from nonmainstream cultures. All cultures do
not value the individual, competitive, conspicuous achievement valued by the dominant culture in the United States (Peterson, 1997). In fact, some cultures do not
value placing anyone above others or displaying what one knows (Peterson, 1999a),
instead valuing elements such as quietly serving one's community, being able to
inspire others, listening, teaching, overcoming adversity, and having wisdom, rather
than "book" knowledge. Counselors can encourage teachers to affirm those values
in nonpatronizing ways, thereby helping adolescents from nondominant cultures to
feel comfortable and respected in the inherently competitive school environment.
Confronting judgmental attitudes of dominant-culture educators, which may reflect
the belief that dominant-culture values are the standard by which other values and
cultures are measured, may also be warranted.

Advocacy

Students Who Don't Fit the Stereotypes
One of a school counselor's many roles, as currently conceived, is advocacy
(Baker & Gerler, 2004), and counselor educators need to educate graduate students

broadly about that role. Because they are grounded in coursework related to raising multicultural awareness, and possibly also related to special education, counselors can offer support not only to gifted students from nonmainstream cultural and ethnic groups, but also to gifted students with varied learning styles, learning disabilities, physical disabilities, and emotional disabilities. They can help to create and support complex *programs* for gifted students, as well. They should certainly recognize that gifted adolescents may be truant, delinquent, addicted, abused, depressed, or gay and may suffer from any of a variety of psychiatric disorders. Counselors can play important roles in the lives of troubled gifted adolescents, including, for example, serving as referral agents for therapy or other outpatient treatment outside of school, being involved with aftercare when students return to school after drug or psychiatric treatment, and monitoring students who are adjusting to medication, experiencing personal crises, or experiencing depression.

Counselors should also be uniquely aware of student struggles related to lack of differentiated instruction and confer with teachers on behalf of, or with, students. In case meetings, when adults meet to discuss a problematic situation of a gifted student, counselors need to be objective voices of advocacy for the student, perhaps also helping the group to be sensitive to parental needs. If a student is twice-exceptional, a counselor's role is to help educators understand that a student can have the double burden of giftedness and a learning disability, for instance. Because gifted students may be able to compensate for such a disability enough to maintain average academic performance, they may not have appropriate services from either special education or the gifted program.

Interpretation of Assessments

In some situations, counselors explain assessment results, including scores on group ability or achievement tests. Counselors usually have had significant training in measurement, but counselor educators should be aware that knowledge *about* intelligence testing and other common assessments is also important for school counselors, since test performance is usually related to identification for programs. Knowledge about the purposes and limitations of tests of intelligence is important. Awareness of Gardner's (1983) theory of multiple intelligences is also helpful, as well as thoughtful consideration of intelligence as a theoretical construct, one which continues to be "reshaped, redefined, and challenged yet again, which gives rise to the ironic quip that intelligence is what intelligence tests measure" (Young, 1999, p. 206). Counselors can also help underachievers or nonmainstream gifted students to affirm their high ability in ways that fit these students' cultural context, as well as affirm abilities that are valued in a particular cultural context, but not necessarily in the dominant culture (Peterson, 1999a).

In addition to the career-exploration activities described earlier in this chapter, counselors should be prepared to administer and interpret assessments related to interests, personality, and values (Kerr & Erb, 1991; Kerr & Sodano, 2003), all of which are important during career-oriented self-assessment. Counselors should also be knowledgeable about the concept of multipotentiality (Greene, 2003) and the challenges associated with choosing one direction from many. Counselors may need to counter parental insistence that direction should be firm during high school or that parental financial support for college will not be available until direction is firm.

In addition, counselors are currently being trained to use school data to demonstrate effectiveness of various programs and interventions. School counselors might offer research assistance to gifted education personnel or administrators to determine if, for example, affective curriculum has an impact on gifted students.

Prevention

The kinds of services and advocacy just described may help prevent major personal or academic problems in gifted students. School counselors are actually being trained to a considerable extent in prevention (Baker & Gerler, 2004). Prevention means conducting large- and small-group psychoeducational work related to supporting students during normal developmental and other life transitions. Parent and teacher education about developmental concerns also serves to prevent or contain problems. For adolescents, normal developmental challenges include establishing identity, including sexual identity; finding direction; achieving emotional and functional autonomy; learning to negotiate peer and family relationships; and moving toward relationship maturity (Papalia, Olds, & Feldman, 2004). Yet, adult preoccupation with performance may preclude conversation about moodiness, sexuality and sexual behavior, gender roles, responding to authority, differentiation issues, and problems with peer relationships, for instance. A counselor can help compensate for that lack, while also encouraging parents to see their adolescent as more than a performer or nonperformer and understand the intersection of giftedness and development.

Counselor educators should encourage school counselors to work in tandem with the gifted education teacher. In fact, a well-trained counselor might be able to, and need to, advocate for a program for gifted adolescents that includes significant attention to affective development. A counselor might also cofacilitate discussion groups for gifted adolescents, offer suggestions for speakers who can offer psychoeducational mental health information, guide discussion of social and emotional issues related to literature in a language arts class, offer instruction in stress reduction to teams preparing for academic competitions, or offer brief training in listening skills for gifted education teachers and gifted students. When appropriate, counselors can offer information about learning styles, teaching styles, and learning disabilities to students confused about their poor fit in school. Counselors might also help gifted education and other teachers to process (i.e., using *process* as a verb) experiences, including academic experiences, thereby providing opportunities to gain skills in articulating concerns (e.g., "How did that feel when you were giving your strong opinions?" "How might your personality fit the environment we observed today at the engineering firm?" "Let's just sit back for a moment and consider the atmosphere here.").

In addition, teachers should be encouraged to refer gifted students to the counselor when there appear to be emotional concerns. The counselor can then confer with the student, arrange a joint meeting with student and parents if appropriate, or refer the teen or family to a community professional who has special expertise in working with gifted youth and their families. Counselors have the potential to help sensitive gifted adolescents be receptive to counseling, including helping them learn to articulate concerns prior to working with an outside professional. Fundamentally, the school counselor can help de-mystify counseling for parents, teachers, and gifted students themselves by explaining what counselors do. Then all can comfortably approach a counselor when needed.

Counselor educators should provide literature about giftedness to counselors-in-training and encourage them to continue to educate themselves about pertinent research developments in the field. Knowing that underachievers can become academic achievers even before leaving high school (Emerick, 1992; Peterson & Colangelo, 1996), but also during the next decade of their life (Peterson, 2000), school counselors can convey hope to gifted adolescents who hear adults "catastrophize" about their future, based on their current underachievement. Simply being aware of characteristics associated with giftedness enables counselors to help gifted adolescents make sense of confusing and frightening feelings and behaviors. Colangelo and Davis' (2002) handbook offers several pertinent readings for counselors. Kerr's (1994), Kerr and Kurpius' (2004), and Reis' (2002a, 2002b, 2003) work related to gifted girls and Kerr and Cohn's (2001) and Hébert's (2002) work related to gifted boys provide important information not only for educators, but also for individual gifted students, including in psychoeducational group work at the high school level. Neihart (1998, 1999), too, has offered insights over several years related to counseling and guidance of gifted students, including profiles of various types of gifted students (Betts & Neihart, 1988) and a summary of research related to giftedness and delinquency (Neihart, 2002). Counselors coleading small groups might use portions from such literature to generate discussion with gifted high school students. In addition, awareness of local and residential summer academic experiences for gifted adolescents may help counselors provide critical outlets for gifted students who do not have "mind mates" at school.

Conveying information about normal developmental tasks can also help gifted adolescents gain a sense of cognitive control. Readily available psychoeducational materials on a variety of topics can serve as bibliotherapy for gifted students, and counselors can provide opportunities to discuss the materials subsequently. In their preparatory programs, counselor educators need to include in-depth experiences related to human development across the lifespan, since counselors may actually spend much of their day interacting with various adults on behalf of students. These adults are also developing, as are couples and families. The fact that everyone is continuously developing in family and school systems raises the possibility of complex developmental interactions, which counselors should be prepared to articulate to all players.

Table 1
Facilitating Secondary Gifted Education

Superintendents
Provide financial support for, and encourage, pertinent professional development
Insist on appropriate programming in and outside of the classroom
Ensure adequate staffing for gifted education
Recognize cognitive and affective concerns of gifted students

Principals
Support staff development geared to building a pertinent knowledge base
Raise own awareness of cognitive and affective concerns
Create a safe school climate for gifted students
Examine own attitudes regarding gifted students
Encourage affective curriculum and creative programming to meet needs of gifted students

Counselors
Examine own attitudes and raise own awareness regarding giftedness and gifted students
Be alert to school safety issues related to giftedness
Advocate for equitable services for nonmainstream gifted students
Serve as a referral resource for mental health concerns
Serve as a liaison between gifted students and classroom teachers when appropriate
Create appropriate career-development programming for gifted students
Make prevention of social and emotional problems a priority
Provide literature related to giftedness to teachers
Be a clearinghouse for information about extra-school opportunities for gifted students

---

CONCLUSION

Administrators and school counselors, with broad responsibilities in the school environment but differing roles, can have significant impact on the lives of gifted adolescents. Supported by knowledge of gifted students' affective and academic concerns, both administrators and counselors can be advocates for appropriate programming, including opportunities to attend to developmental concerns beyond academics. Principals, especially, can make staff development a priority, ensuring that faculty have a current base of knowledge from which to create appropriately differentiated curricula and respond to affective concerns. Principals can also develop effective strategies for countering bullying and harassment, knowing that gifted adolescents are not immune to these and other common interpersonal difficulties during secondary level education. Table 1 provides a summary of admonitions and recommendations related to potential contributions by these professionals, as discussed in this chapter.

Special education for exceptional learners at the high end of bell curves of various kinds of abilities is indeed appropriate education, the kind promoted and protected by the Individuals with Disabilities Education Act (1990). Regular classrooms may not be the least restrictive environment for gifted students, unless instruction is well differentiated. Administrators and counselors, as members of the school leadership team, can help ensure that critical needs of gifted adolescents are met. More than just gifted students potentially benefit when they thrive during the secondary-level school years.

REFERENCES

American Psychiatric Association. (1994). *Diagnostic and statistical manual of mental disorders* (4th ed.). Washington, DC: Author.

Assouline, S. (1997). Assessment of gifted children. In N. Colangelo & G. A. Davis (Eds.), *Handbook of gifted education* (2nd ed., pp. 89–108). Boston: Allyn & Bacon.

Baker, S. B., & Gerler, E. R. (2004). *School counseling for the twenty-first century* (4th ed.). Upper Saddle River, NJ: Pearson/Prentice Hall.

Berthold, K. A., & Hoover, J. H. (2000). Correlates of bullying and victimization among intermediate students in the Midwestern USA. *School Psychology International, 21,* 65–78.

Betts, G. T., & Neihart, M. (1988). Profiles of the gifted and talented. *Gifted Child Quarterly, 32,* 248–253.

Bireley, M., & Genshaft, J. (1991). Adolescence and giftedness: A look at the issues. In M. Bireley & J. Genshaft (Eds.), *Understanding the gifted adolescent* (pp. 1–17). New York: Columbia University, Teachers College Press.

Bosworth, K., Espelage, D. L., & Simon, T. R. (1999). Factors associated with bullying behavior in middle school students. *Journal of Early Adolescence, 19,* 341–362.

Cohn, S. J. (2002). Gifted students who are gay, lesbian, or bisexual. In M. Neihart, S. M. Reis, N. M. Robinson, & S. M. Moon (Eds.), *The social and emotional development of gifted children: What do we know?* (pp. 145–153). Waco, TX: Prufrock Press.

Colangelo, N., & Davis, G. A. (Eds.). (2002). *Handbook on gifted education* (3rd ed.). Boston: Allyn & Bacon.

Dixon, F. A., Lapsley, D. K, & Hanchon, T. A. (2004). An empirical typology of perfectionism in gifted adolescents. *Gifted Child Quarterly, 48,* 95–106.

Dweck, C. S. (1992). Motivational processes affecting learning. In J. S. DeLoache (Ed.), *Current readings in child development* (pp. 147–157). Boston: Allyn & Bacon.

Elkind, D. (1981). *The hurried child.* Reading, MA: Addison-Wesley.

Emerick, L. (1992). Academic underachievement among the gifted: Students' perceptions of factors that reverse the pattern. *Gifted Child Quarterly, 36,* 140–146.

Feldhusen, J. F. (2003). Talented youth at the secondary level. In N. Colangelo & G. A. Davis, (Eds.), *Handbook of gifted education* (pp. 229–237). Boston: Pearson Education/Allyn & Bacon.

Feldhusen, J. F., Hoover, S. M., & Sayler, M. F. (1990). *Identification and education of the gifted and talented at the secondary level.* Monroe, NY: Trillium Press.

Fontaine, J. H., & Hammond, N. L. (1996). Counseling issues with gay and lesbian adolescents. *Adolescence, 31,* 817–830.

Gallagher, J. J. (1997). Issues in the education of gifted students. In N. Colangelo & G. A. Davis (Eds.), *Handbook of gifted education* (2nd ed., pp. 10-23). Boston: Allyn & Bacon.

Gardner, H. (1983). *Frames of mind: The theory of multiple intelligences.* New York: Basic Books.

Gonzales, G. M., & Myrick, R. D. (2000). The teacher as student advisors program (TAP): An effective approach for drug education and other developmental guidance activities. In J. Wittmer (Ed.),

Managing your school counseling program: K–12 developmental strategies (2nd ed., pp. 243–252). Minneapolis, MN: Educational Media Corporation.

Greene, M. J. (2003). Gifted adrift? Career counseling of the gifted and talented. *Roeper Review, 25*, 66–72.

Greenspon, T. S. (2000). "Healthy perfectionism" is an oxymoron! Reflections on the psychology of perfectionism and the sociology of science. *Journal of Secondary Gifted Education, 11,* 197–208.

Gregorc, A. (1985). *Gregorc style delineator*. Columbia, CT: Gregorc Associates.

Gross, M. U. M. (2002). Social and emotional issues for exceptionally intellectually gifted students. In M. Neihart, S. M. Reis, N. M. Robinson, & S. M. Moon (Eds.), *The social and emotional development of gifted children: What do we know?* Waco, TX: Prufrock Press.

Guilford, J. P. (1987). Creativity research: Past, present and future. In S. Isaksen (Ed.), *Frontiers of creativity research* (pp. 33–66). Buffalo, NY: Bearly Ltd.

Harbeck, K. M. (1994). Invisible no more: Addressing the needs of gay, lesbian, and bisexual youth and their advocates. *High School Journal, 77,* 169–176.

Haynie, D. L., Nansel, T., Eitel, P., Crump, A. D., Saylor, K., Yu, K., et al. (2001). Bullies, victims, and bully/victims: Distinct groups of at-risk youth. *Journal of Early Adolescence, 21*, 29–49.

Hébert, T. P. (2002). Gifted males. In M. Neihart, S. M. Reis, N. M. Robinson, & S. M. Moon (Eds.), *The social and emotional development of gifted children: What do we know?* (pp. 137–144). Waco, TX: Prufrock Press.

Higgins, G. O. (1994). *Resilient adults: Overcoming a cruel past*. San Francisco: Jossey-Bass.

Hoover, J. (2003, February). *Angry words, angry minds: Bullying and teasing at school*. Western Canadian Association for Student Teachers (WestCAST) convention, The University of Winnipeg.

Huegel, K. (2003). *GLBTQ: The survival guide for queer and questioning teens*. Minneapolis: Free Spirit.

Hunter, S. C., & Boyle, J. M. E. (2002). Perceptions of control in the victims of bullying: The importance of early intervention. *Educational Research, 44,* 323–336.

Individuals With Disabilities Education Act, 20 U.S.C. §1401 et seq. (1990).

Jackson, N. E., & Klein, E. J. (1997). Gifted performance in young children. In N. Colangelo & G. A. Davis (Eds.), *Handbook of gifted education* (2nd ed., pp. 460–474). Boston: Allyn & Bacon.

Juvonen, J., Graham, S., & Schuster, M. A. (2003). Bullying among young adolescents: The strong, the weak, and the troubled. *Pediatrics, 112,* 1231–1237.

Kerr, B. A. (1994). *Smart girls two: A new psychology of girls, women, and giftedness*. Dayton, OH: Ohio Psychology Press.

Kerr, B. A., & Cohn. S. J. (2001). *Smart boys: Talent, manhood, and the search for meaning*. Scottsdale, AZ: Great Potential Press.

Kerr, B., & Erb, C. (1991). Career counseling with academically talented students: Effects of a value-based intervention. *Journal of Counseling Psychology, 38,* 309–314.

Kerr, B., & Kurpius, S. E. R. (2004). Encouraging talented girls in math and science: Effects of a guidance intervention. *High Ability Studies, 15,* 85–102.

Kerr, B., & Sodano, S. (2003). Career assessment of intellectually gifted students. *Journal of Career Assessment, 11,* 168–186.

Littrell, J. M., & Peterson, J. S. (2005). *Portrait and model of a school counselor*. Boston: Houghton Mifflin/Lahaska Press.

Lovecky, D. V. (1992). Exploring social and emotional aspects of giftedness in children. *Roeper Review, 15,* 18–25.

National Institute of Mental Health Policy Research Institute. (2004). *NAMI policy research institute task force report: Children and psychotropic medications*. Arlington, VA: National Institute of Mental Health.

Neihart, M. (1998). Preserving the true self of the gifted child. *Roeper Review, 20,* 187–191.

Neihart, M. (1999). The impact of giftedness on psychological well-being: What does the empirical literature say? *Roeper Review, 22,* 10–17.

Neihart, M. (2002). Delinquency and gifted children. In M. Neihart, S. M. Reis, N. M. Robinson, & S. M. Moon (Eds.), *The social and emotional development of gifted children: What do we know?* (pp. 103–112). Waco, TX: Prufrock Press.

Newman-Carlson, D., & Horne, A. M. (2004). Bully-busters: A psychoeducational intervention for reducing bullying behavior in middle school students. *Journal of Counseling & Development, 82,* 259–267.

No Child Left Behind Act, 20 U.S.C. §6301 (2001).

Olweus, D. (1973). *Hackkylingar och oversittare.* Stockholm: Almqvist & Wicksell Forlag AB.

Olweus, D. (2003). A profile of bullying at school. *Educational Leadership, 60*(6), 12–17.

Papalia, D. S., Olds, S. W., & Feldman, R. D. (2004). *Human development* (9th ed.). New York: McGraw-Hill.

Peterson, J. S. (1990). Noon-hour discussion groups: Dealing with the burdens of capability. *Gifted Child Today, 13*(4), 17–22.

Peterson, J. S. (1993). Peeling off the elitist label: Smart politics. *Gifted Child Today, 16*(2), 31–33.

Peterson, J. S. (1995). *Talk with teens about feelings, family, relationships, and the future: 50 guided discussions for school and counseling groups.* Minneapolis, MN: Free Spirit.

Peterson, J. S. (1997). Bright, touch, and resilient—and not in a gifted program. *Journal of Secondary Gifted Education, 8,* 121–136.

Peterson, J. S. (1998). The burdens of capability. *Reclaiming Children and Youth, 6,* 194–198.

Peterson, J. S. (1999a). Gifted—through whose cultural lens? An application of the postpositivistic mode of inquiry. *Journal for the Education of the Gifted, 22,* 354–383.

Peterson, J. S. (1999b). When it's hard to leave home. *Reclaiming Children and Youth, 8,* 14–19.

Peterson, J. S. (2000). A follow-up study of one group of achievers and underachievers four years after high school graduation. *Roeper Review, 22,* 217–224.

Peterson, J. S. (2003). An argument for proactive attention to affective concerns of gifted adolescents. *Journal of Secondary Gifted Education, 14,* 62–71.

Peterson, J. S., & Colangelo, N. (1996). Gifted achievers and underachievers: A comparison of patterns found in school files. *Journal of Counseling and Development, 74,* 399–407.

Peterson, J. S., & Ray, K. E. (in press-a). Bullying among the gifted: The subjective experience. *Gifted Child Quarterly.*

Peterson, J. S., & Ray, K. E. (in press-b). Bullying and the gifted: Victims, perpetrators, prevalence, and effects. *Gifted Child Quarterly.*

Peterson, J. S., & Rischar, H. (2000). Gifted and gay: A study of the adolescent experience. *Gifted Child Quarterly, 44,* 149–164.

Piechowski, M. M. (1997). Emotional giftedness: The measure of intrapersonal intelligence. In N. Colangelo & G. A. Davis (Eds.), *Handbook of gifted education* (2nd ed., pp. 366–381). Boston: Allyn & Bacon.

Reis, S. M. (2002a). Gifted females in elementary and secondary school. In M. Neihart, S. M. Reis, N. M. Robinson, & S. M. Moon (Eds.), *The social and emotional development of gifted children: What do we know?* (pp. 125–135). Waco, TX: Prufrock Press.

Reis, S. M. (2002b). Toward a theory of creativity in diverse creative women. *Creativity Research Journal, 14,* 305–316.

Reis, S.M. (2003). Gifted girls, twenty-five years later: Hopes realized and new challenges found. *Roeper Review, 25, 154–157.*

Schuler, P. (2001). Perfection and the gifted adolescent. *Journal of Secondary Gifted Education, 11*, 183–196.

Shearer, C. B. (1999). *Multiple Intelligences Developmental Assessment Scales (MIDAS)*. Kent, OH: Multiple Intelligences Research & Consulting.

Silverman, L. K. (2002). Asynchronous development. In M. Neihart, S. M. Reis, N. M. Robinson, & S. M. Moon (Eds.), *The social and emotional development of gifted children: What do we know?* (pp. 31–37). Waco, TX: Prufrock Press.

Swiatek, M. A., & Dorr, R. M. (1998). Revision of the social coping questionnaire: Replication and extension of previous findings. *Journal of Secondary Gifted Education, 10*, 252–259.

Tannenbaum, A. J. (1997). The meaning and making of giftedness. In N. Colangelo & G. A. Davis (Eds.), *Handbook of gifted education* (2nd ed., pp. 27–42). Boston: Allyn & Bacon.

Tolan, S. (1997). Sex and the highly gifted adolescent. *Counseling and Guidance, 6*(3), 2, 5, 8.

Will, J. D., & Neufeld, P. J. (2002, December). Keep bullying from growing into greater violence. *Principal Leadership, 3*, 51–54.

Young, D. W. (1999). *Wayward kids: Understanding and treating antisocial youth*. Northvale, NJ: Jason Aronson.

ABOUT THE AUTHORS

Editors

Felicia A. Dixon is associate professor of educational psychology at Ball State University. She directs the master's degree program in educational psychology and the license/endorsement in gifted education. She received her doctorate from Purdue University and specializes in gifted education. Author of more than 30 articles and chapters, Dr. Dixon received the Early Scholar Award from NAGC in 2004. She is a member of the board of directors of NAGC and is chairperson of the Task Force on Secondary Gifted Education of NAGC. Her research interests include critical thinking, cognitive abilities, self-concept of gifted adolescents, perfectionism, and curriculum. Her special interest is in the advancement of gifted education for secondary students. Correspondence should be addressed to Felicia A. Dixon, Department of Educational Psychology, Teachers College #508, Ball State University, Muncie, IN 47306-0595 or e-mail: fdixon@bsu.edu.

Sidney M. Moon is director of the Gifted Education Resource Institute (http://purdue.edu/geri) and associate dean for learning and engagement in the College of Education at Purdue University. She has been active in the field of gifted education for 30 years. In that time, she has contributed more than 60 books, articles, and chapters to the field. Sidney is active in the National Association for Gifted Children, where she has served as chair of the Research and Evaluation Division and as a member of the Board of Directors. Her research interests include talent development in the STEM disciplines (science, technology, engineering, and mathematics), secondary gifted education, underserved populations, and personal talent development. Correspondence should be addressed to Sidney M. Moon, Purdue University, Gifted Education Resource Institute, Beering Hall of Liberal Arts and Education, 100 North University Street, West Lafayette, IN 47907-2098 or geri@purdue.edu.

Contributors

Cheryll M. Adams is the director of the Center for Gifted Studies and Talent Development at Ball State University and project director for Project CLUE. She is past-president of the Indiana Association for the Gifted, a former member of the board of directors of NAGC, and a current member of the board of directors of TAG.

Her interests include gifted students in science and math, curriculum development, and identification of gifted students. E-mail: cadams@bsu.edu.

Susan G. Assouline is the Belin-Blank Center's associate director. She received her B.S. in general science with a teaching endorsement, her Ed.S. in school psychology, and her Ph.D. in psychological and quantitative foundations, all from The University of Iowa. Upon completion of her doctorate, she was awarded a 2-year postdoctoral fellowship at the Study of Mathematically Precocious Youth (SMPY) at Johns Hopkins University, and upon completion joined the Belin-Blank Center in 1990. She is especially interested in identification of academic talent in elementary students and is coauthor of *Developing Mathematical Talent: A Guide for Challenging and Educating Gifted Students.* Most recently she coauthored, with Nicholas Colangelo and Miraca U. M. Gross, *A Nation Deceived: How Schools Hold Back America's Brightest Students.* Currently, she is lead investigator on the Belin-Blank Center's national study on twice exceptional children.

Susan Baum is a professor at the College of New Rochelle, where she teaches graduate courses in elementary education and the education of gifted and talented student. She is an international consultant and has published many articles and books about meeting the needs of gifted students. Her latest books include *Multiple Intelligences in the Elementary Classroom: A Teacher's Toolkit,* in collaboration with Howard Gardner, *Keeping in Step: Meeting the Social and Emotional Needs of Adolescents,* and *To Be Gifted & Learning Disabled: Strategies for Meeting the Needs of Gifted Students—LD, ADHD, and More* (Rev. ed.). Dr. Baum served on the board of directors of the National Association for Gifted Students and is the past-secretary for the organization. In addition, Dr. Baum is the past-president and founder of the Association for the Education of Gifted Underachieving Students (AEGUS).

Carolyn M. Callahan, Commonwealth Professor and department chair at the Curry School of Education at the University of Virginia, is currently Director of the University of Virginia site of the National Research Center on the Gifted and Talented. She has written more than 160 articles and 40 book chapters on a broad range of topics in gifted education, including the areas of the identification of gifted students, the evaluation of gifted programs, the development of performance assessments, issues facing gifted females, and gifted program options. She has received the Distinguished Scholar and Service Award from the National Association for Gifted Children and the Outstanding Faculty Award from the Commonwealth of Virginia.

Eric Calvert is a gifted education consultant in the Office for Exceptional Children at the Ohio Department of Education. Calvert earned an M.S. in educational psychology at Purdue University, where he also directed Saturday enrichment and residential summer programs for the Gifted Education Resource Institute. Calvert earned a B.S. at Central Missouri State University, and is a former high school teacher and speech, debate, and mock trial coach. He is currently pursuing a doctorate in leadership at Bowling Green State University.

Scott Chamberlin is an assistant professor of elementary and early childhood education at the University of Wyoming. His Ph.D. in educational psychology was earned in 2002 from Purdue University under the direction of Dr. Sidney Moon. His research interests include mathematical problem solving with gifted students, and Dr. Chamberlin's teaching responsibilities are math and science instruction for elementary education teachers and learning theories with graduate students.

Eric Cleveland is a Ph.D. student in the Educational Studies Department at Purdue University. Cleveland has conducted research on implicit views of creativity, a model initiative to involve urban minority students in residential summer programs, and cross-cultural comparisons of Korean and American gifted youth. Cleveland has also conducted evaluations of university- and school-based gifted programs. His research interests include creativity, populations underrepresented in gifted education, and poverty-related educational barriers. A nontraditional, lifelong learner, Cleveland also enjoys animal training and home remodeling.

Nicholas Colangelo is the Myron & Jacqueline Blank Professor of Gifted Education at The University of Iowa. He is also director of The Connie Belin & Jacqueline N. Blank International Center for Gifted Education and Talent Development. He is author of numerous articles on counseling gifted students and the affective development of gifted, and he has edited two texts: *New Voices in Counseling the Gifted* (with Ronald Zaffrann) and *Handbook of Gifted Education, Editions I, II, and III* (with Gary Davis). He has authored *Nation Deceived: How Schools Hold Back America's Brightest Students* (with Susan Assouline and Miraca Gross). He has served on the editorial boards of major journals, including *Counseling and Development, Gifted Child Quarterly, Journal of Creative Behavior, Journal for the Education of the Gifted*, and *Roeper Review*. In 2002, he received the President's Award from the National Association for Gifted Children. Dr. Colangelo was elected President of the Iowa Academy of Education for 2004–2005, and in 2004, he was appointed by Governor Tom Vilsack (Iowa) to the Iowa Learns Council.

Peggy Dettmer is professor emeritus at Kansas State University, where she taught courses in education of gifted students, educational assessment, creativity in education, and collaborative school consultation. Dr. Dettmer is a past-president of the Professional Development Division of the National Association for Gifted Children and coauthor of the NAGC service publication *Staff Development: The Key to Effective Gifted Education Programs*. She served as guest editor for topical issues of *Gifted Child Quarterly* on staff development and on advocacy and support for gifted programs. Other books include *Assessment for Effective Teaching*, and *Consultation, Collaboration, and Teamwork for Students With Special Needs*.

Donna Y. Ford is Betts Chair of Education and Human Development at Vanderbilt University and teaches in the Department of Special Education. Donna earned her Ph.D. in urban education (educational psychology) from Cleveland State University. Professor Ford conducts research primarily in gifted education and multicultural/urban education. Specifically, her work focuses on: (1) recruiting and retaining culturally diverse students in gifted education; (2) multicultural and urban education; (3) minority student achievement and underachievement; and (4) family involvement. She is the author of *Reversing Underachievement Among Gifted Black Students* (1996) and coauthor of *Multicultural Gifted Education* (1999) and *In Search of the Dream: Designing Schools and Classrooms That Work for High Potential Students From Diverse Cultural Backgrounds* (2004). Donna is a board member of the National Association for Gifted Children, and has served on numerous editorial boards

Dr. Françoys Gagné was born and raised in Montréal, Québec. He obtained his Ph.D. in Psychology at the Université de Montréal in 1966. After devoting the first decade of his career to the study of students' perceptions of teaching, Dr. Gagné made the study of giftedness and talent the center of his professional activities. His main research interests include definitions and developmental models of gifts and talents, the interplay between various causal factors of confirmed talent, accelerative enrichment, peer nominations, the prevalence of giftedness, and the phenomenon of multitalent. He has authored a book (in French) reviewing the literature on acceleration, and published numerous articles and book chapters in both French and English. He is better known in the U.S. and abroad for his Differentiated Model of Giftedness and Talent (DMGT), as well as his psychometric studies of peer nominations (Tracking Talents). Dr. Gagné recently retired from his full professorship in the Department of Psychology (Educational Psychology) at the Université du Québec à Montréal. He has retained the status of Honorary professor.

Shelagh A. Gallagher is associate professor in the Department of Special Education and Child Development at the University of North Carolina at Charlotte. In this position, she is integrally involved in coordinating the doctoral, masters', and licensure programs in education for the gifted. She also directs Project Insights, a Javits grant implementing a new model middle school program for gifted disadvantaged students. Dr. Gallagher was also director for Project P-BLISS (Problem-Based Learning in the Social Sciences) and project manager of the Science Grant at the College of William and Mary, where she oversaw the development of seven PBL science units. She first learned about PBL while at the IMSA, where she was a part of the Science, Society, and the Future project. Dr. Gallagher has served on the board of directors of the National Association for Gifted Children and the North Carolina Association for the Gifted and Talented, and she is coauthor of *Teaching the Gifted Child*.

Marcia Gentry serves as associate professor and associate director of the Gifted Education Resource Institute at Purdue University. A member of the NAGC board of directors and recipient of its Early Scholar Award, Marcia frequently contributes to the gifted education literature, serves on editorial boards, and participates in regional, state, national and international venues for gifted education and educational research. Her work focuses on the use of cluster grouping and differentiation, the development of student attitude measures that assess constructs central to meaningful learning, using gifted education ideas as a means of improving general education, learning about the experiences of gifted students, and the role of student perceptions in teaching and learning.

Thomas P. Hébert is an associate professor of educational psychology in the College of Education at the University of Georgia in Athens, GA, where he teaches graduate courses in gifted education and qualitative research methods. He has been a teacher for 13 years, 10 of which were spent working with gifted students at the elementary, middle, and high school levels. Dr. Hébert is a member of the board of directors of the National Association for Gifted Children (NAGC). He is also the recipient of the National Association for Gifted Children's 2000 Early Scholar Award. His research interests include social and emotional development of gifted students, underachievement, and problems faced by gifted young men.

Linda Jarvin is a research scientist in the Yale University Department of Psychology, and the associate director of the Center for Psychology of Abilities, Competencies, and Expertise (PACE). Her main research focus is on the development and implementation of theory-driven instruction and assessment, with a special interest in individual differences.

Kevin Kelly is a professor and head of the Department of Educational Studies at Purdue University. He received his Ph.D. in counseling psychology from the University of Iowa in 1985. He has authored more than 50 journal articles and book chapters related to career choice and development and is the past-editor of the *Journal of Mental Health Counseling*. Professor Kelly also coordinates a career and academic planning course taken by hundreds of undecided first-year college students each year.

Penny Britton Kolloff is associate professor emerita at Illinois State University. She served two terms on the NAGC board of directors and was president of the Illinois Association for Gifted Children. She is currently a member of several advisory boards and frequently consults, speaks, and writes on topics related to gifted education.

Mary Landrum is an associate professor at the College of Education at James Madison University. Mary has taught in higher education for 15 years, teaching in teacher education, special education, and gifted education. Previously she was an elementary and middle school teacher. Dr. Landrum is a member of the board of directors of the National Association for Gifted Children, and won the Early Leader Award from that organization in 1997. Over the past 15 years, Mary has presented over 175 in-services to educators in Pre-K–12 education, and published widely. Mary is coauthor of a staff development book and coeditor of *Aiming for Excellence: The NAGC Pre-K-12 Gifted Program Standards*, both published collaboratively by Prufrock Press and NAGC. Mary is author of a book on consultation and gifted education published by Creative Learning Press.

Teresa Miller is associate professor in educational leadership at Kansas State University. Her experiences in education include positions as high school principal, elementary school principal, gifted program facilitator at the secondary level, and high school English teacher. Dr. Miller's publications feature leadership factors in schools and administrator leadership in school improvement models. Her research interests focus on historical, biographical, and social factors affecting educational organizations through change; longitudinal analysis of one district's school board performance and outcomes across several decades; and the principalship and other leadership roles in elementary and secondary schools.

James L. Moore III is an assistant professor in counselor education and is also the coordinator of the school counseling program in the College of Education at The Ohio State University. His research focuses on the following topics: (a) studying how educational professionals, such as school counselors, influence the educational/career aspirations and school experiences of students of color (particularly African American males); (b) exploring socio-cultural, familial, school, and community factors that support, enhance, and impede academic outcomes for K–16 African American students; (c) examining recruitment and retention issues of students of color in gifted education and college students in science, technology, engineering, and mathematics (STEM) majors; and (d) exploring social, emotional, and psychological consequences of racial oppression for African American males and other people of color in various domains in society (e.g., education, counseling, workplace, athletics, etc.). He has written nearly 50 publications on these topics.

Steve V. Owen retired in 1999 and began a new career as a biostatistician, after a long stint in educational psychology at the University of Connecticut. He is currently in the School of Medicine at the University of Texas Health Science Center at San Antonio. He has not forgotten his previous life or earlier collaborators, which is why he appears in this volume.

Helen Patrick is an associate professor of educational psychology in the Department of Educational Studies, Purdue University. Her research involves investigating student motivation and learning, especially links between teacher practices, students' perceptions of their classroom environment, and student motivation. She also teaches classes in motivation and educational psychology.

Jean Sunde Peterson is a counselor educator and coordinator of the school counseling program at Purdue University. She is a former classroom and gifted education teacher and is a licensed mental health counselor. She has received national group-work and research awards and has also received teaching and service awards at Purdue. Her *Talk With Teens* books are frequently used as affective curriculum in gifted education. Her research focuses on the social and emotional development of gifted youth and on understudied gifted populations.

Rebecca L. Pierce is an associate professor of mathematical sciences at Ball State University, teaching undergraduate and graduate statistics courses. Most recently, she has been an integral part of two Jacob K. Javits Grants. Her roles include serving as the mathematics curriculum specialist, providing professional development for teachers, and assisting in the statistical analysis of the data. E-mail: rpierce@bsu.edu.

Karen E. Ray is a doctoral student in counseling psychology and graduate assistant with the Gifted Education Resource Institute (http://www.geri.soe.purdue.edu) at Purdue University. She has been active in the field of gifted education since 1986. She is a member of the National Association for Gifted Children and participates in SENG (Supporting Emotional Needs of the Gifted). Her research interests include career development, gifted individuals, social and emotional development, spirituality, and attachment theory. Correspondence should be addressed to Karen E. Ray, Purdue University, Gifted Education Resource Institute, Beering Hall of Liberal Arts and Education, 100 North University Street, West Lafayette, IN 47907-2098 or geri@purdue.edu.

Sally M. Reis is department head and a professor of educational psychology at the University of Connecticut, where she also serves as principal investigator of The National Research Center on the Gifted and Talented. She was a teacher for 15 years, 11 of which were spent working with gifted students on the elementary, junior high, and high school levels. She has authored more than 100 articles, eight books, 30 book chapters, and numerous monographs and technical reports. She has traveled extensively across the country conducting workshops and providing professional development for school districts on enrichment programs and gender equity programs. She is coauthor of *The Schoolwide Enrichment Model, The Secondary Triad Model, Dilemmas in Talent Development in the Middle Years,* and a book published in 1998 about talent development in females entitled *Work Left Undone*: *Choices and Compromises of Talented Females*. Sally serves on the editorial board of the *Gifted Child Quarterly*, and is a past-president of the National Association for Gifted Children.

Sara J. Renzulli graduated from Miss Porter's School in Farmington, CT, in 2003 and is currently a junior at Union College in New York. She is majoring in European history and plans on pursuing in a master's degree in public history in the future.

Mary G. Rizza is an associate professor and coordinator of gifted programs at Bowling Green State University, Ohio. She has been associated with the field of gifted education for more than 15 years in a variety of teaching, counseling, and administrative positions. Currently she directs the Office of Gifted Programs at BGSU, which offers programs, courses, and services to gifted children, their parents, and teachers. She teaches courses in gifted education pedagogy, school psychology, and general education theory. Dr. Rizza's research interests include the use technology in classrooms, issues related to identification/programming for the twice-exceptional, and social/emotional needs of gifted children.

Julia Link Roberts is the Mahurin Professor of Gifted Studies and the director of The Center for Gifted Studies at Western Kentucky University. Dr. Roberts has spent 5 weeks for more than 20 summers directing residential programming for middle and high school young people who are gifted and talented. She is a member of the board of *Gifted Child Today*, the Kentucky Association for Gifted Education, and the Kentucky Advisory Board for Gifted and Talented Education, and she has served on the boards of the National Association for Gifted Children and The Association for the Gifted, an affiliate of the Council for Exceptional Children. Dr. Roberts has been recognized as a Distinguished Professor at Western Kentucky University, the first recipient of the National Association for Gifted Children David W. Belin Advocacy Award, and one of the 55 individuals in *Profiles of Influence in Gifted Education: Historical Perspectives and Future Directions* (2004). She is a graduate of the University of Missouri with a B.A. and Oklahoma State University with an Ed.D.

Ann Robinson is the founding director of the Center for Gifted Education at the University of Arkansas at Little Rock, where she coordinates the licensure, masters', and doctoral specializations in gifted education. Ann served at the editor of the *Gifted Child Quarterly* and is currently the finance secretary for the National Association for Gifted Children. A former high school English teacher, Ann is an enthusiastic reader of biography.

F. Robert Sabol is an associate professor of art and design at Purdue University and chair of art education. He teaches graduate and undergraduate art education courses. His research interests include curriculum studies, assessment, multicultural education, art education in rural and urban contexts, and gifted and talented visual arts education. He has received numerous grants in support of his research and his publication record includes a book, book chapters, and articles in scholarly journals. He is the National Art Education Association Western Region vice president-elect and president of the NAEA Public Policy and Arts Administration Issues Group. He has been recognized by the NAEA with its Manuel Barkan Memorial Award and as Western Region Higher Education Art Educator of the Year.

Michael Sayler is director of gifted education at the University of North Texas (UNT). He is an associate professor in the Department of Technology and Cognition and is associate dean for the College of Education. He serves on the placement committee for the Texas Academy of Mathematics and Science (TAMS) at UNT. Dr. Sayler has served in leadership positions for many national and state gifted education groups.

William C. Stepien's degrees are in teaching social studies and teaching and leadership. He is currently doing postgraduate studies in instructional technology at Northern Illinois University and teaching history at St. Charles North High School in St. Charles, IL. Bill is a frequent conference presenter and professional development trainer in Problem-Based Learning. He is coauthor of *Using the Internet for Problem-Based Learning*.

William J. Stepien's degrees are in history and education, with an emphasis in economics. Bill has been teaching in middle school through college classrooms for more than 40 years. He was a founding faculty member at the Illinois Mathematics and Science Academy, a state-wide high school for gifted students, senior social studies author at Scott Foresman, and consultant/writer in Problem-Based Learning for ASCD, NASA, *Wall Street Journal*, and more than 100 other organizations and schools. Bill is currently the middle school social studies teacher at Trinity Episcopal School in Charlotte, NC.

Rena F. Subotnik is director of the Center for Gifted Education Policy at the American Psychological Association. The Center's mission is to generate public awareness, advocacy, clinical applications, and cutting-edge research ideas that will enhance the achievement and performance of children and adolescents with special gifts and talents in all domains (including the academic disciplines, the performing arts, sports, and the professions). She is coauthor or coeditor of six books and principal investigator on grants with the Institute for Education Sciences, Jack Kent Cooke Foundation, Camille and Henry Dreyfus Foundation, the American Psychological Foundation, and the McDonnell Foundation.

Jacques van Rossum, originally educated as a developmental psychologist, holds a Ph.D. in movement sciences on a motor learning topic. He is staff member at the Faculty of Human Movement Sciences (Vrije Universiteit, Amsterdam, the Netherlands), where he is mainly involved in teaching and executing research on talent development in athletics. For 10 years, he has studied the development of talent in young preprofessional dancers, after having been invited by the Dance Department of The Amsterdam Theatre School to help them determine aspects of load and loadability in young dancers.

Joyce VanTassel-Baska is the Jody and Layton Smith Professor of Education and executive director of the Center for Gifted Education at the College of William and Mary in Virginia, where she has developed a graduate program and a research and development center in gifted education. She has also served as the state director of gifted programs for Illinois, as a regional director of a gifted service center in the

Chicago area, as coordinator of gifted programs for the Toledo, OH, public school system, and as a teacher of gifted high school students in English and Latin. She has worked as a consultant on gifted education in all 50 states and for key national groups, including the U.S. Department of Education, National Association of Secondary School Principals, and American Association of School Administrators. She is past-president of The Association for the Gifted of the Council for Exceptional Children, and the Northwestern University Chapter of Phi Delta Kappa. She is currently president-elect of the National Association for Gifted Children. Dr. VanTassel-Baska has published widely including 15 books and over 300 refereed journal articles, book chapters, and scholarly reports.

Index